CENTAUR CLASSICS
GENERAL EDITOR: J. M. COHEN

The Sacred Theory
of the Earth

The
Sacred Theory
of the
EARTH.

The Sacred Theory
of the Earth

BY THOMAS BURNET

WITH AN INTRODUCTION BY BASIL WILLEY

SOUTHERN ILLINOIS UNIVERSITY PRESS

CARBONDALE   ILLINOIS

© *Centaur Press Ltd.* 1965

Library of Congress Catalog Card No 65.10027.

First published in the United States of America
by the Southern Illinois University Press
Printed in Great Britain

INTRODUCTION

THOMAS BURNET (1635?-1715), successively pupil of Tillotson at Clare, friend of Cudworth, Fellow of Christ's, Master of the Charterhouse, and finally Chaplain-in-Ordinary to William III, deserves to be read, if only for his stately prose, which no less than his theory of the world places him unmistakably within the seventeenth-century penumbra rather than in the period of Newtonian illumination. The *Sacred Theory*, for all its eccentricity, has about it a certain epic grandeur both in conception and style, and Burnet might be described as a kind of prose Milton thirty years nearer to Addison.

Burnet grants, with the physico-theologians (e.g. John Ray, William Derham and others), that in the general economy of Nature there is enough—and more than enough—evidence of design to prove a Deity. Where he differs from them is in not regarding the world in its present state as the best of possible worlds. The world, as we know it, is not the world as God designed it, and it is therefore both unscientific and blasphemous to ground our devotion upon its alleged perfections. On the contrary, the world is a mighty ruin, a damaged paradise— majestic, no doubt (the work of the divine architect could scarcely be otherwise, even in decay), but a ruin none the less. It may furnish evidence of God's anger, but not of his original intention; disproportion'd sin has jarred against Nature's chime. Burnet rests his argument upon three main points: the chaotic state of the terraqueous globe as it presents itself to the unflinching eye, the certainty that this condition arose from sin, and the theory that the cataclysm which produced it was the Flood. It will be seen, then, that Burnet's high argument is blended of aesthetic, moral, theological, and pseudo-scientific ingredients. Indeed (as I hope to show in a moment), his belief in the parallel and synchronized working of the scientific laws along with God's dispensations is one of the most significant points in the book.

Casting his eye, then, over the physical world, Burnet (not unlike Pascal contemplating the stellar scene) is appalled by what he sees.

Oratours and Philosophers treat Nature after a very different manner; Those represent her with all her graces and ornaments, and if there be anything which is not capable of that, they dissemble it, or pass it over slightly. But Philosophers view Nature with a more impartial eye, and without favour or prejudice give a just and free account, how they find all the parts of the Universe, some more, some less perfect. *

If we are to describe the earth as it really is,

though it be handsome and regular enough to the eye in certain parts of it, single tracts and single Regions; yet if we consider the whole surface of it, or the whole Exteriour Region, 'tis as a broken and confus'd heap of bodies, plac'd in no order to one another, nor with any correspondency or regularity of parts: And such a body as the Moon

* *Theory of the Earth* (1684 ed.), p. 109.

5

appears to us, when 'tis look'd upon with a good Glass, rude and ragged. . . . They are both in my judgement the image or picture of a great Ruine, and have the true aspect of a World lying in its rubbish.

Still greater would be our horror if we could descend into the hideous catacombs below the surface of the earth, 'some filled with smoak and fire, some with water, and some with vapours and mouldy Air'; if we saw all this, 'we should not easily believe that God created it into this form immediately out of nothing; It would have cost no more to have made things in better order; nay, it had been more easie and more simple; and accordingly we are assured that all things were made at first in Beauty and proportion.' *

Or again, consider the sea: how aesthetically unsatisfying is its arrangement! How unlike what we should have supposed to be the taste of the divine artificer in world-planning!

If the Sea had been drawn round the Earth in regular figures and borders, it might have been a great Beauty to our Globe, and we should have reasonably concluded it a work of the first Creation, or of Nature's first production; but finding on the contrary all the marks of disorder and disproportion in it, we may as reasonably conclude, that it did not belong to the first order of things, but was something succedaneous, when the degeneracy of mankind, and the judgements of God had destroy'd the first World, and subjected the Creation to some kind of Vanity. †

And the very idea of the ocean-bed, with all its slimy circumstance, fills Burnet with disgust; such things must not be put down to divine omnipotence. 'Nature doth not fall into disorder till mankind be first degenerate and leads the way.' Occasionally, it is true, Burnet slips into a mood of admiration even of our lost planet, and he writes then more in the tone of a *Spectator*-reverie on the Sublime or on the ruins of antiquity. Mountains, for example, move him strongly (and perhaps rather unexpectedly), and he gives us a passage which Derham could quote in support of his own very different argument:

The greatest objects of Nature are, methinks, the most pleasing to behold; and next to the great Concave of the Heavens, and those boundless Regions where the Stars inhabit, there is nothing that I look upon with more pleasure than the wide Sea and the Mountains of the Earth. There is something august and stately in the Air of these things that inspires the mind with great thoughts and passions; We do naturally upon such occasions think of God, and his greatness, and whatsoever hath but the shadow and appearance of Infinite, as all things have that are too big for our comprehension, they fill and over-bear the mind with their Excess, and cast it into a pleasing kind of stupor and admiration. ‡

Almost all that Addison, Gray, Burke, or even Wordsworth could claim for mountains, one might reflect. Yet this mood, so akin, apparently, to that in which Gray wrote of Gordale Scar or 'that huge creature of God Ingleborough', soon deserts him, and he returns to his point. The mountains are majestic ruins, and he receives from them only a sense of awe 'as from old Temples and broken Amphitheaters of the Romans we collect the greatness of that people'. Burnet has crossed the Alps and the Apennines, and the sight of 'those wild, vast and indigested heaps of Stones and Earth' seems to have been what first set him upon devising a theory to account for such prodigies. Apparently there were no

---

* *Theory of the Earth*, p. 125.   † ibid., p. 129.   ‡ ibid, p. 139.

6

'physical' maps in those days—only 'political', for Burnet deplores the absence of the former. He also desiderates rough Globes (i.e. with mountains shown in relief) instead of the smooth ones used in the schools, for then we should see 'what a rude lump our World is which we are so apt to dote upon'.

How, then, was the world formed when fresh from the hands of God? and how did it fall into its present state? Burnet's answers to these questions may be briefly indicated for the sake of their 'period' interest. When the earth was formed from chaos the elements were arranged in their 'proper' order, with Earth as the centre, surrounded by the Water and this in turn by the Air. 'Water', however, includes all fluids, and consequently the watery surface of the globe had a top coating of oil. Further, before the process of creation had quite settled down, the air was full of particles of dust—earthy matter which had not yet found its true location. All this sifted down, and formed a thick crust by mixing with the oily matter on the surface. This became the first crust of the world, and was absolutely smooth, as befitted the paradise which God had designed for man. Paradise was not confined to one spot of ground; it covered the whole earth. Burnet refutes with great composure and surprising resourcefulness all the possible scientific objections which might be raised against his theory. The earth was originally in a 'right posture' to the sun, and so it enjoyed perpetual equinox. How was the earth watered, if there were no seas and no mountains? Vapours arose, he replies, from the waters below the crust, passed through the surface into the air, and then condensed at the Poles. Thence the precipitated water ran in radiating streams towards the equator (why? because the earth being slightly oval, the Poles were 'higher' than the equator) and there evaporated. In this beautifully geometrical world, then so much worthier of its divine original than the 'torn troubled form we know' today, man lived awhile in peace and innocence, enjoying the tranquil climate and attaining great longevity. This was the true Golden Age dreamed of by the poets, and Burnet, like all 'primitivists' who have sung or discoursed of such an age, tells us that it was a time of 'great easiness and simplicity', whereas now we have to endure 'a more pompous, forc'd and artificial method'. Let no one think this paradise fabulous or 'unnatural': 'Tis we that have left the tract of Nature, that are wrought and screw'd up into artifices, that have disguis'd our selves; and 'tis in our World that the Scenes are chang'd, and become more strange and fantastical. *

What, then, of the cataclysm which shattered this spherical and world-wide Eden? It was the Flood, of course, which produced the heavy change; that must be unquestioned. But it is precisely here that Burnet produces his most triumphant pseudo-scientific hypothesis. The Flood? Yes; but Burnet, strongly tinged with the scientific curiosity of his age, is dissatisfied with what Browne had called the 'popular exposition of Moses'. Assuming that the earth was in its present state at that time, how could the available waters have covered the earth, even granting the most torrential downpour of rain throughout the specified forty days and nights? It was inconceivable; there was simply not enough water for the purpose. What really happened was this: in the fulness of time the earth's crust, which had

* ibid, p. 249.

been imperceptibly drying and shrinking through the patriarchal period, began to crack. And when sin had gathered sufficient head, parts of the crust collapsed and fell inwards upon the waters below, forcing them out over all the earth. Here, says Burnet, is the true explanation of that mysterious phrase 'the fountains of the great deep were opened'—a phrase insufficiently regarded by the holders of the rainfall theory. When the force of the convulsion had abated, and the water found its level again, the world was left as we now see it, the collapsed portions constituting the ocean-beds, and the rest the dry land with its fretted coast-lines and broken surfaces. The blend in Burnet of the theologian and the follower of the 'new philosophy' is well seen in his ingenious way of linking together the laws of matter and the decrees of God. How was the world ruined? By the operation of natural causes which, one might suppose, would have produced their result even if man had retained his first innocence. But the things which come to pass in the ordinary course of Nature are no less 'providential' than special interpositions; on the contrary, the regular mechanism of second causes is the best evidence of God's wisdom. And Burnet actually postulates a kind of pre-established harmony between the material and the moral worlds:

This seems to me to be the great Art of Divine Providence, so to adjust the two Worlds, Humane and Natural, Material and Intellectual, as seeing through the possibilities and futuritions of each, according to the first state and circumstances he puts them under, they should all along correspond and fit one another, and especially in their great Crises and Periods. *

For once at least, it would seem, disproportion'd sin chimed punctually with Nature's crash.

Burnet's eschatology (Books III and IV, 'The Burning of the World' and 'The New Heavens and New Earth') may be mentioned, in conclusion, to complete the picture. The last conflagration, like the Flood, will have natural causes. All the volcanoes and more will vomit at once, aided by 'fiery meteors' from above. And if you desire further inflammable material, consider 'our British Soyl', which contains so much coal that England will be a particularly hot corner when the catastrophe arrives. The fire will, however, *begin* at Rome, as being the seat of Antichrist. After the fire, the precipitation of the elements from the vast smoke-cloud begins, and the original paradisal earth is reproduced. The thousand years' reign of Christ and the Saints follows (Satan being in chains), and at the end of this period Gog and Magog, and the 'earth-born' (a second race produced from the new Earth), will arise in a final conflict, in which Satan and the giants will be destroyed, and the saints translated to heaven. The Earth will become a fixed star.

This theory, of which its author seems justly proud, carried many difficulties in its wake, but Burnet tackles them all with that intrepidity which later brought his orthodoxy into suspicion and lost him his Clerkship to William III. For instance, how does he account for the diffusion of Noah's progeny after the Flood? How was America peopled from Ararat? Perhaps each continent had its Noah's Ark, he replies; we may only have been apprised by Moses of the particular Ark which concerns our own part of the world. He is excused by his

* *Theory of the Earth*, p. 107

own theory from assuming more than one Adam, though he is ready to surmise that other planets have had their floods, and so, presumably, their original sins. But the point which, when later developed in his *Archaeologiae philosophicae* (1692), cost him his preferment, is already touched upon in the *Review* of the *Theory* (dated 1690). What explanation was to be offered to anyone who should object that, after all, Moses described a terraqueous globe, and not Burnet's paradise? Moses, replies Burnet, did not 'Philosophize or Astronomize in that description'; ''tis a narration suited to the capacity of the people, and not to the strict and physical nature of things.' Moses must be interpreted so as not to be 'repugnant to clear and uncontested science'. ''Tis a dangerous thing to ingage the authority of Scripture in disputes about the Natural World, in opposition to Reason, lest Time, which brings all things to light, should discover that to be evidently false which we had made Scripture to assert.' * This argument (no new one even in Burnet's time) was worthy, one may feel, of a better kind of 'science' than Burnet's.

BASIL WILLEY

* ibid., Preface.

PUBLISHER'S NOTE:—All plates and cuts appearing in this book have been taken from the 1690/91 edition. The orthography of the original has in general been retained, but indisputable errors, omissions, etcetera, have been corrected.

THE
THEORY
OF THE
EARTH:

Containing an Account

OF THE

Original of the Earth,

AND OF ALL THE

GENERAL CHANGES

Which it hath already undergone,

OR

IS TO UNDERGO

Till the CONSUMMATION of all Things.

THE TWO FISRT BOOKS

Concerning The DELUGE,

AND

Concerning PARADISE.

The Second Edition.

LONDON,

Printed by *R. Norton,* for *Walter Kettilby,* at the Bishops-
Head in S. *Paul*'s Church-Yard, 1 6 9 1.

TO THE

TO THE
KING'S
MOST
Excellent Majesty

SIR,

*N*EW-*found Lands and Countries accrew to the Prince, whose Subject makes the first Discovery; And having retriev'd a World that had been lost, for some thousands of Years, out of the Memory of Man, and the Records of Time, I thought it my Duty to lay it at Your Majesty's Feet. 'Twill not enlarge Your Dominions, 'tis past and gone; nor dare I say it will enlarge Your Thoughts; But I hope it may gratifie Your Princely curiosity to read the Description of it, and see the Fate that attended it.*

We have still the broken Materials of that first World, and walk upon its Ruines; while it stood, there was the Seat of Paradise, *and the Scenes of the* Golden Age; *when it fell, it made the Deluge; And this unshapen Earth we now inhabit, is the Form it was found in when the Waters had retir'd, and the dry Land appear'd. These things, Sir, I propose and presume to prove in the following Treatise, which I willingly submit to Your Majesty's Judgment and Censure; being very well satisfied, that if I had sought a Patron in all the List of Kings, Your Contemporaries: Or in the Roll of Your Nobles, of either Order: I could not have found a more competent Judge in a Speculation of this Nature. Your Majesty's Sagacity, and happy Genius for Natural History, for Observations and Remarks upon the Earth, the Heavens, and the Sea, is a better preparation for Inquiries of this kind, than all the dead Learning of the Schools.*

Sir, This Theory, in the full extent of it, is to reach to the last Period of the Earth, and the End of all things; But this first Volume takes in only so much as is already past, from the Origin of the Earth, to this present time and state of Nature. To describe in like manner the Changes and Revolutions of Nature that are to come, and see thorough all succeeding Ages, will require a steddy and attentive Eye, and a retreat from the noise of the World; Especially so to connect the parts, and present them all under one view, that we may see, as in a Mirrour, the several faces of Nature, from First to Last, throughout all the Circle of Successions.

Your Majesty having been pleas'd to give encouragement to this Translation, I humbly present it to Your Gracious Acceptance. And 'tis our Interest, as well as Duty, in Disquisitions of this Nature, to Address our selves to Your Majesty, as the Defender of our Philosophick *Liberties; against those that would usurp upon the*

Fundamental priviledge and Birth-right of Mankind, The Free use of Reason. *Your Majesty hath always appear'd the Royal Patron of Learning and the Sciences, and 'tis suitable to the Greatness of a Princely Spirit, to favour and promote whatsoever tends to the enlargement of Humane Knowledge, and the improvement of Humane Nature. To be Good and Gracious, and a Lover of Knowledge, are, methinks, two of the most amiable things in this World; And that Your Majesty may always bear that Character, in present and future Ages, and after a long and prosperous Reign, enjoy a blessed Immortality, is the constant Prayer of*

Your MAJESTY'S

Most Humble and most

Obedient Subject,

THOMAS BURNET.

PREFACE
TO THE
READER

HAVING given an account of this whole Work in the first Chapter, and of the method of either Book, whereof this Volume consists, in their proper places, there remains not much to be said here to the Reader. This Theory of the Earth may be call'd *Sacred*, because it is not the common Physiology of the Earth, or of the Bodies that compose it, but respects only the great Turns of Fate, and the Revolutions of our Natural World; such as are taken notice of in the Sacred Writings, and are truly the Hinges upon which the Providence of this Earth moves; or whereby it opens and shuts the several successive Scenes whereof it is made up. This *English* Edition is the same in substance with the *Latin*, though, I confess, 'tis not so properly a Translation, as a new Composition upon the same ground, there being several additional Chapters in it, and several new-moulded.

As every Science requires a peculiar Genius, so likewise there is a Genius peculiarly improper for every one; and as to Philosophy, which is the Contemplation of the works of Nature, and the Providence that governs them, there is no temper or Genius, in my mind, so improper for it, as that which we call a *mean* and *narrow Spirit*; and which the *Greeks* call *Littleness of Soul*. This is a defect in the first make of some Men's minds, which can scarce ever be corrected afterwards, either by Learning or Age. And as Souls that are made little and incapacious cannot enlarge their thoughts to take in any great compass of Times or Things; so what is beyond their compass, or above their reach, they are apt to look upon as Fantastical, or at least would willingly have it pass for such in the World. Now as there is nothing so great, so large, so immense, as the works of Nature, and the methods of Providence, men of this complexion must needs be very unfit for the contemplation of them. Who would set a purblind man at the top of the Mast to discover Land? or upon an high Tower to draw a Landskip of the Country round about? for the same reason, short-sighted minds are unfit to make Philosophers, whose proper business it is to discover and describe in comprehensive Theories the *Phænomena* of the World, and the Causes of them.

This original disease of the Mind is seldom cur'd by Learning, which cures many others; 'Tis like a fault in the first *Stamina* of the Body, which cannot easily be rectified afterwards. 'Tis a great mistake to think that every sort of Learning makes a Man a competent Judge of Natural Speculations; We see unhappy examples to the contrary amongst the Christian Fathers, and particularly in St. *Austin*, who was unquestionably a Man of Parts and Learning, but interposing in a controversie where his Talent did not lie, show'd his zeal against the

Antipodes to very ill purpose, though he drew his Reasons partly from Scripture. And if within a few Years, or in the next Generation, it should prove as certain and demonstrable, that the *Earth is mov'd*, as it is now, that there are *Antipodes*; those that have been zealous against it, and ingag'd the Scripture in the Controversie, would have the same reason to repent of their forwardness, that St. *Austin* would have now, if he was alive. 'Tis a dangerous thing to ingage the authority of Scripture in disputes about the Natural World, in opposition to Reason; lest Time, which brings all things to light, should discover that to be evidently false which we had made Scripture to assert: And I remember St. *Austin* in his Exposition upon *Genesis*, hath laid down a rule to this very purpose, though he had the unhappiness, it seems, not to follow it always himself. The reason also, which he gives there for his rule, is very good and substantial: *For, saith He, *if the Unbelievers or Philosophers shall certainly know us to be mistaken, and to erre in those things that concern the Natural World, and see that we alledge our (Sacred) Books for such vain opinions, how shall they believe those same Books when they tell them of the RESURRECTION of the Dead, and the World to come, if they find them to be fallaciously writ in such things as lie within their certain knowledge?*

We are not to suppose that any truth concerning the Natural World can be an Enemy to Religion; for Truth cannot be an Enemy to Truth, God is not divided against himself; and therefore we ought not upon that account to condemn or censure what we have not examin'd or cannot disprove; as those that are of this narrow Spirit we are speaking of, are very apt to do. Let every thing be tri'd and examin'd in the first place, whether it be *True* or *False*; and if it be found false, 'tis then to be consider'd, whether it be such a falsity as is prejudicial to Religion or no. But for every new Theory that is propos'd, to be alarum'd, as if all Religion was falling about our Ears, is to make the World suspect that we are very ill assur'd of the foundation it stands upon. Besides, do not all Men complain, even These as well as others, of the great ignorance of Mankind? how little we know, and how much is still unknown? and can we ever know more, unless something new be Discover'd? It cannot be old when it comes first to light, when first invented, and first propos'd. If a Prince should complain of the poorness of his Exchequer, and the scarcity of Money in his Kingdom, would he be angry with his Merchants, if they brought him home a *Cargo* of good Bullion, or a Mass of Gold out of a foreign Countrey? and give this reason only for it, *He* would have no *new Silver*; neither should any be Currant in his Dominions but what had his own Stamp and Image upon it: How should this Prince or his People grow rich? To complain of want, and yet refuse all offers of a supply, looks very sullen, or very fantastical.

I might mention also upon this occasion another Genius and disposition in Men, which often makes them improper for Philosophical Contemplations; not so

---

* *Gen. ad lit. lib.* 1, *c.* 19. *Plerumque accidit ut aliquid de Terrâ, de Cœlo, de cæteris hujus mundi elementis, &c. Cùm enim quenquam Christianorum in eâ re quam optimé nôrunt, errare deprehenderint, & vanam sententiam suam ex nostris libris asserere, quo pacto illis libris credituri sunt de Resurrectione Mortuorum, & spe vita æternæ regnóque cælorum, quando de his rebus quas jam experiri vel indubitatis numeris percipere potuerunt, fallaciter putaverint esse conscriptos?*

much, it may be, from the narrowness of their Spirit and Understanding, as because they will not take time to extend them. I mean Men of Wit and Parts, but of short Thoughts, and little Meditation, and that are apt to distrust every thing for a Fancy or Fiction that is not the dictate of Sense, or made out immediately to their Senses. Men of this Humour and Character call such Theories as these, Philosophick Romances, and think themselves witty in the expression; They allow them to be pretty amusements of the Mind, but without Truth or reality. I am afraid if an Angel should write the Theory of the Earth, they would pass the same judgment upon it; Where there is variety of Parts in a due Contexture, with something of surprising aptness in the harmony and correspondency of them, this they call a Romance; but such Romances must all Theories of Nature, and of Providence be, and must have every part of that Character with advantage, if they be well represented. There is in them, as I may so say, a *Plot* or *Mystery* pursued through the whole Work, and certain Grand Issues or Events upon which the rest depend, or to which they are subordinate; but these things we do not make or contrive our selves, but find and discover them, being made already by the Great Author and Governour of the Universe: And when they are clearly discover'd, well digested, and well reason'd in every part, there is, methinks, more of beauty in such a Theory, at least a more masculine beauty, than in any Poem or Romance; And that solid truth that is at the bottom, gives a satisfaction to the Mind, that it can never have from any Fiction, how artificial soever it be.

To enter no farther upon this matter, 'tis enough to observe, that when we make Judgments and Censures upon general presumptions and prejudices, they are made rather from the temper and model of our own Spirits, than from Reason; And therefore, if we would neither impose upon ourselves, nor others, we must lay aside that lazy and fallacious method of Censuring by the Lump, and must bring things close to the test of *True* or *False*, to explicit proof and evidence; And whosoever makes such Objections against an *Hypothesis*, hath a right to be heard, let his Temper and Genius be what it will. Neither do we intend that any thing we have said here, should be understood in another sence.

To conclude, This Theory being writ with a sincere intention to justifie the Doctrines of the *Universal Deluge*, and of a *Paradisiacal* state, and protect them from the Cavils of those that are no well-wishers to Sacred History, upon that account it may reasonably expect fair usage and acceptance with all that are well-dispos'd; And it will also be, I think, a great satisfaction to them to see those pieces of most ancient History, which have been chiefly preserv'd in Scripture, confirm'd anew, and by another Light, that of Nature and Philosophy; and also freed from those misconceptions or misrepresentations which made them sit uneasie upon the Spirits even of the best Men, that took time to think. Lastly, In things purely Speculative, as these are, and no ingredients of our Faith, it is free to differ from one another in our Opinions and Sentiments; and so I remember St. *Austin* hath observ'd upon this very subject of *Paradise*; Wherefore as we desire to give no offence our selves, so neither shall we take any at the difference of Judgment in others; provided this liberty be mutual, and that we all agree to study *Peace, Truth*, and a *good Life*.

CONTENTS
OF THE
CHAPTERS

THE FIRST BOOK

CHAPTER I

THE Introduction; An account of the whole Work, of the extent and general Order of it.

CHAPTER II

A general account of Noah's *Flood. A computation what quantity of Water would be necessary for the making of it; That the common Opinion and Explication of that Flood is not intelligible.*

CHAPTER III

All Evasions concerning the Flood answered; That there was no new Creation of Waters at the Deluge; and that it was not particular or National, but extended throughout the whole Earth. A prelude and preparation to the true account and explication of it. The method of the first Book.

CHAPTER IV

That the Earth and Mankind had an Original, and were not from Eternity; Prov'd against Aristotle. *The first proposition of our Theory laid down, viz. That the Ante-diluvian Earth was of a different Form and Construction from the present. This is prov'd from Divine Authority, and from the Nature and Form of the Chaos, out of which the Earth was made.*

CHAPTER V

The Second Proposition is laid down, viz. That the face of the Earth before the Deluge was smooth, regular and uniform; without Mountains, and without a Sea. *The Chaos out of which the World rise is fully examin'd, and all its motions observ'd, and by what steps it wrought it self into an habitable World. Some things in Antiquity relating to the first state of the Earth are interpreted, and some things in the Sacred Writings. The Divine Art and Geometry in the construction of the first Earth is observ'd and celebrated.*

CHAPTER VI

The Dissolution of the First Earth: The Deluge ensuing thereupon. And the form of the present Earth rising from the Ruines of the First.

CHAPTER VII

That the Explication we have given of an Universal Deluge is not an IDEA only, but an account of what really came to pass in the Earth, and the true explication of Noah's Flood. An examination of Tehom-Rabba, or the Great Abysse, and that by it the Sea cannot be understood, nor the Subterraneous Waters as they are at present; What the true Notion and Form of it was, collected from Moses and other Sacred Writers. Observations on Deucalion's Deluge.

CHAPTER VIII

The particular History of Noah's Flood is explain'd in all the material parts and circumstances of it, according to the preceding Theory. Any seeming difficulties remov'd, and the whole Section concluded with a Discourse how far the Deluge may be lookt upon as the effect of an Ordinary Providence, and how far of an Extraordinary.

CHAPTER IX

The Second Part of this Discourse, proving the same Theory from the Effects and the present Form of the Earth. First, by a general Scheme of what is most remarkable in this Globe, and then by a more particular induction; beginning with an account of Subterraneous Cavities and Subterraneous Waters.

CHAPTER X

Concerning the Chanel of the Sea, and the Original of it; The causes of its irregular form and unequal depths: As also of the Original of Islands, their situation, and other properties.

CHAPTER XI

Concerning the Mountains of the Earth, their greatness and irregular Form, their Situation, Causes and Origin.

CHAPTER XII

A short review of what hath been already treated of, and in what manner. All methods, whether Philosophical or Theological, that have been offer'd by others for the explication of the Form of the Earth, are examin'd and refuted. A conjecture concerning the other Planets, their Natural Form and State compar'd with ours; Especially concerning Jupiter and Saturn.

THE SECOND BOOK

CHAPTER I

THE Introduction and Contents of the Second Book. The general state of the Primæval Earth, and of Paradise.

CHAPTER II

The great change of the World since the Flood from what it was in the first Ages. The Earth under its present Form could not be Paradisiacal, nor any part of it.

CHAPTER III

The Original differences of the Primitive Earth from the present Post-diluvian. The three Characters of Paradise and the Golden Age found in the Primitive Earth. A particular explication of each Character.

CHAPTER IV

A Digression, concerning the Natural Causes of Longævity. That the Machine of an Animal consists of Springs, and which are the two principal. The Age of the Ante-diluvians to be computed by Solar, not Lunar Years.

CHAPTER V

Concerning the Waters of the Primitive Earth: What the state of the Regions of the Air was then, and how all Waters proceeded from them. How the Rivers arose, what was their Course, and how they ended. Several things in Sacred Writ that confirm this Hydrography of the first Earth, especially the Post-diluvian Origin of the Rain-bow.

CHAPTER VI

A Recollection and review of what hath been said concerning the Primitive Earth, with a more full Survey of the state of the first World, Natural and Civil, and the comparison of it with the present World.

CHAPTER VII

Concerning the place of Paradise; It cannot be determin'd from the Theory only, nor from Scripture only; What the sense of Antiquity was concerning it, as to the Jews and Heathens, and especially as to the Christian Fathers; That they generally plac'd it out of this Continent, in the Southern Hemisphere.

CHAPTER VIII

The uses of this Theory for the illustration of Antiquity; The Chaos of the Ancients explain'd; The inhabitability of the Torrid Zone; The change of the Poles of the World; The Doctrine of the Mundane Egg; How America was first peopled; How Paradise within the Circle of the Moon.

CHAPTER IX

A general Objection against this Theory, viz. That if there had been such a Primitive Earth, *as we pretend, the fame of it would have sounded throughout all Antiquity. The Eastern and Western Learning consider'd, the most considerable Records of both are lost; what foot steps remain relating to this subject. The Jewish and Christian Learning consider'd, how far lost as to this Argument, and what Notes or Traditions remain. Lastly, How far the Sacred Writings bear witness to it. The Providential conduct of Knowledge in the World. A Recapitulation and state of the Theory.*

CHAPTER X

Concerning the AUTHOR *of* NATURE.

CHAPTER XI

Concerning Natural Providence. *Several misrepresentations of it, and false methods of Contemplation; Preparatives to the true Method, and a true representation of the Universe. The Mundane* Idea, *and the Universal System of Providence; Several subordinate Systems, That of our Earth and Sublunary World; The Course and Periods of it; How much of this is already treated of, and what remains. Conclusion.*

THE
THEORY
OF THE
EARTH

Book I
Concerning the Deluge, and the Dissolution of the Earth.

CHAPTER I

THE INTRODUCTION
An Account of the whole Work; of the Extent and general Order of it.

SINCE I was first inclin'd to the Contemplation of Nature, and took pleasure to trace out the Causes of Effects, and the dependance of one thing upon another in the visible Creation, I had always, methought, a particular curiosity to look back into the first Sources and ORIGINAL of Things; and to view in my mind, so far as I was able, the Beginning and Progress of a RISING WORLD.

And after some Essays of this Nature, and, as I thought, not unsuccessful, I carried on my enquiries further, to try whether this *Rising World*, when form'd and finisht, would continue always the same; in the same form, structure, and consistency; or what changes it would successively undergo, by the continued action of the same Causes that first produc'd it; And, lastly, what would be its final Period and Consummation. This whole Series and compass of things taken together, I call'd a COURSE OF NATURE, or a SYSTEM OF NATURAL PROVIDENCE; and thought there was nothing belonging to the External World more fit or more worthy our study and meditation, nor any thing that would conduce more to discover the ways of Divine Providence, and to show us the grounds of all true knowledge concerning Nature. And therefore to clear up the several parts of this Theory, I was willing to lay aside a great many other Speculations, and all those dry subtleties with which the Schools, and the Books of Philosophers, are usually fill'd.

But when we speak of a *Rising World*, and the Contemplation of it, we do not mean this of the *Great Universe*; for who can describe the Original of that? But we speak of the *Sublunary World*, This Earth and its dependencies, which rose out of a Chaos about six thousand years ago; And seeing it hath faln to our lot to act upon this Stage, to have our present home and residence here, it seems most reasonable, and the place design'd by Providence, where we should first imploy our thoughts to understand the works of God and Nature. We have accordingly therefore design'd in this Work to give an account of the Original of the Earth, and of all the great and general changes that it hath already undergone, or is hence forwards to undergo, till the Consummation of all things. For if from those Principles we have here taken, and that Theory we have begun in these two first Books, we can deduce with success and clearness the Origin of the Earth, and those States of it that are already past; Following the same Thred, and by the conduct of the same Theory, we will pursue its Fate and History through future Ages, and mark all the great Changes and Conversions that attend it *while Day and Night shall last*; that is, so long as it continues an Earth.

By the States of the Earth that are already past, we understand chiefly *Paradise* and the *Deluge*; Names well known, and as little known in their Nature. By the Future States we understand the *Conflagration*, and what new Order of Nature may follow upon that, till the whole Circle of Time and Providence be compleated. As to the first and past States of the Earth, we shall have little help from the Ancients, or from any of the Philosophers, for the discovery or description of them; We must often tread unbeaten paths, and make a way where we do not find one; but it shall be always with a Light in our hand, that we may see our steps, and that those that follow us may not follow us blindly. There is no Sect of Philosophers that I know of that ever gave an account of the Universal Deluge, or discover'd, from the contemplation of the Earth, that there had been such a thing already in Nature. 'Tis true, they often talk of an alternation of *Deluges* and *Conflagrations* in this Earth, but they speak of them as things to come; at least they give no proof or argument of any that hath already destroyed the World. As to *Paradise*, it seems to be represented to us by the *Golden Age*; whereof the Ancients tell many stories, sometimes very luxuriant, and sometimes very defective: For they did not so well understand the difference betwixt the New-made Earth and the Present, as to see what were the just grounds of the Golden Age, or of Paradise: Tho' they had many broken Notions concerning those things. As to the *Conflagration* in particular, This hath always been reckon'd One amongst the Opinions or Dogmata of the Stoicks, *That the World was to be destroy'd by Fire*, and their Books are full of this Notion; but yet they do not tell us the Causes of the Conflagration, nor what preparations there are in Nature, or will be, towards that great Change. And we may generally observe this of the *Ancients*, that their Learning or Philosophy consisted more in Conclusions, than in Demonstrations; They had many truths among them, whereof they did not know themselves the premisses or the proofs: Which is an argument to me, that the knowledge they had, was not a thing of their own invention, or which they came to by fair reasoning and observations upon Nature, but was delivered to them from others by Tradition and Ancient fame, sometimes more publick, sometimes more secret: These Conclusions they kept in mind, and communicated to those of their School, or Sect, or Posterity, without knowing, for the most part, the just grounds and reasons of them.

'Tis the Sacred writings of Scripture that are the best monuments of Antiquity, and to those we are chiefly beholden for the History of the first Ages, whether Natural History or Civil. 'Tis true, the Poets, who were the most ancient Writers amongst the *Greeks*, and serv'd them both for Historians, Divines, and Philosophers, have deliver'd some things concerning the first Ages of the World, that have a fair resemblance of truth, and some affinity with those accounts that are given of the same things by sacred Authors, and these may be of use in due time and place; but yet, lest any thing fabulous should be mixt with them, as commonly there is, we will never depend wholly upon their credit, nor assert any thing upon the authority of the Ancients which is not first prov'd by natural Reason, or warranted by Scripture.

It seems to me very reasonable to believe, that besides the precepts of Religion, which are the principal subject and design of the Books of holy Scripture, there may be providentially conserv'd in them the memory of things and times so remote, as could not be retriev'd, either by History, or by the light of Nature; and yet were of great importance to be known, both for their own excellency, and also to rectifie the knowledge of men in other things consequential to them: Such points may be, *Our great Epocha* or the Age of the Earth, The Origination of mankind, The first and Paradisiacal state, The destruction of the Old World by an universal Deluge, The longevity of its inhabitants, The manner of their preservation, and of their peopling the Second Earth; and lastly, The Fate and Changes it is to undergo. These I always lookt upon as the Seeds of great knowledge, or heads of Theories fixt on purpose to give us aim and direction how to pursue the rest that depend upon them. But these heads, you see, are of a mixt order, and we propose to our selves in this Work only such as belong to the Natural World; upon which I believe the trains of Providence are generally laid; And we must first consider how God hath order'd Nature, and then now the Oeconomy of the Intellectual World is adapted to it; for of these two parts consists the full System of Providence. In the mean time, what subject can be more worthy the thoughts of any serious person, than to view and consider the Rise and Fall, and all the Revolutions, not of a Monarchy or an Empire, of the *Grecian* or *Roman* State, but of an intire World.

The obscurity of these things, and their remoteness from common knowledge will be made an argument by some, why we should not undertake them; And by others, it may be, the very same thing will be made an argument why we should; for my part I think *There is nothing so secret that shall not be brought to Light*, within the compass of *Our World*; for we are not to understand that of the whole Universe, nor of all Eternity, our capacities do not extend so far; But whatsoever concerns this Sublunary World in the whole extent of its duration, from the Chaos to the last period, this I believe Providence hath made us capable to understand, and will in its due time make it known. All I say, betwixt the first Chaos and the last Completion of Time and all things temporary, This was given to the disquisitions of men; On either hand is Eternity, before the World and after, which is without our reach: But that little spot of ground that lies betwixt those two great Oceans, this we are to cultivate, this we are Masters of, herein we are to exercise our thoughts, to understand and lay open the treasures of the Divine Wisdom and Goodness hid in this part of Nature and of Providence.

As for the difficulty or obscurity of an argument, that does but add to the pleasure of contesting with it, when there are hopes of victory; and success does more than recompence all the pains. For there is no sort of joy more grateful to the mind of man, than that which ariseth from the invention of Truth; especially when 'tis hard to come by. Every man hath a delight suited to his Genius, and as there is pleasure in the right exercise of any faculty, so especially in that of Right-reasoning; which is still the greater, by how much the consequences are more clear, and the chains of them more long: There is no Chase so pleasant, methinks, as to drive a Thought, by good conduct, from one end of the World to the other; and never to lose sight of it till it fall into Eternity, where all things are lost as to our knowledge.

This Theory being chiefly Philosophical, Reason is to be our first Guide; and where that falls short, or any other just occasion offers itself, we may receive further light and confirmation from the Sacred writings. Both these are to be lookt upon as of Divine Original, God is the Author of both; He that made the Scripture made also our Faculties, and 'twere a reflection upon the Divine Veracity, for the one or the other to be false when rightly us'd. We must therefore be careful and tender of opposing these to one another, because that is, in effect, to oppose God to himself. As for Antiquity and the Testimonies of the Ancients, we only make general reflections upon them, for illustration rather than proof of what we propose; not thinking it proper for an English Treatise to multiply citations out of Greek or Latin Authors.

I am very sensible it will be much our interest, that the Reader of this Theory should be of an ingenuous and unprejudic'd temper; neither does it so much require Book-learning and Scholarship, as good natural sence to distinguish *True* and *False*, and to discern what is well prov'd, and what is not. It often happens that Scholastick Education, like a Trade, does so fix a man in a particular way, that he is not fit to judge of any thing that lies out of that way; and so his Learning becomes a clog to his natural parts, and makes him more indocile, and more incapable of new thoughts and new improvements, than those that have only the Talents of Nature. As Masters of exercise had rather take a Scholar that never learn'd before, than one that hath had a bad Master; so generally one would rather chuse a Reader without art, than one ill-instructed; with learning, but opinionative and without judgment: yet it is not necessary they should want either, and Learning well plac'd strengthens all the powers of the mind. To conclude, just reasoning and a generous love of Truth, whether with or without Erudition, is that which makes us most competent Judges what is true; and further than this, in the perusal and examination of this Work, as to the Author as much candor as you please, but as to the Theory we require nothing but attention and impartiality.

CHAPTER II

A general account of Noah's *Flood; A computation what quantity of Water would be necessary for the making of it; that the common Opinion and Explication of that Flood is not intelligible.*

'TIS now more than Five Thousand years since our World was made, and though it would be a great pleasure to the mind, to recollect and view at this distance those first Scenes of Nature: what the face of the Earth was when fresh and new, and how things differ'd from the state we now find them in, the speculation is so remote, that it seems to be hopeless, and beyond the reach of Humane Wit. We are almost the last Posterity of the first Men, and faln into the dying Age of the World; by what footsteps, or by what guide, can we trace back our way to those first Ages, and the first order of things? And yet, methinks, it is reasonable to believe, that Divine Providence, which sees at once throughout all the Ages of the World, should not be willing to keep Mankind finally and fatally ignorant of that part of Nature, and of the Universe, which is properly their Task and Province to manage and understand. We are the Inhabitants of the Earth, the Lords and Masters of it; and we are endow'd with Reason and Understanding; doth it not then properly belong to us to examine and unfold the works of God in this part of the Universe, which is faln to our lot, which is our heritage and habitation? And it will be found, it may be, upon a stricter Enquiry, that in the present form and constitution of the Earth, there are certain marks and Indications of its first State; with which if we compare those things that are recorded in Sacred History, concerning the first Chaos, Paradise, and an universal Deluge, we may discover, by the help of those Lights, what the Earth was in its first Original, and what Changes have since succeeded in it.

And though we shall give a full account of the Origin of the Earth in this Treatise, yet that which we have propos'd particularly for the Title and Subject of it, is to give an account of the primæval PARADISE, and of the universal DELUGE: Those being the two most important things that are explain'd by the Theory we propose. And I must beg leave in treating of these two, to change the order, and treat first of the Deluge, and then of Paradise: For though the State of Paradise doth precede that of the Flood in Sacred History, and in the nature of the thing, yet the explication of both will be more sensible, and more effectual, if we begin with the Deluge; there being more Observations and Effects, and those better known to us, that may be refer'd to this, than to the other; and the Deluge being once truly explain'd, we shall from thence know the form and Quality of the Ante-diluvian Earth. Let us then proceed to the explication of that great and fatal Inundation, whose History is well known; and according to *Moses*, the best of Historians, in a few words is this—

Sixteen Hundred and odd years after the Earth was made, and inhabited, it was over-flow'd, and destroy'd in a Deluge of water. Not a Deluge that was National only, or over-run some particular Country or Region, as *Judea* or *Greece*, or any other, but it overspread the face of the whole Earth, from Pole to Pole, and from East to West, and that in such excess, that the Floods over-reacht the Tops of the highest Mountains; the Rains descending after an unusual manner, and the fountains of the *Great Deep* being broke open; so as a general destruction and devastation was brought upon the Earth, and all things in it, Mankind and other living Creatures; excepting only *Noah* and his Family, who by a special Providence of God were preserv'd in a certain Ark, or Vessel made like a Ship, and such kinds of living Creatures as he took in to him. After these waters had rag'd for some time on the Earth, they began to lessen and shrink, and the great waves and fluctuations of this *Deep* or *Abysse*, being quieted by degrees, the waters retir'd into their Chanels and Caverns within the Earth; and the Mountains and Fields began to appear, and the whole habitable Earth in that form and shape wherein we now see it. Then the World began again, and from that little Remnant preserv'd in the Ark, the present race of Mankind, and of Animals, in the known parts of the Earth, were propagated. Thus perisht the old World, and the present arose from the ruines and remains of it.

This is a short story of the greatest thing that ever yet hapned in the world, the greatest revolution and the greatest change in Nature; and if we come to reflect seriously upon it, we shall find it extremely difficult, if not impossible, to give an account of the waters that compos'd this Deluge, whence they came or whither they went. If it had been only the Inundation of a Country, or of a Province, or of the greatest part of a Continent, some proportionable causes perhaps might have been found out; but a Deluge overflowing the whole Earth, the whole Circuit and whole Extent of it, burying all in water, even the greatest Mountains, in any known parts of the Universe, to find water sufficient for this Effect, as it is generally explained and understood, I think is impossible. And what we may the better judge of the whole matter, let us first compute how much water would be requisite for such a Deluge, or to lay the Earth, consider'd in its present form, and the highest Mountains, under water. Then let's consider whether such a quantity of water can be had out of all the stores that we know in Nature: And from these two we will take our Ground and Rise, and begin to reflect, whether the World hath not been hitherto mistaken in the common opinion and explication of the general Deluge.

To discover how much water would be requisite to make this Deluge, we must first suppose enough to cover the plain surface of the Earth, the Fields and lower Grounds; then we must heap up so much more upon this as will reach above the tops of the highest Mountains; so as drawing a Circle over the tops of the highest Mountains quite round the Earth, suppose from Pole to Pole, and another to meet it about the middle of the Earth, all that space or capacity contain'd within these Circles is to be fill'd up with water. This I confess will make a prodigious mass of water, and it looks frightfully to the imagination; 'tis huge and great, but 'tis extravagantly so, as a great Monster: It doth not look like the work of God or Nature: However let's compute a little more particularly how much this will amount to, or how many Oceans of water would be necessary to compose this great Ocean rowling in the Air, without bounds or banks.

If all the Mountains were par'd off the Earth, and so the surface of it lay even, or in an equal convexity every where with the surface of the Sea, from this surface of the Sea let us suppose that the height of the Mountains may be a mile and an half; or that we may not seem at all to favour our own opinion or calculation, let us take a mile only for the perpendicular height of the Mountains. Let us on the other side suppose the Sea to cover half the Earth, as 'tis generally believ'd to do; and the common depth of it, taking one place with another, to be about a quarter of a mile or 250 paces. I say, taking one place with another, for though the middle Chanel of the great Ocean be far deeper, we may observe, that there is commonly a descent or declivity from the shore to the middle part of the Chanel, so that one comes by degrees into the depth of it; and those shory parts are generally but some fathoms deep. Besides, in arms of the Sea, in Straits and among Islands, there is commonly no great depth, and some places are plain shallows. So as upon a moderate computation, one place compar'd with another, we may take a quarter of a mile, or about an hundred fathoms, for the common measure of the depth of the Sea, if it were cast into a Chanel of an equal depth every where. This being suppos'd, there would need four Oceans to lie upon this Ocean, to raise it up to the top of the Mountains, or so high as the waters of the Deluge rise; then four Oceans more to lie upon the Land, that the water there might swell to the same height; which together make eight Oceans for the proportion of the water requir'd in the Deluge.

'Tis true, there would not be altogether so much water requir'd for the Land as for the Sea, to raise them to an equal height; because Mountains and Hills would fill up part of that space upon the Land, and so make less water requisite. But to compensate this, and confirm our computation, we must consider in the first place, that we have taken a much less height of the Mountains than is requisite, if we respect the Mediterraneous Mountains, or those that are at a great distance from the Sea; For their height above the surface of the Sea, computing the declivity of the Land all along from the Mountains to the Sea-side (and that there is such a declivity is manifest from the course and descent of the Rivers) is far greater than the proportion we have taken: For the height of Mountains is usually taken from the foot of them, or from the next plain, which if it be far from the Sea, we may reasonably allow as much for the declension of the Land from that place to the Sea, as for the immediate height of the Mountain; So, for instance, the Mountains of the Moon in *Africa*, whence the *Nile* flows, and after a long course falls into the Mediterranean Sea by *Egypt*, are so much higher than the surface of that Sea, first, as the Ascent of the Land is from the Sea to the foot of the Mountains, and then as the height of the Mountains is from the bottom to the top: For both these are to be computed when you measure the height of a Mountain, or of a mountainous Land, in respect of the Sea: And the height of Mountains to the Sea being thus computed, there would be need of six or eight Oceans to raise the Sea alone as high as the highest In-land Mountains; And this is more than enough to compensate the less quantity of water that would be requisite upon the Land. Besides, we must consider the Regions of the Air upwards to be more capacious than a Region of the same thickness in or near the Earth, so as if an Ocean pour'd upon the surface of the dry Land, supposing it were all smooth, would rise to the height of half a quarter of a mile every where; the like quantity of water pour'd again at the height of the Mountains, would not have altogether the same effect, or would not there raise the mass half a quarter of a mile higher; for the surfaces of a Globe, the farther they are from their Center, are the greater; and so accordingly the Regions that belong to them. And, lastly, we must consider that there are some Countries or Valleys very low, and also many Caverns or Cavities within the Earth, all which in this case were to be first fill'd with water. These things being compar'd and estimated, we shall find that notwithstanding the room that Hills and Mountains take up on the dry Land, there would be at least eight Oceans requir'd, or a quantity of water eight times as great as the Ocean, to bring an universal Deluge upon the Earth, as that Deluge is ordinarily understood and explained.

The proportion of water for the Deluge being thus stated, the next thing to be done, is to enquire where this water is to be found; if any part of the Sublunary World will afford us so much: Eight Oceans floating in the Air, make a great bulk of water, I do not know what possible Sources to draw it from. There are the Clouds above, and the Deeps below, and in the bowels of the Earth; and these are all the stores we have for water; and *Moses* directs us to no other for the causes of the Deluge. *The Fountains* (he saith) *of the great Abysse were broken up, or burst asunder*, and the Rain descended for forty days, the *Cataracts* or *Floodgates* of Heaven being open'd. And in these two, no doubt, are contain'd the causes of the great Deluge, as according to *Moses*, so also according to reason and necessity; for our World affords no other treasures of water. Let us therefore consider how much this Rain of forty days might amount to, and how much might flow out of the Abysse, that so we may judge whether these two in conjunction would make up the Eight Oceans which we want.

As for the Rains, they would not afford us one Ocean, nor half an Ocean, nor the tenth part of an Ocean, if we may trust to the Observations made by others concerning the quantity of water that falls in Rain. *Mersennus* gives us this

Cog. Phys. Mech., p. 221.

account of it. "It appears by our Observations, that a Cubical Vessel of Brass, "whereof we made use, is fill'd an inch and an half in half an hours time; but "because that sucks up nothing of the moisture as the Earth doth, let us take an "inch for half an hours Rain; whence it follows, that in the space of 40 days and

At 4 feet in 24 hours.

"nights Rain, the waters in the Deluge would rise 160 feet, if the Rains were "constant and equal to ours, and that it rain'd at once throughout the face of the "whole Earth. But the Rain of the Deluge, saith he, should have been 90 times greater than this, to cover, for instance, the Mountains of *Armenia*, or to reach 15 Cubits above them. So that according to his computation, the 40 days Rain would supply little more than the hundredth part of the water requisite to make the Deluge. 'Tis true, he takes the heighth of the Mountains higher than we do; but, however, if you temper the Calculation on all sides as much as you please, the water that came by this Rain would be a very inconsiderable part of what was necessary for a Deluge. If it rain'd 40 days and 40 nights throughout the face of the whole Earth, in the Northern and Southern Hemisphere all at once, it might be sufficient to lay all the lower grounds under water, but it would signifie very little as to the overflowing of the Mountains. Whence another Author upon the

Auct. cat. in Gen. 7. 3.

same occasion hath this passage. "If the Deluge had been made by Rains only, "there would not have needed 40 days, but 40 years Rain to have brought it to "pass. And if we should suppose the whole middle Region condens'd into water, it would not at all have been sufficient for this effect, according to that proportion some make betwixt Air and Water; for they say, Air turn'd into Water takes up a hundred times less room than it did before. The truth is, we may reasonably suppose, that all the vapours of the middle Region were turn'd into water in this 40 days and 40 nights Rain, if we admit, that this Rain was throughout the whole

Earth at once, in either Hemisphere, in every Zone, in every Climate, in every Country, in every Province, in every Field; and yet we see what a small proportion all this would amount to.

Having done then with these Superiour Regions, we are next to examine the Inferiour, and the treasures of water that may be had there. *Moses* tells us, that the Fountains of the great Abysse were broke open, or *clove asunder*, as the word there us'd doth imply; and no doubt in this lay the great mystery of the Deluge, as will appear when it comes to be rightly understood and explain'd; but we are here to consider what is generally understood by the *great Abysse*, in the common explication of the Deluge; and 'tis commonly interpreted either to be the Sea, or Subterraneous waters hid in the bowels of the Earth: These, they say, broke forth and rais'd the waters, caus'd by the Rain, to such an height, that together they overflowed the highest Mountains. But whether or how this could be, deserves to be a little examin'd.

And in the first place; the Sea is not higher than the Land, as some have formerly imagin'd; fansying the Sea stood, as it were, upon a heap, higher than the shore; and at the Deluge a relaxation being made, it overflow'd the Land. But this conceit is so gross, and so much against reason and experience, that none I think of late have ventur'd to make use of it. And yet on the other hand, if the Sea lie in an equal convexity with the Land, or lower generally than the shore, and much more than the mid-land, as it is certainly known to do, what could the Sea contribute to the Deluge? It would keep its Chanel, as it doth now, and take up the same place. And so also the Subterraneous waters would lie quiet in their Cells; whatsoever Fountains or passages you suppose, these would not issue out upon the Earth, for water doth not ascend, unless by force. But let's imagine then that force us'd and appli'd, and the waters both of the Sea and Caverns under ground drawn out upon the surface of the Earth, we shall not be any whit the nearer for this; for if you take these waters out of their places, those places must be fill'd again with other waters in the Deluge; so as this turns to no account upon the whole. If you have two Vessels to fill, and you empty one to fill the other, you gain nothing by that, there still remains one Vessel empty; you cannot have these waters both in the Sea and on the Land, both above ground and under; nor can you suppose the Chanel of the Sea would stand gaping without water, when all the Earth was overflow'd, and the tops of the Mountains cover'd. And so for Subterraneous Cavities, if you suppose the water pumpt out, they would suck it in again when the Earth came to be laid under water; so that upon the whole, if you thus understand the *Abysse* or *great Deep*, and the breaking open its *Fountains* in this manner, it doth us no service as to the Deluge, and where we expected the greatest supply, there we find none at all.

What shall we do then? whither shall we go to find more than seven Oceans of water that we still want? We have been above and below; we have drain'd the whole middle Region, and we have examin'd the Deeps of the Earth; they must want for themselves, they say, if they give us any; And, besides, if the Earth should disgorge all the water that it hath in its bowels, it would not amount to above half an Ocean, which would not at all answer our occasions. Must we not then conclude, that the common explication of the Deluge makes it impossible ? there being no such quantity of water in Nature as they make requisite for an universal Deluge. Yet to give them all fair play, having examin'd the waters above the Earth, or in the Air, the waters upon the Earth, and the waters under the Earth; let us also consider if there be not waters above the Heavens, and if those might not be drawn down for the Deluge. *Moses* speaks of waters above the firmament, which though it be generally understood of the middle Region of the Air, especially as it was constituted before the Deluge, yet some have thought those to be waters plac'd above the highest Heavens, or Super-celestial waters: and have been willing to make use of them for a supply, when they could not find materials enough under the Heavens to make up the great mass of the Deluge. But the Heavens above, where these waters lay, are either solid, or fluid; if solid, as Glass or Crystal, how could the waters get through 'em to descend upon the Earth ? If fluid, as the Air or Æther, how could the waters rest upon them ? For Water is heavier than Air or Æther; So that I am afraid those pure Regions will prove no fit place for that Element, upon any account. But supposing these waters there, how imaginary soever, and that they were brought down to drown the World in that vast quantity that would be necessary, what became of them when the Deluge ceas'd ? Seven or eight Oceans of water, with the Earth wrapt up in the middle of them, how did it ever get quit of them ? how could they be dispos'd of when the Earth was to be dri'd, and the World renew'd ? It would be a hard task to lift them up again among the Spheres, and we have no room for them here below. The truth is, I mention this opinion of the Heavenly waters, because I would omit none that had ever been made use of to make good the common explication of the Deluge; but otherwise, I think, since the System of the World hath been better known, and the Nature of the Heavens, there are none that would seriously assert these Super-celestial waters, or, at least, make use of them so extravagantly, as to bring them down hither for causes of the Deluge.

We have now employ'd our last and utmost endeavours to find out waters for the vulgar Deluge, or for the Deluge as commonly understood; and you see with how little success; we have left no corner unsought, where there was any appearance or report of water to be found, and yet we have not been able to collect the eighth part of what was necessary upon a moderate account. May we not then with assurance conclude, that the World hath taken wrong measures hitherto in their notion and explication of the general Deluge ? They make it impossible and unintelligible upon a double account, both in requiring more water than can be found, and more than can be dispos'd of, if it was found: or could any way be withdrawn from the Earth when the Deluge should cease. For if the Earth was encompass'd with eight Oceans of water heapt one upon another, how these should retire into any Chanels, or be drain'd off, or the Earth any way disengag'd from them, is not intelligible; and that in so short a time as some months: For the violence of the Deluge lasted but four or five months, and in as many months after the Earth was dry and habitable. So as upon the whole enquiry, we can neither find source nor issue, beginning nor ending, for such an excessive mass of waters as the Vulgar Deluge requir'd; neither where to have them, nor if we had them, how to get quit of them. And I think men cannot do a greater injury or injustice to Sacred History, than to give such representations of things recorded there, as to make them unintelligible and incredible; As on the other hand, we cannot deserve better of Religion and Providence, than by giving such fair accounts of all things propos'd by them, or belonging to them, as may silence the Cavils of Atheists, satisfie the inquisitive, and recommend them to the belief and acceptance of all reasonable persons.

CHAPTER III

All Evasions answered; That there was no new Creation of waters at the Deluge: And that it was not particular or National, but extended throughout the whole Earth. A prelude and preparation to the true Account and Explication of it: The method of the first Book.

THOUGH in the preceeding Chapter we may seem to have given a fair trial to the common opinion concerning the state of the Deluge, and might now proceed to sentence of condemnation; yet having heard of another plea, which some have us'd in its behalf, and another way found out by recourse to the Supream Power, to supply all defects, and to make the whole matter intelligible, we will proceed no further till that be consider'd; being very willing to examine whatsoever may be offer'd, in that or any other way, for resolving that great difficulty which we have propos'd, concerning *the quantity of water requisite for such a Deluge.* And to this they say in short, that *God Almighty created waters on purpose to make the Deluge, and then annihilated them again when the Deluge was to cease;* And this, in a few words, is the whole account of the business. This is to cut the knot when we cannot loose it; They show us the naked arm of Omnipotency; such Arguments as these come like lightning, one doth not know what Armour to put on against them, for they pierce the more, the more they are resisted: We will not therefore oppose any thing to them that is hard and stubborn, but by a soft answer deaden their force by degrees.

And I desire to mind those persons in the first place of what St. *Austin* hath said upon a like occasion, speaking concerning those that disprov'd the opinion of waters above the Heavens (which we mentioned before) by natural Reasons. "We are not, saith he, to refute those persons, by saying, that according to the "Omnipotence of God, to whom all things are possible, we ought to believe "there are waters there as heavy as we know and feel them here below; for our "business is now to enquire according to his Scripture, how God hath constituted "the Nature of things, and not what he could do or work in these things by a "miracle of Omnipotency. I desire them to apply this to the present argument for the first answer.

Secondly, let them consider, that *Moses* hath assign'd causes of the Deluge; *Forty days Rain, and the disruption of the Abysse;* and speaks nothing of a new

C

creation of water upon that occasion. Those were causes in Nature which Providence had then dispos'd for this extraordinary effect, and those the Divine Historian refers us to, and not to any productions out of nothing. Besides, *Moses* makes the Deluge increase by degrees with the Rain, and accordingly makes it cease by degrees, and that the waters *going and returning*, as the waves and great commotions of the Sea use to do, retir'd leisurely from the face of the Earth, and setled at length in their Chanels. Now this manner of the beginning or ceasing of the Deluge doth not at all agree with the instantaneous actions of Creation and Annihilation.

2 *Pet.* 3. 6. Thirdly, let them consider, that St. *Peter* hath also assign'd *Causes* of the Deluge; namely the particular constitution of the Earth and Heavens before the Flood; "by *reason whereof*, he saith, *the World that was then, perisht in a Deluge* "*of water*. And not by reason of a new creation of water. His words are these, "The Heavens and the Earth were of old, consisting of water, and by water; "whereby, or by reason whereof, the World that then was, being overflowed "with water, perished.

Fourthly, they are to consider, that as we are not rashly to have recourse to the Divine Omnipotence upon any account, so especially not for new Creations; and least of all for the creation of new matter. The matter of the Universe was created many Ages before the Flood, and the Universe being full, if any more was created, then there must be as much annihilated at the same time to make room for it; for Bodies cannot penetrate one anothers dimensions, nor be two or more within one and the same space. Then on the other hand, when the Deluge ceas'd, and these waters were annihilated, so much other matter must be created again to take up their places: And methinks they make very bold with the Deity, when they make him do and undo, go forward and backwards by such countermarches and retractions, as we do not willingly impute to the wisdom of God Almighty.

Lastly, I shall not think my labour lost, if it be but acknowledg'd, that we have so far clear'd the way in this controversie, as to have brought it to this issue; That either there must be new waters created on purpose to make a Deluge, or there could be no Deluge, as 'tis vulgarly explain'd; there not being water sufficient in Nature to make a Deluge of that kind. This, I say, is a great step, and, I think, will satisfie all parties, at least all that are considerable; for those that have recourse to a new Creation of waters, are of two sorts, either such as do it out of laziness and ignorance, or such as do it out of necessity, seeing they cannot be had otherwise; as for the first, they are not to be valu'd or gratifi'd; and as for the second, I shall do a thing very acceptable to them, if I free them and the argument from that necessity, and show a way of making the Deluge fairly intelligible, and accountable without the creation of new waters; which is the design of this Treatise. For we do not tye this knot with an Intention to puzzle and perplex the Argument finally with it, but the harder it is ty'd, we shall feel the pleasure more sensibly when we come to loose it.

It may be when they are beaten from this new Creation of water, they will say the Element of Air was chang'd into water, and that was the great storehouse for the Deluge. Forty days Rain we allow, as *Moses* does, but if they suppose any other transelementation, it neither agrees with *Moses*'s Philosophy, nor St. *Peter*'s; for then the *opening of the Abysse* was needless, and the form and constitution of the Ante-diluvian *Heavens* and *Earth*, which St. *Peter* refers the Deluge to, bore no part in the work; it might have been made, in that way, indifferently under any Heavens or Earth. Besides, they offend against St. *Austin*'s rule in this method too; for I look upon it as no less a miracle to turn Air into Water, than to turn Water into Wine. *Air*, I say, for Vapours indeed are but water made volatile, but pure Air is a body of another Species, and cannot by any compression or condensation, so far as is yet known, be chang'd into water. And lastly, if the whole Atmosphere was turn'd into water, 'tis very probable it would make no more than 34 foot or thereabouts; for so much Air or Vapours as is of the same weight with any certain quantity of water, 'tis likely, if it was chang'd into water, would also be of the same bulk with it, or not much more: Now according to the doctrine of the Gravitation of the Atmosphere, 'tis found that 34 foot of water does counterbalance a proportionable Cylinder of Air reaching to the top of the Atmosphere; and consequently, if the whole Atmosphere was converted into water, it would make no more than eleven or twelve yards water about the Earth; Which the cavities of the Earth would be able in a good measure to suck up, at least this is very inconsiderable as to our eight Oceans. And if you would change the higher Regions into water too, what must supply the place of that Air which you transform into water, and bring down upon the Earth? There would be little but Fire and Æther betwixt us and the Moon, and I am afraid it would endanger to suck down the Moon too after it. In a word, such an explication as this, is both purely imaginary, and also very operose, and would affect a great part of the Universe; and after all, they would be as hard put to't to get rid of this water, when the Deluge was to cease, as they were at first to procure it.

Having now examin'd and answered all the pleas, from first to last, for the vulgar Deluge, or the old way of explaining it, we should proceed immediately to propose another method, and another ground for an universal Deluge, were it not that an opinion hath been started by some of late, that would in effect supplant both these methods, old and new, and take away in a great measure the subject of the question. Some modern Authors observing what straits they have been put to in all Ages, to find out water enough for *Noah*'s Flood, have ventur'd upon an expedient more brisk and bold, than any of the Ancients durst venture upon: They say, *Noah*'s Flood was not Universal, but a National Inundation, confin'd to *Judæa*, and those Countries thereabouts; and consequently, there would not be so much water necessary for the cause of it, as we have prov'd to be necessary for an Universal Deluge of that kind. Their inference is very true, they have avoided that rock, but they run upon another no less dangerous; to avoid an objection from reason, they deny matter of fact, and such matter of fact as is well attested by History, both Sacred and prophane. I believe the Authors that set up this opinion, were not themselves satisfied with it: but seeing insuperable difficulties in the old way, they are the more excusable in chusing, as they thought, of two evils the less.

But the choice, methinks, is as bad on this hand, if all things be considered; *Moses* represents the Flood of *Noah* as an overthrow and destruction of the whole Earth; and who can imagine, that in sixteen or seventeen hundred years time (taking the lower Chronology) that the Earth had then stood, mankind should be propagated no further than *Judæa*, or some neighbouring Countries thereabouts. After the Flood, when the World was renew'd again by eight persons, they had made a far greater progress in *Asia*, *Europe* and *Africa*, within the same space of years, and yet 'tis likely they were more fruitful in the first Ages of the World, than after the Flood; and they liv'd six, seven, eight, nine hundred years a piece, getting Sons and Daughters. Which longevity of the first Inhabitants of the Earth seems to have been providentially design'd for the quicker multiplication and propagation of mankind; and mankind thereby would become so numerous within sixteen hundred years, that there seems to me to be a greater difficulty from the multitude of the people that would be before the Flood, than from the want of people. For if we allow the first couple at the end of one hundred years, or of the first Century, to have left ten pair of Breeders, which is no hard supposition, there would arise from these, in fifteen hundred years, a greater number than the Earth was capable of; allowing every pair to multiply in the same decuple proportion the first pair did. But because this would rise far beyond the capacities of this Earth, let us suppose them to increase, in the following Centuries, in a quintuple proportion only, or, if you will, only in a quadruple; and then the Table of the multiplication of mankind from the Creation to the Flood, would stand thus;

Century					
1	..	10	9	..	655360
2	..	40	10	..	2621440
3	..	160	11	..	10485760
4	..	640	12	..	41943040
5	..	2560	13	..	167772160
6	..	10240	14	..	671088640
7	..	40960	15	..	2684354560
8	..	163840	16	..	10737418240

This product is too excessive high, if compar'd with the present number of men upon the face of the Earth, which I think is commonly estimated to be betwixt three and four hundred millions; and yet this proportion of their increase seems to be low enough, if we take one proportion for all the Centuries; for, in reality, the same measure cannot run equally through all the Ages, but we have taken this as moderate and reasonable betwixt the highest and the lowest; but if we had taken only a triple proportion, it would have been sufficient (all things consider'd) for our purpose. There are several other ways of computing this number, and some more particular and exact than this is, but which way soever you try, you will find the product great enough for the extent of this Earth; and if you follow the Septuagint Chronology it will still be far higher. I have met with three or four different Calculations, in several Authors, of the number of mankind before the Flood, and never met with any yet, but what exceeded the number of the people that are at present upon the face of the Earth. So as it seems to me a very groundless and forc'd conceit to imagine, that *Judæa* only, and some parts about it in *Asia*, were stor'd with people when the Deluge was brought upon the old World. Besides, if the Deluge was confin'd to those Countries, I do not see but the Borderers might have escap'd, shifting a little into the adjoining places where the Deluge did not reach. But especially what needed so much a-do to build an Ark to save *Noah* and his family, if he might have sav'd himself, and them, only by retiring into some neighbouring Countrey; as *Lot* and his family sav'd themselves, by withdrawing from *Sodom*, when the City was to be destroyed? Had not this been a far easier thing, and more compendious, than the great preparations he made of a large Vessel, with Rooms for the reception and accommodation of Beasts and Birds? And now I mention Birds, why could not they at least have flown into the next dry Country; they might have pearch'd upon the Trees and the tops of the Mountains by the way to have rested themselves if they were weary, for the waters did not all of a sudden rise to the Mountains tops.

I cannot but look upon the Deluge as a much more considerable thing than these Authors would represent it, and as a kind of dissolution of Nature. *Moses* calls it a destroying of the *Earth*, as well as of mankind, *Gen.* 6. 13. And the Bow was set in the Cloud to seal the Covenant, *that he would destroy the Earth no more, Gen.* 9. 11. or that there should be no more a Flood *to destroy the Earth.* And 'tis said, *verse* 13. that the Covenant was made between God and the Earth, or this frame of Nature, that it should perish no more by water. And the Rainbow, which was a token and pledge of this Covenant, appears not only in *Judæa*, or some other *Asiatick* Provinces, but to all the Regions of the Earth, who had an equal concern in it. *Moses* saith also the Fountains of the great Abysse were burst asunder to make the Deluge, and what means this Abysse and the bursting of it, if restrain'd to *Judæa*, or some adjacent Countries? What appearance is there of this disruption there more than in other places? Furthermore, St. *Peter* plainly implies, that the Antediluvian Heavens and Earth perisht in the Deluge; and opposeth the present Earth and Heavens to them, as different and of another constitution: and saith, that these shall perish by Fire, as the other perisht by water. So he compares the Conflagration with the Deluge, as two general dissolutions of Nature, and one may as well say, that the Conflagration shall be only National, and but two or three Countries burnt in that last Fire, as to say that the Deluge was so. I confess that discourse of St. *Peter*, concerning the several States of the World, would sufficiently convince me, if there was nothing else, that the Deluge was not a particular or National Inundation, but a *mundane* change, that extended to the whole Earth, and both to the Heavens and the Earth.

All Antiquity, we know, hath spoke of these mundane Revolutions or Periods, that the World should be successively destroy'd by Water and Fire; and I do not doubt but that this Deluge of *Noah*'s, which *Moses* describes, was the first and leading instance of this kind: And accordingly we see that after this Period, and after the Flood, the blessing for multiplication, and for replenishing the Earth with Inhabitants, was as solemnly pronounc'd by God Almighty, as at the first Creation of man, *Gen.* 9. 1. with *Gen.* 1. 28. These considerations, I think, might

2 Epist. c. 5. 6.

be sufficient to give us assurance from Divine Writ of the universality of the Deluge, and yet *Moses* affords us another argument as demonstrative as any, when in the History of the Deluge, he saith, *Hen.* 7. 19. *The waters exceedingly prevailed upon the Earth, and all the high Hills that were under the whole Heavens were covered.* All the high Hills, he saith, *under the whole Heavens,* then quite round the Earth; and if the Mountains were cover'd quite round the Earth, sure the Plains could not scape. But to argue with them upon their own grounds; Let us suppose only the *Asiatick* and *Armenian* Mountains covered with these waters, this they cannot deny; then unless there was a miracle to keep these waters upon heaps, they would flow throughout the Earth; for these Mountains are high enough to make them fall every way, and make them joyn with our Seas that environ the Continent. We cannot imagine Hills and Mountains of water to have hung about *Judæa,* as if they were congeal'd, or a mass of water to have stood upon the middle of the Earth like one great drop, or a trembling Jelly, and all the places about it dry and untouch'd. All liquid bodies are diffusive; for their parts being in motion have no tye or connexion one with another, but glide and fall off any way, as gravity and the Air presseth them; so the surface of water doth always conform into a Spherical convexity with the rest of the Globe of the Earth, and every part of it falls as near to the Center as it can; wherefore when these waters began to rise at first, long before they could swell to the heighth of the Mountains, they would diffuse themselves every way, and thereupon all the Valleys and Plains, and lower parts of the Earth would be filled throughout the whole Earth, before they could rise to the tops of the Mountains in any part of it: And the Sea would be all raised to a considerable heighth before the Mountains could be covered. For let's suppose, as they do, that this water fell not throughout the whole Earth, but in some particular Country, and there made first a great Lake; this Lake when it begun to swell would every way discharge it self by any descents or declivities of the ground, and these issues and derivations being once made, and supplied with new waters pushing them forwards, would continue their course till they arriv'd at the Sea; just as other Rivers do, for these would be but so many Rivers rising out of this Lake, and would not be considerably deeper and higher at the Fountain than in their progress or at the Sea. We may as well then expect that the *Leman*-Lake, for instance, out of which the *Rhone* runs, should swell to the tops of the *Alpes* on the one hand, and the Mountains of *Switzerland* and *Burgundy* on the other, and then stop, without overflowing the plainer Countries that lie beyond them; as to suppose that this Diluvian Lake should rise to the Mountains tops in one place, and not diffuse it self equally into all Countries about, and upon the surface of the Sea: in proportion to its heighth and depth in the place where it first fell or stood.

Thus much for Sacred History. The universality of the Deluge is also attested by profane History; for the fame of it is gone through the Earth, and there are Records or Traditions concerning it, in all parts of this and the new-found World. The *Americans* do acknowledge and speak of it in their Continent, as *Acosta* witnesseth, and *Laet* in their Histories of them. The *Chineses* have the Tradition of it, which is the farthest part of our Continent; and the nearer and Western

Mart.
Mart.

parts of *Asia* is acknowledg'd the proper seat of it. Not to mention *Deucalion*'s Deluge in the *European* parts, which no question is the same under a disguise: So as you may trace the Deluge quite round the Globe in profane History; and which is remarkable, every one of these people have a tale to tell, some one way, some another, concerning the restauration of mankind; which is an argument that they thought all mankind destroy'd by that Deluge. In the old dispute between the *Scythians* and the *Ægyptians* for Antiquity, which *Justin* mentions, they refer to a former destruction of the World by Water or Fire, and argue whether Nation first rise again, and was original to the other. So the *Babylonians*, *Assyrians*, *Phœnicians* and others, mention the Deluge in their stories. And we cannot without offering violence to all Records and Authority, Divine and Humane, deny that there hath been an universal Deluge upon the Earth; and if there was an universal Deluge, no question it was that of *Noah*'s, and that which *Moses* describ'd, and that which we treat of at present.

These considerations I think are abundantly sufficient to silence that opinion, concerning the limitation and restriction of the Deluge to a particular Country or Countries. It ought rather to be lookt upon as an Evasion indeed than Opinion, seeing the Authors do not offer any positive argument for the proof of it, but depend only upon that negative argument, that an universal Deluge is a thing unintelligible. This stumbling-stone we hope to take away for the future, and that men shall not be put to that unhappy choice, either to deny matter of fact well attested, or admit an effect, whereof they cannot see any possible causes. And so having stated and propos'd the whole difficulty, and try'd all ways offer'd by others, and found them ineffectual, let us now apply our selves by degrees to unty the knot.

The excessive quantity of water is the great difficulty, and the removal of it afterwards. Those eight Oceans lay heavy upon my thoughts, and I cast about every way to find an expedient, or to find some way whereby the same effect might be brought to pass with less water, and in such a manner, that that water might afterwards conveniently be discharg'd. The first thought that came into my mind upon that occasion, was concerning the form of the Earth, which I thought might possibly at that time be different from what it is at present, and might come nearer to plainness and equality in the surface of it, and so might the more easily be overflow'd, and the Deluge perform'd with less water. This opinion concerning the plainness of the first Earth, I also found in Antiquity, mention'd and refer'd to by several Interpreters in their Commentaries upon *Genesis*, either upon occasion of the Deluge, or of that Fountain which is said, *Gen.* 2. 6. to have watered the face of the whole Earth: And a late eminent person, the honour of this profession for Integrity and Learning, in his discourse concerning the *Origination of mankind*, hath made a like judgment of the State of the Earth before the Deluge, that the face of it was more smooth and regular than it is now. But yet upon second thoughts, I easily see that this alone would not be sufficient to explain the Deluge, nor to give an account of the present form of the Earth, unequal and Mountainous as it is. 'Tis true this would give a great advantage to the waters, and the Rains that fell for forty days together would have a great power over the Earth, being plain and smooth; but how would these waters be dispos'd of when the Deluge ceas'd? or how could it ever cease? Besides, what means the disruption of the great *Deep*, or the *great Abysse*, or what answers to it upon this supposition? This was assuredly of no less consideration than the Rains, nay I believe the Rains were but preparatory in some measure, and that the violence and consummation of the Deluge depended upon the disruption of the great Abysse. Therefore I saw it necessary, to my first thought, concerning the smoothness and plainness of the Ante-diluvian Earth, to add a second, concerning the disruption and dissolution of it; for as it often happens in Earthquakes, when the exteriour Earth is burst asunder, and a great Flood of waters issues out, according to the quantity and force of them, an Inundation is made in those parts, more or less; so I thought, if that Abysse lay under ground and round the Earth, and we should suppose the Earth in this manner to be broken, in several places at once, and as it were a general dissolution made, we might suppose that to make a general Deluge, as well as a particular dissolution often makes a particular. But I will not anticipate here the explication we intend to give of the universal Deluge in the following Chapters, only by this previous intimation we may gather some hopes, it may be, that the matter is not so desperate as the former representation might possibly make us fancy it.

Give me leave to add farther in this place, that it hath been observ'd by several, from the contemplation of Mountains and Rocks and Precipices, of the Chanel of the Sea, and of Islands, and of Subterraneous Caverns, that the surface of the Earth, or the exteriour Region which we inhabit, hath been broke, and the parts of it dislocated: And one might instance more particularly in several parcels of Nature, that retain still the evident marks of fraction and ruine; and by their present form and posture show, that they have been once in another state and situation one to another. We shall have occasion hereafter to give an account of these *Phænomena*, from which several have rightly argu'd and concluded some general rupture or ruine in the superficial parts of the Earth. But this ruine, it is true, they have imagin'd and explain'd several ways, some thinking that it was made the *third day* after the foundation of the Earth; when they suppose the Chanel of the Sea to have been form'd, and Mountains and Caverns at the same time; by a violent depression of some parts of the Earth, and an extrusion and elevation of others to make them room. Others suppose it to have come not all at once, but by degrees, at several times, and in several Ages, from particular and accidental causes, as the Earth falling in upon Fires under ground, or water eating away the lower parts, or Vapours and Exhalations breaking out, and tearing the Earth. 'Tis true, I am not of their opinion in either of these Explications; and we shall show at large hereafter, when we have propos'd and stated our own Theory, how incompetent such causes are to bring the Earth into that form and condition we now find it in. But in the mean time, we may so far make use of these Opinions in general, as not to be startled at this Doctrine, concerning the breaking or dissolution of the exteriour Earth; for in all Ages the face of Nature hath provok'd men to think of and observe such a thing. And who can do otherwise, to see the Elements displac'd and disordered, as they seem to lie at present; the heaviest and grossest bodies in the highest places, and the liquid and volatile kept below; an huge mass of Stone or Rock rear'd into the Air, and the water creeping at its feet; whereas this is the more light and active body, and by the law of Nature should take place of Rocks and Stones? So we see, by the like disorder, the Air thrown down into Dungeons of the Earth, and the Earth got up among the Clouds; for there are the tops of the Mountains, and under their roots in holes and Caverns the Air is often detain'd. By what regular action of Nature can we suppose things first produc'd in this posture and form? not to mention how broke and torn the inward substance of the Earth is, which of it self is an uniform mass, close and compact: but in the condition we see it, it lies hollow in many places, with great vacuities intercepted betwixt the portions of it; a thing which we see happens in all ruines more or less, especially when the parts of the ruines are great and inflexible. Then what can have more the figure and mien of a ruine, than Crags and Rocks and Cliffs, whether upon the Sea shore, or upon the sides of Mountains; what can be more apparently broke, than they are; and those lesser Rocks, or great bulky Stones that lie often scatter'd near the feet of the other, whether in the Sea, or upon the Land, are they not manifest fragments, and pieces of those greater masses? Besides, the posture of these Rocks, which is often leaning or recumbent, or prostrate, shows to the eye, that they have had a fall, or some kind of dislocation from their Natural site. And the same thing may be observed in the Tracts and Regions of the Earth, which very seldom for ten miles together have any regular surface or continuity one with another, but lie high and low, and are variously inclin'd sometimes one way, sometimes another, without any rule or order. Whereas I see no reason but the surface of the Land should be as regular as that of the water, in the first production of it. This I am sure of, that this disposition of the Elements, and the parts of the Earth, outward and inward, hath something irregular and unnatural in it, and manifestly shews us the marks or footsteps of some kind of ruine and dissolution; which we shall shew you, in its due place, happen'd in such a way, that at the same time a general Flood of waters would necessarily over-run the face of the whole Earth. And by the same fatal blow, the Earth fell out of that regular form, wherein it was produc'd at first, into all these irregularities which we see in its present form and composition; so that we shall give thereby a double satisfaction to the mind, both to shew it a fair and intelligible account of the general Deluge, how the waters came upon the Earth, and how they return'd into their Chanels again, and left the Earth habitable; and likewise to shew it how the Mountains were brought forth, and the Chanel of the Sea discover'd: How all those inequalities came in the body or face of the Earth, and those empty Vaults and Caverns in its bowels; which things are no less matter of admiration than the Flood it self.

But I must beg leave to draw a Curtain before the work for a while, and to keep your patience a little in suspence, till materials are prepar'd, and all things ready to represent and explain what we have propos'd. Yet I hope in the mean time to entertain the mind with scenes no less pleasing, though of quite another face and order: for we must now return to the beginning of the World, and look upon the first rudiments of Nature, and that dark, but fruitful womb, out of which all things sprang, I mean the *Chaos*: For this is the matter which we must now work upon, and it will be no unpleasing thing to observe, how that rude mass will shoot it self into several forms, one after another, till it comes at length to make an habitable World. The steddy hand of Providence, which keeps all things in weight and measure, being the invisible guide of all its motions. These motions we must examine from first to last, to find out what was the form of the Earth, and what was the place or situation of the Ocean, or the great Abysse, in that first state of Nature: Which two things being determin'd, we shall be able to make a certain judgment, what kind of dissolution that Earth was capable of, and whether from that dissolution an Universal Deluge would follow, with all the consequences of it.

In the mean time, for the ease and satisfaction of the Reader, we will here mark the order and distribution of the first Book, which we divide into three Sections; whereof the first is these three Chapters past: In the second Section we will shew, that the Earth before the Deluge was of a different frame and form from the present Earth; and particularly of such a form as made it subject to a dissolution: And to such a dissolution, as did necessarily expose it to an universal Deluge. And in this place we shall apply our discourse particularly to the explication of *Noah*'s Flood, and that under all its conditions, of the height of the waters, of their universality, of the destruction of the World by them, and of their retiring afterwards from the Earth; and this Section will consist of the Fourth, Fifth, Sixth, Seventh and Eighth Chapters. In the third Section we prove the same dissolution from the effects and consequences of it, or from the contemplation of the present face of the Earth: And here an account is given of the Origin of Mountains, of subterraneous Waters and Caverns, of the great Chanel of the Sea, and of the first production of Islands; and those things are the Contents of the Ninth, Tenth and Eleventh Chapters. Then, in the last Chapter, we make a general review of the whole Work, and a general review of Nature; that, by comparing them together, their full agreement and correspondency may appear. Here several collateral arguments are given for confirmation of the preceeding Theory, and some reflections are made upon the state of the other Planets compar'd with the Earth. And lastly, what accounts soever have been given by others of the present form and irregularities of the Earth, are examin'd and shew'd insufficient. And this seemeth to be all that is requisite upon this subject.

CHAPTER IV

That the Earth and Mankind had an Original, and were not from Eternity: Prov'd against Aristotle. *The first proposition of our Theory laid down,* viz. *That the Ante-diluvian Earth was of a different form and construction from the present. This is prov'd by Divine Authority, and from the nature and form of the Chaos, out of which the Earth was made.*

WE are now to enquire into the Original of the Earth, and in what form it was built at first, that we may lay our foundation for the following Theory, deep and sure. It hath been the general opinion and consent of the Learned of all Nations, that the Earth arose from a Chaos. This is attested by History, both Sacred and Profane; only *Aristotle*, whom so great a part of the Christian world have made their Oracle or Idol, hath maintain'd the Eternity of the Earth, and the Eternity of mankind; that the Earth and the World were from Everlasting, and in that very form they are in now, with Men and Women and all living Creatures. Trees and Fruit, Metals and Minerals, and whatsoever is of Natural production. We say all these things arose and had their first existence or production not six thousand years ago; He saith, they have subsisted thus for ever, through an infinite Series of past Generations, and shall continue as long, without first or last: And if so, there was neither Chaos, nor any other beginning to the Earth. This takes away the subject of our discourse, and therefore we must first remove this stone out of the way, and prove that the Earth had an Original, and that from a Chaos, before we show how it arose from a Chaos, and what was the first habitable form that it setled into.

We are assur'd by Divine Authority, that the Earth and Mankind had a beginning; *Moses* saith, *In the beginning God made the Heavens and the Earth.* Speaking it as of a certain Period or Term from whence he counts the Age of the World. And the same *Moses* tells us, that *Adam* was the first Man, and *Eve* the first Woman, from whom sprung the race of Mankind; and this within the compass of six thousand years. We are also assured from the Prophets, and our Christian Records, that the world shall have an end, and that by a general Conflagration, when all Mankind shall be destroy'd, with the form and all the furniture of the Earth. And as this proves the second part of *Aristotle*'s Doctrine to be false immediately, so doth it the first, by a true consequence: for what hath an end had a beginning, what is not immortal, was not Eternal; for what exists by the strength of its own Nature at first, the same Nature will enable it to exist for ever; and indeed what exists of it self, exists necessarily; and what exists necessarily, exists eternally.

Having this infallible assurance of the Origin of the Earth and of Mankind, from Scripture, we proceed to refute the same Doctrine of *Aristotle*'s by natural Reason. And we will first consider the form of the Earth, and then Mankind; and shew from plain evidence and observation, neither of them to have been Eternal. 'Tis natural to the mind of man to consider that which is compound, as having been once more simple; whether that composition be a mixture of many ingredients, as most Terrestrial bodies are, or whether it be Organical; but especially if it be Organical; For a thing that consists of a multitude of pieces aptly joyn'd, we cannot but conceive to have had those pieces, at one time or another, put together. 'Twere hard to conceive an eternal Watch, whose pieces were never separate one from another, nor ever in any other form than that of a Watch. Or an eternal House, whose materials were never a-sunder, but always in the form of an House. And 'tis as hard to conceive an *eternal Earth*, or an *eternal World:* These are made up of more various substances, more ingredients, and a far greater composition; and the living part of the World, Plants and Animals, have far more variety of parts and multifarious construction, than any House, or any other artificial thing: So that we are led as much by Nature and necessity to conceive this great machine of the World, or of the Earth, to have been once in a state of greater simplicity than now it is, as to conceive a Watch, an House, or any other structure, to have been once in its first and simple materials. This I speak without reference to immediate Creation, for *Aristotle* did not own any such thing, and therefore the argument stands good against him, upon those grounds and notions that he goes. Yet I guess what answer would be made by him or his followers to this argumentation; They would say there is not the same reason for Natural things, as for Artificial, though equally compounded. Artificial things could not be from Eternity, because they suppose Man, by whose Art they were made, pre-existent to them; the workman must be before the work, and whatsoever hath any thing before it, is not Eternal. But may not the same thing be said of Natural things? do not most of them require the action of the Sun, and the influence of the Heavens for their production, and longer preparations than any Artificial things do? Some Years or Ages would be necessary for the concoction and maturation of Metals and Minerals; Stones themselves, at least some sorts of them, were once liquors or fluid masses; and all Vegetable productions require the heat of the Sun, to pre-dispose and excite the Earth, and the Seeds. Nay, according to *Aristotle*, 'tis not Man by himself that begets a Man, but the Sun is his Coadjutor. You see then 'twas as necessary that the Sun, that great workman of Nature, should pre-exist to Natural things, produc'd in or upon the Earth, as that Man should pre-exist to Artificial. So that the Earth under that form and constitution it now hath, could no more be Eternal, than a Statue or Temple, or any work of Art.

Besides, that form, which the Earth is under at present, is in some sort preternatural, like a Statue made and broken again; and so hath still the less appearance or pretence of being Eternal. If the Elements had lain in that order to one another, as *Aristotle* hath dispos'd them, and as seems to be their first disposition, the Earth altogether in a mass in the middle, or towards the Center; then the Water in a Spherical mass about that; the Air above the Water, and then a Sphere of Fire, as he fansied, in the highest Circle of the Air: If they had lain, I say, in this posture, there might have been some pretence that they had been Eternally so; because that might seem to be their Original posture, in which Nature had first plac'd them. But the form and posture we find them in at present is very different, and according to his Doctrine must be lookt upon as unnatural and violent; and no violent state by his own Maxim, can be perpetual, or can have been so.

But there is still a more pressing consideration against this Opinion. If this present state and form of the Earth had been from Eternity, it would have long ere this destroy'd it self, and chang'd it self: the Mountains sinking by degrees into the Valleys, and into the Sea, and the Waters rising above the Earth; which form it would certainly have come into sooner or later, and in it continu'd drown'd and uninhabitable, for all succeeding Generations. For 'tis certain, that the Mountains and higher parts of the Earth grow lesser and lesser from Age to Age; and that from many causes, sometimes the roots of them are weaken'd and eaten by Subterraneous Fires, and sometimes they are torn and tumbled down by

Earthquakes, and fall into those Caverns that are under them; and though those violent causes are not constant, or universal, yet if the Earth had stood from Eternity, there is not a Mountain would have escap'd this fate in one Age or other. The course of these exhalations or Fires would have reach'd them all sooner or later, if through infinite Ages they had stood expos'd to them. But there are also other causes that consume them insensibly, and make them sink by degrees; and those are chiefly the Winds, Rains, and Storms, and heat of the Sun without; and within, the soaking of Water and Springs, with streams and Currents in their veins and crannies. These two sorts of causes would certainly reduce all the Mountains of the Earth, in tract of time, to equality; or rather lay them all under Water: For whatsoever moulders or is washt away from them, is carried down into the lower grounds, and into the Sea, and nothing is ever brought back again by any circulation: Their losses are not repair'd, nor any proportionable recruits made from any other parts of Nature. So as the higher parts of the Earth being continually spending, and the lower continually gaining, they must of necessity at length come to an equality; and the Waters that lie in the lower parts and in the Chanels, those Chanels and Valleys being fill'd up with Earth, would be thrust out and rise every where upon the surface of the Earth; Which new post when they had once seiz'd on, they would never quit it, nor would any thing be able to dispossess them; for 'tis their natural place and situation which they always tend to, and from which there is no progress nor regress in a course of Nature. So that the Earth would have been, both now, and from innumerable Generations before this, all under water and uninhabitable; if it had stood from everlasting, and this form of it had been its first original form.

Nor can he doubt of this argumentation, that considers the coherence of it, and will allow time enough for the effect. I do not say the Earth would be reduc'd to this uninhabitable form in ten thousand years time, though I believe it would: but take twenty, if you please, take an hundred thousand, take a million, 'tis all one, for you may take the one as easily as the other out of Eternity; and they make both equally against their supposition. Nor is it any matter how little you suppose the Mountains to decrease, 'tis but taking more time, and the same effect still follows. Let them but waste as much as a grain of Mustardseed every day, or a foot in an Age, this would be more than enough in ten thousand Ages to consume the tallest Mountain upon Earth. The Air alone, and the little drops of Rain have defac'd the strongest and the proudest monuments of the *Greeks* and *Romans*; and allow them but time enough, and they will of themselves beat down the Rocks into the Sea, and the Hills into the Valleys. But if we add to these all those other foremention'd causes that work with more violence, and the weight of the Mountains themselves, which upon any occasion offer'd, is ready to sink them lower, we shall shorten the time, and make the effect more sure.

We need add no more here in particular, against this *Aristotelian* Doctrine, that makes the present form of the Earth to have been from Eternity, for the truth is, this whole Book is one continued argument against that Opinion; shewing that it hath *de facto* chang'd its form; both in that we have prov'd that it was not capable of an universal Deluge in this form, and consequently was once under another; and also in that we shall prove at large hereafter, throughout the Third and Fourth Sections, that it hath been broken and dissolv'd. We might also add one consideration more, that if it had stood always under this form, it would have been under Fire, if it had not been under Water; and the Conflagration, which it is to undergo, would have overtaken it long ere this. For St. *Peter* saith, the Heavens and the Earth that are now, as oppos'd to the Ante-diluvian, and considered in their present form and constitution, are fitted to be consum'd by Fire. And whosoever understands the progress and revolutions of Nature, will see that neither the present form of the Earth, nor its first form, were permanent and immutable forms, but transient and temporary by their own frame and constitution; which the Author of Nature, after certain periods of time, had design'd for change and for destruction.

Thus much for the body of the Earth, that it could not have been from Eternity, as *Aristotle* pretended, in the form it hath. Now let's consider the Origination of Mankind; and that we shall find could much less be Eternal than the other; for whatsoever destroy'd the form of the Earth, would also destroy Mankind; and besides, there are many particular marks and arguments, that the Generations of Men have not been from Everlasting. All History, and all monuments of Antiquity of what kind soever, are but of a few thousand of years date; we have still the memory of the golden Age, of the first state of Nature, and how mortals liv'd then in innocency and simplicity. The invention of Arts, even those that are necessary or useful to humane life, hath been within the knowledge of Men: How imperfect was the Geography of the Ancients, how imperfect their knowledge of the Earth, how imperfect their Navigation? Can we imagine, if there had been Men from Everlasting, a Sea as now, and all materials for Shipping as much as we have, that men could have been so ignorant, both of the Land and of the Sea, as 'tis manifest they have been till of late Ages? They had very different fansies concerning the figure of the Earth? They knew no Land beyond our Continent, and that very imperfectly too; and the Torrid Zone they thought utterly uninhabitable. We think it strange, taking that short date of the World, which we give it, that Men should not have made more progress in the knowledge of these things; But how impossible is it then, if you suppose them to have been from Everlasting? They had the same wit and passions that we have, the same motives that we have, can we then imagine, that neither the ambition of Princes, nor Interest or gain in private persons, nor curiosity and the desire of Knowledge, nor the glory of discoveries, nor any other passion or consideration could ever move them in that endless time, to try their fortunes upon the Sea, and know something more of the World they inhabited? Though you should suppose them generally stupid, which there is no reason to do, yet in a course of infinite Generations, there would be some great Genio's, some extraordinary persons that would attempt things above the rest. We have done more within the compass of our little World, which we can but count, as to this, from the general Deluge, than those Eternal Men had done in their innumerable Ages foregoing.

You will say, it may be, they had not the advantages and opportunities for Navigation as we have, and for discoveries; because the use of the Loadstone, and the Mariners Needle was not then known. But that's the wonder, that either that invention, or any other should not be brought to light till t'other day, if the World had stood from Eternity. I say this or any other practical invention; for such things when they are once found out and known, are not easily lost again, because they are of daily use. And 'tis in most other practical Arts as in Navigation, we generally know their Original and History: who the Inventors, and by what degrees improv'd, and how few of them brought to any perfection till of late Ages. All the Artificial and Mechanical World is, in a manner, new; and what you may call the *Civil World* too is in a great measure so. What relates to Government, and Laws; to Wars and Discipline; we can trace these things to their Origin, or very near it. The use of Money and of Coins, nay the use of the very Elements; for they tell us of the first invention of Fire by *Prometheus*, and the imploying of Wind or Water to turn the Mills and grind their Corn was scarce known before the *Romans*; and that we may think nothing Eternal here, they tell us the Ages and Genealogies of their very Gods. The measures of Time for the common uses of life, the dividing it into Hours, with the Instruments for those purposes, are not of an unknown date: Even the Arts for preparing Food and Clothing, Medicines and medicaments, Building, Civil and Military, Letters and Writing, which are the foundations of the World Civil: These, with all their retinue of lesser Arts and Trades that belong to them, History and Tradition tell us, when they had their beginning, or were very imperfect; and how many of their Inventors and Inventresses were deifi'd. The World hath not stood so long but we can still run it up to those Artless Ages, when mortals liv'd by plain Nature; when there was but one Trade in the World, one Calling, to look to their Flocks; and afterwards to Till the Ground, when Nature grew less liberal: And may we not reasonably think this the beginning of Mankind, or very near it? If Man be a creature both naturally sagacious to find out its own conveniencies, and naturally sociable and inclin'd to live in a Community, a little time would make them find out and furnish themselves with what was necessary in these two kinds, for the conveniencies of single life, and the conveniencies of Societies; they would not have liv'd infinite Ages unprovided of them. If you say *Necessity* is the Mother of Arts and Inventions, and there was no necessity before, and therefore these things were so slowly invented. This is a good answer upon our supposition, that the World began but some Ages before these were found out, and was abundant with all things at first; and Men not very numerous, and therefore were not put so much to the use of their wits for living commodiously. But this is no answer upon their supposition; for if the World was Eternal and Men too, there were no first Ages, no new and fresh Earth; Men were never less numerous, nor the Earth more fruitful; and consequently there was never less necessity at any time than is now. This also brings to mind another argument against this opinion (*viz.*) from the gradual increase of Mankind. 'Tis certain the World was not so populous one or two thousand years since, as it is now, seeing 'tis observ'd, in particular Nations, that within the space of two or three hundred years, notwithstanding all casualties, the number of Men doubles. If then the Earth had stood from Everlasting, it had been over-stockt long ere this,

Plin. l. 7. c. 56.

and would not have been capable to contain its Inhabitants many Ages and Millions of Ages ago. Whereas we find the Earth is not yet sufficiently Inhabited, and there is still room for some Millions. And we must not flie to universal Deluges and Conflagrations to destroy Mankind; for besides that the Earth was not capable of a Deluge in this present form, nor would have been in this form after a Conflagration, *Aristotle* doth not admit of these universal changes, nor any that hold the form of the Earth to be Eternal. But to return to our Arts and Inventions.

We have spoken of practical Arts and Inventions useful in humane life; then for Theoretical Learning and Sciences, there is nothing yet finish'd or compleat in these; and what is known hath been chiefly the production of latter Ages. How little hath been discover'd till of late, either of our own Bodies, or of the body of the Earth, and of the functions or motions of Nature in either? What more obvious, one would think, than the Circulation of the Bloud? What can more excite our curiosity than the flowing and ebbing of the Sea? Than the nature of Metals and Minerals? These are either yet unknown, or were so at least till this last Age; which seems to me to have made a greater progress than all Ages before put together, since the beginning of the World. How unlikely is it then that these Ages were Eternal? That the Eternal studies of our Forefathers could not effect so much as a few years have done of late? And the whole mass of knowledge in this Earth doth not seem to be so great, but that a few Ages more, with two or three happy Genius's in them, may bring to light all that we are capable to understand in this state of mortality.

To these arguments concerning the novelty of the Earth, and the Origin of Mankind, I know there are some shuffling excuses made, but they can have little effect upon those instances we have chosen. And I would ask those Eternalists one fair question, What mark is there that they could expect or desire of the novelty of a World, that is not found in this? Or what mark is there of Eternity that is found in this? If then their opinion be without any positive argument, and against all appearances in Nature, it may be justly rejected as unreasonable upon all accounts. 'Tis not the bold asserting of a thing that makes it true, or that makes it credible against evidence. If one should assert that such an one had liv'd from all Eternity, and I could bring witnesses that knew him a sucking Child, and others that remembred him a School-boy, I think it would be a fair proof, that the Man was not Eternal. So if there be evidence, either in Reason or History, that it is not very many Ages since Nature was in her minority, as appears by all those instances we have given above; some whereof trace her down to her very infancy: This, I think, may be taken for a good proof that she is not Eternal. And I do not doubt, but if the History of the World was writ Philosophically, giving an account of the several states of Mankind in several Ages, and by what steps or degrees they came from their first rudeness or simplicity to that order of things, both Intellectual and Civil, which the World is advanc'd to at present, that alone would be a full conviction, that the Earth and Mankind had a beginning. As the story of *Rome*, how it rise from a mean Original, by what degrees it increas'd, and how it chang'd its form and government till it came to its greatness, doth satisfie us very well, that the *Roman* Empire was not Eternal.

Thus much concerning the Temporal Original of the Earth. We are now to consider the manner of it, and to shew how it rise from a Chaos. I do not remember that any of the Ancients that acknowledge the Earth to have had an Original, did deny that Original to have been from a Chaos. We are assur'd of both from the authority of *Moses*, who saith, that in the beginning the Earth was *Tohu Bohu*, without form and void; a fluid, dark, confus'd mass, without distinction of Elements; made up of all variety of parts, but without Order, or any determinate Form; which is the true description of a Chaos: And so it is understood by the general consent of Interpreters, both Hebrew and Christian. We need not therefore spend any time here to prove, that the Origin of the Earth was from a Chaos, seeing that is agreed on by all that give it any Origin. But we will proceed immediately to examine into what form it first rise when it came out of that Chaos; or what was the primæval form of the Earth, that continued till the Deluge, and how the Deluge depended upon it, and upon its dissolution.

And that we may proceed in this enquiry by such easie steps as any one may readily follow, we will divide it into three Propositions, whereof the first is this in general; *That the Form of the Ante-diluvian Earth, or of the Earth that rise first from the Chaos, was different from the Form of the present Earth.* I say *different in general*, without specifying yet what its particular form was, which shall be exprest in the following Proposition.

The first Proposition we have in effect prov'd in the Second Chapter; where we have shewn, that if the Earth had been always in this form, it would not have been capable of a Deluge; seeing that could not have been effected without such an infinite mass of water as could neither be brought upon the Earth, nor afterwards any way removed from it. But we will not content our selves with that proof only, but will prove it also from the nature of the Chaos, and the manifest consequences of it. And because this is a leading Proposition, we think it not improper to prove it also from Divine authority, there being a pregnant passage to this purpose in the writings of St. *Peter*. Where treating of this very subject, the Deluge, He manifestly puts a difference between the Ante-diluvian Earth and present Earth, as to their form and constitution. The Discourse is in the Second Epistle of St. *Peter*, the Third Chapter, where certain Deists, as they seem to have been, laught at the prophecy of the day of Judgment, and of the Conflagration of the World, using this argument against it, *That since the Fathers fell asleep, all things have continued as they were from the beginning.* All external Nature hath continued the same without any remarkable change or alteration, and why should we believe (say they) there will be any? what appearance or what foundation is there of such a revolution, that all Nature will be dissolv'd, and the Heavens and the Earth consum'd with Fire, as your prophecies pretend? So from the permanency and immutability of Nature hitherto, they argu'd its permanency and immutability for the future. To this the *Apostle* answers, that they are willing to forget that the Heavens and the Earth of old had a particular form and constitution as to Water, by reason whereof the World that then was, perisht by a

D

Deluge. And the Heavens and the Earth that are now, or since the Deluge, have a particular constitution in reference to Fire, by reason whereof they are expos'd to another sort of destruction or dissolution, namely by Fire, or by an universal Conflagration. The words of the Apostle are these; *For this they are willingly ignorant of, that by the Word of God the Heavens were of old, and the Earth, consisting of Water, and by Water; or (as we render it) standing out of the Water, and in the Water; whereby the World that then was, being overflow'd with Water, perisht. But the Heavens and the Earth that are now, by the same Word are kept in store, reserv'd unto Fire against the day of Judgment.* We shall have occasion, it may be, hereafter to give a full illustration of these words; but at present we shall only take notice of this in general, that the Apostle here doth plainly intimate some difference that was between the Old World and the present World, in their form and constitution; or betwixt the Ante-diluvian and the present Earth, by reason of which difference, that was subject to perish by a Deluge, as this is subject to perish by Conflagration. And as this is the general Air and importance of this discourse of the Apostles, which every one at first sight would discover; so we may in several particular ways prove from it our first Proposition, which now we must return to; (*viz.*) *That the form and constitution of the Ante-diluvian Earth was different from that of the present Earth.* This may be infer'd from the Apostle's discourse, first, because he makes an opposition betwixt these two Earths, or these two natural Worlds; and that not only in respect of their fate, the one perishing by Water, as the other will perish by Fire, but also in respect of their different disposition and constitution leading to this different fate, for otherwise his *fifth verse* is superfluous, and his Inference in the *sixth* ungrounded; you see he premiseth in the *fifth verse* as the ground of his discourse, what the constitution of the Ante-diluvian Heavens and Earth was, and then infers from it in the *sixth* verse, that they therefore perisht in a Deluge of water. Now if they had been the same with ours, there had neither been any ground for making an opposition betwixt them, nor any ground of making a contrary inference as to their fate. Besides, in that he implies, that the constitution of the Ante-diluvian Earth was such, as made it subject to a Deluge; he shews, that it was different from the constitution of the present Earth; for the form of that is such, as makes it rather incapable of a Deluge, as we have shewn in the second Chapter. Then we are to observe further, that when he saith (*verse* 6.) that the first World perish'd in a Deluge, or was destroy'd by it; this is not to be understood of the Animate world only, Men and living Creatures, but of the Natural world, and the frame of it; for he had describ'd it before by the Heavens and the Earth, which make the Natural world. And the objection of the Atheists, or Deists rather, which he was to answer, proceeded upon the Natural world. And lastly, this perishing of the World in a Deluge, is set against, or compar'd with the perishing of the world in the Conflagration, when the frame of Nature will be dissolv'd. We must therefore, according to the tenor of the Apostle's arguing, suppose, that the Natural world was destroy'd or perisht in the Deluge; and seeing it did not perish as to matter and substance, it must be as to the form, frame, and composition of it, that it perisht; and consequently, the present Earth is of another form and frame from what it had before the Deluge; which was the thing to be proved.

Lastly, let us consider what it is the Apostle tells these Scoffers that they were ignorant of: not that there was a Deluge, they could not be ignorant of that; nor doth he tell them that they were; But he tells them that they were ignorant that the Heavens and the Earth of old were so and so constituted, after a different manner than they are now, and that the state of Nature was chang'd at the Deluge. If they had known or attended to this, they had made no such objection, nor us'd any such argument as they did against the future Conflagration of the world. They pretended that there had been no change in Nature since the beginning, and the Apostle in answer tells them, that they are willingly ignorant of the first constitution of the Heavens, and the Earth, and of that change and dissolution that happen'd to them in the Deluge; and how the present Heavens and Earth have another constitution, whereby in like manner they are expos'd, in God's due time, to be consum'd or dissolv'd by Fire. This is the plain, easie and natural import of the Apostles discourse; thus all the parts of it are coherent, and the sence genuine and apposite, and this is a full confirmation of our first and general assertion, That *the Ante-diluvian Earth was of another form from the present Earth.* This hath been observ'd formerly by some of the Ancients from this Text, but that it hath not been generally observ'd, was, partly because they had no Theory to back such an interpretation, and make it intelligible; and partly because they did not observe, that the Apostle's discourse here was an argumentation, and not a bare affirmation, or simple contradiction to those that rais'd the scruple; 'tis an answer upon a ground taken, he premiseth and then infers; in the *fifth* and *sixth* Verses, concerning the Deluge; and in the *seventh*, concerning the Conflagration. And when I had discover'd in my thoughts from the consideration of the Deluge, and other natural reasons, that the Earth was certainly once in another form, it was a great assurance and confirmation to me, when I reflected on this place of St. *Peter*'s; which seems to be so much directed and intended for the same purpose, or to teach us the same conclusion, that though I design'd chiefly a Philosophical Theory of these things, yet I should not have thought we had been just to Providence, if we had neglected to take notice of this passage and Sacred evidence; which seems to have been left us on purpose, to excite our enquiries, and strengthen our reasonings, concerning the first state of things. Thus much from Divine Authority: We proceed now to prove the same Proposition from Reason and Philosophy, and the contemplation of the Chaos, from whence the first Earth arose.

We need not upon this occasion make a particular description of the Chaos, but only consider it as a Fluid Mass, or a Mass of all sorts of little parts and particles of matter, mixt together, and floating in confusion, one with another. 'Tis impossible that the surface of this mass should be of such a form and figure, as the surface of our present Earth is. Or that any concretion or consistent state which this mass could flow into immediately, or first settle in, could be of such a form and figure as our present Earth. The first of these Assertions is of easie proof; for a fluid body, we know, whether it be water or any other liquor, always casts it self into a smooth and spherical surface; and if any parts, by chance, or by some agitation, become higher than the rest, they do not continue so, but glide down again every way into the lower places, till they all come to make a surface of the same height, and of the same distance every where from the center of their gravity. A mountain of water is a thing impossible in Nature, and where there are no Mountains, there are no Valleys. So also a Den or Cave within the water, that hath no walls but the liquid Element, is a structure unknown to Art or Nature; all things there must be full within, and even and level without, unless some External force keep them by violence in another posture. But is this the form of our Earth, which is neither regularly made within nor without? The surface and exteriour parts are broken into all sorts of inequalities, Hills and Dales, Mountains and Valleys; and the plainer tracts of it lie generally inclin'd or bending one way or other, sometimes upon an easie descent, and other times with a more sensible and uneasie steepiness; and though the great Mountains of the Earth were taken all away, the remaining parts would be more unequal than the roughest Sea; whereas the face of the Earth should resemble the face of the calmest Sea, if it was still in the form of its first mass. But what shall we say then to the huge Mountains of the Earth, which lie sometimes in lumps or clusters heapt up by one another, sometimes extended in long ridges or chains for many hundred miles in length? And 'tis remarkable, that in every Continent, and in every ancient and original Island, there is either such a cluster, or such a chain of Mountains. And can there be any more palpable demonstrations than these are, that the surface of the Earth is not in the same form that the surface of the Chaos was, or that any fluid mass can stand or hold it self in?

Then for the form of the Earth within or under its surface, 'tis no less impossible for the Chaos to imitate that; for 'tis full of cavities and empty places, of dens and broken holes, whereof some are open to the Air, and others cover'd and enclosed wholly within the ground. These are both of them unimitable in any liquid substance, whose parts will necessarily flow together into one continued mass, and cannot be divided into apartments and separate rooms, nor have vaults or caverns made within it; the walls would sink, and the roof fall in: For liquid bodies have nothing to sustain their parts, nor any thing to cement them; they are all loose and incoherent, and in a perpetual flux: Even an heap of Sand, or fine Powder will suffer no hollowness within them, though they be dry substances, and though the parts of them being rough, will hang together a little, and stand a little upon an heap; but the parts of liquors being glib, and continually in motion, they fall off from one another, which way soever gravity inclines them, and can neither have any hills or eminencies on their surface, nor any hollowness within their substance.

You will acknowledge, it may be, that this is true, and that a liquid mass or Chaos, while it was liquid, was incapable of either the outward or inward form of the Earth; but when it came to a concretion, to a state of consistency and firmness, then it might go, you'll say, into any form. No, not in its first concretion, nor in its first state of consistence; for that would be of the same form that the surface of it was when it was liquid; as water, when it congeals, the surface of the Ice is smooth and level, as the surface of the water was before; so

Metals, or any other substances melted, or Liquors that of themselves grow stiff and harden, always settle into the same form which they had when they were last liquid, and are always solid within, and smooth without, unless they be cast in a mould, that hinders the motion and flux of the parts. So that the first concrete state or consistent surface of the Chaos, must be of the same form or figure with the last liquid state it was in; for that is the mould, as it were, upon which it is cast; as the shell of an Egg is of the like form with the surface of the liquor it lies upon. And therefore by analogy with all other liquors and concretions, the form of the Chaos, whether liquid or concrete, could not be the same with that of the present Earth, or like it: And consequently, that form of the first or primigenial Earth which rise immediately out of the Chaos, was not the same, nor like to that of the present Earth. Which was the first and preparatory Proposition we laid down to be prov'd. And this being prov'd by the authority both of our Reason and our Religion, we will now proceed to the Second which is more particular.

CHAPTER V

The Second Proposition is laid down, viz. *That* the face of the Earth before the Deluge was smooth, regular and uniform; without Mountains, and without a Sea. *The Chaos out of which the World rise is fully examin'd, and all its motions observ'd, and by what steps it wrought it self into an habitable World. Some things in Antiquity relating to the first state of the Earth are interpreted, and some things in the Sacred Writings. The Divine Art and Geometry in the construction of the first Earth is observ'd and celebrated.*

WE have seen it prov'd, in the foregoing Chapter, That the form of the first or Ante-diluvian Earth, was not the same, nor like the form of the present Earth; this is our first discovery at a distance, but 'tis only general and negative, tells us what the form of that Earth was not, but tells us not expressly what it was; that must be our next enquiry, and advancing one step further in our Theory, we lay down this Second Proposition: *That the face of the Earth before the Deluge was smooth, regular, and uniform; without Mountains, and without a Sea.* This is a bold step, and carries us into another World, which we have never seen nor ever yet heard any relation of; and a World, it seems, of very different scenes and prospects from ours, or from any thing we have yet known. An Earth without a Sea, and plain as the *Elysian* fields; if you travel it all over, you will not meet with a Mountain or a Rock, yet well provided of all things requisite for an habitable World; and the same indeed with the Earth we still inhabit, only under another form. And this is the great thing that now comes into debate, the great Paradox which we offer to be examin'd, and which we affirm, That the Earth in its first rise and formation from a Chaos, was of the form here describ'd, and so continu'd for many hundreds of years.

To examine and prove this, we must return to the beginning of the World, and to that Chaos out of which the Earth and all Sublunary things arose: 'Tis the motions and progress of this which we must now consider, and what form it setled into when it first became an habitable World.

Neither is it perhaps such an intricate thing as we imagine at first sight, to trace a Chaos into an habitable World; at least there is a particular pleasure to see things in their Origin, and by what degrees and successive changes they rise into that order and state we see them in afterwards, when compleated. I am sure, if ever we would view the paths of Divine Wisdom, in the works and in the conduct of Nature, we must not only consider how things are, but how they came to be so. 'Tis pleasant to look upon a Tree in the Summer, cover'd with its green Leaves, deckt with Blossoms, or laden with Fruit, and casting a pleasing shade under its spreading Boughs; but to consider how this Tree with all its furniture, sprang from a little Seed; how Nature shap'd it, and fed it, in its infancy and growth; added new parts, and still advanc'd it by little and little, till it came to this greatness and perfection, this, methinks, is another sort of pleasure, more rational, less common, and which is properly the contemplation of Divine Wisdom in the works of Nature. So to view this Earth, and this Sublunary World, as it is now compleat, distinguisht into the several orders of bodies of which it consists, every one perfect and admirable in its kind; this is truly delightful, and a very good entertainment of the mind; But to see all these in their first Seeds, as I may so say; to take in pieces this frame of Nature, and melt it down into its first principles; and then to observe how the Divine Wisdom wrought all these things out of confusion into order, and out of simplicity into that beautiful composition we now see them in; this, methinks, is another kind of joy, which pierceth the mind more deep, and is more satisfactory. And to give out selves and others this satisfaction, we will first make a short representation of the Chaos, and then shew, how, according to Laws establisht in Nature by the Divine Power and Wisdom, it was wrought by degrees from one form into another, till it setled at length into an habitable Earth; and that of such a frame and structure, as we have describ'd in this second Proposition.

By the Chaos I understand the matter of the Earth and Heavens, without form or order; reduc'd into a fluid mass, wherein are the materials and ingredients of all bodies, but mingled in confusion one with another. As if you should suppose all sorts of Metals, Gold, Silver, Lead &c. melted down together in a common mass, and so mingled, that the parts of no one Metal could be discern'd as distinct from the rest, this would be a little metallick Chaos: Suppose then the Elements thus mingled, Air, Water and Earth, which are the principles of all Terrestrial bodies; mingled, I say, without any order of higher or lower, heavier or lighter, solid or volatile, in such a kind of confus'd mass as is here represented in this first Scheme.

Let this then represent to us the Chaos; in which the first change that we should imagine to happen would be this, that the heaviest and grossest parts would sink down towards the middle of it, (for there we suppose the center of its gravity) and the rest would float above. These grosser parts thus sunk down and compress'd more and more, would harden by degrees, and constitute the interiour parts of the Earth. The rest of the mass, which swims above, would be also

Page 54   Fig. 1

divided by the same principle of gravity into two orders of Bodies, the one Liquid like Water, the other Volatile like Air. For the more fine and active parts disentangling themselves by degrees from the rest, would mount above them; and having motion enough to keep them upon the wing, would play in those open places where they constitute that body we call AIR. The other parts being grosser than these, and having a more languid motion could not fly up and down separate from one another, as these did, but setled in a mass together, under the Air, upon the body of the Earth, composing not only Water strictly so call'd, but the whole mass of liquors, or liquid bodies, belonging to the Earth. And these first separations being thus made, the body of the Chaos would stand in that form which it is here represented in by the second Scheme.

The liquid mass which encircled the Earth, was not, as I noted before, the meer Element of Water, but a collection of all Liquors that belong to the Earth.

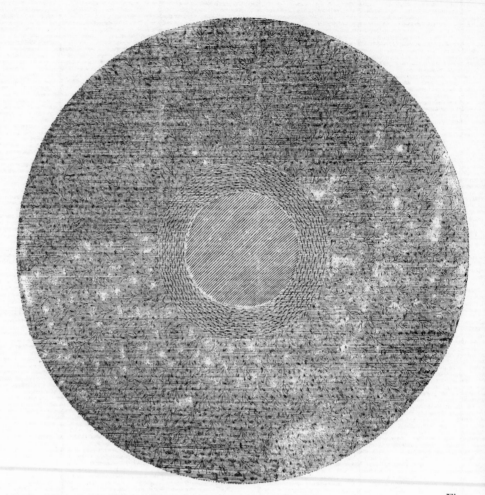

Page 55   Fig. 2

I mean of all that do originally belong to it. Now seeing there are two chief kinds
of Terrestrial liquors, those that are fat, oily, and light; and those that are lean
and more Earthy, like common Water; which two are generally found in compound liquors; we cannot doubt but there were of both sorts in this common
mass of liquids. And it being well known, that these two kinds mixt together,
if left to themselves and the general action of Nature, separate one from another
when they come to settle, as in Cream and thin Milk, Oil and Water, and such
like; we cannot but conclude, that the same Effect would follow here, and the
more oily and light part of this mass would get above the other, and swim upon
it. The whole mass being divided into two lesser masses, and so the Globe would
stand as we see it in this third Figure.

Hitherto the changes of the Chaos are easie and unquestionable, and would be
dispatcht in a short time; we must now look over again these two great masses

56

Page 56   Fig. 3

of the *Air* and *Water*, and consider how their impurities or grosser parts would
be dispos'd of; for we cannot imagine but they were both at first very muddy
and impure: And as the Water would have its sediment, which we are not here
concern'd to look after, so the great Regions of the Air would certainly have
their sediment too; for the Air was as yet thick, gross, and dark; there being an
abundance of little Terrestrial particles swimming in it still, after the grossest
were sunk down; which, by their heaviness and lumpish figure, made their way
more easily and speedily. The lesser and lighter which remain'd, would sink too,
but more slowly, and in a longer time: so as in their descent they would meet
with that oily liquor upon the face of the Deep, or upon the watery mass, which
would entangle and stop them from passing any further; whereupon mixing
there with that unctious substance, they compos'd a certain slime, or fat, soft,
and light Earth, spread upon the face of the Waters; as 'tis represented in this
fourth Figure.

57

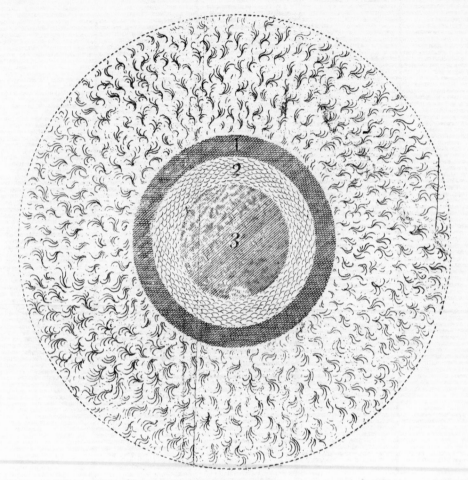

Page 57   Fig. 4

This thin and tender Orb of Earth increas'd still more and more, as the little Earthy parts that were detain'd in the Air could make their way to it. Some having a long journey from the upper Regions, and others being very light would float up and down a good while, before they could wholly disengage themselves and descend. But this was the general rendezvous, which sooner or later they all got to, and mingling more and more with that oily liquor, they suckt it all up at length, and where wholly incorporate together, and so began to grow more stiff and firm, making both but one substance, which was the first concretion, or firm and consistent substance that rise upon the face of the Chaos. And the whole Globe stood in this posture, as in Fig. the fifth.

It may be, you will say, we take our liberty, and our own time for the separation of these two liquors, the Oily and the Earthy, the lighter and the heavier; and suppose that done before the Air was clear'd of Earthy particles, that so they might be catcht and stopt there in their descent. Whereas if all these particles were fallen out of the Air before that separation was made in the liquid mass, they would fall down through the Water, as the first did, and so no concretion would be made, nor any Earthy crust form'd upon the face of the Waters, as we here suppose there was. 'Tis true, there could be no such Orb of Earth form'd there, if the Air was wholly purg'd of all its Earthy parts before the Mass of liquids began to purifie it self, and to separate the Oily parts from the more heavy: But this is an unreasonable and incredible supposition, if we consider,

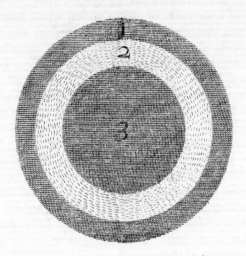

Page 58   Fig. 5

that the mass of the Air was many thousand times greater than the Water, and would in proportion require a greater time to be purified; The particles that were in the Regions of the Air having a long way to come before they reacht the Watery mass, and far longer than the Oily particles had to rise from any part of that mass to the surface of it. Besides, we may suppose a great many degrees of littleness and lightness in these Earthy particles, so as many of them might float in the Air a good while, like Exhalations, before they fell down. And lastly, we do not suppose the separation of these two liquors wholly made and finisht before the purgation of the Air began, though we represent them so for distinction sake; Let them begin to purifie at the same time, if you please, these parts rising upwards, and those falling downwards, they will meet in the middle, and unite and grow into one body, as we have describ'd. And this body or new concretion would be increas'd daily, being fed and suppli'd both from above and below; and having done growing, it would become more dry by degrees, and of a temper of greater consistency and firmness, so as truly to resemble and be fit to make an habitable Earth, such as Nature intended it for.

But you will further object, it may be, that such an effect as this would indeed be necessary in some degree and proportion, but not in such a proportion, and in such quantity as would be sufficient to make this crust or concrete Orb an habitable Earth. This I confess appear'd to me at first a real difficulty, till I consider'd better the great disproportion there is betwixt the Regions of the Air and the Circumference of the Earth, or of that exteriour Orb of the Earth, we are now a making; which being many thousand times less in depth and extent than the Regions of the Air, taken as high as the Moon, though these Earthy particles, we speak of, were very thinly dispers'd through those vast tracts of the Air, when they came to be collected and amass'd together upon the surface of a far lesser Sphere, they would constitute a body of a very considerable thickness and solidity. We see the Earth sometimes cover'd with Snow two or three feet deep, made up only of little flakes or pieces of Ice, which falling from the middle Region of the Air, and meeting with the Earth in their descent, are there stopt and heapt up one upon another. But if we should suppose little particles of Earth to shower down, not only from the middle Region, but from the whole capacity and extent of those vast spaces that are betwixt us and the Moon, we could not imagine but these would constitute an Orb of Earth some thousands of times deeper than the greatest Snow; which being increas'd and swoln by that oily liquor it fell into, and incorporated with, it would be thick, strong, and great enough in all respects to render it an habitable Earth.

We cannot doubt therefore but such a body as this would be form'd, and would be sufficient in quantity for an habitable Earth. Then for the quality of it, it will answer all the purposes of a *Rising World*. What can be a more proper Seminary for Plants and Animals, than a soil of this temper and composition? A finer and lighter sort of Earth mixt with a benign Juice, easie and obedient to the action of the Sun, or of what other causes were imploy'd by the Author of Nature, for the production of things in the new-made Earth. What sort or disposition of matter could be more fit and ready to catch life from Heaven, and to be drawn into all forms that the rudiments of life, or the bodies of living Creatures would require? What soil more proper for Vegetation than this warm moisture, which could have no fault, unless it was too fertile and luxuriant? and that is no fault neither at the beginning of a World. This I am sure of, that the learned amongst the Ancients, both *Greeks*, *Egyptians*, *Phœnicians*, and others, have describ'd the primigenial soil, or the temper of the Earth, that was the first subject for the Generation and Origin of Plants and Animals, after such a manner, as is truly express'd, and I think with advantage, by this draught of the primigenial Earth.

Thus much concerning the matter of the first Earth. Let us reflect a little upon the form of it also, whether External or Internal; whereof both do manifestly shew themselves from the manner of its production or formation. As to the External form, you see it is according to the Proposition we were to prove, *smooth, regular and uniform, without Mountains, and without a Sea*. And the proof we have given of it is very easie; The Globe of the Earth could not possibly rise immediately from a Chaos into the irregular form in which it is at present. The Chaos being a fluid mass, which we know doth necessarily fall into a Spherical surface, whose parts are equi-distant from the Center, and consequently in an equal and even convexity one with another. And seeing upon the distinction of a Chaos and separation into several Elementary masses, the Water would naturally

'Ιλὺς ωροτος
γενῆς.

have a superiour place to the Earth, 'tis manifest, that there could be no habitable Earth form'd out of the Chaos, unless by some concretion upon the face of the Water. Then lastly, seeing this concrete Orb of Earth upon the face of the Water would be of the same form with the surface of the Water it was spread upon, there being no causes, that we know of, to make any inequality in it, we must conclude it equal and uniform, and without Mountains; as also without a Sea; for the Sea and all the mass of Waters was enclos'd within this exteriour Earth, which had no other basis or foundation to rest upon.

The contemplation of these things, and of this posture of the Earth upon the Waters, doth so strongly bring to mind certain passages of Scripture, that we cannot, without injury to truth, pass them by in silence. Passages that have such a manifest resemblance and agreement to this form and situation of the Earth, that it is not possible to believe, but that they allude to it, or rather literally express it; such are those expressions of the Psalmist, *God hath founded the Earth upon the Seas.* And in another Psalm, speaking of the wisdom and power of God in the Creation, he saith, *To him who alone doth great wonders; to him that by wisdom made the Heavens; to him that extended or stretched out the Earth above the Waters.* What can be more plain and positive to denote that form of the Earth that we have describ'd, and to express particularly the inclosure of the Waters within the Earth, as we have represented them? He saith in another place; *By the Word of the Lord were the Heavens made; be shut up the Waters of the Sea as in Bags,* (for so the word is to be render'd, and is render'd by all, except the *English*) *and laid up the Abysse as in store-houses.* We cannot easily imagine any thing more express, or more conformable to that System of the Earth and Sea, which we have propos'd here. Yet there is something more express than all this in that remarkable place in the *Proverbs* of *Solomon*, where *Wisdom* declaring her Antiquity and Existence before the foundation of the Earth, amongst other things, saith; *When he prepared the Heavens, I was there: When he drew an Orb over the surface of the Abysse;* or when he set an Orb upon the face of the Abysse. We render it in the *English* a *Compass*, or *Circle*, but 'tis more truly rendred an Orb or Sphere; and what Orb or Spherical body was this, which at the formation of the Earth was built and plac'd round about the Abysse; but that wonderful Arch, whose form and production we have describ'd, encompassing the mass of Waters, which in Scripture is often call'd the Abysse or Deep? Lastly, this Scheme of the first Earth gives light to that place we mention'd before of St. *Peter*'s, where the first Earth is said to *consist of Water and by Water:* and by reason thereof was obnoxious to a Deluge. The first part of this character is plain from the description now given: and the second will appear in the following Chapter. In the mean time, concerning these passages of Scripture, which we have cited, we may truly and modestly say, that though they would not, it may be, without a Theory premis'd, have been taken or interpreted in this sence, yet this Theory being premis'd, I dare appeal to any unprejudic'd person, if they have not a fairer and easier, a more full and more emphatical sence, when appli'd to that form of the Earth and Sea, we are now speaking of, than to their present form, or to any other we can imagine.

Prov. 8. 27.

Vid. Fig. 5, *p.* 59
This Orb is re-
presented by the
Circle 1, and the
Abysse by the
Region 2.

Thus much concerning the external form of the first Earth. Let us now reflect a little upon the Internal form of it, which consists of several Regions, involving one another like Orbs about the same Center, or of the several Elements cast circularly about each other; as it appears in the Fourth and Fifth Figure. And as we have noted the External form of this primæval Earth, to have been markt and celebrated in the Sacred Writings; so likewise in the Philosophy and Learning of the Ancients, there are several remains and indications of this Internal form and composition of it. For 'tis observable, that the Ancients in treating of the Chaos, and in raising the World out of it, rang'd it into several Regions or Masses, as we have done; and in that order successively, rising one from another, as if it was a Pedigree or Genealogy. And those Parts and Regions of Nature, into which the Chaos was by degrees divided, they signifi'd commonly by dark and obscure names, as the *Night, Tartarus, Oceanus,* and such like, which we have express'd in their plain and proper terms. And whereas the Chaos, when it was first set on work, ran all into divisions, and separations of one Element from another, which afterwards were all in some measure united and associated in this primigenial Earth; the Ancients accordingly made *Contention* the principle that reign'd in the Chaos at first, and then *Love:* The one to express the divisions, and the other the union of all parties in this middle and common bond. These, and such like notions which we find in the writings of the Ancients figuratively and darkly deliver'd, receive a clearer light, when compar'd with this Theory of the Chaos; which representing every thing plainly, and in its natural colours, is a *Lib.* 2. Key to their thoughts, and in allustration of their obscurer Philosophy, con- *Chap.* 7. cerning the Original of the World; as we have shewn at large in the *Latin* Treatise.

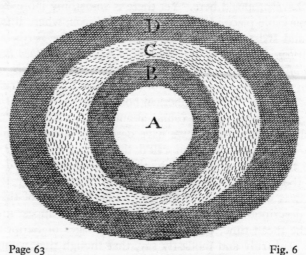

Page 63   Fig. 6

There is another thing in Antiquity, relating to the form and construction of the Earth, which is very remarkable, and hath obtain'd throughout all learned Nations and Ages. And that is the comparison or resemblance of the Earth to an *Egg.* And this is not so much for its External Figure, though that be true too: as for the inward composition of it; consisting of several Orbs, one including another, and in that order, as to answer the several Elementary Regions of which the new-made Earth was constituted. For if we admit for the *Yolk* a Central fire (which, though very reasonable, we had no occasion to take notice of in our Theory of the Chaos) and suppose the Figure of the Earth *Oval*, and a little extended towards the Poles, as probably it was; those two bodies do very naturally represent one another; as in this Scheme, which represents the Interiour faces of both, a divided *Egg*, or Earth. Where, as the two inmost Regions A. B. represent the Yolk and the Membrane that lies next about it; so the Exteriour Region of the Earth (D) is as the Shell of the Egg, and the Abysse (C) under it as the White that lies under the Shell. And considering that this notion of the *Mundane Egg*, or that the World was *Oviform*, hath been the sence and Language of all Antiquity, *Latins*, *Greeks*, *Persians*, *Egyptians*, and others, as we have shew'd elsewhere; I thought it worthy our notice in this place; seeing it receives such a clear and easie explication from that Origin and Fabrick we have given to the first Earth, and also reflects light upon the Theory it self, and confirms it to be no fiction: This notion, which is a kind of Epitome or Image of it, having been conserv'd in the most ancient Learning.

*Tell. Theor. Sac.
lib. 2, c. 10.*

    Thus much concerning the first Earth, its production and form; and concerning our Second Proposition relating to it: Which being prov'd by Reason, the laws of Nature, and the motions of the Chaos; then attested by Antiquity, both as to the matter and form of it; and confirm'd by Sacred Writers, we may take it now for a well establish'd truth, and proceed upon this supposition, *That the Ante-diluvian Earth was smooth and uniform, without Mountains or Sea*, to the explication of the universal Deluge.

    Give me leave only before we proceed any further, to annex here a short Advertisement, concerning the causes of this wonderful structure of the first Earth. 'Tis true, we have propos'd the Natural Causes of it, and I do not know wherein our Explication is false or defective; but in things of this kind we may easily be too credulous. And this structure is so marvellous, that it ought rather to be consider'd as a particular effect of the Divine Art, than as the work of Nature. The whole Globe of the Water vaulted over, and the Exteriour Earth hanging above the Deep, sustain'd by nothing but its own measures and manner of construction: A Building without foundation or corner-stone. This seems to be a piece of Divine Geometry or Architecture; and to this, I think, is to be refer'd that magnificent challenge which God Almighty made to *Job; Where wast thou when I laid the foundations of the Earth? declare if thou hast understanding; Who hath laid the measures thereof, if thou knowest; or who hath stretched the line upon it? Whereupon are the foundations thereof fastned, or who laid the corner-stone thereof? When the morning Stars sang together, and all the sons of God shouted for joy. Moses* also when he had describ'd the Chaos, saith, *The spirit of God mov'd upon*, or sat brooding upon, *the face of the waters;* without all doubt to produce some effects there. And S. *Peter*, when he speaks of the form of the Ante-diluvian Earth, how it stood in reference to the Waters, adds, *By the Word of God*, or by the Wisdom of God it was made so. And this same *Wisdom* of God,

Job 38. 4, 5, 6,
7, &c.

Τῷ λόγῳ τοῦ
Θεοῦ.

in the *Proverbs*, as we observed before, takes notice of this very piece of work in the formation of the Earth. *When he set an Orb over the face of the Deep I was there.* And lastly, the Ancient Philosophers, or at least the best of them, to give them their due, always brought in *Mens* or *Amor*, as a Supernatural principle to unite and consociate the parts of the Chaos; which was first done in the composition of this wonderful Arch of the Earth. *Wherefore* to the great Architect, who made the boundless Universe out of nothing, and form'd the Earth out of a Chaos, let the praise of the whole Work, and particularly of this Master-piece, for ever with all honour be given.

*Λόγος &
Ἔρως.*

CHAPTER VI

The dissolution of the First Earth: The Deluge ensuing thereupon. And the form of the present Earth rising from the Ruines of the First.

*Vid. Fig. 5, & 6.
pag. 59, & 62.*

WE have now brought to light the Ante-diluvian Earth out of the dark mass of the Chaos; and not only described the surface of it, but laid open the inward parts, to shew in what order its Regions lay. Let us now close it up, and represent the Earth entire, and in larger proportions, more like an habitable World; as in this Figure, where you see the smooth convex of the Earth, and may imagine the great Abysse spread under it*; which two are to be the only subject of our further contemplation.

In this smooth Earth were the first Scenes of the World, and the first Generations of Mankind; it had the beauty of Youth and blooming Nature, fresh and fruitful, and not a wrinkle, scar or fracture in all its body; no Rocks nor Mountains, no hollow Caves, nor gaping Chanels, but even and uniform all over. And the smoothness of the Earth made the face of the Heavens so too; the Air was calm and serene; none of those tumultuary motions and conflicts of vapours, which the Mountains and the Winds cause in ours: 'Twas suited to a golden Age, and to the first innocency of Nature.

All this you'll say is well, we are got into a pleasant World indeed, but what's this to the purpose? what appearance of a Deluge here, where there is not so much as a Sea, nor half so much water as we have in this Earth? or what appearance of Mountains, or Caverns, or other irregularities of the Earth, where all is level and united? So that instead of loosing the Knot, this ties it the harder. You pretend to shew us how the Deluge was made, and you lock up all the Waters within the womb of the Earth, and set Bars and Doors, and a Wall of impenetrable strength and thickness to keep them there. And you pretend to shew us the original of Rocks and Mountains, and Caverns of the Earth, and bring us to a wide and endless plain, smooth as the calm Sea.

This is all true, and yet we are not so far from the sight and discovery of those things as you imagine; draw but the curtain and these Scenes will appear, or something very like them. We must remember that St. *Peter* told us, that the Ante-diluvian Earth perish'd, or was demolish'd; and *Moses* saith, the *great Abysse*

---

* *As at the aperture a. a.*

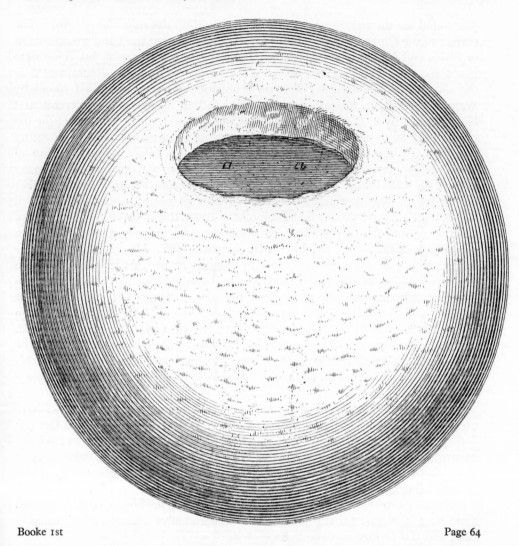

was broken open at the Deluge. Let us then suppose, that at a time appointed by Divine Providence, and from Causes made ready to do that great execution upon a sinful World, that this *Abysse* was open'd, or that the frame of the Earth broke and fell down into the *Great Abysse*. At this one stroke all Nature would be chang'd, and this single action would have two great and visible Effects. The one Transient, and the other permanent. First an universal Deluge would overflow all the parts and Regions of the broken Earth, during the great commotion and agitation of the Abysse, by the violent fall of the Earth into it. This would be the first and unquestionable effect of this dissolution, and all that World would be destroyed. Then when the agitation of the Abysse was asswag'd, and the Waters by degrees were retir'd into their Chanels, and the dry land appear'd,

E

65

you would see the true image of the present Earth in the ruines of the first. The surface of the Globe would be divided into Land and Sea; the Land would consist of Plains and Valleys and Mountains, according as the pieces of this ruine were plac'd and dispos'd: Upon the banks of the Sea would stand the Rocks, and near the shoar would be Islands, or lesser fragments of Earth compass'd round by Water. Then as to Subterraneous Waters, and all Subterraneous Caverns and hollownesses, upon this supposition those things could not be otherwise; for the parts would fall hollow in many places in this, as in all other ruines: And seeing the Earth fell into this Abysse, the Waters at a certain height would flow into all those hollow places and cavities; and would also sink and insinuate into many parts of the solid Earth. And though these Subterraneous Vaults or holes, whether dry or full of Water, would be more or less in all places, where the parts fell hollow; yet they would be found especially about the roots of the Mountains, and the higher parts of the Earth; for there the sides bearing up one against the other, they could not lie so close at the bottoms, but many vacuities would be intercepted. Nor are there any other inequalities or irregularities observable in the present form of the Earth; whether in the surface of it, or interiour construction, whereof this *hypothesis* doth not give a ready, fair, and intelligible account; and doth at one view represent them all to us, with their causes, as in a glass: And whether that Glass be true, and the Image answer to the Original, if you doubt of it, we will hereafter examine them piece by piece. But in the first place, we must consider the General Deluge, how easily and truly this supposition represents and explains it, and answers all the properties and conditions of it.

I think it will be easily allow'd, that such a dissolution of the Earth as we have propos'd, and fall of it into the Abysse, would certainly make an universal Deluge; and effectually destroy the old World, which perish'd in it. But we have not yet particularly prov'd this dissolution, and in what manner the Deluge follow'd upon it: And to assert things in gross never makes that firm impression upon our understandings, and upon our belief, as to see them deduc'd with their causes and circumstances; And therefore we must endeavour to shew what preparations there were in Nature for this great dissolution, and after what manner it came to pass, and the Deluge in consequence of it.

We have noted before, that *Moses* imputed the Deluge to the disruption of the Abysse; and St. *Peter*, to the particular constitution of that Earth, which made it obnoxious to be absorpt in Water, so as our explication so far is justifi'd. But it was below the dignity of those Sacred Pen-men, or the Spirit of God that directed them, to shew us the causes of this disruption, or of this absorption; this is left to the enquiries of men. For it was never the design of Providence, to give such particular explications of Natural things, that should make us idle, or the use of Reason unnecessary; but on the contrary, by delivering great conclusions to us, to excite our curiosity and inquisitiveness after the methods, by which such things were brought to pass: And it may be there is no greater trial or instance of Natural wisdom, than to find out the Chanel, in which these great revolutions of Nature, which we treat on, flow and succeed one another.

Let us therefore resume that System of the Ante-diluvian Earth, which we have deduc'd from the Chaos, and which we find to answer St. *Peter*'s description, and *Moses* his account of the Deluge. This Earth could not be obnoxious to a Deluge, as the Apostle supposeth it to have been, but by a dissolution; for the Abysse was enclos'd within its bowels. And *Moses* doth in effect tell us, there was such a dissolution, when he saith, *The fountains of the great Abysse were broken open.* For fountains are broken open no otherwise than by breaking up the ground that covers them: We must therefore here enquire in what order, and from what causes the frame of this exteriour Earth was dissolv'd, and then we shall soon see how, upon that dissolution, the Deluge immediately prevail'd and overflow'd all the parts of it.

I do not think it in the power of humane wit to determine how long this frame would stand, how many Years, or how many Ages; but one would soon imagine, that this kind of structure would not be perpetual, nor last indeed many thousands of Years, if one consider the effect that the heat of the Sun would have upon it, and the Waters under it; drying and parching the one, and rarifying the other into vapours. For we must consider, that the course of the Sun at that time, or the posture of the Earth to the Sun, was such, that there was no diversity or alternation of seasons in the Year, as there is now; by reason of which alternation, our Earth is kept in an equality of temper, the contrary seasons balancing one another; so as what moisture the heat of the Summer sucks out of the Earth, 'tis repaid in the Rains of the next Winter; and what chaps were made in it, are fill'd up again, and the Earth reduc'd to its former constitution. But if we should imagine a continual Summer, the Earth would proceed in driness still more and more, and the cracks would be wider and pierce deeper into the substance of it: And such a continual Summer there was, at least an equality of seasons in the Ante-diluvian Earth, as shall be prov'd in the following Book, concerning *Paradise*. In the mean time this being suppos'd, let us consider what effect it would have upon this Arch of the exteriour Earth, and the Waters under it.

We cannot believe, but that the heat of the Sun, within the space of some hundreds of years, would have reduc'd this Earth to a considerable degree of driness in certain parts; and also have much rarifi'd and exhal'd the Waters under it: And considering the structure of that Globe, the exteriour crust, and the Waters lying round under it, both expos'd to the Sun, we may fitly compare it to an *Æolipile*, or an hollow Sphere with Water in it, which the heat of the Fire rarifies and turns into Vapours and Wind. The Sun here is as the Fire, and the exteriour Earth is as the Shell of the *Æolipile*, and the Abysse as the Water within it; now when the heat of the Sun had pierced through the Shell and reacht the Waters, it began to rarifie them, and raise them into Vapours; which rarefaction made them require more space and room than they needed before, while they lay close and quiet. And finding themselves pen'd in by the exteriour Earth, they press'd with violence against that Arch, to make it yield and give way to their dilatation and eruption. So we see all Vapours and Exhalations enclos'd within the Earth, and agitated there, strive to break out, and often shake the ground with their attempts to get loose. And in the comparison we us'd of an

Æolipile, if the mouth of it be stopt that gives the vent, the Water rarifi'd will burst the Vessel with its force. And the resemblance of the Earth to an Egg, which we us'd before, holds also in this respect; for when it heats before the Fire, the moisture and Air within being rarifi'd, makes it often burst the Shell. And I do the more willingly mention this last comparison, because I observe that some of the Ancients, when they speak of the doctrine of the *Mundane Egg*, say, that after a certain period of time it was broken.

But there is yet another thing to be consider'd in this case; for as the heat of the Sun gave force to these Vapours more and more, and made them more strong and violent; so on the other hand, it also weaken'd more and more the Arch of the Earth, that was to resist them; sucking out the moisture that was the cement of its parts, drying it immoderately, and chapping it in sundry places. And there being no Winter then to close up and unite its parts, and restore the Earth to its former strength and compactness, it grew more and more dispos'd to a dissolution. And at length, these preparations in Nature being made on either side, the force of the Vapours increas'd, and the walls weaken'd, which should have kept them in, when the appointed time was come, that All-wise Providence had design'd for the punishment of a sinful World, the whole fabrick brake, and the frame of the Earth was torn in pieces, as by an Earthquake; and those great portions or fragments, into which it was divided, fell down into the Abysse, some in one posture, and some in another.

This is a short and general account how we may conceive the dissolution of the first Earth, and an universal Deluge arising upon it. And this manner of dissolution hath so many examples in Nature every Age, that we need not insist farther upon the Explication of it. The generality of Earthquakes arise from like causes, and often end in a like effect, a partial Deluge, or Inundation of the place or Country where they happen; and of these we have seen some instances even in our own times: But whensoever it so happens, that the Vapours and Exhalations shut up in the caverns of the Earth, by rarefaction or compression come to be straitned, they strive every way to set themselves at liberty, and often break their prison, or the cover of the Earth that kept them in; which Earth upon that disruption falls into the Subterraneous Caverns that lie under it: And if it so happens that those Caverns are full of Water, as generally they are, if they be great or deep, that City or tract of Land is drown'd. And also the fall of such a mass of Earth, with its weight and bulk, doth often force out the Water so impetuously, as to throw it upon all the Country round about. There are innumerable examples in History (whereof we shall mention some hereafter) of Cities and Countries thus swallow'd up, or overflow'd, by an Earthquake, and an Inundation arising upon it. And according to the manner of their fall or ruine, they either remain'd wholly under water, and perpetually drown'd, as *Sodom* and *Gomorrha*, *Plato*'s *Atlantis*, *Bura* and *Helice*, and other Cities and Regions in *Greece* and *Asia*; or they partly emerg'd, and became dry Land again; when (their situation being pretty high) the Waters, after their violent agitation was abated, retir'd into the lower places, and into their Chanels.

Now if we compare these partial dissolutions of the Earth with an universal dissolution, we may as easily conceive an universal Deluge from an universal

Dissolution, as a partial Deluge from a partial Dissolution. If we can conceive a City, a Country, an Island, a Continent thus absorpt and overflown; if we do but enlarge our thought and imagination a little, we may conceive it as well of the whole Earth. And it seems strange to me, that none of the Ancients should hit upon this way of explaining the universal Deluge; there being such frequent instances in all Ages and Countries of Inundations made in this manner, and never of any great Inundation made otherwise, unless in maritim Countries, by the irruption of the Sea into grounds that lie low. 'Tis true, they would not so easily imagine this Dissolution, because they did not understand the true form of the Ante-diluvian Earth; but, methinks, the examination of the Deluge should have led them to the discovery of that: For observing the difficulty, or impossibility of an universal Deluge, without the Dissolution of the Earth; as also frequent instances of these Dissolutions accompani'd with Deluges, where the ground was hollow, and had Subterraneous Waters; this, methinks, should have prompted them to imagine, that those Subterraneous Waters were universal at that time, or extended quite round the Earth; so as a dissolution of the exteriour Earth could not be made any where, but it would fall into Waters, and be more or less overflow'd. And when they had once reacht this thought, they might conclude both what the form of the Ante-diluvian Earth was, and that the Deluge came to pass by the dissolution of it. But we reason with ease about the finding out of things, when they are once found out; and there is but a thin paper-wall sometimes between the great discoveries and a perfect ignorance of them. Let us proceed now to consider, whether this supposition will answer all the conditions of an universal Deluge, and supply all the defects which we found in other Explications.

The great difficulty propos'd, was to find Water sufficient to make an universal Deluge, reaching to the tops of the Mountains; and yet that this Water should be transient, and after some time should so return into its Chanels, that the dry Land would appear, and the Earth become again habitable. There was that double impossibility in the common opinion, that the quantity of water necessary for such a Deluge was no where to be found, or could no way be brought upon the Earth; and then if it was brought, could no way be remov'd again. Our explication quite takes off the edge of this Objection; for, performing the same effect with a far less quantity of Water, 'tis both easie to be found, and easily remov'd when the work is done. When the exteriour Earth was broke, and fell into the Abysse, a good part of it was cover'd with water by the meer depth of the Abysse it fell into, and those parts of it that were higher than the Abysse was deep, and consequently would stand above it in a calm water, were notwithstanding reacht and overtop'd by the waves, during the agitation and violent commotion of the Abysse. For it is not imaginable what the commotion of the Abysse would be upon this dissolution of the Earth, nor to what height its waves would be thrown, when those prodigious fragments were tumbled down into it. Suppose a stone of ten thousand weight taken up into the Air a mile or two, and then let fall into the middle of the Ocean, I do not believe but that the dashing of the water upon that impression, would rise as high as a Mountain. But suppose a mighty Rock or heap of Rocks to fall from that height, or a great Island, or a

69

Continent; these would expel the waters out of their places, with such a force and violence, as to fling them among the highest Clouds.

'Tis incredible to what height sometimes great Stones and Cinders will be thrown, at the eruptions of fiery Mountains; and the pressure of a great mass of Earth falling into the Abysse, though it be a force of another kind, could not but impel the water with so much strength, as would carry it up to a great height in the Air; and to the top of any thing that lay in its way, any eminency, or high fragment whatsoever: And then rowling back again, it would sweep down with it whatsoever it rusht upon, Woods, Buildings, living Creatures, and carry them all headlong into the great gulf. Sometimes a mass of water would be quite struck off and separate from the rest, and tost through the Air like a flying River; but the common motion of the waves was to climb up the hills, or inclin'd fragments, and then return into the valleys and deeps again, with a perpetual fluctuation going and coming, ascending and descending, till the violence of them being *Psal.* 104. 6, 7, spent by degrees, they setled at last in the places allotted for them; where *bounds* 8, 9. *are set that they cannot pass over, that they return not again to cover the Earth.*

Neither is it to be wonder'd, that the great Tumult of the waters, and the extremity of the Deluge lasted for some months; for besides, that the first shock and commotion of the Abysse was extremely violent, from the general fall of the Earth, there were ever and anon some secondary ruines; or some parts of the great ruine, that were not well setled, broke again, and made new commotions: And 'twas a considerable time before the great fragments that fell, and their lesser dependencies could be so adjusted and fitted, as to rest in a firm and immoveable posture: For the props and stays whereby they lean'd one upon another, or upon the bottom of the Abysse, often fail'd, either by the incumbent weight, or the violent impulses of the water against them; and so renew'd, or continu'd the disorder and confusion of the Abysse. Besides, we are to observe, that these great fragments falling hollow, they inclos'd and bore down with them under their concave surface a great deal of Air; and while the water compass'd these fragments, and overflow'd them, the Air could not readily get out of those prisons, but by degrees, as the Earth and Water above would give way; so as this would also hinder the settlement of the Abysse, and the retiring of the Water into those Subterraneous Chanels, for some time. But at length, when this Air had found a vent, and left its place to the Water, and the ruines, both primary and secondary, were setled and fixt, then the Waters of the Abysse began to settle too, and the dry Land to appear; first the tops of the Mountains, then the high Grounds, then the Plains and the rest of the Earth. And this gradual subsidency of the Abysse (which *Moses* also hath particularly noted) and discovery of the several parts of the Earth, would also take up a considerable time.

Thus a new World appear'd, or the Earth put on its new form, and became divided into Sea and Land; and the Abysse, which from several Ages, even from the beginning of the World, had lain hid in the womb of the Earth, was brought to light and discover'd; the greatest part of it constituting our present Ocean, and the rest filling the lower cavities of the Earth: Upon the Land appear'd the Mountains and the Hills, and the Islands in the Sea, and the Rocks upon the shore. And so the Divine Providence, having prepar'd Nature for so great a change, at one stroke dissolv'd the frame of the old World, and made us a new one out of its ruines, which we now inhabit since the Deluge. All which things being thus explain'd, deduc'd, and stated, we now add and pronounce our Third and last Proposition; *That the disruption of the Abysse, or dissolution of the primæval Earth and its fall into the Abysse, was the cause of the Universal Deluge, and of the destruction of the old World.*

CHAPTER VII

That the Explication we have given of an Universal Deluge is not an Idea *only, but an account of what really came to pass in this Earth, and the true Explication of* Noah's *Flood; as is prov'd by Argument and from History. An Examination of* Tehom-Rabba, *or the great Abysse, and that by it the Sea cannot be understood, nor the Subterraneous Waters, as they are at present. What the true Notion and Form of it was, collected from* Moses *and other Sacred Writers; The frequent allusions in Scripture to the opening and shutting the Abysse, and the particular stile of Scripture in its reflections on the Origin, and the Formation of the Earth. Observations on* Deucalion's *Deluge.*

WE have now given an account of the first great revolution of Nature, and of the Universal Deluge, in a way that is intelligible, and from causes that answer the greatness of the effect; We have suppos'd nothing but what is also prov'd, both as to the first form of the Earth, and as to the manner of its Dissolution: and how far from that would evidently and necessarily arise a general Deluge; which was that, which put a period to the old World, and the first state of things. And though all this hath been deduc'd in due order, and with connexion and consequence of one thing upon another, so far as I know, which is the true evidence of a Theory; yet it may not be sufficient to command the Assent and Belief of some persons, who will allow, it may be, and acknowledge, that this is a fair *Idea* of a possible Deluge in general, and of the destruction of a World by it; but this may be only an *Idea*, they'll say; we desire it may be prov'd from some collateral arguments, taken either from Sacred History, or from observation, that this hath really been exemplified upon the Earth, and that *Noah*'s Flood came to pass this way. And seeing we have design'd this first Book chiefly for the Explication of *Noah*'s Deluge, I am willing to add here a Chapter or two extraordinary upon this occasion; to shew, that what we have deliver'd is more than an *Idea*, and that it was in this very way that *Noah*'s Deluge came to pass. But they who have not this doubt, and have a mind to see the issue of the Theory, may skip these two Chapters, if they please, and proceed to the following.

To satisfie then the doubtful in this particular, let us lay down in the first place that conclusion which they seem to admit, *viz.* That this is a possible and consistent Explication of an Universal Deluge; and let's see how far this would go, if well consider'd, towards the proof of what they desire, or towards the demonstration of *Noah*'s Deluge in particular. It is granted on both hands, that there hath been an Universal Deluge upon the Earth, which was *Noah*'s Deluge; and it is also granted, that we have given a possible and consistent *Idea* of an Universal Deluge; Now we have prov'd *Chap. II.* and *III.* that all other ways assign'd for the Explication of *Noah*'s Flood are false or impossible; therefore it came to pass in that possible way which we have propos'd. And if we have truly prov'd, in the foremention'd Chapters, the impossibility of it in all other ways, this argumentation is undeniable. Besides, we may argue thus, As it is granted that there hath been an Universal Deluge upon the Earth; so I suppose it will be granted that there hath been but one: Now the dissolution of the Earth, whensoever it happen'd, would make one universal Deluge, and therefore the only one, and the same with *Noah*'s. That such a Dissolution as we have describ'd, would make an universal Deluge, I think, cannot be question'd; and that there hath been such a dissolution, besides what we have already alledg'd, shall be prov'd at large from natural Observations upon the Form and Figure of the present Earth, in the *Third* Section and last *Chap.* of this Book; In the mean time we will proceed to History, both Sacred and Profane, and by comparing our Explication with those, give further assurance of its truth and reality.

In the first place, it agrees, which is most considerable, with *Moses*'s Narration of the Deluge; both as to the matter and manner of it. The matter of the Deluge *Moses* makes to be the Waters from above, and the Waters from below; or he distinguishes the causes of the Deluge, as we do, into Superiour and Inferiour; and the Inferiour causes he makes to be the disruption of the Abysse, which is the principal part, and the great hinge of our Explication. Then as to the manner of the Deluge, the beginning and the ending, the increase and decrease, he saith it increas'd gradually, and decreast gradually, by *going* and *coming*; that is after many repeated fluctuations and reciprocations of the waves, the waters of the Abysse began to be more compos'd, and to retire into their Chanels, whence they shall never return to cover the Earth again. This agrees wholly with our Theory; we suppose the Abysse to have been under an extream commotion and agitation by the fall of the Earth into it, and this at first encrease more and more, till the whole Earth was faln; Then continuing for some time at the height of its rage, overwhelming the greatest Mountains, it afterwards decrease by the like degrees, leaving first the tops of the Mountains, then the Hills and the Fields, till the Waters came to be wholly drawn off the Earth into their Chanels.

It was no doubt a great oversight in the Ancients, to fancy the Deluge like a great standing Pool of water, reaching from the bottom of the Valleys to the tops of the Mountains, every where alike, with a level and uniform surface; by reason of which mistaken notion of the Deluge, they made more water necessary to it than was possible to be had, or being had, than it was possible to get quit of again; for there are no Chanels in the Earth that could hold so much water, either to give it, or to receive it. And the *Psalmist* speaking of the Deluge, as it seems to me, notes this violent commotion of the Abysse. *The Waters went up by the Mountains, came down by the Valleys unto the place which thou hast founded for them.* I know some interpret that passage of the state of the waters in the beginning, when they cover'd the face of the whole Earth, *Gen.* 1. 2. but that

Gen. 7. 11.

Vers. 17, 18, 19, 20. *Chap.* 8. 3, 5.

vid. St. *Austin* in loc.

Psal. 104. *vers.* 8, 9.

cannot be, because of what follows in the next Verse; *Thou hast set a bound that they may not pass over; that they turn not again to cover the Earth.* Which is not true, if the preceding words be understood of the state of the waters at the beginning of the World; for they did pass those bounds, and did return since that time to cover the Earth, namely at the Deluge: But if these words be refer'd to the time of the Deluge, and the state of the waters then, 'tis both a just description of the motion of the Abysse, and certainly true, that the waters since that time are so setled in their Chanels, that they shall never overflow the Earth again. As we are assured by the promise made to *Noah,* and that illustrious pledge and confirmation of it, the *Rainbow,* that the Heavens also shall never pour out so much waters again; their state being chang'd as well as that of the Earth, or Sea, from what they were before the Deluge.

But before we leave *Moses*'s Narration of the Deluge, we must examine further, what is, or can be understood by his TEHOM-RABBA, or *great Abysse,* which he saith was broken up at the Deluge; for this will help us to discover, whether our Explication be the same with his, and of the same Flood. And first we must consider, whether by the *Tehom-Rabba,* or Mosaical Abysse can be understood the Sea or Ocean, under that form we see it in at present; and 'tis plain, methinks, that the Sea cannot be understood by this great Abysse, both because the Sea is not capable upon any disruption to make such an universal Deluge; and because the Narration of *Moses,* and his expressions concerning this Abysse, do not agree to the Sea. Some of the Ancients indeed did imagine, that the waters of the Sea were much higher than the Land, and stood, as it were, on an heap; so as when these waters were let loose, they overflow'd the Earth, and made a Deluge. But this is known to be a gross mistake; the Sea and the Land make one Globe, and the Waters couch themselves, as close as may be, to the Center of this Globe in a Spherical convexity; so that if all the Mountains and Hills were scal'd, and the Earth made even, the Waters would not overflow its smooth surface; much less could they overflow it in the form that it is now in, where the Shores are higher than the Sea, the Inland parts than the Shores, and the Mountains still far above all: So as no disruption of the Sea could make an universal Deluge, by reason of its situation. But besides that, the quantity of Water contain'd in the Sea is no way sufficient to make a Deluge in the present form of the Earth; for we have shewn before, *Chap.* 2. that Eight such Oceans as ours would be little enough for that purpose. Then as to the expressions of *Moses* concerning this Abysse, if he had meant the Sea by it, and that the Deluge was made by the disruption of the Sea, why did he not say so? There is no mention of the Sea in all the History of the Deluge: *Moses* had mention'd the Sea before, *Gen.* 1. 10. and us'd a word that was common and known to signifie the Sea; And if he had a mind to express the same thing here, why should he not use the same word and the same term? In an Historical relation we use terms that are most proper and best known; but instead of that he useth the same term here that he did, *Gen.* 1. 2. when he saith, *Darkness was upon the face of the Abysse, or of the Deep,* as we render it; there the Abysse was open, or cover'd with darkness only, namely before the exteriour Earth was form'd; Here the same Abysse is mention'd again,

Gen. 7. 11.

but cover'd, by the formation of the Earth upon it; and the covering of this Abysse was broken or *cloven asunder*, and the Waters gusht out that made the Deluge. This I am sure is the most natural interpretation or signification of this word, according as it is us'd in *Moses*'s writings. Furthermore, we must observe what *Moses* saith concerning this Abysse, and whether that will agree with the Sea or no; he saith the *Fountains of the great Abysse were broken open*; now if by the great Abysse you understand the Sea, how are its Fountains broken open? To break open a Fountain, is to break open the ground that covers it, and what ground covers the Sea? So that upon all considerations, either of the word that *Moses* here useth, *Tehom-Rabba*, or of the thing affirmed concerning it, *breaking open its Fountains*; or of the effect following the breaking open its Fountains, *drowning of the Earth*; from all these heads it is manifest, that the Sea cannot be understood by the great Abysse, whose disruption was the cause of the Deluge.

And as the *Mosaical* Abysse cannot be the Sea, so neither can it be those Subterraneous waters that are disperst in the Cells and Caverns of the Earth; for as they are now lodg'd within the Earth, they are not one *Abysse*, but several Cisterns and Receptacles of water, in several places, especially under the roots of Mountains and Hills; separate one from another, sometimes by whole Regions and Countries interpos'd. Besides what Fountains, if they were broken up, could let out this water, or bring it upon the face of the Earth? When we sink a Mine, or dig a Well, the waters, when uncover'd, do not leap out of their places, or out of those Cavities, and flow upon the Earth; 'Tis not as if you open'd a Vein, where the Bloud spirts out, and riseth higher than its Source; but as when you take off the cover of a Vessel, the water doth not fly out for that: So if we should imagine all the Subterraneous Caverns of the Earth uncover'd, and the waters laid bare, there they would lie unmov'd in their beds, if the Earth did not fall into them to force them up. Furthermore, if these waters were any way extracted and laid upon the surface of the ground, nothing would be gain'd as to the Deluge by that, for as much water would run into these holes again when the Deluge begun to rise; so that this would be but an useless labour, and turn to no account. And lastly, these waters are no way sufficient for quantity to answer to the *Mosaical* Abysse, or to be the principal cause of the Deluge, as that was.

Now seeing neither the Sea, as it is at present, nor the Subterraneous waters, as they are at present, can answer to the *Mosaical Abysse*, we are sure there is nothing in this present Earth that can answer to it. Let us then on the other hand compare it with that Subterraneous Abysse, which we have found in the Ante-diluvian Earth, represented 2 *Fig.* 5, and examine their characters and correspondency: First, *Moses*'s Abysse was cover'd, and Subterraneous, for the *Fountains* of it are said to have been cloven or burst open; then it was vast and capacious; and thirdly, it was so dispos'd, as to be capable of a disruption, that would cause an universal Deluge to the Earth. Our Ante-diluvian Abysse answers truly to all these characters; 'twas in the womb of the Earth; the Earth was founded upon those *Waters*, as the *Psalmist* saith; or they were enclos'd within the Earth *as in a Bag*. Then for the capacity of it, it contained both all the waters now in the Ocean, and all those that are dispers'd in the Caverns of the Earth: And

p. 59.

74

lastly, it is manifest its situation was such, that upon a disruption or dissolution of the Earth which cover'd it, an universal Deluge would arise. Seeing then this answers the description, and all the properties of the *Mosaical* Abysse, and nothing else will, how can we in reason judge it otherwise than the same, and the very thing intended and propos'd in the History of *Noah*'s Deluge under the name of *Tehom-Rabba*, or the great Abysse, at whose disruption the World was overflow'd. And as we do not think it an unhappy discovery to have found out (with a moral certainty) the seat of the *Mosaical* Abysse, which hath been almost as much sought for, and as much in vain, as the seat of *Paradise*; so this gives us a great assurance, that the Theory we have given of a general Deluge, is not a meer *Idea*, but is to be appropriated to the Deluge of *Noah*, as a true explication of it.

And to proceed now from *Moses* to other Divine writers; That our Description is a reality, both as to the Ante-diluvian Earth, and as to the Deluge, we may further be convinc'd from St. *Peter*'s discourse concerning those two things. St. *Peter* saith, that the constitution of the Ante-diluvian Earth was such, in reference to the Waters, that by reason of that it was obnoxious to a Deluge; we say these Waters were the great *Abysse* it stood upon, by reason whereof that World was really expos'd to a Deluge, and overwhelm'd in it upon the disruption of this Abysse, as *Moses* witnesses. 'Tis true, St. *Peter* doth not specifie what those waters were, nor mention either the Sea, or the Abysse; but seeing *Moses* tells us, that it was by the waters of the Abysse that the Earth was overwhelm'd, St. *Peter*'s waters must be understood of the same Abysse, because he supposeth them the cause of the same Deluge. And, I think, the Apostle's discourse there cannot receive a better illustration, than from *Moses*'s History of the Deluge. *Moses* distinguishes the causes of the Flood into those that belong to the Heavens, and those that belong to the Earth; the Rains and the Abysse: St. *Peter* also distinguisheth the causes of the Deluge into the constitution of the Heavens, in reference to its waters; and the constitution of the Earth, in reference to its waters; and no doubt they both aim at the same causes, as they refer to the same effect; only *Moses* mentions the immediate causes, the Rains and the Waters of the Abysse; and St. *Peter* mentions the more remote and fundamental causes, that constitution of the Heavens, and that constitution of the Earth, in reference to their respective waters, which made that world obnoxious to a Deluge: And these two speaking of *Noah*'s Deluge, and agreeing thus with one another, and both with us, or with the Theory which we have given of a General Deluge, we may safely conclude, that it is no imaginary *Idea*, but a true account of that Ancient Flood, whereof *Moses* hath left us the History.

And seeing the right understanding of the *Mosaical Abysse* is sufficient alone to prove all we have deliver'd concerning the Deluge, as also concerning the frame of the Ante-diluvian Earth, give me leave to take notice here of some other places of Scripture that seem manifestly to describe this same form of the Abysse with the Earth above it, *Psal.* 24. 2. *He founded the Earth upon the Seas, and establish'd it upon the Floods;* and *Psal.* 136. 6. *He stretched out the Earth above the Waters.* Now this Foundation of the Earth upon the Waters, or *extension of*

2 *Epist.* 3. 6.

4 *Esdr.* 16. 58.

it above the Waters, doth most aptly agree to that structure and situation of the Abysse and the Ante-diluvian Earth, which we have assign'd them, and which we have before describ'd; but very improperly and forc'dly to the present form of the Earth and the Waters. In that second place of the *Psalmist*, the word may be render'd either, he *stretch'd*, as we read it, or he *fixt and consolidated* the Earth above the Waters, as the Vulgate and Septuagint translate it: For 'tis from the same word with that which is used for the *Firmament*, *Gen.* 1. So that as the Firmament was extended over and around the Earth, so was the Earth extended over and about the Waters, in that first constitution of things; and I remember some of the Ancients use this very comparison of the Firmament and Earth, to express the situation of the *Paradisiacal* Earth in reference to the Sea or Abysse.

There is another remarkable place in the *Psalms*, to shew the disposition of the Waters in the first Earth; *Psal.* 33. 7. *He gathereth the Waters of the Sea as in a Bag, he layeth up the Abysses in storehouses.* This answers very fitly and naturally to the place and disposition of the Abysse which it had before the Deluge, inclos'd within the vault of the Earth, as in a *Bag* or in a *Storehouse*. I know very well what I render here in a *Bag*, is render'd in the *English*, *as an heap*; but that translation of the word seems to be grounded on the old Error, that the Sea is higher than the Land, and so doth not make a true sence. Neither are the two parts of the Verse so well suited and consequent one to another, if the first express an high situation of the Waters, and the second a low one. And accordingly the Vulgate, Septuagint, and Oriental Versions and Paraphrase, as also *Symmachus*, St. *Jerome*, and *Basil*, render it as we do here, *in a Bag*, or by terms equivalent.

To these passages of the *Psalmist*, concerning the form of the Abysse and the first Earth, give me leave to add this general remark, that they are commonly ushered in, or followed, with something of Admiration in the Prophet. We observ'd before, that the formation of the first Earth, after such a wonderful manner, being a piece of Divine Architecture, when it was spoken of in Scripture, it was usually ascrib'd to a particular Providence, and accordingly we see in these places now mention'd, that it is still made the object of praise and admiration: In that 136 *Psalm* 'tis reckon'd among the wonders of God, *Vers.* 4, 5, 6. *Give praise to him who alone doth great wonders; To him that by wisdom made the Heavens: To him that stretched out the Earth above the Waters.* And in like manner, in that 33 *Psalm*, 'tis joyn'd with the forming of the Heavens, and made the subject of the Divine Power and Wisdom: *Vers.* 6, 7, 8, 9. *By the word of the Lord were the Heavens made, and all the Host of them by the breath of his mouth; He gathereth the Waters of the Sea together, as in a Bag, he layeth up the Abysse in Storehouses. Let all the Earth fear the Lord; Let all the Inhabitants of the World stand in awe of him; For he spake, and it was; he commanded, and it stood fast.* Namely, all things stood in that wonderful posture in which the *Word* of his Power and Wisdom had establisht them. *David* often made the works of Nature, and the External World, the matter of his Meditations, and of his praises and Philosophical Devotions; reflecting sometimes upon the present form of the World, and sometimes upon the primitive form of it: And though Poetical expressions, as the *Psalms* are, seldom are so determinate and distinct, but that they may be interpreted more than one way, yet, I think, it cannot but be acknowledg'd, that those expressions and passages that we have instanc'd in, are more fairly and aptly understood of the Ancient form of the Sea, or the Abysse, as it was enclos'd within the Earth, than of the present form of it in an open Chanel.

There are also in the book of *Job* many noble reflections upon the works of Nature, and upon the formation of the Earth and the Abysse; whereof that in *Chap.* 26. 7. *He stretcheth out the North over the Empty places, and hangeth the Earth upon nothing,* seems to parallel the expression of *David; He stretched out the Earth upon the Waters;* for the word we render the *empty place* is TOHU, which is appli'd to the Chaos and the first Abysse, *Gen.* 1. 2. and *the hanging the Earth upon nothing* is much more wonderful, if it be understood of the first habitable Earth, that hung over the Waters, sustain'd by nothing but its own peculiar form, and the libration of its parts, than if it be understood of the present Earth, and the whole body of it; for if it be in its Center or proper place, whither should it sink further, or whither should it go? But this passage, together with the foregoing and following Verses, requires a more critical examination than this Discourse will easily bear.

There is another remarkable discourse in *Job,* that contains many things to our present purpose, 'tis *Chap.* 38. where God reproaches *Job* with his ignorance of what pass'd at the beginning of the World, and the formation of the Earth, *Vers.* 4, 5, 6. *Where was thou when I laid the foundations of the Earth? Declare if thou hast understanding: Who hath laid the measures thereof, if thou knowest; or who hath stretched the line upon it? Whereupon are the foundations thereof fastned, or who laid the corner-stone?* All these questions have far more force and Emphasis, more propriety and elegancy, if they be understood of the first and Ante-diluvian form of the Earth, than if they be understood of the present; for in the present form of the Earth there is no Architecture, no structure, no more than in a ruine; or at least none comparatively to what was in the first form of it. And that the exteriour and superficial part of the Earth is here spoken of, appears by the *rule* and *line* appli'd to it; but what rule or regularity is there in the surface of the present Earth? what line was us'd to level its parts? But in its original construction when it lay smooth and regular in its surface, as if it had been drawn by rule and line in every part; and when it hung pois'd upon the Deep, without pillar or foundation stone, then just proportions were taken, and every thing plac'd by weight and measure: And this, I doubt not, was that artificial structure here alluded to, and when this work was finisht, then *the morning Stars sang* *Vers.* 7. *together, and all the sons of God shouted for joy.*

Thus far the questions proceed upon the form and construction of the first Earth; in the following *verses* (8, 9, 10, 11.) they proceed upon the demolition of that Earth, the opening the Abysse, and the present state of both. *Or who shut up the Sea with doors when it brake forth, as if it had issu'd out of a womb?* Who can doubt but this was at the breaking open of the *Fountains of the Abysse, Gen.* 7. 11. when the waters gusht out, as out of the great womb of Nature; and by reason of that confusion and perturbation of Air and Water that rise upon it, a thick mist and darkness was round the Earth, and all things as in a second Chaos,

When I made the cloud the garment thereof, and thick darkness a swadling band for it, and brake up for it my decreed place, and made bars and doors. Namely, (taking the words as thus usually render'd) the present Chanel of the Sea was made when the Abysse was broke up, and at the same time were made the shory Rocks and Mountains which are the bars and boundaries of the Sea. *And said hitherto shalt thou come and no further, and here shall thy proud waves be stay'd.* Which last sentence shows, that this cannot be understood of the first disposition of the waters as they were before the Flood, for their proud waves broke those bounds, whatsoever they were, when they overflow'd the Earth in the Deluge. And that the *womb* which they broke out of was the great Abysse, The *Chaldee* Paraphrase in this place doth expressly mention; and what can be understood by *the womb of the Earth*, but that Subterraneous capacity in which the Abysse lay? Then that which followeth, is a description or representation of the great Deluge that ensu'd, and of that disorder in Nature, that was then, and how the Waters were setled and Bounded afterwards. Not unlike the description in the 104 *Psalm*, *vers.* 6, 7, 8, 9. and thus much for these places in the book of *Job*.

תְּהוֹמָה מִן

There remains a remarkable discourse in the *Proverbs* of *Solomon*, relating to the *Mosaical* Abysse, and not only to that, but to the Origin of the Earth in general; where *Wisdom* declares her antiquity and pre-existence to all the works of this Earth, *Chap.* 8. *vers.* 23, 24, 25, 26, 27, 28. *I was set up from everlasting, from the beginning, ere the Earth was. When there were no Deeps or Abysses, I was brought forth; when no fountains abounding with water.* Then in the 27. verse, *When he prepared the Heavens, I was there; when he set a Compass upon the face of the Deep or Abysse. When he established the Clouds above, when he strengthned the fountains of the Abysse.* Here is mention made of the *Abysse*, and of *the Fountains of the Abysse*, and who can question, but that the Fountains of the Abysse here, are the same with the fountains of the Abysse which *Moses* mentions, and were broken open, as he tells us, at the Deluge? Let us observe therefore what form *Wisdom* gives to this Abysse, and consequently to the *Mosaical:* And here seem to be two expressions that determine the form of it, *verse* 28. *He strengthned the fountains of the Abysse*, that is, the cover of those Fountains, for the Fountains could be strengthned no other way than by making a strong cover or Arch over them. And that Arch is exprest more fully and distinctly in the foregoing *verse*, *When he prepar'd the Heavens, I was there; when he set a* Compass *on the face of the Abysse*; we render it *Compass*, the word signifies a Circle or Circumference, or an Orb or Sphere. So there was in the beginning of the World a Sphere, Orb or Arch set round the Abysse, according to the testimony of *Wisdom*, who was then present. And this shews us both the form of the *Mosaical* Abysse, which was included within this Vault: and the form of the habitable Earth, which was the outward surface of this Vault, or the cover of the Abysse that was broke up at the Deluge.

And thus much, I think, is sufficient to have noted out of Scripture, concerning the *Mosaical* Abysse, to discover the form, place, and situation of it; which I have done the more largely, because that being determin'd, it will draw in easily all the rest of our Theory concerning the Deluge. I will now only add one or two general Observations, and so conclude this discourse; The first Observation is concerning the Abysse; Namely, that the *opening and shutting of the Abysse*, is the great hinge upon which Nature turns in this Earth: This brings another face of things, other Scenes and a new World upon the stage: And accordingly it is a thing often mention'd and alluded to in Scripture, sometimes in a Natural, sometimes in a Moral or Theological sence; and in both sences, our Saviour shuts and opens as he pleaseth.   Our Saviour, who is both Lord of Nature and of Grace, whose Dominion is both in Heaven and in Earth, hath a double Key; that of the Abysse, whereby Death and Hell are in his power, and all the revolutions of Nature are under his Conduct and Providence; And the Key of *David*, whereby he admits or excludes from the City of God and the Kingdom of Heaven whom he pleaseth.   Of those places that refer to the shutting and opening the Abysse in a natural sence, I cannot but particularly take notice of that in *Job. Chap.* 12. *vers.* 14, 15. *God breaketh down, and it cannot be built again: he shutteth up man, and there can be no opening: Behold, he withholdeth the waters, and they dry up; also he sendeth them out, and they overturn the Earth.*   Though these things be true of God in lesser and common instances, yet to me it is plain, that they principally refer to the Deluge, the opening and shutting the Abysse, with the dissolution or subversion of the Earth thereupon; and accordingly they are made the great effects of the Divine Power and Wisdom in the foregoing Verse, *With God is wisdom and strength, he hath counsel and understanding; Behold, he breaketh down*, &c.   And also in the conclusion 'tis repeated again, *With him is strength and wisdom*; which solemnity would scarce have been us'd for common instances of his power.   When God is said to build or pull down, and no body can build again, 'tis not to be understood of an House or a Town, God builds and unbuilds Worlds; and who shall build up that Arch that was broke down at the Deluge? Where shall they lay the Foundation, or how shall the Mountains be rear'd up again to make part of the Roof?   This is the Fabrick, which when God breaketh down, none can build up again.   *He withholdeth the waters and they dry up:* As we shew'd the Earth to have been immoderately chapt and parcht before its dissolution.   *He sendeth them forth and they overturn the Earth.*   What can more properly express the breaking out of the waters at the disruption of the Abysse? and the subversion or dissolution of the Earth in consequence of it?   'Tis true this last passage may be applied to the breaking out of waters in an ordinary Earthquake, and the subversion of some part of the Earth, which often follows upon it; but it must be acknowledg'd, that the sence is more weighty, if it be refer'd to the great Deluge, and the great Earthquake which laid the World in ruines and in water.   And Philosophical descriptions in Sacred writings, like Prophecies, have often a lesser and a greater accomplishment and interpretation.

I could not pass by this place without giving this short Explication of it.   We proceed now to the second Observation, which is concerning the stile of Scripture, in most of those places we have cited, and others upon the same subject.   The reflections that are made in several parts of the Divine writings, upon the Origin of the World, and the formation of the Earth, seem to me to be writ in a stile something approaching to the nature of a Prophetical stile, and to have more of

Job. 11. 10, **12**, 14.
Apoc. 1. 18.
20. 1, 2, 3.
21. 1.
Apoc. 3. 7.
Isa. 22. 22.

& Chap. 11. 10.

Vers. 13.

Vers. 6.

a Divine Enthusiasm and Elocution in them, than the ordinary text of Scripture; the expressions are lofty, and sometimes abrupt, and often figurative and disguis'd, as may be observ'd in most of those places we have made use of, and particularly in that speech of *Wisdom, Prov.* 8. where the 26. *verse* is so obscure, that no two Versions that I have yet met with, whether Ancient or Modern, agree in the Translation of that Verse. And therefore though I fully believe that the construction of the first Earth is really intended in those words, yet seeing it could not be made out clear without a long and critical discussion of them, I did not think it proper to be insisted upon here. We may also observe, that whereas there is a double form or composition of the Earth, that which it had at first, or till the Deluge, and that which it hath since; sometimes the one, and sometimes the other may be glanc'd upon in these Scripture phrases and descriptions; and so there may be in the same discourse an intermixture of both. And it commonly happens so in an Enthusiastick or Prophetick stile, that by reason of the eagerness and trembling of the Fancy, it doth not always regularly follow the same even thread of discourse, but strikes many times upon some other thing that hath relation to it, or lies under or near the same view. Of this we have frequent examples in the *Apocalypse*, and in that Prophecy of our Saviour's, *Matth.* 24. concerning the destruction of *Jerusalem*, and of the World. But notwithstanding any such unevenness or indistinctness in the stile of those places which we have cited concerning the Origin and form of the Earth, we may at least make this remark, that if there never was any other form of the Earth but the present, nor any other state of the Abysse, than what it is in now, 'tis not imaginable what should give occasion to all those expressions and passages that we have cited; which being so strange in themselves and paradoxical, should yet so much favour, and so fairly comply with our suppositions. What I have observ'd in another

Tell. Theor. lib.
2. c. 6.

place, in treating of *Paradise*, that the expressions of the Ancient Fathers were very extravagant, if *Paradise* was nothing but a little plot of ground in *Mesopotamia*, as many of late have fansied; may in like manner be observ'd concerning the ancient Earth and Abysse, if they were in no other form, nor other state than what they are under now, the expressions of the Sacred Writers concerning them are very strange and inaccountable, without any sufficient ground, or any just occasion for such uncouth representations. If there was nothing intended or refer'd to in those descriptions, but the present form and state of the Earth, that is so well known, that in describing of it there would be nothing dark or mysterious, nor any occasion for obscurity in the stile or expression, whereof we find so much in those. So as, all things consider'd, what might otherwise be made an exception to some of these Texts alledg'd by us, *viz.* that they are too obscure, becomes an argument for us: as implying that there is something more intended by them, than the present and known form of the Earth. And we having propos'd another form and structure of the Earth, to which those characters suit and answer more easily, as this opens and gives light to those difficult places, so it may be reasonably concluded to be the very sence and notion intended by the holy Writers.

And thus much, I think, is sufficient to have observ'd out of Scripture, to verifie our Explication of the Deluge, and our Application of it to *Noah*'s Flood, both according to the *Mosaical* History of the Flood, and according to many occasional reflections and discourses dispers'd in other places of Scripture, concerning the same Flood, or concerning the Abysse and the first form of the Earth. And though there may be some other passages of a different aspect, they will be of no force to disprove our conclusions, because they respect the present form of the Earth and Sea; and also because expressions that deviate more from the common opinion, are more remarkable and more proving; in that there is nothing could give occasion to such, but an intention to express the very truth. So, for instance, if there was one place of Scripture that said *the Earth was mov'd*, and several that seem'd to imply, that the *Sun* was mov'd, we should have more regard to that one place for the motion of the Earth, than to all the other that made against it; because those others might be spoken and understood according to common opinion and common belief, but that which affirm'd the motion of the Earth, could not be spoke upon any other ground, but only for truth and instruction sake. I leave this to be appli'd to the present subject.

Thus much for the Sacred writings. As to the History of the ancient Heathens, we cannot expect an account or Narration of *Noah*'s Flood, under that name and notion; but it may be of use to observe two things out of that History. First, that the Inundations recorded there came generally to pass in the manner we have describ'd the Universal Deluge; namely, by Earthquakes and an eruption of Subterraneous waters, the Earth being broken and falling in: and of this we shall elsewhere give a full account out of their Authors. Secondly, that *Deucalion*'s Deluge in particular, which is suppos'd by most of the Ancient Fathers to represent *Noah*'s Flood, is said to have been accompanied with a gaping or disruption of the Earth; *Apollodorus* saith, that the Mountains of *Thessaly* were divided *Bibl. lib.* 1. asunder, or separate one from another at that time: And *Lucian* (*de deâ Syriâ*) tells a very remarkable story to this purpose, concerning *Deucalion*'s Deluge, and a ceremony observ'd in the Temple of *Hieropolis*, in commemoration of it; which ceremony seems to have been of that nature, as impli'd that there was an opening of the Earth at the time of the Deluge, and that the waters subsided into that again when the Deluge ceast. He saith, that this Temple at *Hieropolis* was built upon a kind of Abysse, or has a bottomless pit, or gaping of the Earth in one part of it, and the people of *Arabia* and *Syria*, and the Countries thereabouts twice a year repair'd to this Temple, and brought with them every one a vessel of water, which they pour'd out upon the floor of the Temple, and made a kind of an Inundation there in memory of *Deucalion*'s Deluge; and this water sunk by degrees into a Chasm or opening of a Rock, which the Temple stood upon, and so left the floor dry again. And this was a rite solemnly and religiously perform'd both by the Priests and by the People. If *Moses* had left such a Religious rite among the *Jews*, I should not have doubted to have interpreted it concerning his Abysse, and the retiring of the waters into it; but the actual disruption of the Abysse could not well be represented by any ceremony. And thus much concerning the present question, and the true application of our Theory to *Noah*'s Flood.

CHAPTER VIII

The particular History of Noah's *Flood is explain'd in all the material parts and circumstances of it, according to the preceding Theory. Any seeming difficulties removed, and the whole Section concluded, with a Discourse how far the Deluge may be lookt upon as the effect of an ordinary Providence, and how far of an extraordinary.*

WE have now proved our Explication of the Deluge to be more than an *Idea*, or to be a true piece of Natural History; and it may be the greatest and most remarkable that hath yet been since the beginning of the World. We have shown it to be the real account of *Noah*'s Flood, according to Authority both Divine and Humane; and I would willingly proceed one step further, and declare my thoughts concerning the manner and order wherein *Noah*'s Flood came to pass; in what method all those things happen'd and succeeded one another, that make up the History of it, as causes or effects, or other parts or circumstances: As how the Ark was born upon the waters, what effect the Rains had, at what time the Earth broke, and the Abysse was open'd; and what the condition of the Earth was upon the ending of the Flood, and such like. But I desire to propose my thoughts concerning these things only as conjectures, which I will ground as near as I can upon Scripture and Reason, and am very willing they should be rectifi'd where they happen to be amiss. I know how subject we are to mistakes in these great and remote things, when we descend to particulars; but I am willing to expose the Theory to a full trial, and to shew the way for any to examine it, provided they do it with equity and sincerity. I have no other design than to contribute my endeavours to find out the truth in a subject of so great importance, and wherein the World hath hitherto had so little satisfaction: And he that in an obscure argument proposeth an *Hypothesis* that reacheth from end to end, though it be not exact in every particular, 'tis not without a good effect; for it gives aim to others to take their measures better, and opens their invention in a matter which otherwise, it may be, would have been impenetrable to them: As he that makes the first way through a thick Forest, though it be not the streightest and shortest, deserves better, and hath done more, than he that makes it streighter and smoother afterwards.

Providence that ruleth all things and all Ages, after the Earth had stood above sixteen hundred Years, thought fit to put a period to that World, and accordingly, it was reveal'd to *Noah*, that for the wickedness and degeneracy of men, God would destroy mankind with the *Earth* (*Gen.* 6. 13) in a Deluge of water; whereupon he was commanded, in order to the preserving of Himself and Family, as a stock for the new World, to build a great Vessel or Ark, to float upon the waters, and had instructions given him for the building of it both as to the matter and as to the form. *Noah* believed the word of God, though against his senses, and all external appearances, and set himself to work to build an Ark, according to the directions given, which after many years labour was finish'd; whilst the incredulous World, secure enough, as they thought, against a Deluge, continu'd still in their excesses and insolencies, and laught at the admonition of *Noah*, and at the folly of his design of building an extravagant machine, a floating house, to save himself from an imaginary Inundation; for they thought it no less, seeing it was to be in an Earth where there was no Sea, nor any Rain neither in those parts, according to the ordinary course of Nature; as shall be shown in the second Book of this Treatise.

But when the appointed time was come, the Heavens began to melt, and the Rains to fall, and these were the first surprizing causes and preparatives to the Deluge; They fell, we suppose, throughout the face of the whole Earth; which could not but have a considerable effect on that Earth, being even and smooth, without Hills and eminencies, and might lay it all under water to some depth; so as the Ark, if it could not float upon those Rain-waters, at least taking the advantage of a River, or of a Dock or Cistern made to receive them, it might be a-float before the Abysse was broken open. For I do not suppose the Abysse broken open before any rain fell; And when the opening of the Abysse and of the Flood-gates of Heaven are mention'd together, I am apt to think those Flood-gates were distinct from the common rain, and were something more violent and impetuous. So that there might be preparatory Rains before the disruption of the Abysse: and I do not know but those Rains, so covering up and enclosing the Earth on every side, might providentially contribute to the disruption of it; not only by softning and weakning the Arch of the Earth in the bottom of those cracks and Chasms which were made by the Sun, and which the Rain would first run into, but especially by stopping on a sudden all the pores of the Earth, and all evaporation, which would make the Vapours within struggle more violently, as we get a Fever by a Cold; and it may be in that struggle, the Doors and the Bars were broke, and the great Abysse gusht out, as out of a womb.

However, when the Rains were faln, we may suppose the face of the Earth cover'd over with water; and whether it was these waters that St. *Peter* refers to, or that of the Abysse afterwards, I cannot tell, when he saith in his first Epistle, *Chap. 3. 20. Noah* and his Family *were sav'd by water*; so as the water which destroy'd the rest of the World, was an instrument of their conservation, in as much as it bore up the Ark, and kept it from that impetuous shock, which it would have had, if either it had stood upon dry land when the Earth fell, or if the Earth had been dissolv'd without any water on it or under it. However, things being thus prepar'd, let us suppose the great frame of the exteriour Earth to have broke at this time, or the Fountains of the great Abysse, as *Moses* saith, to have been then open'd, from thence would issue, upon the fall of the Earth, with an unspeakable violence, such a Flood of waters as would over-run and overwhelm for a time all those fragments which the Earth broke into, and bury in one common Grave all Mankind, and all the Inhabitants of the Earth. Besides, if the *Flood-gates* of Heaven were any thing distinct from the Forty days Rain, their effusion, 'tis likely, was at this same time when the Abysse was broken open; for the sinking of the Earth would make an extraordinary convulsion of the Regions of the Air, and that crack and noise that must be in the falling World, and in the collision of the Earth and the Abysse, would make a great and universal Concussion above, which things together, must needs so shake, or so squeeze the

Atmosphere, as to bring down all the remaining Vapours; But the force of these motions not being equal throughout the whole Air, but drawing or pressing more in some places than in other, where the Center of the convulsion was, there would be the chiefest collection, and there would fall, not showers of Rain, or single drops, but great spouts or caskades of water; and this is that which *Moses* seems to call, not improperly, the *Cataracts* of Heaven, or the *Windows of Heaven being set open.*

Thus the Flood came to its height; and 'tis not easie to represent to our selves this strange Scene of things, when the Deluge was in its fury and extremity; when the Earth was broken and swallow'd up in the Abysse, whose raging waters rise higher than the Mountains, and fill'd the Air with broken waves, with an universal mist, and with thick darkness, so as Nature seem'd to be in a second Chaos; and upon this Chaos rid the distrest Ark, that bore the small remains of Mankind. No Sea was ever so tumultuous as this, nor is there any thing in present Nature to be compar'd with the disorder of these waters; All the Poetry, and all the Hyperboles that are us'd in the description of Storms and raging Seas, were literally true in this, if not beneath it. The Ark was really carri'd to the tops of the highest Mountains, and into the places of the Clouds, and thrown down again into the deepest Gulfs; and to this very state of the Deluge and of the Ark, which was a Type of the Church in this World, *David* seems to have alluded in the name of the Church, *Psal.* 42. 7. *Abysse calls upon Abysse at the noise of thy Cataracts or water-spouts; all thy waves and billows have gone over me.* It was no doubt an extraordinary and miraculous Providence, that could make a Vessel, so ill man'd, live upon such a Sea; that kept it from being dasht against the Hills, or overwhelm'd in the Deeps. That Abysse which had devour'd and swallow'd up whole Forests of Woods, Cities, and Provinces, nay the whole Earth, when it had conquer'd all, and triumph'd over all, could not destroy this single Ship. I

Dion. Argonaut.
li. 1. *v.* 47.

remember in the story of the *Argonauticks,* when *Jason* set out to fetch the Golden Fleece, the Poet saith, all the Gods that day look'd down from Heaven, to view the Ship; and the *Nymphs* stood upon the Mountain-tops to see the noble Youth of *Thessaly* pulling at the Oars; We may with more reason suppose the good Angels to have lookt down upon this Ship of *Noah*'s; and that not out of curiosity, as idle spectators, but with a passionate concern for its safety and deliverance. A Ship whose *Cargo* was no less than a whole World; that carri'd the fortune and hopes of all posterity, and if this had perisht, the Earth, for any thing we know, had been nothing but a Desert, a great ruine, a dead heap of Rubbish, from the Deluge to the Conflagration. But Death and Hell, the Grave, and Destruction have their bounds. We may entertain our selves with the consideration of the face of the Deluge, and of the broken and drown'd Earth, in this Scheme, with the floating Ark, and the guardian Angels.

Thus much for the beginning and progress of the Deluge. It now remains only that we consider it in its decrease, and the state of the Earth after the waters were retir'd into their Chanels, which makes the present state of it. *Moses* saith, God brought a wind upon the waters, and the tops of the Hills became bare, and then the lower grounds and Plains by degrees; the waters being sunk into the

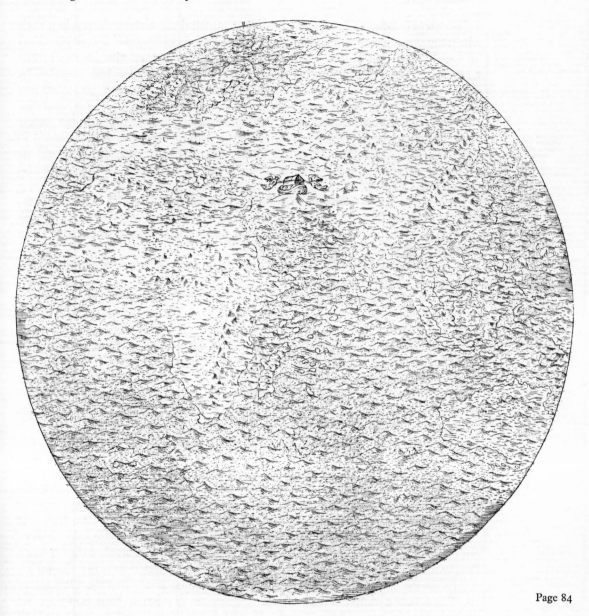

Page 84

Chanels of the Sea, and the hollowness of the Earth, and the whole Globe
appearing in the form it is now under. There needs nothing be added for explication of this, 'tis the genuine consequence of the Theory we have given of the
Deluge; and whether this wind was a descending wind to depress and keep down
the swellings and inequalities of the Abysse, or whether it was only to dry the
Land as fast as it appear'd, or might have both effects, I do not know; But as
nothing can be perpetual that is violent, so this commotion of the Abysse abated

85

after a certain time, and the great force that impell'd the waters, decreasing, their natural gravity began to take effect, and to reduce them into the lowest places, at an equal height, and in an even surface, and level one part with another: That is, in short, the Abysse became our Sea, fixt within its Chanel, and bounded by Rocks and Mountains: *Then was the decreed place establisht for it, and Bars and Doors were set; then it was said, hitherto shalt thou come, and no further, and here shall thy proud waves be stopt.* And the Deluge being thus ended, and the waters setled in their Chanels, the Earth took such a broken Figure as is represented in those larger Schemes, *p.* 118. And this will be the form and state of it till its great change comes in the Conflagration, when we expect *a new Heaven and a new Earth.*

Job. 38. 10, 11.

But to pursue this prospect of things a little further; we may easily imagine, that for many years after the Deluge ceast, the face of the Earth was very different from what it is now, and the Sea had other bounds than it hath at present. I do not doubt but the Sea reach'd much further in-land, and climb'd higher upon the sides of the Mountains; And I have observ'd in many places, a ridge of Mountains some distance from the Sea, and a Plain from their roots to the shore; which Plain no doubt was formerly cover'd by the Sea, bounded against those Hills as its first and natural Ramparts, or as the ledges or lips of its Vessel. And it seems probable, that the Sea doth still grow narrower from Age to Age, and sinks more within its Chanel and the bowels of the Earth, according as it can make its way into all those Subterraneous Cavities, and crowd the Air out of them. We see whole Countries of Land gain'd from it, and by several indications, as ancient Sea-ports left dry and useless, old Sea-marks far within the Land, pieces of Ships, Anchors, &c. left at a great distance from the present shores; from these signs, and such like, we may conclude that the Sea reach'd many places formerly that now are dry Land, and at first I believe was generally bound on either side with a chain of Mountains. So I should easily imagine the Mediterranean Sea, for instance, to have been bounded by the continuation of the *Alps* through *Dauphiné* and *Languedock* to the *Pyreneans*, and at the other end by the *Darmatick* Mountains almost to the Black Sea. Then *Atlas major* which runs along with the Mediterranean from *Ægypt* to the *Atlantick* Ocean, and now parts *Barbary* and *Numidia*, may possibly have been the Ancient Barriere on the *Africk* side. And in our own Island I could easily figure to my self, in many parts of it, other Sea-bounds than what it hath at present; and the like may be observ'd in other Countries.

And as the Sea had much larger bounds for some time after the Deluge, so the Land had a different face in many respects to what it hath now; for we suppose the Valleys and lower grounds, where the descent and derivation of the water was not so easie, to have been full of Lakes and Pools for a long time; and these were often converted into Fens and Bogs, where the ground being spongy, suckt up the water, and the loosen'd Earth swell'd into a soft and pappy substance; which would still continue so, if there was any course of water sensible or insensible, above or within the ground, that fed this moist place: But if the water stood in a more firm Basin, or on a soil which for its heaviness or any other reason would not mix with it, it made a Lake or clear Pool. And we may easily imagine there were innumerable such Lakes, and Bogs and fastnesses for many years after the Deluge, till the world begun to be pretty well stockt with people, and humane industry cleans'd and drain'd those unfruitful and unhabitable places. And those Countries that have been later cultivated, or by a lazier people, retain still, in proportion to their situation and soil, a greater number of them.

Neither is it at all incongruous or inconvenient to suppose, that the face of the Earth stood in this manner for many years after the Deluge; for while Mankind was small and few, they needed but a little ground for their seats or sustenance; and as they grew more numerous, the Earth proportionably grew more dry, and more parts of it fit for habitation. I easily believe that *Plato*'s observation or tradition is true, that Men at first, after the Flood, liv'd in the Up-lands and sides of the Mountains, and by degrees sunk into the Plains and lower Countries, when Nature had prepar'd them for their use, and their numbers requir'd more room. The History of *Moses* tells us, that sometime after the Deluge, *Noah* and his posterity, his Sons and his Grand-children, chang'd their quarters, and fell down into the Plains of *Shiner*, from the sides of the Hills where the Ark had rested; and in this Plain was the last general rendezvous of Mankind; so long they seem to have kept in a body, and from thence they were divided and broken into companies, and disperst, first, into the neighbouring Countries, and then by degrees throughout the whole Earth; the several successive Generations, like the waves of the Sea when it flows, over-reaching one another, and striking out further and further, upon the face of the Land. Not that the whole Earth was peopled by an uniform propagation of Mankind every way, from one place, as a common center: like the swelling of a Lake upon a Plain, for sometimes they shot out in length, like Rivers: and sometimes they flew into remote Countries in Colonies, like swarms from the Hive, and setled there, leaving many places uninhabited betwixt them and their first home. Sea-shores and Islands were generally the last places inhabited: for while the memory or story of the Deluge was fresh amongst them, they did not care for coming so near their late Enemy: or, at least, to be enclos'd and surrounded by his forces.

And this may be sufficient to have discourst concerning all the parts of the Deluge, and the restitution of the Earth to an habitable form, for the further union of our Theory with the History of *Moses*; There rests only one thing in that History to be taken notice of, which may be thought possibly not to agree so well with our account of the Deluge; namely, that *Moses* seems to shut up the Abysse again at the end of the Deluge, which our Explication sypposeth to continue open. But besides that half the Abysse is still really cover'd, *Moses* saith the same thing of the *windows of Heaven*, that they were shut up too; and he seemeth in both to express only the cessation of the Effect which proceeded from their opening: For as *Moses* had ascrib'd the Deluge to the opening of these two, so when it was to cease, he saith, these two were shut up; as they were really put into such a condition, both of them, that they could not continue the Deluge any longer, nor ever be the occasion of a second; and therefore in that sence, and as to that effect were for ever shut up. Some may possibly make that also an Objection against us, that *Moses* mentions and supposes the *Mountains* at the Deluge,

De Leg. li. 3.

Gen. 11.

for he saith, the waters reached fifteen Cubits above the tops of them; whereas we suppose the Ante-diluvian Earth to have had a plain and uniform surface, without any inequality of Hills and Valleys. But this is easily answer'd, 'twas in the height of the Deluge that *Moses* mention'd the Mountains, and we suppose them to have risen then or more towards the beginning of it, when the Earth was broke; and these Mountains continuing still upon the face of the Earth, *Moses* might very well take them for a standard to measure and express to Posterity the height of the waters, though they were not upon the Earth when the Deluge begun. Neither is there any mention made, as is observ'd by some, of Mountains in Scripture, or of Rain, till the time of the Deluge.

We have now finisht our account of *Noah*'s Flood, both generally and particularly; and I have not wittingly omitted or conceal'd any difficulty that occur'd to me, either from the History, or from abstract reason: Our Theory, so far as I know, hath the consent and authority of both: And how far it agrees and is demonstrable from natural observation, or from the form and *Phænomena* of this Earth, as it lies at present, shall be the subject of the remaining part of this First Book. In the mean time I do not know any thing more to be added in this part, unless it be to conclude with an Advertisement to prevent any mistake or misconstruction, as if this Theory, by explaining the Deluge in a natural way, or by natural causes, did detract from the power of God, by which that great judgment was brought upon the World in a Providential and miraculous manner.

To satisfie all reasonable and intelligent persons in this particular, I answer and declare, first, That we are far from excluding Divine Providence, either ordinary or extraordinary, from the causes and conduct of the Deluge. I know a Sparrow doth not fall to the ground without the will of our Heavenly Father, much less doth the great World fall in pieces without his good pleasure and superintendency. In him all things live, move, and have their being; Things that have Life and Thought have it from him, he is the Fountain of both: Things that have motion only, without Thought, have it also from him: And what hath only naked Being, without Thought or Motion, owe still that Being to him. And these are not only deriv'd from God at first, but every moment continued and conserv'd by him. So intimate and universal is the dependance of all things upon the Divine Will and Power.

In the second place, they are guilty, in my Judgment, of a great Error or indiscretion, that oppose the course of Nature to Providence. St. *Paul* says (*Act.* 14. 17.) God hath not left us without witness, in that he *gives us Rain from Heaven*; yet Rains proceed from natural causes, and fall upon the Sea as well as upon the

Mat. 6. 28.
Land. In like manner, our Saviour makes those things instances of Divine Providence, which yet come to pass in an ordinary course of Nature; In that part of his excellent Sermon upon the Mount, that concerns Providence, He bids them *Consider the Lilies how they grow, they toil not, neither do they spin, and yet*
Luk. 12. 24.
Solomon in all his glory was not arrayed like one of these; He bids them also *consider the Ravens, they neither sow nor reap, neither have they Storehouse nor Barn, and God feedeth them.* The Lilies grow, and the Ravens are fed according to the ordinary course of Nature, and yet they are justly made arguments of Providence

by our Saviour; nor are these things less Providential, because constant and regular; on the contrary, such a disposition or establishment of second causes, as will in the best order, and for a long succession, produce the most regular effects, assisted only with the ordinary concourse of the first cause, is a greater argument of wisdom and contrivance, than such a disposition of causes as will not in so good an order, or for so long a time produce regular effects, without an extraordinary concourse and interposition of the First cause. This, I think, is clear to every man's judgment. We think him a better Artist that makes a Clock that strikes regularly at every hour from the Springs and Wheels which he puts in the work, than he that hath so made his Clock that he must put his finger to it every hour to make it strike: And if one should contrive a piece of Clock-work so that it should beat all the hours, and make all its motions regularly for such a time, and that time being come, upon a signal given, or a Spring toucht, it should of its own accord fall all to pieces; would not this be look'd upon as a piece of greater Art, than if the Workman came at that time prefixt, and with a great Hammer beat it into pieces? I use these comparisons to convince us, that it is no detraction from Divine Providence, that the course of Nature is exact and regular, and that even in its greatest changes and revolutions it should still conspire and be prepar'd to answer the ends and purposes of the Divine Will in reference to the *Moral* World. This seems to me to be the great Art of Divine Providence, so to adjust the two Worlds, Humane and Natural, Material and Intellectual, as seeing thorough the possibilities and futuritions of each, according to the first state and circumstances he puts them under, they should all along correspond and fit one another, and especially in their great Crises and Periods.

Thirdly, Besides the ordinary Providence of God in the ordinary course of Nature, there is doubtless an extraordinary Providence that doth attend the greater Scenes and the greater revolutions of Nature. This, methinks, besides all other proof from the Effects, is very rational and necessary in it self; for it would be a limitation of the Divine Power and Will so to be bound up to second causes, as never to use, upon occasion, an extraordinary influence or direction: And 'tis manifest, taking any Systeme of Natural causes, if the best possible, that there may be more and greater things done, if to this, upon certain occasions you joyn an extraordinary conduct. And as we have taken notice before, that there was an extraordinary Providence in the formation or composition of the first Earth, so I believe there was also in the dissolution of it; And I think it had been impossible for the Ark to have liv'd upon the raging Abysse, or for *Noah* and his Family to have been preserv'd, if there had not been a miraculous hand of Providence to take care of them. But 'tis hard to separate and distinguish an ordinary and extraordinary Providence in all cases, and to mark just how far one goes, and where the other begins. And writing a Theory of the Deluge here, as we do, we were to exhibit a Series of causes whereby it might be made intelligible, or to shew the proximate Natural causes of it; wherein we follow the example both of *Moses* and St. *Peter*; and with the same veneration of the Divine Power and Wisdom in the government of Nature, by a constant ordinary Providence, and an occasional extraordinary.

So much for the Theory of the Deluge, and the second Section of this Discourse.

CHAPTER IX

The Second Part of this Discourse, proving the same Theory from the Effects and present Form of the Earth. First, by a general Scheme of what is most remarkable in this Globe, and then by a more particular Induction; beginning with an Account of Subterraneous Cavities and Subterraneous Waters.

WE have now finisht our explication of the Universal Deluge, and given an account, not only of the possibility of it, but of its Causes; and of that form and structure of the Earth, whereby the *Old World* was subject to that sort of Fate. We have not beg'd any Principles or Suppositions for the proof of this, but taking that common ground, which both *Moses* and all Antiquity presents to us, *viz. That this Earth rose from a Chaos*; We have from that deduc'd, by an easie train of consequences, what the first Form of it would be; and from that Form, as from a nearer ground, we have by a second train of consequences made it appear, that at some time or other that first Earth would be subject to a dissolution, and by that dissolution to a Deluge. And thus far we have proceeded only by the intuition of causes, as is most proper to a Theory; but for the satisfaction of those that require more sensible arguments, and to compleat our proofs on either hand, we will now argue from the Effects; And from the present state of Nature, and the present form of the Earth, prove that it hath been broken, and undergone such a dissolution as we have already describ'd, and made the immediate occasion of the Deluge. And that we may do this more perspicuously and distinctly, we will lay down this Proposition to be prov'd, *viz. That the present form and structure of the Earth, both as to the surface and as to the Interiour parts of it, so far as they are known and accessible to us, doth exactly answer to our Theory concerning the form and dissolution of the first Earth, and cannot be explained upon any other Hypothesis.*

Oratours and Philosophers treat Nature after a very different manner; Those represent her with all her graces and ornaments, and if there be any thing that is not capable of that, they dissemble it, or pass it over slightly. But Philosophers view Nature with a more impartial eye, and without favour or prejudice give a just and free account, how they find all the parts of the Universe, some more, some less perfect. And as to this Earth in particular, if I was to describe it as an Oratour, I would suppose it a beautiful and regular Globe, and not only so, but that the whole Universe was made for its sake; that it was the darling and favourite of Heaven, that the Sun shin'd only to give it light, to ripen its Fruit, and make fresh its Flowers; And that the great Concave of the Firmament, and all the Stars in their several Orbs, were design'd only for a spangled Cabinet to keep this Jewel in. This *Idea* I would give of it as an Oratour; But a Philosopher that overheard me, would either think me in jest, or very injudicious, if I took the Earth for a body so regular in it self, or so considerable, if compar'd with the rest of the Universe. This, he would say, is to make the great World like one of the Heathen Temples, a beautiful and magnificent structure, and of the richest materials, yet built only for a little brute Idol, a Dog, or a Crocodile, or some deformed Creature, plac'd in a corner of it.

We must therefore be impartial where the Truth requires it, and describe the Earth as it is really in it self; and though it be handsome and regular enough to the eye in certain parts of it, single tracts and single Regions; yet if we consider the whole surface of it, or the whole Exteriour Region, 'tis as a broken and con-fus'd heap of bodies, plac'd in no order to one another, nor with any correspondency or regularity of parts: And such a body as the Moon appears to us, when 'tis look'd upon with a good Glass, rude and ragged; as it is also represented in the modern Maps of the Moon; such a thing would the Earth appear if it was seen from the Moon. They are both in my judgment the image or picture of a great Ruine, and have the true aspect of a World lying in its rubbish.

Vide Fig. pag. 116.

Our Earth is first divided into Sea and Land, without any regularity in the portions, either of the one or the other; In the Sea lie the Islands, scatter'd like limbs torn from the rest of the body; great Rocks stand rear'd up in the waters; The Promontories and Capes shoot into the Sea, and the Sinus's and Creeks on the other hand run as much into the Land; and these without any order or uniformity. Upon the other part of our Globe stand great heaps of Earth or stone, which we call Mountains; and if these were all plac'd together, they would take up a very considerable part of the dry Land; In the rest of it are lesser Hills, Valleys, Plains, Lakes, and Marishes, Sands and Desarts, &c. and these also without any regular disposition. Then the inside of the Earth, or inward parts of it, are generally broken or hollow, especially about the Mountains and high Lands, as also towards the shores of the Sea, and among the Rocks. How many Holes and Caverns, and strange Subterraneous passages do we see in many Countries; and how many more may we easily imagine, that are unknown and unaccessible to us?

This is the pourtraicture of our Earth, drawn without flattery; and as oddly as it looks, it will not be at all surprizing to one that hath consider'd the foregoing Theory; For 'tis manifest enough, that upon the dissolution of the first Earth, and its fall in to the Abysse, this very face and posture of things, which we have now describ'd, or something extreamly like it, would immediately result. The Sea would be open'd, and the face of the Globe would be divided into Land and Water: And according as the fragments fell, some would make Islands or Rocks in the Sea, others would make Mountains or Plains upon the Land; and the Earth would generally be full of Caverns and hollownesses, especially in the Mountainous parts of it. And we see the resemblance and imitation of this in lesser ruines, when a Mountain sinks and falls into Subterraneous water; or which is more obvious, when the Arch of a Bridge is broken, and falls into the water, if the water under it be not so deep as to overflow and cover all its parts, you may see there the image of all these things in little Continents, and Islands, and Rocks under water: And in the parts that stand above the water, you may see Mountains, and Precipices, and Plains, and most of the varieties that we see and admire in the parts of the Earth. What need we then seek any further for the Explication of these things? Let us suppose this Arch as the great Arch of the Earth, which once it had, and the water under it as the Abysse, and the parts of this ruine to represent the parts of the Earth; There will be scarce any difference but of lesser and greater, the same things appearing in both. But we have naturally that weakness or prejudice, that we think great things are not to be explain'd from easie and familiar instances; We think there must be something difficult and operose in the explication of them, or else we are not satisfied; whether it is that we are asham'd to see our ignorance and admiration to have been so groundless, or whether we fancy there must be a proportion between the difficulty of the explication, and the greatness of the thing explain'd; but that is a very false Judgment, for let things be never so great, if they be simple, their explication must be simple and easie; And on the contrary, some things that are mean, common, and ordinary, may depend upon causes very difficult to find out; for the difficulty of explaining an effect doth not depend upon its greatness or littleness, but upon the simplicity or composition of its causes. And the effects and *Phænomena* we are here to explain, though great, yet depending upon causes very simple, you must not wonder if the Explication, when found out, be familiar and very intelligible.

And this is so intelligible, and so easily deducible from the forementioned causes, that a Man born blind or brought up all his life in a Cave, that had never seen the face of the Earth, nor ever heard any description of it, more than that it was a great Globe, having this Theory propos'd to him, or being instructed what the form of the first Earth was, how it stood over the waters, and then how it was broke and fell into them, he would easily of his own accord foretel what changes would arise upon this dissolution; and what the new form of the Earth would be. As in the first place he would tell you, that this second Earth would be distinguish'd and checker'd into Land and Water; for the Orb which fell being greater than the circumference it fell upon, all the fragments could not fall flat and lie drown'd under water; and those that stood above, would make the dry Land or habitable part of the Earth. Then in the second place, he would plainly discern that these fragments that made the dry Land, could not lie all plain and smooth and equal, but some would be higher and some lower, some in one posture and some in another, and consequently would make Mountains, Hills, Valleys, and Plains, and all other varieties we have in the situation of the parts of the Earth. And lastly, a blind man would easily divine that such a great ruine could not happen but there would be a great many holes and cavities amongst the parts of it, a great many intervals and empty places in the rubbish, as I may so say; for this we see happens in all ruines more or less; and where the fragments are great and hard, 'tis not possible they should be so adjusted in their fall, but that they would lie hollow in many places, and many unfill'd spaces would be intercepted amongst them; some gaping in the surface of the Earth, and others hid within; so as this would give occasion to all sorts of fractures and cavities either in the skin of the Earth, or within its body. And these Cavities, that I may add that in the last place, would be often fill'd with Subterraneous waters, at least at such a depth; for the foundations of the Earth standing now within the waters, so high as those waters reach'd they would more or less propagate themselves every way.

Thus far our Blind man could tell us what the new World would be, or the form of the Earth upon the great dissolution; and we find his reasonings and inferences very true, these are the chief lineaments and features of our Earth; which appear indeed very irregular and very inaccountable when they are lookt upon naked in themselves, but if we look upon them through this Theory, we see as in a glass all the reasons and causes of them. There are different Genius's of men, and different conceptions, and every one is to be allow'd their liberty as to things of this nature; I confess, for my own part, when I observe how easily and naturally this *Hypothesis* doth apply it self to all the particularities of this Earth, hits and falls in so luckily and surprizingly with all the odd postures of its parts, I cannot, without violence, bear off my mind from fully assenting to it: And the more odd and extravagant, as I may so say, and the more diversifi'd the effects and appearances are, to which an *Hypothesis* is to be appli'd, if it answers them all and with exactness, it comes the nearer to a moral certitude and infallibility. As a Lock that consists of a great deal of workmanship, many Wards, and many odd pieces and contrivances, if you find a Key that answers to them all, and opens it readily, 'tis a thousand to one that 'tis the true Key, and was made for that purpose.

An eminent Philosopher of this Age, *Monsieur des Cartes*, hath made use of the like *Hypothesis* to explain the irregular form of the present Earth; though he never dream'd of the Deluge, nor thought that first Orb built over the Abysse, to have been any more than a transient crust, and not a real habitable World that lasted for more than sixteen hundred years, as we suppose it to have been. And though he hath, in my opinion, in the formation of that first Orb, and upon the dissolution of it, committed some great oversights, whereof we have given an account in the Latin Treatise; however he saw a necessity of such a thing, and of the disruption of it, to bring the Earth into that form and posture wherein we now find it. *C. 7. & lib. 2. c. 4.*

Thus far we have spoken in general concerning the agreement and congruity of our supposition with the present face of the Earth, and the easie account it gives of the causes of it. And though I believe to ingenuous persons that are not prejudic'd by the forms and opinions of the Schools against every thing that looks like a novelty or invention, thus much might be sufficient; yet for the satis-faction of all, we will, as a farther proof of our Theory, or that part of it which concerns the dissolution of the Earth, descend to a particular explication of three or four of the most considerable and remarkable things that occur in the fabrick of this present Earth; namely, *the great Chanel of the Ocean; Subterraneous Cavities and Subterraneous Waters;* and lastly, *Mountains and Rocks.* These are the wonders of the Earth as to the visible frame of it; and who would not be pleas'd to see a rational account of these? of their Origin, and of their properties; Or who would not approve of that *Hypothesis*, when they see that Nature in her greatest and strangest works may easily be understood by it, and is in no other way intelligible.

We will speak first of Subterraneous Cavities and Waters, because they will be of easier dispatch, and an introduction to the rest.

That the inside of the Earth is hollow and broken in many places, and is not one firm and united mass, we have both the Testimony of Sence and of easie Observations to prove: How many Caves and Dens and hollow passages into the ground do we see in many Countries, especially amongst Mountains and Rocks; and some of them endless and bottomless so far as can be discover'd. We have many of these in our own Island, in *Derbishire, Somersetshire, Wales*, and other Counties, and in every Continent or Island they abound more or less. These hollownesses of the Earth the Ancients made prisons, or storehouses for the winds, and set a God over them to confine them, or let them loose at his pleasure. For some Ages after the Flood, as all Antiquity tells us, These were the first houses men had, at least in some parts of the Earth; here rude mortals shelter'd themselves, as well as they could, from the injuries of the Air, till they were beaten out by wild beasts that took possession of them. The Ancient Oracles also us'd to be given out of these Vaults and recesses under ground, the *Sibyls* had their Caves, and the *Delphick* Oracle, and their Temples sometimes were built upon an hollow Rock. Places that are strange and solemn strike an awe into us, and incline us to a kind of superstitious timidity and veneration, and therefore they thought them fit for the seats and residences of their Deities. They fansied also that streams rise sometimes, or a sort of Vapour in those hollow places, that gave a kind of Divine fury or inspiration. But all these uses and employments are now in a great measure worn out, we know no use of them but to make the places talkt on where they are, to be the wonders of the Countrey, to please our curiosity to gaze upon and admire; but we know not how they came, nor to what purpose they were made at first.

It would be very pleasant to read good descriptions of these Subterraneous places, and of all the strange works of Nature there; how she furnisheth these dark neglected Grottoes; they have often a little Brook runs murmuring through them, and the roof is commonly a kind of petrefi'd Earth or Icy fret-work; proper enough for such rooms. But I should be pleas'd especially to view the Sea-caves, or those hollow Rocks that lie upon the Sea, where the waves roll in a great way under ground, and wear the hard Rock into as many odd shapes and figures as we see in the Clouds. 'Tis pleasant also to see a River in the middle of its course throw it self into the mouth of a Cave, or an opening of the Earth, and run under ground sometimes many miles; still pursuing its way through the dark pipes of the Earth, till at last it find an out-let. There are many of these Rivers taken notice of in History in the several parts of the Earth, as the *Rhone* in *France*, *Guadiana* in *Spain*, and several in *Greece*, *Alpheus, Lycus*, and *Eracinus*; then *Niger* in *Africa*, *Tigris* in *Asia*, *&c.* And I believe if we could turn *Derwent*, or any other River into one of the holes of the Peak, it would groap its way till it found an issue, it may be in some other County. These subterraneous Rivers that emerge again, shew us that the holes of the Earth are longer and reach farther than we imagine, and if we could see into the ground, as we ride or walk, we should be affrighted to see so often Waters or Caverns under us.

But to return to our dry Caves; these commonly stand high, and are sometimes of a prodigious greatness: *Strabo* mentions some in the Mountains towards *Arabia*, that are capable to receive four thousand men at once. The Cave of *Engedi* hid *David* and six hundred men, so as *Saul*, when he was in the mouth of it, did not perceive them. In the Mountains of the *Traconites* there are many

Geo. l. 16.

1 *Sam.* 24. 3, 4.

94

of these vast dens and recesses, and the people of that Country defended themselves a long time in those strong Holds against *Herod* and his Army; They are plac'd among such craggy Rocks and Precipices, that, as *Josephus* tells us, *Herod* was forc't to make a fort of open chests, and in those by chains of Iron he let down his Souldiers from the top of the Mountains to go fight them in their dens. I need add no more instances of this kind; In the Natural History of all Countries, or the Geographical descriptions of them, you find such places taken notice of, more or less; yet if there was a good collection made of the chief of them in several parts, it might be of use, and would make us more sensible how broken and torn the body of the Earth is.

Ant. Jud. li. 14. *ch.* 27.

There are subterraneous Cavities of another nature, and more remarkable, which they call *Volcano*'s, or fiery Mountains; that belch out flames and smoke and ashes, and sometimes great stones and broken Rocks, and lumps of Earth, or some metallick mixture; and throw them to an incredible distance by the force of the eruption. These argue great vacuities in the bowels of the Earth, and magazines of combustible matter treasur'd up in them. And as the Exhalations within these places must be copious, so they must lie in long Mines or Trains to do so great execution, and to last so long. 'Tis scarce credible what is reported concerning some eruptions of *Vesuvius* and *Ætna*. The Eruptions of *Vesuvius* seem to be more frequent and less violent of late; The flame and smoke break out at the top of the Mountain, where they have eaten away the ground and made a great hollow, so as it looks at the top, when you stand upon the brims of it, like an *Amphitheater*, or like a great Caldron, about a mile in circumference, and the burning Furnace lies under it. The outside of the Mountain is all spread with Ashes, but the inside much more; for you wade up to the mid-leg in Ashes to go down to the bottom of the Cavity, and 'tis extreamly heavy and troublesome to get up again. The inside lies sloping, and one may safely go down if it be not in a raging fit; but the middle part of it or center, which is a little rais'd like the bottom of a Platter, is not to be ventur'd upon, the ground there lies false and hollow, there it always smoaks, and there the Funnel is suppos'd to be; yet there is no visible hole or gaping any where when it doth not rage. *Naples* stands below in fear of this fiery Mountain, which hath often cover'd its Streets and Palaces with its Ashes; and in sight of the Sea (which lies by the side of them both) and as it were in defiance to it, threatens at one time or another, to burn that fair City. History tells us, that some eruptions of *Vesuvius* have carri'd Cinders and Ashes as far as *Constantinople*; this is attested both by *Greek* and *Latin* Authors; particularly, that they were so affrighted with these Ashes and darkness, that the Emperor left the City, and there was a day observ'd yearly for a memorial of this calamity or prodigy.

Ætna is of greater fame than *Vesuvius*, and of greater fury, all Antiquity speaks of it; not only the *Greeks* and *Romans*, but as far as History reacheth, either real or fabulous, there is something recorded of the Fires of *Ætna*. The Figure of the Mountain is inconstant, by reason of the great consumptions and ruines it is subject to; The Fires and Æstuations of it are excellently describ'd by *Virgil*, upon occasion of *Æneas* his passing by those Coasts.

——Horrificis juxta tonat Ætna ruinis;
Interdumque atram prorumpit ad æthera nubem,
Turbine fumantem piceo & candente favillâ;
Attollítque globos flammarum & sydera lambit;
Interdum scopulos, avolsáque viscera Montis
Erigit eructans, liquefactáque saxa sub auras
Cum gemitu glomerat, fundóque exæstuat imo.

Fama est Enceladi *semustum fulmine corpus*
Urgeri mole hâc, ingentémque insuper Ætnam
Impositam, ruptis flammam expirare caminis.
Et fessum quoties mutet latus, intremere omnem
Murmure Trinacriam *& cœlum subtexere fumo.*

*——*Ætna, *whose ruines make a thunder;*
Sometimes black clouds of smoak, that rowl about
Mingled with flakes of fire, it belches out.
And sometimes Balls of flame it darts on high,
Or its torn bowels flings into the Sky.
Within deep Cells under the Earth, a store
Of fire-materials, molten Stones, and Ore,
It gathers, then spews out, and gathers more.

Enceladus *when thunder-struck by* Jove,
Was buri'd here, and Ætna *thrown above;*
And when, to change his wearied side, he turns,
The Island trembles and the Mountain burns.

Not far from *Ætna* lies *Strombolo*, and other adjacent Islands, where there are also such magazines of Fire; and throughout all Regions and Countries in the *West-Indies* and in the *East*, in the Northern and Southern parts of the Earth, there are some of these *Volcano's*, which are sensible evidences that the Earth is incompact and full of Caverns; besides the roarings, and bellowings that use to be heard before an eruption of these *Volcano's*, argue some dreadful hollowness in the belly or under the roots of the Mountain, where the Exhalations struggle before they can break their prison.

The subterraneous Cavities that we have spoke of hitherto, are such as are visible in the surface of the Earth, and break the skin by some gaping Orifice; but the Miners and those that work under ground, meet with many more in the bowels of the Earth, that never reach to the top of it: Burrows, and Chanels, and Clefts, and Caverns, that never had the comfort of one beam of light since the great fall of the Earth. And where we think the ground is firm and solid, as upon Heaths and Downs, it often betrays its hollowness, by sounding under the Horses feet and the Chariot-wheels that pass over it. We do not know when and where we stand upon good ground, if it was examin'd deep enough; and to make us further sensible of this, we will instance in two things that argue the unsoundness and hollowness of the Earth in the inward recesses of it, though the surface be

96

intire and unbroken; These are *Earthquakes* and the communication of *Subterraneous waters and Seas*: Of which two we will speak a little more particularly.

Earthquakes are too evident demonstrations of the hollowness of the Earth, being the dreadful effects or consequences of it; for if the body of the Earth was sound and compact, there would be no such thing in Nature as an Earthquake. They are commonly accompanied with an heavy dead sound, like a dull thunder, which ariseth from the Vapours that are striving in the womb of Nature when her throes are coming upon her. And that these Caverns where the Vapours lie are very large and capacious, we are taught sometimes by sad experience; for whole Cities and Countries have been swallow'd up into them, as *Sodom* and *Gomorrha*, and the Region of *Pentapolis*, and several Cities in *Greece*, and in *Asia*, and other parts. Whole Islands also have been thus absorpt in an Earthquake; the pillars and props they stood upon being broken, they have sunk and faln in as an house blown up. I am also of opinion that those Islands that are made by divulsion from a Continent, as *Sicily* was broken off from *Italy*, and Great *Britain*, as some think, from *France*, have been made the same way; that is, the Isthmus or necks of Land that joyn'd these Islands with their Continents before, have been hollow, and being either worn by the water, or shak'd by an Earthquake, have sunk down, and so made way for the Sea to overflow them, and of a Promontory to make an Island. For it is not at all likely that the neck of Land continu'd standing, and the Sea overflow'd it, and so made an Island; for then all those passages between such Islands, and their respective Continents would be extreamly shallow and unnavigable, which we do not find them to be. Nor is it any more wonder if such a neck of Land should fall, than that a Mountain should sink, or any other tract of Land, and a Lake rise in its place, which hath often happen'd. *Plato* supposeth his *Atlantis* to have been greater than *Asia* and *Africa* together, and yet to have sunk all into the Sea; whether that be true or no, I do not think it impossible that some arms of the Sea or Sinus's might have had such an original as that; and I am very apt to think, that for some years after the Deluge, till the fragments were well setled and adjusted, great alterations would happen as to the face of the Sea and the Land; many of the fragments would change their posture, and many would sink into the water that stood out before, the props failing that bore them up, or the joynts and corners whereby they lean'd upon one another; and thereupon a new face of things would arise, and a new Deluge for that part of the Earth. Such removes and interchanges, I believe, would often happen in the first Ages after the Flood; as we see in all other ruines there happen lesser and secondary ruines after the first, till the parts be so well pois'd and setled, that without some violence they scarce change their posture any more.

But to return to our Earthquakes, and to give an instance or two of their extent and violence: *Pliny* mentions one in the Reign of *Tiberius Cæsar* that struck down twelve Cities of *Asia* in one night, And *Fournier* gives us an account of one in *Peru*, that reacht three hundred leagues along the Sea-shore, and seventy leagues in-land; and level'd the Mountains all along as it went, threw down the Cities, turn'd the Rivers out of their Chanels, and made an universal havock and confusion; And all this, he saith, was done within the space of seven or eight minutes.

There must be dreadful Vaults and Mines under that Continent, that gave passage to the Vapours, and liberty to play for nine hundred miles in length, and above two hundred in breadth. *Asia* also hath been very subject to these desolations by Earthquakes; and many parts in *Europe*, as *Greece*, *Italy*, and others. The truth is, our Cities are built upon ruines, and our Fields and Countries stand upon broken Arches and Vaults, and so does the greatest part of the outward frame of the Earth, and therefore it is no wonder if it be often shaken; there being quantities of Exhalations within these Mines, or Cavernous passages, that are capable of rarefaction and inflammation; and, upon such occasions, requiring more room, they shake or break the ground that covers them. And thus much concerning Earthquakes.

A second observation that argues the hollowness of the Earth, is the communication of the Seas and Lakes under ground. The *Caspian* and *Mediterranean* Seas, and several Lakes, receive into them great Rivers, and yet have no visible out-let: These must have subterraneous out-lets, by which they empty themselves, otherwise they would redound and overflow the brims of their Vessel. The *Mediterranean* is most remarkable in this kind, because 'tis observ'd that at one end the great Ocean flows into it through the straits of *Gibralter*, with a sensible current, and towards the other end about *Constantinople* the *Pontus* flows down into it with a stream so strong, that Vessels have much ado to stem it; and yet it neither hath any visible evacuation or out-let, nor overflows its banks. And besides that it is thus fed at either end, it is fed by the navel too, as I may so say; it sucks in, by their Chanels, several Rivers into its belly, whereof the *Nile* is one very great and considerable. These things have made it a great Problem, *What becomes of the water of the Mediterranean Sea?* And for my part, I think, the solution is very easie, namely, that it is discharg'd by Subterraneous passages, or convey'd by Chanels under the ground into the Ocean. And this manner of discharge or conveyance is not peculiar to the *Mediterranean*, but is common to it with the *Caspian* Sea, and other Seas and Lakes, that receive great Rivers into them, and have no visible issue.

I know there have been propos'd several other ways to answer this difficulty concerning the efflux or consumption of the waters of the *Mediterranean*; some have suppos'd a double current in the strait of *Gibralter*, one that carri'd the water in, and another that brought it out; like the Arteries and Veins in our Body, the one exporting our bloud from the heart, and the other re-importing it: So they suppos'd one current upon the surface, which carri'd the water into the *Mediterranean*, and under it at a certain depth a counter-current, which brought the water back into the Ocean. But this hath neither proof nor foundation; for unless it was included in pipes, as our bloud is, or consisted of liquors very different, these cross currents would mingle and destroy one another. Others are of opinion, that all the water that flows into the *Mediterranean*, or a quantity equal to it, is consum'd in Exhalations every day; This seems to be a bolder supposition than the other, for if so much be consum'd in Vapours and Exhalations every day as flows into this Sea, what if this Sea had an out-let, and discharg'd by that, every day, as much as it receiv'd; in a few days the Vapours would have consum'd all the rest; and yet we see many Lakes that have as free an out-let as an in-let, and are not consum'd, or sensibly diminisht by the Vapours. Besides, this reason is a Summer-reason, and would pass very ill in Winter, when the heat of the Sun is much less powerful: At least there would be a very sensible difference betwixt the height of the waters in Summer and Winter, if so much was consum'd every day as this Explication supposeth. And the truth is, this want of a visible out-let is not a property belonging only to the *Mediterranean* Sea, as we noted before, but is also in other Seas and great Lakes, some lying in one Climat and some in another, where there is no reason to suppose such excessive Exhalations; And though 'tis true some Rivers in *Africk*, and in other parts of the Earth, are thus exhal'd and dri'd up, without ever flowing into the Sea (as were all the Rivers in the first Earth) yet this is where the sands and parch'd ground suck up a great part of them; the heat of the Climat being excessively strong, and the Chanel of the River growing shallower by degrees, and, it may be, divided into lesser branches and rivulets; which are causes that take no place here. And therefore we must return to our first reason, which is universal, for all seasons of the Year and all Climats; and seeing we are assur'd that there are Subterraneous Chanels and passages, for Rivers often fall into the ground, and sometimes rise again, and sometimes never return; why should we doubt to ascribe this effect to so obvious a cause? Nay, I believe the very Ocean doth evacuate it self by Subterraneous out-lets; for considering what a prodigious mass of water falls into it every day from the wide mouths of all the Rivers of the Earth, it must have out-lets proportionable; and those *Syrtes* or great Whirlpools that are constant in certain parts or Sinus's of the Sea, as upon the Coast of *Norway* and of *Italy*, arise probably from Subterraneous out-lets in those places, whereby the water sinks, and turns, and draws into it whatsoever comes within such a compass; and if there was no issue at the bottom, though it might by contrary currents turn things round, within its Sphere, yet there is no reason from that why it should suck them down to the bottom. Neither does it seem improbable, that the currents of the Sea are from these in-draughts, and that there is always a submarine inlet in some part of them, to make a circulation of the Waters. But thus much for the Subterraneous communication of Seas and Lakes.

And thus much in general concerning subterraneous Cavities, and concerning the hollow and broken frame of the Earth. If I had now magick enough to show you at one view all the inside of the Earth, which we have imperfectly describ'd; if we could go under the roots of the Mountains, and into the sides of the broken rocks; or could dive into the Earth with one of those Rivers that sink under ground, and follow its course and all its windings till it rise again, or led us to the Sea, we should have a much stronger and more effectual *Idea* of the broken form of the Earth, than any we can excite by these faint descriptions collected from Reason. The Ancients I remember us'd to represent these hollow Caves and Subterraneous Regions in the nature of a *World* under-ground, and suppos'd it inhabited by the *Nymphs*, especially the *Nymphs* of the waters and the Sea-Goddesses; so *Orpheus* sung of old; and in imitation of him *Virgil* hath made a description of those Regions; feigning the Nymph *Cyrene* to send for her son to come down to her, and made her a visit in those shades where mortals were not admitted.

Virgil

Duc age, duc ad nos, fas illi limina Divûm
Tangere, ait: Simul alta jubet discedere latè
Flumina, quà juvenis gressus inferret, at illum
Curvata in montis faciem circumstitit unda,
Accepítque sinu vasto, misítque sub amnem.
Jámque domum mirans Genetricis & humida regna,
Speluncísque lacos clausos, lucósque sonantes,
Ibat, & ingenti motu stupefactus aquarum
Omnia sub magnâ labentia flumina terrâ
Spectabat diversa locis; Phasímque Licúmque, *&c.*
Et Thalami matris pendentia pumice tecta, &c.

Come lead the Youth below, bring him to me,
The Gods are pleas'd our Mansions he should see;
Streight she commands the floods to make him way,
They open their wide bosom and obey;
Soft is the path, and easie is his tread,
A watry Arch bends o'er his dewy head;
And as he goes he wonders, and looks round,
To see this new-found Kingdom under ground.
The silent Lakes in hollow Caves he sees,
And on their banks an echoing grove of Trees;
The fall of waters 'mongst the Rocks below
He hears, and sees the Rivers how they flow:
All the great Rivers of the Earth are there,
Prepar'd, as in a womb, by Nature's care.
Last, to his mother's bed-chamber he's brought,
Where the high roof with Pumice-stone is wrought, &c.

If we now could open the Earth as this *Nymph* did the Water, and go down into the bosom of it, see all the dark Chambers and Apartments there, how ill contriv'd, and how ill kept, so many holes and corners, some fill'd with smoak and fire, some with water, and some with vapours and mouldy Air; how like a ruine it lies gaping and torn in the parts of it; we should not easily believe that God created it into this form immediately out of nothing; It would have cost no more to have made things in better order; nay, it had been more easie and more simple; and accordingly we are assured that all things were made at first in Beauty and proportion. And if we consider Nature and the manner of the first formation of the Earth, 'tis evident that there could be no such holes and Caverns, nor broken pieces, made then in the body of it; for the grosser parts of the Chaos falling down towards the Center, they would there compose a mass of Earth uniform and compact, the water swimming above it; and this first mass under the water could have no Caverns or vacuities in it; for if it had had any, the Earthy parts, while the mass was liquid or semiliquid, would have sunk into them and fill'd them up, expelling the Air or Water that was there; And when afterwards there came to be a crust or new Earth form'd upon the face of the Waters, there could be no Cavities, no dens, no fragments in it, no more than in the other; And for the same general reason, that is, passing from a liquid form into a concrete or solid leisurely and by degrees, it would flow and settle together in an entire mass; There being nothing broken, nor any thing hard, to bear the parts off from one another, or to intercept any empty spaces between them.

'Tis manifest then that the Earth could not be in this Cavernous form originally, by any work of nature; nor by any immediate action of God, seeing there is neither use nor beauty in this kind of construction: Do we not then, as reasonably, as aptly, ascribe it to that desolation that was brought upon the Earth in the general Deluge? When its outward frame was dissolv'd and fell into the great Abysse: How easily doth this answer all that we have observ'd concerning the Subterraneous Regions? That hollow and broken posture of things under ground, all those Caves and holes, and blind recesses, that are otherwise so inaccountable, say but that they are a *Ruine*, and you have in one word explain'd them all. For there is no sort of Cavities, interior or exterior, great or little, open or shut, wet or dry, of what form or fashion soever, but we might reasonably expect them in a ruine of that nature. And as for the Subterraneous waters, seeing the Earth fell into the Abysse, the pillars and foundations of the present (exteriour) Earth must stand immers'd in water, and therefore at such a depth from the surface every where, there must be water found, if the soil be of a nature to admit it. 'Tis true, all Subterraneous waters do not proceed from this original, for many of them are the effects of Rains and melted Snows sunk into the Earth; but that in digging any where you constantly come to water at length, even in the most solid ground this cannot proceed from these Rains or Snows, but must come from below, and from a cause as general as the effect is; which can be no other in my judgment than this, that the roots of the exteriour Earth stand within the old Abysse, whereof, as a great part lies open in the Sea, so the rest lies hid and cover'd among the fragments of the Earth; sometimes dispers'd and only moistning the parts, as our bloud lies in the flesh, and in the habit of the body; sometimes in greater or lesser masses, as the bloud in our Vessels. And this I take to be the true account of Subterraneous waters as distinguish'd from Fountains and Rivers, and from the matter and causes of them.

Thus much we have spoke to give a general *Idea* of the inward parts of the Earth, and an easie Explication of them by our *Hypothesis*; which whether it be true or no, if you compare it impartially with Nature, you will confess at least, that all these things are just in such a form and posture as if it was true.

CHAPTER X

Concerning the Chanel of the Sea, and the Original of it: The Causes of its irregular form and unequal depths: As also of the Original of Islands, their situation, and other properties.

WE have hitherto given an account of the Subterraneous Regions, and of their general form; We now come above ground to view the surface of the Globe, which we find *Terraqueous*, or divided into Sea and Land: These we must survey, and what is remarkable in them as to their frame and structure, we must give an account of from our *Hypothesis*, and shew to be inaccountable from any other.

As for the Ocean, there are two things considerable in it, the Water and the Chanel that contains it. The Water, no doubt is as ancient as the Earth and contemporary with it, and we suppose it to be part of the great Abysse wherein the World was drown'd; the rest lying cover'd under the hollow fragments of Continents and Islands. But that is not so much the subject of our present discourse as the Chanel of the Ocean, that vast and prodigious Cavity that runs quite round the Globe, and reacheth, for ought we know, from Pole to Pole, and in many places is unsearchably deep: When I present this great Gulf to my imagination, emptied of all its waters, naked and gaping at the Sun, stretching its jaws from one end of the Earth to another, it appears to me the most ghastly thing in Nature. What hands or instruments could work a Trench in the body of the Earth of this vastness, and lay Mountains and Rocks on the side of it, as Ramparts to enclose it?

But as we justly admire its greatness, so we cannot at all admire its beauty or elegancy, for 'tis as deform'd and irregular as it is great. And there appearing nothing of order or any regular design in its parts, it seems reasonable to believe that it was not the work of Nature, according to her first intention, or according to the first model that was drawn in measure and proportion, by the Line and by the Plummet, but a secondary work, and the best that could be made of broken materials. And upon this supposition 'tis easie to imagine, how upon the dissolution of the primæval Earth the Chanel of the Sea was made, or that huge Cavity that lies between the several Continents of the Earth; which shall be more particularly explain'd after we have view'd a little better the form of it, and the Islands that lie scatter'd by its shores.

There is no Cavity in the Earth, whether open or Subterraneous, that is comparably so great as that of the Ocean, nor would any appear of that deformity if we could see it empty. The inside of a Cave is rough and unsightly; The beds of great Rivers and great Lakes when they are laid dry, look very raw and rude; The Valleys of the Earth, if they were naked, without Trees and without Grass, nothing but bare ground and bare stones, from the tops of their Mountains would have a ghastly aspect; but the Sea-chanel is the complex of all these; here Caves, empty Lakes, naked Valleys are represented as in their original, or rather far exceeded and out-done as to all their irregularities; for the Cavity of the Ocean is universally irregular, both as to the shores and borders of it; as to the uncertain breadth and the uncertain depth of its several parts, and as to its ground and bottom and the whole mould: If the Sea had been drawn round the Earth in regular figures and borders, it might have been a great beauty to our Globe, and we should reasonably have concluded it a work of the first Creation, or of Nature's first production; but finding on the contrary all the marks of disorder and disproportion in it, we may as reasonably conclude, that it did not belong to the first order of things, but was something succedaneous, when the degeneracy of Mankind, and the judgments of God had destroy'd the first World, and subjected the Creation to some kind of Vanity.

Nor can it easily be imagin'd, if the Sea had been always, and the Earth, in this *Terraqueous* form, broke into Continents and Islands, how Mankind could have been propagated at first through the face of the Earth, all from one head and from one place. For Navigation was not then known, at least as to the grand Ocean, or to pass from Continent to Continent; And, I believe, *Noah*'s Ark was the first Ship, or Vessel of bulk, that ever was built in the World; how could then the Posterity of *Adam* overflow the Earth, and stock the several parts of the World, if they had been distant or separate then, as they are now, by the interposal of the great Ocean? But this consideration we will insist upon more largely in another place; let us reflect upon the irregularities of the Sea-chanel again, and the possible causes of it.

If we could imagine the Chanel of the Sea to have been made as we may imagine the Chanels of Rivers to have been, by long and insensible attrition, the water wearing by degrees the ground under it, by the force it hath from its descent and course, we should not wonder at its irregular form; but 'tis not possible it should have had any such original; whence should its waters have descended, from what Mountains, or from what Clouds? Where is the spring-head of the Sea? what force could eat away half the surface of the Earth, and wear it hollow to an immeasurable depth? This must not be from feeble and lingring causes, such as the attrition of waters, but from some great violence offer'd to Nature, such as we suppose to have been in the general Deluge, when the frame of the Earth was broken. And after we have a little survey'd the Sea-coast, and so far as we can, the form of the Sea-chanel, we shall the more easily believe that they could have no other original than what we assign.

The shores and coasts of the Sea are no way equal or uniform, but go in a line uncertainly crooked and broke; indented and jag'd as a thing torn, as you may see in the Maps of the Coasts and the Sea-charts; and yet there are innumerable more inequalities than are taken notice of in those draughts; for they only mark the greater Promontories and Bays; but there are besides those a multitude of Creeks and out-lets, necks of Land and Angles, which break the evenness of the shore in all manner of ways. Then the height and level of the shore is as uncertain as the line of it; 'Tis sometimes high and sometimes low, sometimes spread in sandy Plains, as smooth as the Sea it self, and of such an equal height with it, that the waves seem to have no bounds but the meer figure and convexity of the Globe; In other places 'tis rais'd into banks and ramparts of Earth, and in others 'tis wall'd in with Rocks; And all this without any order that we can observe, or any other reason than that this is what might be expected in a ruine.

As to the depths and soundings of the Sea, they are under no rule nor equality any more than the figures of the Shores; Shallows in some places, and Gulfs in others; beds of Sands sometimes, and sometimes Rocks under water; as Navigators have learn'd by a long and dangerous experience: And though we that are upon dry Land, are not much concern'd how the Rocks and the Shelves lie in the Sea, yet a poor Ship-wreckt Mariner, when he hath run his Vessel upon a Rock in the middle of the Chanel, expostulates bitterly with Nature, who it was that plac'd that Rock there, and to what purpose? was there not room enough, saith he, upon the Land, or the Shore, to lay your great Stones, but they must be thrown into the middle of the Sea, as it were in spite to Navigation? The best Apology that can be made for Nature in this case, so far as I know, is to confess that the whole business of the Sea-chanel is but a ruine, and in a ruine things tumble uncertainly, and commonly lie in confusion: Though to speak the truth, it seldom happens, unless in narrow Seas, that Rocks or Banks or Islands lie in the middle of them, or very far from the Shores.

Having view'd the more visible parts of the Chanel of the Sea, we must now descend to the bottom of it, and see the form and contrivance of that; but who shall guide us in our journey, while we walk, as *Job* saith, in the search of the deep? Or who can make a description of that which none hath seen? It is reasonable to believe, that the bottom of the Sea is much more rugged, broken and irregular than the face of the Land; There are Mountains, and Valleys, and Rocks, and ridges of Rocks, and all the common inequalities we see upon Land; besides these, 'tis very likely there are Caves under water, and hollow passages into the bowels of the Earth, by which the Seas circulate and communicate one with another, and with Subterraneous waters; Those great *Eddees* and infamous *Syrtes* and Whirlpools that are in some Seas, as the *Baltick* and the *Mediterranean*, that suck into them and overwhelm whatever comes within their reach, show that there is something below that sucks from them in proportion, and that drinks up the Sea as the Sea drinks up the Rivers. We ought also to imagine the Shores within the water to go inclin'd and sloping, but with great inequality; there are many Shelves in the way, and Chambers, and sharp Angles; and many broken Rocks and great Stones lie tumbled down to the bottom.

Chap. 38. 16.

'Tis true these things affect us little, because they are not expos'd to our senses; and we seldom give our selves the trouble to collect from reason what the form of the invisible and inaccessible parts of the Earth is; Or if we do sometimes, those *Idea*'s are faint and weak, and make no lasting impression upon our imagination and passions; but if we should suppose the Ocean dry, and that we lookt down from the top of some high Cloud upon the empty Shell, how horridly and barbarously would it look? And with what amazement should we see it under us like an open Hell, or a wide bottomless pit? So deep, and hollow, and vast; so broken and confus'd, so every way deform'd and monstrous. This would effectually waken our imagination, and make us inquire and wonder how such a thing came in Nature; from what causes, by what force or engines could the Earth be torn in this prodigious manner? did they dig the Sea with Spades, and carry out the molds in hand-baskets? where are the entrails laid? and how did they cleave the Rocks asunder? if as many Pioneers as the Army of *Xerxes*, had been at work ever since the beginning of the World, they could not have made a ditch of this greatness. According to the proportions taken before in the *Second Chapter*, the Cavity or capacity of the Sea-chanel will amount to no less than 4639090 cubical miles. Nor is it the greatness only, but that wild and multifarious confusion which we see in the parts and fashion of it, that makes it strange and inaccountable; 'tis another Chaos in its kind, who can paint the Scenes of it? Gulfs, and Precipices, and Cataracts; Pits within Pits, and Rocks under Rocks, broken Mountains and ragged Islands, that look as if they had been Countries pull'd up by the roots, and planted in the Sea.

If we could make true and full representations of these things to our selves, I think we should not be so bold as to make them the immediate product of Divine Omnipotence; being destitute of all appearance of Art or Counsel. The first orders of things are more perfect and regular, and this *Decorum* seems to be observ'd afterwards, Nature doth not fall into disorder till Mankind be first degenerate and leads the way. Monsters have been often made an argument against Providence; if a Calf have two heads, or five legs, streight there must not be a God in Heaven, or at least not upon Earth; and yet this is but a chance that happens once in many years, and is of no consequence at all to the rest of the World: but if we make the standing frame of Nature monstrous, or deform'd and disproportion'd, and to have been so not by corruption and degeneracy, but immediately by Divine Creation or Formation, it would not be so easie to answer that objection against Providence. Let us therefore prevent this imputation, and supposing, according to our Theory, that these things were not originally thus, let us now explain more distinctly how they came to pass at the Deluge, or upon the dissolution of the first Earth.

And we will not content our selves with a general answer to these observations concerning the Sea-chanel, as if it was a sufficient account of them to say they were the effects of a ruine; there are other things to be consider'd and explain'd besides this irregularity, as the vast hollowness of this Cavity, bigger incomparably than any other belonging to the Earth; and also the declivity of the sides of it, which lie shelving from top to bottom; For notwithstanding all the inequalities we have taken notice of in the Chanel or the Sea, it hath one general form, which may, though under many differences, be observ'd throughout, and that is, that the shores and sides within the water lie inclin'd, and you descend by degrees to the deepest part, which is towards the middle. This, I know, admits of many exceptions, for sometimes upon a rocky shore, or among rocky Islands the Sea is very deep close to the Rocks, and the deeper commonly the higher and steeper the Rocks are. Also where the descent is more leisurely, 'tis often after a different manner, in some Coasts more equal and uniform, in others more broken and interrupted, but still there is a descent to the Chanel or deepest part, and this in the deep Ocean is fathomless; And such a deep Ocean, and such a deep Chanel there is always between Continents. This, I think, is a property as determinate as any we can pitch upon in the Chanel of the Sea, and with those other two mention'd, its vast Cavity and universal irregularity, is all one can desire an account of as to the form of it; we will therefore from this ground take our rise and first measures for the Explication of the Sea-chanel.

Let us suppose then in the dissolution of the Earth when it began to fall, that it was divided only into three or four fragments, according to the number of our Continents; but those fragments being vastly great could not descend at their full

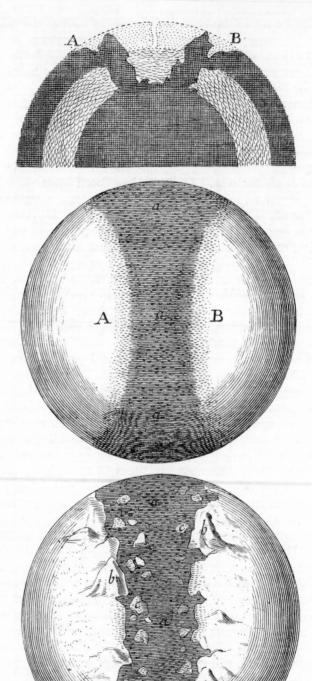

Fig. 1

Fig. 2

Fig. 3

breadth and expansion, or at least could not descend so fast in the middle as towards the extremities; because the Air about the edges would yield and give place easily, not having far to go to get out of the way; but the Air that was under the middle of the fragment could not without a very swift motion get from under the concave of it, and consequently its descent there would be more resisted and suspended; but the sides in the mean time would continually descend, bending the fragment with their weight, and so making it of a lesser compass and expansion than it was before: And by this means there would be an interval and distance made between the two falling fragments, and a good part of the Abysse, after their descent, would lie uncover'd in the middle betwixt them; as may be seen in this Figure, where the fragments A. B. bending downwards in their extremities, separate as they go, and after they are faln leave a good space in the Abysse betwixt them, altogether uncover'd; This space is the main Chanel of the great Ocean, lying betwixt two Continents; and the inclining sides shew the declivity of the Shores.

This we have represented here only in a Ring or Circle of the Earth, in the first Figure; but it may be better represented in a broader surface, as in the second Figure, where the two fragments A. B. that are to make the two opposite Continents, fall in like double Doors opening downwards, the Hinges being towards the Land on either side, so as at the bottom they leave in the middle betwixt them a deep Chanel of water, a. a. a. such as is betwixt all Continents; and the Water reaching a good height upon the Land on either side, makes Sea there too, but shallower, and by degrees you descend into the deepest Chanel.

This gives an account of two things that we mention'd to be consider'd and explain'd as to the Sea, how the great Cavity of its Chanel was made, and how it was made in that general form of declivity in its sides from the Land: The third thing was the irregularities of it, both as to its various depths, and as to the form of the shores and of the bottom. And this is as easily and naturally explain'd from the same supposition as the former two; for though we have hitherto represented the fragments A. B. as even and regular after their fall, because that was most simple, and there was no occasion then to represent them otherwise, yet we must suppose that as soon as in their fall they hit upon the top or bottom of the Abysse, that great force and weight with which they descended broke off all the Edges and extremities, and so made innumerable ruptures and inequalities in the shores, and as many within the Sea and at the bottom; where the broken Rocks and lumps of Earth would lie in all imaginable disorder; as you may conceive from the *third Figure*. For when the motion came on a sudden to be obstructed, the load of the fragment still pressing it forwards, such a concussion arise as made thousands of lesser fragments, of all shapes and magnitudes, and in all postures and forms, and most of them irregular. And by these fractions and secondary ruines the line of the shores was broken, and the level of them too; In some places they would stand high, in others low, sometimes rough and sometimes even, and generally crooked, with Angles and in-lets, and uncertain windings. The bottom also, by the same stroke, was diversifi'd into all manner of forms, sometimes Rocky with Pits and Gulfs, and sometimes spread in plain beds, sometimes shallow and sometimes deep; for those differences would depend only upon the situation of the secondary fragments; and so it might come to pass, that some places near the shore might be excessive deep when a Rock or Rocks stood in a steep posture, as (*Figure* 3.) b. b. b. and, on the contrary, sometimes places much more advanc'd into the Ocean, might be less deep, where a fragment of Earth lay under water, or one bore up another, as c. c. c. but these cases would not be very frequent. To conclude, there are no properties of the Sea-chanel, that I know of, nor differences or irregularities in the form of it, which this *Hypothesis* doth not give a fair account of: And having thus far open'd the way, and laid down the general grounds for their Explication, other things that are more minute, we leave to the curiosity of particular Genius's; being unwilling to clog the Theory at first with things that may seem unnecessary. We proceed now to the consideration of Islands.

We must in the first place distinguish between *Original* Islands and *Factitious* Islands; Those I call factitious, that are not of the same date and Antiquity with the Sea, but have been made some at one time, some at another, by accidental causes, as the aggestion of Sands and Sand-beds, or the Sea leaving the tops of some shallow places that lie high, and yet flowing about the lower skirts of them; These make sandy and plain Islands, that have no high Land in them, and are but mock-Islands in effect. Others are made by divulsion from some Continent, when an Isthmus or the neck of a Promontory running into the Sea, sinks or falls in, by an Earthquake or otherwise, and the Sea entring in at the gap passeth through, and makes that Promontory or Country become an Island. Thus the Island *Sicily* is suppos'd to have been made, and all *Africa* might be an Island, if the Isthmus between the *Mediterranean* and the red Sea should sink down. And these Islands may have Rocks and Mountains in them, if the Land had so before. Lastly, there are Islands that have been said to rise from the bottom of the Sea; History mentions such in both the *Archipelago's*, *Ægæan* and *Indian*; and this seems to argue that there are great fragments or tracts of Earth that lie loose at the bottom of the Sea, or that are not incorporated with the ground; which agrees very well with our Explication of the Sea-chanel.

But besides these Islands and the several sorts of them, there are others which I call *Original*; because they could not be produc'd in any of the forementioned ways, but are of the same Origin and Antiquity with the Chanel of the Sea; and such are the generality of our Islands; They were not made of heaps of Sands, nor torn from any Continent, but are as ancient as the Continents themselves, namely, ever since the Deluge, the common Parent of them both. Nor is there any difficulty to understand how Islands were made at the dissolution of the Earth, any more than how Continents were made; for Islands are but lesser Continents, or Continents greater Islands; and according as Continents were made of greater masses of Earth or greater fragments standing above the Water, so Islands were made of less, but so big always, and in such a posture, as to bear their tops above the water. Yet though they agree thus far, there is a particular difference to be taken notice of as to their Origin; for the Continents were made of those three or four primary masses into which the falling Orb of the Earth was divided, but the Islands were made of the fractures of these, and broken off by the fall from the skirts and extremities of the Continents; We noted before, that when those great masses and primary fragments came to dash upon the Abysse in their fall, the sudden stop of the motion, and the weighty bulk of the descending fragment broke off all the edges and extremities of it, which edges and extremities broken off made the Islands; And accordingly we see that they generally lie scatter'd along the sides of the Continents, and are but splinters, as it were, of those greater bodies. 'Tis true, besides these, there were an infinite number of other pieces broke off that do not appear, some making Rocks under water, some shallows and banks in the Sea; but the greatest of them when they fell either one upon another, or in such a posture as to prop up one another, their heads and higher parts would stand out of the water and make Islands.

Thus I conceive the Islands of the Sea were at first produc'd; we cannot wonder therefore that they should be so numerous, or far more numerous than the Continents; These are the Parents, and those are the Children; Nor can we wonder to see along the sides of the Continents several Islands or sets of Islands, sown, as it were, by handfuls, or laid in trains; for the manner of their generation would lead us to think they would be so plac'd. So the *American* Islands lie scatter'd upon the Coast of that Continent; the *Maldivian* and *Philipine* upon the *East-Indian* shore, and the *Hesperides* upon the *Africk*; and there seldom happen to be any towards the middle of the Ocean, though, by an accident, that also might come to pass. Lastly, it suits very well with out Explication, that there should be Mountains and Rocks, sometimes in clusters, sometimes in long chains, in all Islands; (as we find there are in all that are true and Original) for 'tis that makes them high enough to appear above the water, and strong enough to continue and preserve themselves in that high situation.

And thus much may suffice for a summary Explication of the causes of the Sea-chanel and Islands, according to our *Hypothesis*.

CHAPTER XI

Concerning the Mountains of the Earth, their greatness and irregular Form, their Situation, Causes, and Origin.

WE have been in the hollows of the Earth, and the Chambers of the Deep, amongst the damps and steams of those lower Regions; let us now go air our selves on the tops of the Mountains, where we shall have a more free and large Horizon, and quite another face of things will present it self to our observation.

The greatest objects of Nature are, methinks, the most pleasing to behold; and next to the great Concave of the Heavens, and those boundless Regions where the Stars inhabit, there is nothing that I look upon with more pleasure than the wide Sea and the Mountains of the Earth. There is something august and stately in the Air of these things, that inspires the mind with great thoughts and passions; We do naturally, upon such occasions, think of God and his greatness: and whatsoever hath but the shadow and appearance of INFINITE, as all things have that are too big for our comprehension, they fill and over-bear the mind with their Excess, and cast it into a pleasing kind of stupor and admiration.

And yet these Mountains we are speaking of, to confess the truth, are nothing but great ruines; but such as show a certain magnificence in Nature; as from old Temples and broken Amphitheaters of the *Romans* we collect the greatness of that people. But the grandeur of a Nation is less sensible to those that never see the remains and monuments they have left, and those who never see the mountainous parts of the Earth, scarce ever reflect upon the causes of them, or what power in Nature could be sufficient to produce them. The truth is, the generality of people have not sence and curiosity enough to raise a question concerning these things, or concerning the Original of them. You may tell them that Mountains grow out of the Earth like Fuzz-balls, or that there are Monsters under ground that throw up Mountains as Moles do Mole-hills; they will scarce raise one objection against your doctrine; or if you would appear more Learned, tell them that the Earth is a great Animal, and these are Wens that grow upon its body. This would pass current for Philosophy; so much is the World drown'd in stupidity and sensual pleasures, and so little inquisitive into the works of God and Nature.

There is nothing doth more awaken our thoughts or excite our minds to enquire into the causes of such things, than the actual view of them; as I have had experience my self when it was my fortune to cross the *Alps* and *Appennine* Mountains; for the sight of those wild, vast and indigested heaps of Stones and Earth, did so deeply strike my fancy, that I was not easie till I could give my self some tolerable account how that confusion came in Nature. 'Tis true, the height of Mountains compar'd with the Diameter of the Earth is not considerable, but the extent of them and the ground they stand upon, bears a considerable proportion to the surface of the Earth; and if from *Europe* we may take our measures for the rest, I easily believe, that the Mountains do at least take up the tenth part of the dry land. The Geographers are not very careful to describe or note in their Charts, the multitude or situation of Mountains; They mark the bounds of Countries, the site of Cities and Towns, and the course of Rivers, because these are things of chief use to civil affairs and commerce, and that they design to serve, and not Philosophy or Natural History. But *Cluverius* in his description of *Ancient Germany*, *Switzerland* and *Italy*, hath given Maps of those Countries more approaching to the natural face of them, and we have drawn (at the end of this Chapter) such a Map of either Hemisphere, without marking Countries or Towns, or any such artificial things; distinguishing only Land and Sea, Islands and Continents, Mountains and not Mountains; and 'tis very useful to imagine the Earth in this manner, and to look often upon such bare draughts as shew us Nature undrest; for then we are best able to judge what her true shapes and proportions are.

'Tis certain that we naturally imagine the surface of the Earth much more regular than it is; for unless we be in some Mountainous parts, there seldom occur any great inequalities within so much compass of ground as we can, at once, reach with our Eye; and to conceive the rest, we multiply the same *Idea*, and extend it to those parts of the Earth that we do not see; and so fancy the whole Globe much more smooth and uniform than it is. But suppose a man was carri'd asleep out of a Plain Country, amongst the *Alps,* and left there upon the top of one of the highest Mountains, when he wak'd and look'd about him, he would think himself in an inchanted Country, or carri'd into another World; Every thing would appear to him so different to what he had ever seen or imagin'd before. To see on every hand of him a multitude of vast bodies thrown together in confusion, as those Mountains are; Rocks standing naked round about him; and the hollow Valleys gaping under him; and at his feet it may be, an heap of frozen Snow in the midst of Summer. He would hear the thunder come from below, and see the black Clouds hanging beneath him; Upon such a prospect, it would not be easie to him to perswade himself that he was still upon the same Earth; but if he did, he would be convinc'd, at least, that there are some Regions of it strangely rude, and ruine-like, and very different from what he had ever thought of before. But the inhabitants of these wild places are even with us; for those that live amongst the *Alps* and the great Mountains, think that all the rest of the Earth is like their Country, all broken into Mountains, and Valleys, and Precipices; They never see other, and most people think of nothing but what they have seen at one time or another.

These *Alps* we are speaking of are the greatest range of Mountains in *Europe*; and 'tis prodigious to see and to consider of what extent these heaps of Stones and Rubbish are; one way they overspread *Savoy* and *Dauphiné,* and reach through *France* to the *Pyrenean* Mountains, and so to the Ocean. The other way they run along the skirts of *Germany,* through *Stiria, Pannonia,* and *Dalmatia,* as far as *Thrace* and the Black Sea. Then backwards they cover *Switzerland* and the parts adjacent; and that branch of them which we call the *Appennines,* strikes through *Italy,* and is, as it were, the back-bone of that Country. This must needs be a large space of ground which they stand upon; Yet 'tis not this part of *Europe* only that is laden with Mountains, the Northern part is as rough and rude in the face of the Country, as in the manners of the people; *Bohemia, Silesia, Denmark, Norway, Sweedland, Lapland,* and *Iseland,* and all the coasts of the *Baltick Sea,* are full of Clifts, and Rocks, and Crags of Mountains: Besides the *Riphean* Mountains in *Muscovy,* which the Inhabitants there use to call the *Stone-girdle,* and believe that it girds the Earth round about.

Nor are the other parts of our Continent more free from Mountains than *Europe,* nor other parts of the Earth than our Continent: They are in the New World as well as the Old; and if they could discover two or three New Worlds or Continents more, they would still find them there. Neither is there any Original Island upon the Earth, but is either all a Rock, or hath Rocks and Mountains in it. And all the dry Land, and every Continent, is but a kind of Mountain: though that Mountain hath a multitude of lesser ones, and Valleys, and Plains, and Lakes, and Marshes, and all variety of grounds.

In *America,* the *Andes,* or a ridge of Mountains so call'd, are reported to be higher than any we have, reaching above a thousand Leagues in length, and twenty in breadth, where they are the narrowest. In *Africk* the Mountain *Atlas,* that for its height was said to bear the Heavens on its back, runs all along from the Western Sea to the borders of *Ægypt*, parallel with the *Mediterranean*. There also are the Mountains of the *Moon*, and many more whereof we have but an imperfect account, as neither indeed of that Country in the remote and inner parts of it. *Asia* is better known, and the Mountains thereof better describ'd: *Taurus*, which is the principal, was adjudg'd by the ancient Geographers the greatest in the World. It divides *Asia* into two parts, which have their denomination from it: And there is an *Anti-Taurus* the greater and the less, which accordingly divide *Armenia* into greater and less. Then the *Cruciform* Mountains of *Imaus*, the famous *Caucasus*, the long Chains of *Tartary* and *China*, and the Rocky and Mountainous *Arabia*. If one could at once have a prospect of all these together, one would be easily satisfied, that the Globe of the Earth is a more rude and indigested Body than 'tis commonly imagin'd; If one could see, I say, all the Kingdoms and Regions of the Earth at one view, how they lie in broken heaps; The Sea hath overwhelm'd one half of them, and what remains are but the taller parts of a ruine. Look upon those great ranges of Mountains in *Europe* or in *Asia*, whereof we have given a short survey, in what confusion do they lie? They have neither form nor beauty, nor shape, nor order, no more than the Clouds in the Air. Then how barren, how desolate, how naked are they? how they stand neglected by Nature? neither the Rains can soften them, nor the Dews from Heaven make them fruitful.

I have given this short account of the Mountains of the Earth, to help to remove that prejudice we are apt to have, or that conceit, That the present Earth *is regularly form'd*. And to this purpose I do not doubt but that it would be of very good use to have *natural* Maps of the Earth, as we noted before, as well as *civil*; and done with the same care and judgment. Our common Maps I call *Civil*, which note the distinction of Countries and of Cities, and represent the Artificial Earth as inhabited and cultivated: But *natural* Maps leave out all that, and represent the Earth as it would be if there was not an Inhabitant upon it, nor ever had been; the Skeleton of the Earth, as I may so say, with the site of all its parts. Methinks also every Prince should have such a Draught of his own Country and Dominions, to see how the ground lies in the several parts of them, which highest, which lowest; what respect they have to one another, and to the Sea; how the Rivers flow, and why; how the Mountains stand, how the Heaths, and how the Marches are plac'd. Such a Map or Survey would be useful both in time of War and Peace, and many good observations might be made by it, not only as to Natural History and Philosophy, but also in order to the perfect improvement of a Countrey. But to return to our Mountains.

As this Survey of the multitude and greatness of them may help to rectifie our mistakes about the form of the Earth, so before we proceed to examine their causes, it will be good to observe farther, that these Mountains are plac'd in no order one with another, that can either respect use or beauty; And if you consider them singly, they do not consist of any proportion of parts that is referrable to any design, or that hath the least footsteps of Art or Counsel. There is nothing in Nature more shapeless and ill-figur'd than an old Rock or a Mountain, and all that variety that is among them, is but the various modes of irregularity; so as you cannot make a better character of them, in short, than to say they are of all forms and figures, except regular. Then if you could go within these Mountains, (for they are generally hollow,) you would find all things there more rude, if possible, than without: And lastly, if you look upon an heap of them together, or a Mountainous Country, they are the greatest examples of confusion that we know in Nature; no Tempest or Earthquake puts things into more disorder. 'Tis true, they cannot look so ill now as they did at first; a ruine that is fresh looks much worse than afterwards, when the Earth grows discolour'd and skin'd over. But I fancy if we had seen the Mountains when they were new-born and raw, when the Earth was fresh broken, and the waters of the Deluge newly retir'd, the fractions and confusions of them would have appear'd very gastly and frightful.

After this general Survey of the Mountains of the Earth and their properties, let us now reflect upon the causes of them. There is a double pleasure in Philosophy, first that of Admiration, whilst we contemplate things that are great and wonderful, and do not yet understand their Causes; for though admiration proceed from ignorance, yet there is a certain charm and sweetness in that passion. Then the second pleasure is greater and more intellectual, which is that of distinct knowledge and comprehension, when we come to have the Key that unlocks those secrets, and see the methods wherein those things come to pass that we admir'd before; The reasons why the World is so or so, and from what causes Nature, or any part of Nature, came into such a state; and this we are now to enquire after as to the Mountains of the Earth, what their original was, how and when the Earth came into this strange frame and structure? In the beginning of our World, when the Earth rise from a Chaos, 'twas impossible it should come immediately into this Mountainous form; because a mass that is fluid, as a Chaos is, cannot lie in any other figure than what is regular; for the constant laws of Nature do certainly bring all Liquors into that form: And a Chaos is not call'd so from any confusion or brokenness in the form of it, but from a confusion and mixture of all sorts of ingredients in the composition of it. So we have already produc'd, in the precedent Chapters, a double argument that the Earth was not originally in this form, both becaute it rise from a Chaos, which could not of it self, or by any immediate concretion, settle into a form of this nature, as hath been shown in the Fourth and Fifth Chapters; as also because if it had been originally made thus, it could never have undergone a Deluge, as hath been prov'd in the Second and Third Chapters. If this be then a secondary and succedaneous form, the great question is from what causes it arises.

Some have thought that Mountains, and all other irregularities in the Earth, have rise from Earthquakes, and such like causes; others have thought that they came from the universal Deluge; yet not from any dissolution of the Earth that was then, but only from the great agitation of the waters, which broke the ground into this rude and unequal form. Both these causes seem to me very incompetent and insufficient. Earthquakes seldom make Mountains, they often take them away, and sink them down into the Caverns that lie under them; Besides, Earthquakes are not in all Countries and Climates as Mountains are; for, as we have observ'd more than once, there is neither Island that is original, nor Continent any where in the Earth, in what latitude soever, but hath Mountains and Rocks in it. And lastly, what probability is there, or how is it credible, that those vast tracts of Land which we see fill'd with Mountains both in *Europe, Asia* and *Africa,* were rais'd by Earthquakes, or any eruptions from below. In what Age of the World was this done, and why not continued? As for the Deluge, I doubt not but Mountains were made in the time of the general Deluge, that great change and transformation of the Earth happen'd then, but not from such causes as are pretended, that is, the bare rowling and agitation of the waters; For if the Earth was smooth and plain before the Flood, as they seem to suppose as well as we do, the waters could have little or no power over a smooth surface to tear it any way in pieces, no more than they do a meadow or low ground when they lie upon it; for that which makes Torrents and Land-floods violent, is their fall from the Mountains and high Lands, which our Earth is now full of, but if the Rain fell upon even and level ground, it would only sadden and compress it; there is no possibility how it should raise Mountains in it. And if we could imagine an universal Deluge as the Earth is now constituted, it would rather throw down the Hills and Mountains than raise new ones; or by beating down their tops and loose parts, help to fill the Valleys, and bring the Earth nearer to evenness and plainness.

Seeing then there are no hopes of explaining the Origin of Mountains, either from particular Earthquakes, or from the general Deluge, according to the common notion and Explication of it; these not being causes answerable to such vast effects; Let us try our *Hypothesis* again; which hath made us a Chanel large enough for the Sea, and room for all subterraneous Cavities, and I think will find us materials enough to raise all the Mountains of the Earth. We suppose the great Arch or circumference of the first Earth to have fallen into the Abyss at the Deluge, and seeing that was larger than the surface it fell upon, 'tis absolutely certain, that it could not all fall flat, or lie under the water: Now as all those parts that stood above the water made dry Land, or the present habitable Earth, so such parts of the dry Land as stood higher than the rest, made Hills and Mountains; And this is the first and general account of them, and of all the inequalities of the Earth. But to consider these things a little more particularly; There is a double cause and necessity of Mountains, first this now mention'd, because the exteriour Orb of the Earth was greater than the interiour which it fell upon, and therefore it could not all fall flat; and secondly, because this exteriour Orb did not fall so flat and large as it might, or did not cover all the bottom of the Abyss, as it was very capable to do; but as we shewed before in explaining the Chanel of the Ocean, it left a gaping in the middle, or an *Abysschanel,* as I should call it; and the broader this Abyss-chanel was, the more Mountains there would be upon the dry Land; for there would be more Earth, or more of the falling Orb left, and less room to place it in, and therefore it must stand more in heaps.

In what parts of the Earth these heaps would lie, and in what particular manner, it cannot be expected that we should tell; but all that we have hitherto observ'd concerning Mountains, how strange soever and otherwise unaccountable, may easily be explain'd, and deduc'd from this original; we shall not wonder at their greatness and vastness, seeing they are the ruines of a broken World; and they would take up more or less of the dry Land, according as the Ocean took up more or less space of our Globe: Then as to their figure and form, whether External or Internal, 'tis just such as answers our expectation, and no more than what the *Hypothesis* leads us to; For you would easily believe that these heaps would be irregular in all manner of ways, whether consider'd apart, or in their situation to one another. And they would lie commonly in Clusters and in Ridges, for those are two of the most general postures of the parts of a ruine, when they fall inwards. Lastly, we cannot wonder that Mountains should be generally hollow; For great bodies falling together in confusion, or bearing and leaning against one another, must needs make a great many hollownesses in them, and by their unequal Applications empty spaces will be intercepted. We see also from the same reason, why mountainous Countries are subject to Earthquakes; and why Mountains often sink and fall down into the Caverns that lie under them; their joynts and props being decay'd and worn, they become unable to bear their weight. And all these properties you see hang upon one and the same string, and are just consequences from our supposition concerning the dissolution of the first Earth. And there is no surer mark of a good *Hypothesis*, than when it doth not only hit luckily in one or two particulars, but answers all that it is to be appli'd to, and is adequate to Nature in her whole extent.

But how fully or easily soever these things may answer Nature, you will say, it may be, that all this is but an *Hypothesis*; that is, a kind of fiction or supposition that things were so and so at first, and by the coherence and agreement of the Effects with such a supposition, you would argue and prove that they were really so. This I confess is true, this is the method, and if we would know any thing in Nature further than our senses go, we can know it no otherwise than by an *Hypothesis*. When things are either too little for our senses, or too remote and inaccessible, we have no way to know the inward Nature, and the causes of their sensible properties, but by reasoning upon an *Hypothesis*. If you would know, for example, of what parts Water, or any other Liquor consists, they are too little to be discern'd by the Eye, you must therefore take a supposition concerning their invisible figure and form, and if that agrees and gives the reason of all their sensible qualities, you understand the nature of Water. In like manner, if you would know the nature of a Comet, or of what matter the Sun consists, which are things inaccessible to us, you can do this no otherwise than by an *Hypothesis*; and if that *Hypothesis* be easie and intelligible, and answers all the *Phænomena* of those two bodies, you have done as much as a *Philosopher* or as *Humane reason* can do. And this is what we have attempted concerning the Earth and concerning the Deluge; We have laid down an *Hypothesis* that is easie and perspicuous, consisting of a few things, and those very intelligible, and from this we have given an account how the Old World was destroy'd by a Deluge of water, and how the Earth came into this present form; so distinguish'd and interrupted with Sea and Land, Mountains and Valleys, and so broken in the surface and inward parts of it.

Fig. 1

But to speak the Truth, this Theory is something more than a bare *Hypothesis*; because we are assur'd that the general ground that we go upon is true, namely, that the Earth rise at first from a Chaos; for besides Reason and Antiquity, Scripture it self doth assure as of that; and that one point being granted, we have deduc'd from it all the rest by a direct chain of consequences, which I think cannot be broken easily in part part or link of it. Besides, the great hinge of this Theory upon which all the rest turns, is the distinction we make of the Ante-diluvian Earth and Heavens from the Post-diluvian, as to their form and con-

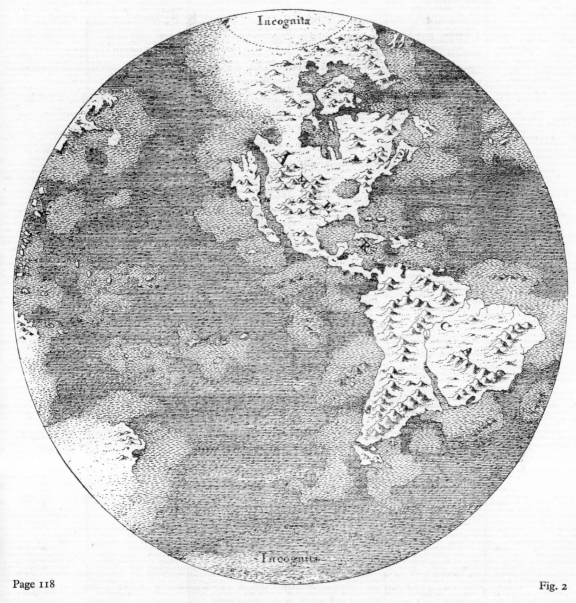

Page 118

Fig. 2

stitution. And it will never be beaten out of my head, but that St. *Peter* hath made the same distinction sixteen hundred years since, and to the very same purpose; so that we have sure footing here again, and the Theory riseth above the character of a bare *Hypothesis*. And whereas an *Hypothesis* that is clear and proportion'd to Nature in every respect, is accounted morally certain, we must in equity give more than a moral certitude to this Theory. But I mean this only as to the general parts of it; for as to particularities, I look upon them only as problematical, and accordingly I affirm nothing therein but with a power of revocation,

2 *Ep. Chap.* 3. 5, 6.

117

and a liberty to change my opinion when I shall be better inform'd. Neither do I know any Author that hath treated a matter new, remote, and consisting of a multitude of particulars, who would not have had occasion, if he had liv'd to have seen his *Hypothesis* fully examin'd, to have chang'd his mind and manner of explaining things, in many material instances.

To conclude both this Chapter and this Section, we have here added a Map or Draught of the Earth, according to the Natural face of it, as it would appear from the Moon, if we were a little nearer to her; or as it was at first after the Deluge, before Cities were built, distinctions of Countries made, or any alterations by humane industry. 'Tis chiefly to expose more to view the Mountains of the Earth, and the proportions of Sea and Land, to shew it as it lies in it self, and as a Naturalist ought to conceive and consider it. 'Tis true, there are far more Mountains upon the Earth than what are here represented, for more could not conveniently be plac'd in this narrow Scheme; But the best and most effectual way of representing the body of the Earth as it is by Nature, would be, not in plain Tables, but by a *rough Globe*, expressing all the considerable inequalities that are upon the Earth. The smooth Globes that we use, do but nourish in us the conceit of the Earth's regularity, and though they may be convenient enough for Geographical purposes, they are not so proper for Natural Science; nothing would be more useful, in this respect, than a rough Globe of the largest dimensions, wherein the Chanel of the Sea should be really hollow, as it is in Nature, with all its unequal depths according to the best soundings, and the shores exprest both according to matter and form, little Rocks standing where there are Rocks, and Sands and Beaches in the places where they are found; And all the Islands planted in the Sea-chanel in a due form, and in their solid dimensions. Then upon the Land should stand all the ranges of Mountains, in the same order or disorder that Nature hath set them there; And the in-land Seas, and great Lakes, or rather the beds they lie in, should be duly represented; as also the vast desarts of Sand as they lie upon the Earth. And this being done with care and due Art, would be a true Epitome or true model of our Earth. Where we should see, besides other instructions, what a rude Lump our World is, which we are so apt to dote upon.

CHAPTER XII

A short review of what hath been already treated of, and in what manner. The several faces and Schemes under which the Earth would appear to a Stranger, that should view it first at a distance, and then more closely, and the Application of them to our subject. All methods, whether Philosophical or Theological, that have been offer'd by others for the Explication of the Form of the Earth, are examin'd and refuted. A conjecture concerning the other Planets, their Natural Form and State compared with ours.

WE have finisht the Three Sections of this Book, and in this last Chapter we will make a short review and reflection upon what hath been hitherto treated of, and add some further confirmations of it. The Explication of the

Universal Deluge was the first proposal and design of this Discourse, to make that a thing credible and intelligible to the mind of Man: And the full Explication of this drew in the whole Theory of the Earth: Whose original we have deduc'd from its first Source, and shew'd both what was its Primæval Form, and how it came into its present Form. The summ of our *Hypothesis* concerning the Universal Deluge was this; That it came not to pass, as was vulgarly believ'd, by any excess of Rains, or any Inundation of the Sea, nor could ever be effected by a meer abundance of Waters; unless we suppose some dissolution of the Earth at the same time, namely when the *Great Abyss* was broken open. And accordingly we shewed that without such a dissolution, or if the Earth had been always in the same form it is now, no mass of water, any where to be found in the World, could have equal'd the height of the Mountains, or made such an universal Deluge. Secondly, we shewed that the form of the Earth at first, and till the Deluge, was such as made it capable and subject to a Dissolution: And thirdly, that such a dissolution being suppos'd, the Doctrine of the universal Deluge is very reasonable and intelligible; And not only the doctrine of the Deluge, but the same supposition is a Key to all Nature besides, shewing us how our Globe became Terraqueous, what was the original of Mountains, of the Sea-chanel, of Islands, of subterraneous Cavities; Things, which without this supposition, are as unintelligible as the universal Flood it self. And these things reciprocally confirming one another, our *Hypothesis* of the Deluge is arm'd both breast and back, by the causes and by the effects.

It remains now, that, as to confirm our Explication of the Deluge, we shew'd all other accounts that had been given of it to be ineffectual or impossible, so to confirm our doctrine concerning the dissolution of the Earth, and concerning the original of Mountains, Seas, and all inequalities upon it, or within it, we must examine what causes have been assign'd by others, or what accounts given of these things: That seeing their defectiveness, we may have the more assurance and satisfaction in our own method.

And in order to this, let us observe first the general forms under which the Earth may be consider'd, or under which it doth appear accordingly as we view it more nearly or remotely; And the first of these and the most general is that of a *Terraqueous Globe*. If a Philosopher should come out of another World out of curiosity to see our Earth, the first discovery or observation he would make would be this, that it was a Terraqueous Globe; Thus much he might observe at a great distance when he came but near the borders of our World. This we discern in the Moon and most of the Planets, that they are divided into Sea and Land, and how this division came, would be his first remark and inquiry concerning our Earth; and how also those subdivisions of Islands, or little Earths which lie in the Water, how these were form'd, and that great Chanel that contains them both.

The second form that the Earth appears under, is that of an uneven and *Mountainous Globe*. When our Traveller had got below the Circle of the Moon, he would discern the bald tops of our Mountains, and the long ranges of them upon our Continents. We cannot from the Earth discern Mountains and Valleys in the Moon, directly, but from the motion of the light and shadows which we see there, we easily collect that there are such inequalities: And accordingly we suppose that our Mountains would appear at a great distance, and the shady Valleys lying under them; and that this curious person that came to view our Earth, would make that his second Enquiry, how those Mountains were form'd ? and how our Globe came to be so rude and irregular ? for we may justly demand how any irregularity came into Nature, seeing all her first motions and her first forms are regular, and whatsoever is not so is but secondary, and the consequence of some degeneracy, or of some decay.

The third visible form of our Earth is that of *a broken Globe*; not broken throughout, but in the outward parts and Regions of it. This, it may be, you will say, is not a visible form; it doth not appear to the eye, without reasoning, that the surface of the Earth is so broken. Suppose our new Visitant had now pass'd the middle Region of the Air, and was alighted upon the top of Pick *Teneriffe* for his first resting place, and that sitting there he took a view of the great Rocks, the wide Sea, and of the shores of *Africk* and *Europe*; for we'll suppose his piercing Eye to reach so far; I will not say that at first sight he would pronounce that the surface of this Globe was broken, unless he knew it to be so by comparison with some other Planet like to it; but the broken form and figure of many parts of the Rocks, and the posture in which they lay, or great portions of them, some inclin'd, some prostrate, some erected, would naturally lead him to that thought, that they were a ruine; He would see also the Islands tore from the Continents, and both the shores of the Continents and their in-land parts in the same disorder and irregular situation. Besides, he had this great advantage in viewing the Earth at a distance, that he could see a whole Hemisphere together, which, as he made his approaches through the Air, would have much what the same aspect and countenance as 'tis represented with in the great

Pag. 118.

Scheme; And if any man should accidentally hit upon that Scheme, not knowing or thinking that it was the Earth, I believe his first thought of it would be, that it was some great broken body, or ruin'd frame of matter; and the original, I am sure, is more manifestly so. But we'll leave our Strange-Philosopher to his own observations, and with him good Guides and Interpreters in his Survey of the Earth, and that he would make a favourable report at his return home, of our little dirty Planet.

In the mean time, let us pursue, in our own way, this Third *Idea* of the Earth a little further, as it is a *broken Globe*. Nature I know hath dissembled and cover'd this form as much as may be, and time hath helpt to repair some of the old breaches, or fill them up; besides, the changes that have been made by Art and Humane industry, by Agriculture, Planting, and Building Towns, hath made the face of the Earth quite another thing from what it was in its naked rudeness. As mankind is much alter'd from its Pristine state, from what it was four thousand years ago, or towards the first Ages after the Flood, when the Nations liv'd in simplicity or barbarousness; So is the Earth too, and both so disguis'd and transform'd, that if one of those Primitive Fathers should rise from the dead, he would scarce know this to be the same World which he liv'd in before. But to discern the true form of the Earth, whether intire or broken, regular or disorder'd, we must in the first place take away all those ornaments or additions made by Art or Nature, and view the bare carcass of the Earth, as it hath nothing on it but Rocks and Mountains, Desarts and Fields, and hollow Valleys, and a wide Sea. Then secondly, we must in our imagination empty this Chanel of the Sea, take out all the Waters that hinder the sight of it, and look upon the dry Ditch, measure the depth and breadth of it in our mind, and observe the manner of its construction, and in what a wild posture all the parts of it lie; according as it hath been formerly represented. And lastly, we must take off the cover of all Subterraneous places and deep Caverns, to see the inside of the Earth; and lay bare the roots of Mountains, to look into those holes and Vaults that are under them, fill'd sometimes with Fire, sometimes with Water, and sometimes with thick Air and Vapours. The object being thus prepar'd, we are then to look fix'dly upon it, and to pronounce what we think of this disfigur'd mass, whether this Exteriour frame doth not seem to be shatter'd; and whether it doth more aptly resemble a new-made World, or the ruines of one broken. I confess when this *Idea* of the Earth is present to my thoughts, I can no more believe that this was the form wherein it was first produc'd, than if I had seen the Temple of *Jerusalem* in its ruines, when defac'd and sack'd by the *Babylonians,* I could have perswaded my self that it had never been in any other posture, and that *Solomon* had given orders for building it so.

Chap. 10.

So much for the form of the Earth: It remains now that we examine what causes have been assign'd by others of these irregularities in the form of the Earth, which we explain by the dissolution of it; what accounts any of the Ancients have given or attempted to give, how the Earth swell'd into Mountains in certain places, and in others was deprest into low Valleys, how the body of it was so broken, and how the Chanel of the Sea was made. The Elements naturally lie in regular forms one above another, and now we find them mixt, confounded and transpos'd, how comes this disturbance and disordination in Nature? The Explications of these things that have been given by others, may be reduc'd to two general sorts, *Philosophical* or *Theological,* and we will try them both for our satisfaction.

Of Philosophers none was more concern'd to give an account of such things than *Epicurus,* both because he acknowledg'd the Origin of the Earth to have been from a *Chaos,* and also admitted no causes to act in Nature but Matter and Motion: Yet all the account we have from the *Epicureans* of the form of the Earth, and the great inequalities that are in it, is so slight and trivial, that methinks it doth not deserve the name of a Philosophical Explication. They say that the Earth and Water were mix'd at first, or rather the Earth was above the Water, and as the Earth was condens'd by the heat of the Sun, and the Winds, the Water was squeez'd out in certain places, which either it found hollow or made so; and so was the Chanel of the Sea made. Then as for Mountains, while some parts of the Earth shrunk and sunk in this manner, others would not sink, and these standing still while the others fell lower, made the Mountains. How the subterraneous Cavities were made according to them, I do not find.

This is all the Account that *Monsieur Gassendi* (who seems to have made it his business, as well as his pleasure, to embellish that Philosophy) can help us to out of the *Epicurean* Authors, how the Earth came into this form; And he that can content himself with this, is, in my mind, of an humour very easie to be pleas'd. Do the Sun and the Wind use to squeaze pools of Water out of the Earth, and that in such a quantity as to make an Ocean? They dry the Earth, and the Waters too, and rarifie them into vapours, but I never knew them to be the causes of pressing Water out of the Earth by condensation. Could they compress the Earth any otherwise, than by drying it and making it hard? and in proportion, as it was more dry, would it not the more imbibe and suck up the Water? and how were the great Mountains of the Earth made, in the North and in the South, where the influence of the Sun is not great? what sunk the Earth there, and made the flesh start from the bones? But 'tis no wonder that *Epicurus* should give such a mean account of the Origin of the Earth, and the form of its parts, who did not so much as understand the general Figure of the Body of it, that it was Spherical, or that the Heavens encompast it round. One must have a blind love for that Philosophy, and for the conclusions it drives at, not to see its lameness and defects in those first and fundamental parts.

Aristotle, though he was not concern'd to give an account how the Earth came into this present form, as he suppos'd it, Eternal; yet upon another consideration he seems oblig'd to give some reason how the Elements came into this disorder; seeing he supposeth, that, according to the order of Nature, the Water should lie above the Earth in a Sphere, as the Air doth above the Water, and his Fire above the Air. This he toucheth upon in his Meteors, but so gently and fearfully, as if he was handling hot coals. He saith the Sea is to be consider'd as the Element, or body of Waters that belongs to this Earth, and that these Waters change places, and the Sea is some Ages in one part of the Globe, and some Ages in another; but that this is at such great distances of time that there can be no memory or record of it. And he seems willing to suppose that the Water was once all over the Earth, but that it dri'd up in certain places, and continuing in others, it there made the Sea.

What a miserable account is this? As to his change or removal of the Sea-chanel in several Ages, as it is without all proof or probability, if he mean it of the Chanel of the great Ocean, so 'tis nothing to the purpose here; for the question is not why the Chanel of the Sea is in such a part of the Earth, rather than in another, but why there is any such prodigious Cavity in or upon the Earth any where. And if we take his supposition, that the Element of Water was once higher than the Earth, and lay in a Sphere about it, then let him tell us in plain terms how the Earth got above, or how the Cavity of the Ocean was made, and how the Mountains rise; for this Elementary Earth which lay under the Water, was, I suppose, equal and smooth when it lay there; and what reason was there, that the Waters should be dri'd in one part of it, more than another, if they were every where of an equal depth, and the ground equal under them? It was not the Climates made any distinction, for there is Sea towards the Poles, as well as under the Æquator; but suppose they were dri'd up in certain places, that would make no Mountains, no more than there are Mountains in our dri'd Marches: And the places where they were not dri'd, would not therefore become as deep and hollow as the Sea-chanel, and tear the Earth and Rocks in pieces. If you should say that this very Elementary Earth, as it lay under the Waters, was unequal, and was so originally, form'd into Mountains and Valleys, and great Cavities; besides that the supposition is altogether irrational in it self, you must suppose a prodigious mass of Water to cover such an Earth; as much as we found requisite for the vulgar Deluge, namely, eight Oceans; and what then is become of the other seven? Upon the whole I do not see that either in *Epicurus*'s way, who seems to suppose that the Waters were at first within the Earth; nor in *Aristotle*'s way, who seems to suppose them upon the Earth, any rational or tolerable account can be given of the present form of the Earth.

Wherefore some modern Authors, dissatisfied, as very well they might be, with these Explications given us by the Ancients concerning the form of the Earth, have pitch'd upon other causes, more true indeed in their kind, and in their degree, but that fall as much short of those effects to which they would apply them. They say that all the irregularities of the body of the Earth have risen from Earthquakes in particular places, and from Torrents and Inundations, and from eruptions of Fire, or such like causes, whereof we see some instances more or less every Age; And these have made that havock upon the face of the Earth, and turn'd things up-side down, raising the Earth in some places, and making great Cavities or Chasms in others, so as to have brought it at length into that torn, broken, and disorderly form in which we now see it.

These Authors do so far agree with us, as to acknowledge that the present irregular form of the Earth must have proceeded from ruines and dissolutions of one sort or other, but these ruines they make to have been partial only, in this or in that Country, by piece-meal, and in several Ages, and from no other causes but such as still continue to act in Nature, namely, accidental Earthquakes and eruptions of Fires and Waters. These causes we acknowledge as readily as they do, but not as capable to produce so great effects as they would ascribe to them: The surface of the Earth may be a little changed by such accidents as these, but for the most part they rather sink the Mountains than raise new ones: As when Houses are blown up by Mines of powder, they are not set higher, but generally fall lower and flatter: Or suppose they do sometimes raise an Hill, or a little Mount, what's that to the great Mountains of our World, to those long and vast piles of Rocks and Stones, which the Earth can scarce bear? What's that to strong-backt *Taurus* or *Atlas*, to the *American Andes*, or to a Mountain that reacheth from the *Pyreneans* to the *Euxine* Sea? There's as much difference between these and those factitious Mountains they speak of, as betwixt them and Mole-hills.

And to answer more distinctly to this opinion, as before in speaking of Islands we distinguish'd betwixt Factitious and Original Islands, so if you please we may distinguish here betwixt Factitious and Original Mountains; and allowing some few, and those of the fifth or sixth magnitude, to have risen from such accidental causes, we enquire concerning the rest and the greatest, what was their Original?

If we should suppose that the seven Hills upon which *Rome* stands, came from ruines or eruptions, or any such causes, it doth not follow that the *Alps* were made so too. And as for Mountains, so for the Cavities of the Earth, I suppose there may be disruptions sometimes made by Earthquakes, and holes worn by subterraneous Fires and Waters; but what's that to the Chanel of the *Atlantick Ocean*, or of the *Pacifick Ocean*, which is extended an hundred and fifty degrees under the Æquator, and towards the Poles still further. He that should derive such mighty things from no greater causes, I should think him a very credulous Philosopher. And we are too subject indeed to that fault of credulity in matter of Philosophizing; Many when they have found out causes that are proper for certain effects within such a compass, they cannot keep them there, but they will make them do every thing for them; and extend them often to other effects of a superiour nature or degree, which their activity can by no means reach to. *Ætna* hath been a burning Mountain ever since and above the memory of Man, yet it hath not destroy'd that Island, nor made any new Chanel to the Sea, though it stands so near it. Neither is *Vesuvius* above two or three miles distant from the Sea-side, to the best of my remembrance, and yet in so many Ages it hath made no passage to it, neither open nor subterraneous. 'Tis true some *Isthmus*'s have been thrown down by Earthquakes, and some Lakes have been made in that manner, but what's this to a Ditch nine thousand miles broad? such an one we have upon the Earth, and of a depth that is not measurable; what proportion have these causes to such an instance? and how many thousand Ages must be allow'd to them to do their work, more than the Chronology of our Earth will bear?

Besides, when were these great Earthquakes and disruptions, that did such great execution upon the body of the Earth? was this before the Flood or since? If before, then the old difficulty returns, how could there be a Flood, if the Earth was in this Mountainous form before that time? This, I think, is demonstrated impossible in the Second and Third Chapters. If since the Flood, where were the Waters of the Earth before these Earthquakes made a Chanel for them? Besides, where is the History or Tradition that speaks of these strange things, and of this great change of the Earth? hath any writ of the Origins of the *Alps*? In what year of *Rome*, or what *Olympiad* they were born? or how they grew from little ones? how the Earth groan'd when it brought them forth, when its bowels were torn by the ragged Rocks? Do the Chronicles of the Nations mention these things, or ancient fame, or ancient Fables? were they made all at once, or in successive Ages? These causes continue still in Nature, we have still Earthquakes and subterraneous Fires and Waters, why should they not still operate and have the same effects? We often hear of Cities thrown down by Earthquakes, or Countries swallow'd up, but whoever heard of a new chain of Mountains made upon the Earth, or a new Chanel made for the Ocean? We do not read that there hath been so much as a new *Sinus* of the Sea ever since the memory of man: Which is far more feasible than what they pretend. And things of this nature being both strange and sensible, excite admiration and great attention when they come to pass, and would certainly have been remembred or propagated in some way or other, if they had ever happen'd since the Deluge. They have recorded the foundation of Cities and Monarchies, the appearance of blazing-Stars, the eruptions of fiery Mountains, the most remarkable Earthquakes and Inundations, the great Eclipses or obscurations of the Sun, and any thing that look'd strange or prodigy-like, whether in the Heavens or on Earth, and these which would have been the greatest prodigies and greatest changes that ever happen'd in nature, would these have escap'd all observation and memory of men? that's as incredible as the things themselves are.

Lastly, to comprehend all these opinions together, both of the Ancient and Modern Authors, they seem all to agree with us in this, *That* the Earth was once under another form; otherwise why do they go about to shew the causes how it came into this form. I desire then to know what form they suppose the Earth to have been under before the Mountains were made, the Chanel of the Sea, or subterraneous Cavities. Either they must take that form which we have assign'd it before the Deluge, or else they must suppose it cover'd with Water, till the Sea-chanels were made, and the Mountains brought forth; As in that Fig. *pag. 55.* *Fig. 2. p. 56.* And no doubt it was once in this form, both reason and the authority of *Moses* assures us of it; and this is the Test which every opinion must be brought to, *how* the Earth emerg'd out of that watery form? and in particular, as to that opinion which we are now examining, the question is, *how* by Earthquakes, and fiery eruptions, subterraneous Waters, and such like causes, the body of the Earth could be wrought from that form to this present form? And the thing is impossible at first sight; for such causes as these could not take place in such an Earth. As for subterraneous Waters, there could be none at that time, for they were all above ground; and as for subterraneous Exhalations, whether Fiery or Aery, there was no place for them neither, for the Earth when it lay under the Water was a solid uniform mass, compact and close united in its parts, as we have shewn before upon several occasions; no Mines or hollow Vaults for the Vapours to be lodg'd in, no Store-houses of Fire, nothing that could make Earth-quakes, nor any sort of ruines or eruptions: These are Engines that cannot play but in an Earth already broken, hollow, and cavernous. Therefore the Authors of this opinion do in effect beg the question; they assign such causes of the present form of the Earth, as could not take place, nor have any activity until the Earth was in this form: These causes may contribute something to increase the rudeness and inequalities of the Earth in certain places, but they could not be the original causes of it: And that not only because of their disproportion to such effects, but also because of their incapacity, or non-existence at that time when these effects were to be wrought.

Thus much concerning the Philosophical opinions, or the natural Causes that have been assign'd for the irregular form of this present Earth. Let us now consider the Theological opinions, how Mountains were made at first, and the wonderful Chanel of the Sea: And these Authors say, God Almighty made them immediately when he made the World; and so dispatch the business in a few words. This is a short account indeed, but we must take heed that we do not derogate from the perfection of God, by ascribing all things promiscuously to his immediate action. I have often suggested that the first order of things is regular and simple, according as the Divine Nature is; and continues so till there is some degeneracy in the moral World; I have also noted upon several occasions, especially in the *Lat. Treat. Chap.* II the deformity and incommodiousness of the present Earth; and from these two considerations we may reasonably infer, that the present state of the Earth was not Original, but is a state of subjection to Vanity, wherein it must continue till the redemption and restitution of all things.

But besides this general consideration, there are many others, both Natural and Theological against this opinion, which the Authors of it, I believe, will find unanswerable. As first, St. *Peter*'s distinction betwixt the present Earth and the Ante-diluvian; and that in opposition to certain profane persons, who seem to have been of the same opinion with these Authors, namely, that the Heavens and the Earth were the same now that they had been from the beginning, and that there had been no change in Nature, either of late, or in former Ages; These St. *Peter* confutes and upbraids them with ignorance or forgetfulness of the change that was brought upon Nature at the Deluge, or that the Ante-diluvian Heavens and Earth were of a different form and constitution from the present, whereby that World was obnoxious to a Deluge of Water, as the present is to a Deluge of Fire. Let these Authors put themselves in the place of those Objectors, and see what answer they can make to the Apostle, whom I leave to dispute the case with them. I hope they will not treat this Epistle of St. *Peter*'s so rudely as *Didymus Alexandrinus* did, an ancient Christian, and one of St. *Jerom*'s Masters, he was of the same opinion with these Theological Authors, and so fierce in it, that seeing St. *Peter*'s doctrine here to be contrary, he said this Epistle of St. *Peter*'s was corrupted, and was not to be receiv'd into the Canon. And all this because it taught that the Heavens and the Earth had chang'd their form, and would do so again at the Conflagration; so as the same World would be Triform in success of time. We acknowledge his Exposition of St. *Peter*'s words to be very true, but what he makes an argument of the corruption of this Epistle, is rather, in my mind, a peculiar argument of its Divine Inspiration. In the second place, these writers dash upon the old rock, the impossibility of explaining the Deluge; if there were Mountains from the beginning, and the Earth then in the same form as it is now. Thirdly, they make the state of *Paradise* as unintelligible as that of the Deluge; For those properties that are assign'd to *Paradise* by the Ancients, are inconsistent with the present form of the Earth: As will appear in the Second Book. Lastly, they must answer, and give an account of all those marks which we have observ'd in Nature (both in this Chapter, and the Ninth, Tenth, and Eleventh), of fractions, ruines, and dissolutions that have been on the Earth, and which we have shewn to be inexplicable, unless we admit that the Earth was once in another form.

These arguments being premis'd, let us now bring their opinion close to the Test, and see in what manner these Mountains must have been made according to them, and how the Chanel of the Sea, and all other Cavities of the Earth. Let us to this purpose consider the Earth again in that transient incompleat form which it had when the Abysse encompast the whole body of it; we both agree

2 Ep. Chap. 3. 5, 6.

Fig. 2. p. 56.

that the Earth was once in this state, and they say that it came immediately out of this state into its present form, there being made by a supernatural Power a great Chanel or Ditch in one part of it, which drew off the Waters from the rest, and the Earth which was squeez'd and forc'd out of this Ditch made the Mountains. So there is the Chanel of the Sea made, and the Mountains of the Earth; how the subterraneous Cavities were made according to these Authors, I do not well know. This I confess seems to me a very gross thought, and a way of working very un-God-like; but however let's have patience to examine it.

And in the first place, if the Mountains were taken out of the Chanel of the Sea, then they are equal to it, and would fill it up if they were thrown in again. But these proportions upon examination will not agree; for though the Mountains of the Earth be very great, yet they do not equal by much the great Ocean. The Ocean extends to half the surface of the Earth; and if you suppose the greatest depth of the Ocean to answer the height of the greatest Mountains, and the middle depth to the middle sort of Mountains, the Mountains ought to cover all the dry Land to make them answer to all the capacity of the Ocean; whereas we suppos'd them upon a reasonable computation to cover but the tenth part of the dry Land; and consequently, neither they, nor the Sea-chanel, could have been produc'd in this manner, because of their great disproportion to one another. And the same thing appears, if we compare the Mountains with the Abyss, which cover'd the Earth before this Chanel was made; for this Chanel being made great enough to contain all the Abyss, the Mountains taken out of it must also be equal to all the Abyss, but the aggregate of the Mountains will not answer this by many degrees; for suppose the Abyss was but half as deep as the deep Ocean, to make this Calculus answer, all the dry Land ought to be cover'd with Mountains, and with Mountains as high as the Ocean is deep, or doubly high to the depth of the Abyss, because they are but upon one half of the Globe. And this is the first argument against the reciprocal production of Mountains and the Sea, their incongruency or disproportion.

Secondly, we are to consider that a great many Mountains of the Earth are far distant from any Seas, as the great in-land Mountains of *Asia* and of *Africk*, and the *Sarmatick* Mountains, and others in *Europe*, how were these great bodies flung thorough the Air from their respective Seas, whence they were taken, to those places where they stand? What appearance is there in common reason, or credibility, that these huge masses of Earth and Stone that stand in the middle of Continents, were dug out of any Seas? We think it strange, and very deservedly, that a little Chapel should be transported from *Palestine* to *Italy* over Land and Sea, much more the transportation of Mount *Atlas* or *Taurus* thorough the Air, or of a range of Mountains two or three thousand miles long, would surely upon all accounts appear incongruous and incredible: Besides, neither the hollow form of Mountains, nor the stony matter whereof they commonly consist, agrees with that supposition, that they were prest or taken out of the Chanel of the Sea.

Lastly, We are to consider that the Mountains are not barely laid upon the Earth, as a Tomb-stone upon a Grave, nor stand as Statues do upon a Pedestal, as this opinion seems to suppose; but they are one continu'd substance with the body of the Earth, and their roots reach into the Abyss; As the Rocks by the Sea-side go as deep as the bottom of the Sea in one continu'd mass: And 'tis a ridiculous thing to imagine the Earth first a plain surface, then all the Mountains set upon it, as Hay-cocks in a Field, standing upon their flat bottoms. There is no such common surface in Nature, nor consequently any such super-additions, 'tis all one frame or mass, only broken and disjoynted in the parts of it. To conclude, 'tis not only the Mountains that make the inequalities of the Earth, or the irregularity of its surface, every Country, every Province, every Field hath an unequal and different situation, higher or lower, inclin'd more or less, and sometimes one way, sometimes another, you can scarce take a miles compass in any place where the surface of the ground continues uniform; and can you imagine that there were Moulds or Stones brought from the Sea-chanel to make all those inequalities? Or that Earthquakes have been in every Country, and in every Field? The inner Veins and Lares of the Earth are also broken as well as the surface. These must proceed from universal causes, and all those that have been alledg'd, whether from Philosophy or Theology, are but particular or Topical. I am fully satisfied, in contemplation of these things, and so I think every unprejudic'd person may be, that to such an irregular variety of situation and construction, as we see every where in the parts of the Earth, nothing could answer but some universal concussion or dislocation, in the nature of a general ruine.

We have now finisht this first part of our Theory, and all that concerns the Deluge or dissolution of the Earth; and we have not only establisht our own *Hypothesis* by positive arguments, but also produc'd and examin'd all suppositions that have been offer'd by others, whether Philosophical or Theological, for the Explication of the same things; so as nothing seems now to remain further upon this subject. For a conclusion of all, we will consider, if you please, the rest of the Earths, or of the Planets within our Heavens, that appertain to the same common Sun; to see, so far as we can go by rational conjectures, if they be not of the same Fabrick, and have undergone the like fate and forms with our Earth. It is now acknowledg'd by the generality of Learned Men, that the Planets are Opake bodies, and particularly our next neighbour, the Moon, is known to be a Terraqueous Globe, consisting of Mountains and Valleys, as our Earth does; and we have no reason to believe but that she came into that form by a dissolution, or from like causes as our Earth did. *Mercury* is so near the Sun, that we cannot well discern his face, whether spotted or no, nor make a judgment of it. But as for *Venus* and *Mars*, if the spots that be observed in them be their Waters or their Sea, as they are in the Moon, 'tis likely They are also Terraqueous Globes, and in much what a like form with the Moon and the Earth, and, for ought we know, from like causes. Particularly as to *Venus*, 'tis a remarkable passage that St. *Austin* hath preserv'd out of *Varro*, he saith, That *about the time of the great Deluge there was a wonderful alteration or Catastrophe happen'd to the Planet Venus, and that she chang'd her colour, form, figure, and magnitude.* This is a great presumption that she suffer'd her dissolution about the same time that our Earth did. I do not know that any such thing is recorded concerning any of the other Planets, but the body of *Mars* looks very rugged, broken, and much disorder'd.

De civ. Dei lib.
21. c. 8.

Saturn and *Jupiter* deserve a distinct consideration, as having something particular and different from the rest of the Planets. *Saturn* is remarkable for his *Hoop* or Ring, which seems to stand off from his body, and would strongly induce one to believe, that the exteriour Earth of that Planet, at its dissolution, did not all fall in, but the Polar parts sinking into the Abyss, the middle or *Æquinoctial* parts still subsisted, and bore themselves up in the nature of an Arch about the Planet, or of a Bridge, as it were, built over the Sea of *Saturn*. *Jupiter* of all the Planets I take to be most intire, and in an Ante-diluvian state; His *Fasciæ* or *Belts*, as they call them, I should guess to be Waters, or the two frigid Zones, where his Waters fall and make two Canals in those parts; such as we shall show to have been in our Earth before it was broke. This Planet without all doubt is turn'd about its *Axis*, otherwise how should its Four Moons be carri'd about it ? And this is also collected from the motion of that (permanent) spot that is upon its body; which spot I take to be either a Lake, or a Chasm and *Hiatus* into the Abysse of the Planet; that is part of the Abysse open or uncover'd, like the Aperture we made in the Seventh Figure. And this might either have been left so, by Providence, at first, for some reasons fitting that Earth, or it may have faln in afterwards, as *Plato*'s *Atlantis*, or as *Sodom* and *Gomorrha*, as some judgment upon part of that World. However that be, as to the Belts of *Jupiter*, which are the most remarkable *Phænomenon* of that Planet, I take them to be his Zones, and to lie parallel with one another, and I believe also with his *Æquator*: But we must first know how his Poles lie, and in what situation with the Ecliptick, and in what Aspect to us, before such things can be certainly determin'd. In the mean time, if we have guest aright, that *Jupiter* is in an Ante-diluvian state, I should rather expect to find the Figure of his Body, than of any other of the Planets, to be *Oval* or Oblong, such as our Earth was before its Deluge. To conclude, seeing all the Planets that are plac'd in this Heaven, and are the foster-children of this Sun, seem to have some affinity one with another, and have much-what the same countenance, and the same general *Phænomena*; It seems probable that they rise much-what the same way, and after the like manner as our Earth, each one from its respective Chaos; And that they had the same Elementary Regions at first, and an exteriour Orb form'd over their Abyss: And lastly, that every one of them hath suffer'd, or is to suffer its Deluge, as our Earth hath done. These, I say, are probable conjectures according to the Analogy of Reason and Nature, so far as we can judge concerning things very remote and inaccessible.

And these things being thus, and our Theory of the Deluge, and the Dissolution which brought it, having such a general agreement both with our Heavens and our Earth, I think there is nothing but the uncouthness of the thing to some mens understandings, the custom of thinking otherwise, and the uneasiness of entring into a new sett of thoughts, that can be a bar or hindrance to its reception.

2 *Book. c.* 9. *Fig.* 3

Chap. 6. *pag.* 67.

I

THE THEORY OF THE EARTH:

Containing an Account
OF THE
Original of the Earth,
AND OF ALL THE
GENERAL CHANGES
Which it hath already undergone,

OR

IS TO UNDERGO

Throughout the whole Course of its Duration.

THE SECOND BOOK

Concerning the *PRIMÆVAL EARTH,*

AND

Concerning *PARADISE.*

LONDON,
Printed by *R. Norton,* for *Walter Kettilby,* at the Bishops-
Head in S. *Paul's* Church-Yard, 1 6 9 1.

THE
THEORY
OF THE
EARTH

BOOK II
Concerning the Primæval Earth, and concerning *Paradise*.

CHAPTER I

The Introduction and Contents of the Second Book. The general state of the Primæval Earth, and of Paradise.

WE have already seen a World begin and perish; An Earth rais'd from the rudiments of a Chaos, and dissolv'd and destroy'd in an Universal Deluge. We have given also an imperfect description of that Primæval Earth, so far as was necessary to show the causes and manner of its dissolution. But we must not content our selves with this; Seeing that Earth was the first Theater upon which mortals appear'd and acted, and continued so for above Sixteen hundred Years; and that with Scenes, as both Reason and History tell us, very extraordinary and very different from these of our present Earth, 'tis reasonable we should endeavour to make a more full discovery and description of it; Especially seeing *Paradise* was there; that seat of pleasure which our first Parents lost, and which all their posterity have much ado to find again.

In the First Book we so far describ'd This new-found World, as to shew it very different in form and fabrick from the present Earth; there was no Sea there, no Mountains, nor Rocks, nor broken Caves, 'twas all one continued and regular mass, smooth, simple and compleat, as the first works of Nature use to be. But to know thus much only, doth rather excite our curiosity than satisfie it; what were the other properties of this World? how were the Heavens, how the Elements? what accommodation for humane life? why was it more proper to be the seat of *Paradise* than the present Earth? Unless we know these things, you will say, it will seem but an aery *Idea* to us; and 'tis certain that the more properties and particularities that we know concerning any thing, the more real it appears to be.

As it was our chief design therefore in the precedent Book, to give an account of the Universal Deluge, by way of a just Theory; so we propose to our selves chiefly in this Book, from the same Theory to give a just account of *Paradise*; and in performing of this, we shall be led into a more full examination and display of that first Earth, and of its qualities. And if we be so happy, as by the conduct of the same principles and the same method, to give as fair an account, and as intelligible of the state of *Paradise* in that Original Earth, as we have done of the Deluge by the dissolution of it, and of the form of this Earth which succeeded, one must be very morose or melancholy to imagine that the grounds we go upon, all this while, are wholly false or fictitious. A foundation which will bear the weight of two Worlds without sinking, must surely stand upon a firm Rock. And I am apt to promise my self that this Theory of the Earth will find acceptance and credit, more or less, with all but those, that think it a sufficient answer to all arguments, to say *it is a Novelty.*

But to proceed in our disquisition concerning *Paradise,* we may note, in the first place, two opinions to be avoided, being both extreams; one that placeth *Paradise* in the extra-mundane Regions, or in the Air, or in the Moon; and the other that makes it so inconsiderable, as to be confin'd to a little spot of ground in *Mesopotamia,* or some other Country of *Asia,* the Earth being now as it was then. This offends as much in the defect, as the other in the excess. For it is not any single Region of the Earth that can be *Paradisiacal,* unless all Nature conspire and a certain Order of things proper and peculiar for that state. Nor is it of less importance to find out this peculiar Order of things, than to find out the particular feat of *Paradise,* but rather pre-requisite to it: We will endeavour therefore to discover and determine both, so far as a Theory can go, beginning with that which is more general.

'Tis certain there were some qualities and conditions of *Paradise* that were not meerly Topical, but common to all the rest of the Earth at that time; and these we must consider in the first place, examine what they were, and upon what they depended. History, both Sacred and Profane, must tell us what they were, and our Theory must show us upon what causes they depended. I had once, I confess, propos'd to my self another method, independent upon History or Effects; I thought to have continued the description of the Primitive or Ante-diluvian Earth from the contemplation of its causes only, and then left it to the judgment of others to determine, whether that was not the Earth where the Golden Age was past, and where *Paradise* stood. For I had observ'd three conditions or characters of it, which I thought were sufficient to answer all that we knew concerning that first state of things, *viz. The regularity of its surface; The situation or posture of its Body to the Sun; and the Figure of it:* From these three general causes, I thought might be deduc'd all the chief differences of that Earth from the present, and particularly those that made it more capable of being *Paradisiacal.*

But upon second thoughts I judg'd it more useful and expedient to lay aside the Causes at present, and begin with the Effects, that we might have some sensible matter to work upon. Bare *Idea*'s of things are lookt upon as Romantick till Effects be propos'd, whereof they are to give an account; that makes us value the Causes when necessity puts us upon enquiry after them; and the reasons of things are very acceptable, when they ease the mind, anxious, and at a loss, how to understand Nature without their help. We will therefore, without more ado, premise those things that have been taken notice of as extraordinary and peculiar to the first Ages of the World, and to *Paradise,* and which neither do, nor can, obtain in the present Earth; whereof the first is a *perpetual Spring or Equinox;* The second, the *Longevity of Animals;* the and third *Their production out of the Earth,* and the great fertility of the soil in all other things.

These difficulties guard the way to *Paradise* like the flaming Sword, and must be remov'd before we can enter; these are general Preliminaries which we must explain before we proceed to enquire after the particular place of this Garden of Pleasure. The Ancients have taken notice of all these in the first Ages of the World, or in their *Golden Age*, as they call it; and I do not doubt but what they ascrib'd to the Golden Age, was more remarkably true of *Paradise*; yet was not so peculiar to it, but that it did in a good measure extend to other parts of the Earth at that time. And 'tis manifest that their Golden Age was contemporary with our *Paradise*; for they make it begin immediately after the production and inhabitation of the Earth (which They, as well as *Moses*, raise from the Chaos) and to degenerate by degrees till the Deluge; when the World ended and begun again.

That this parallel may the better appear, we may observe, that as we say that the whole Earth was, in some sence, Paradisiacal in the first Ages of the World, and that there was besides, one Region or Portion of it that was peculiarly so, and bore the denomination of *Paradise*; So the Ancients besides their Golden Age, which was common to all the Earth, noted some parts of it that were more Golden, if I may so say, than the rest, and which did more particularly answer to *Paradise*; as their *Elysian* Fields, Fortunate Islands, Gardens of *Hesperides*, *Alcinous*, &c. these had a double portion of pleasantness, and besides the advantages which they had common with the rest of the Earth at that time, had something proper and singular, which gave them a distinct consideration and character from the rest.

Having made this observation, let us proceed, and see what Antiquity saith concerning that first and Paradisiacal state of things, upon those three Heads forementioned; First that there was a perpetual Spring, and constant serenity of the Air; This is often repeated by the Ancient Poets, in their description of the Golden Age:

> *Non alios primâ crescentis origine mundi*   *Virgil*
> *Illuxisse dies, aliumve habuisse tenorem,*
> *Crediderim: Ver illud erat, Ver magnus agebat*
> *Orbis, & hybernis parcebant flatibus Euri.*

> *Such days the new-born Earth enjoy'd of old,*
> *And the calm Heavens in this same tenour rowl'd:*
> *All the great World had then one constant Spring,*
> *No cold East-winds, such as our Winters bring.*

For I interpret this in the same sence with *Ovid*'s Verses of the Golden Age:

> *Ver erat Æternum: placidique tepentibus auris*
> *Mulcebant Zephyri natos sine semine flores.*

> *The Spring was constant, and soft Winds that blew*
> *Rais'd, without Seed, Flow'rs always sweet and new.*

And then upon the expiration of the Golden Age, He says,

Jupiter antiqui contraxit tempora Veris, &c.

When Jove *begun to reign he chang'd the Year,*
And for one Spring four Seasons made appear.

The Ancients suppos'd, that in the reign of *Saturn*, who was an Ante-diluvian God, as I may so call him, Time flow'd with a more even motion, and there was no diversity of Seasons in the Year; but *Jupiter*, they say, first introduc'd that, when he came to manage affairs. This is exprest after their way, who seldom give any severe and Philosophical accounts of the changes of Nature. And as they suppos'd this perpetual Spring in the Golden Age, so they did also in their particular *Elysiums*; as I could show largely from their Authors, if it would not multiply Citations too much in this place.

The Christian Authors have no less celebrated the perpetual Spring and Serenity of the Heavens in *Paradise*; such expressions or descriptions you will find in *Justin Martyr*, St. *Basil, Damascen, Isadore Hispalensis*, and others; inso-
De Grat. prim. much that *Bellarmine*, I remember, reflecting upon those Characters of *Paradise*,
hom. which many of the Fathers have given in these respects, saith, such things could not be, unless the Sun had then another course from what he hath now; or which is more easie, the Earth another situation. Which conjecture will hereafter appear to have been well-grounded. In the mean time, let us see the Christian Poetry upon this subject, as we have seen the *Roman* upon the other. *Alcimus Avitus* hath thus describ'd *Paradise* in his Notes upon *Genesis:*

Non hîc alterni succedit temporis unquam
Bruma, nec æstivi redeunt post frigora Soles;
Hîc Ver assiduum Cœli clementia servat.
Turbidus Auster abest, sempérque sub aere sudo
Nubila diffugiunt, jugi cessura sereno.
Nec poscit Natura loci, quos non habet, imbres,
Sed contenta suo dotantur germina rore.
Perpetuò viret omne solum, terræque benignæ
Blanda nitet facies: Stant semper collibus herbæ,
Arboribúsque comæ, &c.

No change of Seasons or excess was there,
No Winter chill'd, nor Summer scorch'd the Air,
But, with a constant Spring, Nature was fresh and fair.
Rough Winds or Rains that Region never knew,
Water'd with Rivers and the morning Dew;
The Heav'ns still clear, the Fields still green and gay,
No Clouds above, nor on the Earth decay;
Trees kept their leaves and verdure all the Year,
And Fruits were never out of Season there.

And as the Christian Authors, so likewise the *Jewish* have spoken of *Paradise* in the same manner; they tell us also that the days there were always of the same length throughout the whole Year; and that made them fancy *Paradise* to lie under the Æquinoctial; as we shall see in its due place. 'Tis true, we do not find these things mention'd expresly in the Sacred writings, but the effects that flow'd from them are recorded there, and we may reasonably suppose Providence to have foreseen, that when those Effects came to be scan'd and narrowly lookt into, they would lead us to a discovery of the Causes, and particularly of this great and general Cause, that *perpetual Æquinox* and unity of seasons in the Year, till the Deluge. The Longævity of the Ante-diluvians cannot be explain'd upon any other supposition, as we shall have occasion to show hereafter; and that you know is recorded carefully in Scripture: As also that there was no *Rainbow* before the Flood; which goes upon the same ground, that there was no variety of Seasons, nor any Rain: And this by many is thought to be understood by *Moses* his words, *Gen.* 2. 5, 6. which he speaks of the first and Paradisiacal Earth. Lastly, seeing the Earth then brought forth the principles of life and all living Creatures (Man excepted) according to *Moses, Gen.* I. 24. we must suppose that the state of the Heavens was such as favour'd these Conceptions and Births, which could not possibly be brought to perfection, as the Seasons of the Year are at present. The first time that we have mention made in Scripture of Summer and Winter, and the differences of Seasons, is at the ending of the Deluge, *Gen.* 8. 22. *Hence forward all the days of the Earth, Seed-time and Harvest, Heat and Cold, Summer and Winter, Day and Night shall not cease.* 'Tis true these words are so lax, that they may be understood either of a new course of Nature then instituted, or of an old one restor'd; but seeing it doth appear from other arguments and considerations, that there was at that time a new course of Nature constituted, it is more reasonable to interpret the words in that sence; which, as it is agreeable to truth, according to Reason and Antiquity; so it renders that remark of *Moses* of far greater importance, if it be understood as an indication of a new order then setled in Nature, which should continue thence forwards so long as the Earth endur'd. Nor do I at all wonder that such things should not be expresly and positively declar'd in Scripture, for natural mysteries in the Holy writings, as well as Prophetical, are many times, on set purpose, incompleatly deliver'd, so as to awaken and excite our thoughts rather than full resolve them: This being often more suitable to the designs of Providence in the government of the World. But thus much for this first common or general Character of the Golden Age, and of *Paradise*, a *perpetual Serenity and perpetual Æquinox.*

The second Character is the Longævity of men; and, as is probable, of all other Animals in proportion. This, methinks, is as strange and surprising as the other; and I know no difference betwixt the Ante-diluvian World and the present, so apt to affect us, if we reflect upon it, as this wonderful disproportion in the Ages of Men; Our fore-fathers and their Posterity; They liv'd seven, eight, nine hundred Years and upwards, and 'tis a wonder now if a man live to one hundred. Our Oaks do not last so long as their Bodies did; Stone and Iron would scarce out-wear them. And this property of the first Ages, or their Inhabitants, how strange soever, is well attested, and beyond all exception, having the joynt consent of Sacred and Profane History. The Scripture sets down the precise Age of a series of Ante-diluvian Patriarchs, and by that measures the time from the beginning of the World to the Deluge; so as all Sacred Chronology stands upon that bottom. Yet I know some have thought this so improbable and incongruous a thing, that to save the credit of *Moses* and the Sacred History, they interpret these years of *Lunar* years or months; and so the Ages of these Patriarchs are reduc'd to much what the same measure with the common life of man at this time. It may be observ'd in this, as in many other instances, that for want of a Theory to make things credible and intelligible, men of wit and parts have often deprest the sence of Scripture; and that not out of any ill will to Scripture or Religion, but because they could not otherwise, upon the stock of their notions, give themselves a rational account of things recorded there. But I hope when we come to explain the causes of this longævity, we shall show that it is altogether as strange a thing that men should have such short lives as they have now, as that they had such long lives in the first Ages of the World. In the mean time, there are a great many collateral reasons to assure us that *Lunar* years cannot be here understood by *Moses*, for all Antiquity gives the same account of those first Ages of the World, and of the first men, that they were extreamly long-liv'd. We meet with it generally in the description of the Golden Age; and not only so, but in their Topical *Paradises* also they always suppos'd a great vivacity or

Book. I.
Chap. 4.

longævity in those that enjoy'd them. And *Josephus* speaking upon this subject, saith, the Authors of all the learned Nations, *Greeks* or *Barbarians*, bear witness to *Moses*'s doctrine in this particular. And in the *Mosaical* History it self, there are several circumstances and marks that discover plainly, that the years of the Patriarchs cannot be understood of *Lunar* years; as we shall have occasion to

Chap. 4.

show in another place. We proceed in the mean time to the third and last Character, The extraordinary fertility of the Soil, and the production of Animals out of the new-made Earth.

The first part of this Character is unquestionable; All Antiquity speaks of the plenty of the Golden Age, and of their *Paradises*, whether Christian or Heathen. The fruits of the Earth at first were spontaneous, and the ground without being torn and tormented, satisfied the wants or desires of man. When Nature was fresh and full, all things flow'd from her more easily and more pure, like the first running of the Grape, or the Hony-comb; but now she must be prest and squeez'd, and her productions tast more of the Earth and of bitterness. The Ancient Poets have often pleas'd themselves in making descriptions of this happy state, and in admiring the riches and liberality of Nature at that time, but we need not transcribe their Poetry here, seeing this point is not, I think, contested by any. The second part of this Character, concerning the spontaneous Origin of living Creatures out of that first Earth, is not so unquestionable; and as to Man, *Moses* plainly implies that there was a particular action or ministery of Providence in the formation of his Body, but as to other Animals He seems to suppose that the Earth brought them forth as it did Herbs and Plants. (*Gen.* I. 24 compar'd with the II Verse.) And the truth is, there is no such great difference betwixt Vegetable and Animals Egg, or betwixt the Seeds out of which Plants rise, and the Eggs out of which all Animals rise, but that we may conceive, the one as well as the other, in the first Earth: And as some warmth and influence from the Sun is requir'd for the Vegetation of Seeds, so that influence or impregnation which is necessary to make animal Eggs fruitful, was imputed by the Ancients to the *Æther*, or to an active and pure Element which had the same effect upon our great Mother the Earth, as the irradiation of the Male hath upon the Females Eggs.

> *Tum Pater omnipotens fœcundis imbribus Æther*
> *Conjugis in gremium lætæ descendit.*

> *In fruitful show'rs of Æther* Jove *did glide*
> *Into the bosom of his joyful Bride.*

'Tis true, this opinion of the spontaneous Origin of Animals in the first Earth, hath lain under some *Odium*, because it was commonly reckon'd to be *Epicurus*'s opinion peculiarly; and he extended it not only to all brute Creatures, but to Mankind also, whom he suppos'd to grow out of the Earth in great numbers, in several Parts and Countries, like other Animals; which is a notion contrary to the Sacred writings; for they declare, that all Mankind, though diffus'd now through the several parts and Regions of the Earth, rise at first from one Head or single Man and Woman; which is a Conclusion of great importance, and that could not, I think, by the Light of Nature, have ever been discover'd. And this makes the *Epicurean* opinion the more improbable, for why should two rise only, if they sprung from the Earth? or how could they rise in their full growth and perfection, as *Adam* and *Eve* did? But as for the opinion of Animals rising out of the Earth at first, that was not at all peculiar to *Epicurus*; The *Stoicks* were of the same mind, and the *Pythagoreans*, and the *Ægyptians*, and, I think, all that suppos'd the Earth to rise from a Chaos. Neither do I know any harm in that opinion, if duly limited and stated; for what inconvenience is it, or what diminution of Providence, that there should be the principles of Life, as well as the principles of Vegetation, in the new Earth? And unless you suppose all the first Animals, as well as the first man, to have been made at one stroke, in their full growth and perfection, which we have neither reason nor authority sufficient to believe; if they were made young, little and weak, as they come now into the World, there seems to be no way for their production more proper, and decorous, than that they should spring from their great Mother the Earth. Lastly, considering the innumerable little Creatures that are upon the Earth, Insects and Creeping things: and that these were not created out of nothing, but form'd out of the ground: I think that an office most proper for Nature, that can set so many hands to work at once; and that hath hands fit for all those little operations or manufactures, how small soever, that would less become the dignity of Superiour Agents.

Thus much for the Preliminaries, or three general Characters of *Paradise*, which were common to it with the rest of the Primæval Earth; and were the chief ingredients of the Golden Age, so much celebrated by the Ancients. I know there were several other differences betwixt that Earth and this, but these are the original; and such as are not necessary to be premis'd for the general Explication of *Paradise*, we reserve for another place. We may, in the mean time observe, how preposterously they go to work, that set themselves immediately to find out some pleasant place of the Earth to fix *Paradise* in, before they have consider'd, or laid any grounds, to explain the general conditions of it, wheresoever it was. These must be first known and determin'd, and we must take our aim and directions from these, how to proceed further in our enquiries after it; otherwise we sail without a Compass, or seek a Port and know not which way it lies. And as we should think him a very unskilful Pilot that sought a place in the new World, or *America*, that really was in the old; so they commit no less an error, that seek *Paradise* in the present Earth, as now constituted, which could only belong to the former, and to the state of the first World: As will appear more plainly in the following Chapter.

CHAPTER II

The great Change of the World since the Flood, from what it was in the first Ages. The Earth under its present form could not be Paradisiacal, *nor any part of it.*

*T*HE *Scheme of this World passeth away*, saith an holy Author; The mode and form, both of the Natural and Civil World, changeth continually more or less, but most remarkably at certain Periods, when all Nature puts on another face; as it will do at the Conflagration, and hath done already from the time of the Deluge. We may imagine how different a prospect the first World would make from what we see now in the present state of things, if we consider only those generals by which we have describ'd it in the foregoing Chapter, and what their influence would be upon mankind and the rest of Nature. For every new state of Nature doth introduce a new Civil Order, and a new face and Oeconomy of Humane affairs: And I am apt to think that some two Planets, that are under the same state or Period, do not so much differ from one another, as the same Planet doth from it self, in different periods of its duration. We do not seem to inhabit the same World that our first fore-fathers did, nor scarce to be the same race of Men. Our life now is so short and vain, as if we came into the World only to see it and leave it; by that time we begin to understand our selves a little, and to know where we are, and how to act our part, we must leave the stage, and give place to others as meer Novices as we were our selves at our first entrance. And this short life is imploy'd, in a great measure, to preserve our selves from necessity, or diseases, or injuries of the Air, or other inconveniences; to make one man easie, ten must work and do drudgery; The Body takes up so much time, we have little leisure for Contemplation, or to cultivate the mind. The Earth doth not yield us food, but with much labour and industry, and what was her freewill offering before, or an easie liberality can scarce now be extorted from her. Neither are the Heavens more favourable, sometimes in one extream, sometimes in another; The Air often impure or infectious, and, for a great part of the year, Nature her self seems to be sick or dead. To this vanity the external Creation is made subject as well as Mankind, and so must continue till the restitution of all things.

Can we imagine, in those happy Times and Places we are treating of, that things stood in this same posture? are these the fruits of the Golden Age and of *Paradise*, or consistent with their happiness? And the remedies of these evils must be so universal, you cannot give them to one place or Region of the Earth, but all must participate: For these are things that flow from the course of the Heavens, or such general causes as extend at once to all Nature. If there was a perpetual Spring and perpetual Æquinox in *Paradise*, there was at the same time a perpetual Æquinox all the Earth over; unless you place *Paradise* in the middle of the Torrid Zone. So also the long lives of the Ante-diluvians was an universal Effect, and must have had an universal Cause. 'Tis true, in some single parts or Regions of the present Earth, the Inhabitants live generally longer than in others, but do not approach in any measure the Age of their Ante-diluvian fore-fathers; and that degree of longævity which they have above the rest, they owe to the calmness and tranquility of their Heavens and Air; which is but an imperfect participation of that cause which was once Universal, and had its effect through-out the whole Earth. And as to the fertility of this Earth, though in some spots it be eminently more fruitful than in others, and more delicious, yet that of the first Earth was a fertility of another kind, being spontaneous, and extending to the production of Animals, which cannot be without a favourable concourse from the Heavens also.

Thus much in general; We will now go over those three foremention'd Characters more distinctly, to show by their unsuitableness to the present state of Nature, that neither the whole Earth, as it is now, nor any part of it, could be *Paradisiacal*. The perpetual Spring, which belong'd to the Golden Age, and to *Paradise*, is an happiness this present Earth cannot pretend to, nor is capable of, unless we could transfer the Sun from the Ecliptick to the Æquator, or, which is as easie, per-swade the Earth to change its posture to the Sun. If *Archimedes* had found a place to plant his Machines in for removing of the Earth, all that I should have desir'd of him, would have been only to have given it an heave at one end, and set it a little to rights again with the Sun, that we might have enjoy'd the comfort of a perpetual Spring, which we have lost by its dislocation ever since the Deluge. And there being nothing more indispensably necessary to a *Paradisiacal* state than this unity and equality of Seasons, where that cannot be, 'tis in vain to seek for the rest of *Paradise*.

That spontaneous fruitfulness of the ground was a thing peculiar to the primigenial soil, which was so temper'd, as made it more luxuriant at that time than it could ever be afterwards; and as that rich temperament was spent, so by degrees it grew less fertile. The Origin or production of Animals out of the Earth, depended not only upon this vital constitution of the soil at first, but also upon such a posture and aspect of the Heavens, as favour'd, or at least permitted, Nature, to make her best works out of this prepar'd matter, and better than could be made in that manner, after the Flood. *Noah*, we see, had orders given him to preserve the Races of living Creatures in his Ark, when the Old World was destroy'd, which is an argument to me, that Providence foresaw that the Earth would not be capable to produce them under its new form; and that, not only for want of fitness in the soil, but because of the diversity of Seasons which were then to take place, whereby Nature would be disturb'd in her work, and the subject to be wrought upon would not continue long enough in the same due temper. But this part of the second Character concerning the Original of Animals, deserves to be further examin'd and explain'd.

The first principles of life must be tender and ductile, that they may yield to all the motions and gentle touches of Nature; otherwise it is not possible that they should be wrought with that curiosity, and drawn into all those little fine threds and textures, that we see and admire in some parts of the Bodies of Animals. And as the matter must be so constituted at first, so it must be kept in a due temper till the work be finisht, without any excess of heat or cold; and accordingly we see, that Nature hath made provision in all sorts of Creatures, whether Oviparous or Viviparous, that the first rudiments of life should be preserv'd from all injuries of the Air, and kept in a moderate warmth. Eggs are enclos'd in a Shell, or ffilm, and must be cherisht with an equal and gentle heat, to begin formation and continue it, otherwise the work miscarries: And in Viviparous Creatures, the materials of life are safely lodg'd in the Females womb, and conserv'd in a fit temperature 'twixt heat and cold, while the Causes that Providence hath imploy'd, are busie at work, fashioning and placing and joyning the parts, in that due order which so wonderful a Fabrick requires.

Let us now compare these things with the birth of Animals in the new-made World, when they first rose out of the Earth, to see what provision could be made there for their safety and nourishment, while they were a-making, and when newly made; And though we take all advantages we can, and suppose both the Heavens and the Earth favourable, a fit soil and a warm and constant temper of the Air, all will be little enough to make this way of production feasible or probable: But if we suppose there was then the same inconstancy of the Heavens that is now, the same vicissitude of seasons, and the same inequality of heat and cold, I do not think it at all possible that they could be so form'd, or being new-form'd, preserv'd and nourisht. 'Tis true, some little Creatures that are of short dispatch in their formation, and find nourishment enough wheresoever they are bred, might be produc'd and brought to perfection in this way, notwithstanding and inequality of Seasons; because they are made all at a heat, as I may so say, begun and ended within the compass of one Season; But the great question is concerning the more perfect kinds of Animals, that require a long stay in the womb, to make them capable to sustain and nourish themselves when they first come into the World. Such Animals being big and strong, must have a pretty hardness in their bones, and force and firmness in their Muscles and Joynts, before they can bear their own weight, and exercise the common motions of their body: And accordingly we see Nature hath ordain'd for these a longer time of gestation, that their limbs and members might have time to acquire strength and solidity. Besides the young ones of these Animals have commonly the milk of the Dam to nourish them after they are brought forth, which is a very proper nourishment, and like to that which they had before in the womb; and by this means their stomachs are prepar'd by degrees for courser food: Whereas our Terrigenous Animals must have been wean'd as soon as they were born, or as soon as they were separated from their Mother the Earth, and therefore must be allow'd a longer time of continuing there.

These things being consider'd, we cannot in reason but suppose that, these Terrigenous Animals were as long, or longer, a-perfecting, than our Viviparous, and were not separated from the body of the Earth for ten, twelve, eighteen, or more months, according as their Nature was; and seeing in this space of time they must have suffer'd, upon the common *Hypothesis*, all vicissitudes and variety of seasons, and great excesses of heat and cold, which are things incompatible with the tender principles of life and the formation of living Creatures, as we have shown before; we may reasonably and safely conclude, that Nature had not, when the World began, the same course she hath now, or that the Earth was not then in its present posture and constitution: Seeing, I say, these first spontaneous Births, which both the holy Writ, Reason, and Antiquity seem to allow, could not be finisht and brought to maturity, nor afterwards preserv'd and nourisht, upon any other supposition.

Longævity is the last Character to be consider'd, and as inconsistent with the present state of the Earth as any other. There are many things in the story of the first Ages that seem strange, but nothing so prodigy-like as the long lives of those Men; that their houses of Clay should stand eight or nine hundred years and upwards, and those we build of the hardest Stone and Marble will not now last so long. This hath excited the curiosity of ingenious and learned men in all Ages to enquire after the possible Causes of that longævity; and if it had been always in conjunction with innocency of life and manners, and expir'd when that expir'd, we might have thought it some peculiar blessing or reward attending that; but 'twas common to good and bad, and lasted till the Deluge, whereas mankind was degenerate long before. Amongst natural Causes, some have imputed it to the sobriety and simplicity of their diet and manner of living in those days, that they eat no flesh, and had not all those provocations to gluttony which Wit and Vice have since invented. This might have some effect, but not possibly to that degree and measure that we speak of. There are many Monastical persons now that live abstemiously all their lives, and yet they think an hundred years a very great age amongst them. Others have imputed it to the excellency of their Fruits and some unknown vertue in their Herbs and Plants in those days; But they may as well say nothing, as say that which can neither be prov'd nor understood. It could not be either the quantity or quality of their food that was the cause of their long lives, for the Earth was curst long before the Deluge, and probably by that time was more barren and juiceless (for the generality) than ours is now; yet we do not see that their longævity decreast at all, from the beginning of the World to the Flood. *Methusalah* was *Noah*'s Grandfather, but one intire remove from the Deluge, and he liv'd longer than any of his Forefathers. That food that will nourish the parts and keep us in health, is also capable to keep us in long life, if there be no impediments otherwise; for to continue health is to continue life; as that fewel that is fit to raise and nourish a flame, will preserve it as long as you please, if you add fresh fewel, and no external causes hinder: Neither do we observe that in those parts of the present Earth where people live longer than in others, that there is any thing extraordinary in their food, but that the difference is chiefly from the Air and the temperateness of the Heavens; And if the Ante-diluvians had not enjoy'd that advantage in a peculiar manner, and differently from what any parts of the Earth do now, they would never have seen seven, eight, or nine hundred years go over their heads, though they had been nourisht with *Nectar* and *Ambrosia*.

Others have thought that the long lives of those men of the old World proceeded from the strength of their *Stamina*, or first principles of their bodies; which if they were now as strong in us, they think we should still live as long as they did. This could not be the sole and adæquate cause of their longævity, as will appear both from History and Reason. *Shem*, who was born before the Flood, and had in his body all the vertue of the Ante-diluvian *Stamina* and constitution, fell three hundred years short of the age of his fore-fathers, because the greatest part of his life was past after the Flood. That their *Stamina* were stronger than ours are, I am very ready to believe, and that their bodies were greater; and any race of strong men, living long in health, would have children of a proportionably strong constitution with themselves; but then the question is, How was this interrupted? We that are their posterity, why do not we inherit their long lives? how was this constitution broken at the Deluge, and how did the *Stamina* fail so fast when that came? why was there so great a *Crisis* then and turn of life, or why was that the period of their strength?

We see this longævity sunk half in half immediately after the Flood, and after that it sunk by gentler degrees, but was still in motion and declension till it was

Ps. 90. 10. *call'd a Psalm of* Moses.

fixt at length, before *David*'s time, in that which hath been the common standard of man's age ever since: As when some excellent fruit is transplanted into a worse Climate and Soil, it degenerates continually till it comes to such a degree of meanness as suits that Air and Soil, and then it stands. That the age of Man did not fall all on a sudden from the Ante-diluvian measure to the present, I impute it to the remaining *Stamina* of those first Ages, and the strength of that pristine constitution which could not wear off but by degrees. We see the Blacks do not quit their complexion immediately by removing into another Climate, but their posterity changeth by little and little, and after some generations they become altogether like the people of the Country where they are. Thus by the change of Nature that happened at the Flood, the unhappy influence of the Air and unequal Seasons weaken'd by degrees the innate strength of their bodies and the vigour of the parts, which would have been capable to have lasted several more hundreds of years, if the Heavens had continued their course as formerly, or the Earth its position. To conclude this particular, If any think that the Ante-diluvian longævity proceeded only from the *Stamina*, or the meer strength of their bodies, and would have been so under any constitution of the Heavens, let them resolve themselves these Questions; first, why these *Stamina*, or this strength of constitution fail'd? Secondly, why did it fail so much and so remarkably at the Deluge? Thirdly, why in such proportions as it hath done since the Deluge? And lastly, why it hath stood so long immovable, and without any further diminution? Within the compass of five hundred years they sunk from nine hundred to ninety; and in the compass of more than three thousand years since they have not sunk ten years, or scarce any thing at all. Who considers the reasons of these things, and the true resolution of these questions, will be satisfi'd, that to understand the causes of that longævity something more must be consider'd than the make and strength of their bodies; which, though they had been made as strong as the *Behemoth* or *Leviathan*, could not have lasted so many Ages, if there had not been a particular concurrence of external causes, such as the present state of Nature doth not admit of.

By this short review of the three general Characters of *Paradise* and the Golden Age, we may conclude how little consistent they are with the present form and order of the Earth. Who can pretend to assign any place or Region in this Terraqueous Globe, Island or Continent, that is capable of these conditions, or that agrees either with the descriptions given by the ancient Heathens of their *Paradises*, or by the Christian Fathers of Scripture-*Paradise*. But where then, will you say, must we look for it, if not upon this Earth? This puts us more into despair of finding it than ever; 'tis not above nor below, in the Air or in the subterraneous Regions: no, doubtless 'twas upon the surface of the Earth, but of the Primitive Earth, whose form and properties as they were different from this, so they were such as made it capable of being truly *Paradisiacal*, both according to the forementioned Characters, and all other qualities and priviledges reasonably ascrib'd to *Paradise*.

CHAPTER III

The Original differences of the Primitive Earth from the present or Post-diluvian. The three Characters of Paradise *and the Golden Age found in the Primitive Earth. A particular Explication of each Character.*

WE have hitherto only perplext the Argument and our selves, by showing how inexplicable the state of *Paradise* is according to the present order of things, and the present condition of the Earth. We must now therefore bring into view that Original and Ante-diluvian Earth where we pretend its seat was, and show it capable of all those priviledges which we have deny'd to the present; in vertue of which priviledges, and of the order of Nature establisht there, that Primitive Earth might be truly *Paradisiacal*, as in the Golden Age; and some Region of it peculiarly so, according to the *Idea* of the Christian *Paradise*. And this, I think, is all the knowledge and satisfaction that we can expect, or that Providence hath allow'd us in this Argument.

The Primigenial Earth, which in the first Book (*Chap.* 5) we rais'd from a Chaos, and set up in an habitable form, we must now survey again with more care, to observe its principal differences from the present Earth, and what influence they will have upon the question in hand. These differences, as we have said before, were chiefly three; The form of it, which was smooth, even, and regular. The posture and situation of it to the Sun, which was direct, and not, as it is at present, inclin'd and oblique; And the Figure of it, which was more apparently and regularly Oval than it is now. From these three differences flow'd a great many more, inferiour and subordinate; and which had a considerable influence upon the moral World at that time, as well as the natural. But we will only observe here their more immediate effects, and that in reference to those general Characters or properties of the Golden Age and of *Paradise*, which we have instanc'd in, and whereof we are bound to give an account by our *Hypothesis*.

And in this respect the most fundamental of those three differences we mention'd, was, that of the right posture and situation of the Earth to the Sun; for from this immediately follow'd a perpetual Æquinox all the Earth over, or, if you will, a perpetual Spring: And that was the great thing we found awanting in the present Earth to make it *Paradisiacal*, or capable of being so. Wherefore this being now found and establisht in the Primitive Earth, the other two properties, of Longævity and of Spontaneous and Vital fertility, will be of more easie explication. In the mean time let us view a little the reasons and causes of that regular situation in the first Earth.

The truth is, one cannot so well require a reason of the regular situation the Earth had then, for that was most simple and natural; as of the irregular situation it hath now; standing oblique and inclin'd to the Sun or the Ecliptick: Whereby the course of the year is become unequal, and we are cast into a great diversity of Seasons. But however, stating the first aright with its circumstances, we shall have a better prospect upon the second, and see from what causes, and in what manner, it came to pass. Let us therefore suppose the Earth, with the rest of its fellow-Planets, to be carried about the Sun in the Ecliptick by the motion of the liquid Heavens; and being at that time perfectly uniform and regular, having the same Center of its magnitude and gravity, it would by the equality of its libration necessarily have its Axis parallel to the Axis of the same Ecliptick, both its Poles being equally inclin'd to the Sun. And this posture I call a *right situation*, as oppos'd to oblique or inclin'd. Now this is a thing that needs no proof besides its own evidence; for 'tis the immediate result and common effect of gravity or libration, that a Body freely left to it self in a fluid *medium*, should settle in such a posture as best answers to its gravitation; and this first Earth whereof we speak, being uniform and every way equally ballanc'd, there was no reason why it should incline at one end, more than at the other, towards the Sun. As if you should suppose a Ship to stand North and South under the Æquator, if it was equally built and equally ballasted, it would not incline to one Pole or other, but keep its Axis parallel to the Axis of the Earth; but if the ballast lay more at one end, it would dip towards that Pole, and rise proportionably higher towards the other. So those great Ships that sail about the Sun once a year, or once in so many years, whilst they are uniformly built and equally pois'd, they keep steddy and even with the Axis of their Orbit; but if they lose that equality, and the Center of their gravity change, the heavier end will incline more towards the common Center of their motion, and the other end will recede from it: So particularly the Earth, which makes one in that aery Fleet, when it scap'd so narrowly from being shipwrackt in the great Deluge, was however so broken and disorder'd, that it lost its equal poise, and thereupon the Center of its gravity changing, one Pole became more inclin'd towards the Sun, and the other more remov'd from it, and so its right and parallel situation which it had before to the Axis of the Ecliptick, was chang'd into an oblique; in which skew posture it hath stood ever since, and is likely so to do for some Ages to come. I instance in this, as the most obvious cause of the change of the situation of the Earth, tho' it may be, upon this, followed a change in its Magnetism: and that might also contribute to the same effect.

However, This change and obliquity of the Earth's posture had a long train of consequences depending upon it; whereof that was the most immediate, that it alter'd the form of the year, and brought in that inequality of Seasons which hath since obtain'd: As, on the contrary, while the Earth was in its first and natural posture, in a more easie and regular disposition to the Sun, That had also another respective train of consequences, whereof one of the first, and that which we are most concern'd in at present, was, that it made a perpetual Æquinox or Spring to all the World, all the parts of the year had one and the same tenour, face and temper; there was no Winter or Summer, Seed-time or Harvest, but a continual temperature of the Air and Verdure of the Earth. And this fully answers the first and fundamental character of the Golden Age and of *Paradise*; And what Antiquity, whether Heathen or Christian, hath spoken concerning that perpetual serenity and constant Spring that reign'd there, which in the one was accounted fabulous, and in the other hyperbolical, we see to have been really and Philosophically true. Nor is there any wonder in the thing, the wonder is rather on our side, that the Earth should stand and continue in that forc'd posture wherein it is now, spinning yearly about an Axis that doth not belong to the Orbit of its motion; this, I say, is more strange than that it once stood in a posture that was streight and regular; As we more justly admire the Tower at *Pisa,* that stands crook'd, than twenty other streight Towers that are much higher.

Having got this foundation to stand upon, the rest of our work will go on more easily; and the two other Characters which we mention'd, will not be of very difficult explication. The spontaneous fertility of the Earth, and its production of Animals at that time, we have in some measure explain'd before; supposing it to proceed partly from the richness of the Primigenial soil, and partly from this constant Spring and benignity of the Heavens, which we have now establisht; These were always ready to excite Nature, and put her upon action, and never to interrupt her in any of her motions or attempts. We have show'd in the Fifth Chapter of the First Book, how this Primigenial soil was made, and of what ingredients; which were such as compose the richest and fattest soil, being a light Earth mixt with unctuous juices, and then afterwards refresh'd and diluted with the dews of Heaven all the year long, and cherisht with a continual warmth from the Sun. What more hopeful beginning of a World than this? You will grant, I believe, that whatsoever degree or whatsoever kind of fruitfulness could be expected from a Soil and a Sun, might be reasonably expected there. We see great Woods and Forests of Trees rise spontaneously, and that since the Flood (for who can imagine that the ancient Forests, whereof some were so vastly great, were planted by the hand of man?) why should we not then believe that Fruit-trees and Corn rose as spontaneously in that first Earth? That which makes Husbandry and Humane Arts so necessary now for the Fruits and productions of the Earth, is partly indeed the decay of the Soil, but chiefly the diversity of Seasons, whereby they perish, if care be not taken of them; but when there was neither Heat nor Cold, Winter nor Summer, every Season was a Seed-time to Nature, and ever Season an Harvest.

This, it may be, you will allow as to the Fruits of the Earth, but that the same Earth should produce Animals also will not be thought so intelligible. Since it hath been discover'd, that the first materials of all Animals are Eggs, as Seeds are of Plants, it doth not seem so hard to conceive that these Eggs might be in the first Earth, as well as those Seeds; for there is a great analogy and similitude betwixt them; Especially if you compare these Seeds first with the Eggs of Insects or Fishes, and then with the Eggs of Viviparous Animals. And as for those juices which the Eggs of Viviparous Animals imbibe thorough their coats from the womb, they might as well imbibe them, or something analogous to them, from a conveniently temper'd Earth, as Plant-Eggs do; And these things being admitted, the progress is much-what the same in Seeds as Eggs, and in one sort of Eggs as in another.

'Tis true, Animal-Eggs do not seem to be fruitful of themselves, without the influence of the Male; and this is not necessary in Plant-Eggs or Vegetable Seeds. But neither doth it seem necessary in all Animal-Eggs, if there be any Animals *sponte orta*, as they call them, or bred without copulation. And, as we observ'd before, according to the best knowledge that we have of this Male influence, it is reasonable to believe, that it may be supplied by the Heavens or *Æther*. The Ancients, both the *Stoicks* and *Aristotle*, have suppos'd that there was something of an Æthereal Element in the Male-geniture, from whence the vertue of it chiefly proceeded; and if so, why may we not suppose, at that time, some general impression or irradiation of that purer Element to fructifie the new-made Earth? *Moses* saith there was an incubation of the Spirit of God upon the mass, and without all doubt that was either to form or fructifie it, and by the mediation of this active principle; but the Ancients speak more plainly with express mention of this *Æther*, and of the impregnation of the Earth by it, as betwixt Male and Female. As in the place before cited;

> *Tum Pater omnipotens fœcundis imbribus Æther*
> *Conjugis in gremium lætæ descendit; & omnes*
> *Magnus alit magno commixtus corpore, fœtus.*

De Civ. D. lib.
4. c. 10. Which notion, I remember, St. *Austin* saith, *Virgil* did not take from the fictions of the Poets, but out of the Books of the Philosophers. Some of the gravest Authors amongst the *Romans* have reported that this vertue hath been convey'd

into the wombs of some Animals by the Winds or the *Zephyri*; and as I easily believe that the first fresh Air was more impregnated with this Æthereal principle than ours is, so I see no reason but those balmy dews that fell every night in the Primitive Earth, might be the Vehicle of it as well as the Male-geniture is now; and from them the teeming Earth and those vital Seeds which it contain'd, were actuated, and receiv'd their first fruitfulness.

Now this Principle, howsoever convey'd to those rudiments of life which we call Eggs, is that which gives the first stroke towards Animation; And this seems to be by exciting a ferment in those little masses whereby the parts are loosen'd, and dispos'd for that formation which is to follow afterwards. And I see nothing that hinders but that we may reasonably suppose that these Animal productions might proceed thus far in the Primigenial Earth; And as to their progress and the formation of the Body, by what Agents or principles soever that great work is carried on in the womb of the Female, it might by the same be carried on there. Neither would there be any danger of miscarrying by excess of Heat or Cold, for the Air was always of an equal temper and moderate warmth; And all other impediments were remov'd, and all principles ready, whether active or passive; so as we may justly conclude, that as *Eve* was the Mother of all living as to Mankind, so was the Earth the Great Mother of all living Creatures besides.

The third Character to be explain'd, and the most extraordinary in appearance, is that of LONGÆVITY. This sprung from the same root, in my opinion, with the other; though the connexion, it may be, is not so visible. We show'd in the foregoing Chapter, that no advantage of Diet, or of strong Constitutions, could have carried their lives, before the Flood, to that wonderful length, if they had been expos'd to the same changes of Air and of Seasons that our Bodies are: But taking a perpetual Æquinox, and fixing the Heavens, you fix the life of Man too; which was not then in such a rapid flux as it is now, but seem'd to stand still, as the Sun did once, without declension. There is no question but every thing upon Earth, and especially the Animate World, would be much more permanent, if the general course of Nature was more steddy and uniform; A stability in the Heavens makes a stability in all things below; and that change and contrariety of qualities that we have in these Regions, is the fountain of corruption, and suffers nothing to be long in quiet: Either by intestine motions and fermentations excited within, or by outward impressions, Bodies are no sooner well constituted, but they are tending again to dissolution. The *Æther* in their little pores and chinks is unequally agitated, and differently mov'd at different times, and so is the Air in their greater, and the Vapours and Atmosphere round about them: All these shake and unsettle both the texture and continuity of Bodies. Whereas in a fixt state of Nature, where these principles have always the same constant and uniform motion, when they are once suited to the forms and compositions of Bodies, they give them no further disturbance; they enjoy a long and lasting peace without any commotions or violence, within or without.

We find our selves, sensible changes in our Bodies upon the turn of the Year, and the change of Seasons; new fermentations in the Bloud and resolutions of the Humours; which if they do not amount to diseases, at least they disturb

Nature, and have a bad effect not only upon the fluid parts, but also upon the more solid; upon the Springs and Fibres in the Organs of the Body; to weaken them and unfit them by degrees for their respective functions. For though the change is not sensible immediately in these parts, yet after many repeated impressions every year, by unequal heat and cold, driness and moisture, contracting and relaxing the Fibres, their tone at length is in a great measure destroy'd, or brought to a manifest debility; and the great Springs failing, the lesser that depend upon them, fail in proportion, and all the symptoms of decay and old age follow. We see by daily experience, that Bodies are kept better in the same *medium*, as we call it, than if they often change their *medium*, as sometimes in Air, sometimes in Water, moisten'd and dri'd, heated and cool'd; these different states weaken the contexture of the parts: But our Bodies, in the present state of Nature, are put into an hundred different *mediums* in the course of a Year; sometimes we are steept in Water, or in a misty foggy Air for several days together, sometimes we are almost frozen with cold, then fainting with heat at another time of the Year; and the Winds are of a different nature, and the Air of a different weight and pressure, according to the Weather and the Seasons: These things would wear our Bodies, though they were built of Oak, and that in a very short time in comparison of what they would last, if they were always incompast with one and the same *medium*, under one and the same temper, as it was in the Primitive Earth.

The Ancients seem to have been sensible of this, and of the true causes of those long periods of life; for wheresoever they assign'd a great longævity, as they did not only to their Golden Age, but also to their particular and topical *Paradises*, they also assign'd there a constant serenity and equality of the Heavens, and sometimes expresly a constant Æquinox; as might be made appear from their Authors. And some of our Christian Authors have gone farther, and connected these two together, as Cause and Effect; for they say that the Longævity of the Ante-diluvian Patriarchs proceeded from a favourable Aspect and influence of the Heavens at that time; which *Aspect* of the Heavens being rightly interpreted, is the same thing that we call the Position of the Heavens, or the right situation of the Sun and the Earth, from whence came a perpetual Æquinox. And if we consider the present Earth, I know no place where they live longer than in that little Island of the *Bermudas*, where, according to the proportion of time they hold out there, after they are arriv'd from other parts, one may reasonably suppose, that the Natives would live two hundred Years. And there's nothing appears in that Island that should give long life above other places, but the extraordinary steddiness of the Weather, and of the temper of the Air throughout the whole Year, so as there is scarce any considerable difference of Seasons.

But because it would take up too much time to show in this place the full and just reasons why, and how, these long periods of life depend upon the stability of the Heavens: and how on the contrary, from their inconstancy and mutability these periods are shorten'd, as in the present order of Nature; we will set apart the next Chapter to treat upon that subject; yet by way of digression only, so as those that have a mind may pass to the following, where the thred of this discourse is continued. In the mean time, you see, we have prepar'd an Earth for

Paradise, and given a fair and intelligible account of those three general Characters, which, according to the rules of method, must be determin'd before any further progress can be made in this Argument. For in the doctrine of *Paradise* there are two things to be consider'd, the state of it, and the place of it; And as it is first in order of Nature, so it is much more material, to find out the state of it, than the Region where it stood. We need not follow the Windings of Rivers, and the interpretation of hard names, to discover this, we take more faithful Guides, THE unanimous reports of Antiquity, Sacred and Profane, supported by a regular Theory. Upon these grounds we go, and have thus far proceeded on our way; which we hope will grow more easie and pleasant, the nearer we come to our journeys end.

CHAPTER IV

A digression, concerning the Natural Causes of Longævity. That the Machine of an Animal consists of Springs, and which are the two principal. The Age of the Ante-diluvians to be computed by Solar *not* Lunar *Years.*

TO confirm our opinion concerning the reasons of Longævity in the first Inhabitants of the World, it will not be amiss to deduce more at large the Natural Causes of *long* or *short periods of life*. And when we speak of long or short periods of life, we do not mean those little difference of ten, twenty or forty Years which we see amongst men now adays, according as they are of stronger or weaker constitutions, and govern themselves better or worse, but those grand and famous differences of several hundreds of Years, which we have examples of in the different Ages of the World, and particularly in those that liv'd before and since the Flood. Neither do we think it peculiar to this Earth to have such an inequality in the lives of men, but the other Planets, if they be inhabited, have the same property, and the same difference in their different periods; All Planets that are in their Ante-diluvian state, and in their first and regular situation to the Sun, have long-liv'd Inhabitants; and those that are in an oblique situation, have short-liv'd; unless there be some counter-causes that hinder this general rule of Nature from taking place.

We are now so us'd to a short life, and to drop away after threescore or fourscore years, that when we compare our lives with those of the Ante-diluvians, we think the wonder lies wholly on their side, *why* they liv'd so long; and so it doth, popularly speaking; but if we speak Philosophically, the wonder lies rather on our side, *why* we live so little, or so short a time: For seeing our Bodies are such Machines as have a faculty of nourishing themselves, that is, of repairing their lost or decay'd parts, so long as they have good nourishment to make use of, why should they not continue in good plight, and always the same? as a flame does, so long as it is supplied with fewel? And that we may the better see on whether side the wonder lies, and from what causes it proceeds, we will propose this Problem to be examin'd, *Why the frame or Machine of an humane Body, or of another Animal, having that construction of parts and those faculties which* it

hath, lasts so short a time? And though it fall into no disease, nor have any unnatural accident, within the space of eighty years, more or less, fatally and in-
evitably decays, dies and perisheth?

That the state and difficulty of this question may the better appear, let us
consider a man in the prime and vigour of his life, at the age of twenty or twenty
four years, of an healthful constitution, and all his Vitals sound; let him be nourisht
with good food, use due exercise, and govern himself with moderation in all other
things; The Question is, why this Body should not continue in the same plight,
and in the same strength, for some Ages? or at least why it should decay so soon,
and so fast as we see it does? We do not wonder at things that happen daily,
though the causes of them be never so hard to find out; We contract a certain
familiarity with common events, and fancy we know as much of them as can be
known, though in reality we know nothing of them but matter of fact; which the
vulgar knows as well as the Wise or the Learned. We see daily instances of the
shortness of mans life, how soon his race is run, and we do not wonder at it,
because 'tis common, yet if we examine the composition of the Body, it will be
very hard to find any good reasons why the frame of it should decay so soon.

I know 'tis easie to give general and superficial answers and accounts of these
things, but they are such, as being strictly examin'd, give no satisfaction to an
inquisitive mind: You would say, it may be, that the Interiour parts and Organs
of the Body wear and decay by degrees, so as not performing so well their several
offices and functions, for the digestion and distribution of the food and its juices,
all the other parts suffer by it, and that draws on insensibly a decay upon the
whole frame of the Body. This is all true; but why, and how comes this to pass?
from what causes? where is the first failure, and what are the consequences of it?
The inward parts do not destroy themselves, and we suppose that there is no
want of good food, nor any disease, and we take the Body in its full strength
and vigour, why doth it not continue thus, as a Lamp does, if you supply it with
Oil? The causes being the same, why doth not the same effect still follow? why
should not the flame of life, as well as any other flame, if you give it fewel, continue
in its force without languishing or decay?

You will say, it may be, The case is not the same in a simple Body, such as a
Lamp or a Fire, and in an Organical Body; which being variously compounded
of multiplicity of parts, and all those parts put in connexion and dependance one
upon another, if any one fail, it will disorder the whole frame; and therefore it
must needs be more difficult for such a body to continue long in the same state,
than for a simple Body that hath no variety of parts or operations. I acknowledge
such a Body is much more subject to diseases and accidents than a more simple,
but barring all diseases and accidents, as we do, it might be of as long a duration
as any other, if it was suppli'd with nourishment adequately to all its parts: As
this Lamp we speak of, if it consisted of twenty branches, and each of these
branches was to be fed with a different Oil, and these Oils should be all mixt
together in some common Cistern, whence they were to be distributed into the
several branches, either according to their different degrees of lightness, one
rising higher than another; or according to the capacity and figure of the little

pipes they were to pass thorough; such a compounded Lamp, made up of such artifices, would indeed be more subject to accidents, and to be out of order, by the obstruction of some of the little pipes, or some unfit qualities in the Oils, but all these casualties and disorders excepted, as they are in our case, if it was suppli'd with convenient liquors, it would burn as long as any other, though more plain and simple.

To instance yet, for more plainness, in another sort of Machine, suppose a Mill, where the Water may represent the nourishment and humours in our Body, and the frame of Wood and Stone, the solid parts; If we could suppose this Mill to have a power of nourishing it self by the Water it receiv'd, and of repairing all the parts that were worn away, whether of the Wood-work or of the Stone, feed it but with a constant stream, and it would subsist and grind for ever. And 'tis the same thing for all other Artificial Machines of this nature, if they had a faculty of nourishing themselves, and repairing their parts. And seeing those natural Machines we are speaking of, the Body of Man, and of other Animals, have and enjoy this faculty, why should they not be able to preserve themselves beyond that short period of time which is now the measure of their life?

Thus much we have said to shew the difficulty propos'd and inforce it; We must now consider the true answer and resolution of it; and to that purpose bring into view again those causes which we have assign'd, both of the long periods of life before the Flood, and of the short ones since. That there was a perpetual Æquinox and stability of the Heavens before the Flood, we have show'd both from History and reason; neither was there then any thing of Clouds, Rains, Winds, Storms or unequal weather, as will appear in the following Chapter; And to this steddiness of Nature and universal calmness of the external World we have imputed those long periods of life which men enjoy'd at that time: As on the contrary, when that great change and revolution happen'd to Nature at the Deluge, and the Heavens and the Earth were cast in another mould, then was brought in, besides many other new Scenes, that shortness and vanity in the life of Man, and a general instability in all sublunary things, but especially in the Animate World.

It is not necessary to show, more than we have done already, how that Primitive state of Nature contributed to long life; neither is it requir'd that it should actively contribute, but only be permissive, and suffer our Bodies to act their parts; for if they be not disturb'd, nor any harm done them by external Nature, they are built with art and strength enough to last many hundreds of years. And as we observ'd before concerning the posture of the Earth, that that which it had at first, being simple and regular, was not so much to be accounted for, as its present posture, which is irregular; so likewise for the life of Man, the difficulty is not why they liv'd so long in the old World; that was their due and proper course; but why our Bodies being made after the same manner, should endure so short a time now. This is it therefore which we must now make our business to give an account of, namely, how that vissitude of Seasons, inconstancy of the Air, and unequal course of nature which came in at the Deluge, do shorten *Life*; and indeed hasten the dissolution of all Bodies, Animate or Inanimate.

In our Bodies we may consider three several qualities or dispositions, according to each whereof they suffer decay; First, their continuity; Secondly, that disposition whereby they are capable of receiving nourishment, which we may call Nutribility; and Thirdly, the Tone or Tonick disposition of the Organs whereby they perform their several functions. In all these three respects they would decay in any state of Nature, but far sooner and faster in the present state than in the Primæval. As for their Continuity, we have noted before that all consistent Bodies must be less durable now, than under that first order of the World, because of the unequal and contrary motions of the Elements, or of the Air and Æther that penetrate and pervade them; and 'tis part of that vanity which all things now are subject to, to be more perishable than in their first Constitution. If we should consider our Bodies only as breathing Statues, consisting of those parts they do, and of that tenderness, the Air which we breath, and wherewith we are continually incompast, changing so often 'twixt moist and dry, hot and cold, a slow and eager motion, these different actions and restless changes would sooner weaken and destroy the union of the parts, than if they were always in a calm and quiet *medium*.

But it is not the gross and visible Continuity of the parts of our Body that first decays, there are finer Textures that are spoil'd insensibly, and draw on the decay of the rest; such are those other two we mention'd, That disposition and temper of the parts whereby they are fit to receive their full nourishment; and especially that construction and texture of the Organs that are preparatory to this Nutrition. The Nutribility of the Body depends upon a certain temperament in the parts, soft and yielding, which makes them open to the Bloud and Juices in their Circulation and passage through them, and mixing intimately, and universally, hold fast and retain many of their Particles; as muddy Earth doth of the Water that runs into it and mixeth with it: And when these Nutritious Particles retain'd are more than the Body spends, that Body is in its growth; as when they are fewer, 'tis in its decay. And as we compar'd the flesh and tender parts when they are young and in a growing disposition, to a muddy soil, that opens to the Water, swells and incorporates with it; so when they become hard and dry, they are like a sandy Earth, that suffers the Water to glide through it, without incorporating or retaining many of its parts; and the sooner they come to this temper, the sooner follows their decay: For the same Causes that set limits to our Growth, set also limits to our Life; and he that can resolve that Question, *why* the time of our *Growth* is so short, will also be able to resolve the other in a good measure, *why* the time of our *Life* is so short. In both cases, that which stops our progress is external Nature, whose course, while it was even and steddy, and the ambient Air mild and balmy, preserv'd the Body much longer in a fresh and fit temper to receive its full nourishment, and consequently gave larger bounds both to our growth and Life.

But the third thing we mention'd is the most considerable, The decay of the Organick parts; and especially of the Organs preparatory to Nutrition. This is the point chiefly to be examin'd and explain'd, and therefore we will endeavour to state it fully and distinctly. There are several functions in the Body of an

Animal, and several Organs for the conduct of them; and I am of opinion, that all the Organs of the Body are in the nature of Springs, and that their action is Tonical. The action of the Muscles is apparently so, and so is that of the Heart and the Stomach; and as for those parts that make secretions only, as the *Glandules* and *Parenchymata*, if they be any more than meerly passive, as Strainers, 'tis the Tone of the parts, when distended, that performs the separation: And accordingly in all other active Organs, the action proceeds from a Tone in the parts. And this seems to be easily prov'd, both as to our Bodies and all other Bodies, for no matter that is not fluid, hath any motion or action in it, but in vertue of some Tone; If matter be fluid, its parts are actually in motion, and consequently may impel or give motion to other Bodies; but if it be solid or consistent, the parts are not separate or separately mov'd from one another, and therefore cannot impel or give motion to any other, but in vertue of their Tone; they having no other motion themselves. Accordingly we see in Artificial Machines there are but two general sorts, those that move by some fluid or volatile matter, as Water, Wind, Air, or some active Spirit; And those which move by Springs, or by the Tonick disposition of some part that gives motion to the rest: For as for such Machines as act by weights, 'tis not the weight that is the active principle, but the Air or Æther that impels. it 'Tis true, the Body of an Animal is a kind of mixt Machine, and those Organs that are the Primary parts of it, partake of both these principles; for there are Spirits and Liquors that do assist in the motions of the Muscles, of the Heart and of the Stomach; but we have no occasion to consider them at present, but only the Tone of the solid Organs.

This being observ'd in the first place, *Wherein* the force of our Organs consists, we might here immediately subjoyn, how this force is weaken'd and destroy'd by the unequal course of Nature which now obtains, and consequently our Life shorten'd; for the whole state and Oeconomy of the Body depends upon the force and action of these Organs. But to understand the business more distinctly, it will be worth our time to examine, upon which of the Organs of the Body Life depends more immediately, and the prolongation of it; that so reducing our Inquiries into a narrower compass, we may manage them with more ease and more certainty.

In the Body of Man there are several Compages, or setts of parts, some whereof need not be consider'd in this question; There is that Systeme that serves for sence and local-motion, which is commonly call'd the ANIMAL Compages; and that which serves for generation, which is call'd the GENITAL. These have no influence upon long Life, being parts nourished, not nourishing, and that are fed from others as Rivers from their Fountain: Wherefore having laid these aside, there remain two Compages more, the NATURAL and VITAL, which consist of the Heart and Stomach, with their appendages. These are the Sources of Life, and all that is absolutely necessary to the constitution of a Living Creature; what parts we find more, few or many, of one sort or other, according to the several kinds of Creatures, is accidental to our purpose; The form of an Animal, as we are to consider it here, lies in this little compass, and what is superadded is for some new purposes, besides that of meer Life, as for Sense, Motion, Generation, and such like. As in a Watch, besides the Movement, which is made to tell you the hour of the day, which constitutes a Watch, you may have a fancy to have an Alarum added, or a Minute-motion, or that it should tell you the day of the month; and this sometimes will require a new Spring, sometimes only new Wheels; however if you would examine the Nature of a Watch, and upon what its motion, or, if I may so say, its Life depends, you must lay aside those secondary Movements, and observe the main Spring, and the Wheels that immediately depend upon that, for all the rest is accidental. So for the Life of an Animal, which is a piece of Nature's Clockwork, if we would examine upon what the duration of it depends, we must lay aside those additional parts or Systems of parts, which are for other purposes, and consider only the first principles and fountains of Life, and the causes of their natural and necessary decay.

Having thus reduc'd our Inquiries to these two Organs, The Stomach and the Heart, as the two Master-Springs in the Mechanism of an Animal, upon which all the rest depend, let us now see what their action is, and how it will be more or less durable and constant, according to the different states of external Nature. We determin'd before, that the force and action of all Organs in the Body was Tonical, and of none more remarkable than of these two, the Heart and Stomach; for though it be not clearly determin'd what the particular structure of these Organs, or of their Fibres is, that makes them Tonical, yet 'tis manifest by their actions that they are so. In the Stomach, besides a peculiar ferment that opens and dissolves the parts of the Meat, and melts them into a fluor or pulp, the coats of it, or Fibres whereof they consist, have a motion proper to them, proceeding from their Tone, whereby they close the Stomach, and compress the Meat when it is receiv'd, and when turn'd into Chyle, press it forwards, and squeese it into the Intestines; And the Intestines also partaking of the same motion, push and work it still forwards into those little Veins that convey it towards the Heart. The Heart hath the same general motions with the Stomach, of opening and shutting, and hath also a peculiar ferment which rarifies the Bloud that enters into it; and that bloud by the Spring of the Heart, and the particular Texture of its Fibres, is thrown out again to make its Circulation through the Body. This is, in short, the action of both these Organs; and indeed the mystery of the Body of an Animal, and of its operations and Oeconomy, consists chiefly in Springs and Ferments; The one for the solid parts, the other in the fluid.

But to apply this Fabrick of the Organick parts to our purpose, we may observe and conclude, that whatsoever weakens the Tone or Spring of these two Organs, which are the Bases of all Vitality, weaken the principle of Life, and shorten the Natural duration of it; And if of two Orders or Courses of Nature, the one be favourable and easie to these Tonick principles in the Body, and the other uneasie and prejudicial, that course of Nature will be attended with long periods of Life, and this with short. And we have shewn, that in the Primitive Earth the course of Nature was even, steddy and unchangeable, without either different qualities of the Air, or unequal Seasons of the Year, which must needs be more easie to these principles we speak of, and permit them to continue longer in their strength and vigour, than they can possibly do under all those changes of the Air, of the

Atmosphere, and of the Heavens, which we now suffer yearly, monthly, and daily. And though Sacred History had not acquainted us with the Longævity of the Ante-diluvian Patriarchs, nor profane History with those of the Golden Age, I should have concluded, from the Theory alone, and the contemplation of that state of Nature, that the forms of all things were much more permanent in that World than in ours, and that the lives of Men and all other Animals had longer periods.

I confess, I am of opinion, that 'tis this that makes, not only these living Springs or Tonick Organs of the Body, but all Artificial Springs also, though made of the hardest Metal, decay so fast. The different pressure of the Atmosphere, sometimes heavier, sometimes lighter, more rare or more dense, moist or dry, and agitated with different degrees of motion, and in different manners; this must needs operate upon that nicer contexture of Bodies, which makes them Tonical or Elastick; altering the figure or minuteness of the pores, and the strength and order of the Fibres upon which that propriety depends: bending and unbending, closing and opening the parts. There is a subtle and Æthereal Element that traverseth the pores of all Bodies, and when 'tis straiten'd and pent up there, or stopt in its usual course and passage, its motion is more quick and eager, as a Current of Water, when 'tis obstructed or runs through a narrower Chanel; and that strife and those attempts which these little active Particles make to get free, and follow the same tracts they did before, do still press upon the parts of the Body that are chang'd, to redress and reduce them to their first and Natural posture, and in this consists the force of a Spring. Accordingly we may observe, that there is no Body that is Tonical or Elastick, if it be left to it self, and to that posture it would take naturally; for then all the parts are at ease, and the subtle matter moves freely and uninterruptedly within its pores; but if by distention, or by compression, or by flexion, or any other way, the situation of the parts and pores be so alter'd, that the Air sometimes, but for the most part that subtiler Element, is uneasie and comprest too much, if causeth that renitency or tendency to restitution, which we call the Tone or Spring of a Body. Now as this disposition of Bodies doth far more easily perish than their Continuity, so I think there is nothing that contributes more to its perishing (whether in Natural or Artificial Springs) than the unequal action and different qualities of the Æther, Air, and Atmosphere.

It will be objected to us, it may be, that in the beginning of the Chapter we instanc'd in Artificial things, that would continue for ever, if they had but the power of nourishing themselves, as Lamps, Mills, and such like; why then may not Natural Machines that have that power, last for ever? The case is not the same as to the Bodies of Animals, and the things there instanc'd in, for those were springless Machines, that act only by some external cause, and not in vertue of any Tone or interiour temper of the parts, as our Bodies do; and when that Tone or temper is destroy'd, no nourishment can repair it. There is something, I say, irreparable in the Tonical disposition of matter, which, when lost, cannot be restor'd by Nutrition; Nutrition may answer to a bare consumption of parts, but where the parts are to be preserv'd in such a temperament, or in such a degree of humidity and driness, warmth, rarity or density, to make them capable of that nourishment, as well as of their other operations, as Organs; (which is the case of our Bodies) there the Heavens, the Air, and external Causes will change the qualities of the matter in spite of all Nutrition; and the qualities of the matter being chang'd (in a course of Nature, where the Cause cannot be taken away) that is a fault incorrigible, and irreparable by the nourishment that follows, being hinder'd of its effect by the indisposition or incapacity of the Recipient. And as they say, a fault in the first concoction cannot be corrected in the second; so neither can a fault in the Prerequisites to all the concoctions be corrected by any of them.

I know the Ancients made the decay and term of Life to depend rather upon the humours of the Body, than the solid parts, and suppos'd an *Humidum radicale* and a *Calidum innatum*, as they call them, a Radical moisture and Congenit heat to be in every Body from its birth and first formation; and as these decay'd, life decay'd. But who's wiser for this account, what doth this instruct us in? We know there is heat and moisture in the Body, and you may call the one *Radical*, and the other *Innate* if you please; this is but a sort of Cant, for we know no more of the real Physical Causes of that effect we enquir'd into, than we did before. What makes this heat and moisture fail, if the nourishment be good, and all the Organs in their due strength and temper? The first and original failure is not in the fluid, but in the solid parts, which if they continued the same, the humours would do so too. Besides, what befel this Radical moisture and heat at the Deluge, that it should decay so fast afterwards, and last so long before? There is a certain temper, no doubt, of the juices and humours of the Body, which is more fit than any other to conserve the parts from driness and decay; but the cause of that driness and decay, or other inability in the solid parts, whence is that, if not from external Nature? 'Tis thither we must come at length in our search of the reasons of the Natural decay of our Bodies, we follow the fate and Laws of that: and, I think, by those Causes, and in that order, that we have already describ'd and explain'd.

To conclude this Discourse, we may collect from it what judgment is to be made of those Projectors of Immortality, or undertakes to make Men live to the Age of *Methusalah*, if they will use their methods and medicines; There is but one method for this, To put the Sun into his old course, or the Earth into its first posture; there is no other secret to prolong life; Our Bodies will sympathize with the general course of Nature, nothing can guard us from it, no Elixir, no Specifick, no Philosophers-stone. But there are Enthusiasts in Philosophy, as well as in Religion; men that go by no principles, but their own conceit and fancy, and by a Light within, which shines very uncertainly, and, for the most part, leads them out of the way of truth. And so much for this disquisition, concerning the *Causes* of *Longævity*, or of the long and short periods of Life in the different periods of the World.

That the Age of the Ante-diluvian Patriarchs is to be computed by Solar *or common Years, not by* Lunar *or Months.*

Having made this discourse of the unequal periods of life, only in reference to the Ante-diluvians and their fam'd Longævity, lest we should seem to have proceeded upon an ill-grounded and mistaken supposition, we are bound to take notice of, and confute, that opinion which makes the Years of the Ante-diluvian Patriarchs to have been *Lunar*, not *Solar*, and so would bear us in hand, that they liv'd only so many Months, as Scripture saith they liv'd Years. Seeing there is nothing could drive men to this bold interpretation, but the incredibility of the thing, as they fansied; They having no Notions or *Hypothesis* whereby it could appear intelligible or possible to them; and seeing we have taken away that stumbling-stone, and show'd it not only possible but necessary, according to the constitution of that World, that the periods of Life should be far longer than in this; by removing the ground or occasion of their misinterpretation, we hope we have undeceiv'd them, and let them see that there is no need of that subterfuge, either to prevent an incongruity, or save the credit of the Sacred Historian.

But as this opinion is inconsistent with Nature truly understood, so is it also with common History; for besides what I have already mention'd in the first Chapter of this Book, *Josephus* tells us, that the Historians of all Nations, both *Greeks* and *Barbarians*, give the same account of the first Inhabitants of the Earth; Manetho, *who writ the story of the* Ægyptians, Berosus, *who writ the* Chaldæan *History, and those Authors that have given us an account of the* Phœnician *Antiquities; besides* Molus *and* Hestiæus, *and* Hieronymus *the* Ægyptian; *and amongst the Greeks* Hesiodus, Hecateus, Hellanicus, Acusilaus, Ephorus *and* Nicolaus. *We have the Suffrages of all these, and their common consent, that in the first Ages of the World Men liv'd a thousand Years.* Now we cannot well suppose, that all these Historians meant *Lunar* Years, or that they all conspir'd together to make and propagate a Fable.

Lib. 1. *Jew. Ant. Chap.* 4.

Lastly, as Nature and Profane History do disown and confute this opinion, so much more doth Sacred History; not indeed in profess'd terms, for *Moses* doth not say that he useth *Solar* Years, but by several marks and observations, or collateral Arguments, it may be clearly collected, that he doth not use *Lunar*. As first, because He distinguisheth *Months* and *Years* in the History of the Deluge, and of the life of *Noah*; for *Gen.* 7. 11 he saith in the six hundredth year of *Noah*'s life, in the second month, *&c.* It cannot be imagin'd that in the same verse and sentence these two terms of *Year* and *Month* should be so confounded as to signifie the same thing; and therefore *Noah*'s Years were not the same with Months, nor consequently those of the other Patriarchs, for we have no reason to make any difference. Besides, what ground was there, or how was it proper or pertinent to reckon, as *Moses* does there, first, second, third Month, as so many going to a Year, if every one of them was a Year? And seeing the Deluge begun in the six hundredth year of *Noah*'s life, and in the second Month, and ended in the six hundredth and first Year (*Chap.* 8. 13) the first or second Month, all that was betwixt these two terms, or all the duration of the Deluge, made but one year in *Noah*'s life, or it may be not so much; and we know *Moses* reckons a great many months in the duration of the Deluge; so as this is a demonstration that *Noah*'s years are not to be understood of *Lunar*. And to imagine that his years are to be understood one way, and those of his fellow-Patriarchs another, would be an inaccountable fiction. This Argument therefore extends to all the Ante-diluvians; And *Noah*'s life will take in the Post-diluvians too, for you see part of it runs amongst them, and ties together the two Worlds; so that if we exclude *Lunar* years from his life, we exclude them from all, those of his Fathers, and those of his Children.

Secondly, If *Lunar* years were understood in the Ages of the Ante-diluvian Patriarchs, the interval betwixt the Creation and the Deluge would be too short, and in many respects incongruous. There would be but 1656 months from the beginning of the World to the Flood; which converted into common years, make but 127 years, and five months, for that interval. This perverts all Chronology, and besides, makes the number of people so small and inconsiderable at the time of the Deluge, that destroying of the World was not so much as destroying of a Country Town would be now: For from one couple you cannot well imagine there could arise above five hundred persons in so short a time; but if there was a thousand, 'tis not so many as we have sometimes in a good Country Village. And were the Flood-gates of Heaven open'd, and the great Abysse broken up to destroy such an handful of people? and the Waters rais'd fifteen Cubits above the highest Mountains throughout the face of the Earth, to drown a Parish or two? is not this more incredible than our Age of the Patriarchs? Besides, this short interval doth not leave room for Ten generations, which we find from *Adam* to the Flood, nor allows the Patriarchs age enough at the time when they are said to have got Children. One hundred twenty seven years for Ten genera-tions is very strait; and of these you must take off forty six years for one Generation only, or for *Noah*, for he liv'd six hundred years before the Flood, and if they were *Lunar*, they would come however to forty six of our years; so that for the other nine Generations you would have but eighty one years, that is, nine years a-piece; at which Age they must all be suppos'd to have begun to get Children; which you cannot but think a very absurd supposition. Thus it would be, if you divide the whole time equally amongst the nine Generations, but if you consider some single instances, as they are set down by *Moses*, 'tis still worse; for *Mahaleel* and his Grandchild *Enoch* are said to have got Children at sixty five years of Age, which if you suppose months, they were but five years old at that time; now I appeal to any one, Whether it is more incredible that men should live to the age of nine hundred years, or that they should beget Children at the age of five years.

You will say, it may be, 'tis true these inconveniences follow, if our *Hebrew* Copies of the Old Testament be Authentick; but if the *Greek* Translation by the *Septuagint* be of better Authority, as some would have it to be, that gives a little relief in this case; for the *Septuagint* make the distance from the Creation to the Flood six hundred years more than the *Hebrew* Text does, and so give us a little more room for our Ten Generations: And not only so, but they have so con-veniently dispos'd those additional years, as to salve the other inconvenience too, of the Patriarchs having Children so young: for what Patriarchs are found to have got Children sooner than the rest, and so soon, that upon a computation by *Lunar* years, they would be but meer Children themselves at that time, to these, more years are added and plac'd opportunely, before the time of their getting Children; so as one can scarce forbear to think that it was done on purpose to cure that inconvenience, and to favour and protect the computation by *Lunar* years. The thing looks so like an artifice, and as done to serve a turn, that one cannot but have a less opinion of that Chronology for it.

But not to enter upon that dispute at present, methinks they have not wrought the cure effectually enough; for with these six hundred *Lunar* years added, the summ will be only one hundred seventy three common years and odd months; and from these deducting, as we did before, for *Noah*, forty six years, and for *Adam*, or the first Generation, about eighteen, (for he was two hundred and thirty years old, according to the *Septuagint*, when he begot *Seth*) there will remain but one hundred and nine years for eight Generations; which will be thirteen years a-piece and odd months; a low age to get Children in, and to hold for eight Generations together. Neither is the other inconvenience we mention'd, well cur'd by the *Septuagint* account, namely, the small number of people that would be in the World at the Deluge; for the *Septuagint* account, if understood of *Lunar* years, adds but forty six common years to the *Hebrew* account, and to the age of the World at the Deluge, in which time there could be but a very small accession to the number of Mankind. So as both these incongruities continue, though not in the same degree, and stand good in either account, if it be understood of *Lunar* years.

Thirdly, 'tis manifest from other Texts of Scripture, and from other considerations, that our first Fathers liv'd very long, and considerably longer than men have done since; whereas if their years be interpreted *Lunar*, there is not one of them that liv'd to the age that men do now; *Methusalah* himself did not reach threescore and fifteen years, upon that interpretation: Which doth depress them not only below those that liv'd next to the Flood, but below all following Generations to this day; and those first Ages of the World, which were always celebrated for strength and vivacity, are made as weak and feeble as the last dregs of Nature. We may observe, that after the Flood for some time, till the pristine *Crasis* of the Body was broken by the new course of Nature, they liv'd five, four, three, two hundred years, and the Life of Men shortn'd by degrees; but before the Flood, when the liv'd longer, there was no such decrease or gradual declension in their lives. For *Noah*, who was the last, liv'd longer than *Adam*; and *Methusalah* who was last but two, liv'd the longest of all: So that it was not simply their distance from the beginning of the World that made them live a shorter time, but some change which happen'd in Nature after such a period of time; namely, at the Deluge, when the declension begun. Let's set down the Table of both states.

A Table of the Ages of the Ante-diluvian Fathers.		*A Table of the Ages of the Post-diluvian Fathers, from* Shem *to* Joseph	
	Years.		Years.
Adam	930	Shem	600
Seth	912	Arphaxad	438
Enos	905	Salah	433
Cainan	910	Eber	464
Mahaleel	895	Peleg	239
Jared	962	Reu	239
Enoch	365	Serug	230
Methusalah	969	Nahor	148
Lamech	777	Terah	205
Noah	950	Abraham	175
		Isaac	180
		Jacob	147
		Joseph	110

From these Tables we see that Mens Lives were much longer before the Flood, and next after it, than they are now; which also is confirm'd undiniably by *Jacob*'s complaint of the shortness of his life, in comparison of his Fore-fathers, when he had liv'd one hundred and thirty years, *Gen. 47. 9. The days of the years of my pilgrimage are an hundred and thirty years; few and evil have the days of the years of my life been, and have not attained unto the days of the years of the life of my Fathers.* There was then, 'tis certain, long-liv'd men in the World before *Jacob*'s time; when were they, before the Flood or after? We say both, according as the Tables shew it: But if you count by *Lunar* years, there never were any, either before or after, and *Jacob*'s complaint was unjust and false; for he was the oldest Man in the World himself, or at least there was none of his Fore-fathers that liv'd so long as he.

The Patrons of this opinion must needs find themselves at a loss, how or where to break off the account of *Lunar* years in Sacred History, if they once admit it. If they say, that way of counting must only be extended to the Flood, then they make the Post-diluvian Fathers longer liv'd than the Ante-diluvian; did the Flood bring in Longævity? how could that be the cause of such an effect? Besides, if they allow the Post-diluvians to have liv'd six hundred (common) years, that being clearly beyond the standard of our lives, I should never stick at two or three hundred years more for the first Ages of the World. If they extend their *Lunar* account to the Post-diluvians too, they will still be intangled in worse absurdities; for they must make their lives miserably short, and their Age of getting Children altogether incongruous and impossible. *Nahor*, for example, when he was but two years and three months old must have begot *Terah, Abraham*'s Father: And all the rest betwixt him and *Shem* must have had Children before they were three years old: A pretty race of Pigmies. Then their lives were pro-portionably short, for this *Nahor* liv'd but eleven years and six months at this rate; and his Grandchild *Abraham*, who is said to have died *in a good old age, and full of years,* (*Gen.* 25. 8) was not fourteen years old. What a ridiculous account this gives of Scripture-Chronology and Genealogies? But you'll say, it may be, these *Lunar* years are not to be carried so far as *Abraham* neither; tell us then where you'll stop, and why you stop in such a place rather than another. If you once take in *Lunar* years, what ground is there in the Text, or in the History, that you should change your way of computing, at such a time, or in such a place? All our Ancient Chronology is founded upon the Books of *Moses*, where the terms and periods of time are exprest by years, and often by Genealogies, and the Lives of Men; now if these years are sometimes to be interpreted *Lunar*, and sometimes *Solar*, without any distinction made in the Text, what light or certain rule have we to go by? let these Authors name to us the parts and places where, and only where, the *Lunar* years are to be understood, and I dare undertake to show, that their method is not only arbitrary, but absurd and incoherent.

To conclude this Discourse, we cannot but repeat what we have partly observ'd before, How necessary it is to understand Nature, if we would rightly understand those things in holy Writ that relate to the Natural World. For without this knowledge, as we are apt to think some things consistent and credible that are really impossible in Nature; so on the other hand, we are apt to look upon other things as incredible and impossible that are really founded in Nature. And seeing every one is willing so to expound Scripture, as it may be to them good sence, and consistent with their Notions in other things, they are forc'd many times to go against the easie and natural importance of the words, and to invent other interpretations more compliant with their principles, and, as they think, with the nature of things. We have, I say, a great instance of this before us in the Scripture-History of the long lives of the Ante-diluvians, where without any ground or shadow of ground in the Narration, only to comply with a mistaken Philosophy, and their ignorance of the Primitive World, many men would beat down the Scripture account of years into months, and sink the lives of those first Fathers below the rate of the worst of Ages. Whereby that great Monument, which Providence hath left us of the first World, and of its difference from the Second, would not only be defac'd, but wholly demolisht. And all this sprung only from the seeming incredibility of the thing; for they cannot show in any part of Scripture, New or Old, that these *Lunar* years are made use of, or that any computation, literal or Prophetical, proceeds upon them: Nor that there is any thing in the Text or Context of that place, that argues or intimates any such account. We have endeavour'd, upon this occasion, effectually to prevent this misconstruction of Sacred History, for the future; both by showing the incongruities that follow upon it, and also that there is no necessity from Nature of any such shift or evasion, as that is: But rather on the contrary, that we have just and necessary reasons to conclude, That as the Forms of all things would be far more permanent and lasting in that Primitive state of the Heavens and the Earth; so particularly the Lives of Men, and of other Animals.

CHAPTER V

Concerning the Waters of the Primitive Earth: What the state of the Regions of the Air was then, and how all Waters proceeded from them; how the Rivers arose, what was their course, and how they ended. Several things in Sacred Writ that confirm this Hydrography of the first Earth; especially the Origin of the Rainbow.

HAVING thus far clear'd our way to *Paradise*, and given a rational account of its general properties; before we proceed to discourse of the place of it, there is one affair of moment, concerning this Primitive Earth, that must first be stated and explain'd; and that is, *How* it was water'd; from what causes, and in what manner. How could Fountains rise, or Rivers flow in an Earth of that Form and Nature? We have shut up the Sea with thick walls on every side, and taken away all communication that could be 'twixt it and the external Earth; and we have remov'd all the Hills and the Mountains where the Springs use to rise, and whence the Rivers descend to water the face of the ground: And lastly, we have left no issue for these Rivers, no Ocean to receive them, nor any other place to disburden themselves into: So that our New-found World is like to be a dry and barren Wilderness, and so far from being *Paradisiacal*, that it would scarce be habitable.

I confess there was nothing in this whole Theory that gave so rude a stop to my thoughts, as this part of it, concerning the Rivers of the first Earth; how they rise, how they flow'd, and how they ended. It seem'd at first, that we had wip'd away at once the Notion and whole Doctrine of Rivers; we had turn'd the Earth so smooth, that there was not an Hill or rising for the head of a Spring, nor any fall or descent for the course of a River: Besides, I had suckt in the common opinion of Philosophers, That all Rivers rise from the Sea, and return to it again; and both those passages, I see, were stopt up in that Earth. This gave me occasion to reflect upon the modern, and more solid opinion, concerning the Origin of Fountains and Rivers, That they rise chiefly from Rains and melted Snows, and not from the Sea alone; and as soon as I had undeceiv'd my self in that particular, I see it was necessary to consider, and examine, how the Rains fell in that first Earth, to understand what the state of their Waters and Rivers would be.

And I had no sooner appli'd my self to that Inquiry, but I easily discover'd, that the Order of Nature in the Regions of the Air, would be then very different from what it is now, and the Meteorology of that World was of another sort from that of the present. The Air was always calm and equal, there could be no violent Meteors there, nor any that proceeded from extremity of Cold; as Ice, Snow or Hail; nor Thunder neither; for the Clouds could not be of a quality and consistency fit for such an effect, either by falling one upon another, or by their disruption. And as for Winds, they could not be either impetuous or irregular in that Earth; seeing there were neither Mountains nor any other inequalities to obstruct the course of the Vapours; nor any unequal Seasons, or unequal action of the Sun, nor any contrary and struling motions of the Air: Nature was then a stranger to all those disorders. But as for watery Meteors, or those that rise from watery Vapours more immediately, as Dews and Rains, there could not but be plenty of these, in some part or other of that Earth; for the action of the Sun in raising Vapours, was very strong and very constant, and the Earth was at first moist and soft, and according as it grew more dry, the Rays of the Sun would pierce more deep into it, and reach at length the great Abysse which lay underneath, and was an unexhausted storehouse of new Vapours. But, 'tis true, the same heat which extracted these Vapours so copiously, would also hinder them from condensing into Clouds or Rain, in the warmer parts of the Earth; and there being no Mountains at that time, nor contrary Winds, nor any such causes to stop them or compress them, we must consider which way they would tend, and what their course would be, and whether they would any where meet with causes capable to change or condense them; for upon this, 'tis manifest, would depend the Meteors of that Air, and the Waters of that Earth.

And as the heat of the Sun was chiefly towards the middle parts of the Earth, so the copious Vapours rais'd there were most rarified and agitated; and being once in the open Air, their course would be that way, where they found least resistance to their motion; and that would certainly be towards the Poles, and the colder Regions of the Earth. For East and West they would meet with as warm an Air, and Vapours as much agitated as themselves, which therefore would not yield to their progress that way; but towards the North and the South, they would find a more easie passage, the Cold of those parts attracting them, as we call it, that is, making way to their motion and dilatation without much resistance, as Mountains and Cold places usually draw Vapours from the warmer. So as the regular and constant course of the Vapours of that Earth, which were rais'd chiefly about the Æquinoctial and middle parts of it, would be towards the extream parts of it, or towards the Poles.

And in consequence of this, when these Vapours were arriv'd in those cooler Climats, and cooler parts of the Air, they would be condens'd into Rain; for wanting there the cause of their agitation, namely the heat of the Sun, their motion would soon begin to languish, and they would fall closer to one another in the form of Water. For the difference betwixt Vapours and Water is only gradual, and consists in this, that Vapours are in a flying motion, separate and distant each from another; but the parts of Water are in a creeping motion, close to one another, like a swarm of Bees, when they are setled; as Vapours resemble the same Bees in the Air before they settle together. Now there is nothing puts these Vapours upon the wing, or keeps them so, but a strong agitation by Heat; and when that fails, as it must do in all colder places and Regions, they necessarily return to Water again. Accordingly therefore we must suppose they would soon, after they reacht these cold Regions, be condens'd, and fall down in a continual Rain or Dew upon those parts of the Earth. I say a *continual* Rain; for seeing the action of the Sun, which rais'd the Vapours, was (at that time) always the same, and the state of the Air always alike, nor any cross Winds, nor any thing else that could hinder the course of the Vapours towards the Poles, nor their condensation when arriv'd there; 'tis manifest there would be a constant Source or store-house of Waters in those parts of the Air, and in those parts of the Earth.

And this, I think, was the establisht order of Nature in that World, this was the state of the Ante-diluvian Heavens and Earth; all their Waters came from above, and that with a constant supply and circulation; for when the croud of Vapours, rais'd about the middle parts of the Earth, found vent and issue this way towards the Poles, the passage being once open'd, and the Chanel made, the Current would be still continued without intermission; and as they were dissolv'd and spent there, they would suck in more and more of those which followed, and came in fresh streams from the hotter Climates. *Aristotle*, I remember, in his *Meteors*, speaking of the course of the Vapours, saith, there is a River in the Air, constantly flowing betwixt the Heavens and the Earth, made by the ascending and descending Vapours; This was more remarkably true in the Primitive Earth, where the state of Nature was more constant and regular; there was indeed an uninterrupted flood of Vapours rising in one Region of the Earth, and flowing to another, and there continually distilling in Dews and Rain, which made this Aereal River. As may be easily apprehended from this Scheme of the Earth and Air.

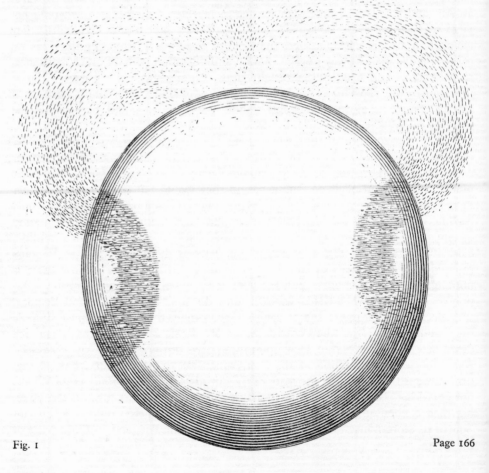

Fig. 1   Page 166

Thus we have found a Source for Waters in the first Earth, which had no communication with the Sea; and a Source that would never fail, neither diminish or overflow, but feed the Earth with an equal supply throughout all the parts of the year. But there is a second difficulty that appears at the end of this, *How* these Waters would flow upon the even surface of the Earth, or form themselves into Rivers; there being no descent or declivity for their course. There were no Hills, nor Mountains, nor high Lands in the first Earth, and if these Rains fell in the Frigid Zones, or towards the Poles, there they would stand, in Lakes and Pools, having no descent one way more than another; and so the rest of the Earth would be no better for them. This, I confess, appear'd as great a difficulty as the former, and would be unanswerable, for ought I know, if that first Earth had been exactly Spherical; but we noted before, that it was Oval or Oblong; and in such a Figure, 'tis manifest, the Polar parts are higher than the Æquin-octial, that is, more remote from the Center, as appears to the eye in this Scheme. This affords us a present remedy, and sets us free of the second difficulty; for by this means the Waters which fell about the extream parts of the Earth, would have a continual descent towards the middle parts of it; this Figure gives them motion and distribution; and many Rivers and Rivulets would flow from those Mother-Lakes to refresh the face of the Earth, bending their course still towards the middle parts of it.

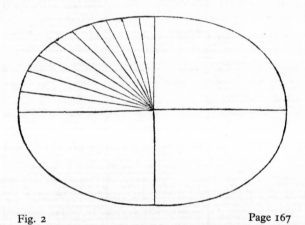

Fig. 2   Page 167

'Tis true, these derivations of the Waters at first would be very irregular and diffuse, till the Chanels were a little worn and hollowed; and though that Earth was smooth and uniform, yet 'tis impossible upon an inclining surface, but that Waters should find a way of creeping downwards, as we see upon a smooth Table, or a flagg'd Pavement, if there be the least inclination, Water will flow from the higher to the lower parts of it, either directly, or winding to and fro: So the smoothness of that Earth would be no hinderance to the course of the Rivers, provided there was a general declivity in the site and libration of it, as 'tis plain there was from the Poles towards the Æquator. The Current indeed would be easie and gentle all along, and if it chanc'd in some places to rest or be stopt, it would spread it self into a pleasant Lake, till by fresh supplies it had rais'd its Waters so high, as to overflow and break loose again; then it would pursue its way, with many other Rivers its companions, through all the temperate Climates, as far as the Torrid Zone.

But you'll say, when they were got thither, what would become of them then? *How* would they end or finish their course? This is the third difficulty, *concerning* the ending of the Rivers in that Earth; what issue could they have when they were come to the middle parts of it, whither, it seems, they all tended. There was no Sea to lose themselves in, as our Rivers do; nor any Subterraneous passages to throw themselves into; how would they die, what would be their fate at last? I answer, The greater Rivers, when they were come towards those parts of the Earth, would be divided into many branches, or a multitude of Rivulets; and those would be partly exhal'd by the heat of the Sun, and partly drunk up by the dry and sandy Earth. But how and in what manner this came to pass, requires a little further Explication.

We must therefore observe in the first place, that those Rivers as they drew nearer to the Æquinoctial parts, would find a less declivity or descent of ground than in the beginning or former part of their course; that is evident from the Oval Figure of the Earth, for near the middle parts of an Oval, the Semidiameters, as I may call them, are very little shorter one than another; and for this reason the Rivers, when they were advanc'd towards the middle parts of the Earth, would begin to flow more slowly, and by that weakness of their Current, suffer themselves easily to be divided and distracted into several lesser streams and Rivulets; or else, having no force to wear a Chanel, would lie shallow upon the ground like a plash of Water; and in both cases their Waters would be much more expos'd to the action of the Sun, than if they had kept together in a deeper Chanel, as they were before.

Secondly, we must observe, that seeing these Waters could not reach to the middle of the Torrid Zone, for want of descent; that part of the Earth having the Sun always perpendicular over it, and being refresht by no Rivers, would become extreamly dry and parch'd, and be converted at length into a kind of sandy Desart; so as all the Waters that were carried thus far, and were not exhal'd and consum'd by the Sun, would be suckt up, as in a Spunge, by these Sands of the Torrid Zone. This was the common Grave wherein the Rivers of the first Earth were buried; and this is nothing but what happens still in several parts of the present Earth, especially in *Africk*, where many Rivers never flow into the Sea, but expire after the same manner as these did, drunk up by the Sun and the Sands. And one arm of *Euphrates* dies, as I remember, amongst the Sands of *Arabia*, after the manner of the Rivers of the first Earth.

Thus we have conquer'd the greatest difficulty, in my apprehension, in this whole Theory, *To* find out the state of the Rivers in the Primitive and Antediluvian Earth, their Origin, course, and period. We have been forc'd to win our ground by Inches, and have divided the difficulty into parts, that we might encounter them single with more ease. The Rivers of that Earth, you see, were in most respects different, and in some contrary to ours; and if you could turn

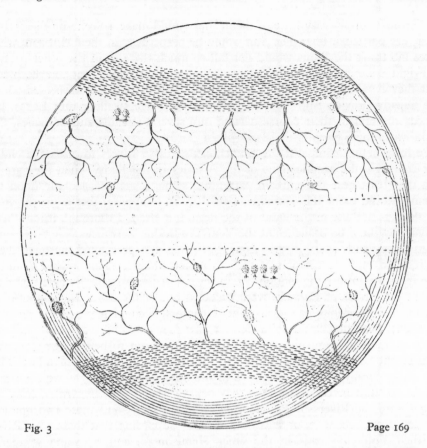

Fig. 3   Page 169

our Rivers backwards, to run from the Sea towards their Fountain-heads, they would more resemble the course of those Ante-diluvian Rivers; for they were greatest at their first setting out, and the Current afterwards, when it was more weak, and the Chanel more shallow, was divided into many branches, and little Rivers; like the Arteries in our Body, that carry the Bloud, they are greatest at first, and the further they go from the Heart, their Source, the less they grow and divide into a multitude of little branches, which lose themselves insensibly in the habit of the flesh, as these little Floods did in the Sands of the Earth.

Because it pleaseth more, and makes a greater impression upon us, to see things represented to the Eye, than to read their description in words, we have ventur'd to give a model of the Primæval Earth, with its Zones or greater Climates, and the general order and tracts of its Rivers: Not that we believe things to have been in the very same form as here exhibited, but this may serve as a general *Idea* of that Earth, which may be wrought into more exactness, according as we are able to enlarge or correct our thoughts hereafter. And as the Zones here represented resemble the *Belts* or *Fasciæ* of *Jupiter,* so we suppose them to proceed from like causes, that Planet being, according to our judgment, in an Ante-diluvian state, as the Earth we here represent. As for the Polar parts in that

169

our Earth, I can say very little of them, they would make a Scene by themselves, and a very particular one; The Sun would be perpetually in their Horizon, which makes me think the Rains would not fall so much there as in the other parts of the Frigid Zones, where accordingly we have made their chief seat and receptacle. That they flow'd from thence in such a like manner as is here represented, we have already prov'd; And sometimes in their passage swelling into Lakes, and towards the end of their course parting into several streams and branches, they would water those parts of the Earth like a Garden.

We have before compar'd the branchings of these Rivers towards the end of their course to the ramifications of the Arteries in the Body, when they are far from the Heart near the extream parts; and some, it may be, looking upon this Scheme, would carry the comparison further, and suppose, that as in the Body the Bloud is not lost in the habit of the flesh, but strain'd thorough it, and taken up again by the little branches of the Veins; so in that Earth the Waters were not lost in those Sands of the Torrid Zone, but strain'd or percolated thorough them, and receiv'd into the Chanels of the other Hemisphere. This indeed would in some measure answer the Notion which several of the Ancient Fathers make use of, that the Rivers of *Paradise* were trajected out of the other Hemisphere into this, by Subterraneous passages. But, I confess, I could never see it possible, how such a trajection could be made, nor how they could have any motion, being arriv'd in another Hemisphere; and therefore I am apt to believe, that doctrine amongst the Ancients arose from an intanglement in their principles; They suppos'd generally, that *Paradise* was in the other Hemisphere, as we shall have occasion to show hereafter; and yet they believ'd that *Tigris, Euphrates, Nile,* and *Ganges* were the Rivers of *Paradise,* or came out of it; and these two opinions they could not reconcile, or make out, but by supposing that these four Rivers had their Fountain-heads in the other Hemisphere, and by some wonderful trajection broke out again here. This was the expedient they found out to make their opinions consistent one with another; but this is a method to me altogether unconceivable; and, for my part, I do not love to be led out of my depth, leaning only upon Antiquity. How there could be any such communication, either above ground, or under ground, betwixt the two Hemispheres, does not appear, and therefore we must still suppose the Torrid Zone to have been the Barrier betwixt them, which nothing could pass either way.

We have now examin'd and determin'd the state of the Air, and of the Waters in the Primitive Earth, by the light and consequences of reason; and we must not wonder to find them different from the present order of Nature; what things are said of them, or relating to them in holy Writ, do testifie or imply as much; and it will be worth our time to make some reflection upon those passages for our further confirmation. *Moses* tells us, that the *Rainbow* was set in the Clouds after the Deluge; those Heavens then that never had a Rainbow before, were certainly of a constitution very different from ours. And St. *Peter* doth formally and expresly tell us, that the *Old Heavens,* or the Ante-diluvian Heavens had a different constitution from ours, and particularly, that they were compos'd or constituted of Water; which Philosophy of the Apostle's may be easily understood, if we attend to two things, first, that the Heavens he speaks of, were not the Starry Heavens, but the Aerial Heavens, or the Regions of our Air, where the Meteors are; Secondly, that there were no Meteors in those Regions, or in those Heavens, till the Deluge, but watery Meteors, and therefore, he says, they consisted of Water. And this shows the foundation upon which that description is made, how coherently the Apostle argues, and how justly he distinguisheth the first Heavens from the present Heavens, or rather opposeth them one to another; because as those were constituted of Water and watery Meteors only, so the present Heavens, he saith, have treasures of Fire, fiery Exhalations and Meteors, and a disposition to become the Executioners of the Divine wrath and decrees in the final Conflagration of the Earth.

This minds me also of the *Celestial Waters*, or the Waters above the Firmaments, which Scripture sometimes mentions, and which, methinks, cannot be explain'd so fitly and emphatically upon any supposition as this of ours. Those who place them above the Starry Heavens, seem neither to understand Astronomy nor Philosophy; and, on the other hand, if nothing be understood by them, but the Clouds and the middle Region of the Air, as it is at present, methinks that was no such eminent and remarkable thing, as to deserve a particular commemoration by *Moses* in his six days work; but if we understand them, not as they are now, but as they were then, the only Source of Waters, or the only Source of Waters upon that Earth, (for they had not one drop of Water but what was Celestial,) this gives it a new force and Emphasis: Besides, the whole middle Region having no other sort of Meteors but them, that made it still the greater singularity, and more worthy commemoration. As for the Rivers of *Paradise*, there is nothing said concerning their Source, or their issue, that is either contrary to this, or that is not agreeable to the general account we have given of the Waters and Rivers of the first Earth. They are not said to rise from any Mountain, but from a great River, or a kind of Lake in *Eden*, according to the custom of the Rivers of that Earth: And as for their end and issue, *Moses* doth not say, that they disburthen'd themselves into this or that Sea, as they usually do in the description of great Rivers, but rather implies, that they spent themselves in compassing and watering certain Countries, which falls in again very easily with our *Hypothesis*.

But to return to the Rainbow, which we mention'd before, and is not to be past over so slightly. This we say, is a Creature of the modern World, and was not seen nor known before the Flood. *Moses* (*Gen.* 9. 12, 13) plainly intimates as much, or rather directly affirms it; for he says, The Bow was set in the Clouds after the Deluge, as a confirmation of the promise or Covenant which God made with *Noah*, that he would drown the World no more with Water. And how could it be a sign of this, or given as a pledge and confirmation of such a promise, if it was in the Clouds before, and with no regard to this promise? and stood there, it may be, when the World was going to be drown'd. This would have been but cold comfort to *Noah*, to have had such a pledge of the Divine veracity. You'll say, it may be, that it was not a sign or pledge that signified naturally, but voluntarily only, and by Divine institution; I am of opinion, I confess, that it signifi'd naturally, and by connexion with the effect, importing thus much, that the state of Nature was chang'd from what it was before, and so chang'd, that the Earth was no more in a condition to perish by Water. But however, let us grant that it signified only by institution; to make it significant in this sence, it must be something new, otherwise it could not signifie any new thing, or be the confirmation of a new promise. If God Almighty had said to *Noah*, I make a promise to you, and to all living Creatures, that the World shall never be destroy'd by Water again, and for confirmation of this, Behold, *I set the Sun in the firmament:* Would this have been any strengthning of *Noah's* faith, or any satisfaction to his mind? Why, says *Noah*, the Sun was in the Firmament when the Deluge came, and was a spectator of that sad Tragedy; why may it not be so again? what sign or assurance is this against a second Deluge? When God gives a sign in the Heavens, or on the Earth, of any Prophecy or Promise to be fulfill'd, it must be by something new, or by some change wrought in Nature; whereby God doth testifie to us, that he is able and willing to stand to his promise.

Isa. 7. God says to *Ahaz, Ask a sign of the Lord; Ask it either in the depth, or in the height above:* And when *Ahaz* would ask no sign, God gives one unaskt, *Behold, a Virgin shall conceive and bear a Son.* So when *Zachary* was promis'd a Son, he

Luke 1. asketh for a sign, *Whereby shall I know this? for I am old, and my Wife well stricken in years;* and the sign given him was, that he became dumb, and continued so till the promise was fulfill'd. So in other instances of signs given in external

Isa. 38.
Judg. 7. Nature, as the sign given to King *Hezekiah* for his recovery, and to *Gideon* for his victory; to confirm the promise made to *Hezekiah*, the shadow went back ten degrees in *Ahaz* Dial: And for *Gideon, his Fleece was wet, and all the ground about it dry;* and then to change the trial, *it was dry, and all the ground about it wet.* These were all signs very proper, significant, and satisfactory, having something surprising and extraordinary, yet these were signs by institution only; and to be such they must have something new and strange, as a mark of the hand of God, otherwise they can have no force or significancy. If every thing be as it was before, and the face of Nature, in all its parts, the very same, it cannot signifie any thing new, nor any new intention in the Author of Nature; and consequently, cannot be a sign or pledge, a token or assurance of the accomplishment of any new Covenant or promise made by him.

This, methinks, is plain to common Sense, and to every mans Reason; but because it is a thing of importance, to prove that there was no Rainbow before the Flood, and will confirm a considerable part of this Theory, by discovering what the state of the Air was in the Old World, give me leave to argue it a little further, and to remove some prejudices that may keep others from assenting to clear Reason. I know 'tis usually said, that signs, like words, signifie any thing by institution, or may be appli'd to any thing by the will of the Imposer; as hanging out a white Flag is calling for mercy, a Bush at the door, a sign of Wine to be sold, and such like. But these are instances nothing to our purpose, these are signs of something present, and that signifie only by use and repeated experience; we are speaking of signs of another nature, given in confirmation of a promise, or threatning, or prophecy, and given with design to cure our unbelief, or to excite and beget in us Faith in God, in the Prophet, or in the Promiser; such signs, I say, when they are wrought in external Nature, must be some new Appearance, and must thereby induce us to believe the effect, or more to believe it, than if there had been no sign, but only the affirmation of the Promiser; for otherwise the pretended sign is a meer Cypher and superfluity. But a thing that obtain'd before, and in the same manner (even when that came to pass, which we are now promis'd shall not come to pass again) signifies no more, than if there had been no sign at all: it can neither signifie another course in Nature, nor another purpose in God; and therefore is perfectly insignificant. Some instance in the Sacraments, Jewish or Christian, and make them signs in such a sence as the Rainbow is: But those are rather Symbolical representations or commemorations; and some of them, marks of distinction and consecration of our selves to God in such a Religion; They were also new, and very particular when first instituted; but all such instances fall short and do not reach the case before us; we are speaking of signs confirmatory of a promise, when there is something affirm'd *de futuro,* and to give us a further argument of the certainty of it, and of the power and veracity of the Promiser, a sign is given: This we say, must indispensably be something new, otherwise it cannot have the nature, vertue, and influence of a sign.

We have seen how incongruous it would be to admit that the Rainbow appear'd before the Deluge, and how dead a sign that would make it, how forc'd, fruitless and ineffectual, as to the promise it was to confirm; Let us now on the other hand suppose, that it first appear'd to the Inhabitants of the Earth after the Deluge, How proper, and how apposite a sign would this be for Providence to pitch upon, to confirm the Promise made to *Noah* and his posterity, *That* the World should be no more destroy'd by Water? It had a secret connexion with the effect it self, and was so far a natural sign; but however appearing first after the Deluge, and in a watery Cloud, there was, methinks, a great easiness, and propriety of application for such a purpose. And if we suppose, that while God Almighty was declaring his promise to *Noah,* and the sign of it, there appear'd at the same time in the Clouds a fair Rainbow, that marvellous and beautiful Meteor, which *Noah* had never seen before; it could not but make a most lively impression upon him, quickning his Faith, and giving him comfort and assurance, that God would be stedfast to his promise.

Nor ought we to wonder, that Interpreters have commonly gone the other way, and suppos'd that the Rainbow was before the Flood; This, I say, was no wonder in them, for they had no *Hypothesis* that could answer to any other interpretation: And in the interpretation of the Texts of Scripture that concern natural things, they commonly bring them down to their own Philosophy and Notions: As we have a great instance in that discourse of St. *Peter*'s, concerning   2 *Epist. c.* 3. 5. the Deluge, and the Ante-diluvian Heavens, and Earth, which, for want of a Theory, they have been scarce able to make sence of; for they have forc'dly appli'd to the present Earth, or the present form of the Earth, what plainly respected another. A like instance we have in the *Mosaical* Abysse, or *Tehom-Rabba,* by whose disruption the Deluge was made; this they knew not well what to make of, and so have generally interpreted it of the Sea, or of our subterraneous Waters; without any propriety, either as to the word, or as to the sence. A third instance is this of the Rainbow, where their Philosophy hath misguided them again; for to give them their due, they do not alledge, nor pretend to alledge, any thing from the Text, that should make them interpret thus, or think the Rainbow was before the Flood; but they pretend to go by certain reasons, as that the Clouds were before the Flood, therefore the Rainbow; and if the Rainbow was not before the Flood, then all things were not made within the six days Creation: To whom these reasons are convictive, they must be led into the same belief with them, but not by any thing in the Text, nor in the true Theory, at least if Ours be so; for by that you see that the Vapours were never condens'd into drops, nor into Rain in the temperate and inhabited Climates of that Earth, and consequently there could never be the production or appearance of this Bow in the Clouds. Thus much concerning the Rainbow.

To recollect our selves, and conclude this Chapter, and the whole disquisition concerning the Waters of the Primitive Earth; we seem to have so well satisfied the difficulties propos'd in the beginning of the Chapter, that they have rather given us an advantage; a better discovery, and such a new prospect of that Earth, as makes it not only habitable, but more fit to be *Paradisiacal*. The pleasantness of the site of *Paradise* is made to consist chiefly in two things, its Waters, and its Trees, (*Gen.* 2 and *Chap.* 13. 10. *Ezek.* 31. 8) and considering the richness of that first soil in the Primitive Earth, it could not but abound in Trees, as it did in Rivers and Rivulets; and be wooded like a Grove, as it was water'd like a Garden, in the temperate Climates of it; so as it would not be, methinks, so difficult, to find one *Paradise* there, as not to find more than one.

CHAPTER VI

A Recollection and Review of what hath been said concerning the Primitive Earth; with a more full Survey of the State of the first World, Natural and Civil, and the comparison of it with the present World.

WE have now, in a good measure, finisht our description of the first and Ante-diluvian Earth; And as Travellers, when they see strange Countries, make it part of their pleasure and improvement, to compare them with their own, to observe the differences, and wherein they excel, or come short of one another: So it will not be unpleasant, nor unuseful, it may be, having made a discovery, not of a new Country, but of a new World, and travell'd it over in our thoughts and fancy, now to sit down and compare it with our own: And 'twill be no hard task, from the general differences which we have taken notice of already, to observe what lesser would arise, and what the whole face of Nature would be.

'Tis also one fruit of travelling, that by seeing variety of places and people, of humours, fashions, and forms of living, it frees us, by degrees, from that pedantry and littleness of Spirit, whereby we are apt to censure every thing for absurd and ridiculous, that is not according to our own way, and the mode of our own

Country; But if instead of crossing the Seas, we could waft our selves over to our neighbouring Planets, we should meet with such varieties there, both in Nature and Mankind, as would very much enlarge our thoughts and Souls, and help to cure those diseases of little minds, that make them troublesome to others, as well as uneasie to themselves.

But seeing our heavy Bodies are not made for such Voyages, the best and greatest thing we can do in this kind, is to make a Survey and reflection upon the Ante-diluvian Earth, which in some sence was another World from this, and it may be, as different as some two Planets are from one another. We have declar'd already the general grounds upon which we must proceed, and must now trace the consequences of them, and drive them down into particulars, which will show us in most things, wherein that Earth, or that World, differ'd from the present. The form of that Earth, and its situation to the Sun, were two of its most fundamental differences from ours; As to the form of it, 'twas all one smooth Continent, one continued surface of earth, without any Sea, any Mountains, or Rocks; any Holes, Dens or Caverns: And the situation of it to the Sun was such as made a perpetual Æquinox. These two joyn'd together, lay the foundation of a new Astronomy, Meteorology, Hydrography and Geography; such as were proper and peculiar to that World. The Earth by this means having its Axis parallel to the Axis of the Ecliptick, the Heavens would appear in another posture: And their diurnal motion, which is imputed to the *Primum Mobile*, and suppos'd to be upon the Poles of the Æquator, would then be upon the same Poles with the second and Periodical motions of the Orbs and Planets, namely, upon the Poles of the Ecliptick; by which means the *Phænomena* of the Heavens would be more simple and regular, and much of that intangledness and perplexity, which we find now in Astronomy, would be taken away. Whether the Sun and the Moon would suffer any Eclipses then, cannot well be determin'd, unless one knew what the course of the Moon was at that time, or whether she was then come into our neighbourhood: Her presence seems to have been less needful when there were no long Winter-nights, nor the great Pool of the Sea to move or govern.

As for the Regions of the Air and the Meteors, we have in the preceding Chapter set down what the state of them would be, and in how much a better order, and more peaceable, that Kingdom was, till the Earth was broken and displac'd, and the course of Nature chang'd: Nothing violent, nothing frightful, nothing troublesome or incommodious to Mankind, came from above, but the countenance of the Heavens was always smooth and serene. I have often thought it a very desirable piece of power, if a man could but command a fair day, when he had occasion for it, for himself, or for his friends; 'tis more than the greatest Prince or Potentate upon Earth can do; yet they never wanted one in that World, nor ever see a foul one. Besides, they had constant breezes from the motion of the Earth, and the course of the Vapours, which cool'd the open Plains, and made the weather temperate, as well as fair. But we have spoken enough in other places upon this subject of the Air and the Heavens, Let us now descend to the Earth.

The Earth was divided into two Hemispheres, separated by the Torrid Zone, which at that time was uninhabitable, and utterly unpassable; so as the two Hemispheres made two distinct Worlds, which, so far as we can judge, had no manner of commerce or communication one with another. The Southern Hemisphere the Ancients call'd *Antichthon, the Opposite Earth*, or the *Other World*. And this name and notion remain'd long after the reason of it had ceast. Just as the Torrid Zone was generally accounted uninhabitable by the Ancients, even in their time, because it really had been so once, and the Tradition remain'd uncorrected, when the causes were taken away; namely, when the Earth had chang'd its posture to the Sun after the Deluge.

This may be lookt upon as the first division of that Primæval Earth, into two Hemispheres, naturally sever'd and disunited: But it was also divided into five Zones, two Frigid, two Temperate, and the Torrid betwixt them. And this distinction of the Globe into five Zones, I think, did properly belong to that Original Earth, and Primitive Geography, and improperly, and by translation only, to the present. For all the Zones of our Earth are habitable, and their distinctions are in a manner but imaginary, not fixt by Nature; whereas in that Earth where the Rivers fail'd, and the Regions became uninhabitable, by reason of driness and heat, there begun the Torrid Zone; and where the Regions became uninhabitable, by reason of cold and moisture, there begun the Frigid Zone; and these being determin'd, they became bounds on either side to the Temperate. But all this was alter'd when the posture of the Earth was chang'd; and chang'd for that very purpose, as some of the Ancients have said, *That the uninhabitable parts of the Earth might become habitable*. Yet though there was so much of the first Earth uninhabitable, there remain'd as much to be inhabited as we have now; for the Sea, since the breaking up of the Abysse, hath taken away half of the Earth from us, a great part whereof was to them good Land. Besides, we are not to suppose, that the Torrid Zone was of that extent we make it now, twenty three degrees and more on either side of the Æquator; these bounds are set only by the Tropicks, and the Tropicks by the obliquity of the course of the Sun, or of the posture of the Earth, which was not in that World. Where the Rivers stopt, there the Torrid Zone would beign, but the Sun was directly perpendicular to no part of it, but the middle.

How the Rivers flow'd in the first Earth we have before explain'd sufficiently, and what parts the Rivers did not reach, were turn'd into Sands and Desarts by the heat of the Sun; for I cannot easily imagine, that the Sandy Desarts of the Earth were made so at first, immediately and from the beginning of the World; from what causes should that be, and to what purpose? But in those Tracts of the Earth that were not refresht with Rivers and moisture, which cement the parts, the ground would moulder and crumble into little pieces, and then those pieces by the heat of the Sun were bak'd into Stone. And this would come to pass chiefly in the hot and scorch'd Regions of the Earth, though it might happen sometimes where there was not that extremity of heat, if by any chance a place wanted Rivers and Water to keep the Earth in due temper; but those Sands would not be so early or ancient as the other. As for greater loose Stones, and rough Pebbles, there were none in that Earth; *Deucalion* and *Pyrrha*, when the Deluge was over, found new-made Stones to cast behind their backs; the bones of their mother Earth, which then were broken in pieces, in that great ruine.

As for Plants and Trees, we cannot imagine but that they must needs abound in the Primitive Earth, seeing it was so well water'd, and had a soil so fruitful; A new unlabour'd soil, replenisht with the Seeds of all Vegetables; and a warm Sun that would call upon Nature early for her First-fruits, to be offer'd up at the beginning of her course. Nature had a wild luxuriancy at first, which humane industry by degrees gave form and order to; The Waters flow'd with a constant and gentle Current, and were easily led which way the Inhabitants had a mind, for their use, or for their pleasure; and shady Trees, which grow best in moist and warm Countries, grac'd the Banks of their Rivers or Canals. But that which was the beauty and crown of all, was their perpetual Spring, the Fields always green, the Flowers always fresh, and the Trees always cover'd with Leaves and Fruit: But we have occasionally spoken of these things in several places, and may do again hereafter, and therefore need not inlarge upon them here.

As for Subterraneous things, Metals and Minerals, I believe they had none in the first Earth; and the happier they; no Gold, nor Silver, nor courser Metals. The use of these is either imaginary, or in such works, as, by the constitution of their World, they had little occasion for. And Minerals are either for Medicine, which they had no need of further than Herbs; or for Materials to certain Arts, which were not then in use, or were suppli'd by other ways. These Subterraneous things, Metals and metallick Minerals, are Factitious, not Original bodies, coeval with the Earth; but are made in process of time, after long preparations and concoctions, by the action of the Sun within the bowels of the Earth. And if the *Stamina* or principles of them rise from the lower Regions that lie under the Abysse, as I am apt to think they do, it doth not seem probable, that they could be drawn through such a mass of Waters, or that the heat of the Sun could on a sudden penetrate so deep, and be able to loosen them, and raise them into the exterior Earth. And as the first Age of the World was call'd *Golden*, though it knew not what Gold was; so the following Ages had their names from several Metals, which lay then asleep in the dark and deep womb of Nature, and see not the Sun till many Years and Ages afterwards.

Having run through the several Regions of Nature, from top to bottom, from the Heavens to the lower parts of the Earth, and made some observations upon their order in the Ante-diluvian World; Let us now look upon Man and other living Creatures, that make the Superiour and Animate part of Nature. We have observ'd, and sufficiently spoken to that difference betwixt the men of the old World, and those of the present, in point of Longævity, and given the reasons of it; but we must not imagine, that this long life was peculiar to Man, all other Animals had their share of it, and were in their proportion longer-liv'd than they are now. Nay, not only Animals, but also Vegetables, and the forms of all living things were far more permanent; The Trees of the Field and of the Forest, in all probability, out-lasted the lives of Men; and I do not know but the first Groves of Pines and Cedars that grew out of the Earth, or that were planted in the Garden *Ezek.* 31. 8.

M　　　　　　　　　　　　　　　　　　　　　　　　　　177

of God, might be standing when the Deluge came, and see, from first to last, the entire course and period of a World.

Civ. Dei lib. 15. *c.* 9. We might add here, with St. *Austin,* another observation, both concerning Men and other lving Creatures in the first World, that They were greater, as well as longer-liv'd, than they are at present. This seems to be a very reasonable conjecture, for the state of every thing that hath life, is divided into the time of its growth, its consistency, and its decay; and when the whole duration is longer, every one of these parts, though not always in like proportions, will be longer. We must suppose then, that the growth both in Men and other Animals lasted longer in that World than it doth now, and consequently carried their Bodies both to a greater height and bulk. And in like manner, their Trees would be both taller, and every way bigger than ours; neither were they in any danger there to be blown down by Winds and Storms, or struck with Thunder, though they had been as high as the *Ægyptian* Pyramids; and whatsoever their height was, if they had Roots and Trunks proportionable, and were streight and well pois'd, they would stand firm, and with a greater majesty. *The Fowls of Heaven making their Nests in their Boughs, and under their shadow the Beasts of the Field bringing forth their Young.* When things are fairly possible in their causes, and possible in several degrees, higher or lower, 'tis weakness of Spirit in us, to think there is nothing in Nature, but in that one way, or in that one degree, that we are us'd to. And whosoever believes those accounts given us, both by the Ancients* and Moderns,† of the *Indian* Trees, will not think it strange that those of the first Earth, should much exceed any that we now see in this World. That Allegorical description of the glory of *Assyria* in *Ezekiel* (*Chap.* 31) by allusion to Trees, and particularly to the Trees of *Paradise,* was chiefly for the greatness and stateliness of them; and there is all fairness of reason to believe, that in that first Earth, both the Birds of the Air, and the Beasts of the Field, and the Trees, and their Fruit, were all, in their several kinds, more large and goodly than Nature produces any now.

So much in short concerning the Natural World, Inanimate or Animate; We should now take a prospect of the Moral World of that time, or of the Civil and Artificial World; what the order and Oeconomy of these was, what the manner of living, and how the Scenes of humane life were different from ours at present. The Ancients, especially the Poets, in their description of the Golden Age, exhibit to us an Order of things, and a Form of life, very remote from any thing we see in our days; but they are not to be trusted in all particulars, many times they exaggerate matters on purpose, that they may seem more strange, or more great, and by that means move and please us more. A *Moral* or *Philosophick History* of the World well writ, would certainly be a very useful work, to observe and relate how the Scenes of Humane life have chang'd in several Ages, the Modes and Forms of living, in what simplicity Men begun at first, and by what degrees they came out of that way, by luxury, ambition, improvement, or changes in Nature; then what new forms and modifications were superadded by the invention of Arts, what by Religion, what by Superstition. This would be a view

* *Plin. li.* 7, *c.* 2. *Strab. l.* 17. † *Hort. Malabr. vol.* 3.

of things more instructive, and more satisfactory, than to know what Kings Reign'd in such an Age, and what Battles were fought; which common History teacheth, and teacheth little more. Such affairs are but the little underplots in the Tragi-comedy of the World; the main design is of another nature, and of far greater extent and consequence. But to return to the subject;

As the Animate World depends upon the Inanimate, so the Civil World depends upon them both, and takes its measures from them: Nature is the foundation still, and the affairs of Mankind are a superstructure that will be always proportion'd to it. There fore wemust look back upon the model or picture of their natural World, which we have drawn before, to make our conjectures or judgment of the Civil and Artificial that were to accompany it. We observ'd from their perpetual Æquinox, and the smoothness of the Earth, that the Air would be always calm, and the Heavens fair, no cold or violent Winds, Rains, or Storms, no extremity of weather in any kind, and therefore they would need little protection from the injuries of the Air in that state; whereas now one great part of the affairs of life, is to preserve our selves from those inconveniences, by building and cloathing. How many Hands, and how many Trades are imploy'd about these two things, which then were in a manner needless, or at least in such plainness and simplicity, that every man might be his own workman. Tents and Bowers would keep them from all incommodities of the Air and weather, better than Stone-walls, and strong Roofs defend us now; and men are apt to take the easiest ways of living, till necessity or vice put them upon others that are more laborious, and more artificial. We also observ'd and prov'd, that they had no Sea in the Primitive and Ante-diluvian World, which makes a vast difference 'twixt us and them; This takes up half of our Globe, and a good part of Mankind is busied with Sea-affairs and Navigation. They had little need of Merchandizing then, Nature suppli'd them at home with all necessaries, which were few, and they were not so greedy of superfluities as we are. We may add to these what concern'd their Food and Diet; Antiquity doth generally suppose that men were not Carnivorous in those Ages of the World, or did not feed upon Flesh, but only upon Fruit and Herbs. And this seems to be plainly confirm'd by Scripture; for after the Deluge God Almighty gives *Noah* and his Posterity a Licence to eat Flesh, (*Gen.* 9. 2, 3.) *Every moving thing that liveth shall be meat for you.* Whereas before in the new-made Earth God had prescrib'd them Herbs and Fruit for their Diet, *Gen.* 1. 29. *Behold, I have given you every Herb bearing Seed, which is upon the face of all the Earth; and every Tree, in the which is the Fruit of a Tree yielding Seed, to you it shall be for meat.* And of this Natural Diet they would be provided to their hands, without further preparation, as the Birds and the Beasts are.

Upon these general grounds we may infer and conclude, that the Civil World then, as well as the Natural, had a very different face and aspect from what it hath now; for of these Heads, Food and Cloathing, Building and Traffick, with that train of Arts, Trades and Manufactures that attend them, the Civil order of things is in a great measure constituted and compounded: These make the business of life, the several occupations of Men, the noise and hurry of the World;

These fill our Cities, and our Fairs, and our Havens and Ports; Yet all these fine things are but the effects of indigency and necessitousness, and were, for the most part, needless and unknown in that first state of Nature. The Ancients have told us the same things in effect, but telling us them without their grounds, which they themselves did not know, they lookt like Poetical stories, and pleasant fictions, and with most men past for no better. We have shewn them in another light, with their Reasons and Causes, deduc'd from the state of the natural World, which is the Basis upon which they stand; and this doth not only give them a just and full credibility, but also lays a foundation for after-thoughts, and further deductions, when they meet with minds dispos'd to pursue Speculations of this Nature.

As for Laws, Government, natural Religion, Military and Judicial affairs, with all their Equipage, which make an higher order of things in the Civil and Moral World, to calculate these upon the grounds given, would be more difficult, and more uncertain; neither do they at all belong to the present Theory. But from what we have already observ'd, we may be able to make a better judgment of those Traditional accounts which the Ancients have left us concerning these things, in the early Ages of the World, and the Primitive state of Nature. No doubt in these, as in all other particulars, there was a great easiness and simplicity in comparison of what is now, we are in a more pompous, forc'd, and artificial method, which partly the change of Nature, and partly the Vices and Vanities of men have introduc'd and establisht. But these things, with many more, ought to be the subject of a *Philosophick History* of the World, which we mention'd before.

This is a short and general Scheme of the Primæval World, compar'd with the Modern; yet these things did not equally run through all the Parts and Ages of it, there was a declension and degeneracy, both Natural and Moral, by degrees, and especially towards the latter end; but the principal form of Nature remaining till the Deluge and the dissolution of that Heavens and Earth, till then also this Civil frame of things would stand in a great measure. And though such a state of Nature, and of Mankind, when 'tis propos'd crudely, and without its grounds, appear fabulous or imaginary, yet 'tis really in it self a state, not only possible, but more easie and natural, than what the World is in at present. And if one of the old Ante-diluvian Patriarchs should rise from the dead, he would be more surpris'd to see our World in that posture it is, than we can be by the story and description of his. As an *Indian* hath more reason to wonder at the *European* modes, than we have to wonder at their plain manner of living. 'Tis we that have left the tract of Nature, that are wrought and screw'd up into artifices, that have disguis'd our selves; and 'tis in our World that the Scenes are chang'd, and become more strange and Fantastical.

I will conclude this Discourse with an easie remark, and without any particular Application of it. 'Tis a strange power that custom hath upon weak and little Spirits; whose thoughts reach no further than their Senses; and what they have seen and been us'd to, they make the standard and measure of Nature, of Reason, and of all *Decorum*. Neither are there any sort of men more positive and tenacious of their petty opinions, than they are; nor more censorious, even to bitterness and malice. And 'tis generally so, that those that have the least evidence for the truth of their beloved opinions, are most peevish and impatient in the defence of them. This sort of men are the last that will be made wise men, if ever they be; for they have the worst of diseases that accompany ignorance, and do not so much as know themselves to be sick.

CHAPTER VII

The place of Paradise *cannot be determin'd from the Theory only, nor from Scripture only; what the sence of Antiquity was concerning it, both as to the Jews and Heathens, and especially as to the Christian Fathers; That they generally plac'd it out of this Continent, in the Southern Hemisphere.*

WE have now prepar'd our work for the last finishing stroaks; describ'd the first Earth, and compar'd it with the Present; and not only the two Earths, but in a good measure the whole State and Oeconomy of those two Worlds. It remains only to determine the place of *Paradise* in that Primæval Earth; I say, in that Primæval Earth, for we have driven the point so far already, that the seat of it could not be in the present Earth, whose Form, Site, and Air are so dispos'd, as could not consist with the first and most indispensable properties of *Paradise:* And accordingly, we see with what ill success our modern Authors have rang'd over the Earth, to find a fit spot of ground to plant *Paradise* in; some would set it on the top of an high Mountain, that it might have good Air and fair weather, as being above the Clouds, and the middle Region; but then they were at a loss for Water, which made a great part of the pleasure and beauty of that place; Others therefore would seat it in a Plain, or in a River-Island, that they might have Water enough, but then it would be subject to the injuries of the Air, and foul weather at the seasons of the Year, from which, both Reason and all Authority have exempted *Paradise*. 'Tis like seeking a perfect beauty in a mortal Body, there are so many things requir'd to it, as to complexion, Features, Proportions and Air, that they never meet altogether in one person; neither can all the properties of a Terrestrial *Paradise* ever meet together in one place, though never so well chosen, in this present Earth.

But in the Primæval Earth, which we have describ'd, 'tis easie to find a Seat that had all those beauties and conveniences; we have every where, through the temperate Climates, a clear and constant Air, a fruitful Soil, pleasant Waters, and all the general characters of *Paradise*; so that the trouble will be rather, in that competition, what part or Region to pitch upon in particular. But to come as near it as we can, we must remember in the first place, how that Earth was divided into two Hemispheres, distant and separated from one another, not by an imaginary line, but by a real boundary that could not be past; so as the first inquiry will be, in whether of these Hemispheres was the Seat of *Paradise*. To answer this only according to our Theory, I confess, I see no natural reason or occasion to place it in one Hemisphere more than in another, I see no ground of difference

or pre-eminence, that one had above the other; and I am apt to think, that depended rather upon the will of God, and the Series of Providence that was to
follow in this Earth, than upon any natural incapacity in one of these two Regions
more than in the other, for planting in it the Garden of God. Neither doth
Scripture determine, with any certainty, either Hemisphere for the place of it;
for when 'tis said to be in *Eden*, or to be the Garden of *Eden*, 'tis no more than
the Garden of *pleasure* or *delight*, as the word signifies: And even the *Septuagint*,
who render this word *Eden*, as a proper name twice, (*Gen.* 2. *ver*. 8 & 10) do in
the same story render it twice as a common name, signifying τρυφὴ, *pleasure*,
(*Chap.* 2. 15 and *Chap.* 3. 24) and so they do accordingly render it in *Ezekiel*
(*Chap.* 31. 9, 16, 18) where this Garden of *Eden* is spoken of again. Some have
thought that the word *Mekiddim* (*Geb.* 2. 8) was to be render'd *in the East*, or
Eastward, as we read it, and therefore determin'd the site of *Paradise*; but 'tis
only the *Septuagint* Translate it so, all the other *Greek* Versions, and St. *Jerom*,
the *Vulgate*, the *Chaldee* Paraphrase, and the *Syriack* render it *from the beginning*,
or *in the beginning*, or to that effect. And we that do not believe the *Septuagint*
to have been infallible, or inspir'd, have no reason to prefer their single authority
above all the rest. Some also think the place of *Paradise* may be determin'd by
the four Rivers that are named as belonging to it, and the Countries they ran
thorough; but the names of those Rivers are to me uncertain, and two of them
altogether unintelligible. Where are there four Rivers in our Continent that
come from one Head, as these are said to have done, either at the entrance or
issue of the Garden. 'Tis true, if you admit our *Hypothesis*, concerning the
fraction and disruption of the Earth at the Deluge, then we cannot expect to
find Rivers now as they were before, the general Source is chang'd, and their
Chanels are all broke up; but if you do not admit such a dissolution of the Earth,
but suppose the Deluge to have been only like a standing Pool, after it had once
cover'd the surface of the Earth, I do not see why it should make any great havock
or confusion in it; and they that go that way, are therefore the more oblig'd to
show us still the Rivers of *Paradise*. Several of the Ancients, as we shall show
hereafter, suppos'd these four Rivers to have their Heads in the other Hemisphere,
and if so, the Seat of *Paradise* might be there too. But let them first agree amongst
themselves, concerning these Rivers, and the Countries they run thorough, and
we will undertake to show, that there cannot be any such in this Continent.

Seeing then neither the Theory doth determine, nor Scripture, where the place
of *Paradise* was, nor in whether Hemisphere, we must appeal to Antiquity, or
the opinions of the Ancients; for I know no other Guide, but one of these three,
Scripture, Reason, and ancient Tradition; and where the two former are silent, it
seems very reasonable to consult the third. And that our Inquiries may be comprehensive enough, we will consider what the *Jews*, what the *Heathens*, and what the
Christian Fathers have said or determin'd concerning the Seat of *Paradise*. The
Jews and *Hebrew* Doctors place it in neither Hemisphere, but betwixt both,
under the Æquinoctial, as you may see plainly in *Abravanel*, *Manasses Ben-Israel*,
Maimonides, *Aben Ezra*. and others. But the reason why they carried it no further
than the Line, is because they suppos'd it certain, as *Aben Ezra* tells us, that the

days and nights were always equal in *Paradise*, and they did not know how that could be, unless it stood under the Æquinoctial. But we have shown another method, wherein that perpetual Æquinox came to pass, and how it was common to all the parts and Climates of that Earth, which if they had been aware of, and that the Torrid Zone at that time was utterly uninhabitable, having remov'd their *Paradise* thus far from home, they would probably have remov'd it a little further, into the temperate Climates of the other Hemisphere.

The Ancient Heathens, Poets and Philosophers, had the notion of *Paradise*, or rather of several *Paradises* in the Earth; and 'tis remarkable, that they plac'd them generally, if not all of them, out of this Continent; in the Ocean, or beyond it, or in another Orb or Hemisphere. The Garden of the *Hesperides*, the Fortunate *Islands*, the *Elysian Fields*, *Ogygia* and *Toprabane*, as it is describ'd by *Diodorus Siculus*, with others such like; which as they were all characteriz'd like so many *Paradises*, so they were all seated out of our Continent by their Geography and descriptions of them.

Thus far Antiquity seems to incline to the other Hemisphere, or to some place beyond the bounds of our Continent for the Seat of *Paradise*; But that which we are most to depend upon in this affair, is Christian Antiquity, the Judgment and Tradition of the Fathers upon this Argument. And we may safely say in the first place, negatively, that none of the Christian Fathers, *Latin* or *Greek*, ever plac'd *Paradise* in *Mesopotamia*; that is a conceit and invention of some modern Authors, which hath been much incouraged of late, because it gave men ease and rest as to further inquiries, in an argument they could not well manage. Secondly, we may affirm, that none of the Christian Fathers have plac'd *Paradise* in any determinate Region of our Continent, *Asia Africk* or *Europe*. I have read of one or two Authors, I think, that fansied *Paradise* to have been at *Jerusalem*, but 'twas a meer fancy, that no body regarded or pursu'd. The controversie amongst the Fathers concerning *Paradise*, was quite another thing from what it is now of late: They disputed and controverted, whether *Paradise* was Corporeal, or Intellectual only, and Allegorical; This was the grand point amongst them. Then of those that thought it Corporeal, some plac'd it high in the Air, some inaccessible by Desarts or Mountains, and many beyond the Ocean, or in another World; And in these chiefly consisted the differences and diversity of opinions amongst them; nor do we find that they nam'd any particular place or Country in the known parts of the Earth for the Seat of *Paradise*, or that one contested for one spot of ground, and another for another, which is the vain temerity of modern Authors; as if they could tell to an Acre of Land where *Paradise* stood, or could set their foot upon the Center of the Garden. These have corrupted and misrepresented the notion of our *Paradise*, just as some modern Poets have the notion of the *Elysian Fields*, which *Homer* and the Ancients plac'd remote on the extremities of the Earth, and these would make a little green Meadow in *Campania Felix* to be the fam'd *Elysium*.

Thus much concerning the Fathers, negatively; but to discover as far as we can, what their positive Assertions were in this Argument, we may observe, that though their opinions be differently exprest, they generally concenter in this, that

the *Southern Hemisphere* was the Seat of *Paradise*. This, I say, seems manifestly
to be the sence of Christian Antiquity and Tradition, so far as there is any thing
definitive in the remains we have upon that subject. Some of the Fathers did
not believe *Paradise* to be Corporeal and Local, and those are to be laid aside in
the first place, as to this point; Others that thought it Local, did not determine
any thing (as most of them indeed did not) concerning the particular place of it;
But the rest that did, though they have exprest themselves in various ways, and
under various forms, yet, upon a due interpretation, they all meet in one common
and general conclusion, That *Paradise* was seated beyond the Æquinoctial, or in
the other Hemisphere.

And to understand this aright, we must reflect, in the first place, upon the
form of the Primæval Earth, and of the two Hemispheres of which it consisted,
altogether incommunicable one with another, by reason of the Torrid Zone
betwixt them; so as those two Hemispheres were then as two distinct Worlds, or
distinct Earths, that had no commerce with one another. And this Notion or
Tradition we find amongst Heathen Authors, as well as Christian, this Opposite
Earth being call'd by them *Antichthon*, and its Inhabitants *Antichthones*: For
those words comprehend both the *Antipodes* and *Antœci*, or all beyond the Line,
as is manifest from their best Authors, as *Achilles Tatius*, and *Cæsar Germanicus*
upon *Aratus, Probus Grammaticus, Censorinus, Pomponius Mela*, and *Pliny*. And
these were call'd another World, and lookt upon as another stock and race of

Mankind, as appears from *Cicero* and *Macrobius*; But as the latter part was their
mistake, so the former is acknowledg'd by Christian Authors, as well as others;
and particularly St. *Clement*, in his Epistle to the *Corinthians*, mentions a *World*,
or *Worlds beyond the Ocean, subject to Divine Providence, and the great Lord of
Nature, as well as ours*. This passage of St. *Clement* is also cited by St. *Jerom*, in

his Commentary upon *Ephes.* 2. 2 and by *Origen Periarchon*, where the Inhabit-
tants of that other World are call'd *Antichthones*.

I make this remark in the first place, that we may understand the true sence
and importance of those phrases and expressions amongst the Ancients, when
they say *Paradise* was in *another World*. Which are not to be so understood, as
if they thought *Paradise* was in the Moon, or in *Jupiter*, or hung above like a
Cloud or a Meteor, they were not so extravagant; but that *Paradise* was in another
Hemisphere, which was call'd *Antichthon*, another *Earth*, or another *World* from
Ours; and justly reputed so, because of an impossibility of commerce or intercourse betwixt their respective Inhabitants. And this remark being premis'd, we
will now distribute the Christian Authors and Fathers that have deliver'd their
opinion concerning the place of *Paradise*, into three or four ranks or orders; and
though they express themselves differently, you will see, when duly examin'd
and expounded, they all conspire and concur in the forementioned conclusion,
That the Seat of *Paradise* was in the other Hemisphere.

In the first rank then we will place and reckon those that have set *Paradise* in
another *World*, or in another *Earth*; seeing, according to the foregoing Explication,
that is the same thing, as to affirm it seated beyond the Torrid Zone in the other
Hemisphere. In this number are *Ephrem Syrus, Moses Bar Cepha, Tatianus*, and

of later date *Jacobus de Valentia*. To these are to be added again such Authors as say, that *Adam*, when he was turn'd out of *Paradise*, was brought into *our Earth*, or into our Region of the Earth; for this is tantamount with the former; And this seems to be the sence of St. *Jerom* in several places against *Jovinian*, as also of *Constantine*, in his Oration in *Eusebius*, and is positively asserted by *Sulpitius Severus*. And lastly, those Authors that represent *Paradise* as remote from our World, and inaccessible, so St. *Austin*, *Procopius Gazeus*, *Beda*, *Strabus Fuldensis*, *Historia Scholiastica*, and others, these, I say, pursue the same notion of Antiquity; for what is remote from our World (that is, from our Continent, as we before explain'd it) is to be understood to be that *Antichthon*, or Anti-hemisphere which the Ancients oppos'd to ours.

Οἰκουμένη.

Another sett of Authors, that interpret the *Flaming Sword* that guarded *Paradise* to be the *Torrid Zone*, do plainly intimate, that *Paradise* in their opinion lay beyond the Torrid Zone, or in the Anti-hemisphere; And thus *Tertullian* interprets the Flaming Sword, and in such words as fully confirm our sence: *Paradise*, He says, *by the Torrid Zone, as by a wall of Fire, was sever'd from the communication and knowledge of our World*. It lay then on the other side of this Zone. And St. *Cyprian*, or the ancient Author that passeth under his name, in his Comment upon *Genesis*, expresseth himself to the same effect; so also St. *Austin* and *Isidore Hispalensis* are thought to interpret it: And *Aquinas*, who makes *Paradise* inaccessible, gives this reason for it, *Propter vehementiam æstûs in locis intermediis ex propinquitate Solis, & hoc significatur per Flammeum Gladium: Because of that vehement heat in the parts betwixt us and that, arising from the nearness of the Sun, and this is signified by the Flaming Sword*. And this interpretation of the *Flaming Sword* receives a remarkable force and Emphasis from our Theory and description of the Primæval Earth, for there the Torrid Zone was as a wall of Fire indeed, or a Region of flame which none could pass or subsist in, no more than in a Furnace.

There is another form of expression amongst the Ancients concerning *Paradise*, which, if deciphered, is of the same force and signification with this we have already instanc'd in; They say sometimes, *Paradise* was *beyond the Ocean*, or that the Rivers of *Paradise* came from beyond the Ocean. This is of the same import with the former Head, and points still at the other Hemisphere; for, as we noted before, some of them fixt their *Antichthon* and *Antichthones* beyond the Ocean; that is, since there was an Ocean, Since the form of the Earth was chang'd, and the Torrid Zone become habitable, and consequently could not be a boundary or separation betwixt the two Worlds. Wherefore, as some run still upon the old division by the Torrid Zone, others took the new division by the Ocean. Which Ocean they suppos'd to lie from East to West betwixt the Tropicks; as may be seen in ancient Authors, *Geminus*, *Herodotus*, *Cicero de Republicâ*, and *Clemens Romanus*, whom we cited before. St. *Austin* also speaks upon the same supposition, when he would confute the doctrine of the *Antipodes*, or *Antichthones*; and *Macrobius*, I remember, makes it an Argument of Providence, that the Sun and the Planets, in what part of their course soever they are betwixt the two Tropicks, have still the Ocean under them, that they may be cool'd and nourisht by its

De Civ. Dei lib.
16. c. 9.

moisture. They thought the Sea, like a Girdle, went round the Earth, and the temperate Zones on either side were the habitable Regions, whereof this was call'd the *Oicouméne*, and the other *Antichthon*.

This being observ'd, 'tis not material, whether their Notion was true or false, it shows us what their meaning was, and what part of the Earth they design'd, when they spoke of any thing beyond the Ocean; namely, that they meant beyond the Line, in the other Hemisphere, or in the *Antichthon*; and accordingly, when they say *Paradise*, or the Fountains of its Rivers were beyond the Ocean, they say the same thing in other terms with the rest of those Authors we have cited. In *Moses Bar Cepha* above mention'd, we find a Chapter upon this subject, *Quomodo trajecerint Mortales inde ex Paradisi terrâ in hanc Terram?* How Mankind past out of that Earth or Continent where Paradise *was, into that where we are?* Namely, how they past the Ocean, *that lay betwixt them,* as the answer there given explains it. And so *Ephrem Syrus* is cited often in that Treatise, placing *Paradise* beyond the Ocean. The *Essenes* also, who were the most Philosophick Sect of the *Jews*, plac'd *Paradise*, according to *Josephus*, beyond the Ocean, under a perfect temperature of Air. And that passage in *Eusebius*, in the Oration of *Constantine*, being corrected and restor'd to the true reading, represents *Paradise*, in like manner, as in another Continent, from whence *Adam* was brought, after his transgression, into this. And lastly, there are some Authors, whose testimony and authority may deserve to be consider'd, not for their own Antiquity, but because they are profess'dly transcribers of Antiquity and Traditions, such as *Strabus, Comestor*, and the like, who are known to give this account or report of *Paradise* from the Ancients, that it was *interposito Oceano ab Orbe nostro vel à Zonâ nostrâ habitabili secretus, Separated from our Orb or Hemisphere by the interposition of the Ocean.*

It is also observable, that many of the Ancients that took *Tigris, Euphrates, Nile* and *Ganges* for the Rivers of *Paradise*, said that those Heads or Fountains of them which we have in our Continent, are but their *Capita secunda*, their second Sources, and that their first Sources were in another Orb where *Paradise* was; and thus *Hugo de Sancto Victore* says, *Sanctos communiter sensisse*, that the Holy men of old were generally of that opinion. To this sence also *Moses Bar Cepha* often expresseth himself; as also *Epiphanius, Procopius Gazeus*, and *Severianus in Catenâ*. Which notion amongst the Ancients, concerning the trajection or passage of the Paradisiacal Rivers under-ground, or under-Sea, from one Continent into another, is to me, I confess, unintelligible, either in the first or second Earth; but however it discovers their sence and opinion of the Seat of *Paradise*, that it was not to be sought for in *Asia* or in *Africk*, where those Rivers rise to us, but in some remoter parts of the World, where they suppos'd their first Sources to be.

This is a short account of what the Christian Fathers have left us, concerning the Seat of *Paradise*; and the truth is, 'tis but a short and broken account; yet 'tis no wonder it should be so, if we consider, as we noted before, that several of them did not believe *Paradise* to be Local and Corporeal; Others that did believe it so, yet did not offer to determine the place of it, but left that matter wholly untoucht and undecided; And the rest that did speak to that point, did it commonly both in general terms, and in expressions that were disguis'd, and needed interpretation; but all these differences and obscurities of expression, you see, when duly stated and expounded, may signifie one and the same thing, and terminate all in this common Conclusion, *That Paradise* was without our Continent, according to the general opinion and Tradition of Antiquity. And I do not doubt but the Tradition would have been both more express and more universal, if the Ancients had understood Geography better; for those of the Ancients that did not admit or believe, that there were *Antipodes* or *Antichthones*, as *Lactantius*, St. *Austin*, and some others, these could not joyn in the common opinion about the place of *Paradise*, because they thought there was no Land, nor any thing habitable ἔξω τ᾽ οἰκουμγύης, or besides this Continent. And yet St. *Austin* was so cautious, that as he was bounded on the one hand by his false *Idea* of the Earth, that he could not joyn with Antiquity as to the place of *Paradise*; so on the other hand he had that respect for it, that he would not say any thing to the contrary; therefore being to give his opinion, he says only, *Terrestrem esse Paradisum, & locum ejus ab hominum cognitione esse remotissimum: That it is somewhere upon the Earth, but the place of it very remote from the knowledge of Men.*

And as their ignorance of the Globe of the Earth was one reason, why the doctrine of *Paradise* was so broken and obscure, so another reason why it is much more so at present is, because the chief ancient Books writ upon that subject, are lost; *Ephrem Syrus*, who liv'd in the Fourth Century, writ a Commentary *in Genesin sive de Ortu rerum*, concerning the Origin of the Earth; and by those remains that are cited from it, we have reason to believe, that it contain'd many things remarkable concerning the first Earth, and concerning *Paradise*, *Tertullian* also writ a Book *de Paradiso*, which is wholly lost; and we see to what effect it would have been, by his making the Torrid Zone to be the *Flaming Sword*, and the partition betwixt this Earth and *Paradise*; which two Earths he more than once distinguisheth as very different from one another. The most ancient Author that I know upon this subject, at least of those that writ of it literally, is *Moses Bar Cepha*, a *Syrian* Bishop, who liv'd about seven hundred years since, and his Book is translated into *Latin*, by that Learned and Judicious man, *Andreas Masius*. *Bar Cepha* writes upon the same Views of *Paradise* that we have here presented, that it was beyond the Ocean, in another tract of Land, or another Continent from that which we inhabit: As appears from the very Titles of his Eighth, Tenth, and Fourteenth Chapters. But we must allow him for his mistaken Notions about the form of the Earth; for he seems to have fansied the Earth plain, (not only as oppos'd to rough and Mountainous, for so it was plain; but as oppos'd to Spherical) and the Ocean to have divided it in two parts, an Interiour, and an Exteriour, and in that Exteriour part was *Paradise*. Such allowances must often be made for Geographical mistakes, in examining and understanding the writings of the Ancients. The rest of the *Syrian* Fathers, as well as *Ephrem* and *Bar Cepha*, incline to the same doctrine of *Paradise*, and seem to have retain'd more of the ancient Notions concerning it, than the *Greek* and *Latin* Fathers have; and yet there is in all some fragments of this doctrine, and but fragments in the best.

Cont. Marc. lib. 2. c. 2. c. 5.

We might add in that last place, that as the most ancient Treatises concerning *Paradise* are lost, so also the ancient *Glosses* and *Catenæ* upon Scripture, where we might have found the Traditions and Opinions of the Ancients upon this subject, are many of them either lost or unpublisht; And upon this consideration we did not think it improper to cite some Authors of small Antiquity, but such as have transcrib'd several things out of ancient Manuscript-glosses into their Commentaries: They living however before Printing was invented, or Learning well restor'd, and before the Reformation. I add that also *before the Reformation,* for since that time the Protestant Authors having lessen'd the authority of Traditions, the Pontificial Doctors content themselves to insist only upon such as they thought were useful or necessary, left by multiplying others that were but matter of curiosity, they should bring the first into question, and render the whole doctrine of Traditions more dubious and exceptionable; And upon this account, there are some Authors that writ an Age or two before the Reformation, that have with more freedom told us the Tenets and Traditions of the Ancients in these Speculations, that are but collateral to Religion, than any have done since. And I must confess, I am apt to think that what remains concerning the doctrine of *Paradise,* and the Primæval Earth, is in a good measure Traditional; for one may observe, that those that treat upon these subjects, quote the true Opinions, and tell you some of the Ancients held so and so, as That *Paradise* was in another Earth, or higher than this Earth, That there were no Mountains before the Flood, nor any Rain, and such like: yet they do not name those ancient Authors that held these Opinions; which makes me apt to believe, either that they were convey'd by a Traditional communication from one to another, or that there were other Books extant upon those subjects, or other Glosses, than what are now known.

Finally, to conclude this Discourse concerning the Seat of *Paradise,* we must mind you again upon what Basis it stands. We declar'd freely, that we could not by our Theory alone determine the particular place of it, only by that we are assur'd that it was in the Primæval Earth, and not in the present; but in what Region, or in whether Hemisphere of that Earth it was seated, we cannot define from Speculation only. 'Tis true, if we hold fast to that Scripture-conclusion, That all Mankind rise from one Head, and from one and the same Stock and Lineage, (which doth not seem to be according to the sentiments of the Heathens) we must suppose they were born in one Hemisphere, and after some time translated into the other, or a Colony of them; But this still doth not determine, in whether of the two they begun, and were first seated before their translation; and I am apt to think that depended rather, as we noted before, upon the Divine pleasure, and the train of affairs that was to succeed, than upon Natural causes and differences. Some of the Ancients, I know, made both the Soil and the Stars more noble in the Southern Hemisphere, than in ours, but I do not see any proof or warrant for it; wherefore laying aside all natural Topicks, we are willing, in this particular, to refer our selves wholly to the report and majority of Votes amongst the Ancients; who yet do not seem to me to lay much stress upon the notion of a particular and topical Paradise, and therefore use general and remote expressions concerning it. And finding no place for it in this Continent, they are willing to quit their hands of it, by placing it in a Region some-where far off, and inaccessible. This, together with the old Tradition, that Paradise was in another Earth, seems to me to give an account of most of their Opinions concerning the Seat of Paradise.

CHAPTER VIII

The uses of this Theory for the illustration of Antiquity; The ancient Chaos explain'd; The inhabitability of the Torrid Zone; The change of the Poles of the World; The doctrine of the Mundane Egg; How America was first peopled; How Paradise within the Circle of the Moon.

WE have now dispatch'd the Theory of the Primæval Earth, and reviv'd a forgotten World; 'Tis pity the first and fairest works of Nature should be lost out of the memory of Man, and that we should so much dote upon the Ruines, as never to think upon the Original Structure. As the modern Artists from some broken pieces of an ancient Statue, make out all the other parts and proportions; so from the broken and scatter'd limbs of the first World we have shown you how to raise the whole Fabrick again; and renew the prospect of those pleasant Scenes that first see the light, and first entertain'd Man, when he came to act upon this new-erected Stage.

We have drawn this Theory chiefly to give an account of the Universal Deluge, and of *Paradise*; but as when one lights a Candle to look for one or two things which they want, the light will not confine it self to those two objects, but shows all the other in the room; so, methinks, we have unexpectedly cast a light upon all Antiquity, in seeking after these two things, or in retrieving the Notion and Doctrine of the Primæval Earth, upon which they depended. For in ancient Learning there are many Discourses, and many Conclusions deliver'd to us, that are so obscure and confus'd, and so remote from the present state of things, that one cannot well distinguish, whether they are fictions or realities; and there is no way to distinguish with certainty, but by a clear Theory upon the same subjects; which showing us the truth directly, and independently upon them, shows us also by reflection, how far they are true or false, and in what sence they are to be interpreted and understood. And the present Theory being of great extent, we shall find it serviceable in many things, for the illustration of such dubious and obscure doctrines in Antiquity.

To begin with their Ancient CHAOS, what a dark story have they made of it, both their Philosophers and Poets; and how fabulous in appearance? 'Tis deliver'd as confus'dly as the Mass it self could be, and hath not been reduc'd to order, nor indeed made intelligible by any. They tell us of *moral* principle sin the Chaos instead of *natural*, of *strife*, and *discord*, and *division* on the one hand, and *Love*, *Friendship*, and *Venus* on the other; and, after a long contest, Love got the better of Discord, and united the disagreeing principles: This is one part of their story. Then they make the forming of the World out of the Chaos a kind of

Genealogie or Pedigree; *Chaos* was the common Parent of all, and from Chaos sprung, first, *Night,* and *Tartarus,* or *Oceanus*; Night was a teeming Mother, and of her were born *Æther* and the *Earth*; The Earth conceiv'd by the influences of Æther, and brought forth Man and all Animals.

This seems to be a Poetical fiction rather than Philosophy; yet when 'tis set in a true light, and compar'd with our Theory of the Chaos, 'twill appear a pretty regular account, how the World was form'd at first, or how the Chaos divided it self successively into several Regions, rising one after another, and propagated one from another, as Children and Posterity from a common Parent. We show'd in the first Book, *Chap.* 5, how the Chaos, from an uniform mass, wrought it self into several Regions or Elements; the grossest part sinking to the Center, upon this lay the mass of Water, and over the Water was a Region of dark, impure, caliginous Air; This impure, caliginous Air is that which the Ancients call *Night,* and the mass of Water *Oceanus* or *Tartarus,* for those two terms with them are often of the like force, *Tartarus* being *Oceanus* inclos'd and lock'd up: Thus we have the first off-spring of the Chaos, or its first-born twins, *Nox* and *Oceanus.* Now this turbid Air purifying it self by degrees, as the more subtle parts flew upwards, and compos'd the Æther; so the earthy parts that were mixt with it dropt down upon the surface of the Water, or the liquid mass; and that mass on the other hand sending up its lighter and more oily parts towards its surface, these two incorporate there, and by their mixture and union compose a Body of Earth quite round the mass of Waters: And this was the first habitable Earth, which as it was, you see, the Daughter of *Nox* and *Oceanus,* so it was the Mother of all other things, and all living Creatures, which at the beginning of the World sprung out of its fruitful womb.

This doctrine of the Chaos, for the greater pomp of the business, the Ancients call'd their *Theogonia,* or the Genealogy of the Gods; for they gave their Gods, at least their Terrestrial Gods, an original and beginning; and all the Elements and greater portions of Nature they made Gods and Goddesses, or their Deities presided over them in such a manner, that the names were us'd promiscuously for one another. We also mention'd before some moral principles, which they plac'd in the Chaos, *Eris* and *Eros*; Strife, discord, and disaffection which prevail'd at first, and afterward *Love,* kindness and union got the upper hand, and in spite of those factious and dividing principles gather'd together the separated Elements, and united them into an habitable World. This is all easily understood, if we do but look upon the Schemes of the rising World, as we have set them down in that fifth Chapter; for in the first commotion of the Chaos, after an intestine struggle of all the parts, the Elements separated from one another into so many distinct bodies or masses, and in this state and posture things continued a good while, which the Ancients, after their Poetick or Moral way, call'd the Reign of *Eris* or Contention, of hatred, flight and disaffection; and if things had always continued in that System, we should never have had an habitable World. But Love and good Nature conquer'd at length, *Venus* rise out of the Sea, and receiv'd into her bosom, and intangled in her imbraces the falling Æther, *viz.* The parts of lighter earth, which were mixt with the Air in that first separation, and gave it the name of *Night*, fell down upon the oily parts of the Sea-mass, which lay floating upon the surface of it, and by that union and conjunction, a new Body, and a new World was produc'd, which was the first habitable Earth. This is the interpretation of their mystical Philosophy of the Chaos, and the resolution of it into plain natural History: Which you may see more fully discust in the *Latin* Treatise.   *Lib. 2. c. 7.*

We have already explain'd, in several places, the *Golden Age* of the Ancients, and laid down such grounds as will enable us to discern what is real, and what Poetical, in the reports and characters that Antiquity hath given of those first Ages of the World. And if there be any thing amongst the Ancients that refers to another Earth, as *Plato*'s *Atlantis*, which he says, was absorpt by an Earth-quake, and an inundation, as the Primæval Earth was; or his *Æthereal* Earth mention'd in his *Phædo*, which he opposeth to this broken hollow Earth; makes it to have long-liv'd inhabitants, and to be without Rains and Storms, as that first Earth was also; or the pendulous *Gardens* of *Alcinous*, or such like, to which nothing answers in present Nature, by reflecting upon the state of the first Earth, we find an easie explication of them. We have also explain'd what the *Antichthon* and *Antichthones* of the Ancients were, and what the true ground of that distinction was. But nothing seems more remarkable than the *inhabitability of the Torrid Zone*, if we consider what a general fame and belief it had amongst the Ancients, and yet in the present form of the Earth we find no such thing, nor any foundation for it. I cannot believe that this was so universally receiv'd upon a slight presumption only, because it lay under the course of the Sun, if the Sun had then the same latitude from the Æquator in his course and motion that he hath now, and made the same variety of seasons; whereby even the hottest parts of the Earth have a Winter, or something equivalent to it. But if we apply this to the Primæval Earth, whose posture was direct to the Sun, standing always fixt in its Equinoctial, we shall easily believe that the Torrid Zone was then uninhabitable by extremity of heat, there being no difference of seasons, noge ofr any chan weather, the Sun hanging always over head at the same distance, and in the same direction. Besides this, the descent of the Rivers in that first Earth was such, that they could never reach the Equinoctial parts, as we have shown before; by which means, and the want of Rain, that Region must necessarily be turn'd into a dry Desart. Now this being really the state of the first Earth, the fame and general belief that the Torrid Zone was uninhabitable had this true Original, and continued still with posterity after the Deluge, though the causes then were taken away; for they being ignorant of the change that was made in Nature at that time, kept up still the same Tradition and opinion currant, till observation and experience taught later Ages to correct it. As the true miracles that were in the Christian Church at first, occasion'd a fame and belief of their continuance long after they had really ceast.

This gives an easie account, and, I think, the true cause, of that opinion, amongst the Ancients generally receiv'd, *That the Torrid Zone was uninhabitable*. I say generally receiv'd; for not only the Poets, both *Greek* and *Latin*, but their Philosophers, Astronomers and Geographers, had the same notion, and deliver'd the same doctrine; as *Aristotle, Cleomedes, Achilles Tatius, Ptolomy, Cicero, Strabo, Mela, Pliny, Macrobius, &c.* And to speak truth, the whole doctrine of the Zones is calculated more properly for the first Earth, than for the present; for the divisions and bounds of them now, are but arbitrary, being habitable all over, and having no visible distinction; whereas they were then determin'd by Nature, and the Globe of the Earth was really divided into so many Regions of a very different aspect and quality; which would have appear'd at a distance, if they had been lookt upon from the Clouds, or from the Moon, as *Jupiter*'s Belts, or as so many Girdles or Swathing-bands about the body of the Earth: And so the word imports, and so the Ancients use to call them *Cinguli* and *Fasciæ*. But in the present form of the Earth, if it was seen at a distance, no such distinction would appear in the parts of it, nor scarce any other but that of Land and Water, and of Mountains and Valleys, which are nothing to the purpose of Zones. And to add this note further, When the Earth lay in this regular form, divided into Regions or Walks, if I may so call them, as this gave occasion of its distinction by Zones, so if we might consider all that Earth as a *Paradise*, and *Paradise* as a Garden, (for it is always call'd so in Scripture, and in *Jewish* Authors) as this Torrid Zone, bare of Grass and Trees, made a kind of Gravel-walk in the middle: so there was a green Walk on either hand of it, made by the temperate Zones;

See Fig. 3. *c.* 5. and beyond those lay a Canal, which water'd the Garden from either side.

But to return to Antiquity; We may add under this Head another observation or doctrine amongst the Ancients, strange enough in appearance, which yet receives an easie explication from the preceding Theory; They say, *The Poles* of the World did once change their situation, and were at first in another posture from what they are in now, till that inclination happen'd; This the ancient Philo-

See the Lat. Treat. lib. 2. *c.* 10. sophers often make mention of, as *Anaxagoras, Empedocles, Diogenes, Leucippus, Democritus*; as may be seen in *Laertius*, and in *Plutarch*; and the Stars, they say, at first were carried about the Earth in a more uniform manner. This is no more than what we have observ'd and told you in other words, namely, that the Earth chang'd its posture at the Deluge, and thereby made these seeming changes in the Heavens; its Poles before pointed to the Poles of the Ecliptick, which now point to the Poles of the Æquator, and its Axis is become parallel with that Axis; and this is the mystery and interpretation of what they say in other terms; this makes the different aspect of the Heavens, and of its Poles: And I am apt to think, that those changes in the course of the Stars, which the Ancients some-times speak of, and especially the *Ægyptians*, if they did not proceed from defects in their Calendar, had no other Physical account than this

And as they say the Poles of the World were in another situation at first, so first they say, there was no variety of seasons in the Year, as in their Golden Age. Which is very coherent with all the rest, and still runs along with the Theory. And you may observe, that all these things we have instanc'd in hitherto, are but links of the same chain, in connexion and dependance upon one another. When the Primæval Earth was made out of the Chaos, its form and posture was such, as, of course, brought on all those Scenes which Antiquity hath kept the remembrance of: though now in another state of Nature they seem very strange;

especially being disguis'd, as some of them are, by their odd manner of representing them. *That* the Poles of the World stood once in another posture; That the Year had no diversity of Seasons; That the Torrid Zone was uninhabitable; That the two Hemispheres had no possibility of intercourse, and such like: These all hang upon the same string; or lean one upon another as Stones in the same Building; whereof we have, by this Theory, laid the very foundation bare, that you may see what they all stand upon, and in what order.

There is still one remarkable Notion or Doctrine amongst the Ancients, which we have not spoken to; 'tis partly Symbolical, and the propriety of the Symbol, or of the Application of it, hath been little understood; 'Tis their doctrine of the *Mundane Egg*, or their comparing the World to an Egg, and especially in the original composition of it. This seems to be a mean comparison, the World and an Egg, what proportion, or what resemblance betwixt these two things? And yet I do not know any Symbolical doctrine, or conclusion, that hath been so universally entertain'd by the *Mystæ*, or Wise and Learned, of all Nations; as hath been noted before in the Fifth Chapter of the First Book, and at large in the *Latin* Treatise. 'Tis certain, that by the *World* in this similitude, they do not   *Lib.* 2. *c.* 10.
mean the Great Universe, for that hath neither Figure, nor any determinate form of composition, and it would be a great vanity and rashness in any one to compare this to an Egg; The works of God are immense, as his nature is infinite, and we cannot make any image or resemblance of either of them; but this comparison is to be understood of the *Sublunary World*, or of the *Earth*; And for a general key to Antiquity upon this Argument, we may lay this down as a Maxim or Canon, *That what the Ancients have said concerning the form and figure of the World, or concerning the Original of it from a Chaos, or about its periods and dissolution, are never to be understood of the Great Universe, but of our Earth, or of this Sublunary and Terrestrial World.* And this observation being made, do but reflect upon our Theory of the Earth, the manner of its composition at first, and the figure of it, being compleated, and you will need no other interpreter to understand this mystery. We have show'd there, that the figure of it, when finisht, was Oval, and the inward form of it was a frame of four Regions incom-   *Book* 1. *c.* 5.
passing one another, where that of Fire lay in the middle like the Yolk, and a shell of Earth inclos'd them all. This gives a solution so easie and natural, and shows such an aptness and elegancy in the representation, that one cannot doubt, upon a view, and compare of circumstances, but that we have truly found out the Riddle of the Mundane Egg.

To these illustrations of Antiquity in things Natural and Geographical, give me leave to add, and to resolve from the same Theory, one Historical difficulty; and 'twill seem, 'tis likely, of no less moment than any we have hitherto insisted upon, and I am sure hath exercis'd the Pens of many Learned men with small or no success. 'Tis to give an account of the Original of the people of *America*, how that Continent was first peopled and inhabited, or any other Continent distinct from ours, wherein we suppose *Adam* to have liv'd, and to have propagated his posterity. 'Tis certain, that all Mankind came from one Head, or from one common Parent; *Certain*, I say, according to the History of *Moses*, confirm'd

N   193

Acts 17. 26.
by Apostolical authority; and 'tis also admitted on all hands that *Adam* after his expulsion out of *Paradise*, wheresoever he was before, liv'd in this Continent, which being encompass'd with great Seas, and separate from *America* on either side, how could the children of *Adam* pass the wide Ocean, to hunt out remote habitations in *America*? How easie is the answer to this great Question, which hath imploy'd the time of so many Learned men to resolve? Or rather how suddenly doth it vanish at the sight of truth, as a phantom at the approach of light? The ground sinks under it that it seem'd to stand upon; *Adam*'s Earth was not broken into Continents and Islands, as ours is, nor the parts of it separated by Seas and Mountains; 'twas one continued and smooth surface, and gave free and easie passage from the rising to the setting Sun: So according as his progeny increast, and new swarms were ready to go abroad, they might spread themselves on either hand, East and West, without any interruption or impediment; neither Sea, Mountain, nor Desart would stand in their way. 'Tis true, the passage was not so free North and South, they could not go out of one Hemisphere into another, but Providence seems to have made provision for that, in transplanting *Adam* into this Hemisphere, after he had laid the foundation of a World in the Other.

We see then the great difficulty concerning the peopling the several Continents and Islands of the Earth, and particularly of *America*, easily remov'd by this *Hypothesis*; The propagation of Mankind, and of all sorts of Animals into those several portions of the World, may readily be understood, if you admit the true form of the first Earth: But without that 'tis an endless controversie, as those commonly are that proceed upon a false supposition. I will not examine here the several projects and methods that have been propos'd, some by one Author, and some by another, for getting people into *America*; they confute one another, methinks, very well; and to show, as we have done, that the ground they go upon is imaginary, is a compendious way of confuting them all together. However, those that will not admit our *Hypothesis*, concerning the continuity and uniformity of the first Earth, stand oblig'd still to give us an account of the propagation of Mankind from one Head, and how the posterity of *Adam* got into *America*.

'Twill be said, possibly, that this doth not intirely remove the difficulty, because it returns again after the Flood; and then we suppose the Earth broken into Continents and Islands, in the same manner that it is now; How then did the posterity of *Noah* get into *America*, to people it after the Flood? I do not know that ever they got into *America* till *Columbus* went thither in the last Age, who, for any thing I know, was the first of *Noah*'s progeny that ever set foot in that Continent. Scripture tells us, that all Mankind rise from one Head, namely, from *Adam*, and his fault was derived to posterity, but no where that *Noah* was the common Head of Mankind that hath been since his time, nor does any doctrine of faith, that I know of, depend upon that supposition. When the great frame of the Earth broke at the Deluge, Providence fore-see into how many Continents it would be divided after the ceasing of the Flood, and accordingly, as we may reasonably suppose, made provision to save a remnant in every Continent, that the race of Mankind might not be quite extinct in any of them. What provision he made in our Continent we know from Sacred History, but as that takes notice of no other Continent but ours, so neither could it take notice of any method that was us'd there for saving of a remnant of men; but 'twere great presumption, methinks, to imagine that Providence had a care of none but us, or could not find out ways of preservation in other places, as well as in that where our habitations were to be. *Asia*, *Africk* and *Europe* were repeopled by the Sons of *Noah*, *Shem*, *Ham*, and *Japhet*, but we read nothing of their going over into *America*, or sending any Colonies thither; and that World which is near as big as ours, must have stood long without people, or any thing of Humane race in it, after the Flood, if it stood so till this was full, or till men navigated the Ocean, and by chance discovered it: It seems more reasonable to suppose, that there was a stock providentially reserv'd there, as well as here, out of which they sprung again; but we do not pretend in an Argument of this nature to define or determine any thing positively. To conclude, as this is but a secondary difficulty, and of no great force, so neither is it any thing peculiar to us, or to our *Hypothesis*, but alike common to both; and if they can propose any reasonable way, whereby the Sons of *Noah* might be transplanted into *America*, with all my heart; but all the ways that I have met with hitherto, have seem'd to me meer fictions, or meer presumptions. Besides, finding Birds and Beasts there, which are no where upon our Continent, nor would live in our Countries if brought hither, 'tis a fair conjecture that they were not carried from us, but originally bred and preserv'd there.

Thus much for the illustration of Antiquity in some points of Humane literature, by our Theory of the Primæval Earth; There is also in *Christian Antiquity* a Tradition or Doctrine, that appears as obscure and as much a Paradox as any of these, and better deserves an illustration, because it relates more closely and expressly to our present subject: 'Tis that Notion or Opinion amongt the Ancients concerning *Paradise*, that it was seated as high as the Sphere of the Moon, or *within the Lunar Circle*. This looks very strange, and indeed extravagantly, at first sight, but the wonder will cease, if we understand this not of *Paradise* taken apart from the rest of the Earth, but of the whole Primæval Earth, wherein the Seat of *Paradise* was; That was really seated much higher than the present Earth, and may be reasonably suppos'd to have been as much elevated as the tops of our Mountains are now. And that phrase of reaching to *the Sphere of the Moon*, signifies no more than those other expressions of *reaching to Heaven*, or *reaching above the Clouds*, which are phrases commonly us'd to express the height of Buildings, or of Mountains, and such like things: So the Builders of *Babel* said, they would make a Tower should reach to Heaven; *Olympus* and *Parnassus* are said by the Poets to reach to Heaven, or to rise above the Clouds; And *Pliny* and *Solinus* use this very expression of the *Lunar Circle*, when they describe the height of Mount *Atlas*, *Eductus in viciniam Lunaris Circuli*. The Ancients, I *Solin. c. 17.* believe, aim'd particularly by this phrase, to express an height above the middle Region, or above our Atmosphere, that *Paradise* might be serene; and where our Atmosphere ended, they reckon'd the Sphere of the Moon begun, and therefore said it reach'd to the Sphere of the Moon. Many of the Christian Fathers exprest their opinion concerning the high situation of *Paradise* in plain and formal terms, as St. *Basil, Damascen, Moses Bar Cepha, &c.* but this phrase of reaching to the *Lunar Circle* is repeated by several of them, and said to be of great Antiquity. *Aquinas, Albertus,* and others, ascribe it to *Bede,* but many to St. *Austin;* and therefore *Ambrosius Catharinus* is angry with their great School-man, that he should derive it from *Bede,* seeing St. *Austin* writing to *Orosius,* deliver'd this doctrine, which surely, says He, St. *Austin neither feign'd nor dream'd only, but had received it from Antiquity:* And from so great Antiquity, that it was no less than Apostolical, if we credit *Albertus Magnus,* and the ancient Books he appeals to; for He says this Tradition was deriv'd as high as from St. *Thomas* the Apostle. His words are these, after he had deliver'd his own opinion. *Hoc tamen dico,* &c. *But this I say, without prejudice to the better opinion, for I have found it in some most ancient Books, that* Thomas *the Apostle was the Author of that opinion, which is usually attributed to* Bede *and* Strabus, *namely, that* Paradise *was so high as to reach to the Lunar Circle.* But thus much concerning this Opinion, and concerning Antiquity.

Com. in Gen. c. 2

Sum. Theol. par.
2. tract. 13. q. 79

To conclude all, we see this Theory, which was drawn only by a thred of Reason, and the Laws of Nature, abstractly from all Antiquity, notwithstanding casts a light upon many passages there, which were otherwise accounted fictions, or unintelligible truths; and though we do not alledge these as proofs of the Theory, for it carries its own light and proof with it, yet whether we will or no, they do mutually confirm, as well as illustrate, one another; And 'tis a pleasure also, when one hath wrought out truth by meer dint of thinking, and examination of causes, and propos'd it plainly and openly, to meet with it again amongst the Ancients, disguis'd, and in an old fashion'd dress: scarce to be known or discover'd, but by those that before-hand knew it very well. And it would be a further pleasure and satisfaction, to have render'd those Doctrines and Notions, for the future, intelligible and useful to others, as well as delightful to our selves.

CHAPTER IX

A general objection against this Theory, viz. That if there had been such a Primitive Earth, *as we pretend, the fame of it would have sounded throughout all Antiquity. The Eastern and Western Learning consider'd, the most considerable Records of both are lost; what footsteps remain relating to this Subject. The* Jewish *and* Christian *Learning consider'd; how far lost as to this Argument, and what Notes or Traditions remain. Lastly, how far the Sacred Writings bear witness to it. The Providential conduct of Knowledge in the World. A recapitulation and state of the Theory.*

HAVING gone through the two first Parts, and the two first Books of this Theory, that concern the Primitive World, the Universal Deluge, and the state of *Paradise,* We have leizure now to reflect a little, and consider what may probably be objected against a Theory of this nature. I do not mean single objections against single parts, for those may be many, and such as I cannot fore-see; but what may be said against the body and substance of the Theory, and the credibility of it, appearing new and surprising, and yet of great extent and importance. This, I fancy, will induce many to say, surely this cannot be a reality; for if there had been such a Primitive Earth, and such a Primitive World as is here represented, and so remarkably different from the present, it could not have been so utterly forgotten, or lain hid for so many Ages; all Antiquity would have rung of it; the memory of it would have been kept fresh by Books or Traditions. Can we imagine, that it should lie buried for some thousands of years in deep silence and oblivion; and now only when the second World is drawing to an end, we begin to discover that there was a first, and that of another make and order from this?

To satisfie this objection, or surmise rather, it will be convenient to take a good large scope and compass in our Discourse; We must not suppose, that this Primitive World hath been wholly lost out of the memory of man, or out of History, for we have some History and Chronology of it preserv'd by *Moses*, and likewise in the Monuments of the Ancients, more or less; for they all suppos'd a World before the Deluge. But 'tis the Philosophy of this Primitive World that hath been lost in a great measure, what the state of Nature was then, and wherein it differ'd from the present or Post-diluvian order of things. This, I confess, hath been little taken notice of; it hath been generally thought or presum'd, that the World before the Flood was of the same form and constitution with the present World; This we do not deny, but rather think it design'd and Providential, that there should not remain a clear and full knowledge of that first state of things; and we may easily suppose how it might decay and perish, if we consider how little of the remote Antiquities of the World have ever been brought down to our knowledge.

The *Greeks* and *Romans* divided the Ages of the World into three periods or intervals, whereof they call'd the first the *Obscure* Period, the second the *Fabulous*, and the third *Historical*. The dark and obscure Period was from the beginning of the World to the Deluge; what pass'd then, either in Nature or amongst Men, they have no Records, no account, by their own confession; all that space of time was cover'd with darkness and oblivion; so that we ought rather to wonder at those remains they have, and those broken notions of the Golden Age, and the conditions of it, how they were sav'd out of the common shipwrack, than to expect from them the Philosophy of that World, and all its differences from the present. And as for the other Nations that pretend to greater Antiquities, to more ancient History and Chronology, from what is left of their Monuments many will allow only this difference, that their fabulous Age begun more high, or that they had more ancient Fables.

But besides that our expectations cannot be great from the learning of the *Gentiles*, we have not the means or opportunity to inform our selves well what Notions they did leave us concerning the Primitive World; for their Books and Monuments are generally lost, or lie hid unknown to us. The Learning of the World may be divided into the Eastern learning and the Western; and I look upon the Eastern as far more considerable for Philosophical Antiquities, and Philosophical Conclusions; I say *Conclusions*, for I do not believe either of them had any considerable Theory, or Contexture of Principles and Conclusions together: But 'tis certain, that in the East, from what Source soever it came, Humane or Divine, they had some extraordinary Doctrines and Notions disperst amongst them. Now as by the Western learning we understand that of the *Greeks* and *Romans*; so by the Eastern, that which was amongst the *Ægyptians*, *Phœnicians*, *Chaldæans*, *Assyrians*, and *Persians*; and of the Learning of these Nations, how little have we now left? except some fragments and Citations in *Greek* Authors, what do we know of them? But if we had, not only those Books intire, whereof we have now the gleanings and reversions only, but all that have perisht besides, especially in that famous Library at *Alexandria*; if these, I say, were all restor'd to the World again, we might promise our selves the satisfaction of seeing more of the Antiquities, and Natural History of the first World, than we have now left, or can reasonably expect. That Library we speak of, at *Alexandria*, was a Collection, besides *Greek* Books, of *Ægyptian*, *Chaldæan*, and all the Eastern Learning; and *Cedrenus* makes it to consist of an hundred thousand Volumes: But *Josephus* saith, when the Translation of the Bible by the *Septuagint* was to be added to it, *Demetrius Phalereus* (who was Keeper or Governour of it) told the King then, that he had already two hundred thousand Volumes, and that he hop'd to make them up five hundred thousand; And he was better than his word, or his Successors for him, for *Ammianus Marcellinus*, and other Authors, report them to have increas'd to seven hundred thousand. This Library was unfortunately burnt in the sacking of *Alexandria* by *Cæsar*, and considering that all these were ancient Books, and generally of the Eastern wisdom, 'twas an inestimable and irreparable loss to the Commonwealth of Learning. In like manner we are told of a vast Library of Books of all Arts and Sciences, in *China*, burnt by the command or caprice of one of their Kings. Wherein, the *Chineses*, according to their vanity, were us'd to say, greater riches were lost, than will be in the last Conflagration.

As for the Western Learning, we may remember what the *Ægyptian* Priest says to *Solon* in *Plato*'s *Timæus*, *You Greeks are always Children*, and know nothing of Antiquity; And if the *Greeks* were so, much more the *Romans*, who came after them in time, and for so great a People, and so much civiliz'd, never any had less Philosophy, and less of the Sciences amongst them than the *Romans* had; They studied only the Art of Speaking, of Governing, and of Fighting: and left the rest to the *Greeks* and Eastern Nations, as unprofitable. Yet we have reason to believe, that the best Philosophical Antiquities that the *Romans* had, perisht with the Books of *Varro*, of *Numa Pompilius*, and of the ancient *Sibyls*. *Varro* writ, as St. *Austin* tells us, a multitude of Volumes, and of various sorts, and I had rather retrieve his works, than the works of any other *Roman* Author; not his Etymologies and Criticisms, where we see nothing admirable, but his *Theologia Physica*, and his *Antiquitates*; which in all probability would have given us more light into remote times, and the Natural History of the past World, than all the *Latin* Authors besides have done. He has left the foremention'd distinction of three Periods of time; He had the doctrine of the *Mundane Egg*, as we see in *Probus Grammaticus*; and he gave us that observation of the Star *Venus*, concerning the great change she suffer'd about the time of our Deluge.

De Civ. Dei lib. 6
Dion. Halic. Ant.
Rom. lib. 4.

Numa Pompilius was doubtless a contemplative man, and 'tis thought that he understood the true System of the World, and represented the Sun by his *Vestal Fire*; though, methinks, *Vesta* does not so properly refer to the Sun, as to the Earth, which hath a Sacred fire too, that is not to be extinguisht. He order'd his Books to be buried with him, which were found in a Stone-Chest by him, four hundred years after his death; They were in all twenty-four, whereof twelve contain'd Sacred Rites and Ceremonies, and the other twelve the Philosophy and Wisdom of the *Greeks*; The *Romans* gave them to the *Prætor Petilius* to peruse; and to make his report to the Senate, whether they were fit to be publisht or no: The *Prætor* made a wise politick report, that the Contents of them might be of dangerous consequence to the establisht Laws and Religion; and thereupon they were condemn'd to be burnt, and Posterity was depriv'd of that ancient treasure, whatsoever it was. What the nine Books of the *Sibyl* contain'd, that were offer'd to King *Tarquin*, we little know; She valued them high, and the higher still, the more they seem'd to slight or neglect them; which is a piece of very natural indignation or contempt, when one is satisfied of the worth of what they offer. 'Tis likely they respected, besides the fate of *Rome*, the fate and several periods of the World, both past and to come, and the most mystical passages of them. And in these Authors and Monuments are lost the greatest hopes of Natural and Philosophick Antiquities, that we could have had from the *Romans*.

And as to the *Greeks*, their best and Sacred Learning was not originally their own; they enrich themselves with the spoils of the East, and the remains we have of that Eastern Learning, is what we pick out of the *Greeks*; whose works, I believe, if they were intirely extant, we should not need to go any further for witnesses to confirm all the principal parts of this Theory. With what regret does one read in *Laertius*, *Suidas*, and others, the promising titles of Books writ by the *Greek* Philosophers, hundreds or thousands, whereof there is not one now extant; and those that are extant are generally but fragments: Those Authors also that have writ their Lives, or collected their Opinions, have done it confus'dly and injudiciously. I should hope for as much light and instruction, as to the Original of the World, from *Orpheus* alone, if his works had been preserv'd, as from all that is extant now of the other *Greek* Philosophers. We may see from what remains of him, that he understood in a good measure, how the Earth rise from a Chaos, what was its external Figure, and what the form of its inward structure; The opinion of the *Oval* Figure of the Earth is ascrib'd to *Orpheus* and his Disciples; and the doctrine of the *Mundane Egg* is so peculiarly his, that 'tis call'd by *Proclus*, The *Orphick Egg*; not that he was the first Author of that doctrine, but the first that brought it into *Greece*.

Thus much concerning the Heathen Learning, Eastern and Western, and the small remains of it in things Philosophical; 'tis no wonder then if the account we have left us from them of the Primitive Earth, and the Antiquities of the natural World be very imperfect. And yet we have trac'd (in the precedent Chapter, and more largely in our *Latin* Treatise) the foot-steps of several parts of this Theory amongst the writings and Traditions of the Ancients: and even of those parts that seem the most strange and singular, and that are the Basis upon which the rest

Tell. Theor. lib.
2. c. 7.

Ibid. Cap. 10.

Ibid.

stand. We have shown there, that their account of the Chaos, though it seem'd to many but a Poetical Rhapsody, contain'd the true mystery of the formation of the Primitive Earth. We have also shown upon the same occasion, that both the external Figure and internal form of that Earth was compriz'd and signified in their ancient doctrine of the Mundane Egg, which hath been propagated through all the Learned Nations. And lastly, as to the situation of that Earth, and the change of its posture since, that the memory of that has been kept up, we have brought several testimonies and indications from the *Greek* Philosophers. And these were the three great and fundamental properties of the Primitive Earth, upon which all the other depend, and all its differences from the present Order of Nature. You see then, though Providence hath suffer'd the Heathen Learning and their Monuments, in a great part, to perish, yet we are not left wholly without witnesses amongst them, in a speculation of this great importance.

You will say, it may be, though this account, as to the Books and Learning of the Heathen, may be lookt upon as reasonable, yet we might expect however, from the *Jewish* and *Christian* Authors, a more full and satisfactory account of that Primitive Earth, and of the Old World. First, as to the *Jews*, 'tis well known that they have no ancient Learning, unless by way of Tradition, amongst them. There is not a Book extant in their Language, excepting the Canon of the Old Testament, that hath not been writ since our Saviour's time. They are very bad Masters of Antiquity, and they may in some measure be excus'd, because of their several captivities, dispersions, and desolations. In the *Babylonish* captivity their Temple was ransack'd, and they did not preserve, as is thought, so much as the Autograph or original Manuscript of the Law, nor the Books of those of their Prophets that were then extant, and kept in the Temple; And at their return from the Captivity after seventy years, they seem to have had forgot their Native Language so much, that the Law was to be interpreted to them in *Chaldee*, after it was read in *Hebrew*;
C. 8. 7, 8.
for so I understand that interpretation in *Nehemiah*. 'Twas a great Providence, methinks, that they should any way preserve their Law, and other Books of Scripture, in the Captivity, for so long a time; for 'tis likely they had not the liberty of using them in any publick worship, seeing they return'd so ignorant of their own Language, and, as 'tis thought, of their Alphabet and Character too. And if their Sacred Books were hardly preserv'd, we may easily believe all others perisht in that publick desolation.

Yet there was another destruction of that Nation, and their Temple, greater than this, by the *Romans*; and if there were any remains of Learning preserv'd in the former ruine, or any recruits made since that time, this second desolation would sweep them all away. And accordingly we see they have nothing left in their Tongue, besides the Bible, so ancient as the destruction of *Jerusalem*. These and other publick calamities of the *Jewish* Nation, may reasonably be thought to have wasted their Records of ancient Learning, *if they had any*; for, to speak truth, the *Jews* are a people of little curiosity, as to Sciences and Philosophical enquiries: They were very tenacious of their own customs, and careful of those Traditions that did respect them, but were not remarkable, that I know of, or thought great Proficients in any other sort of Learning. There has been a great fame, 'tis true, of the *Jewish Cabala*, and of great mysteries contain'd in it; and, I believe, there was once a Traditional doctrine amongst some of them, that had extraordinary Notions and Conclusions: But where is this now to be found? The *Essenes* were the likeliest Sect, one would think, to retain such doctrines, but 'tis probable they are now so mixt with things fabulous and fantastical, that what one should alledge from thence would be of little or no authority. One Head in this *Cabala* was the doctrine of the *Sephiroth*, and though the explication of them be uncertain, the Inferiour *Sephiroth* in the Corporeal World cannot so well be appli'd to any thing, as to those several Orbs and Regions, infolding one another, whereof the Primigenial Earth was compos'd. Yet such conjectures, I know, are of no validity, but in consort with better Arguments. I have often thought also, that their first and second Temple represented the first and second Earth or World; and that of *Ezekiel*'s, which is the third, is still to be erected, the most beautiful of all, when this second Temple of the World shall be burnt down. If the Prophecies of *Enoch* had been preserv'd, and taken into the Canon by *Ezra*, after their return from *Babylon*, when the Collection of their Sacred Books is suppos'd to have been made, we might probably have had a considerable account there, both of times past and to come, of Antiquities and Futuritions; for those Prophecies are generally suppos'd to have contain'd both the first and second fate of this Earth, and all the Periods of it. But as this Book is lost to us, so I look upon all others that pretend to be Ante-Mosaical or Patriarchal, as Spurious and Fabulous.

Vid. Men. ben Isr. de Creat. probl. 28.

Thus much concerning the *Jews*. As for *Christian* Authors, their knowledge must be from some of these fore-mention'd, *Jews* or *Heathens*; or else by Apostolical Tradition: For the *Christian* Fathers were not very speculative, so as to raise a Theory from their own thoughts and contemplations, concerning the Origin of the Earth. We have instanc'd, in the last Chapter, in a *Christian* Tradition, concerning *Paradise*, and the high situation of it, which is fully consonant to the site of the Primitive Earth, where *Paradise* stood, and doth seem plainly to refer to it, being unintelligible upon any other supposition. And 'twas, I believe, this elevation of *Paradise*, and the pensile structure of that *Paradisiacal* Earth, that gave occasion to *Celsus*, as we see by *Origen*'s answer, to say, that the *Christian Paradise* was taken from the pensile Gardens of *Alcinous*: But we may see now what was the ground of such expressions or Traditions amongst the Ancients, which Providence left to keep mens minds awake; not fully to instruct them, but to confirm them in the truth, when it should come to be made known in other methods. We have noted also above, that the ancient Books and Authors amongst the *Christians*, that were most likely to inform us in this Argument, have perisht, and are lost out of the World, such as *Ephrem Syrus de ortu rerum*, and *Tertullian de Paradiso*; and that piece which is extant, of *Moses Bar Cepha*'s upon this subject, receives more light from our *Hypothesis*, than from any other I know; for correcting some mistakes about the Figure of the Earth, which the Ancients were often guilty of, the obscurity or confusion of that Discourse in other things, may be easily rectifi'd, if compar'd with this Theory.

Of this nature also is that Tradition that is common both to *Jews* and *Christians*, and which we have often mention'd before, that there was a perpetual serenity, and perpetual Equinox in *Paradise*; which cannot be upon this Earth, not so much as under the Equinoctial; for they have a sort of Winter and Summer there, a course of Rains at certain times of the Year, and great inequalities of the Air, as to heat and cold, moisture and drought. They had also Traditions amongst them, *That there was no Rain from the beginning of the World till the Deluge*, and that *there were no Mountains till the Flood*, and such like; These, you see, point directly at such an Earth, as we have describ'd. And I call these *Traditions*, because we cannot find the Original Authors of them; The ancient *ordinary Gloss* (upon *Genesis*) which some make Eight hundred years old, mentions both these Opinions; so does *Historia Scholastica, Alcuinus, Rabanus Maurus, Lyranus*, and such Collectors of Antiquity. *Bede* also relates that of the *plainness* or smoothness of the *Ante-diluvian* Earth. Yet these are reported Traditionally, as it were, naming no Authors or Books from whence they were taken; Nor can it be imagin'd that they feign'd them themselves; to what end or purpose? it serv'd no interest; or upon what ground? seeing they had no Theory that could lead them to such Notions as these, or that could be strengthen'd and confirm'd by them. Those opinions also of the Fathers, which we recited in the seventh Chapter, placing *Paradise* beyond the Torrid Zone, and making it thereby inaccessible, suit very well to the form, qualities, and bipartition of the Primæval Earth, and seem to be grounded upon them.

Lat. Treat. lib. 2. c. 10.

Thus much may serve for a short Survey of the ancient Learning, to give us a reasonable account, why the memory and knowledge of the Primitive Earth should be so much lost out of the World; and what we retain of it still; which would be far more, I do not doubt, if all Manuscripts were brought to light, that are yet extant in publick or private Libraries. The truth is, one cannot judge with certainty, neither what things have been recorded and preserv'd in the monuments of Learning, nor what are still; not what have been, because so many of those Monuments are lost: The *Alexandrian* Library, which we spoke of before, seems to have been the greatest Collection that ever was made before Christianity, and the *Constantinopolitan* (begun by *Constantine*, and destroy'd in the Fifth Century, when it was rais'd to the number, as is said, of one hundred twenty thousand Volumes) the most valuable that was ever since, and both these have been permitted by Providence to perish in the merciless Flames. Besides those devastations of Books and Libraries that have been made in Christendom, by the *Northern* barbarous Nations overflowing *Europe*, and the *Saracens* and *Turks* great parts of *Asia* and *Africk*. It is hard therefore to pronounce what knowledge hath been in the World, or what accounts of Antiquity; Neither can we well judge what remain, or of what things the memory may be still latently conserv'd; for besides those Manuscripts that are yet unexamin'd in these parts of Christendom, and those that have been scarce view'd in the great *Abyssine* or *Æthiopick* Library, there are many, doubtless, of good value in other parts; and we know particularly of two fam'd Libraries, that of *Buda*, and that of *Fez*, both in the hands of *Mahometans*; who keep them as the Dragon did the Golden Apples, will neither make use of them themselves, nor suffer others to peruse them. The Library of *Fez* is said to contain thirty two thousand Volumes in

Arabick; and though the *Arabick* Learning was mostwhat *Western*, and therefore of less account, yet they did deal in *Eastern* Learning too; for *Avicenna* writ a Book with that Title, *Philosophia Orientalis*. There may be also in the *East* thousands of Manuscripts unknown to us, of greater value than most books we have: And as to those subjects we are treating of, I should promise my self more light and confirmation from the *Syriack* Authors than from any others. These things being consider'd, we can make but a very imperfect estimate, what evidences are left us, and what accounts of the Primitive Earth; and if these deductions and defalcations be made, both for what Books are wholly lost, and for what lie asleep or dead in Libraries, we have reason to be satisfied in a Theory of this nature, to find so good attestations as we have produc'd for the several parts of it; which we purpose to inlarge upon considerably at another time and occasion.

But to carry this Objection as far as may be, let us suppose it to be urg'd still in the last place, that though these Humane writings have perisht, or be imperfect, yet in the Divine writings at least, we might expect, that the memory of the Old World, and of the Primitive Earth should have been preserv'd. To this I answer in short, That we could not expect in the Scriptures any Natural Theory of that Earth, nor any account of it, but what was general; and this we have, both by the *Tehom-Rabba* of *Moses*, and the description of the same Abysse in other places of Scripture, as we have shown at large in the First Book, *Chap.* 7. And also by the description which St. *Peter* hath given of the Ante-diluvian Heavens and Earth, and their different constitution from the present. You will say, it may be, that that place of St. *Peter* is capable of another interpretation; so are most places of Scripture, if you speak of a bare capacity; they are capable of more than one interpretation; but that which is most natural, proper and congruous, suitable to the words, suitable to the Argument, and suitable to the Context, wherein is nothing superfluous or impertinent, that we prefer and accept of as the most reasonable interpretation. Besides, in such Texts as relate to the Natural World, if of two interpretations propos'd, one agrees better with the Theory of Nature than the other, *cæteris paribus*, that ought to be prefer'd. And by these two rules we are willing to be tri'd, in the exposition of that remarkable Discourse of St. *Peter*'s, and to stand to that sence which is found most agreeable to them.

2 Pet. 3. 5, 6, &c.

Give me leave to conclude the whole Discourse with this general Consideration; 'Tis reasonable to suppose, that there is a Providence in the conduct of *Knowledge*, as well as of other affairs on the Earth; and that it was not design'd that all the mysteries of Nature and Providence should be plainly and clearly understood throughout all the Ages of the World; but that there is an Order establisht for this, as for other things, and certain Periods and Seasons; And what was made known to the Ancients only by broken Conclusions and Traditions, will be known (in the later Ages of the World) in a more perfect way, by Principles and Theories. The increase of Knowledge being that which changeth so much the face of the World, and the state of Humane affairs, I do not doubt but there is a particular care and superintendency for the conduct of it; by what steps and degrees it should come to light, at what Seasons and in what Ages; what evidence should be left, either in Scripture, Reason, or Tradition, for the grounds of it; how clear or obscure, how disperst or united; all these things were weigh'd and consider'd, and such measures taken as best suit the designs of Providence, and the general project and method propos'd in the government of the World. And I make no question but the state both of the Old World, and of that which is to come, is exhibited to us in Scripture in such a measure and proportion, as is fit for this foremention'd purpose; not as the Articles of our Faith, or the precepts of a good Life, which he that runs may read; but to the attentive and reflexive, to those that are unprejudic'd, and to those that are inquisitive, and have their minds open and prepar'd for the discernment of mysteries of such a nature.

Thus much in answer to that general Objection which might be made against this Theory, *That* it is not founded in Antiquity. I do not doubt but there may be many particular Objections against Parts and Sections of it, and the exposing it thus in our own Tongue may excite some or other, it may be, to make them; but if any be so minded, I desire (if they be Scholars) that it may rather be in *Latin*, as being more proper for a subject of this nature; and also that they would keep themselves close to the substance of the Theory, and wound that as much as they can; but to make excursions upon things accidental or collateral, that do not destroy the *Hypothesis*, is but to trouble the World with impertinencies. Now the substance of the Theory is this, THAT there was a *Primitive Earth* of another form from the present, and inhabited by Mankind till the Deluge; That it had those properties and conditions that we have ascrib'd to it, namely, a perpetual Equinox or Spring, by reason of its *right* situation to the Sun; Was of an Oval Figure, and the exteriour face of it smooth and uniform, without Mountains or a Sea. That in this Earth stood *Paradise*; the doctrine whereof cannot be understood but upon supposition of this Primitive Earth, and its properties. Then that the disruption and fall of this Earth into the Abysse, which lay under it, was that which made the Universal Deluge, and the destruction of the Old World; And that neither *Noah*'s Flood, nor the present form of the Earth can be explain'd in any other method that is rational, nor by any other Causes that are intelligible. These are the Vitals of the Theory, and the primary Assertions, whereof I do freely profess my full belief: and whosoever by solid reasons will show me in an Errour, and undeceive me, I shall be very much oblig'd to him. There are other lesser Conclusions which flow from these, and may be call'd Secondary, as that the Longævity of the Ante-diluvians depended upon their perpetual Equinox, and the perpetual equality and serenity of the Air; That the Torrid Zone in the Primitive Earth was uninhabitable; And that all their Rivers flow'd from the extreme parts of the Earth towards the Equinoctial; there being neither Rain, nor Rainbow, in the temperate and habitable Regions of it; And lastly, that the place of *Paradise*, according to the opinion of Antiquity, was in the Southern Hemisphere. These, I think, are all truly deduc'd and prov'd in their several ways, though they be not such essential parts of the Theory, as the former. There are also besides, many particular Explications that are to be consider'd with more liberty and latitude, and may be perhaps upon better thoughts, or better observations, corrected, without any prejudice to the general Theory.

Those places of Scripture which we have cited, I think, are all truly appli'd; and I have not mention'd *Moses*'s *Cosmopœia*, because I thought it deliver'd by him as a Lawgiver, not as a Philosopher; which I intend to show at large in another Treatise, not thinking that discussion proper for the Vulgar Tongue. Upon the whole, we are to remember, that some allowances are to be made for every *Hypothesis* that is new-propos'd and untri'd: and that we ought not out of levity of wit, or any private design, discountenance free and fair Essays: nor from any other motive, but the only love and concern of Truth.

CHAPTER X

Concerning the Author of Nature.

SEEING the Theory which we have propos'd in this Work is of that extent and comprehension, that it begins with the first foundation of this World, and is to reach to the last Period of it, in one continued Series or chain of Nature; It will not be improper, before we conclude, to make some reflections and remarks what *Nature* is, and upon what Superiour Causes she depends in all her Motions and Operations: And this will lead us to the discovery of the *Author* of Nature, and to the true Notion and state of *Natural Providence*, which seems to have been hitherto very much neglected, or little understood in the World. And 'tis the more reasonable and fitting, that we should explain these Notions before we shut up this Treatise, lest those Natural Explications which we have given of the Deluge, and other things, should be mistaken or misappli'd; Seeing some are apt to run away with pieces of a Discourse, which they think applicable to their purpose, or which they can maliciously represent, without attending to the scope or just limitations of what is spoken.

By *Nature* in general is understood All the Powers of Finite Beings, with the Laws establisht for their action and conduct, according to the ordinary course of things. And this extends both to Intellectual Beings and Corporeal; but seeing 'tis only the Material World that hath been the subject of our Discourse, Nature, as to that, may be defin'd, The Powers of *Matter*, with the Laws establisht for their action and conduct. Seeing also Matter hath no action, whether from it self, or imprest upon it, but Motion, as to the Corporeal World Nature is no more than The powers and capacities of Matter, with the Laws that govern the Motions of it. And this definition is so plain and easie, that, I believe, all parties will agree in it; There will also be no great controversie what these Laws are, As that one part of Matter cannot penetrate another, nor be in several places at once; That the greater Body overcomes the less, and the swifter the slower; That all Motion is in a right line, till something obstruct it or divert it; which are points little disputed as to the matter of fact; but the points concerning which the controversie ariseth, and which are to lead us to the Author of Nature, are these, *Who* or *what* is the Author of these *Laws*? of this *Motion*? and even of *Matter* it self; and of all those modes and forms of it which we see in Nature?

The Question useth chiefly to be put concerning *Motion*, how it came into the World; what the first Source of it is, or how Matter came at first to be mov'd? For the simple notion of Matter, not divided into parts, nor diversified, doth not imply Motion, but Extension only; 'Tis true, from Extension there necessarily follows *mobility*, or a capacity of being mov'd by an External power, but not actual or necessary Motion springing from it self. For dimensions, or length, breadth, and depth, which is the *Idea* of Matter, or of a Body, do no way include local Motion, or translation of parts; on the contrary, we do more easily and naturally conceive simple Extension as a thing steddy and fixt, and if we conceive Motion in it, or in its parts, we must superadd something to our first thought, and something that does not flow from Extension. As when we conceive a Figure, a Triangle, Square, or any other, we naturally conceive it fixt or quiescent, and if afterwards we imagine it in Motion, that is purely accidental to the Figure; in like manner it is accidental to Matter, that there should be Motion in it, it hath no inward principle from whence that can flow, and its Nature is compleat without it; Wherefore if we find Motion and Action in Matter, which is of it self a dead inactive mass, this should lead us immediately to the Author of Nature, or to some External power distinct from Matter, which is the Cause of all Motion in the World.

In single Bodies, and single parts of Matter, we readily believe and conclude, that they do not move, unless something move them, and why should we not conclude the same thing of the whole mass? If a Rock or Mountain cannot move it self, nor divide it self, either into great gobbets, or into small powder, why should it not be as impossible for the whole mass of Matter to do so? 'Tis true, Matter is capable both of motion and rest, yet to conceive it undivided, undiversified and unmov'd, is certainly a more simple Notion, than to conceive it divided and mov'd; and this being first in order of Nature, and an adequate conception too, we ought to inquire and give our selves an account how it came out of this state, and by what Causes, or, as we said before, how *Motion came first into the World.*

In the second place, That diversity which we see in Nature, both as to the qualities of Matter, and the compositions of it, being one step further than bare Motion, ought also to be a further indication of the Author of Nature, and to put us upon inquiry into the Causes of this diversity. There is nothing more uniform than simple Extension, nothing more the same throughout, all of a piece, and all of a sort, similar, and like to it self every where, yet we find the matter of the Universe diversified a thousand ways, into Heavens and Earth, Air and Waters, Stars, Meteors, Light, Darkness, Stones, Wood, Animals, and all Terrestrial Bodies; These diversifications are still further removes from the natural unity and identity of Matter, and a further argument of some external and superiour power that hath given these different forms to the several portions of Matter by the intervention of Motion. For if you exclude the Author of Nature, and suppose nothing but Matter in the World, take whether *Hypothesis* you will, either that Matter is without Motion of it self, or that it is of it self in Motion, there could not arise this diversity, and these compositions in it. If it was without

Motion, then the case is plain, for it would be nothing but an hard inflexible lump of impenetrable extension, without any diversity at all. And if you suppose it mov'd of it self, or to have an innate Motion, that would certainly hinder all sort of natural concretions and compositions, and in effect destroy all Continuity. For Motion, if it be essential to Matter, it is essential to every Atome of it, and equally diffus'd throughout all its parts; and all those parts or Atomes would be equal to one another, and as little as possible; For if Matter was divided into parts by its own innate Motion, that would melt it down into parts as little as possible, and consequently all equal to one another, there being no reason why you should stop those divisions, or the effect of this innate *impetus* in any one part sooner than in another, or in any part indeed till it was divided as much as was possible; Wherefore upon this principle, or in this method, all the Matter of the Universe would be one liquid or volatile mass, smaller than pin-dust, nay, than Air or Æther: And there would be no diversity of forms, only another sort of identity from the former. And so, upon the whole, you see, that Matter, whether we allow it Motion, or no Motion, could not come into that variety of tempers and compositions in which we find it in the World, without the influence and direction of a Superior external Cause, which we call the Author of Nature.

But there is still a further and stronger Argument from this Head, if we consider not only the diversity of Bodies, that the mass of Matter is cut into, but also that that diversity is *regular*, and in some parts of it admirably artful and ingenious. This will not only lead us to an Author of Nature, but to such an Author as hath Wisdom as well as Power. Matter is a brute Being, stupid and senseless, and though we should suppose it to have a force to move it self, yet that it should be able to meditate and consult, and take its measures how to frame a World, a regular and beautiful structure, consisting of such and such parts and Regions, and adapted to such and such purposes, this would be too extravagant to imagine; to allow it not only Motion from it self, but Wit and Judgment too; and that before it came into any Organical or Animate composition.

You'll say, it may be, The Frame of the World was not the result of counsel and consultation, but of *necessity*; Matter being once in Motion under the conduct of those Laws that are essential to it, it wrought it self by degrees from one state into another, till at length it came into the present form which we call the World. These are words thrown out at random, without any pretence of ground, only to see if they can be confuted; And so they may easily be, for we have shown already, that if Matter had innate Motion, it would be so far from running into the orderly and well dispos'd frame of the World, that it would run into no frame at all, into no forms, or compositions, or diversity of Bodies; but would either be all fluid, or all solid; either every single particle in a separate Motion, or all in one continued mass with an universal tremor, or inclination to move without actual separation; And either of these two states is far from the form of a World. Secondly, as to the Laws of Motion, as some of them are essential to Matter, so others are not demonstrable, but upon supposition of an Author of Nature. And thirdly, though all the Laws of Motion be admitted, they cannot bring Matter into the form of a World, unless some measures be taken at first by an intelligent

Being; I say some measures be taken to determine the primary Motions upon which the rest depend, and to put them in a way that leads to the formation of a World. The mass must be divided into Regions, and Centers fixt, and Motions appropriated to them; and it must be consider'd of what magnitude the first Bodies, or the first divisions of Matter should be, and how mov'd: Besides, there must be a determinate proportion, and certain degree of motion imprest upon the universal Matter, to qualifie it for the production of a World; if the dose was either too strong or too weak, the work would miscarry; And nothing but infinite Wisdom could see thorough the effects of every proportion, or every new degree of Motion, and discern which was best for the beginning, progress, and perfection of a World. So you see the Author of Nature is no way excluded, or made useless by the Laws of Motion, nor if Matter was promiscuously mov'd would these be sufficient causes of themselves to produce a World, or that regular diversity of Bodies that compose it.

But 'tis hard to satisfie men against their inclinations, or their interest: And as the regularity of the Universe was always a great stumbling-stone to the *Epicuræans*; so they have endeavour'd to make shifts of all sorts to give an account and answer to it, without recourse to an intelligent Principle; And for their last refuge, they say, that Chance might bring that to pass, which Nature and Necessity could not do; The Atoms might hit upon a lucky sett of Motions, which though it were casual and fortuitous, might happily lead them to the forming of a World. A lucky hit indeed, for Chance to frame a World: But this is a meer shuffle and collusion; for if there was nothing in Nature but Matter, there could be no such thing as Chance, all would be pure mechanical necessity; and so this answer, though it seem very different, is the same in effect with the former, and *Epicurus* with his Atomists are oblig'd to give a just mechanical account, how all the parts of Nature, the most compound and elaborate parts not excepted, rise from their Atoms by pure necessity: There could be no accidental concourse or coalition of them, every step, every motion, every composition was fatal and necessary. And therefore 'tis non-sence for an *Epicuræan* to talk of Chance, as Chance is oppos'd to Necessity; And if they oppose it to *Counsel* and *Wisdom*, 'tis little better than non-sence, to say the World and all its furniture rise by Chance, in that notion of it. But it will deserve our patience a little to give a more full and distinct answer to this, seeing it reacheth all their pleas and evasions at once.

What proof or demonstration of Wisdom and Counsel can be given, or can be desir'd, that is not found in some part of the World, Animate or Inanimate? We know but a little portion of the Universe, a meer point in comparison, and a broken point too, and yet in this broken point, or some small parcels of it, there is more of Art, Counsel and Wisdom shewn, than in all the works of men taken together, or than in all our *Artificial* World. In the construction of the Body of an Animal, there is more of thought and contrivance, more of exquisite invention, and fit disposition of parts, than is in all the Temples, Palaces, Ships, Theaters, or any other pieces of Architecture the World ever yet see: And not Architecture only, but all other Mechanism whatsoever, Engines, Clockwork, or any other, is not comparable to the Body of a living Creature. Seeing then we acknowledge these artificial works, wheresoever we meet with them, to be the effects of Wit, Understanding and Reason, is it not manifest partiality, or stupidity rather, to deny the works of Nature, which excel these in all degrees, to proceed from an intelligent Principle? Let them take any piece of Humane Art, or any Machine fram'd by the wit of Man, and compare it with the body of an Animal, either for diversity and multiplicity of workmanship, or curiosity in the minute parts, or just connexion and dependance of one thing upon another, or fit subserviency to the ends propos'd, of life, motion, use and ornament to the Creature, and if in all these respects they find it superiour to any work of Humane production, as they certainly must do, why should it be thought to proceed from inferiour and sense-less Causes? ought we not in this, as well as in other things, to proportion the Causes to the Effect? and to speak truth, and bring in an honest Verdict for Nature as well as Art.

In the composition of a perfect Animal, there are four several frames or Com-pages joyn'd together, The Natural, Vital, Animal, and Genital; Let them examine any one of these apart, and try if they can find any thing defective or superfluous, or any way inept, for matter or form. Let them view the whole Compages of the Bones, and especially the admirable construction, texture and disposition of the Muscles, which are joyn'd with them for moving the Body, or its parts. Let them take an account of the little Pipes and Conduits for the Juices and the Liquors, of their form and distribution; Or let them take any single Organ to examine, as the Eye, or the Ear, the Hand or the Heart; In each of these they may discover such arguments of Wisdom, and of Art, as will either convince them, or confound them; though still they must leave greater undiscover'd. We know little the in-sensible form and contexture of the parts of the Body, nor the just method of their Action; We know not yet the manner, order, and causes of the Motion of the Heart, which is the chief Spring of the whole Machine; and with how little exactness do we understand the Brain, and the parts belonging to it? why of that temper and of that form? how Motions are propagated there, and how conserv'd? how they answer the several operations of the Mind? why such little discom-posures of it disturb our Senses, and upon what little differences in this the great differences of Wits and Genius's depend. Yet seeing in all these Organs, whose make and manner of action we cannot discover, we see however by the Effects, that they are truly fitted for those offices to which Nature hath design'd them, we ought in reason to admire that Art which we cannot penetrate; At least we cannot but judge it a thing absurd, that what we have not wit enough to find out or comprehend, we should not allow to be an argument of wit and understanding in the Author, or Inventor of it. This would be against all Logick, common Sense, and common *Decorum*. Neither do I think it possible to the mind of man, while we attend to evidence, to believe that these, and such like works of Nature came by *Chance*, as they call it, or without Providence, forecast and wisdom, either in the first Causes, or in the proximate; in the design, or in the execution; in the preparation to them, or in the finishing of them.

Wherefore, in my judgment, if any be of this perswasion, it cannot be so much the effect of their understanding, as of their disposition and inclination; and in

o

moral things, mens opinions do as often spring from the one as from the other. For my part, I do generally distinguish of two sorts of opinions in all men, *Inclination-opinions*, and *Reason'd-opinions*; Opinions that grow upon mens Complexions, and Opinions that are the results of their Reason; and I meet with very few that are of a temperament so equal, or a constitution so even pois'd, but that they incline to one sett of Opinions rather than another, antecedently to all proofs of Reason: And when they have espous'd their opinions from that secret sympathy, then they find out as good Reasons as they can to maintain them, and say, nay think sometimes, that 'twas for the sake of those Reasons that they first imbrac'd them. We may commonly distinguish these Inclination-opinions from the Rational, because we find them accompanied with more Heat than Light, a great deal of eagerness and impatience in defending of them, and but slender arguments. One might give instances of this, both in Sects of Religion and Philosophy, in *Platonists*, *Stoicks*, and *Epicuræans*, that are so by their temper more than their reason, but to our purpose it will be sufficient to instance in one hearty *Epicuræan*, *Lucretius*, who is manifestly such, more from his inclination, and the bent of his Spirit, than from the force of Argument. For though his suppositions be very precarious, and his reasonings all along very slight, he will many times strut and triumph, as if he had wrested the Thunder out of *Jove*'s right hand; and a Mathematician is not more confident of his demonstration, than he seems to be of the truth of his shallow Philosophy. From such a principle of natural Complexion as this, I allow a man may be Atheistical, but never from the calm dictate of his Reason; yet he may be as confident, and as tenacious of his Conclusion, as if he had a clear and distinct evidence for it. For I take it to be a true Maxim in Humane Nature, that *A strong inclination, with a little evidence, is equivalent to a strong evidence*. And therefore we are not to be surpris'd, if we find men confident in their opinions many times far beyond the degree of their evidence, seeing there are other things, besides evidence, that incline the Will to one Conclusion rather than another. And as I have instanc'd in Natural Complexion, so *Interest* hath the same effect upon Humane Nature, because it always begets an inclination to those opinions that favour our interest, and a disinclination to the contrary; And this principle may be another ingredient, and secret perswasive to Atheism; for when men have run themselves so deep into Vice and Immorality, that they expect no benefit from a God, 'tis in a manner necessary to their quiet, and the ease of their mind, that they should fansie there is none; for they are afraid, if there be a God, that he will not stand neuter, and let them alone in another World. This, I say, is necessary to the quiet of their mind, unless they can attain that great Art, which many labour after, of *non-reflection*, or an *unthinking faculty*, as to God and a World to come. But to return to our Argument, after this short digression . . .

As that regular diversity which we see in the forms of Nature, and especially in the Bodies of Animals, could not be from any blind principle, either of Necessity or of Chance; So, in the last place, that *Subordination* which we see in the parts of Nature, and subserviency to one another, the less Noble to the more Noble, the Inanimate to the Animate, and all things upon Earth unto Man, must needs have been the effect of some Being higher than Matter; that did wisely dispose all things so at first, and doth still conserve them in the same order. If Man had been born into the World, and a numerous host of Creatures, without any provision or accommodation made for their subsistence and conveniences, we might have suspected that they had come by Chance, and therefore were so ill provided for; but which of them can complain? through their various Kinds and Orders, what is there awanting? They are all fitted to their several Elements, and their ways of living, Birds, Beasts, and Fishes, both by the form and shape of their Bodies, the manner of their covering, and the quality of their food. Besides, they are instructed in little Arts and Instincts for their conservation; and not only for their proper conservation, but also to find a way to make and bring up young ones, and leave behind them a Posterity; And all this in so fit a method, and by such a pretty train of actions, as is really admirable.

Man is the Master of all, and of him a double care is taken; that he should neither want what Nature can afford, nor what Art can supply. He could not be provided of all conveniences by Nature only, especially to secure him against the injuries of the Air; but in recompence, Nature hath provided materials for all those Arts which she see would be needful in Humane Life; as Building, Cloathing, Navigation, Agriculture, &c. that so Mankind might have both wherewithal to answer their occasions, and also to imploy their time, and exercise their ingenuity. This Oeconomy of Nature, as I may call it, or well ordering of the great Family of living Creatures, is an argument both of Goodness and of Wisdom, and is every way far above the powers of brute Matter. All regular administration we ascribe to conduct and judgment; If an Army of men be well provided for in things necessary both for Food, Cloaths, Arms, Lodging, Security and Defence, so as nothing is awanting in so great a multitude, we suppose it the effect of care and forcast in those persons that had the charge of it; they took their measures at first, computed and proportion'd one thing to another, made good regulations, and gave orders for convenient supplies. And can we suppose the great Army of Creatures upon Earth manag'd and provided for with less fore-thought and Providence, nay, with none at all, by meer Chance? This is to recede from all rules and analogy of Reason, only to serve a turn, and gratifie an unreasonable humour.

To conclude this Argument; There are two general Heads of things, if I recollect aright, which we make the marks and characters of Wisdom and Reason, Works of Art, and the Conduct of affairs or direction of means to an end; and wheresoever we meet, either with regular material works, or a regular ordination of affairs, we think we have a good title and warrant to derive them from an intelligent Author; Now these two being found in the Natural World, and that in an eminent degree, the one in the Frame of it, and the other in the Oeconomy of it, we have all the evidence and ground that can be in arguing from things visible to things invisible, that there is an Author of Nature, Superiour both to Humane Power and Humane Wisdom.

Before we proceed to give any further proofs or discoveries of the Author of Nature, let us reflect a little upon those we have already insisted upon; which have been taken wholly from the Material World, and from the common course of Nature. The very existence of Matter is a proof of a Deity, for the *Idea* of it hath no connexion with existence, as we shall show hereafter; however we will take leave now to set it down with the rest, in order as they follow one another.

1. *The existence of Matter.*
2. *The Motion of Matter.*
3. *The just quantity and degree of that Motion.*
4. *The first form of the Universe upon Motion imprest; both as to the Divisions of Matter, and the Leading Motions.*
5. *The Laws for communication and regulation of that Motion.*
6. *The regular effects of it, especially in the Animate World.*
7. *The Oeconomy of Nature, and fit Subordination of one part of the World to another.*

The five first of these Heads are prerequisites, and preparatives to the formation of a World, and the two last are as the image and character of its Maker, of his Power, Goodness and Wisdom, imprest upon it. Every one of them might well deserve a Chapter to it self, if the subject was to be treated on at large; but this is only an occasional dissertation, to state the Powers of Matter, lest they should be thought boundless, and the Author of Nature unnecessary, as the *Epicuræans* pretend; but notwithstanding their vain confidence and credulity, I defie them, or any man else, to make sence of the Material World, without placing a God at the Center of it.

To these considerations taken wholly from the Corporeal World, give me leave to add one of a mixt nature, concerning the *Union of our Soul and Body*. This strange effect, if rightly understood, doth as truly discover the Author of Nature, as many Effects that are accounted more Supernatural. The Incarnation, as I may so say, of a Spiritual substance, is to me a kind of standing miracle; That there should be such an union and connexion reciprocally betwixt the motions of the Body, and the actions and passions of the Soul: betwixt a substance Intellectual, and a parcel of organiz'd Matter: can be no effect of either of those substances; being wholly distinct in themselves, and remote in their natures from one another. For instance, when my Finger is cut, or when 'tis burnt, that my Soul thereupon should feel such a smart and violent pain, is no consequence of Nature, or does not follow from any connexion there is betwixt the Motion or Division of that piece of Matter, I call my Finger, and the passion of that Spirit I call my Soul; for these are two distinct Essences, and in themselves independent upon one another, as much as the Sun and my Body are independent; and there is no more reason in strict Nature, or in the essential chain of Causes and Effects, that my Soul should suffer, or be affected with this Motion in the Finger, than that the Sun should be affected with it; nay, there is less reason, if less can be, for the Sun being Corporeal, as the finger is, there is some remote possibility that there might be communication of Motion betwixt them; but Motion cannot beget a thought, or a passion by its own force; Motion can beget nothing but Motion, and if it should produce a thought, the Effect would be more noble than the Cause. Wherefore this Union is not by any necessity of Nature, but only from a positive Institution, or Decree establisht by the Author of Nature, that there should be such a communication betwixt these two substances for a time, *viz.* during the Vitality of the Body.

'Tis true indeed, if Thought, Apprehension, and Reason, was nothing but Corporeal Motion, this Argument would be of no force; but to suppose this, is to admit an absurdity to cure a difficulty; to make a Thought out of a local Motion, is like making a God out of a Stock, or a Stone; for these two are as remote in their Nature, and have as different *Idea*'s in the Mind, as any two disparate things we can propose or conceive; Number and Colour, a Triangle and Vertue, Free-will and a Pyramid are not more unlike, more distant, or of more different forms, than Thought and local Motion. Motion is nothing but a Bodies changing its place and situation amongst other Bodies, and what affinity or resemblance hath that to a *Thought*? how is that like to Pain, or to a doubt of the Mind? to Hope or to Desire? to the *Idea* of God? to any act of the Will or Understanding, as judging, consenting, reasoning, remembring, or any other? These are things of several orders, that have no similitude, nor any mixture of one another. And as this is the nature of Motion, so, on the other hand, in a *Thought* there are two things, *Consciousness*, and a *Representation*; Consciousness is in all Thoughts indifferently, whether distinct or confusd', for no man thinks but he is conscious that he thinks, nor perceives any thing but he is conscious that he perceives it; there is also in a Thought, especially if it be distinct, a representation; 'tis the image of that we think upon, and makes its Object present to the Mind. Now what hath local Motion to do with either of these two, Consciousness, or Representativeness? how doth it include either of them, or hold them any way affixt to its Nature? I think one may with as good sence and reason ask of what colour a Thought is, green or scarlet, as what sort of Motion it is; for Motion of what sort soever, can never be conscious, nor represent things as our Thoughts do. I have noted thus much in general, only to show the different nature of Motion and Cogitation, that we may be the more sensible that they have no mutual connexion in us, nor in any other Creature, from their essence or essential properties, but by a supervenient power from the Author of Nature, who hath thus united the Soul and the Body in their operations.

We have hitherto only consider'd the ordinary course of Nature, and what indications and proofs of its Author, that affords us; There is another remarkable Head of Arguments from effects extraordinary and supernatural, such as Miracles, Prophecies, Inspirations, Prodigies, Apparitions, Witchcraft, Sorceries, *&c.* These, at one step, lead us to something above Nature, and this is the shortest way, and the most popular; several Arguments are suited to several tempers, and God hath not left himself without a proper witness to every temper that is not wilfully blind. Of these witnesses we now speak of, the most considerable are Miracles, and the most considerable Records of them are the Books of Scripture; which if we consider only as an History, and as having nothing Sacred in them more than other good Histories, that is, truth in matter of fact, we cannot doubt but there have been miracles in the World; That *Moses* and the Prophets, our Saviour and his Apostles, wrought Miracles, I can no more question, than that

Cæsar and *Alexander* fought Battles, and took Cities. So also that there were true Prophecies and Inspirations, we know from Scripture, only consider'd as a true History. But as for other supernatural effects that are not recorded there, we have reason to examine them more strictly before we receive them, at least as to particular instances; for I am apt to think they are like Lotteries, where there are ten or twenty Blanks for one Prize; but yet if there were no Prizes at all, the Lottery would not have credit to subsist, and would be cri'd down as a perfect Cheat; So if amongst those many stories of Prodigies, Apparitions, and Witch-crafts, there were not some true, the very fame and thought of them would die from amongst men, and the first broachers of them would be hooted at as Cheats. As a false Religion that hath nothing true and solid mixt with it, can scarce be fixt upon Mankind; but where there is a mixture of true and false, the strength of the one supports the weakness of the other. As for Sorcery, the instances and examples of it are undeniable; not so much those few scatter'd instances that happen now and then amongst us, but such as are more constant, and in a manner National, in some Countries, and amongst barbarous people. Besides, the Oracles, and the Magick that was so frequent amongst the Ancients, show us that there have been always some Powers more than Humane tampering with the affairs of Mankind. But this Topick from effects Extraordinary and Supernatural, being in a great measure Historical, and respecting evil Spirits as well as the Author of Nature, is not so proper for this place.

There is a third Sett or Head of Arguments, that to some tempers are more cogent and convictive than any of these, namely, Arguments *abstract* and *Metaphysical*; And these do not only lead us to an Author of Nature in general, but show us more of his properties and perfections; represent him to us as a supream Deity, infinitely perfect, the fountain of all Being, and the steddy Center of all things. But reasons of this order, being of a finer thred, require more attention, and some preparation of Mind to make us discern them well, and be duly sensible of them. When a man hath withdrawn himself from the noise of this busie World, lock'd up his Senses and his Passions, and every thing that would unite him with it: commanded a general silence in the Soul, and suffers not a Thought to stir, but what looks inwards; Let him then reflect seriously, and ask himself, *What am I*, and *How came I into Being?* If I was Author and Original to my self, surely I ought to feel that mighty Power, and enjoy the pleasure of it; but, alas, I am conscious of no such force or Vertue, nor of any thing in my Nature, that should give me necessary existence; It hath no connexion with any part of me, nor any faculty in me, that I can discern. And now that I do exist, from what Causes soever, *Can I secure my self in Being?* now that I am in possession, am I sure to keep it? am I certain, that three minutes hence I shall still exist? I may or I may not, for ought I see; Either seems possible in it self, and either is contingent as to me; I find nothing in my Nature that can warrant my subsistence for one day, for one hour, for one moment longer. I am nothing but Thoughts, fleeting Thoughts, that chase and extinguish one another; and my Being, for ought I know, is successive, and as dying as they are, and renew'd to me every moment. This I am sure of, that so far as I know my self, and am conscious what I am, there is no principle of immutability, or of necessary and indefectible existence in my Nature; and therefore I ought in reason to believe, that I stand or fall at the mercy of other Causes, and not by my own will, or my own sufficiency.

Besides, I am very sensible, and in this I cannot be mistaken, that my Nature is, in several respects, weak and imperfect; both as to Will and Understanding. I *will* many things in vain, and without effect, and I wish often what I have no ability to execute or obtain. And as to my Understanding, how defective is it? how little or nothing do I know in comparison of what I am ignorant of? Almost all the Intellectual World is shut up to me, and the far greatest part of the Corporeal; And in those things that fall under my cognizance, how often am I mistaken? I am confin'd to a narrow sphere, and yet within that sphere I often erre; my conceptions of things are obscure and confus'd, my reason short-sighted; I am forc'd often to correct my self, to acknowledge that I have judg'd false, and consented to an errour. In summ, all my powers I find are limited, and I can easily conceive the same kind of perfections in higher degrees than I possess them, and consequently there are Beings, or may be, greater and more excellent than my self, and more able to subsist by their own power. Why should I not therefore believe that my Original is from those Beings rather than from my self? For every Nature, the more great and perfect it is, the nearer it approacheth to necessity of existence, and to a power of producing other things. Yet, the truth is, it must be acknowledg'd, that so long as the perfections of those other Beings are limited and finite, though they be far superiour to us, there is no necessity ariseth from their Nature that they should exist; and the same Arguments that we have us'd against our selves, they may, in proportion, use against themselves; and therefore we must still advance higher to find a self-originated Being, whose existence must flow immediately from his essence, or have a necessary connexion with it.

Τὸ τέλοιον πρότερον τῇ ουσει τοῦ ἀτελοῦς. *Arist.*

And indeed all these different degrees of higher and higher perfections lead us directly to an highest, or Supream degree, which is Infinite and unlimited Perfection. As subordinate causes lead to the first, so Natures more perfect one than another lead us to a Nature infinitely perfect, which is the Fountain of them all. Thither we must go, if we will follow the course of Reason, which cannot stop at one more than another, till it arrive there; And being arriv'd there, at that Soveraign and Original Perfection, it finds a firm and immoveable ground to stand upon; the steddy Center of all Being, wherein the Mind rests and is satisfied. All the scruples or objections that we mov'd against our selves, or other Creatures, take no place here; This Being is conscious of an All-sufficiency in it self, and of immutability as to any thing else, including in it all the causes of existence, or, to speak more properly, all necessity of existence. Besides, that *we exist our selves*, notwithstanding the imperfection and insufficiency of our Nature, is a just, collateral proof of the existence of this Supream Being; for such an effect as this cannot be without its cause, and it can have no other competent cause but that we mention. And as this Being is its own Origin, so it must needs be capable of producing all Creatures; for whatsoever is possible, must be possible to it; and that Creatures or finite Beings are possible, we both see by experience, and may also discern by Reason; for those several degrees of perfection, or limitations of it, which we mention'd before, are all consistent Notions, and consequently make consistent Natures, and such as may exist; but contingently indeed, and in dependance upon the first Cause.

Thus we are come at length to a fair resolution of that great Question, *Whence we are*, and *how* we continue in Being? And this hath led us by an easie ascent to the Supream Author of Nature, and the first Cause of all things; and presents us also with such a Scheme and Draught of the Universe, as is clear and rational; every thing in its order, and in its place, according to the dignity of its Nature, and the strength of its principles. When the Mind hath rais'd it self into this view of a Being infinitely perfect, 'tis in a Region of Light, hath a free prospect every way, and sees all things from top to bottom, as pervious and transparent. Whereas without God and a First Cause, there is nothing but darkness and confusion in the Mind, and in Nature; broken views of things, short interrupted glimpses of Light, nothing certain or demonstrative, no Basis of Truth, no extent of Thought, no Science, no Contemplation.

You will say, it may be, 'Tis true, something must be *Eternal*, and of *necessary existence*, but why may not *Matter* be this Eternal necessary Being? Then our Souls and all other Intellectual things must be parts and parcels of Matter; and what pretensions can Matter have to those properties and perfections that we find in our Souls, how limited soever? much less to *necessary existence*, and those perfections that are the foundation of it? What exists Eternally, and from it self, its existence must flow immediately from its essence, as its cause, reason or ground; for as Existence hath always something antecedent to it in order of Nature, so that which is antecedent to it must infer it by a necessary connexion, and so may be call'd the cause, ground, or reason of it. And nothing can be such a ground, but what is a perfection; nor every perfection neither, it must be Sovereign and Infinite perfection; for from what else can necessary existence flow, or be inferr'd? Besides, if that Being was not infinitely perfect, there might be another Being more powerful than it, and consequently able to oppose and hinder its existence; and what may be hinder'd is contingent and arbitrary. Now *Matter* is so far from being a Nature infinitely perfect, that it hath no perfection at all, but that of bare *substance*; neither Life, Sense, Will or Understanding; nor so much as Motion, from it self; as we have show'd before. And therefore this brute inactive mass, which is but, as it were, the Drudge of Nature, can have no right or title to that Sovereign prerogative of Self-existence.

We noted before, as a thing agreed upon, *That something or other must needs be Eternal*. For if ever there was a time or state, when there was no Being, there never could be any. Seeing *Nothing* could not produce *Something*. Therefore 'tis undeniably true on all hands, That there was some Being from Eternity. Now, according to our understandings, *Truth* is *Eternal*: therefore, say we, some intellect or intelligent Being. So also the reasons of *Goodness* and *Justice* appear to us Eternal, and therefore some Good and Just Being is Eternal. Thus much is plain, that these perfections which bear the signatures of Eternity upon them, are things that have no relation to *Matter*, but relate immediately to an Intellectual Being: therefore some such Being, to whom they originally belong, must be that *Eternal.* Besides, we cannot possibly but judge such a Being more perfect than Matter; Now every Nature, the more perfect it is, the more remote it is from *Nothing:* and the more remote it is from nothing, the more it approaches to necessity of existence, and consequently to Eternal existence.

Thus we have made a short Survey, so far as the bounds of a Chapter would permit, of those evidences and assurances which we have, from abstract Reason, and the external World, that there is an Author of Nature; and That, a Being infinitely perfect, which we call *God.* We may add to these, in the last place, that universal consent of Mankind, or natural instinct of Religion, which we see, more or less, throughout all Nations, Barbarous or Civil. For though this Argument, 'tis true, be more disputable than the rest, yet having set down just grounds already from whence this Natural judgment or perswasion might spring, we have more reason to impute it to some of those, and their insensible influence upon the Mind, than to the artifices of Men, or to make it a weakness, prejudice, or errour of our Nature. That there is such a propension in Humane Nature, seems to be very plain; at least so far as to move us to implore, and have recourse to invisible Powers in our extremities. Prayer is natural in certain cases, and we do at the meer motion of our natural Spirit, and indeliberately, invoke God and Heaven, either in case of extream danger, to help and assist us; or in case of injustice and oppression, to relieve or avenge us; or in case of false accusation, to vindicate our innocency; and generally in all cases desperate and remediless as to Humane power, we seem to appeal, and address our selves to something higher. And this we do by a sudden impulse of Nature, without reflexion or deliberation. Besides, as witnesses of our Faith and Veracity, we use to invoke the Gods, or Superiour Powers, by way of imprecation upon our selves, if we be false and perjur'd; And this hath been us'd in most Nations and Ages, if not in all. These things also argue, that there is a Natural Conscience in Man, and a distinction of moral *Good* and *Evil*; and that we look upon those invisible Powers as the Guardians of Vertue and Honesty. There are also few or no People upon the Earth but have something of External Religion, true or false; and either of them is an argument of this natural anticipation, or that they have an opinion that there is something above them, and above visible Nature; though what that *something* was, they seldom were able to make a good judgment. But to pursue this Argument particularly, would require an Historical deduction of Times and Places, which is not suitable to our present design.

To conclude this Chapter and this Subject; If we set Religion apart, and consider the Deist and Atheist only as two Sects in Philosophy, or their doctrine as two different *Hypotheses* propos'd for the explication of Nature, and in competition with one another, whether should give the more rational account of the Universe, of its Origin and *Phænomena*; I say, if we consider them only thus, and make an impartial estimate, whether System is more reasonable, more clear, and more satisfactory, to me there seems to be no more comparison, than betwixt light and darkness. The *Hypothesis* of the Deist reacheth from top to bottom, both thorough the Intellectual and Material World, with a clear and distinct light every where; is genuine, comprehensive, and satisfactory; hath nothing forc'd, nothing confus'd, nothing precarious; whereas the *Hypothesis* of the Atheist is strain'd and broken, dark and uneasie to the Mind, commonly precarious, often incongruous and irrational, and sometimes plainly ridiculous. And this judgment I should make of them abstractly from the interest of Religion, considering them only as matter of Reason and Philosophy; *And* I dare affirm with assurance, if the faculties of our Souls be true, that no Man can have a System of Thoughts reaching thorough Nature, coherent and consistent in every part, without a Deity for the Basis of it.

CHAPTER XI
Concerning NATURAL PROVIDENCE.

Several incroachments upon Natural Providence, or misrepresentations of it, and false methods of Contemplation; A true method propos'd, and a true representation of the Universe. The Mundane Idea, *and the Universal System of Providence; Several subordinate Systems, That of our Earth and Sublunary World; The course and Periods of it; How much of this is already treated of, and what remains. The Conclusion.*

WE have set bounds to Nature in the foregoing Chapter, and plac'd her Author and Governour upon his Throne, to give Laws to her Motions, and to direct and limit her Power in such ways and methods as are most for his honour. Let us now consider Nature under the conduct of Providence, or consider *Natural Providence,* and the extent of it; And as we were cautious before not to give too much power or greatness to Nature, consider'd apart from Providence, so we must be careful now, under this second consideration, not to contract her bounds too much; lest we should by too mean and narrow thoughts of the Creation, Eclipse the glory of its Author, whom we have so lately own'd as a Being infinitely perfect.

And to use no further Introduction, In the *first place,* we must not by any means admit or imagine, that all Nature, and this great Universe, was made only for the sake of Man, the meanest of all Intelligent Creatures that we know of; Nor that this little Planet where we sojourn for a few days, is the only habitable part of the Universe; These are Thoughts so groundless and unreasonable in themselves, and also so derogatory to the infinite Power, Wisdom, and Goodness of the First Cause, that as they are absurd in Reason, so they deserve far better to be mark'd and censur'd for Heresies in Religion, than many Opinions that have been censur'd for such, in former Ages. How is it possible that it should enter into the thoughts of vain Man, to believe himself the principal part of God's Creation: or that all the rest was ordain'd for him, for his service or pleasure? Man, whose follies we laugh at every day, or else complain of them; whose pleasures are vanity, and his Passions stronger than his Reason; Who sees himself every way weak and impotent, hath no power over external Nature, little over himself; cannot execute so much as his own good resolutions; mutable, irregular, prone to evil. Surely if we made the least reflection upon our selves with impartiality, we should be asham'd of such an arrogant Thought. How few of these Sons of Men, for whom, they say, all things were made, are the Sons of Wisdom? how few find the paths of Life? They spend a few days in folly and sin, and then go down to the Regions of death and misery. And is it possible to believe, that all Nature, and all Providence, are only, or principally for their sake? Is it not a more reasonable character or conclusion which the Prophet hath made, *Surely every Man is vanity?* Man that comes into the World at the pleasure of another, and goes out by an hundred accidents; His Birth and Education generally determine his fate here, and neither of those are in his own power; His wit also is as uncertain as his fortune; He hath not the moulding of his own Brain: however a knock on the Head makes him a Fool, stupid as the Beasts of the Field; and a little excess of passion or melancholy makes him worse, Mad and frantick. In his best Senses, he is shallow, and of little understanding: and in nothing more blind and ignorant than in things Sacred and Divine; He falls down before a stock or a stone, and says, Thou art my God; He can believe nonsence and contradictions, and make it his Religion to do so. And is this the great Creature which God hath made *by the might of his Power, and for the honour of his Majesty?* upon whom all things must wait, to whom all things must be subservient? Methinks we have noted weaknesses and follies enough in the Nature of Man, this need not be added as the top and accomplishment, *That with all these he is so Vain, as to think that all the rest of the World was made for his sake.*

And as due humility and the consideration of our own meanness, ought to secure us from any such vain opinion of our selves, so the perfection of other Beings ought to give us more respect and honour for them. With what face can we pretend, that Creatures far superiour to us, and more excellent both in Nature and condition, should be made for our sake and service? How preposterous would it be to ascribe such a thing to our Maker, and how intolerable a vanity in us to affect it? We that are next to the Brutes that perish, by a sacrilegious attempt, would make our selves more considerable than the highest Dignities. It is thought to have been the crime of *Lucifer*, who was thrown down from Heaven to Hell, that he affected an equality with the Almighty; and to affect to be next to the Almighty is a crime next to that. We have no reason to believe, but that there are, at least, as many orders of Beings above us, as there are ranks of Creatures below us; there is a greater distance sure betwixt us and God Almighty, than there is betwixt us and the meanest Worm: and yet we should take it very ill, if the Worms of the Earth should pretend that we were made for them. But to pass from the invisible World to the visible and Corporeal, ...

Was that made only for our sake? King *David* was more wise, and more just both to God and man, in his *8th* Psalm; where he says, He wonders, when he considers the Heavens, that the Maker of them could think on Man. He truly supposes the Celestial Bodies and the Inhabitants of them, much more considerable than we are, and reckons up only Terrestrial things as put in subjection to Man. Can we then be so fond as to imagine all the Corporeal Universe made for our use? 'Tis not the millioneth part of it that is known to us, much less useful; We can neither reach with our Eye, nor our imagination, those Armies of Stars that lie far and deep in the boundless Heavens. If we take a good Glass, we discover innumerably more Stars in the Firmament than we can with our single Eye; And yet if you take a second Glass, better than the first, that carries the sight to a greater distance, you see more still lying beyond the other; And a third Glass that pierceth further, still make new discoveries of Stars; and so forwards, indefinitely and inexhaustedly for any thing we know, according to the immensity of the Divine Nature and Power. Who can reckon up the Stars of the Galaxy, or direct us in the use of them? And can we believe that those and all the rest were made for us? Of those few Stars that we enjoy, or that are visible to the Eye, there is not a tenth part that is really useful to Man; And no doubt if the principal end of them had been our pleasure or conveniency, they would have been put in some better order in respect of the Earth; They lie carelessly scatter'd, as if they had been sown in the Heaven, like Seed, by handfuls; and not by a skilful hand neither. What a beautiful Hemisphere they would have made, if they had been plac'd in rank and order, if they had been all dispos'd into regular figures, and the little ones set with due regard to the greater, Then all finisht and made up into one fair piece or great Composition, according to the rules of Art and Symmetry. What a surprizing beauty this would have been to the Inhabitants of the Earth? what a lovely Roof to our little World? This indeed might have given one some temptation to have thought that they had been all made for us; but lest any such vain imagination should now enter into our thoughts, Providence (besides more important Reasons) seems on purpose to have left them under that negligence or disorder which they appear in to us.

The second part of this opinion supposeth this Planet, where we live, to be the only habitable part of the Universe; And this is a natural consequence of the former; If all things were made to serve us, why should any more be made than what is useful to us. But 'tis only our ignorance of the System of the World, and of the grandeur of the works of God, that betrays us to such narrow thoughts.

See the Lat. Treat. lib. I. c. 10, p. 108, 109, &c.

If we do but consider what this Earth is, both for littleness and deformity, and what its Inhabitants are, we shall not be apt to think that this miserable Atome hath engross'd and exhausted all the Divine favours, and all the riches of his goodness, and of his Providence. But we will not inlarge upon this part of the opinion, lest it should carry us too far from the subject, and it will fall, of its own accord, with the former. Upon the whole we may conclude, that it was only the Sublunary World that was made for the sake of Man, and not the Great Creation, either Material or Intellectual; and we cannot admit or affirm any more, without manifest injury, depression, and misrepresentation of Providence, as we may be easily convinc'd from these four Heads; *The* meanness of Man and of this Earth, *The* excellency of other Beings, *The* immensity of the Universe, And *The* infinite perfection of the first Cause. Which I leave to your further meditation, and pass on to the second rule, concerning Natural Providence.

In the second place then, if we would have a fair view and right apprehensions, of Natural Providence, we must not cut the chains of it too short, by having recourse, without necessity, either to the First Cause, in explaining the Origins of things: or to Miracles, in explaining particular effects. This, I say, breaks the chains of Natural Providence, when it is done without necessity, that is, when things are otherwise intelligible from second Causes. Neither is any thing gain'd by it to God Almighty; for 'tis but, as the Proverb says, to rob *Peter* to pay *Paul*, to take so much from his ordinary Providence, and place it to his extraordinary. When a new Religion is brought into the World, 'tis very reasonable and decorous that it should be usher'd in with Miracles, as both the *Jewish* and *Christian* were; but afterwards things return into their Chanel, and do not change or overflow again, but upon extraordinary occasions or revolutions. The power *Extraordinary* of God is to be accounted very Sacred, not to be touch'd or expos'd for our pleasure or conveniency; but I am afraid we often make use of it only to conceal our own ignorance, or to save us the trouble of inquiring into Natural Causes. Men are generally unwilling to appear ignorant, especially those that make profession of knowledge, and when they have not skill enough to explain some particular effect in a way of Reason, they throw it upon the First Cause, as able to bear all; and so placing it to that account, they excuse themselves, and save their credit; for all men are equally wise, if you take away Second Causes; as we are all of the same colour, if you take away the Light.

But to state this matter, and see the ground of this rule more distinctly, we must observe and consider, that *The Course of Nature is truly the Will of God*; and as I may so say, his first Will; from which we are not to recede, but upon clear evidence and necessity. And as in matter of Religion, we are to follow the known reveal'd will of God, and not to trust to every impulse or motion of Enthusiasm, as coming from the Divine Spirit, unless there be evident marks that it is Supernatural, and cannot come from our own; So neither are we, without necessity, to quit the known and ordinary Will and Power of God establisht in the course of Nature, and fly to Supernatural Causes, or his extraordinary Will; for this is a kind of Enthusiasm or Fanaticism, as well as the other: And no doubt that great prodigality and waste of Miracles which some make, is no way to the honour of God or Religion. 'Tis true, the other extream is worse than this, for to deny all Miracles, is in effect to deny all reveal'd Religion; therefore due measures are to be taken betwixt these two, fo as neither to make the Divine Power too mean and cheap, nor the Power of Nature illimited and all-sufficient.

See Book 1. *c.* 8. *at the end.*

In the Third Place, To make the Scenes of Natural Providence considerable, and the knowledge of them satisfactory to the Mind, we must take a true Philosophy, or the true principles that govern Nature, which are Geometrical and Mechanical. By these you discover the footsteps of the Divine Art and Wisdom, and trace the progress of Nature step by step, as distinctly as in Artificial things, where we see how the Motions depend upon one another, in what order and by what necessity. God made all things in *Number*, *Weight* and *Measure*, which are Geometrical and Mechanical Principles; He is not said to have made things by *Forms* and *Qualities*, or any combination of qualities, but by these three principles, which may be conceiv'd to express the subject of three Mathematical Sciences, *Number*, of *Arithmetick*; Weight, of *Staticks*; and *Measure* and Proportion, of *Geometry*; If then all things were made according to these principles, to understand the manner of their construction and composition, we must proceed in the search of them by the same principles, and resolve them into these again. Besides, the nature of the subject does direct us sufficiently; for when we contemplate or treat of Bodies, and the Material World, we must proceed by the modes of Bodies and their real properties, such as can be represented, either to Sense or Imagination, for these faculties are made for Corporeal things; but Logical Notions, when appli'd to particular Bodies, are meer shadows of them, without light or substance. No man can raise a Theory upon such grounds, nor calculate any revolutions of Nature; nor render any service, or invent any thing useful in Humane Life: And accordingly we see, that for these many Ages, that this dry Philosophy hath govern'd Christendom, it hath brought forth no fruit, produc'd nothing good, to God or Man, to Religion or Humane Society.

To these true principles of Philosophy, we must joyn also the true System of the World. That gives scope to our thoughts, and rational grounds to work upon; but the vulgar System, or that which *Aristotle* and others have propos'd, affords no matter of contemplation. All above the Moon, according to him, is firm as Adamant, and as immutable; no change or variation in the Universe, but in those little removes that happen here below, one quality or form shifting into another; there would therefore be no great exercise of Reason or Meditation in such a World, no long Series's of Providence; The Regions above being made of a kind of immutable Matter, they would always remain in the same form, structure, and qualities: so as we might lock up that part of the Universe as to any further Inquiries, and we should find it ten thousand years hence in the same form and state wherein we left it. Then in this Sublunary World there would be but very small doings neither, things would lie in a narrow compass, no great revolution of Nature, no new Form of the Earth, but a few anniversary *Corruptions* and *Generations*, and that would be the short and the long of Nature, and of Providence, according to *Aristotle*. But if we consider the Earth, as one of those many Planets that move about the Sun, and the Sun as one of those innumerable fixt Stars that adorn the Universe, and are the Centers of its greatest Motions; and all this subject to fate and change, to corruptions and renovations; This opens a large Field for our Thoughts, and gives a large subject for the exercise and expansion of the Divine Wisdom and Power, and for the glory of his Providence.

In the last place, Having thus prepar'd your Mind, and the subject, for the Contemplation of *Natural Providence*, do not content yourself to consider only the present face of Nature, but look back into the first *Sources* of things, into their more simple and original states; and observe the progress of Nature from one form to another, through various modes and compositions. For there is no single Effect, nor any single state of Nature, how perfect soever, that can be such an argument and demonstration of Providence, as a Period of Nature, or a revolution of several states consequential to one another; and in such an order and dependance, that as they flow and succeed, they shall still be adjusted to the periods of the moral World; so as to be ready always to be the ministers of the Divine Justice or beneficence to Mankind. This shows the manifold riches of the Wisdom and Power of God in Nature. And this may give us just occasion to reflect again upon *Aristotle*'s System and method, which destroys Natural Providence in this respect also; for he takes the World as it is now, both for Matter and Form, and supposeth it to have been in this posture from all Eternity, and that it will continue to Eternity in the same; so as all the great turns of Nature, and the principal scenes of Providence in the Natural World are quite struck out; and we have but this one Scene for all, and a pitiful one too, if compar'd with the infinite Wisdom of God, and the depths of Providence. We must take things in their full extent, and from their Origins, to comprehend them well, and to discover the mysteries of Providence, both in the Causes and in the Conduct of them. That method which *David* followed in the contemplation of the Little World, or in the Body of Man, we should also follow in the Great; take it in its first mass, in its tender principles and rudiments, and observe the progress of it to a compleat form; In these first stroaks of Nature are the secrets of her Art; The Eye must be plac'd in this point to have a right prospect, and see her works in a true light.   *David* admires the Wisdom of God in the Origin and formation of his Body; *My Body*, says He, *was not hid from thee, when I was made in secret, curiously*   Psal. 139. 15, 16. *wrought in the lower parts of the Earth; Thine eyes did see my substance being yet unperfect, and in thy Book all my members were written; which in continuance were fashioned, when as yet there was none of them*, or being at first in no form. *How precious are thy Thoughts to me, O God*, &c. This was the subject of *David*'s Meditations, how his Body was wrought from a shapeless mass into that marvellous composition which it had when fully fram'd; and this, he says, was under the Eye of God all along, and the model of it, as it were, was design'd and delineated in the Book of Providence, according to which it was by degrees fashion'd and wrought to perfection. *Thine eyes did see my substance yet being imperfect, in thy Book all my members were drawn*, &c. *Job* also hath aptly exprest those first rudiments of the Body, or that little Chaos out of which it riseth, *Hast thou not poured*   Job 10. 10, 11. *me out as Milk, and crudled me like Cheese? Thou hast cloathed me with Skin and Flesh, and fenced me with Bones and Sinews.* Where he notes the first Matter and the last Form of his Body, its compleat and most incompleat state. According to these examples we must likewise consider the Greater Bodies of Nature, The Earth and the Sublunary World; we must go to the Origin of them, the Seminal Mass, the Chaos out of which they rise; Look upon the World first as an Embryo-world, without form or shape, and then consider how its Members were fashion'd, how by degrees it was brought into that diversity of parts and Regions, which it consists of, with all their furniture, and with all their ornaments. The *Idea* of all which was beforehand, according to *David*'s expression, written in the Divine Mind; and we partake of that wisdom, according to our capacity, in seeing and admiring the methods of it.

These seem to be necessary preparatives or directions to those that would contemplate, with profit, Natural Providence, and the great works of God in the visible Creation. We consider'd Nature in the precedent Chapter abstractly, and in her self, and now we consider her under the Conduct of Providence, which we therefore call Natural Providence; And as we have endeavour'd to remove those false notions and suppositions that lay as Clouds upon her face, so we must now endeavour to represent her in a better light, and in a fuller beauty. By *Natural Providence* therefore we understand, *The Form or Course of Universal Nature, as actuated by the Divine Power:* with all the changes, Periods, and vicissitudes, that attend it, according to the method and establishment made at first, by the Author of it. I said of *Universal Nature,* through all the orders of Beings in the Intellectual World, and all the Regions and Systems of Matter in the Corporeal. For, having prov'd in the foregoing Chapter, that there is an Author of Nature, A Being infinitely Perfect, by whose power and influence alone all finite Natures exist and act, we have an assured ground to conclude, that nothing can come to pass, throughout the whole Creation, without the prescience and permission of its Author; and as it is necessary to suppose, that there is an *Idea* in the Divine Understanding of all the mass of Beings produc'd or Created, according to the several ranks and orders wherein they stand; so there is also an *Idea* there, according to which this great Frame moves, and all the parts of it, in beauty and harmony

And these two things, The *Essences* of all Beings, and the Series of their *Motions,* compose the MUNDANE IDEA, as I may so call it; or that great All-comprehensive Thought in the Divine Understanding, which contains the System of Universal Providence, and the state of all things, past, present, or to come. This glorious *Idea* is the express Image of the whole Creation, of all the works of God, and the disposition of them; here lie the mysteries of Providence, as in their Original; The successive Forms of all Nature; and herein, as in a Glass, may be view'd all the Scenes of Time or Eternity. This is an Abysse of Sacred Wisdom, The inexhausted treasure of all Science, The Root of Truth, and Fountain of Intellectual Light; And in the clear and full contemplation of this is perfect happiness, and a truly beatifick Vision.

But what concerns the Intellectual World in this *Idea,* and the Orders or Natures that compose it, is not our present business to pursue; We are to speak of the Corporeal Universe, whereof we will make now a short and general Survey, as it lies under Providence. The Corporeal Universe, how immense soever it be, and divided into innumerable Regions, may be consider'd all as one System, made up of several subordinate Systems. And there is also one immense design of Providence co-extended with it, that contains all the fate, and all the revolutions of this great Mass. This, I say, is made up of several subordinate Systems, involving one another, and comprehending one another, in greater and greater Orbs and Compositions; and the Aggregate of all these is that which we call the *Universe.* But what the Form of these Compositions is, and what the Design of Providence that runs thorough them all, and comprehends them all, this is unsearchable, not only to Humane Understanding, but even to Angels and Archangels.

Wherefore leaving those greater Systems and Compositions of the Universe, as matter of our admiration, rather than of our knowledge, There are two or three kinds of lesser Systems that are visible to us, and bring us nearer to our subject, and nearer home. *That* of a Fixt Star, single; *That* of a Fixt Star with its Planets, and *That* of a single Planet, Primary or Secondary. These three Systems we see and enjoy more or less. No doubt there are Fixt Stars single, or that have no Planets about them, as our Sun hath; nay, 'tis probable, that at first the whole Universe consisted only of such; Globes of liquid Fire, with Spheres about them of pure Light and Æther: Earths are but the dirt and skum of the Creation, and all things were pure as they came at first out of the hands of God. But because we have nothing particular taught us, either by the light of Nature or Revelation, concerning the Providence that governs these single Stars, of what use they are to Intellectual Beings, how animated by them, what diversity there is amongst those Æthereal Worlds, what Periods they have, what Changes or Vicissitudes they are capable to undergo; because such Inquiries would seem too remote, and carry us too far from our subject, we leave these Heavenly Systems to the enjoyment and contemplation of higher and more noble Creatures.

The Sun, with all the Planets that move about him, and depend upon him, make a second sort of System; not considerable indeed, if compar'd with the whole Universe, or some of the greater Compositions in it, but in respect of us, the System of the Sun is of vast extent; We cannot measure the greatness of his Kingdom, and his Dominion is without end. The distance from the highest Planet to the nearest fixt Star in the Firmament is unmeasurable, and all this belongs to the Empire of the Sun; besides the several Planets and their Orbs, which cast themselves closer about his Body, that they may receive a warmer and stronger influence from him; for by him they may be said to *live* and *move*. But those vast spaces that lie beyond these opake Bodies, are Regions of perpetual light; One Planet may eclipse the Sun to another, and one Hemisphere of a Planet to the other Hemisphere makes night and darkness, but nothing can eclipse the Sun, or intercept the course of his light to these remote Æthereal Regions; They are always luminous, and always pure and serene. And if the worst and Planetary parts of his Dominions be replenisht with Inhabitants, we cannot suppose the better to lie as Desarts, uninjoy'd and uninhabited; his Subjects then must be numerous, as well as his Dominions large; And in both respects, this System of a Fixt Star, with its Planets (of which kind we may imagine innumerable in the Universe, besides this of the Sun, which is near and visible to us) is of a noble Character and Order, being the habitation of Angels and glorified Spirits, as well as of mortal Men.

A Planetary System is the last and lowest; And of these, no doubt, there is great variety, and great differences; not only of Primary and Secondary, or of the principal Planet, and its Moons or Attendants, but also amongst Planets of the same rank; for they may differ both in their original constitution, and according to the form and state they are under at present; of which sort of differences we have noted* some amongst our Planets, though they seem to be all of muchwhat the same original constitution. Besides, according to external circumstances, their distance, manner of motion, and posture to the Sun, which is the Heart of the whole System, they become different in many things. And we may observe, that those leading differences, though they seem little, draw after them innumerable others, and so make a distinct face of Nature, and a distinct World; which still shows the riches and fecundity of Divine Providence, and gives new matter of contemplation to those that take pleasure in studying the works and ways of

---

* *Book* I, *chap. last, p.* 128, *&c.*

God. But leaving all other Planets or Planetary Systems to our meditations only, we must particularly consider our own.

Having therefore made this general Survey of the great Universe, run thorough the boundless Regions of it, and with much ado found our way home to that little Planet where our concerns lie, This Earth or Sublunary World, we must rest here as at the end of our course; And having undertaken to give the general Theory of this Earth, to conclude the present Treatise, we'll reflect upon the whole work, and observe what progress we have hitherto made in this Theory, and what remains to be treated of hereafter. This Earth, though it be a small part or particle of the Universe, hath a distinct System of Providence belonging to it, or an Order establisht by the Author of Nature for all its *Phænomena* (Natural or Moral) throughout the whole Period of its duration, and every interval of it; for as there is nothing so great as to be above the Divine care, so neither is there any thing so little as to be below it. All the Changes of our World are fixt, How, or how often to be destroy'd, and how renew'd; What different faces of Nature, and what of Mankind, in every part of its Course; What new Scenes to adorn the Stage, and what new parts to be Acted; What the Entrance, and what the Consummation of all. Neither is there any sort of knowledge more proper, or of more importance to us that are the Inhabitants of this Earth, than to understand this its Natural and Sacred History, as I may so call it, both as to what is past, and what is to come. And as those greater Volumes and Compositions of the Universe are proportion'd to the understanding of Angels and Superiour Beings, so these little Systems are *Compendium*'s of the Divine Wisdom, more fitted to our capacity and comprehension.

The Providence of the Earth, as of all other Systems, consists of two parts, Natural, and Sacred or Theological. I call that Sacred or Theological that respects Religion, and the dispensations of it; the government of the Rational World, or of Mankind, whether under the light of Nature only, or of a Revelation; the method and terms of their happiness and unhappiness in a future life; The State, Oeconomy, and Conduct of this, with all the Mysteries contain'd in it, we call Theological Providence; in the head whereof stands the Soul of the Blessed *Messiah,* who is Lord of both Worlds, Intellectual and Material. When we call the other part of Providence *Natural,* we use that word in a restrain'd sence, as respecting only the Material World; and accordingly this part of Providence orders and superintends the state of the Earth, the great Vicissitudes and Mutations of it; for we must not imagine, but that these are under the eye of Providence, as well as Humane affairs, or any revolutions of States and Empires. Now seeing both in the Intellectual and Corporeal World there are certain Periods, Fulnesses of Time, and fixt Seasons, either for some great Catastrophe, or some great Instauration, 'Tis Providence that makes a due harmony or Synchronism betwixt these two, and measures out the concurrent fates of both Worlds, so as Nature may be always a faithful minister of the Divine pleasure, whether for rewards or punishments, according as the state of Mankind may require. But Theological Providence not being the subject of this work, we shall only observe, as we said before, what account we have hitherto given of the Natural state of the Earth, and what remains to be handled in another Treatise, and so conclude.

226

I did not think it necessary to carry the story and original of the Earth, higher than the Chaos, as *Zoroaster* and *Orpheus* seem to have done; but taking That for our Foundation, which Antiquity Sacred and Profane doth suppose, and Natural Reason approve and confirm, we have form'd the Earth from it. But when we say the Earth rise from a Fluid Mass, it is not to be so crudely understood, as if a rock of Marble, suppose, was fluid immediately before it became Marble; no, Things had a gradual progression from one form to another, and came at length to those more permanent forms they are now setled in: Stone was once Earth, and Earth was once Mud, and Mud was once fluid. And so other things may have another kind of progression from fluidity; but all was once fluid, at least all the exteriour Regions of this Earth. And even those Stones and Rocks of Marble which we speak of, seem to confess they were once soft or liquid, by those mixtures we find in them of Heterogeneous Bodies, and those spots and Veins disperst thorough their substance; for these things could not happen to them after they were hard and impenetrable, in the form of Stone or Marble. And if we can soften Rocks and Stones, and run them down into their first Liquors, as these observations seem to do, we may easily believe that other Bodies also that compose the Earth, were once in a fluid Mass, which is that we call a Chaos.

We therefore watch'd the motions of that Chaos, and the several transformations of it, while it continued Fluid; and we found at length what its first Concretion would be, and how it setled into the form of an habitable Earth. But that form was very different from the present form of the Earth, which is not deducible from a Chaos, by any known laws of Nature, or by any wit of Man; as every one, that will have patience to examine it, may easily be satisfied. That first Earth was of a smooth regular surface, as the Concretions of Liquors are, before they are disturb'd or broken; under that surface lay the Great Abysse, which was ready to swallow up the World that hung over it, and about it, whensoever God should give the command, and the Vault should break; And this constitution of the Primæval Earth gave occasion to the first Catastrophe of this World, when it perisht in a Deluge of Water. For that Vault did break, as we have shown at large, and by the dissolution and fall of it, the Great Deep was thrown out of its bed, forc'd upwards into the Air, and overflow'd, in that impetuous Commotion, the highest tops of the Fragments of the ruin'd Earth, which now we call its Mountains. And as this was the first great and fatal Period of Nature; so upon the issue of this, and the return of the Waters into their Chanels, the second face of Nature appear'd, or the present broken form of the Earth, as it is *Terraqueous, Mountainous,* and *Cavernous.* These things we have explain'd fully in the first Book, and have thereby setled two great Points, given a rational account of the *Universal Deluge,* And shown the Causes of the irregular form of the present or *Post-diluvian Earth.* This being done, we have appli'd our selves, in the Second Book, to the description of the *Primæval Earth,* and the examination of its properties; And this hath led us by an easie tract to the discovery of *Paradise,* and of the true Notion and Mystery of it; which is not so much a spot of ground where a fine Garden stood, as a course of Nature, or a peculiar state of the Earth; *Paradisiacal* in many parts, but especially in one Region of it; which place or Region we have also endeavour'd to determine, though not so much from the Theory, as from the suffrages of Antiquity.

THUS much is finisht, and this contains the Natural Theory of the Earth till this present time; for since the Deluge all things have continued in the same state, or without any remarkable change. We are next to enter upon new Matter and new Thoughts, and not only so, but upon a Series of *Things and Times to come*, which is to make the Second part of this Theory. Dividing the duration of the World into two parts, Past and Future, we have dispatch'd the first and far greater part, and come better half our way; And if we make a stand here, and look both ways, backwards to the Chaos, and the Beginning of the World, and forwards to the End and consummation of all things, though the first be a longer prospect, yet there are as many general Changes and Revolutions of Nature in the remaining part as have already happen'd; and in the Evening of this long Day the Scenes will change faster, and be more bright and illustrious. From the Creation to this Age the Earth hath undergone but one Catastrophe, and Nature hath had two different faces; The next Catastrophe is the CONFLAGRATION, to which a new face of Nature will accordingly suceed, *New Heavens* and a *New Earth*, *Paradise* renew'd, and so it is call'd the *Restitution* of things, or *Regeneration* of the World. And that Period of Nature and Providence being expir'd, then follows the *Consummation of all things*, or the General *Apotheosis*; *when Death and Hell shall be swallowed up in victory*; When the great Circle of Time and Fate is run; or according to the language of Scripture, *When the Heavens and the Earth shall pass away, and Time shall be no more.*

MAY we, in the mean time, by a true Love of God above all things, and a contempt of this Vain World which passeth away; By a careful use of the Gifts of God and Nature, the Light of Reason and Revelation, prepare our selves, and the state of things, for the great Coming of our Saviour. To whom be Praise and Honour for evermore.

'Ατοκατά ζασις, ναλιγζενεσία.

Effigies Authoris.

THE
THEORY
OF THE
EARTH:

Containing an Account
OF THE
Original of the Earth,

AND OF ALL THE
GENERAL CHANGES

Which it hath already undergone,

OR

IS TO UNDERGO,

Till the CONSUMMATION of all Things.

THE TWO LAST BOOKS,

Concerning the BURNING *of the* WORLD,

AND

Concerning the NEW HEAVENS and NEW EARTH.

LONDON,

Printed by *R. Norton*, for *Walter Kettilby*, at the Bishop's
Head in St. *Paul's* Church-Yard. 1690.

TO THE
QUEEN'S
MOST
Excellent Majesty

MADAM,

*H*AVING *had the honour to present the first part of this Theory to Your ROYAL UNCLE, I presume to offer the Second to Your Majesty. This part of the Subject, I hope, will be no less acceptable, for certainly 'tis of no less importance. They both indeed agree in this, That there is a WORLD made and destroy'd in either Treatise. But we are more concern'd in what is to come, than in what is past. And as the former Books represented to us the Rise and Fall of the First World; so These give an account of the present Frame of Nature labouring under the last Flames, and of the Resurrection of it in the* New Heavens *and* New Earth: *which, according to the Divine Promises, we are to expect.*

Cities that are burnt, are commonly rebuilt more beautiful and regular than they were before. And when this World is demolish'd by the last Fire, He that undertakes to rear it up again, will supply the defects, if there were any, of the former Fabrick. This Theory supposes the present Earth to be little better than an Heap of Ruines: where yet there is room enough for Sea and Land, for Islands and Continents, for several Countries and Dominions: But when these are all melted down, and refin'd in the general Fire, they will be cast into a better mould, and the Form and Qualities of the Earth will become Paradisiacal.

But, I fear, it may be thought no very proper address, to shew Your Majesty a World laid in ashes, where You have so great an interest Your Self, and such fair Dominions; and then, to recompence the loss by giving a Reversion in a Future Earth. But if that future Earth be a second Paradise, to be enjoyed for a Thousand Years; with Peace, Innocency, and constant health: An Inheritance there will be an happy exchange for the best Crown in this World.

I confess, I could never perswade my self, that the Kingdom of Christ and of his Saints, which the Scripture speaks of so frequently, was design'd to be upon this present Earth. But however, upon all suppositions, They that have done some eminent Good in this Life, will be sharers in the happiness of that State. To humble the Oppressors, and rescue the Oppressed, is a work of Generosity and Charity that cannot want its reward; Yet, MADAM, *They are the greatest Benefactors to Mankind, that dispose the World to become Vertuous: and by their example, Influence, and Authority, retrieve that* TRUTH *and* JUSTICE, *that have been lost, amongst* men, for many Ages. *The School-Divines tell us, Those that act or suffer great things for the Publick Good, are distinguish'd in Heaven by a Circle of Gold about their Heads. One would not willingly vouch for that: but one may safely for what the Prophet says, which is far greater: namely, that They shall shine like Stars in the Firmament,* that turn many to Righteousness. *Which is not to be understood, so much, of the Conversion of single Souls, as of the turning of Nations and People, The turning of the World to Righteousness. They that lead on that great and happy Work, shall be distinguish'd in Glory from the rest of Mankind.*

We are sensible, MADAM, *from Your Great Example, that Piety and Vertue seated upon a Throne, draw many to imitation, whom ill Principles, or the course of the World, might have led another way. These are the best, as well as easiest Victories, that are gain'd without Contest. And as Princes are the Vicegerents of God upon Earth, so when their Majesty is in Conjunction with Goodness, it hath a double Character of Divinity upon it: and we owe them a double Tribute, of Fear and Love. Which, with constant Prayers for Your* MAJESTY'S *present and future Happiness, shall be always Dutifully paid, by*

Your MAJESTY'S

Most Humble and most

Obedient Subject,

T. BURNET.

PREFACE

TO THE

READER

I HAVE not much to say to the Reader in this Preface to the Third Part of the Theory: seeing it treats upon a Subject own'd by all, and out of dispute: *The Conflagration of the World*. The question will be only about the bounds and limits of the Conflagration, the Causes and the Manner of it. These I have fix'd according to the truest measures I could take from Scripture, and from Nature. I differ, I believe, from the common Sentiment in this, that, in following St. *Peter*'s Philosophy, I suppose, that the burning of the Earth will be a true Liquefaction or dissolution of it, as to the exteriour Region. And that this lays a foundation for *New Heavens* and a *New Earth*; which seems to me as plain a doctrine in Christian Religion, as the Conflagration it self.

I have endeavour'd to propose an intelligible way, whereby the Earth may be consum'd by Fire. But if any one can propose another, more probable and more consistent, I will be the first man that shall give him thanks for his discovery. He that loves Truth for its own sake, is willing to receive it from any hand: as he that truly loves his Country, is glad of a Victory over the Enemy, whether himself, or any other, has the glory of it. I need not repeat here, what I have already said upon several occasions, That 'tis the substance of this Theory, whether in this part or in other parts, that I mainly regard and depend upon. Being willing to suppose that many single explications and particularities may be rectified, upon further thoughts and clearer light. I know our best writings, in this life, are but *Essays*, which we leave to Posterity to review and correct.

As to the Style, I always endeavour to express my self, in a plain and perspicuous manner: that the Reader may not lose time, nor wait too long, to know my meaning. To give an Attendant quick dispatch, is a civility, whether you do his business or no. I would not willingly give any one the trouble of reading a period twice over, to know the sence of it: lest when he comes to know it, he should not think it a recompence for his pains. Whereas, on the contrary, if you are easie to your Reader, he will certainly make you an allowance for it, in his censure.

You must not think it strange however, that the Author sometimes, in meditating upon this subject, is warm in his thoughts and expressions. For to see a World perishing in Flames, Rocks melting, the Earth trembling, and an Host of Angels in the clouds, one must be very much a Stoick, to be a cold and unconcerned Spectator of all this. And when we are mov'd our selves, our words will have a tincture of those passions which we feel. Besides, in moral reflections which are designed for use, there must be some heat, as well as dry reason, to inspire this cold clod of clay, this dull body of earth, which we carry about with us; and you must soften and pierce that crust, before you can come at the Soul. But especially when things future are to be represented, you cannot use too strong Colours, if you would give them life, and make them appear present to the mind. Farewel.

CONTENTS
OF THE
CHAPTERS

___

THE THIRD BOOK

CHAPTER I

*T*HE *Introduction; with the Contents and Order of this Treatise.*

CHAPTER II

The true state of the Question is propos'd. 'Tis the general doctrine of the Ancients, That the present World, or the present Frame of Nature, is mutable and perishable: To which the Sacred Books agree: And natural Reason can alledge nothing against it.

CHAPTER III

That the World will be destroy'd by Fire, is the doctrine of the Ancients, especially of the Stoicks. That the same doctrine is more ancient than the Greeks, and deriv'd from the Barbarick *Philosophy, and That probably from* Noah, *the Father of all Traditionary Learning. The same doctrine expresly authoriz'd by Revelation, and inroll'd into the Sacred Canon.*

CHAPTER IV

Concerning the Time of the Conflagration, and the End of the World. What the Astronomers say upon this Subject, and upon what they ground their Calculations. The true notion of the Great Year, or of the Platonick Year, stated and explain'd.

CHAPTER V

Concerning Prophecies that determine the End of the World; Of what order soever, Prophane or Sacred: Jewish *or Christian. That no certain judgment can be made from any of them, at which distance we are from the Conflagration.*

CHAPTER VI

Concerning the Causes of the Conflagration. The difficulty of conceiving how this Earth can be set on fire. With a general answer to that difficulty. Two suppos'd Causes of the Conflagration, by the Sun's drawing nearer to the Earth, or the Earth's throwing out the Central Fire, examin'd and rejected.

CHAPTER VII

The true bounds of the last Fire, and how far it is Fatal. The natural Causes and Materials of it, cast into three ranks. First, such as are exteriour and visible upon Earth. Where the Volcano's of this Earth, and their Effects are consider'd. Secondly, such Materials as are within the Earth. Thirdly, such as are in the Air.

CHAPTER VIII

Some new dispositions towards the Conflagration, as to the Matter, Form, and Situation of the Earth. Concerning miraculous Causes, and how far the ministery of Angels may be engag'd in this work.

CHAPTER IX

How the Sea will be diminish'd and consum'd. How the Rocks and Mountains will be thrown down and melted, and the whole exteriour Frame of the Earth dissolv'd into a Deluge of Fire.

CHAPTER X

Concerning the beginning and progress of the Conflagration, what part of the Earth will first be burnt. The manner of the future destruction of Rome. *The last state and consummation of the general Fire.*

CHAPTER XI

An Account of those Extraordinary Phænomena and Wonders in Nature, that, according to Scripture, will precede the coming of Christ, and the Conflagration of the World.

CHAPTER XII

An imperfect description of the coming of our Saviour, and of the World on fire.

The Conclusion.

THE FOURTH BOOK

CHAPTER I

*T*HE *Introduction: That the World will not be annihilated in the last fire. That we are to expect, according to Scripture, and the Christian doctrine, New Heavens and a New Earth, when these are dissolv'd or burnt up.*

CHAPTER II

The Birth of the New Heavens and the New Earth, from the second Chaos, or the remains of the old World. The form, order and qualities of the new Earth, according to Reason and Scripture.

CHAPTER III

Concerning the Inhabitants of the New Earth. That natural reason cannot determine this point. That, according to Scripture, The Sons of the first Resurrection, or the heirs of the Millennium, are to be the Inhabitants of the New Earth. The Testimony of the Philosophers, and of the Christian Fathers, for the Renovation of the World. The first Proposition laid down.

CHAPTER IV

The Proof of a Millennium, or of a blessed Age to come, from Scripture. A view of the Apocalypse, and of the Prophecies of Daniel, *in reference to this kingdom of Christ, and of his Saints.*

CHAPTER V

A view of other places of Scripture, concerning the Millennium, or future kingdom of Christ. In what sence all the Prophets have born Testimony concerning it.

CHAPTER VI

The sence and testimony of the Primitive Church, concerning the Millennium, or future kingdom of Christ: from the times of the Apostles to the Nicene Council. *The second Proposition laid down. When, by what means, and for what reasons, that doctrine was afterwards neglected or discountenanc'd.*

CHAPTER VII

The true state of the Millennium, according to Characters taken from Scripture. Some mistakes concerning it rectified.

CHAPTER VIII

The third Proposition laid down, concerning the Time and Place of the Millennium. Several arguments us'd to prove, that it cannot be till after the Conflagration: and that the New Heavens and New Earth are the true Seat of the Blessed Millennium.

CHAPTER IX

The chief employment of the Millennium, DEVOTION and CONTEMPLATION.

CHAPTER X

Objections against the Millennium, answer'd. With some conjectures concerning the state of things after the Millennium: and what will be the final Consummation of this World.

A Review of the whole Theory.

THE
THEORY
OF THE
EARTH

BOOK III
Concerning the Conflagration.

CHAPTER I

THE INTRODUCTION
With the Contents and Order of this Work.

SEEING Providence hath planted in all Men a natural desire and curiosity of knowing things to come; and such things especially as concern our particular Happiness, or the general Fate of mankind: This Treatise may, in both respects, hope for a favourable reception amongst inquisitive persons; seeing the design of it is, to give an account of the greatest revolutions of Nature that are expected in future Ages; and in the first place, of the *Conflagration of the World*. In which Universal Calamity, when all Nature suffers, every man's particular concern must needs be involv'd.

We see with what eagerness men pry into the Stars, to see if they can read there the Death of a King, or the fall of an Empire: 'Tis not the fate of any single Prince or Potentate, that we Calculate, but of all Mankind: Nor of this or that particular Kingdom or Empire, but of the whole Earth. Our enquiries must reach to that great period of Nature, when all things are to be dissolv'd: both humane affairs, and the Stage whereon they are acted. When the Heavens and the Earth will pass away, and the Elements melt with fervent heat. We desire, if possible, to know what will be the face of that Day, that great and terrible Day, when the Regions of the Air will be nothing but mingled Flame and Smoak, and the habitable Earth turn'd into a Sea of molten Fire.

But we must not leave the World in this disorder and confusion, without examining what will be the Issue and Consequences of it. Whether this will be the End of all things, and Nature, by a sad fate, lie eternally dissolv'd and desolate in this manner: or whether we may hope for a Restauration: *New Heavens* and a *New Earth*, which the Holy Writings make mention of, more pure and perfect than the former. As if this was but as a *Refiner's fire*, to purge out the dross and courser parts, and then cast the Mass again into a new and better Mould. These things, with God's assistance, shall be matter of our present enquiry; These make the general subject of this Treatise, and of the remaining parts of this *Theory* of the Earth. Which now, you see, begins to be a kind of Prophecy, or Prognostication of things to come: as it hath been hitherto an History of things pass'd; of such states and changes as Nature hath already undergone. And if that account which we have given of the Origine of the Earth, its first and Paradisiacal form, and the dissolution of it at the universal Deluge, appear fair and reasonable: The Second dissolution by Fire, and the renovation of it out of a second Chaos, I hope will be deduc'd from as clear grounds and suppositions. And Scripture it self will be a more visible Guide to us in these following parts of the Theory, than it was in the former. In the mean time, I take occasion to declare here again, as I have done heretofore, that neither this, nor any other great revolutions of Nature, are brought to pass, by causes purely natural, without the conduct of a particular Providence. And 'tis the Sacred Books of Scripture that are the records of this Providence, both as to times past, and times to come: as to all the signal Changes either of the Natural World, or of Mankind, and the different Oeconomies of Religion. In which respects, these Books, tho' they did not contain a Moral Law, would notwithstanding be, as the most mystical, so also the most valuable Books in the World.

This Treatise, you see, will consist of Two Parts: The former whereof is to give an account of the *Conflagration*; and the latter, of the *New Heavens* and *New Earth* following upon it; together with the state of Mankind in those new Habitations. As to the Conflagration, we first enquire, what the Antients thought concerning the present frame of this World; whether it was to perish or no: whether to be destroyed, or to stand eternally in this posture. Then in what manner they thought it would be destroy'd; by what force or violence; whether by Fire or other ways. And with these opinions of the Antients we will compare the doctrine of the Prophets and Apostles, to discover and confirm the truth of them. In the Second place, We will examine what Calculations or Conjectures have been made concerning the time of this great Catastrophe, or of the end of this World. Whether that period be defineable or no: and whether by natural Arguments, or by Prophecies. Thirdly, We will consider the Signs of the approaching Conflagration: Whether such as will be in Nature, or in the State of humane Affairs; but especially such as are taken notice of and recorded in Scripture. Fourthly, which is the principal point, and yet that wherein the Antients have been most silent, *What Causes* there are in Nature, what preparations, for this Conflagration: Where are the Seeds of this universal Fire, or fewel sufficient for the nourishing of it? Lastly, in what order and by what degrees the Conflagration will proceed: In what manner the frame of the Earth will be dissolv'd: and what will be the dreadful countenance of a *Burning World*.

These heads are set down more fully in the Arguments of each Chapter; and seem to be sufficient for the explication of this whole matter: Taking in some additional discourses, which, in pursuing these heads, enter of their own accord, and make the work more even and intire. In the second Part, we restore the World that we had destroy'd: Build new Heavens and a new Earth, *wherein Righteousness shall dwell*. Establish that new order of things, which is so often celebrated by the Prophets: A Kingdom of Peace and of Justice, where the Enemy of Mankind shall be bound, and the Prince of Peace shall rule. A Paradise without a Serpent, and a Tree of Knowledge, not to wound, but to heal the Nations.

Where will be neither *curse*, nor *pain*, nor *death*, nor *disease*. Where all things
are new, all things are more perfect: both the World it self, and its Inhabitants.
Where the First-born from the Dead, have the First-fruits of glory.

We dote upon this present World, and the enjoyments of it: and 'tis not
without pain, and fear, and reluctancy, that we are torn from them: as if our
hopes lay all within the compass of this life. Yet, I know not by what good fate,
my thoughts have been always fixt upon things to come, more than upon things
present. These I know, by certain experience, to be but trifles; and if there be
nothing more considerable to come, the whole Being of Man is no better than a
trifle. But there is room enough before us in that we call *Eternith*, for great and
noble Scenes: and the mind of Man feels it self lessen'd and straiten'd in this
low and narrow state: wishes and waits to see something greater. And if it could
discern another World a coming, on this side eternal life; a beginning Glory, the
best that Earth can bear, It wou'd be a kind of Immortality to enjoy that prospect
before-hand; To see, when this Theater is dissolv'd, where we shall act next,
and what parts. What Saints and Hero's, if I may so say, will appear upon that
Stage; and with what luster and excellency. How easie would it be, under a view
of these futurities, to despise the little pomps and honours, and the momentary
pleasures of a mortal life. But I proceed to our Subject.

CHAPTER II

The true state of the Question is propos'd.

*'Tis the general doctrine of the Ancients, that the present World, or the present frame
of Nature, is mutable and perishable: To which the Sacred Books agree: and
natural reason can alledge nothing against it.*

WHEN we speak of the End or destruction of the World, whether by Fire
or otherwise, 'Tis not to be imagin'd that we understand this of the *Great
Universe*; Sun, Moon, and Stars, and the highest Heavens: as if these were to
perish or be destroy'd, some few years hence, whether by Fire or any other way.
This Question is only to be understood of the *Sublunary World*, of this Earth
and its Furniture; which had its original about six thousand years ago, according
to the History of *Moses*; and hath once already been destroy'd, when the exteriour region of it broke, and the Abyss issuing forth, as out of a womb, over- *Gen.* 7. 11.
flow'd all the habitable Earth. The next Deluge is that of Fire; which will have *Job* 38. 8.
the same bounds, and overflow the Surface of the Earth much-what in the same
manner. But the celestial Regions, where the Stars and Angels inhabit, are not
concern'd in this fate: Those are not made of combustible matter, nor, if they
were, cou'd our flames reach them. Possibly those Bodies may have changes
and revolutions peculiar to themselves, but in ways unknown to us, and after
long and unknown periods of time. Therefore when we speak of the Conflagration of the World, These have no concern in the question; nor any other part of
the Universe, than the Earth and its dependances. As will evidently appear
when we come to explain the manner and causes of the Conflagration.

And as this Conflagration can extend no further than to the Earth and its Elements, so neither can it destroy the matter of the Earth; but onely the form and fashion of it, as it is an habitable World. Neither Fire, nor any other natural Agent can destroy Matter, that is, reduce it to nothing: It may alter the modes and qualities of it, but the substance will always remain. And accordingly the Apostle, when he speaks of the mutability of this World, says onely, *The figure* or fashion of *this World passes away.* This structure of the Earth and disposition of the Elements: And all the *works* of the Earth, as St. *Peter* says; All its natural productions, and all the works of art or humane industry; these will perish, melted or torn in pieces by the Fire; but without an annihilation of the Matter, any more than in the former Deluge. And this will be further prov'd and illustrated in the beginning of the following Book.

1 *Cor.* 7. 31.

2 *Epist.* 3.

The question being thus stated, we are next to consider the sense of Antiquity upon these two Points: First, whether this Sublunary World is mutable and perishable. Secondly, by the force and action of what causes, and in what manner it will perish: whether by Fire or otherwise. *Aristotle* is very irregular in his Sentiments about the state of the World; He allows it neither beginning nor ending, rise nor fall, but wou'd have it eternal and immutable. And this he understands not onely of the great Universe, but of this Sublunary World, this Earth which we inhabit: wherein he will not admit there ever have been or ever will be, either general Deluges or Conflagrations. And as if he was ambitious to be thought singular in his opinion about the eternity of the World, He says, *All* the *Ancients* before him, gave some beginning or origine to the World: but were not indeed so unanimous as to its future fate. Some believing it immutable, or as the Philosophers call it, incorruptible; Others, that it had its fatal times and periods, as lesser Bodies have; and a term of age prefixt to it, by Providence.

But before we examine this Point any further, it will be necessary to reflect upon that which we noted before, an ambiguity in the use of the word *World*, which gives frequent occasion of mistakes in reading the Ancients: when that which they speak of the *great Universe*, we apply to the *Sublunary World:* or on the contrary, what they speak of this Earth, we extend to the whole Universe. And if some of them, besides *Aristotle*, made the World incorruptible, they might mean that of the *great Universe*, which they thought would never be dissolv'd or perish as to its Mass and bulk: But single parts and points of it (and our Earth is no more) may be variously transform'd, and made habitable and unhabitable, according to certain periods of time, without any prejudice to their Philosophy. So *Plato*, for instance, thinks this World will have no Dissolution: for, being a work so beautiful and noble, the goodness of God, he says, will always preserve it. It is most reasonable to understand this of the Great Universe; for, in our Earth, *Plato* himself admits such dissolutions, as are made by general Deluges and Conflagrations; and we contend for no other. So likewise in other Authors, if they speak of the immortality of the World, you must observe what world they apply it to; and whether to the matter or the form of it: and if you remember that our Discourse proceeds onely upon the Sublunary World, and the dissolution of its form, you will find little in antiquity contrary to this doctrine.

I always except *Aristotle*, (who allow'd of no Providence in this inferiour World) and some *Pythagoreans* falsly so call'd, that were Apostates from the doctrine of their Master. These being excepted, upon a view of the rest, you will find very few dissenters from this general doctrine.

Plato's argument against the dissolution of the world, from the goodness and wisdom of God, wou'd not be altogether unreasonable, tho' apply'd to this Earth, if it was so to be dissolv'd, as never to be restor'd again. But we expect *new Heavens* and a *new Earth* upon the dissolution of these: better in all respects, more commodious and more beautiful. And the several perfections of the divine nature, wisdom, power, goodness, justice, sanctity, cannot be so well display'd and exemplifi'd in any one single state of Nature, as in a succession of States: fitted to receive one another according to the dispositions of the Moral World, and the order of Divine Providence. Wherefore *Plato*'s argument from the Divine Attributes, all things consider'd, doth rather prove a succession of Worlds, than that one single world should remain the same throughout all ages, without change or variation. Next to the *Platonists*, the *Stoicks* were most considerable in matters relating to Morality and Providence: And their opinion, in this case, is well known; they being lookt upon by the Moderns, as the principal authors of the doctrine of the *Conflagration*. Nor is it less known that the School of *Democritus* and *Epicurus* made all their worlds subject to dissolution; and by a new concourse of Atomes restor'd them again. Lastly, The *Ionick* Philosophers, who had *Thales* for their Master, and were the first Naturalists amongst the *Greeks*, taught the same doctrine. We have indeed but an imperfect account left us of this Sect, and 'tis great pity; for as it was one of the most ancient, so it seems to have been one of the most considerable amongst the *Greeks* for Natural Philosophy. In those remains which *Diogenes Laertius* hath preserv'd, of *Anaxagoras*, *Anaximenes*, *Archelaus*, &c. All great men in their time, we find that they treated much of the Origine of the world, and had many extraordinary Notions about it, which come lame and defective to us. The doctrine of their founder, *Thales*, which made all things to consist of Water, seems to have a great resemblance to the doctrine of *Moses* and St. *Peter*, about the constitution of the first Heavens and Earth. But there is little in *Laertius* what their opinion was about the Dissolution of the world. Other Authors inform us more of that. *Stobæus* joyns them with *Leucippus* and the *Epicureans*: *Simplicius* with *Heraclitus* and the *Stoicks*, in this doctrine about the corruptibility of the World. So that all the Schools of the Greek Philosophers, as we noted before, were unanimous in this point, excepting the *Peripateticks*; whose Master, *Aristotle*, had neither modesty enough to follow the doctrine of his Predecessors, not wit enough to invent any thing better.

Besides these Sects of Philosophers, there were Theologers amongst the Greeks, more antient than these Sects, and more mystical. *Aristotle* often distinguisheth the *Naturalists* and the *Theologues*. Such were *Orpheus* and his followers, who had more of the antient Oriental Learning than the succeeding Philosophers. But they writ their Philosophy, or Theology rather, Mythologically and Poetically, in Parables and Allegories, that needed an interpretation. All these Theologers supposed the Earth to rise from a Chaos: and as they said that *Love* was

Gen. 1.
2 *Pet.* 2. 5.

Ecl. Phys. l. 1.
c. 24.

Οἱ φυσικοί,
οἱ θεόλογος.

the principle at first, that united the loose and severed Elements, and formed them into an habitable World: So they supposed that if *Strife* or *Contention* prevail'd, that would again dissolve and disunite them, and reduce things into a Chaos: Such as the Earth will be in, upon the Conflagration. And it further appears, that both these Orders of the Learned in *Greece* suppos'd this present frame of Nature might perish, by their doctrine of *Periodical Revolutions*, or of the Renovation of the World after certain periods of time: which was a doctrine common amongst the learned *Greeks*, and received by them from the ancient Barbarick Nations. As will appear more at large in the following Book. In the mean time we may observe that *Origen* in answering *Celsus*, about the point of the Resurrection, tells him, that Doctrine ought not to appear so strange or ridiculous to him, seeing their own Authors did believe and teach the *Renovation of the World*, after certain Ages or periods. And the truth is, this Renovation of the World, rightly stated, is the same thing with the *first Resurrection* of the Christians. And as to the second and general Resurrection, when the Righteous shall have Celestial bodies; 'tis well known that the *Platonists* and *Pythagoreans* cloath'd the Soul with a Celestial body, or, in their Language, an Ethereal Vehicle, as her last Beatitude or Glorification. So that *Origen* might very justly tell his adversary, he had no reason to ridicule the Christian doctrine of the Resurrection, seeing their own Authors had the main strokes of it in their Traditionary Learning.

Ch. 3.
li. 5.

I will only add one remark more, before we leave this Subject, to prevent a mistake in the word *Immortal* or *Immortality*, when applyed to the World. As I told you before, the equivocation that was in that term *World*, it being us'd sometimes for the whole Universe, sometimes for this inferiour part of it where we live; so likewise we must observe, that when this inferiour World is said to be *immortal*, by the Philosophers, as sometimes it is, that commonly is not meant of any single state of Nature, or any single World, but of a succession of Worlds, consequent one upon another. As a family may be said immortal, not in any single person, but in a succession of Heirs. So as, many times, when the Ancients mention the immortality of the World, they do not thereby exclude the Dissolution or Renovation of it: but suppose a vicissitude, or series of Worlds succeeding one another. This observation is not mine, but was long since made by *Simplicius*, *Stobæus*, and others, who tell us in what sense some of those Philosophers who allowed the World to be perishable, did yet affirm it to be immortal: namely, by successive renovations.

Thus much is sufficient to shew the sence and judgment of Antiquity, as to the changeableness or perpetuity of the World. But ancient learning is like ancient Medals, more esteemed for their rarity, than their real use; unless the Authority of a Prince make them currant. So neither will these testimonies be of any great effect, unless they be made good and valuable by the Authority of Scripture. We must therefore add the Testimonies of the Prophets and Apostles to these of the Greeks and Barbarians, that the evidence may be full and undeniable. That the Heavens and the Earth will perish or be chang'd into another form, is, sometimes, plainly exprest, sometimes supposed and alluded to in Scripture. The Prophet *David*'s testimony is express, both for the beginning and ending of the

World: in the 102. *Psalm, Of old hast thou laid the foundation of the Earth, and*   Ver. 25, 26, 27.
the heavens are the work of thy hands. They shall perish, but thou shalt endure: yea,
all of them shall wax old like a garment; as a Vesture shalt thou change them, and
they shall be changed. But thou art the same, and thy Years shall have no end. The
Prophet *Esay*'s testimony is no less express, to the same purpose. *Lift up your*   Ca. 51. 6.
eyes to the heavens, and look upon the Earth beneath: for the heavens shall vanish
away like smoke, and the Earth shall wax old like a garment, and they that dwell
therein shall die in like manner. These Texts are plain and explicite; And in
allusion to this day of the Lord, and this destruction of the World, the same
Prophet often useth phrases that relate to it. As the *Concussion of the Heavens*   *Isa.* 13. 13. *c.* 24.
and the Earth. The *shaking of the foundations of the World.* The *dissolution of*   18, 19. *c.* 34. 4.
the Host of Heaven. And other Sacred Writers have expressions of the like force,
and relating to the same effect. As the *Hills melting like wax, at the presence of*
the Lord: Psal. 97. 5. Shattering *once more* all the parts of the Creation: *Hagg.*
2. 6. *Overturning the mountains, and making the pillars of the Earth to tremble:*
Job 9. 5, 6. If you reflect upon the explication given of the Deluge in the first
part of this Theory, and attend to the manner of the Conflagration, as it will be
explain'd in the sequel of this Discourse, you will see the justness and fitness of
these expressions: That they are not poëtical hyperboles, or random expressions,
of great and terrible things in general, but a true account of what hath been, or
will be, at that great day of the Lord. 'Tis true, the Prophets sometimes use
such-like expressions figuratively, for commotions in States and Kingdoms, but
that is onely by way of metaphor and accommodation; the true basis they stand
upon, is that ruine, overthrow, and dissolution of the natural World, which was
once at the Deluge, and will be again, after another manner, at the general
Conflagration.

As to the new Testament, our Saviour says, *Heaven and Earth shall pass away,*
but his words shall not pass away: Matt. 24. 35. St. *Paul* says, the *Scheme of this*
world; the fashion, form, and composition of it, *passeth away:* 1 *Cor.* 7. 31. And
when mention is made of *new Heavens* and a *new Earth*, which both the Prophet
Isaiah, and the Apostles, St. *Peter* and St. *John*, mention, 'tis plainly imply'd   *Isa.* 65. 17. &
that the old ones will be dissolv'd. The same thing is also imply'd, when our   66. 22.
Saviour speaks of a *Renascency* or *Regeneration: Matt.* 19. 28. and St. *Peter*, of a   *Rev.* 21. 1.
Restitution of all things: *Act.* 3. 21. For what is now, must be abolish'd, before   2 *Pet.* 3. 13.
any former order of things can be restor'd or reduc'd. In a word, If there was
nothing in Scripture concerning this subject, but that discourse of St. *Peter*'s, in
his 2*d.* Epistle and 3*d.* Chapter, concerning the triple order and succession of the
Heavens and the Earth; past, present, and to come; that alone wou'd be a conviction and demonstration to me, that this present World will be dissolv'd.

You will say, it may be, in the last place, we want still the testimony of natural
reason and Philosophy to make the evidence compleat. I answer, 'tis enough if
They be silent, and have nothing to say to the contrary. Here are witnesses,
humane and divine, and if none appear against them, we have no reason to refuse
their testimony, or to distrust it. Philosophy will very readily yield to this doctrine, that All material compositions are dissolvable: and she will not wonder to

see that die, which she had seen born; I mean, this Terrestrial World. She stood upon the Chaos, and see it rowl it self, with difficulty and after many struglings, into the form of an habitable Earth: And that form she see broken down again at the Deluge; and can as little hope or expect now, as then, that it should be everlasting and immutable. There would be nothing great or considerable in this inferiour World, if there were not such revolutions of nature. The Seasons of the Year, and the fresh Productions of the Spring, are pretty in their way; *Annus Magnus* But when the *Great Year* comes about, with a new order of all things, in the Heavens and on the Earth; and a new dress of nature throughout all her regions, far more goodly and beautiful than the fairest Spring; This gives a new life to the Creation, and shows the greatness of its Author. Besides, These Fatal Catastrophes are always a punishment to degenerate Mankind, that are overwhelm'd in the ruines of these perishing Worlds. And to make nature her self execute the divine vengeance against rebellious Creatures, argues both the power and wisdom of that Providence that governs all things here below. These things Reason and Philosophy approve of; but if you further require that they should shew a *Necessity* of this future destruction of the World, from *Natural Causes*, with the time and all other circumstances of this effect; your demands are unreasonable, seeing these things do not depend solely upon Nature. But if you will content your self to know what dispositions there are in Nature towards such a change, how it may begin, proceed, and be consummate, under the conduct of Providence, be pleased to read the following Discourse for your further satisfaction.

CHAPTER III

That the World will be destroy'd by Fire, is the doctrine of the Ancients, especially of the Stoicks. *That the same doctrine is more ancient than the* Greeks, *and deriv'd from the Barbarick Philosophy, and That probably from* Noah; *the Father of all Traditionary Learning. The same doctrine expresly authoriz'd by Revelation, and inroll'd into the Sacred Canon.*

THAT the present World, or the present frame of Nature, will be destroy'd, we have already shewn. In what manner this destruction will be, by what force or what kind of fate, must be our next enquiry. The Philosophers have always spoken of *Fire* and *Water*, those two unruly Elements, as the only Causes that can destroy the World, and work our ruine; And accordingly they say, all the great and fatal Revolutions of Nature, either past or to come, depend upon the violence of these Two; when they get the mastery, and overwhelm all the rest and the whole Earth, in a Deluge or Conflagration. But as they make these Two the Destroying Elements, so they also make them the Purifying Elements. And accordingly in the Lustrations, or their rites and ceremonies for purging sin, Fire and Water were chiefly made use of, both amongst the *Romans, Greeks* and *Barbarians*. And when these Elements over-run the world, it is not, they say, for a final destruction of it, but to purge Mankind and Nature from their Impurities. As for purgation by Fire and Water, the stile of our Sacred Writings does very much accommodate it self to that sence; and the Holy Ghost, who is the great Purifier of Souls, is compared in his operation upon us, and in our regeneration, to fire or water. And as for the external world, St. *Peter* makes the Flood to have been a kind of *Baptising* or renovation of the world. And St. *Paul* and the Prophet *Malachy* make the last Fire, to be a purging and refining fire. But to return to the Ancients.

1 Ep. 3. 21.
1 Cor. 3. 13.
Mal. 3. 2, 3.

The *Stoicks* especially, of all other Sects amongst the *Greeks*, have preserved the doctrine of the Conflagration, and made it a considerable part of their Philosophy, and almost a character of their order. This is a thing so well known that I need not use any Citations to prove it. But they cannot pretend to have been the first authors of it neither. For, besides that amongst the *Greeks* themselves, *Heraclitus* and *Empedocles*, more ancient than *Zeno*, the Master of the *Stoicks*, taught this doctrine, 'tis plainly a branch of the Barbarick Philosophy, and taken from thence by the *Greeks*. For it is well known that the most ancient and mystick learning amongst the *Greeks*, was not originally their own, but borrowed of the more Eastern Nations, by *Orpheus*, *Pythagoras*, *Plato*, and many more: who travel'd thither, and traded with the Priests for knowledge and Philosophy; and when they got a competent stock, returned home, and set up a School, or a Sect, to instruct their Country-men. But before we pass to the Eastern nations, let us, if you please, compare the *Roman* Philosophy upon this subject, with that of the *Greeks*.

The *Romans* were a great people, that made a shew of Learning, but had little in reality, more than words and Rhetorick. Their curiosity or emulation in Philosophical Studies was so little, that it did not make different Sects and Schools amongst them, as amongst the *Greeks*. I remember no Philosophers they had but such as *Tully*, *Seneca*, and some of their Poets. And of these *Lucretius*, *Lucan* and *Ovid*, have spoken openly of the Conflagration. *Ovid*'s Verses are well known,

> *Esse quoque in fatis reminiscitur, affore tempus,*
> *Quo mare, quo Tellus, correptaque Regia Cœli*
> *Ardeat, & mundi moles operosa laboret.*

> *A Time decreed by Fate, at length will come,*
> *When Heavens and Earth and Seas shall have their doom;*
> *A fiery doom: And Nature's mighty frame*
> *Shall break, and be dissolv'd into a flame.*

We see *Tully*'s sence upon this matter in *Scipio*'s *Dream*. When the old man speaks to his Nephew *Africanus*, and shews him from the clouds, this spot of Earth, where we live; He tells him, tho' our actions shou'd be great, and fortune favour them with success, yet there wou'd be no room for any lasting glory in this World; for the World it self is transient and fugitive. And a Deluge or a Conflagration, which necessarily happen after certain periods of time, sweep away all records of humane actions. As for *Seneca*, he being a profest *Stoick*, we need not doubt of his opinion in this point. We may add here, if you please, the *Sibylline verses*, which were kept with great Religion, in the Capitol at *Rome*, and consulted with much ceremony upon solemn occasions. These *Sibyls* were the Prophetesses of the *Gentiles*, and tho' their writings now have many spurious additions, yet none doubt but that the Conflagration of the World was one of their original Prophecies.

Let us now proceed to the Eastern nations. As the *Romans* receiv'd the small skill they had in the Sciences, from the *Greeks*; so the *Greeks* receiv'd their chief mystick learning from the *Barbarians*: that is, from the *Ægyptians*, *Persians*, *Phœnicians*, and other Eastern Nations: For 'tis not onely the Western or Northern people, that they call'd *Barbarians*, but indeed all Nations besides themselves. For that is commonly the vanity of great Empires, to uncivilize in a manner all the rest of the World; and to account all those People *Barbarous*, that are not subject to their dominion. These however, whom they call'd so, were the most ancient People, and had the first learning that was ever heard of after the Flood. And amongst these, the *Ægyptians* were as famous as any: whose Sentiment in this particular of the Conflagration is well known. For *Plato*, who liv'd amongst them several years, tells us in his *Timæus*, that it was the doctrine of their Priests, that the fatal Catastrophes of the World were by *Fire* and *Water*. In like manner the *Persians* made their beloved God, *Fire*, at length to consume all things that are capable of being consum'd. For that is said to have been the doctrine of *Hydaspes*, one of their great *Magi* or Wise men. As to the *Phœnicians*, I suspect very much that the Stoicks had their Philosophy from them, and amongst other things the Conflagration. We shall take notice of that hereafter.

Just. Mar. Apol.
2.

But to comprehend the *Arabians* also, and *Indians*, give me leave to reflect a little upon the story of the *Phœnix*. A story well known, and related by some ancient Authors, and is in short this. The *Phœnix*, they say, is a Bird in *Arabia*, *India*, and those Eastern parts, single in her kind, never more than one at a time, and very long-liv'd: appearing onely at the expiration of the *Great Year*, as they call it: And then she makes her self a Nest of Spices, which being set on fire by the Sun, or some other secret power, she hovers upon it, and consumes her self in the flames. But, which is most wonderful, out of these ashes riseth a second *Phœnix*; so that it is not so much a death as a renovation. I do not doubt but the story is a fable, as to any such kind of Bird, single in her species, living and dying, and reviving in that manner: But 'tis an Apologue, or a Fable with an interpretation, and was intended as an Emblem of the World: which, after a long age, will be consum'd in the last fire: and from its ashes or remains will arise another world, or a new-form'd Heavens and Earth. This, I think, is the true mystery of the *Phœnix*, under which Symbol the Eastern Nations preserv'd the doctrine of the Conflagration and renovation of the World. They tell somewhat a like story of the Eagle, soaring a-loft so near the Sun, that by his warmth and enlivening rays, she renews her age and becomes young again. To this the *Psalmist* is thought to allude: Psal. 103. 5. *Thy Youth shall be renew'd like the Eagles:* which the *Chaldee* Paraphrast renders, *In mundo venturo renovabis, sicut Aquilæ, juventutem tuam.* These things to me seem plainly to be symbolical, representing that World to come, which the Paraphrast mentions, and the fireing of this. And this is after the manner of the Eastern Wisdom; which always lov'd to go fine, cloath'd in figures and fancies.

And not onely the Eastern *Barbarians*, but the Northern and Western also, had this doctrine of the Conflagration amongst them. The *Scythians*, in their dispute with the *Ægyptians* about antiquity, argue upon both suppositions, of Fire or Water, destroying the last World, or beginning this. And in the West, the *Celts*, the most ancient People there, had the same tradition; for the *Druids*, who were their Priests and Philosophers, deriv'd, not from the *Greeks*, but of the old race of Wise men, that had their Learning traditionally, and, as it were, hereditary from the first ages: These, as *Strabo* tells us, gave the World a kind *l. 4.* of immortality by repeated renovations; and the principle that destroy'd it, according to them, was always Fire or Water. I had forgot to mention in this List, the *Chaldeans*: whose opinion we have from *Berosus* in *Seneca*. They did *Nat. Quæst. 3.* not onely teach the Conflagration, but also fixt it to a certain period of time, *c. 29.* when there should happen a great Conjunction of the Planets in *Cancer*. Lastly, we may add, to close the account, the Modern *Indian* Philosophers, the reliques of the old *Bragmans*; These, as *Maffeus* tells us, declare, that the World will be *l. 16. Hist. Ind.* renew'd, after an Universal Conflagration.

You see of what extent and universality throughout all Nations, this doctrine of the Conflagration hath been. Let us now consider what defects or excesses there are, in these ancient opinions, concerning this fate of the World, and how they may be rectified: That we may admit them no further into our belief, than they are warranted by reason, or by the authority of Christian Religion. The first fault they seem to have commited about this point, is this, That they made these revolutions and renovations of nature, indefinite or endless: as if there would be such a succession of Deluges and Conflagrations to all eternity. This, the *Stoicks* seem plainly to have asserted, as appears from *Eumenius*, *Philo*, *Simplicius*, and Others. St. *Jerome* imputes this Opinion also to *Origen*: but he *Epist. 60.* does not always hit the true sence of that Father, or is not fair and just in the representation of it. Whosoever held this Opinion, 'tis a manifest errour, and may be easily rectified by the Christian Revelation; which teaches us plainly, that there is a final period and consummation of all things that belong to this Sublunary or Terrestrial world. When the *Kingdom shall be deliver'd up to the Father:* and Time shall be no more.

Another Errour they committed in this doctrine, is, the Identity, or sameness, if I may so say, of the worlds, succeeding one another. They are made indeed of the same Lump of matter, but they suppos'd them to return also in the same Form. And, which is worse, that there would be the same face of humane affairs; The same Persons and the same actions over again; So as the second World would be but a bare repetition of the former, without any variety or diversity. Such a revolution is commonly call'd the *Platonick Year:* A period, when all things return to the same posture they had some thousands of years before; As a Play acted over again, upon the same Stage, and to the same Auditory. This is a groundless and injudicious supposition. For, whether we consider the nature of things; The Earth after a dissolution, by Fire or by Water, could not return into the same form and fashion it had before; Or whether we consider Providence, it would no ways suit with the Divine Wisdom and Justice to bring upon the stage again those very Scenes, and that very course of humane affairs, which it had so lately condemn'd and destroy'd. We may be assured therefore, that, upon the dissolution of a World, a new order of things, both as to Nature and Providence, always appears: And what that new order will be, in both respects, after the *Conflagration*, I hope we shall, in the following Book, give a satisfactory account.

   These are the opinions, true or false, of the Ancients; and chiefly of the *Stoicks*, concerning the mystery of the Conflagration. It will not be improper to enquire in the last place, how the *Stoicks* came by this doctrine: whether it was their discovery and invention, or from whom they learned it. That it was not their own invention, we have given sufficient ground to believe, by shewing the antiquity of it beyond the times of the *Stoicks*. Besides, what a man invents himself, he can give the reasons and causes of it, as things upon which he founded his invention: But the *Stoicks* do not this, but according to the ancient traditional way, deliver the conclusion without proof or premisses. We nam'd *Heraclitus* and *Empedocles* amongst the *Greeks* to have taught this doctrine before the *Stoicks*:

De defec. Orac.

And, according to *Plutarch*, *Hesiod* and *Orpheus*, authors of the highest antiquity, sung of this last Fire, in their Philosophick Poetry. But I suspect the *Stoicks* had this doctrine from the *Phœnicians*; for if we enquire into the original of that Sect, we shall find that their Founder *Zeno*, was a Barbarian or Semi-barbarian, deriv'd from the *Phœnicians*, as *Laertius* and *Cicero* give an account of him. And the *Phœnicians* had a great share in the Oriental knowledge, as we see by *Sanchoniathon*'s remains in *Eusebius*. And by their mystical Books which *Suidas* mentions, from whence *Pherecydes*, *Pythagoras* his Master, had his learning. We may therefore reasonably presume that it might be from his Countrey-men, the *Phœnicians*, that *Zeno* had the doctrine of the *Conflagration*. Not that he brought it first into *Greece*, but strongly reviv'd it, and made it almost peculiar to his Sect.

   So much for the *Stoicks* in particular, and the *Greeks* in general. We have also, you see, trac'd these Opinions higher, to the first Barbarick Philosophers: who were the first race of Philosophers after the Flood. But *Josephus* tells a formal story of Pillars set up by *Seth*, before the Flood; implying the foreknowledge of this Fiery destruction of the World, even from the beginning of it. His words

l. 1. c. 3.

are to this effect, give what credit to them you think fit. *Seth and his fellow students having found out the knowledge of the cœlestial Bodies, and the order and disposition of the Universe; and having also receiv'd from* Adam *a Prophecy, that the World should have a double destruction, one by Water, another by Fire; To preserve and transmit their knowledge, in either case, to posterity. They raised two Pillars, one of Brick, another of Stone, and ingrav'd upon them their Philosophy and inventions. And one of these pillars,* the Author says, *was standing in* Syria,

κατὰ τὴν Συριάδα.

even to his time. I do not press the belief of this story; there being nothing, that I know of, in Antiquity Sacred or prophane, that gives a joint testimony with it. And those that set up these Pillars, do not seem to me to have understood the nature of the Deluge or *Conflagration*; if they thought a Pillar, either of Brick or Stone, would be secure, in those great dissolutions of the Earth. But we have pursued this doctrine high enough without the help of these ante-diluvian Antiquities: namely, to the earliest people and the first appearances of Wisdom after the Flood. So that, I think, we may justly look upon it as the doctrine of *Noah*, and of his immediate posterity. And as that is the highest source of learning to the present World; so we should endeavour to carry our Philosophical Traditions to that Original: for I cannot perswade my self but that they had amongst them, even in those early days, the main strokes or conclusions of the best Philosophy: or, if I may so say, a form of sound doctrine concerning Nature and Providence. Of which matter, if you will allow me a short digression, I will speak my thoughts in a few words.

In those first Ages of the World after the Flood, when *Noah* and his Children peopled the Earth again, as he gave them Precepts of morality and piety for the conduct of their manners: which are usually call'd *Præcepta Noachidarum*, the *Precepts* of *Noah*, frequently mention'd both by the Jews and Christians: So also he deliver'd to them, at least, if we judge aright, certain Maximes or Conclusions about Providence, the state of Nature, and the fate of the World: And these, in proportion, may be call'd *Dogmata Noachidarum*, the *Doctrines* of *Noah*, and *his Children*. Which made a Systeme of Philosophy or secret knowledge amongst them, deliver'd by Tradition from Father to Son; but especially preserv'd amongst their Priests and Sacred Persons, or such others as were addicted to Contemplation. This I take to be more ancient than *Moses* himself, or the *Jewish* Nation. But it would lead me too far out of my way, to set down in this place, the reasons of my judgment. Let it be sufficient to have pointed onely at this Fountainhead of knowledge, and so return to our Argument.

We have heard, as it were, a Cry of Fire, throughout all Antiquity, and throughout all the People of the Earth. But those alarums are sometimes false, or make a greater noise than the thing deserves. For my part, I never trust Antiquity barely upon its own account, but always require a second witness, either from Nature, or from Scripture: What the voice of Nature is, we shall hear all along in the following Treatise: Let us then examine at present, what testimony the Prophets and Apostles give to this ancient doctrine of the Conflagration of the World. The Prophets see the World a-fire at a distance and more imperfectly, as a brightness in the Heavens, rather than a burning flame: but St. *Peter* describes it, as if he had been standing by, and seen the Heavens and Earth in a red fire: heard the cracking flames and the tumbling Mountains: 2 *Pet.* 3. 10. In the day of the Lord, *The Heavens shall pass away with a great noise, and the Elements shall melt with fervent heat: The Earth also, and the works that are therein, shall be burnt up.* Then, after a pious Ejaculation, he adds, Ver. 12. *Looking for and hastening the coming of the day of God, wherein the Heavens, being on fire, shall be dissolved; and the Elements shall melt with fervent heat.* This is as lively, as a Man could express it, if he had the dreadful spectacle before his Eyes. St. *Peter* had before taught the same doctrine (*ver.* 5, 6, 7.) but in a more Philosophick way; describing the double fate of the World, by water and fire, with relation to the Nature and Constitution of either World, past or present. *The Heavens and the Earth were of old, consisting of water and by water: whereby, the World that then was, being overflow'd with water, perished. But the Heavens and the Earth which are now, by the same Word are kept in store, reserved unto fire*

against the day of Judgment, and perdition of ungodly, or Atheistical men. This
testimony of St. *Peter* being full, direct, and explicit, will give light and strength
to several other passages of Scripture, where the same thing is exprest obscurely
or by allusion. As when St. *Paul* says, *The fire shall try every mans work in that
day.* And our Saviour says, *The tares shall be burnt in the fire, at the end of the
World.* Accordingly it is said, both by the Apostles and Prophets, that *God* will
come to judgment *in Fire.* St. *Paul* to the *Thessalonians,* promiseth the persecuted
Righteous, rest and ease, *When the Lord shall be revealed from Heaven, with his
mighty Angels, in flaming fire: taking vengeance on them that know not God, &c.*
And so to the *Hebrews,* St. *Paul* says, that for wilful Apostates there remaineth
no more Sacrifice for sin, *but a certain fearful looking for of judgment, and fiery
indignation, which shall devour the adversaries,* or enemies of God. And in the
12*th.* Chapter, he alludes to the same thing, when after he had spoken of *shakeing
the Heavens* and the *Earth* once more, he exhorteth, as St. *Peter* does upon the
same occasion, to *reverence and godly fear, For our God is a consuming Fire.*

    In like manner the Prophets, when they speak of destroying the wicked, and
the Enemies of God and Christ, at the end of the world, represent it as a destruction *by Fire.* Psalm the 11*th.* 6. *Upon the wicked the Lord shall rain coals,
fire, and brimstone, and a burning tempest: This shall be the portion of their Cup.*
And Psal. 50. 3. *Our God shall come, and will not be slow: A fire shall devour
before him,* and it *shall be very tempestuous round about him.* And in the beginning
of those two triumphal Psalms, the sixty-eight, and ninety-seventh, we see plain
allusions to this coming of the Lord in fire. The other Prophets speak in the
same style, Of a fiery indignation against the wicked, in the day of the Lord:
As in *Isaiah* 66. 15. *For behold the Lord will come with fire, and with his Chariots
like a whirlwind, to render his anger with fury, and his rebuke with flames of fire.*
And in *Daniel,* (c. 7. 9, 10.) The Ancient of days is plac'd upon his Seat of Judgment, cover'd in flames. *I beheld till the Thrones were set, and the Ancient of days
did sit, whose garment was white as snow, and the hair of his head like the pure
wool: His Throne was like the fiery flame, his wheels as burning fire. A fiery stream
issued and came forth from before him: Thousand thousands ministred unto him, and
ten thousand times ten thousand stood before him: The judgment was set, and the
Books were opened.* The Prophet *Malachy* (c. 4. 1.) describes the Day of the Lord
to the same effect, and in like colours; *Behold the Day cometh, that shall burn as
an Oven: and all the proud, yea, and all that do wickedly shall be as stubble; and the
day that cometh shall burnt them up, saith the Lord of Hosts, that it shall leave them
neither root nor branch.* And that nature her self, and the Earth shall suffer in
that fire, the Prophet *Zephany* tells us, (c. 3. 8.) *All the Earth shall be devoured
with the fire of my jealousie.* Lastly, this consumption of the Earth by fire, even
to the foundations of it, is exprest livelily by *Moses* in his Song, *Deut.* 32. 22.
*A fire is kindled in my anger, and shall burn unto the lowest Hell: and shall consume
the Earth with her increase, and set on fire the foundations of the Mountains.*

    If we reflect upon these Witnesses; and especially the first and last, *Moses* and
St. *Peter*: at what a great distance of time they writ their Prophecies, and yet
how well they agree, we must needs conclude that they were acted by the same

1 Cor. 3. 12, 13.
Mat. 13. 40, 41,
42.

2 Thess. 2. 7, 8.

ch. 10. 27.

Ver. 26, 27, 28,
29.

and ch. 34. 8, 9,
10.

Spirit: and a Spirit that see thorough all the Ages of the World, from the beginning to the end. These Sacred Writers were so far distant in time from one another, that they could not confer together, nor conspire, either in a false testimony, or to make the same prediction. But being under one common influence and inspiration, which is always consistent with it self, they have dictated the same things, tho' at two thousand years distance sometimes from one another. This besides many other considerations, makes their authority incontestable. And upon the whole account, you see, that the doctrine of the future *Conflagration of the World*, having run through all Ages and Nations, is, by the joynt consent of the Prophets and Apostles, adopted into the Christian Faith.

CHAPTER IV

Concerning the time of the Conflagration, and the end of the World. What the Astronomers say upon this Subject, and upon what they ground their Calculations; The true notion of the Great Year, or of the Platonick Year, stated and explained.

HAVING, in this first Section, laid a sure foundation as to the Subject of our Discourse; the truth and certainty of the *Conflagration* whereof we are to treat; we will now proceed to enquire after the *Time, Causes*, and *Manner* of it. We are naturally more inquisitive after the end of the World, and the time of that fatal revolution, than after the causes of it: for these, we know, are irresistible, whensoever they come, and therefore we are only sollicitous that they should not overtake us, or our near posterity. The *Romans* thought they had the fates of their Empire in the Books of the Sibyls, which were kept by the Magistrates as a Sacred Treasure. We have also our Prophetical Books, more sacred and more infallible than theirs, which contain the fate of all the Kingdoms of the Earth, and of that glorious Kingdom that is to succeed. And of all futurities, there is none can be of such importance to be enquired after, as this last scene and close of all humane affairs.

If I thought it possible to determine the time of the *Conflagration* from the bare intuition of Natural Causes, I would not treat of it in this place, but reserve it to the last; after we had brought into view all those Causes, weigh'd their force, and examin'd how and when they would concur to produce this great effect. But I am satisfied that the excitation and concurse of those Causes does not depend upon Nature only; and tho' the Causes may be sufficient when all united, yet the union of them at such a time, and in such a manner, I look upon as the effect of a particular Providence: and therefore no foresight of ours, or inspection into Nature can discover to us the time of this conjuncture. This method therefore of Prediction from Natural Causes being laid aside as impracticable, all other methods may be treated of in this place, as being independent upon any thing that is to follow in the Treatise; and it will be an ease to the Argument to discharge it of this part, and clear the way by degrees to the principal point, which is, the *Causes* and *Manner* of the Conflagration.

Some have thought it a kind of impiety in a Christian to enquire after the end of the World; because of that check which our Saviour gave his Disciples, when, after his Resurrection, enquiring of him about the time of his Kingdom, He *Act.* 1. 7. answer'd, *It is not for you to know the times or the seasons, which the Father hath put in his own power.* And, before his death, when he was discoursing of the Consummation of all things, He told them expressly, that tho' there should be *Mat.* 24. 36. such and such previous Signs as he had mentioned, yet, *Of that day and hour knoweth no man. No, not the Angels that are in Heaven, but my Father only.* Be it so, that the Disciples deserv'd a reprimand, for desiring to know, by a particular revelation from our Saviour, the state of future times; when many other things were more necessary for their instruction, and for their ministery. Be it also admitted, that the Angels, at that distance of time, could not see thorow all events to the end of the World; it does not at all follow from thence that they do not know it now; when, in the course of Sixteen hundred years, many things are come to pass, that may be marks and directions to them to make a judgment of what remains, and of the last period of all things. However there will be no danger in our enquiries about this matter, seeing they are not so much to discover the certainty, as the uncertainty of that period, as to humane knowledge. Let us therefore consider what methods have been used, by those that have been curious and busie to measure the duration of the World.

The *Stoicks* tell us, *When* the Sun and the Stars have drunk up the Sea, then the Earth shall be burnt. A very fair Prophecy: but how long will they be a drinking? For unless we can determine that, we cannot determine when this Cicer. de Nat. D. l. 2. combustion will begin. Many of the Ancients thought that the Stars were nourish'd by the vapours of the Ocean and of the moist Earth: and when that nourishment was spent, being of a fiery nature, they would prey upon the Body of the Earth it self, and consume that, after they had consum'd the Water. This is old-fashion'd Philosophy, and now, that the nature of those Bodies is better known, will scarce pass for currant. 'Tis true, we must expect some dispositions towards the combustion of the World, from a great drought and desiccation of the Earth: But this helps us nothing on our way; for the question still returns, *When* will this immoderate drought or dryness happen? and that's as ill to re-solve as the former. Therefore, as I said before, I have no hopes of deciding the question by Physiology or Natural Causes; let us then look up from the Earth to the Heavens, To the Astronomers and the Prophets; These think they can define the age and duration of the World; The one by their Art, and the other by Inspiration.

We begin with the Astronomers: whose Calculations are founded either upon the Aspects and Configurations of the Planets, or upon the Revolutions of the Fixt Stars: or lastly upon that which they call *Annus Magnus*, or the *Great Year*, whatsoever that Notion proves to be when it is rightly interpreted. As to the *Sen. Nat. qu.* li. 3. c. 29. Planets, *Berosus* tells us, The *Chaldeans* suppose Deluges to proceed from a great conjunction of the Planets in *Capricorn*: and from a like conjunction in the opposite Sign of *Cancer*, the Conflagration will ensue. So that if we compute by the Astronomical Tables how long it will be to such a Conjunction, we find at the same time how long it will be to the *Conflagration*. This doctrine of the *Chaldeans* some Christian Authors have owned, and followed the same principles and method.

If these Authors would deal fairly with Mankind, they should shew us some connexion betwixt these Causes and the Effects which they make consequent upon them. For 'tis an unreasonable thing to require a man's assent to a Proposition, where he sees no dependance or connexion of Terms; unless it come by Revelation, or from an infallible Authority. If you say, The Conflagration will be at the first great Conjunction of the Planets in *Cancer*, and I say it will be at the next Eclipse of the Moon, if you shew no more reason for your assertion than I do for mine, and neither of us pretend to revelation or infallibility, we may justly expect to be equally credited. Pray what reason can you give why the Planets, when they meet, should plot together, to set on Fire their Fellow-Planet, the Earth, who never did them any harm? But now there is a plausible reason for my opinion; for the Moon, when Eclips'd may think herself affronted by the Earth, interposing rudely betwixt her and the Sun, and leaving her to grope her way in the dark; She therefore may justly take her revenge as she can. But you'l say, 'tis not in the power of the Moon to set the Earth on Fire, if she had malice enough to do it. No, nor, say I, is it in the power of the other Planets, that are far more distant from the Earth than the Moon, and as stark dull lumps of Earth, as she is. The plain truth is, The Planets are so many Earths; and our Earth is as much a Planet as the brightest of them. 'Tis carried about the Sun with the same common stream, and shines with as much lustre to them, as they do to us: neither can they do any more harm to it, than it can do to them. 'Tis now well known, that the Planets are dark opake Bodies, generally made up of Earth and Water, as our Globe is; and have no force or action, but that of reverberating the light which the Sun casts upon them. This blind superstitious fear or reverence for the Stars, had its original from the ancient Idolaters; They thought them Gods, and that they had domination over humane affairs. We do not indeed worship them, as they did; but some men retain still the same opinion of their vertues, of their rule and influence upon us and our affairs, which was the ground of their worship. 'Tis full time now to sweep away these cobwebs of superstition, these reliques of Paganism. I do not see how we are any more concern'd in the postures of the Planets, than in the postures of the Clouds; and you may as well build an art of prediction or divination upon the one as the other. They must not know much of the Philosophy of the Heavens, or little consider it, that think the fate, either of single persons, or of the whole Earth, can depend upon the aspects or figur'd dances of those Bodies.

But you'l say, it may be, tho' no reason can be given for such effects, yet experience does attest the truth of them. In the first place, I answer, no experience can be produc'd for this effect we are speaking of, the conflagration of the World. Secondly, experience fallaciously recorded, or wholly in favour of one side, is no proof. If a publick Register was kept of all Astrological Predictions, and of all the events that followed upon them, right or wrong, agreeing or disagreeing, I could willingly refer the cause to the determination of such a Register, and such experience. But that which they call experience, is so stated, that if one pre-diction of ten, hits right or near right, it shall make more noise, and be more taken notice of, than all the nine that are false. Just as in a Lottery, where many Blanks are drawn for one Prize, yet these make all the noise, and those are for-gotten. If any one be so lucky as to draw a good Lot, then the Trumpet sounds, and his Name is register'd, and he tells his good fortune to every body he meets: whereas those that lose, go silently away with empty Pockets, and are asham'd to tell their losses. Such a thing is the Register of Astrological experiences; they record what makes for their credit, but drop all blank instances, that would dis-cover the vanity or cheat of their Art.

So much for the Planets. They have also a pretended calculation of the end of the World from the fixt Stars and the Firmament. Which in short is this: They suppose these Bodies, besides the hurry of their Diurnal motion from East to West, quite round the Earth in four and twenty hours, to have another retro-grade motion, from West to East; which is more slow and leisurely; And when they have finish'd the Circle of this retrogradation, and come up again to the same place from whence they started at the beginning of the World, then this course of Nature will be at an end; and either the Heavens will cease from all motion, or a new set of motions will be put a foot, and the world begin again. This is a bundle of fictions tied up in a pretty knot. In the first place, there is no such thing as a solid Firmament, in which the Stars are fixt, as nails in a board. The Heavens are as fluid as our air, and the higher we go, the more thin and subtle is the ethereal matter. Then, the fixt Stars are not all in one Surface, as they seem to us, nor at an equal distance from the Earth, but are plac'd in several Orbs higher and higher; there being infinite room in the great Deep of the Heavens, every way, for innumerable Stars and Spheres behind one another, to fill and beautify the immense spaces of the Universe. Lastly, the fixt Stars have no motion common to them all, nor any motion singly, unless upon their own centres; and therefore, never leaving their stations, they can never return to any common station, which they would suppose them to have had at the beginning of the World. So as this period they speak of, whereby they would measure the duration of the World, is meerly imaginary, and hath no foundation in the true nature or motion of the celestial Bodies.

But in the third place, They speak of an ANNUS MAGNUS, a *Great Year*; A revolution so call'd, whatsoever it is, that is of the same extent with the length of the world. This notion, I confess, is more ancient and universal, and therefore I am the more apt to believe that it is not altogether groundless. But the difficulty is, to find out the true notion of this *Great Year*, what is to be understood by it, and then of what length it is. They all agree that it is a time of some grand in-stauration of all things, or a Restitution of the Heavens and the Earth to their former state; that is, to the state and posture they had at the beginning of the world; such therefore as will reduce the Golden age, and that happy state of nature wherein things were at first. If so, if these be the marks and properties of this Revolution, which is call'd the *Great Year*, we need not go so far to find the true notion and interpretation of it. Those that have read the first part of this Theory, may remember that in the second Book we gave an account what the posture of the Earth was at the beginning of the world, and what were the consequences of that posture, *A perpetual Spring* and Equinox throughout all the Earth: And if the Earth was restor'd again to that posture and situation, all that is imputed to the *Great Year*, would immediately follow upon it, without ever disturbing or moving the fix'd Stars, Firmament, or Planets; and yet at the same time all these three would return or be restor'd to the same posture they had at the beginning of the world; so as the whole character of the *Great Year* would be truly fulfill'd, tho' not in that way which they imagin'd; but in another, more compendious, and of easier conception. My meaning is this, If the Axis of the Earth was rectified, and set parallel with the Axis of the Ecliptick, upon which the Planets, Firmament and fix'd Stars are suppos'd to move, all things would be as they were at first; A general harmony and conformity of all the motions of the Universe would presently appear, such, as they say, was in the Golden Age, before any disorder came into the natural or moral World.

As this is an easie, so I do not doubt, but it is a true account of that which was originally call'd the *Great Year*, or the Great Instauration; which nature will bring to pass in this simple method, by rectifying the Axis of the Earth, without those operose revolutions, which some Astronomers have fansied. But however, this account being admitted, how will it help us to define what the Age and duration of the World will be? 'Tis true, many have undertaken to tell us the length of this *Great Year*, and consequently of the World; but, besides that their accounts are very different, and generally of an extravagant length, if we had the true account, it would not assure us when the World would end; because we do not know when it did begin, or what progress we have already made in the line of time. For I am satisfied, the Chronology of the World, whether sacred or prophane, is lost; till Providence shall please to retrieve it by some new discovery. As to prophane Chronology, or that of the *Heathens*, the *Greeks* and the *Romans* knew nothing above the *Olympiads*; which fell short many Ages of the Deluge, much more of the beginning of the World. And the Eastern barbarous Nations, as they disagreed amongst themselves, so generally they run the origine of the World to such a prodigious height, as is neither agreeable to Faith, nor Reason. As to Sacred Chronology, 'tis well known, that the difference there is betwixt the *Greek*, *Hebrew*, and *Samaritan* Copies of the Bible, makes the Age of the World altogether undetermin'd: And there is no way yet found out, how we may certainly discover which of the three Copies is most Authentick, and consequently what the Age of the World is, upon a true computation. Seeing therefore we have no assurance how long the World hath stood already, neither could we be assur'd how long it hath to stand, though, by this *Annus Magnus*, or any other way, the total sum, or whole term of its duration was truly known.

I am sorry to see the little success we have had in our first search after the end of the World, from Astronomical Calculations. But 'tis an useful piece of knowledge to know the bounds of our knowledge; that so we may not spend our time and thoughts about things that lie out of our reach. I have little or no hopes of resolving this point by the Light of Nature, and therefore it only remains now to enquire, Whether Providence hath made it known by any sort of Prophecy or Revelation. Which shall be the Subject of the following Chapter.

CHAPTER V

Concerning Prophecies that determine the end of the World; Of what order soever, Prophane or Sacred: Jewish or Christian. That no certain judgment can be made from any of them, at what distance we are now from the Conflagration.

THE bounds of humane knowledge are so narrow, and the desire of knowing so vast and illimited, that it often puts Mankind upon irregular methods of inlargeing their knowledge. This hath made them find out arts of commerce with evil Spirits, to be instructed by them in such Events as they could not of themselves discover. We meddle not with those mysteries of iniquity: but what hath appear'd under the notion of Divine Prophecy, relating to the Chronology of the World: giving either the whole extent of it, or certain marks of its expiration: these we purpose to examine in this place. How far any thing may, or may not, be concluded from them, as to the resolution of our Problem, *How long the World will last.*

Amongst the Heathens I do not remember any Prophecies of this nature, except the *Sibylline Oracles*, as they are usually call'd. The ancient Eastern Philosophers have left us no account that I can call to mind, about the time of this fatality. They say when the *Phœnix* returns we must expect the Conflagration to follow; but the age of the *Phœnix* they make as various and uncertain, as they do the computation of their *Great Year*: which two things are indeed one and the same in effect. Some of them, I confess, mention Six Thousand years for the whole age of the World: which being the famous Prophecy of the *Jews*, we shall speak to it largely hereafter: and reduce to that head what broken Traditions remain amongst the Heathens of the same thing. As to the Sibylline Oracles, which were so much in reputation amongst the *Greeks* and *Romans*, they have been tamper'd with so much, and chang'd so often, that they are become now of little authority. They seem to have divided the duration of the World into Ten Ages, and the last of these they make a Golden Age, a state of peace, righteousness and perfection: but seeing they have not determin'd, in any definite numbers, what the length of every Age will be, nor given us the summ of all, we cannot draw any conclusion from this account as to the point in question before us. But must proceed to the Jewish and Christian Oracles.

The *Jews* have a remarkable Prophecy, which expresseth both the whole and the parts of the World's duration. The World, they say, will stand Six Thousand Years: *Two thousand before the Law, Two Thousand under the Law, and Two thousand under the Messiah.* This Prophecy they derive from *Elias*; but there were two of the Name, *Elias* the *Thesbite*, and *Elias* the *Rabbin*, or *Cabalist*: and 'tis suppos'd to belong immediately to the later of these. Yet this does not hinder, in my opinion, but that it might come originally from the former *Elias*, and was preserv'd in the School of this *Elias* the *Rabbin*, and first made publick by him.

Symbolum
ἀποκαταζάσεως
πολυχρονίου,
Phœnix. Hor.
Apol. l. 2. c. 57.

258

Or he added, it may be, that division of the time into three parts, and so got a
Title to the whole. I cannot easily imagine that a Doctor that liv'd two hundred
years, or thereabouts, before Christ, when Prophecy had ceas'd for some Ages
amongst the *Jews*, should take upon him to dictate a Prophecy about the duration
of the World, unless he had been supported by some antecedent Cabalistical
Tradition: which, being kept more secret before, he took the liberty to make
publick, and so was reputed the Author of the Prophecy. As many Philosophers
amongst the *Greeks*, were the reputed Authors of such doctrines as were much
more ancient than themselves: But they were the publishers of them in their
Country, or the revivers of them after a long silence; and so, by forgetful posterity,
got the honour of the first invention.

You will think, it may be, the time is too long and the distance too great betwixt
Elias the *Thesbite*, and this *Elias* the *Rabbin*, for a Tradition to subsist all the
while, or be preserv'd with any competent integrity. But it appears from St.
Jude's Epistle, that the *Prophecies of Enoch*, (who liv'd before the Flood) relating
to the day of judgment and the end of the World, were extant in his time, either
in writing or by Tradition: And the distance betwixt *Enoch* and St. *Jude* was
vastly greater than betwixt the two *Elias*'s. Nor was any fitter to be inspir'd
with that knowledge, or to tell the first news of that fatal period, than the old
Prophet *Elias*, who is to come again and bring the alarum of the approaching
Conflagration. But however this conjecture may prove as to the original Author
of this Prophecy, the Prophecy it self concerning the *Sexmillennial* duration of
the World, is very much insisted upon by the Christian Fathers. Which yet I
believe is not so much for the bare Authority of the Tradition, as because they
thought it was founded in the History of the *Six days Creation*, and the *Sabbath*
succeeding: as also in some other Typical precepts and usages in the Law of
Moses. But before we speak of that, give me leave to name some of those Fathers
to you, that were of this judgment, and supposed the great Sabbatism would
succeed after the World had stood Six thousand years. Of this opinion was
St. *Barnabas* in his Catholick Epistle, ch. 15. Where he argues that the Creation
will be ended in Six Thousand years, as it was finish'd in Six Days: Every day
according to the Sacred and mystical account, being a Thousand Years. Of the
same judgment is St. *Irenæus*, both as to the conclusion and the reason of it. He   *Li. 5. c. 28, 29,*
saith, the History of the Creation in six days, *is a narration as to what is pass'd,*   *30.*
and a Prophecy of what is to come. As the Work was said to be consummated in
six days, and the Sabbath to be the seventh: So the consummation of all things
will be in six thousand years, and then the great Sabbatism to come on in the
blessed reign of Christ. *Hippolitus* Martyr, disciple of *Irenæus*, is of the same
judgment, as you may see in *Photius*, ch. 202. *Lactantius* in his *Divine Institutions*,
li. 7. c. 14. gives the very same account of the state and continuance of the World,
and the same proofs for it. And so does St. *Cyprian*, in his *Exhortation to Martyr-
dom, ch.* 11. St. *Jerome* more than once declares himself of the same opinion;
and St. *Austin*, tho' he wavers and was doubtful as to the *Millennium*, or Reign   *C. D. li. 20. c. 7.*
of Christ upon Earth, yet he receives this computation without hesitancy, and
upon the foremention'd grounds. So *Johannes Damascenus de fide Orthodoxâ,*

takes seven Millenaries for the entire space of the World, from the Creation to the general Resurrection, the Sabbatism being included. And that this was a received and approv'd opinion in early times, we may collect from the Author of the *Questions and answers ad Orthodoxos in Justin Martyr*. Who giving an answer to that enquiry about the six thousand-years-term of the World, says, *We may conjecture from many places of Scripture, that those are in the right, that say six thousand years is the time prefixt for the duration of this present frame of the World*. These Authors I have examin'd my self: but there are many others brought in confirmation of this opinion: as St. *Hilary, Anastatius Sinaita*, Sanctus *Gaudentius*, Q. *Julius Hilarion, Junilius Africanus, Isidorus Hispalensis, Cassiodorus, Gregorius Magnus*, and others, which I leave to be examin'd by those that have curiosity and leisure to do it.

In the mean time it must be confest that many of these Fathers were under a mistake in one respect, in that they generally thought, the World was near an end in their time. An errour, which we need not take pains to confute now; seeing we, who live twelve hundred or fourteen hundred years after them, find the World still in being, and likely to continue so for some considerable time. But it is easie to discern whence their mistake proceeded: not from this Prophecy alone, but because they reckon'd this Prophecy according to the Chronology of the Septuagint: which setting back the beginning of the World many Ages beyond the *Hebrew*, these six thousand years were very near expir'd in the time of those Fathers; and that made them conclude that the World was very near an end. We will make no reflections, in this place, upon that Chronology of the Septuagint, lest it should too much interrupt the thred of our discourse. But it is necessary to show how the Fathers grounded this computation of six thousand years, upon Scripture. 'Twas chiefly, as we suggested before, upon the *Hexameron*, or the Creation finish'd in *six days*, and the *Sabbath* ensuing. The Sabbath, they said,

ch. 4. was a type of the Sabbatism, that was to follow at the end of the World, according to St. *Paul* to the *Hebrews*; and then by analogy and consequence, the six days preceding the Sabbath, must note the space and duration of the World. If therefore they could discover how much a Day is reckon'd for, in this mystical computation, the sum of the six days would be easily found out. And they think, that according to the Psalmist, (*Psal*. 90. 4.) and St. *Peter*, (2 *Epist*. 3. 8.) *a Day* may be estimated *a thousand years*; and consequently six days must be counted six thousand years, for the duration of the World. This is their interpretation, and their inference: but it must be acknowledged, that there is an essential weakness in all typical and allegorical argumentations, in comparison of literal. And this being allow'd in diminution of the proof, we may be bold to say, that nothing yet appears, either in nature, or Scripture, or humane affairs, repugnant to this supposition of six thousand years: which hath Antiquity, and the Authority of the Fathers, on its side.

We proceed now to the Christian Prophecies concerning the end of the World. I do not mention those in *Daniel*, because I am not satisfied that any there (excepting that of the fifth kingdom it self) extend so far. But in the *Apocalypse* of St. *John*, which is the last Revelation we are to expect, there are several Prophecies that reach to the Consummation of this World, and the first Resurrection. The *seven Seals*, the *seven Trumpets*, the *seven Vials*, do all terminate upon that great period. But they are rather Historical Prophecies than Chronological: they tell us, in their Language, the Events, but do not measure or express the time wherein they come to pass. Others there are that may be call'd Chronological, as the *Treading under foot the holy City, forty and two months*. Apoc. 11. 2. The *Witnesses* opposing Antichrist, *one thousand two hundred and sixty days*, Apoc. 11. 3. The flight of the *Woman into the Wilderness*, for the same number of days, or for a *Time, Times, and half a Time*. Apoc. 12. 6. & 14. And lastly, the War of the Beast against the Saints, *forty two months*, Apoc. 13. 5. These all, you see, express a time for their completion; And all the same time, if I be not mistaken: but they do not reach to the end of the World. Or if some of them did reach so far, yet because we do not certainly know where to fix their beginning, we must still be at a loss, when, or in what year they will end. As for instance, If the Reign of the Beast, or the preaching of the Witnesses be 1260 years, as is reasonably suppos'd; yet if we do not know certainly when this Reign, or this preaching begun, neither can we tell when it will end. And the Epocha's or beginnings of these Prophecies are so differently calculated, and are things of so long debate, as makes the discussion of them altogether improper for this place. Yet it must be confest, that the best conjectures that can be made concerning the approaching end of the World, must be taken from a judicious examination of these points: and according as we gather up the Prophecies of the Apocalypse, in a successive completion, we see how by degrees we draw nearer and nearer to the conclusion of all. But till some of these enlightening Prophecies be accomplish'd, we are as a Man that awakes in the Night, all is dark about him, and he knows not how far the Night is spent: but if he watch till the light appears, the first glimpses of that will resolve his doubts. We must have a little patience, and, I think, but a little; still eyeing those Prophecies of the *Resurrection* of the *Witnesses*, and the *depression* of *Antichrist*: till by their accomplishment, the day dawn, and the Clouds begin to change their colour. Then we shall be able to make a near guess, when the Sun of righteousness will arise.

So much for Prophecies. There are also *Signs*, which are look'd upon as forerunners of the coming of our Saviour: and therefore may give us some direction how to judge of the distance or approach of that great Day. Thus many of the Fathers thought the *coming* of *Antichrist* would be a sign to give the World notice of its approaching end. But we may easily see, by what hath been noted before, what it was that led the Fathers into that mistake. They thought their six thousand years were near an end, as they truly were, according to that Chronology they followed; and therefore they concluded the Reign of Antichrist must be very short, whensoever he came, and that he could not come long before the end of the World. But we are very well assur'd from the Revelation of St. *John*, that the reign of Antichrist is not to be so short and transient; and from the prospect and history of Christendom, that he hath been already upon his Throne many hundreds of Years. Therefore this Sign wholly falls to the ground; unless you will take it from the fall of Antichrist, rather than from his first entrance.

Others expect the *coming* of *Elias* to give warning of that day, and prepare the way of the Lord. I am very willing to admit that *Elias* will come, according to the sence of the Prophet *Malachi*, but he will not come *with observation*, no more than he did in the Person of *John* the Baptist; He will not bear the name of *Elias*, nor tell us he is the Man that went to Heaven in a fiery Chariot, and is now come down again to give us warning of the last Fire. But some divine person may appear before the second coming of our Saviour, as there did before his first coming: and by giving a new light and life to the Christian Doctrine, may dissipate the mists of error, and abolish all those little controversies amongst good men, and the divisions and animosities that spring from them: enlarging their Spirits by greater discoveries, and uniting them all in the bonds of love and charity, and in the common study of truth and perfection. Such an *Elias*, the Prophet seems to point at; And may he come, and be the great Peace-maker and preparer of the ways of the Lord. But at present, we cannot from this Sign make any judgment when the World will end.

c. 4. 5, 6.

Another Sign preceeding the end of the World, is, *The Conversion of the Jews*; and this is a wonderful sign indeed. St. *Paul* seems expresly to affirm it, *Rom.* 11. 25, 26. But it is differently understood, either of their Conversion only, or of their Restoration to their own Countrey, Liberties and Dominion. The Prophets bear hard upon this sence sometimes, as you may see in *Isaiah, Ezekiel, Hosea, Amos*. And to the same purpose the ancient promise of *Moses* is interpreted, *Deut.* 30. Yet this seems to be a thing very unconceivable; unless we suppose the Ten Tribes to be still in some hidden corner of the World, from whence they may be conducted again into their own Countrey, as once out of *Egypt*, by a miraculous Providence, and establish'd there. Which being known, will give the alarum to all the other *Jews* in the World, and make an universal confluence to their old home. Then our Saviour by an extraordinary appearance to them, as once to St. *Paul*: and by Prophets rais'd up amongst them for that purpose, may convince them that he is the true Messiah, and convert them to the Christian Faith; which will be no more strange, than was the first Conversion of the Gentile World. But if we be content with a Conversion of the *Jews*, without their restoration; and of those Two Tribes only which are now disperst throughout the Christian World and other known parts of the Earth: That these should be Converted to the Christian Faith, and incorporated into the Christian Commonwealth, losing their national character and distinction. If this, I say, will satisfie the Prophecies, it is not a thing very difficult to be conceived. For when the World is reduc'd to a better and purer state of Christianity, and that Idolatry in a great measure, remov'd, which gave the greatest scandal to the *Jews*, they will begin to have better thoughts of our Religion, and be dispos'd to a more ingenuous and unprejudic'd examination of their Prophecies concerning the Messiah: God raising up men amongst them of divine and enlarged Spirits, Lovers of Truth more than of any particular Sect or Opinion; with light to discern it, and courage to profess it. Lastly, it will be a cogent argument upon them, to see the Age of the World so far spent, and no appearance yet of their long expected Messiah. So far spent, I say, that there is no room left, upon any computation

Joh. 19. 37.
Apoc. 1. 7.
Mat. 23. 39.

whatsoever, for the Oeconomy of a Messiah yet to come. This will make them reflect more carefully and impartially upon him whom the Christians propose, *Jesus of Nazareth*, whom their Fathers Crucified at *Jerusalem*. Upon the Miracles he wrought, in his life and after his death: and upon the wonderful propagation of his Doctrine throughout the World, after his Ascension. And lastly, upon the desolation of *Jerusalem*, upon their own scatter'd and forlorn condition, foretold by that Prophet, as a judgment of God upon an ungrateful and wicked People.

This I have said to state the case of the Conversion of the *Jews*, which will be a sign of the approaching reign of Christ. But alas, what appearance is there of this Conversion in our days, or what judgment can we make from a sign that is not yet come to pass? 'Tis ineffectual as to us, but may be of use to posterity. Yet even to them it will not determine at what distance they are from the end of the World, but be a mark only that they **are** not far from it. There will be Signs also, in those last days, in the Heavens, and in the Earth, and in the Sea, fore-runners of the *Conflagration*; as the obscuration of the Sun and Moon, Earth-quakes, roarings of the troubled Sea, and such like disorders in the natural World. 'Tis true, but these are the very pangs of death, and the strugglings of Nature just before her dissolution, and it will be too late then to be aware of our ruine when it is at the door. Yet these being Signs or Prodigies taken notice of by Scripture, we intend, God willing, after we have explained the causes and manner of the *Conflagration*, to give an account also whence these unnatural commotions will proceed, that are the beginnings or immediate introductions to the last Fire.

Thus we have gone through the Prophecies and Signs that concern the last day and the last fate of the World. And how little have we learned from them as to the time of that great revolution? Prophecies rise sometimes with an even gradual light, as the day riseth upon the Horizon: and sometimes break out suddenly like a fire, and we are not aware of their approach till we see them accomplish'd. Those that concern the end of the World are of this latter sort to unobserving men; but even to the most observing, there will still be a latitude; We must not expect to calculate the coming of our Saviour like an Eclipse, to minutes and half-minutes. There are *Times and Seasons which the Father hath put in his own power*. If it was designed to keep these things secret, we must not think to out-wit Providence, and from the Prophecies that are given us, pick out a discovery that was not intended we should ever make. It is determin'd in the Councils of Heaven just how far we shall know these events before-hand, and with what degree of certainty: and with this we must be content whatsoever it is. The *Apocalypse* of St. *John* is the last Prophetical declaration of the Will of God, and contains the fate of the Christian Religion to the end of the World, its purity, degeneracy, and reviviscency. The head of this degeneracy is call'd *The Beast, the false Prophet, the whore of Babylon*, in Prophetical terms: and in an Ecclesi-astical term is commonly call'd *Antichrist*. Those that bear Testimony against this degeneracy, are call'd the *Witnesses*: who, after they have been a long time, in a mean and persecuted condition, are to have their Resurrection and Ascension: that is, be advanc'd to power and Authority. And this Resurrection of the *Wit-nesses* and depression of *Antichrist*, is that which will make the great turn of the

Apoc. c. 9.
Apoc. c. 16.
ch. 11. 14.

World to righteousness, and the great Crisis whereby we may judge of its drawing to an end. 'Tis true, there are other marks, as the passing away of the *Second Woe*: which is commonly thought to be the Ottoman Empire: and the Effusion of the *Vials*. The first of these will be indeed a very conspicuous mark, if it follow upon the Resurrection of the Witnesses, as by the Prophecy it seems to do. But as to the Vials, tho' they do plainly reach in a Series to the end of the World, I am not satisfied with any exposition I have yet met with, concerning their precise time or contents.

In a word, Tho' the sum and general contents of a Prophecy be very intelligible, yet the application of it to Time and Persons may be very lubricous. There must be obscurity in a Prophecy, as well as shadow in a Picture. All its lines must not stand in a full light. For if Prophecies were open and bare-fac'd as to all their parts and circumstances, they would check and obstruct the course of humane affairs; and hinder, if it was possible, their own accomplishment. Modesty and Sobriety are in all things commendable, but in nothing more than in the explication of these Sacred Mysteries; and we have seen so many miscarry by a too close and particular application of them, that we ought to dread the Rock about which we see so many shipwrecks. He that does not err above a Century in calculating the last period of Time, from what evidence we have at present, hath, in my opinion, cast up his accounts very well. But the Scenes will change fast towards the Evening of this long day, and when the Sun is near setting, they will more easily compute how far he hath to run.

CHAPTER VI

Concerning the Causes of the Conflagration.

The difficulty of conceiving how this Earth can be set on fire. With a general answer to that difficulty. Two suppos'd causes of the Conflagration, by the Sun's drawing nearer to the Earth, or the Earth's throwing out the central fire, examin'd and rejected.

WE have now made our way clear to the principal point, *The Causes of the Conflagration:* How the Heavens and the Earth will be set on fire, what materials are prepar'd, or what train of causes, for that purpose. The Ancients, who have kept us company pretty well thus far, here quite desert us. They deal more in Conclusions than Causes, as is usual in all Traditional Learning. And the *Stoicks* themselves, who inculcate so much the doctrine of the Conflagration, and make the strength of it such as to dissolve the Earth into a fiery Chaos, are yet very short and superficial in their explications, how this shall come to pass. The latent seeds of fire, they say, shall every where be let loose, and that Element will prevail over all the rest, and transform every thing into its own nature. But these are general things that give little satisfaction to inquisitive Persons. Neither do the modern Authors that treat of the same subject, relieve us in this particular: They are willing to suppose the Conflagration a supernatural effect, that so they may excuse themselves the trouble of enquiring after causes. 'Tis, no doubt, in a sort, supernatural: and so the Deluge was: yet *Moses* sets down the causes of the Deluge, the rains from above, and the disruption of the Abyss. So there must be treasures of fire provided against that day, by whose eruption this second Deluge will be brought upon the Earth.

To state the case fairly, we must first represent the difficulty of setting the Earth on fire: Tie the knot, before we loose it; that so we may the better judge whether the causes that shall be brought into view, may be sufficient to overcome so great opposition. The difficulty, no doubt, will be chiefly from the great quantity of water that is about our Globe; whereby Nature seems to have made provision against any invasion by fire, and secur'd us from that enemy more than any other. We see half of the Surface of the Earth cover'd with the Seas: whose Chanel is of a vast depth and capacity. Besides innumerable Rivers, great and small, that water the face of the dry Land, and drench it with perpetual moisture. Then within the bowels of the Earth, there are Store-houses of subterraneous waters: which are as a reserve, in case the Ocean and the Rivers should be overcome. Neither is water our onely security, for the hard Rocks and stony Mountains, which no fire can bite upon, are set in long ranges upon the Continents and Islands: and must needs give a stop to the progress of that furious Enemy, in case he should attack us. Lastly, the Earth it self is not combustible in all its parts. 'Tis not every Soyl that is fit fewel for the fire. Clay, and Mire, and such like Soyles will rather choak and stifle it, than help it on its way. By these means one would think the Body of the Earth secur'd; And tho' there may be partial fires, or inundations of fire, here and there, in particular regions, yet there cannot be an universal fire throughout the Earth. At least one would hope for a safe retreat towards the Poles, where there is nothing but Snow, and Ice, and bitter cold. These regions sure are in no danger to be burnt, whatsoever becomes of the other climates of the Earth.

This being the state and condition of the present Earth, one would not imagine by these preparations, 'twas ever intended that it should perish by an universal fire. But such is often the method of Providence, that the exteriour face of things looks one way, and the design lies another; till at length, touching a Spring, as it were, at a certain time, all those affairs change posture and aspect, and shew us which way Providence inclines. We must therefore suppose, before the Conflagration begins, there will be dispositions and preparatives suitable to so great a work: and all antiquity, sacred and prophane, does so far concur with us, as to admit and suppose that a great drought will precede, and an extraordinary heat and driness of the Air, to usher in this fiery doom. And these being things which often happen in a course of nature, we cannot disallow such easie preparations, when Providence intends so great a consequence. The Heavens will be shut up, and the Clouds yield no rain; and by this, with an immoderate heat in the Air, the Springs of water will become dry, the Earth chap'd and parch'd, and the Woods and Trees made ready fewel for the fire. We have instances in history that there have been droughts and heats of this nature, to that degree, that the Woods and Forests have taken fire, and the outward Turf and Surface of the Earth, without any other cause than the driness of the Season, and the vehemency of the Sun. And which is more considerable, the Springs and Fountains being dry'd up, the greater Rivers have been sensibly lessen'd, and the lesser quite emptied and exhal'd. These things which happen frequently in particular Countreys and Climates, may at an appointed time, by the disposition of Providence, be more universal throughout the Earth; and have the same effects every where, that we see by experience they have had in certain places. And by this means we may conceive it as feisible to set the whole Earth on fire in some little space of time, as to burn up this or that Country after a great drought. But I mean this, with exception still to the main Body of the Sea; which will indeed receive a greater diminution from these causes than we easily imagine, but the final consumption of it will depend upon other reasons, whereof we must give an account in the following Chapters.

As to the Mountains and Rocks, their lofty heads will sink when the Earthquakes begin to roar, at the beginning of the Conflagration: as we shall see hereafter. And as to the Earth it self, 'tis true there are several sorts of earth that are not proper fewel for fire; but those Soils that are not so immediately, as clayey Soils, and such like, may by the strength of fire be converted into brick, or stone, or earthen metal, and so melted down and vitrified. For, in conclusion, there is no terrestrial Body that does not finally yield to the force of fire, and may either be converted into flame, incorporated fire, or into a liquor more ardent than either of them. Lastly, as to the polar regions, which you think will be a safe retreat and inaccessible to the fire; 'Tis true, unless Providence hath laid subterraneous treasures of fire there unknown to us, those parts of the Earth will be the last consum'd. But it is to be observ'd, that the cold of those regions proceeds from the length of their Winter, and their distance from the Sun when he is beyond the Æquator; and both these causes will be remov'd at the Confla-

chap. 3. gration. For we suppose the Earth will then return to its primitive situation, which we have explain'd in the 2d. Book of this Theory; and will have the Sun always in its Equator; whereby the several Climates of the Earth will have a perpetual Equinox, and those under the Poles a perpetual day. And therefore all the excess of cold, and all the consequences of it, will soon be abated. However, the Earth will not be burnt in one day, and those parts of the Earth being uninhabited, there is no inconvenience that they should be more slowly consum'd than the rest.

This is a general answer to the difficulty propos'd about the possibility of the Conflagration; and being general onely, the parts of it must be more fully explain'd and confirm'd in the sequel of this discourse. We should now proceed directly to the causes of the Conflagration, and show in what manner they do this great execution upon nature. But to be just and impartial in this enquiry, we ought first to separate the spurious and pretended causes from those that are real and genuine; to make no false musters, nor any show of being stronger than we are; and if we can do our work with less force, it will be more to our credit; as a Victory is more honourable that is gain'd with fewer men.

There are two grand capital causes which some Authors make use of, as the chief Agents in this work, the *Sun*, and the *Central Fire*. These two great Incendiaries, they say, will be let loose upon us at the Conflagration. The one drawing nearer to the Earth, and the other breaking out of its bowels into these upper regions. These are potent causes indeed, more than enough to destroy this Earth, if it was a thousand times bigger than it is. But for that very reason, I suspect they are not the true causes; for God and Nature do not use to employ unnecessary means to bring about their designs. Disproportion and over-sufficiency is one sort of false measures, and 'tis a sign we do not thoroughly understand our work, when we put more strength to it than the thing requires. Men are forward to call in extraordinary powers to rid their hands of a troublesome argument, and so make a short dispatch to save themselves the pains of further enquiries: but such methods, as they commonly have no proof, so they give little satisfaction to an inquisitive mind. This supposition of burning the Earth, by the Sun drawing nearer and nearer to it, seems to be made in imitation of the story of *Phaeton*, who driving the Chariot of the Sun with an unsteddy hand, came so near the Earth, that he set it on fire. But however we will not reject any pretensions without a fair trial; Let us examine therefore what grounds they can have for either of these suppositions, of the Approximation of the Sun to the Earth, or the Eruption of the Central Fire.

As to the Sun, I desire first to be satisfied in present matter of Fact: whether by any instrument or observation it hath or can be discover'd, that the Sun is nearer to the Earth now, than he was in former ages? or if by any reasoning or comparing calculations such a conclusion can be made? If not, this is but an imaginary cause, and as easily deny'd as propos'd. Astronomers do very little agree in their opinions about the distance of the Sun, *Ptolomy*, *Albategnius*, *Copernicus*, *Tycho*, *Kepler*, and others more modern, differ all in their calculations; but not in such a manner or proportion, as should make us believe that the Sun comes nearer to the Earth, but rather goes further from it. For the more modern of them make the distance greater than the more ancient do. *Kepler* says, the distance of the Sun from the Earth lies betwixt 700 and 2000 semidiameters of the Earth: but *Ricciolus* makes it betwixt 700 and 7000. And *Gottefrid Wendeline* hath taken 14656 semidiameters, for a middle proportion of the Sun's distance; to which *Kepler* himself came very near in his later years. So that you see how groundless our fears are from the approaches of an enemy, that rather flies from us, if he change posture at all. And we have more reason to believe the report of the modern Astronomers than of the ancient, in this matter; both because the nature of the Heavens and of the celestial Bodies is now better known, and also because they have found out better instruments and better methods to make their observations.

If the Sun and Earth were come nearer to one another, either the circle of the Suns diurnal arch would be less, and so the day shorter: or the Orbit of the Earths annual course would be less, and so the Year shorter: Neither of which we have any experience of. And those that suppose us in the centre of the World, need not be afraid till they see *Mercury* and *Venus* in a combustion, for they lie betwixt us and danger; and the Sun cannot come so readily at us with his fiery darts, as at them, who stand in his way. Lastly, this languishing death by the gradual approaches of the Sun, and that irreparable ruine of the Earth which at last must follow from it, do neither of them agree with that Idea of the *Confla-gration*, which the Scripture hath given us; for it is to come suddenly and un-expectedly, and take us off like a violent Feaver, not as a lingring Consumption. And the Earth is also so to be destroyed by Fire, as not to take away all hopes of a Resurrection or Renovation. For we are assur'd by Scripture that there will be new Heavens and a new Earth after these are burnt up. But if the Sun should come so near us as to make the *heavens pass away with a noise, and melt the Elements with fervent heat,* and destroy the form and all the works of the Earth, what hopes or possibility would there be of a Renovation while the Sun con-tinued in this posture? He would more and more consume and prey upon the Carcass of the Earth, and convert it at length either into an heap of ashes, or a lump of vitrified metal.

So much for the Sun. As to the *Central Fire,* I am very well satisfied it is no imaginary thing. All Antiquity hath preserv'd some sacred Monument of it. The *Vestal* fire of the *Romans,* which was so religiously attended: The *Prytoneia* of the *Greeks* were to the same purpose, and dedicated to *Vesta:* and the *Pyretheia* of the *Persians,* where fire was kept continually by the *Magi.* These all, in my opinion, had the same origine and the same signification. And tho' I do not know any particular observation, that does directly prove or demonstrate that there is such a mass of fire in the middle of the Earth; yet the best accounts we have of the generation of a Planet, do suppose it; and 'tis agreeable to the whole Oeconomy of Nature; as a fire in the heart, which gives life to her motions and productions. But however the question is not at present, about the existence of this fire, but the eruption of it, and the effect of that Eruption: which cannot be, in my judgment, such a *Conflagration* as is describ'd in Scripture.

This Central Fire must be enclos'd in a shell of great strength and firmness; for being of it self the lightest and most active of all Bodies, it would not be detained in that lowest prison without a strong guard upon it. 'Tis true, we can make no certain judgment of what thickness this shell is, but if we suppose this fire to have a twentieth part of the semidiameter of the Earth, on either side the centre, for its sphere, which seems to be a fair allowance; there would still re-main nineteen parts, for our safeguard and security. And these nineteen parts of the semidiameter of the Earth will make 3268 miles, for a partition-wall betwixt us and this Central Fire. Who wou'd by afraid of an Enemy lock'd up in so strong a prison? But you'l say, it may be, tho' the Central Fire, at the beginning of the World, might have no more room or space than what is mentioned: yet being of that activity that it is, and corrosive nature, it may, in the space of some thousands of years, have eaten deep into the sides of its prison; and so come nearer to the surface of the Earth, by some hundreds or thousands of miles than it was at first. This would be a material exception if it could be made out. But what Phænomenon is there in Nature that proves this? How does it appear by any observation that the Central Fire gains ground upon us? Or is increased in quantity, or come nearer to the surface of the Earth? I know nothing that can be offered in proof of this: and if there be no appearance of a change, nor any sensible effect of it, 'tis an argument there is none, or none considerable. If the quantity of that fire was considerably increas'd, it must needs, besides other effects, have made the Body of the Earth considerably lighter. The Earth having, by this conversion of its own substance into fire, lost so much of its heaviest matter, and got so much of the lightest and most active Element in stead of it: and in both these respects its gravity would be manifestly lessen'd. Which if it really was, in any considerable degree, it would discover it self by some change, either as to the motion of the Earth, or as to its place or station in the Heavens. But there being no external change observable, in this or any other respect, 'tis reasonable to presume that there is no considerable inward change, or no great consumption of its inward parts and substance: and consequently no great increase of the Central Fire.

But if we should admit both an encrease and eruption of this fire, it would not have that effect which is pretended. It might cause some confusion and disorder in those parts of the Earth where it broke out, but it would not make an universal Conflagration, such as is represented to us in Scripture. Let us suppose the Earth to be open or burst in any place, under the Pole, for instance, or under the Æquator: and let it gape as low as the Central Fire. At this chasm or rupture we suppose the fire wou'd gush out; and what then would be the consequence of this when it came to the surface of the Earth? It would either be dissipated and lost in the air, or fly still higher towards the Heavens in a mass of flame. But what execution in the mean time would it do upon the Body of the Earth? 'Tis but like a flash of lightning, or a flame issuing out of a pit, that dies presently. Besides, this Central Fire is of that subtilty and tenuity that it is not able to inflame gross Bodies: no more than those Meteors we call *Lambent Fires*, inflame the bodies to which they stick. Lastly, in explaining the manner of the Conflagration, we must have regard principally to Scripture; for the explications given there are more to the purpose, than all that the Philosophers have said upon that subject. Now, as we noted before, 'tis manifest in Scripture that after the Conflagration there will be a *Restauration, New Heavens* and a *New Earth.* 'Tis the express doctrine of St. *Peter,* besides other Prophets: We must therefore suppose the Earth reduc'd to such a Chaos by this last fire, as will lay the foundation of a new World. Which can never be, if the inward frame of it be broke, the Central Fire exhausted, and the exterior region suck'd into those central vacuities. This must needs make it lose its former poise and libration, and it will thereupon be thrown into some other part of the Universe, as the useless shell of a broken Granado, or as a dead carkass and unprofitable matter.

2 Pet. 3. 12, 13.

These reasons may be sufficient why we should not depend upon those pretended causes of the Conflagration, The Suns advance towards the Earth, or such a rupture of the Earth as will let out the Central Fire. These Causes, I hope, will appear superfluous, when we shall have given an account of the Conflagration without them. But young Philosophers, like young Soldiers, think they are never sufficiently armed; and often take more weapons, than they can make use of, when they come to fight. Not that we altogether reject the influence of the Sun, or of the Central Fire; especially the latter. For in that great estuation of Nature, the Body of the Earth will be much open'd and relaxated; and when the pores are enlarg'd, the steams of that fire will sweat out more plentifully into all its parts; but still without any rupture in the vessels or in the skin. And whereas these Authors suppose the very Veins burst, and the vital blood to gush out, as at open flood-gates, we onely allow a more copious perspiration, and think that sufficient for all purposes in this case.

CHAPTER VII

The true bounds of the Last Fire, and how far it is fatal. The natural Causes and Materials of it, cast into three ranks: First, such as are exteriour and visible upon the Earth; where the Volcano's of the Earth, and their effects, are consider'd. Secondly, such materials as are within the Earth. Thirdly, such as are in the Air.

A S we have, in the preceding Chapter, laid aside those Causes of the Conflagration, which we thought too great and cumbersome; so now we must, in like manner, examine the Effect, and reduce that to its just measures and proportions; that there may be nothing left superfluous on either side: Then, by comparing the real powers with the work they are to do, both being stated within their due bounds, we may the better judge how they are proportion'd to one another.

We noted before, that the Conflagration had nothing to do with the Stars and superiour Heavens, but was wholly confin'd to this Sublunary World. And this Deluge of Fire will have much what the same bounds, that the Deluge of Water had formerly. This is according to St. *Peter*'s doctrine, for he makes the same parts of the Universe to be the subject of both: namely, the inferiour Heavens and the Earth. *The Heavens and the Earth which were then, perish'd in a Deluge of Water: But the Heavens and the Earth that are now, are reserv'd to fire.* The present Heavens and Earth are substituted in the place of those that perish'd at the Deluge, and these are to be over-run and destroy'd by fire, as those were by water. So that the Apostle takes the same Regions, and the same space and compass for the one as for the other, and makes their fate different according to their different constitution, and the different order of Providence. This is the sence St. *Austin* gives us of the Apostle's words, and these are the bounds he sets to the last Fire; whereof a modern Commentator is so well assur'd, that he says, *They neither understand Divinity, nor Philosophy, that would make the Conflagration reach above the Elementary Heavens.*

Let these be then its limits upwards, the Clouds, Air, and Atmosphere of the Earth. But the question seems more doubtful, *How* far it will extend downwards, into the bowels of the Earth. I answer still, to the same depth that the Waters of the Deluge reach'd: To the lowest Abysses and the deepest Caverns within the ground. And seeing no Caverns are deeper or lower, at least according to our Theory, than the bottom of the great Ocean, to that depth, I suppose, the rage of this fire will penetrate, and devour all before it. And therefore we

2 Pet. 3. 5, 6.
Ver. 7

Estius in loc.

270

must not imagine, that onely the outward turf and habitable surface of the Earth will be put into a flame and laid wast; the whole exteriour region of the Earth, to the depth of the deepest part of the Sea, will suffer in this fire; and suffer to that degree, as to be melted down, and the frame of it dissolv'd. For we are not to conceive that the Earth will be onely scorcht or charkt in the last fire, there will be a sort of liquefaction and dissolution; It will become a *molten Sea mingled with fire*, according to the expression of Scripture. And this dissolution may reasonably be suppos'd to reach as low as the Earth hath any hollowednesses, or can give vent to smoak and flame.

Rev. 15. 2.
2 Pet. 3. 10.
Psal. 97. 5.

Wherefore taking these for the bounds and limits of the last great fire, the next thing to be enquir'd into, are the *Natural Causes* of it. How this strange fate will seize upon the Sublunary World, and with an irresistible fury subdue all things to it self. But when I say *Natural Causes*, I would not be so understood, as if I thought the Conflagration was a pure *Natural Fatality*, as the *Stoicks* seem to do. No, 'tis a *mixt Fatality*; The Causes indeed are natural, but the administration of them is from an higher hand. Fire is the Instrument, or the executive power, and hath no more force given it, than what it hath naturally; but the concurrence of these causes, or of these fiery powers, at such a time, and in such a manner, and the conduct of them to carry on and compleat the whole work without cessation or interruption, that I look upon as more than what material Nature could effect of it self, or than could be brought to pass by such a government of matter, as is the bare result of its own laws and determinations. When a Ship sails gently before the wind, the Mariners may stand idle; but to guide her in a storm, all hands must be at work. There are rules and measures to be observ'd, even in these tumults and desolations of Nature, in destroying a World, as well as in making one, and therefore in both it is reasonable to suppose a more than ordinary Providence to superintend the work. Let us not therefore be too positive or presumptuous in our conjectures about these things, for if there be an invisible hand, Divine or Angelical, that touches the Springs and Wheels; it will not be easie for us to determine, with certainty, the order of their motions. However, 'tis our duty to search into the ways and works of God, as far as we can: And we may without offence look into the Magazines of Nature, see what provisions are made, and what preparations for this great Day; and in what method 'tis most likely the design will be executed.

But before we proceed to mark out Materials for this fire, give me leave to observe one condition or property in the Form of this present Earth, that makes it capable of inflammation. 'Tis the manner of its construction, in an hollow cavernous form; By reason whereof, containing much Air in its cavities, and having many inlets and outlets, 'tis in most places capable of ventilation, pervious and passable to the winds, and consequently to the fire. Those that have read the former part of this Theory, know how the Earth came into this hollow and broken form, from what causes and at what time; namely, at the Universal Deluge; when there was a disruption of the exteriour Earth that fell into the Abyss, and so, for a time, was overflow'd with water. These Ruines recover'd from the water, we inhabit, and these Ruines onely will be burnt up; For being

Book 1. *ch.* 6, 7.

not onely unequal in their Surface, but also hollow, loose, and incompact within, as ruines use to be, they are made thereby capable of a second fate, by inflammation. *Thereby*, I say they are made combustible; for if the exteriour Regions of this Earth were as close and compact in all their parts, as we have reason to believe the interiour Regions of it to be, the Fire could have little power over it, nor ever reduce it to such a state as is requir'd in a compleat Conflagration, such as ours is to be.

This being admitted, that the Exteriour region of the Earth stands hollow, as a well set fire, to receive Air freely into its parts, and hath issues for smoke and flame: It remains to enquire what fewel or materials Nature hath fitted to kindle this Pile, and to continue it on fire till it be consum'd; or, in plain words, What are the *natural causes and preparatives for a Conflagration*. The first and most obvious preparations that we see in nature for this effect, are the *Burning Mountains* or Volcano's of the Earth. These are lesser Essays or preludes to the general fire; set on purpose by Providence to keep us awake, and to mind us continually, and forewarn us of what we are to expect at last. The Earth you see is already kindled, blow but the Coal, and propagate the fire, and the work will go on.

Isa. 30. 33. *Tophet is prepar'd of old,* and when the Day of Doom is come, and the Date of the World expir'd, *the breath of the Lord* shall make it burn.

But besides these Burning Mountains, there are Lakes of pitch and brimstone and oily Liquors disperst in several parts of the Earth. These are to enrage the fire as it goes, and to fortifie it against any resistance or opposition. Then all the vegetable productions upon the Surface of the Earth, as Trees, shrubs, grass, corn, and such like; Every thing that grows out of the ground, is fewel for the fire; And tho' they are now accommodated to our use and service, they will then turn all against us; and with a mighty blaze, and rapid course, make a devastation of the outward furniture of the Earth, whether natural or artificial. But these things deserve some further consideration, especially that strange Phænomenon of the *Volcano's* or *Burning Mountains*, which we will now consider more particularly.

There is nothing certainly more terrible in all Nature than Fiery Mountains, to those that live within the view or noise of them; but it is not easie for us, who never see them nor heard them, to represent them to our selves with such just and lively imaginations as shall excite in us the same passions, and the same horrour as they would excite, if present to our senses. The time of their eruption and of their raging, is, of all others, the most dreadful; but, many times, before their eruption, the symptomes of an approaching fit are very frightful to the People. The Mountain begins to roar and bellow in its hollow caverns; cries out, as it were, in pain to be deliver'd of some burthen, too heavy to be born, and too big to be easily discharg'd. The Earth shakes and trembles, in apprehension of the pangs and convulsions that are coming upon her; And the Sun often hides his head, or appears with a discolour'd face, pale, or dusky, or bloudy, as if all Nature was to suffer in this Agony. After these forerunners or symptomes of an eruption, the wide jaws of the Mountain open: And first, clouds of smoke issue out, then flames of fire, and after that a mixture of all sorts of burning matter;

red hot stones, lumps of metal, half-dissolv'd minerals, with coals and fiery ashes. These fall in thick showres round about the Mountain, and in all adjacent parts; and not onely so, but are carried, partly by the force of the expulsion, and partly by the winds, when they are aloft in the Air, into far distant Countries. As from *Italy* to *Constantinople*, and cross the Mediterranean Sea into *Africk*; as the best Historians, *Procopius, Ammianus Marcellinus*, and *Dion Cassius*, have attested.

These Volcano's are planted in several regions of the Earth, and in both Continents, This of ours, and the other of *America*. For by report of those that have view'd that new-found World, there are many Mountains in it that belch out Smoke and Fire; some constantly, and others by fits and intervals. In our Continent Providence hath variously disperst them, without any rule known to us; but they are generally in Islands, or near the Sea. In the Asiatick Oriental Islands they are in great abundance, and Historians tell us of a Mountain in the Island *Java*, that in the year, 1586 at one eruption kill'd ten thousand people in the neighbouring Cities and Countrey. But we do not know so well the History of those remote Volcano's, as of such as are in Europe and nearer home. In *Iseland*, tho' it lye within the Polar circle, and is scarce habitable by reason of the extremity of cold, and abundance of Ice and Snow, yet there are three burning Mountains in that Island; whereof the chief and most remarkable is *Hecla*. This hath its head always cover'd with Snow, and its belly always fill'd with Fire; and these are both so strong in their kind, and equally powerful, that they cannot destroy one another. It is said to cast out, when it rages, besides earth, stones and ashes, a sort of flaming water. As if all contrarieties were to meet in this Mountain to make it the more perfect resemblance of Hell, as the credulous inhabitants fancy it to be.

But there are no Volcano's in my opinion, that deserve our observation so much, as those that are in and about the *Mediterranean Sea*; There is a knot of them called the *Vulcanian Islands*, from their fiery eruptions, as if they were the Forges of *Vulcan*; as *Stombolo, Lipara*, and others, which are not so remarkable now as they have been formerly. However, without dispute, there are none in the Christian World to be compared with *Ætna* and *Vesuvius*; one in the Island of *Sicily*, and the other in *Campania*, overlooking the Port and City of *Naples*. These two, from all memory of man and the most ancient records of History, have been fam'd for their Treasures of subterraneous Fires: which are not yet exhausted, nor diminish'd, so far as is perceivable; for they rage still, upon occasions, with as much fierceness and violence, as they ever did in former Ages; as if they had a continual supply to answer their expences, and were to stand till the last fire, as a type and prefiguration of it, throughout all generations.

Let us therefore take these two Volcano's as a pattern for the rest; seeing they are well known, and stand in the heart of the Christian World, where, 'tis likely the last fire will make its first assault. *Ætna*, of the two, is more spoken of by the ancients, both Poets and Historians; and we should scarce give credit to their relations concerning it, if some later eruptions did not equal or exceed the fame of all that hath been reported from former ages. That it heated the waters of the Sea, and cover'd them over with ashes; crack'd or dissolv'd the neighbouring Rocks; darkened the Sun and the Air; and cast out, not only mighty streams of flame, but a floud of melted Ore and other materials; These things we can now believe, having had experience of greater, or an account of them from such as have been eyewitnesses of these fires, or of the fresh ruines and sad effects of them.

There are two things especially, in these Eruptions of *Ætna*, that are most prodigious in themselves and most remarkable for our purpose. The Rivers of fiery matter that break out of its bowels, or are spew'd out of its mouth; and the vast burning stones which it flings into the Air, at a strange height and distance. As to these fiery rivers or torrents, and the matter whereof they are compounded, we have a full account of them by *Alphonsus Borellus*, a learned Mathematician at *Pisa*; who, after the last great Eruption in the year 1669 went into *Sicily*, while the fact was fresh, to view and survey what *Ætna* had done or suffer'd. And he says the quantity of matter thrown out of the Mountain at that time, upon survey amounted to Ninety three millions, eight hundred thirty eight thousand, seven hundred and fifty cubical paces. So that if it had been extended in length upon the surface of the Earth, at the bredth and depth of 3 foot, it would have reacht further than ninety three millions of paces; which is more than four times the Circuit of the whole Earth, taking a thousand paces to a mile. This is strange to our imagination and almost incredible, that one Mountain should throw out so much fiery matter, besides all the ashes that were disperst through the Air, far and near, and could be brought to no account.

'Tis true, all this matter was not actually inflam'd or liquid fire. But the rest that was sand, stone and gravel, might have run into glass or some melted liquor like to it, if it had not been thrown out before the heat fully reacht it. However, sixty million paces of this matter, as the same Author computes, were liquid fire, or came out of the mouth of the pit in that form. This made a River of fire, sometimes two miles broad, according to his computation; but according to the observation of others who also viewed it, the Torrent of fire was six or seven miles broad, and sometimes ten or fifteen fathoms deep; and forc'd its way into the Sea near a mile, preferving it self alive in the midst of the waters.

This is beyond all the infernal Lakes and Rivers, *Acheron, Phlegeton, Cocytus,* all that the Poets have talkt of. Their greatest fictions about Hell have not come up to the reality of one of our burning Mountains upon Earth. Imagin then all our *Volcano*'s rageing at once in this manner.—But I will not pursue that supposition yet; Give me leave only to add here what I mentioned in the second place, The vast *Burning Stones* which this Mountain, in the time of its rage and estuation, threw into the Air with an incredible force. This same Author tells us of a stone fifteen foot long, that was flung out of the mouth of the pit, to a miles distance. And when it fell, it came from such an height and with such a violence, that it buried it self in the ground eight foot deep. What trifles are our Mortar-pieces and Bombes, when compar'd with these Engines of Nature? When she flings out of the wide throat of a Volcano, a broken Rock, and twirles it in the air like a little bullet; then lets it fall to do execution here below, as Providence shall point and direct it. It would be hard to give an account how so great an impulse can be given to a Body so ponderous, But there's no disputing against matter of fact; and as the thoughts of God are not like our thoughts, so neither are his works like our works.

Thus much for *Ætna*. Let us now give an instance in *Vesuvius*, another *Burning Mountain* upon the coast of the Mediterranean, which hath as frequent Eruptions, and some as terrible as those of *Ætna*. *Dion Cassius* (one of the best writers of the *Roman* History) hath given us an account of one that happened in the time of *Titus Vespatian*; and tho' he hath not set down particulars, as the former Author did, of the quantity of fiery matter thrown out at that time: yet supposing that proportionable to its fierceness in other respects, this seems to me as dreadful an Eruption as any we read of; and was accompanied with such prodigies and commotions in the Heavens and the Earth, as made it look like the beginning of the last Conflagration. As a prelude to this Tragedy, He says there were strange sights in the air, and after that followed an extraordinary drought, *Then the Earth began to tremble and quake, and the Concussions were so great that the ground seem'd to rise and boyl up in some places, and in others the tops of the mountains sunk in or tumbled down. At the same time were great noises and sounds heard, some were subterraneous, like thunder within the Earth; others above ground, like groans or bellowings.* The Sea roar'd, *The heavens ratled with a fearful noise, and then came a sudden and mighty crack, as if the frame of Nature had broke, or all the mountains of the Earth had faln down at once. At length* Vesuvius *burst, and threw out of its womb, first, huge stones, then a vast quantity of fire and smoke, so as the air was all darkned, and the Sun was hid, as if he had been under a great Eclipse. The day was turn'd into night, and light into darkness; and the frighted people thought the Gyants were making war against heaven, and fansied they see the shapes and images of Gyants in the smoak, and heard the sound of their trumpets. Others thought the World was returning to its first Chaos, or going to be all consum'd with fire. In this general confusion and consternation they knew not where to be safe, some run out of the fields into the houses, others out of the houses into the fields; Those that were at Sea hasten'd to Land, and those that were at Land endeavour'd to get to Sea; still thinking every place safer than that where they were. Besides grosser lumps of matter, there was thrown out of the Mountain such a prodigious quantity of ashes, as cover'd the Land and Sea, and fill'd the Air, so as, besides other damages, the Birds, Beasts, and Fishes, with Men, Women and Children, were destroy'd, within such a compass; and two entire Cities,* Herculanium *and* Pompeios, *were overwhelm'd with a showre of ashes, as the People were sitting in the Theater. Nay, these ashes were carried* by the winds *over the Mediterranean into Africk, and into Ægypt and Syria. And at* Rome *they choak'd the Air on a sudden, so as to hide the face of the Sun. Whereupon the People, not knowing the cause, as not having yet got the News from Campania of the Eruption of Vesuvius, could not imagine what the reason should be; but thought the Heavens and the Earth were coming together, The Sun coming down, and the Earth going to take its place above.* Thus far the Historian.

You see what disorders in nature, and what an alarum, the Eruption of one fiery Mountain is capable to make; These things, no doubt, would have made strong impressions upon us, if we had been eye-witnesses of them; But I know,

lib. 66.

representations made from dead history, and at a distance, though the testimony
be never so credible, have a much less effect upon us than what we see our selves,
and what our senses immediately inform us of. I have onely given you an account
of two Volcano's, and of a single Eruption in either of them; These Mountains
are not very far distant from one another: Let us suppose two such Eruptions,
as I have mention'd, to happen at the same time, and both these Mountains to
be raging at once, in this manner; By that violence you have seen in each of them
singly, you will easily imagine what a terrour and desolation they would carry
round about, by a conjunction of their fury and all their effects, in the Air and
on the Earth. Then, if to these two, you should joyn two more, the Sphere of
their activity would still be enlarg'd, and the Scenes become more dreadful.
But, to compleat the supposition, Let us imagine all the Volcano's of the whole
Earth, to be prepar'd and set to a certain time; which time being come, and a
signal given by Providence, all these Mines begin to play at once; I mean, All
these Fiery Mountains burst out, and discharge themselves in flames of fire, tear
up the roots of the Earth, throw hot burning stones, send out streams of flowing
Metals and Minerals, and all other sorts of ardent matter, which Nature hath
lodg'd in those Treasuries. If all these Engines, I say, were to play at once, the
Heavens and the Earth would seem to be in a flame, and the World in an universal
combustion. But we may reasonably presume, that against that great Day of
vengeance and execution, not onely all these will be employ'd, but also new
Volcano's will be open'd, and new Mountains in every Region will break out
into smoke and flame; just as at the Deluge, the Abyss broke out from the Womb
of the Earth, and from those hidden stores sent an immense quantity of water,
which, it may be, the Inhabitants of that World never thought of before. So we
must expect new Eruptions, and also new sulphureous Lakes and Fountains of
Oyl, to boyl out of the ground; And these all united with that Fewel that naturally
grows upon the Surface of the Earth, will be sufficient to give the first onset, and
to lay wast all the habitable World, and the Furniture of it.

But we suppose the Conflagration will go lower, pierce under-ground, and
dissolve the substance of the Earth to some considerable depth; therefore besides
these outward and visible preparations, we must consider all the hidden invisible
Materials within the Veins of the Earth; Such are all Minerals or Mineral juices
and concretions that are igniferous, or capable of inflammation; And these cannot
easily be reckon'd up or estimated. Some of the most common are, Sulphur, and
all sulphureous bodies, and Earths impregnated with Sulphur, Bitumen and
bituminous concretions; inflammable Salts, Coal and other fossiles that are
ardent, with innumerable mixtures and compositions of these kinds, which being
open'd by heat, are unctuous and inflammable; or by attrition discover the latent
seeds of fire. But besides consistent Bodies, there is also much volatile fire within
the Earth, in fumes, steams, and exudations, which will all contribute to this
effect. From these stores under-ground all Plants and Vegetables are fed and
supply'd, as to their oily and sulphureous parts; And all hot Waters in Baths or
Fountains, must have their original from some of these, some mixture or participation of them. And as to the *Brittish* Soyl, there is so much Coal incorporated

with it, that when the Earth shall burn, we have reason to apprehend no small danger from that subterraneous Enemy.

These dispositions, and this Fewel we find, in and upon the Earth, towards the last Fire. The third sort of Provision is in the Air; All fiery Meteors and Exhalations engender'd and form'd in those Regions above, and discharg'd upon the Earth in several ways. I believe there were no fiery Meteors in the ante-diluvian Heavens; which therefore St. *Peter* says, *were constituted of water*; had nothing in them but what was watery. But he says, *the Heavens that are now* have treasures of fire, or are reserv'd for fire, as things laid up in a store-house for that purpose. We have thunder and lightning, and fiery tempests, and there is nothing more vehement, impetuous, and irresistible, where their force is directed. It seems to me very remarkable, that the Holy Writers describe the *coming of the Lord*, and the destruction of the wicked, in the nature of a tempest, or a storm of fire. *Upon the wicked the Lord shall rain coals, fire and brimstone, and a burning tempest, this shall be the portion of their cup.* And in the lofty Song of *David* (*Psal.* 18.) which, in my judgment, respects both the past Deluge and the future Conflagration, 'tis said, *The Lord also thundred in the heavens, and the Highest gave his voice, hail-stones and coals of fire. Yea, he sent forth his arrows and scattered them, and he shot out lightnings and discomfited them. Then the Chanels of waters were seen, and the foundations of the World were discover'd; at thy rebuke, O Lord, at the blast of the breath of thy nostrils.* And a like fiery coming is describ'd in the ninety seventh Psalm, as also by *Isaiah, Daniel,* and St. *Paul.* And lastly, in the *Apocalypse,* when the World draws to a conclusion, as in the seventh Trumpet (ch. 11. 19.) and the seventh Vial (ch. 16. 18.) we have still mention made of this Fiery Tempest of Lightnings and Thunderings.

Psal. 11. 6.

ver. 13, 14, 15.

Isa. 66. 15.
Dan. 7. 9, 10.
2 *Thess.* 1. 8.

We may therefore reasonably suppose, that, before the Conflagration, the air will be surcharg'd every where, (by a precedent drought) with hot and fiery exhalations; And as against the Deluge, those regions were burthened with water and moist vapours, which were pour'd upon the Earth, not in gentle showres, but like rivers and cataracts from Heaven; so they will now be fill'd with hot fumes and sulphureous clouds, which will sometimes flow in streams and fiery impressions through the Air, sometimes make Thunder and Lightnings, and sometimes fall down upon the Earth in flouds of Fire. In general, there is a great analogy to be observed betwixt the two Deluges, of Water and of Fire; not only as to the bounds of them, which were noted before; but as to the general causes and sources upon which they depend, from above and from below. At the Floud, the windows of Heaven were opened above, and the Abyss was opened below; and the Waters of these two joyn'd together to overflow the World. In like manner, at the Conflagration, God will rain down Fire from Heaven, as he did once upon *Sodom*; and at the same time the subterraneous store-houses of Fire will be broken open, which answers to the disruption of the Abyss: And these two meeting and mingling together, will involve all the Heaven and Earth in flames.

This is a short account of the ordinary stores of Nature, and the ordinary preparations for a general Fire; And in contemplation of these, *Pliny* the Naturalist, said boldly. *It was one of the greatest wonders of the World, that the World was not every day set on fire.* We will conclude this Chapter with his words, in the second Book of his *Natural History*; having given an account of some fiery Mountains, and other parts of the Earth that are the seats and sources of Fire, He makes this reflection; *Seeing this Element is so fruitful that it brings forth it self, and multiplies and encreases from the least sparks, what are we to expect from so many fires already kindled on the Earth? How does nature feed and satisfie so devouring an Element, and such a great voracity throughout all the World, without loss or diminution of her self? Add to these fires we have mentioned, the Stars and the Great Sun, then all the fires made for humane uses; fire in stones, in wood, in the clouds and in thunder; IT EXCEEDS ALL MIRACLES, IN MY OPINION, THAT ONE DAY SHOULD PASS WITHOUT SETTING THE WORLD ALL ON FIRE.*

ch. 106, 107.

CHAPTER VIII

Some new dispositions towards the Conflagration, as to the matter, form, and situation of the Earth. Concerning miraculous Causes, and how far the ministery of Angels may be engaged in this Work.

WE have given an account, in the preceding Chapter, of the ordinary preparations of Nature for a general fire; We now are to give an account of the extraordinary, or of any new dispositions, which towards the end of the World, may be superadded to the ordinary state of Nature. I do not, by these, mean things openly miraculous and supernatural, but such a change wrought in Nature as shall still have the face of Natural Causes, and yet have a greater tendency to the Conflagration. As for example, suppose a great Drought, as we noted before, to precede this fate, or a general heat and dryness of the air and of the Earth; because this happens sometimes in a course of Nature, it will not be lookt upon as prodigious. 'Tis true, some of the Ancients speak of a Drought of Forty Years, that will be a forerunner of the Conflagration, so that there will not be a watery Cloud, nor a Rainbow seen in the Heavens, for so long time. And this they impute to *Elias*, who, at his coming, will stop the Rain and shut up the Heavens, to make way for the last Fire. But these are excessive and illgrounded suppositions, for half forty years drought will bring an universal sterility upon the Earth, and thereupon an universal Famine, with innumerable diseases; so that all mankind would be destroyed before the Conflagration could overtake them.

But we will readily admit an extraordinary drought and desiccation of all bodies to usher in this great fatality. And therefore whatsoever we read in Natural History concerning former droughts, of their drying up fountains and rivers, parching the Earth and making the outward Turf take fire in several places; filling the air with fiery impressions, making the Woods and Forests ready fewel, and sometimes to kindle by the heat of the Sun or a flash of Lightning: These and what other effects have come to pass in former droughts, may come to pass again; and that in an higher measure, and so as to be of more general extent. And we must also allow, that by this means, a great degree of inflammability, or easiness to be set on Fire, will be superinduc'd, both into the body of the Earth, and of all things that grow upon it. The heat of the Sun will pierce deeper into its bowels, when it gapes to receive his beams, and by chinks and widened pores makes way for their passage to its very heart. And, on the other hand, it is not improbable, but that upon this general relaxation and incalescency of the Body of the Earth, the *Central Fire* may have a freer efflux, and diffuse it self in greater abundance every way; so as to affect even these exteriour regions of the Earth, so far, as to make them still more catching and more combustible.

From this external and internal heat acting upon the Body of the Earth, all Minerals that have the feeds of fire in them, will be open'd, and exhale their effluvium's more copiously: As Spices, when warm'd, are more odoriferous, and fill the Air with their perfumes; so the particles of fire, that are shut up in several bodies, will easily flie abroad, when by a further degree of relaxation you shake off their chains, and open the Prison-doors. We cannot doubt, but there are many sorts of Minerals, and many sorts of Fire-stones, and of Trees and Vegetables of this nature, which will sweat out their oily and sulphureous atomes, when by a general heat and driness their parts are loosen'd and agitated.

We have no experience that will reach so far, as to give us a full account what the state of Nature will be at that time; I mean, after this drought, towards the end of the world; But we may help our imagination, by comparing it with other seasons and temperaments of the Air. As therefore in the Spring the Earth is fragrant, and the Fields and Gardens are fill'd with the sweet breathings of Herbs and Flowers; especially after a gentle rain, when their Bodies are soften'd, and the warmth of the Sun makes them evaporate more freely; So a greater degree of heat acting upon all the bodies of the Earth, like a stronger fire in the Alembick, will extract another sort of parts or particles, more deeply incorporated and more difficult to be disintangled; I mean oily parts, and such undiscover'd parcels of fire, as lie fix'd and imprison'd in hard bodies. These, I imagine, will be in a great measure set a-float, or drawn out into the Air, which will abound with hot and dry Exhalations, more than with vapours and moisture in a wet season; and by this means, all Elements and elementary Bodies will stand ready, and in a proximate disposition to be inflam'd.

Thus much concerning the last drought, and the general effects of it. In the next place, we must consider the Earth-quakes that will precede the Conflagration, and the consequences of them. I noted before, that the cavernous and broken construction of the present Earth, was that which made it obnoxious to be destroy'd by fire; as its former construction over the Abyss, made it obnoxious to be destroy'd with Water. This hollowness of the Earth is most sensible in mountainous and hilly Countreys, which therefore I look upon as most subject to burning; but the plain Countreys may also be made hollow and hilly by Earth-quakes; when the vapours not finding an easie vent, raise the ground and make a forcible eruption, as at the springing of a Mine. And tho' plain Countreys are not so subject to Earth-quakes as mountainous, because they have not so many cavities and subterraneous vaults to lodge the vapours in; yet every Region hath more or less of them: And after this drought, the vacuities of the Earth being every where enlarg'd, the quantity of exhalations much increas'd, and the motion of them more strong and violent, they will have their effects in many places where they never had any before. Yet I do not suppose that this will raise new ridges of Mountains, like the *Alpes* or *Pyreneans*, in those Countreys that are now plain, but that they will break and loosen the ground, make greater inequalities in the surface, and greater cavities within, than what are at present in those places; And by this means, the fire will creep under them, and find a passage thorough them, with more ease, than if they were compact, and every where continued and unbroken.

But you will say, it may be, how does it appear, that there will be more frequent Earth-quakes towards the end of the World? If this precedent drought be admitted, 'tis plain that fiery exhalations will abound every where within the Earth, and will have a greater agitation than ordinary; and these being the causes of Earth-quakes, when they are rarified or inflam'd, 'tis reasonable to suppose that in such a state of nature, they will more frequently happen, than at other times. Besides, Earth-quakes are taken notice of in Scripture, as signs and fore-runners of the last day, as they usually are of all great changes and calamities. The destruction of *Jerusalem* was a type of the destruction of the World, and the Evangelists aways mention Earth-quakes amongst the ominous Prodigies that were to attend it. But these Earth-quakes we are speaking of at present, are but the beginnings of sorrow, and not to be compar'd with those that will follow afterwards, when Nature is convulst in her last agony, just as the flames are seizing on her. Of which we shall have occasion to speak hereafter.

These changes will happen as to the *matter* and *form* of the Earth, before it is attack't by the last fire; There will be also another change as to the *situation* of it; for that will be rectified, and the Earth restor'd to the posture it had at first, namely, of a right aspect and conversion to the Sun. But because I cannot determine at what time this restitution will be, whether at the beginning, middle, or end of the Conflagration, I will not presume to lay any stress upon it. *Plato* seems to have imputed the Conflagration to this only; which is so far true, that the Revolution call'd *The Great Year*, is this very Revolution, or the Return of the Earth and the Heavens to their first posture. But tho' this may be contemporary with the last fire, or some way concomitant; yet it does not follow that it is the cause of it, much less the onely cause. It may be an occasion of making the fire reach more easily towards the Poles, when by this change of situation, their long Nights and long Winters shall be taken away.

These new dispositions in our Earth which we expect before that great day, may be look'd upon as extraordinary, but not as miraculous, because they may proceed from natural causes. But now in the last place, we are to consider *miraculous causes:* What influence they may have, or what part they may bear, in this great revolution of nature. By *miraculous* causes we understand either God's immediate omnipotency, or the Ministery of Angels; And what may be perform'd by the latter, is very improperly and undecently thrown upon the former. 'Tis a great step to Omnipotency: and 'tis hard to define what miracles, on this side Creation, require an infinite power. We are sure that the Angels are ministring Spirits, and ten thousand times ten thousand stand about the Throne of the Almighty, to receive his commands and execute his judgments. That perfect knowledge they have of the powers of nature, and of conducting those powers to the best advantage, by adjusting causes in a fit subordination one to another, makes them capable of performing, not onely things far above our force, but even above our imagination. Besides, they have a radical inherent power, belonging to the excellency of their nature, of determining the motions of matter, within a far greater sphere than humane Souls can pretend to. We can onely command our spirits, and determine their motions within the compass of our own Bodies; but their activity and empire is of far greater extent, and the outward World is much more subject to their dominion than to ours. From these considerations it is reasonable to conclude, that the generality of miracles may be and are perform'd by Angels; It being less decorous to employ a Sovereign power, where a subaltern is sufficient, and when we hastily cast things upon God, for quick dispatch, we consult our own ease more than the honour of our Maker.

I take it for granted here, that what is done by an Angelical hand, is truly providential, and of divine administration; and also justly bears the character of a miracle. Whatsoever may be done by pure material causes, or humane strength, we account Natural; and whatsoever is above these we call supernatural and miraculous. Now what is supernatural and miraculous is either the effect of an Angelical power, or of a Sovereign and Infinite power. And we ought not to confound these two, no more than Natural and Supernatural; for there is a greater difference betwixt the highest Angelical power and Omnipotency, than betwixt an Humane power and Angelical. Therefore as the first Rule concerning miracles is this, That we must not flie to miracles, where Man and Nature are sufficient; so the second Rule is this, that we must not flie to a sovereign infinite power, where an Angelical is sufficient. And the reason in both Rules is the same, namely, because it argues a defect of Wisdom in all Oeconomies to employ more and greater means than are sufficient.

Now to make application of this to our present purpose, I think it reasonable, and also sufficient, to admit the ministery of Angels in the future Conflagration of the World. If Nature will not lay violent hands upon her self, or is not sufficient to work her own destruction, Let us allow *Destroying Angels* to interest themselves in the work, as the Executioners of the Divine Justice and Vengeance upon a degenerate World. We have examples of this so frequently in Sacred History, how the Angels have executed God's Judgments upon a Nation or a People, that it cannot seem new or strange, that in this last judgment, which by all the Prophets is represented as the *Great Day of the Lord*, the day of his Wrath and of his Fury, the same Angels should bear their parts, and conclude the last scene of that Tragedy which they had acted in all along. We read of the *Destroying Angel* in *Ægypt*; of Angels that presided at the destruction of *Sodom*, which was a Type of the future destruction of the World, (*Jude* 7.) and of Angels that will

Gen. 12. 23.
Gen. 19. 13.
2 *Thess.* 1. 7, 8.

accompany our Saviour when he comes in flames of Fire: Not, we suppose, to be Spectators only, but Actors and Superintendents in this great Catastrophe.

This ministery of Angels may be either in ordering and conducting such Natural Causes as we have already given an account of, or in adding new ones, if occasion be; I mean, encreasing the quantity of Fire, or of fiery materials, in and about the Earth. So as that Element shall be more abundant and more predominant, and overbear all opposition that either Water, or any other Body, can make against it. It is not material whether of these two Suppositions we follow, provided we allow that the Conflagration is a work of Providence, and not a pure Natural Fatality. If it be necessary that there should be an augmentation made of Fiery Matter, 'tis not hard to conceive how that may be done, either from the Heavens or from the Earth. The Prophets sometimes speak of multiplying or strengthning the Light of the Sun, and it may as easily be conceiv'd of his heat as of his light; as if the Vial that was to be pour'd upon it, and *gave it a power to scorch men with fire*, had something of a Natural sence as well as Moral. But there is another stream of Ethereal matter that flows from the Heavens, and recruits the *Central Fire* with continual supplies; This may be encreas'd and strengthned, and its effects convey'd throughout the whole Body of the Earth.

But if an augmentation is to be made of Terrestrial Fire, or of such terrestrial principles as contain it most, as Sulphur, Oyl, and such like, I am apt to believe, these will encrease of their own accord, upon a general drought and desiccation of the Earth. For I am far from the opinion of some Chymists, that think these principles immutable, and incapable of diminution or augmentation. I willingly admit that all such particles may be broken and disfigur'd, and thereby lose their proper and specifick virtue, and new ones may be generated to supply the places of the former. Which supplies, or new productions being made in a less or greater measure, according to the general dispositions of Nature; when Nature is heightned into a kind of Feaver and Ebullition of all her juices and humours, as she will be at that time, we must expect that more parts than ordinary, should be made inflammable, and those that are inflam'd should become more violent. Under these circumstances, when all Causes lean that way, a little help from a superiour power will have a great effect, and make a great change in the state of the World. And as to the power of Angels, I am of opinion that it is very great as to the Changes and Modifications of Natural Bodies; that they can dissolve a Marble as easily as we can crumble Earth and Moulds, or fix any liquor, in a moment, into a substance as hard as Crystal. That they can either make flames more vehement and irresistible to all sorts of Bodies; or as harmless as Lambent Fires, and as soft as Oyl. We see an instance of this last, in *Nebuchadnezzar's* fiery Furnace, where the three Children walk'd unconcern'd in the midst of the Flames, under the charge and protection of an Angel. And the same Angel, if he had pleas'd, could have made the same Furnace seven times hotter than the wrath of the Tyrant had made it.

We will therefore leave it to their ministery to manage this great Furnace, when the Heavens and the Earth are on Fire. To conserve, encrease, direct, or temper the flames, according to instructions given them, as they are to be *Tutelary*

Isa. 30. 26.

Rev. 26. 8.

Dan. 3. 28.

or *Destroying*. Neither let any body think it a diminution of Providence to put things into the hands of Angels; 'Tis the true rule and method of it; For to employ an Almighty power where it is not necessary, is to debase it, and give it a task fit for lower Beings. Some think it devotion and piety to have recourse immediately to the arm of God to salve all things; This may be done sometimes with a good intention, but commonly with little judgment. God is as jealous of the glory of his Wisdom, as of his Power; and Wisdom consists in the conduct and subordination of several causes to bring our purposes to effect; but what is dispatched by an immediate Supreme Power, leaves no room for the exercise of Wisdom. To conclude this point, which I have touch'd upon more than once, We must not be partial to any of God's Attributes, and Providence being a complexion of many, Power, Wisdom, Justice, and Goodness, when we give due place and honour to all these, then we most honour DIVINE PROVIDENCE.

CHAPTER IX

How the Sea will be diminish'd and consum'd. How the Rocks and Mountains will be thrown down and melted, and the whole exteriour frame of the Earth dissolv'd into a Deluge of Fire.

WE have now taken a view of the Causes of the Conflagration, both ordinary and extraordinary: It remains to consider the manner of it; How these Causes will operate, and bring to pass an effect so great and so prodigious. We took notice before that the grand obstruction would be from the Sea, and from the Mountains; we must therefore take these to task in the first place; and if we can remove them out of our way, or overcome what resistance and opposition they are capable to make, the rest of the work will not be uneasie to us.

The Ocean indeed is a vast Body of Waters; and we must use all our art and skill to dry it up, or consume it in a good measure, before we can compass our design. I remember the advice a Philosopher gave *Amasis* King of *Egypt,* when he had a command sent him from the King of *Æthiopia, That he should drink up the Sea. Amasis* being very anxious and solicitous what answer he should make to this strange command, the Philosopher *Bias* advis'd him to make this round answer to the King; *That he was ready to perform his command and to drink up the Sea, provided he would stop the rivers from flowing into his cup while he was drinking.* This answer baffled the King, for he could not stop the rivers; but this we must do, or we shall never be able to drink up the Sea, or burn up the Earth.

Neither will this be so impossible as it seems at first sight, if we reflect upon those preparations we have made towards it, by a general drought all over the Earth. This we suppose will precede the Conflagration, and by drying up the Fountains and Rivers, which daily feed the Sea, will by degrees starve that Monster, or reduce it to such a degree of weakness, that it shall not be able to make any great resistance. More than half an Ocean of Water flows into the Sea every day, from the Rivers of the Earth, if you take them all together. This

I speak upon a moderate computation. *Aristotle* says the Rivers carry more water into the Sea, in the space of a year, than would equal in bulk the whole Globe of the Earth. Nay some have ventur'd to affirm this of one single River, The *Volga*, that runs into the *Caspian* Sea. 'Tis a great River indeed, and hath seventy mouths; and so it had need have, to disgorge a mass of Water equal to the Body of the Earth, in a years time. But we need not take such high measures; There are at least an hundred great Rivers that flow into the Sea, from several parts of the Earth, Islands and Continents, besides several thousands of lesser ones; Let us suppose these, all together, to pour as much water into the Sea-chanel, every day, as is equal to half the Ocean. And we shall be easily convinc'd of the reasonableness of this supposition, if we do but examine the daily expence of one River, and by that make an estimate of the rest. This we find calculated to our hands in the *River Po* in *Italy*; a River of much what the same bigness with our *Thames*, and disburthens it self into the Gulph of *Venice*. *Baptista Riccioli*, hath computed how much water this River discharges in an hour, *viz*. 18 000 000 cubical paces of Water, and consequently 432 000 000 in a day; which is scarce credible to those that do not distinctly compute it. Suppose then an hundred Rivers as great as this or greater, to fall into the Sea from the land; besides thousands of lesser, that pay their tribute at the same time into the great Receit of the Ocean; These all taken together, are capable to renew the Sea every twice four and twenty hours. Which suppositions being admitted, if by a great and lasting drought these Rivers were dryed up, or the Fountains from whence they flow, what would then become of that vast Ocean, that before was so formidable to us?

'Tis likely you will say, These great Rivers cannot be dry'd up, tho' the little ones may; and therefore we must not suppose such an Universal stop of waters, or that they will all fail, by any drought whatsoever. But great Rivers being made up of little ones, if these fail, those must be diminish'd, if not quite drain'd and exhausted. It may be all Fountains and Springs do not proceed from the same causes, or the same original; and some are much more copious than others; for such differences we will allow what is due; but still the driness of the Air and of the Earth continuing, and all the sources and supplies of moisture, both from above and from below, being lessen'd or wholly discontinued, a general decay of all Fountains and Rivers must necessarily follow, and consequently of the Sea, and of its fulness that depends upon them. And that's enough for our present purpose.

The first step therefore towards the Consumption of the Ocean will be the diminution or suspension of the Rivers that run into it. The next will be an Evacuation by Subterraneous passages; And the last, by Eruptions of fires in the very Chanel of it, and in the midst of the waters. As for Subterraneous evacuations, we cannot doubt but that the Sea hath out-lets at the bottom of it; whereby it discharges that vast quantity of water that flows into it every day, and that could not be discharg'd so fast as it comes from the wide mouths of the Rivers, by percolation or straining thorough the Sands. Seas also communicate with one another by these internal passages; as is manifest from those particular

Seas that have no external outlet or issue, tho' they receive into them many great Rivers, and sometimes the influx of other Seas. So the *Caspian* Sea receives not onely *Volga*, which we mention'd before, but several other Rivers, and yet hath no visible issue for its waters. The *Mediterranean* Sea, besides all the Rivers it receives, hath a current flowing into it, at either end, from other Seas; from the *Atlantick* Ocean at the streights of *Gibraltar*, and from the Black Sea, above *Constantinople:* and yet there is no passage above-ground, or visible derivation of the *Mediterranean* waters out of their Chanel; which seeing they do not over-fill, nor overflow the Banks, 'tis certain they must have some secret conveyances into the bowels of the Earth, or subterraneous communication with other Seas. Lastly, from the Whirl-pools of the Sea, that suck in Bodies that come within their reach, it seems plainly to appear, by that attraction and absorption, that there is a descent of waters in those places.

Wherefore when the current of the Rivers into the Sea is stopt, or in a great measure diminish'd; The Sea continuing to empty it self by these subterraneous passages, and having little or none of those supplies that it us'd to have from the Land, it must needs be sensibly lessen'd; and both contract its Chanel into a narrower compass, and also have less depth in the waters that remain. And in this last place, we must expect fiery eruptions in several parts of the Sea-chanel, which will help to suck up or evaporate the remaining waters. In the present state of Nature there have been several instances of such eruptions of fire from the bottom of the Sea; and in that last state of Nature, when Earth-quakes and Eruptions will be more frequent every where, we must expect them also more frequently by Sea, as well as by Land. 'Tis true, neither Earth-quakes nor Eruptions can happen in the middle of the Great Ocean, or in the deepest Abyss, because there are no cavities, or mines below it, for the vapours and exhalations to lodge in; But 'tis not much of the Sea-chanel that is so deep, and in other parts, especially in streights and near Islands, such Eruptions, like Sea-Volcano's, have frequently happen'd, and new Islands have been made by such fiery matter thrown up from the bottom of the Sea. Thus, they say, those Islands in the Mediterranean call'd the *Vulcanian* Islands, had their original; being matter cast up from the bottom of the Sea, by the force of fire; as new Mountains some-times are rais'd upon the Earth. Another Island in the *Archipelago* had the same original, whereof *Strabo* gives an account. The *flames*, he says, *sprung up thorough*   *li.* 1. *the waters, four days together, so as the whole Sea was hot and burning; and they rais'd by degrees, as with Engines, a mass of Earth, which made a new Island, twelve furlongs in compass.* And in the same *Archipelago*, flames and smoak have several times (particularly in the year 1650) rise out of the Sea, and fill'd the Air with sulphureous scents and vapours. In like manner, in the Island of St. *Michel*, one of the *Tercera*'s, there have been, of later years, such eructations of fire and flames; so strong and violent, that, at the depth of an hundred and sixty fathoms, they forc'd their way through the midst of the waters, from the bottom of the Sea into the open Air. As has been related by those that were eye-witnesses.

In these three ways, I conceive, the great force of the Sea will be broken, and the mighty Ocean reduc'd to a standing Pool of putrid waters, without vent and without recruits. But there will still remain in the midst of the Chanel a great mass of troubled liquors, like dregs in the bottom of the vessel; which will not be drunk up till the Earth be all on fire, and torrents of melted and sulphureous matter flow from the Land, and mingle with this Dead Sea. But let us now leave the Sea in this humble posture, and go on to attack the Rocks and Mountains which stand next in our way.

See how scornfully they look down upon us, and bid defiance to all the Elements. They have born the thunder and lightning of Heaven, and all the artillery of the Skies, for innumerable Ages; and do not fear the crackling of thorns and of shrubs that burn at their feet. Let the Towns and Cities of the Earth, say they, be laid in ashes; Let the Woods and Forests blaze away; and the fat Soyl of the Earth fry in its own grease; These things will not affect us; We can stand naked in the midst of a Sea of fire, with our roots as deep as the foundations of the Earth, and our heads above the Clouds of the Air. Thus they proudly defie Nature; and it must be confest, that these, being, as it were, the Bones of the Earth, when the Body is burning, will be the last consum'd; And I am apt to think, if they could keep in the same posture they stand in now, and preserve themselves from falling, the fire could never get an entire power over them. But Mountains are generally hollow, and that makes them subject to a double casualty; first, of Earth-quakes, secondly, of having their roots eaten away by water or by fire; but by fire especially in this case: for we suppose there will be innumerable subterraneous fires smothering under ground, before the general fire breaks out; and these by corroding the bowels of the Earth, will make it more hollow and more ruinous; And when the Earth is so far dissolv'd, that the cavities within the Mountains are fill'd with Lakes of fire, then the Mountains will sink, and fall into those boyling Caldrons; which, in time, will dissolve them, tho' they were as hard as Adamant.

To conclude this point, the Mountains will all be brought low, in that state of nature, either by Earthquakes or subterraneous fires; *Every valley shall be exalted, and every mountain and hill shall be made low.* Which will be literally true at the second coming of our Saviour, as it was figuratively apply'd to his first coming. Now, being once level'd with the rest of the Earth, the question will onely be, how they shall be dissolv'd. But there is no Terrestrial Body indissolvable to Fire, if it have a due strength and continuance; and this last fire will have both, in the highest degrees; So that it cannot but be capable of dissolving all Elementary compositions, how hard or solid soever they be.

Isa. 40. 4.

Luk. 3. 5.

'Tis true, these Mountains and Rocks, as I said before, will have the priviledge to be the last destroy'd. These, with the deep parts of the Sea, and the Polar regions of the Earth, will undergo a slower fate, and be consum'd more leisurely. The action of the last Fire may be distinguish'd into two Times, or two assaults; The first assault will carry off all Mankind, and all the works of the Earth that are easily combustible, and this will be done with a quick and sudden motion. But the second assault, being employ'd about the consumption of such Bodies or such Materials as are not so easily subjected to fire, will be of long continuance, and the work of some years. And 'tis fit it should be so; that this Flaming World may be view'd and consider'd by the neighbouring Worlds about it, as a dreadful spectacle, and monument of God's wrath against disloyal and disobedient Creatures. That by this example, now before their eyes, they may think of their own fate, and what may befal them, as well as another Planet of the same Elements and composition.

Thus much for the Rocks and Mountains; which, you see, according to our Hypothesis, will be level'd, and the whole face of the Earth reduc'd to plainness and equality; nay, which is more, melted and dissolved into a Sea of liquid Fire. And because this may seem a Paradox, being more than is usually supposed, or taken notice of, in the doctrine of the Conflagration, it will not be improper in this place to give an account, wherein our Idea of the Conflagration and its effects, differs from the common opinion and the usual representation of it. 'Tis commonly suppos'd, that the Conflagration of the World is like the burning of a City, where the Walls and materials of the Houses are not melted down, but scorch'd, inflam'd, demolish'd, and made unhabitable. So they think in the Burning of the World; such Bodies, or such parts of Nature, as are fit Fewel for the Fire, will be inflam'd, and, it may be, consum'd, or reduc'd to smoak and ashes; But other Bodies that are not capable of Inflammation, will only be scorch'd and defac'd, the beauty and furniture of the Earth spoil'd, and by that means, say they, it will be laid wast and become unhabitable. This seems to me a very short and imperfect Idea of the Conflagration; neither agreeable to Scripture, nor to the deductions that may be made from Scripture. We therefore suppose that this is but half the work, this destroying of the outward garniture of the Earth is but the first onset, and that the Conflagration will end in a Dissolution and liquefaction of the Elements and all the exteriour region of the Earth; so as to become a true Deluge of Fire, or a Sea of Fire overspreading the whole Globe of the Earth. This state of the Conflagration I think may be plainly prov'd, partly by the expressions of Scripture concerning it, and partly from the *Renovation* of the Earth that is to follow upon it. St. *Peter*, who is our chief Guide in the doctrine of the Conflagration, says, *The Elements will be melted with fervent heat*; besides burning up the works of the Earth. Then adds, *Seeing all these things shall be dissolv'd, &c.* These terms of *Liquefaction* and *Dissolution* cannot, without violence, be restrained to simple devastation and superficial scorching. Such expressions carry the work a great deal further, even to that full sence which we propose. Besides, the Prophets often speak of the melting of the Earth, or of the hills and mountains, at the presence of the Lord, in the day of his wrath. And St. *John* (*Apoc.* 15. 2.) tells us of a *Sea of Glass, mingled with Fire*; where the Saints stood, singing the song of *Moses*, and triumphing over their enemies, the Spiritual *Pharaoh* and his host, that were swallowed up in it. That *Sea of Glass* must be a Sea of *molten* glass; it must be fluid, not solid, if a Sea; neither can a solid substance be said to be *mingled with Fire*, as this was. And to this answers the *Lake of fire and brimstone*, which the Beast and false Prophet were thrown into alive, *Apoc.* 19. 20. These all refer to the end of the World and the last Fire, and also plainly imply, or express rather, that state of Liquefaction which we suppose and assert.

2 *Pet.* 3. 10, 11.

Isa. 34. 3, 4. & 44. 1, 2.
Nah. 1. 5.
Ps. 97. 5.

287

Furthermore, The *Renovation* of the World, or *The New Heavens* and *New Earth*, which St. *Peter*, out of the Prophets, tells us shall spring out of these that are burnt and dissolved, do suppose this Earth reduc'd into a fluid Chaos, that it may lay a foundation for a second World. If you take such a Skeleton of an Earth, as your scorching Fire would leave behind it; where the flesh is torn from the bones, and the Rocks and Mountains stand naked and staring upon you; the Sea, half empty, gaping at the Sun, and the Cities all in ruines and in rubbish; How would you raise a New World from this? and a World fit to be an *habitation for the Righteous*; for so St. *Peter* makes that to be, which is to

2 Pet. 3. 13.
Apoc. 21. 1.

succeed after the Conflagration. And a World also *without a Sea*, so St. *John* describes the New Earth he saw. As these characters do not agree to the present Earth, so neither would they agree to *your* Future one; for if that dead lump could revive and become habitable again, it would however retain all the imperfections of the former Earth, besides some scars and deformities of its own. Wherefore if you would cast the Earth into a new and better mould, you must first melt it down; and the last Fire, being as a *Refiner*'s fire, will make an improvement in it, both as to matter and form. To conclude, it must be reduc'd into a fluid Mass, in the nature of a Chaos, as it was at first; but this last will be a Fiery Chaos, as that was Watery; and from this state it will emerge again into a Paradisiacal World. But this being the Subject of the following Book, we will discourse no more of it in this place.

CHAPTER X

Concerning the beginning and progress of the Conflagration, what part of the Earth will first be Burnt. The manner of the future destruction of Rome. *The last state and consummation of the general Fire.*

HAVING remov'd the chief obstructions to our design, and drawn a method for weakning the strength of Nature, by draining the Trench, and beating down those Bulwarks, wherein she seems to place her greatest confidence: we must now go to work; making choice of the weakest part of Nature for our first attack, where the fire may be the easiest admitted, and the best maintain'd and preserv'd.

And for our better direction, it will be of use to consider what we noted before, *viz.* That the Conflagration is not a pure *Natural Fatality*, but a *mixt Fatality*; or a Divine Judgment supported by Natural Causes. And if we can find some part of the Earth, or of the Christian World, that hath more of these natural dispositions to Inflammation than the rest; and is also represented by Scripture as a more peculiar object of God's Judgments at the comeing of our Saviour, we may justly pitch upon that part of the World as first to be destroyed. Nature and Providence conspiring to make that the first Sacrifice to this Fiery Vengeance.

Now as to Natural dispositions, in any Country or Region of the Earth, to be set on Fire, They seem to be chiefly these two, Sulphureousness of the Soil, and an hollow, mountainous construction of the ground. Where these two dispositions meet in the same tract or territory, (the one as to the quality of the matter, and the other as to the form) it stands like a Pile of fit materials, ready set to have the Fire put to it. And as to Divine Indications where this General Fire will begin, the Scripture points to the Seat of Antichrist wheresoever that is, for the beginning of it. The Scripture, I say, points at this, two ways, First, in telling us that our Saviour at his coming *in flames of Fire shall consume the wicked one,* *The Man of sin, the Son of perdition, with the Spirit of his mouth, and shall destroy him with the brightness of his presence.* Secondly, under the name of *Mystical Babylon*; which is allowed by all to be the Seat of Antichrist, and by Scripture always condemn'd to the Fire. This we find in plain words asserted by St. *John* in the 18*th chap.* of his *Revelations*, and in the 19*th.* (*ver.* 3) under the name of the *Great Whore*; which is the same City and the same Seat, according to the interpretation of Scripture it self. And the Prophet *Daniel* when he had set the *Ancient of Days* upon his fiery Throne, says, *The Body of the Beast was given to the burning flame.* Which I take to be the same thing with what St. *John* says afterwards, (*Apoc.* 19. 20.) *The Beast and the false Prophet were cast alive into a Lake of fire burning with brimstone.* By these places of Scripture it seems manifest, that Antichrist, and the Seat of Antichrist, will be consumed with Fire, at the coming of our Saviour. And 'tis very reasonable and decorous, that the Grand Traitor and Head of the Apostasie should be made the first example of the divine vengeance.

    Thus much being allow'd from Scripture, let us now return to Nature again; to seek out that part of the Christian World, that from its own constitution is most subject to burning; by the sulphureousness of its Soil, and its fiery Mountains and Caverns. This we shall easily find to be the *Roman Territory*, or the Countrey of *Italy*: which, by all accounts, ancient and modern, is a store-house of fire; as if it was condemn'd to that fate by God and Nature, and to be an Incendiary, as it were, to the rest of the World. And seeing *Mystical Babylon*, the Seat of Antichrist, is the same *Rome*, and its Territory; as it is understood by most Interpreters, of former and later Ages; you see both our lines meet in this point; And that there is a fairness, on both hands, to conclude, that, at the glorious appearance of our Saviour, the Conflagration will begin at the City of *Rome* and the *Roman* Territory.

    Nature hath sav'd us the pains of kindling a fire in those parts of the Earth, for, since the memory of man, there have always been subterraneous fires in *Italy*. And the *Romans* did not preserve their Vestal fire with more constancy, than Nature hath done her fiery Mountains in some part or other of that Territory. Let us then suppose, when the fatal time draws near, all these Burning Mountains to be fill'd and replenish'd with fit materials for such a design; and when our Saviour appears in the Clouds, with an Host of Angels, that they all begin to play, as Fire-works at the Triumphal Entry of a Prince. Let *Vesuvius*, *Ætna*, *Strongyle*, and all the *Vulcanian* Islands, break out into flames; and by the Earthquakes, which then will rage, let us suppose new Eruptions, or new Mountains open'd, in the *Apennines*, and near to *Rome*; and to vomit out fire in the same manner as the old Volcano's. Then let the sulphureous ground take fire; **and**

2 Thess. I. 7, *ch.* 2. 8.

ver. 8, *& ver.* 19.

ch. 17. 18.
Dan. 7. 9, 10, 11.

T

seeing the Soil of that Countrey, in several places, is so full of brimstone, that the steams and smoke of it visibly rise out of the Earth; we may reasonably suppose, that it will burn openly, and be inflam'd, at that time. Lastly, the Lightnings of the Air, and the flaming streams of the melting Skies, will mingle and joyn with these burnings of the Earth. And these three Causes meeting together, as they cannot but make a dreadful Scene, so they will easily destroy and consume whatsoever lies within the compass of their fury.

Thus you may suppose the beginning of the General Fire; And it will be carried on by like causes, tho' in lesser degrees, in other parts of the Earth. But as to *Rome*, there is still, in my opinion, a more dreadful fate that will attend it; namely, to be absorpt or swallowed up in a Lake of fire and brimstone, after the manner of *Sodom* and *Gomorrha*. This, in my judgment, will be the fate and final conclusion of *Mystical Babylon*, to sink as a great Milstone into the Sea, and never to appear more. Hear what the Prophet says, *A mighty Angel took up a stone, like a great Milstone, and cast it into the Sea, saying, thus, with violence, shall that great City Babylon be thrown down; and shall be found no more at all.* Simply to be burnt, does not at all answer to this description of its perishing, by *sinking like a Milstone into the Sea, and never appearing more,* nor of, *not having its place ever more found;* that is, leaving no remains or marks of it. A City that is onely burnt, cannot be said to *fall like a Milstone into the Sea*; or that it *can never more be found*: For after the burning of a City, the ruines stand, and its place is well known. Wherefore, in both respects, besides this exteriour burning, there must be an absorption of this *Mystical Babylon*, the Seat of the Beast; and thereupon a total disappearance of it. This also agrees with the suddenness of the judgment, which is a repeated character of it: *Chap.* 18. 8, 10, 17, 19. Now what kind of absorption this will be, into what, and in what manner, we may learn from what St. *John* says afterwards, (ch. 19. 20) *The Beast and the false Prophet were cast alive into a Lake of fire and brimstone.* You must not imagine that they were bound, hand and foot, and so thrown headlong into this Lake, but they were swallowed up alive, they and theirs, as *Corah* and his company. Or, to use a plainer example, after the manner of *Sodom* and *Gomorrha*; which perish't by fire, and at the same time sunk into a Dead Sea, or a Lake of brimstone.

Apoc. 18. 21.

This was a lively type of the fate of *Rome*, or *Mystical Babylon*; and 'tis fit it should resemble *Sodom*, as well in its punishment, as in its crimes. Neither is it a hard thing to conceive how such an absorption may come to pass; That being a thing so usual in Earth-quakes, and Earth-quakes being so frequent in that Region. And lastly, that this should be after the manner of *Sodom*, turn'd into a Lake of fire, will not be at all strange, if we consider, that there will be many subterraneous Lakes of fire at that time, when the bowels of the Earth begin to melt, and the Mountains spew out streams of liquid fire. The ground therefore being hollow and rotten in those parts, when it comes to be shaken with a mighty Earth-quake, the foundations will sink, and the whole frame fall into an Abyss of fire below, as a Milstone into the Sea. And this will give occasion to that Cry, *Babylon the Great is fallen, is fallen,* and shall never more be found.

This seems to be a probable account, according to Scripture and reason, of the beginning of the general fire, and of the particular fate of *Rome*. But it may be propos'd here as an objection against this Hypothesis, that the Mediterranean Sea, lying all along the Coast of *Italy*, must needs be a sufficient guard to that Countrey against the invasion of fire; or at least must needs extinguish it, before it can do much mischief there, or propagate it self into other Countreys. I thought we had in a good measure prevented this objection before, by showing how the Ocean would be diminish'd before the Conflagration, and especially the Arms and Sinus's of the Ocean; and of these none would be more subject to this diminution than the Mediterranean, for receiving its supplies from the Ocean and the Black Sea, if these came to sink in their chanels, they would not rise so high, as to be capable to flow into the Mediterranean, at either end. And these supplies being cut off, it would soon empty it self so far, partly by evaporation, and partly by subterraneous passages, as to shrink from all its shores, and become onely a standing Pool of water in the middle of the Chanel. Nay, 'tis possible, by flouds of fire descending from the many Volcano's upon its shores, it might it self be converted into a Lake of fire, and rather help than obstruct the progress of the Conflagration.

It may indeed be made a question, whether this fiery Vengeance upon the seat of Antichrist, will not precede the general Conflagration, at some distance of time, as a fore-runner and forewarner to the World, that the rest of the People may have space to repent; And particularly the *Jews*, being Spectators of this Tragedy, and of the miraculous appearance of our Saviour, may see the hand of God in it, and be convinc'd of the truth and divine authority of the Christian Religion. I say, this supposition would leave room for these and some other prophetick Scenes, which we know not well where to place; But seeing *The Day of the Lord* is represented in Scripture as one entire thing, without interruption or discontinuation, and that it is to begin with the destruction of Antichrist, we have warrant enough to pursue the rest of the Conflagration from this beginning and introduction.

Let us then suppose the same preparations made in the other parts of the Earth to continue the fire; for the Conflagration of the World being a work of providence, we may be sure such measures are taken, as will effectually carry it on when once begun. The Body of the Earth will be loosen'd and broken by Earthquakes, the more solid parts impregnated with sulphur, and the cavities fill'd with unctuous fumes and exhalations; so as the whole Mass will be but as one great funeral Pile, ready built, and wanting nothing but the hand of a destroying Angel, to give it fire. I will not take upon me to determine which way this devouring Enemy will steer his course from *Italy*, or in what order he will advance and enter the several Regions of our Continent; that would be an undertaking, as uncertain, as useless. But we cannot doubt of his success, which way soever he goes: unless where the Chanel of the Ocean may chance to stop him. But as to that, we allow, that different Continents may have different Fires; not propagated from one another, but of distinct sources and originals; and so likewise in remote Islands; and therefore no long passage or trajection will be requir'd from shore to shore. And even the Ocean it self, will at length be as Fiery as any part of the Land; But that, with its Rocks, like Death, will be the last thing subdued.

As to the Animate World, the Fire will over-run it with a swift and rapid course, and all living Creatures will be suffocated or consumed, at the first assault. And at the same time, the beauty of the Fields and the external decorations of Nature will be defac'd. Then the Cities and the Towns, and all the works of man's hands, will burn like stubble before the wind. These will be soon dispatch'd; but the great burthen of the Work still remains; which is that *Liquefaction* we mention'd before, or a *melting fire*, much more strong and vehement than these transient blazes, which do but sweep the surface of the Earth. This Liquefaction, I say, we prov'd before out of Scripture, as the last state of the fiery Deluge. And 'tis this, which, at length, will make the Sea it self a *Lake of fire and brimstone*. When instead of rivers of Waters which used to flow into it from the Land, there come streams and rivulets of Sulphureous Liquors, and purulent melted matter, which, following the tract of their natural gravity will fall into this great drain of the Earth. Upon which mixture, the remaining parts of sweet water will soon evaporate, and the salt mingling with the Sulphur will make a Dead Sea, an *Asphaltites*, a Lake of *Sodom*, a Cup of the Wine of the fierceness of God's wrath.

ch. 9.

We noted before two remarkable effects of the *Burning Mountains*, which would contribute to the Conflagration of the World; and gave instances of both in former Eruptions of *Ætna* and *Vesuvius*. One was, of those Balls or lumps of Fire, which they throw about in the time of their rage; and the other, of those torrents of liquid Fire, which rowl down their sides to the next Seas or Valleys. In the first respect these Mountains are as so many Batteries, planted by Providence in several parts of the Earth, to fling those fiery Bombs into such places, or such Cities, as are marked out for destruction. And in the second respect, they are to dry up the Waters, and the Rivers, and the Sea it self, when they fall into its chanel. *T. Fazellus*, a *Sicilian*, who writ the History of that Island, tells us of such a River of fire (upon an eruption of *Ætna*) near twenty eight miles long; reaching from the Mountain to Port *Longina*; and might have been much longer if it had not been stopt by the Sea. Many such as these, and far greater, we ought in reason to imagin, when all the Earth begins to melt, and to ripen towards a dissolution. It will then be full of these Sulphureous juices, as Grapes with Wine; and these will be squeez'd out of the Earth into the Sea, as out of a wine-press into the Receiver; to fill up that *Cup with the wine of the fierceness of God's wrath*.

*Annal. Sic. dec.
I, li. 2, c. 4.*

If we may be allow'd to bring Prophetical passages of Scripture to a natural sence, as doubtless some of those must that respect the end of the World, these phrases which we have now suggested, of the *Wine-press of the wrath of God. Drinking the fierceness of his wine, poured, without mixture, into the cup of his indignation*, with expressions of the like nature that occur sometimes in the old Prophets, but especially in the Apocalypse; These, I say, might receive a full and emphatical explication from this state of things which now lies before us. I would not exclude any other explication of less force, as that of alluding to the

Apoc. 14. 10, 19.
c. 16. 19.
c. 19. 15.

bitter cup or *mixt potion* that us'd to be given to malefactors: but that, methinks, is a low sence when applyed to these places in the Apocalypse. That these phrases signifie God's remarkable judgments, all allow, and here they plainly relate to the end of the World, to the last Plagues, and the Last of the last Plagues, chap. 16. 19. Besides, the Angel that presided over this judgment, is said to be an Angel that *had power over fire*; And those who are to drink this potion, are said to be *tormented with fire and brimstone*, ch. 14. 10. This presiding Angel seems to be our Saviour himself (c. 19. 15.) who when he comes to execute Divine Vengeance upon the Earth, gives his orders in these words, *Gather the clusters of the*   *ch.* 14. 18, 19. *Vine of the Earth, for her grapes are fully ripe.* And thereupon the Destroying Angel *thrust in his sickle into the Earth, and gathered the Vine of the Earth, and cast it into the great Wine-press of the Wrath of God.* And this made a potion, *compounded of several ingredients, but not diluted with water*; (ch. 14. 10.) and   τοῦ κεκουρασ- was indeed a potion of fire and brimstone and all burning materials mixt together.   μένου ἀκράτου. The similitudes of Scripture are seldom nice and exact, but rather bold, noble and great; and according to the circumstances which we have observ'd, This *Vineyard* seems to be the *Earth*, and this *Vintage* the end of the World; The pressing of the Grapes into the cup or vessel that receives them, the distillation of burning liquors from all parts of the Earth into the trough of the Sea; and that lake of red Fire, the bloud of those Grapes so flowing into it.

'Tis true, this judgment of the Vintage and Wine-press, and the effects of it, seem to aim more especially at some particular region of the Earth, ch. 14. 20. And I am not against that, provided the substance of the explication be still retained, and the universal Sea of Fire be that which follows in the next Chapter, under the name of a *Sea of Glass, mingled with Fire*; This I think expresses the   *ch.* 16. 2. highest and compleat state of the Conflagration; when the Mountains are fled away, and not only so, but the exteriour region of the Earth quite dissolv'd, like wax before the Sun; The Chanel of the Sea fill'd with a mass of fluid fire, and the same fire overflowing all the Globe, and covering the whole Earth, as the Deluge, or the first Abyss. Then will the Triumphal Songs and Hallelujah's be sung for the Victories of the Lamb over all his Enemies and over Nature it self. *Great and marvellous are thy works, Lord God Almighty: Just and true are thy*   *Apoc.* 15. 3, 4. *ways thou King of Saints. Who shall not fear thee O Lord, and glorifie thy name? for thou only art holy: for all nations shall come and worship before thee; for thy judgments are made manifest.*

CHAPTER XI

An Account of those extraordinary Phænomena and Wonders in Nature, that, according to Scripture, will precede the coming of Christ, and the Conflagration of the World.

IF we reflect upon the History of Burning Mountains, we cannot but observe, that, before their Eruptions, there are usually some changes in the Earth or in the Air, in the Sea or in the Sun it self; as signs and forerunners of the ensuing storm. We may then easily conclude that when the last great Storm is a coming, and all the Vulcano's of the Earth ready to burst, and the frame of the World to be dissolv'd, there will be previous signs, in the Heavens and on the Earth, to introduce this Tragical fate. Nature cannot come to that extremity, without some symptomes of her illness; nor die silently, without pangs or complaint. But we are naturally heavy of belief as to Futurities, and can scarce fancy any other Scenes, or other state of nature, than that is present, and continually before our eyes; we will therefore, to cure our unbelief, take Scripture for our guide, and keep within the limits of its Predictions.

The Scripture plainly tells us of Signs or Prodigies that will precede the coming of our Saviour, and the end of the World; both in the Heavens and on the Earth. The Sun, Moon, and Stars, will be disturb'd in their motion or aspect; The Earth and the Sea will roar and tremble, and the Mountains fall at his Presence. These things both the Prophets and Evangelists have told us; But what we do not understand, we are slow to believe; and therefore those that cannot apprehend how such Changes should come to pass in the Natural World, chuse rather to allegorize all these expressions of Scripture, and to make them signifie no more than political changes of Governments and Empires; and the great confusions that will be amongst the People and Princes of the Earth towards the end of the World. So that *darkning of the Sun, shaking of the Earth*, and such like phrases of Scripture, according to these Interpreters, are to be understood onely in a moral sence.

And they think they have a warrant for this interpretation from the Prophetick style of the old Testament, where the destruction of Cities, and Empires, and great Princes, is often describ'd by such figures, taken from the Natural World. So much is true indeed as to the phrase of the old Prophets in some places; but I take the true reason and design of that, to be a typical adumbration of what was intended should literally come to pass in the great and universal destruction of the World; whereof these partial destructions were onely shadows and pre-figurations. But to determine this case, Let us take the known and approved rule for interpreting Scripture, *Not to recede from the literal sence without necessity*, or where the nature of the subject will admit of a literal interpretation. Now as to those cases in the old Testament, history and matter of fact do show that they did not come to pass literally, therefore must not be so understood; But as for those that concern the end of the World, as they cannot be determin'd in that way, seeing they are yet *future*; So neither is there any Natural repugnancy or improbability that they should come literally to pass: On the contrary, from the intuition of that state of Nature, one would rather conclude the probability or necessity of them. That there may and must be such disorders in the external World before the general dissolution. Besides, if we admit Prodigies in any case, or Providential indications of God's judgments to come, there can be no case suppos'd, wherein it will be more reasonable or proper to admit them, than when they are to be the Messengers of an Universal vengeance and destruction.

Let us therefore consider what signs Scripture hath taken notice of, as destin'd to appear at that time, to publish, as it were, and proclaim the approaching end of the World; And how far they will admit of a natural explication, according to those grounds we have already given, in explaining the causes and manner of the Conflagration. These Signs are chiefly, Earth-quakes, and extraordinary commotions of the Seas. Then the darkness or bloudy colour of the Sun and Moon; The shaking of the Powers of Heaven, the fulgurations of the Air and the falling of Stars. As to Earth-quakes, we have upon several occasions shown, that these will necessarily be multiplied towards the end of the World; when, by an excess of drought and heat, exhalations will more abound within the Earth; and, from the same causes, their inflammation also will be more frequent, than in the ordinary state of nature. And as all Bodies, when dry'd, become more porous and full of Vacuities; so the Body of the Earth will be at that time: And the Mines or Cavities wherein the fumes and exhalations lodge, will accordingly be of greater extent, open into one another, and continued through long tracts and regions; By which means, when an Earth-quake comes, as the shock will be more strong and violent, so it may reach to a vast compass of ground, and whole Islands or Continents be shaken at once, when these trains have taken fire. The effects also of such concussions, will not onely affect Mankind, but all the Elements and the Inhabitants of them.

I do not wonder therefore that frequent and great Earth-quakes should be made a sign of an approaching Conflagration; and the highest expressions of the Prophets concerning the *Day of the Lord*, may be understood in a literal sence, if they be finally referr'd to the general destruction of the World, and not terminated solely upon those particular Countries or People, to whom they are at first directed. Hear what *Ezekiel* says upon this subject: *For in my Jealousy and in the fire of my wrath have I spoken; Surely in that Day there shall be a great shaking in the Land of Israel. So that the Fishes of the Sea, and the Fowls of the Heaven, and the Beasts of the Field, and all creeping things that creep upon the Earth; and all the Men that are upon the face of the Earth, shall shake at my presence; and the Mountains shall be thrown down, and the steep places shall fall, and every wall shall fall to the ground.—And I will rain an over-flowing rain, and great hail-stones, fire and brimstone.* The Prophet *Isaias* describes these judgments in terms as high, and relating to the Natural World: *The Windows from on high are open, and the foundations of the Earth do shake. The Earth is utterly broken down, the Earth is clean dissolv'd, the Earth is moved exceedingly. The Earth shall reel to and fro like a drunkard, and shall be removed like a Cottage, and the transgression thereof shall be heavy upon it, and it shall fall and not rise again.*

Ch. 38. 19, 20, 22.

ch. 24. 18, 19, 20

To restrain all these things to *Judea*, as their adequate and final object, is to force both the words and the sence. Here are manifest allusions and foot-steps of the destruction of the World, and the dissolution of the Earth; partly as it was in the Deluge, and partly as it will be in its last ruine; torn, broken, and shatter'd. But most Men have fallen into that errour, To fancy both the destructions of the World, by water and by fire, quiet, noiseless things; executed without any ruines or ruptures in Nature; That the Deluge was but a great Pool of still waters, made by the rains and inundation of the Sea: and the Conflagration will be onely a superficial scorching of the Earth, with a running fire. These are false Idea's, and unsuitable to Scripture: for as the Deluge is there represented a

Disruption of the Abyss, and consequently of the then habitable Earth; so the future combustion of it, according to the representations of Scripture, is to be usher'd in and accompanied with all sort of violent impressions upon Nature; and the chief instrument of these violences will be Earth-quakes. These will tear the Body of the Earth, and shake its foundations; rend the Rocks, and pull down the tall Mountains; sometimes overturn, and sometimes swallow up Towns and Cities; disturb and disorder the Elements, and make a general confusion in Nature.

ch. 21. 25, 26, 27

Next to Earth-quakes, we may consider the *roarings of a troubled Sea*. This is another sign of a dying World. St. *Luke* hath set down a great many of them together; Let us hear his words: *And there shall be signs in the Sun, and in the Moon, and in the Stars; and upon the Earth, distress of Nations, with perplexity, The Sea and the Waves roaring. Mens hearts failing them for fear, and for looking after those things which are coming on the Earth: for the powers of Heaven shall be shaken. And then shall they see the Son of Man coming in a cloud, with power and great glory,* &c. As some would allegorize these Signs, which we noted before; so others would confine them to the destruction of *Jerusalem*. But 'tis plain, by this *coming of the Son of man in the clouds*, and the *redemption of the faithful*, and at the same time, the *sound of the last trumpet*, which all relate to the end of the World, that something further is intended than the destruction of *Jerusalem*. And though there were Prodigies at the destruction of that City and State, yet not of this force, nor with these circumstances. 'Tis true, those partial destructions and calamities, as we observ'd before, of *Babylon, Jerusalem*, and the *Roman* Empire, being types of an universal and final destruction of all God's Enemies, have, in the pictures of them, some of the same strokes, to show they are all from the same hand; decreed by the same wisdom, foretold by the same Spirit; and the same power and providence that have already wrought the one, will also work the other, in due time, the former being still pledges; as well as prefigurations, of the latter.

Ver. 28.
Mat. 24. 31.

Let us then proceed in our explication of this sign, *The roaring of the Sea, and the Waves*, applying it to the end of the World. I do not look upon this ominous noise of the Sea, as the effect of a tempest, for then it would not strike such a terrour into the Inhabitants of the Earth, nor make them apprehensive of some great evil coming upon the World, as this will do; what proceeds from visible causes, and such as may happen in a common course of Nature, does not so much amaze us, nor affright us. Therefore 'tis more likely these disturbances of the Sea proceed from below; partly by sympathy and revulsions from the Land; by Earth-quakes there, and exhausting the subterraneous cavities of waters, which will draw again from the Seas what supplies they can: And partly by Earth-quakes in the very Sea it self; with exhalations and fiery Eruptions from the bottom of it. Things indeed that happen at other times, more or less, but at this conjuncture, all causes conspiring, they will break out with more violence, and put the whole Body of the Waters into a tumultuary motion. I do not see any occasion, at this time, for high Winds; neither can think a superficial agitation of the Waves would answer this Phænomenon; but 'tis rather from

Contorsions in the bowels of the Ocean, which make it roar, as it were, for pain. Some Causes impelling the Waters one way, and some another, make intestine struglings and contrary motions; from whence proceed unusual noises, and such a troubled state of the Waters, as does not only make the Sea innavigable, but also strikes terror into all the Maritime inhabitants, that live within the view or sound of it.

So much for the Earth and the Sea. The face of the Heavens also will be chang'd in divers respects. The Sun and the Moon darkned, or of a bloudy, or pale countenance; The Celestial Powers shaken, and the Stars unsetled in their Orbs. As to the Sun and Moon, their obscuration or change of colour is no more than what happens commonly before the Eruption of a fiery Mountain; *Dion Cassius*, you see, hath taken notice of it in that Eruption of *Ætna* which he describes; and others upon the like occasions in *Vesuvius*. And 'tis a thing of easie explication; for according as the Atmosphere is more or less clear or turbid, the Luminaries are more or less conspicuous; and according to the nature of those fumes or exhalations that swim in the Air, the face of the Sun is discolour'd, sometimes one way, sometimes another. You see, in an ordinary Experiment, when we look upon one another through the fumes of Sulphur, we appear pale like so many Ghosts; and in some foggy days the Sun hangs in the Firmament as a lump of Bloud. And both the Sun and Moon at their rising, when their light comes to us through the thick vapours of the Earth, are red and fiery. These are not changes wrought in the substance of the Luminaries, but in the modifications of their light as it flows to us. For colours are but Light in a sort of disguise; as it passes through *Mediums* of different qualities, it takes different forms; but the matter is still the same, and returns to its simplicity when it comes again into a pure air.

Now the air may be changed and corrupted to a great degree, tho' there appear no visible change to our eye. This is manifest from infectious airs, and the changes of the air before storms and rains; which we feel commonly sooner than we see, and some other creatures perceive much sooner than we do. 'Tis no wonder then if before this mighty storm the dispositions of the Air be quite alter'd; especially if we consider, what we have so often noted before, that there will be a great abundance of fumes and exhalations through the whole Atmosphere of the Earth, before the last Fire breaks out; whereby the Light of the Sun may be tinctur'd in several ways. And lastly, it may be so order'd providentially, that the Body of the Sun may contract at that time some Spots or *Maculæ* far greater than usual, and by that means be really darkened; not to us only, but to all the neighbouring Planets. And this will have a proportionable effect upon the Moon too, for the diminution of her light. So that upon all suppositions these Phænomena are very intelligible, if not necessary forerunners of the Conflagration.

The next Sign given us, is, that the *powers of heaven will be shaken*. By the *Heavens* in this place is either understood the Planetary Heavens, or that of the *Fix'd Stars*; but this latter being infinitely distant from the Earth, cannot be really affected by the Conflagration. Nor the powers of it, that is, its motions or the Bodies contain'd in it, any way shaken or disorder'd. But in appearance these celestial Bodies may seem to be shaken and their motions disorder'd; as in a tempest by night, when the ship is toss'd with contrary and uncertain motions, the Heavens seem to fluctuate over our heads, and the Stars to reel to and fro, when the motion is only in our own Vessel. So possibly the uncertain motions of the Atmosphere, and sometimes of the Earth it self, may so vary the sight and aspect of this starry Canopy, that it may seem to shake and tremble.

But if we understand this of the *Planetary Heavens*, They may really be shaken. Providence either ordering some great changes in the other Planets previously to the Conflagration of our Planet; as 'tis probable there was a great change in *Venus*, at the time of our *Deluge*. Or the great shakings and concussions of our Globe at that time, affecting some of the neighbouring Orbs, at least that of the Moon, may cause Anomalies and irregularities in their motions. But the sence that I should pitch upon chiefly for explaining this phrase of *shaking the powers of heaven*, comprehends, in a good measure, both these Heavens, of the Fix'd Stars and of the Planets; 'Tis that change of situation in the Axis of the Earth, which we have formerly mention'd; whereby the Stars will seem to change their places, and the whole Universe to take another posture. This is sufficiently known to those that know the different consequences of a strait or oblique posture of the Earth. And as the heavens and the earth were, in this sence, once shaken before; namely at the Deluge, when they lost their first situation; so now they will be shaken again, and thereby return to the posture they had before that
ch. 2. 6.
Hebr. 12. 26. first concussion. And this I take to be the true literal sence of the Prophet *Haggai*, repeated by St. *Paul, Yet once more I shake not the Earth only, but also heaven.*

That last Sign we shall take notice of, is that of *Falling Stars. And the Stars shall fall from Heaven*, says our Saviour, *Matt.* 24. 29. We are sure, from the nature of the thing, that this cannot be understood either of fix'd Stars or Planets; for if either of these should tumble from the Skies, and reach the Earth, they would break it all in pieces, or swallow it up, as the Sea does a sinking ship; and at the same time would put all the inferiour universe into confusion. It is necessary therefore by these Stars to understand either fiery Meteors falling from the middle Region of the Air, or Comets and Blazing Stars. No doubt there will be all sorts of fiery Meteors at that time; and amongst others, those that are call'd *Falling Stars*; which, tho' they are not considerable singly, yet if they were
Isa. 34. 4. multiplyed in great numbers, falling, as the Prophet says, as *leafs from the Vine, or figs from the fig-tree*, they would make an astonishing sight. But I think this expression does chiefly refer to Comets; which are dead Stars, and may truly be said to fall from heaven, when they leave their seats above, and those ethereal regions wherein they were fixt, and sink into this lower World; where they wander about with a blaze in their tail, or a flame about their heads, as if they came on purpose to be the Messengers of some fiery Vengeance. If numbers of these blazing Stars should fall into our heaven together, they would make a dreadful and formidable appearance; And I am apt to think that Providence hath so contriv'd the periods of their motion, that there will be an unusual concourse of them at that time, within the view of the Earth, to be a prelude to this last and most Tragical Scene of the Sublunary World.

I do not know any more in Scripture relating to the last Fire, that, upon the grounds laid down in this discourse, may not receive a satisfactory explication. It reaches, beyond the Signs before mention'd, to the highest expressions of Scripture, As *Lakes of fire and brimstone, a molten Sea mingled with fire, the Liquefaction of Mountains*, and of the Earth it self. We need not now look upon these things as Hyperbolical and Poetical strains, but as barefac'd Prophecies, and things that will literally come to pass as they are predicted. One thing more will be expected in a just hypothesis or Theory of the Conflagration, namely, that it should answer, not only all the conditions and characters belonging to the last Fire, but should also make way and lay the foundation of another World to succeed this, or of *New Heavens* and a *New Earth*. For St. *Peter* hath taught this doctrine of the *Renovation* of the World, as positively and expressly as that of its Conflagration. And therefore they that so explain the destruction of the present World, as to leave it afterwards in an eternal rubbish, without any hopes of restoration, do not answer the Christian doctrine concerning it. But as to our Hypothesis, we are willing to stand this farther trial, and be accountable for the consequences of the Conflagration, as well as the Antecedents and manner of it. And we have accordingly in the following Book, from the Ashes of this, rais'd a New Earth; which we leave to the enjoyment of the Readers. In the mean time, to close our discourse, we will bid farewel to the present World, in a short review of its last flames.

CHAPTER XII

An imperfect description of the Coming of our Saviour, and of the World on Fire.

CERTAINLY there is nothing in the whole course of Nature, or of Humane affairs, so great and so extraordinary, as the two last Scenes of them, THE COMING OF OUR SAVIOUR, and the BURNING OF THE WORLD. If we could draw in our minds the Pictures of these, in true and lively colours, We should scarce be able to attend to any thing else, or ever divert our imagination from these two objects. For what can more affect us than the greatest Glory that ever was visible upon Earth, and at the same time the greatest Terror. A God descending in the Head of an Army of Angels, and a Burning World under his feet.

These are things truly above expression; And not only so, but so different and remote from our ordinary thoughts and conceptions, that he that comes nearest to a true description of them, shall be look'd upon as the most extravagant. 'Tis our unhappiness to be so much used to little trifling things in this life, that when any thing great is represented to us, it appears phantastical: An Idea, made by some contemplative or melancholy person. I will not venture therefore, without premising some grounds out of Scripture, to say any thing concerning This Glorious Appearance. As to the Burning of the World; I think we have already laid a foundation sufficient to support the highest description that can be made of it; But the coming of our Saviour being wholly out of the way of

Natural Causes, it is reasonable we should take all directions we can from Scripture, that we may give a more fitting and just account of that Sacred Pomp.

Matt. 24. 30, 31.
Act. 1. 11. & 3.
20, 21. Apoc. 1.
7. Heb. 9. 28.

I need not mention those places of Scripture that prove the second coming of our Saviour in general, or his return to the Earth again at the end of the World: no Christian can doubt of this, 'tis so often repeated in those Sacred Writings. But the manner and circumstances of this Coming, or of this Appearance, are the things we now enquire into. And in the first place, we may observe that Scripture tells us our Saviour will come in *Flaming Fire*, and with an *Host of mighty Angels*; so says St. *Paul* to the *Thessalonians*, *The Lord Jesus shall be*

1 Ep. 1. 7.

revealed from Heaven with mighty Angels; in flaming fire, taking vengeance on them that know not God, and obey not the Gospel of our Lord Jesus Christ. In the

Matt. 16. 27.

second place, our Saviour says himself, *The Son of man shall come in the glory of his Father with his Angels.* From which two places we may learn, first, that the appearance of our Saviour will be with flames of Fire. Secondly, with an Host of Angels. Thirdly, in the glory of his Father. By which glory of the Father I think is understood that Throne of Glory represented by *Daniel* for the *Ancient of Days.* For our Saviour speaks here to the *Jews*, and probably in a way intelligible to them; And the Glory of the Father which they were most likely to understand, would be either the Glory wherein God appeared at Mount *Sinai*, upon the giving of the Law, whereof the Apostle speaks largely to the *Hebrews*;

ch. 12. 18, 19,
20, 21.

or that which *Daniel* represents Him in at the day of Judgment. And this latter being more proper to the subject of our Saviour's discourse, 'tis more likely this expression refers to it. Give me leave therefore to set down that description of the Glory of the Father upon his Throne, from the Prophet *Daniel*, ch. 7, 9. *And I beheld till the Thrones were *set, and the Ancient of days did sit, whose garment was white as snow, and the hair of his head like the pure wool: His throne was like the fiery flame, and his wheels as burning fire. A fiery stream issued and came forth from before him, thousand thousands ministred unto him, and ten thousand times ten thousand stood before him.* With this Throne of the glory of the Father, let us, if you please, compare the Throne of the Son of God, as it was seen by St. *John* in the Apocalypse, ch. 4. 2, &c. *And immediately I was in the Spirit: and behold a throne was set in heaven, and one sate on the Throne. And he that sat, was to look upon like a Jasper, and a Sardine stone: and there was a Rain-bow round about the Throne, in appearance like unto an Emerald. And out of the Throne proceeded Lightnings, and Thunderings, and Voices, &c. and before the Throne was a Sea of glass like unto Crystal.*

In these representations you have some beams of the glory of the Father and of the Son; which may be partly a direction to us, in conceiving the lustre of our Saviour's appearance. Let us further observe, if you please, how external nature will be affected at the sight of God, or of this approaching glory. The Scripture often takes notice of this, and in terms very high and eloquent. The Psalmist seems to have lov'd that subject above others; to set out the greatness of the day of the Lord, and the consternation of all nature at that time. He throws about his thunder and lightning, makes the Hills to melt like wax at the presence of

---

* 'Tis ill render'd in the English, *cast down.*

the Lord, and the very foundations of the Earth to tremble, as you may see in the 18*th Psalm*, and the 97. and the 104. and several others, which are too long to be here inserted. So the Prophet *Habakkuk*, in his Prophetick prayer, *Chap.* 3*d.* hath many Ejaculations to the like purpose. And the Prophet *Nahum* says, *The mountains quake at him, and the hills melt, and the Earth is burnt at his presence: yea, the world, and all that dwell therein.*

But more particularly, as to the face of Nature just before the coming of our Saviour, that may be best collected from the signs of his coming mention'd in the precedent Chapter. Those all meeting together, help to prepare and make ready a Theater, fit for an angry God to come down upon. The countenance of the Heavens will be dark and gloomy; and a Veil drawn over the face of the Sun. The Earth in a disposition every where to break into open flames. The tops of the Mountains smoaking; the Rivers dry; Earth-quakes in several places; the Sea sunk and retir'd into its deepest Chanel, and roaring, as against some mighty storm. These things will make the day dead and melancholy, but the Night-Scenes will have more of horrour in them. When the *Blazing-Stars* appear, like so many Furies, with their lighted Torches, threatning to set all on fire. For I do not doubt but the Comets will bear a part in this Tragedy, and have something extraordinary in them, at that time; either as to number, or bigness, or nearness to the Earth. Besides, the Air will be full of flaming Meteors, of unusual forms and magnitudes; Balls of fire rowling in the Skie, and pointed lightnings darted against the Earth; mixt with claps of thunder, and unusual noises from the Clouds. The Moon and the Stars will be confus'd and irregular, both in their light and motions; as if the whole frame of the Heavens was out of order, all the laws of Nature were broken or expir'd.

When all things are in this languishing or dying posture, and the Inhabitants of the Earth under the fears of their last end; The Heavens will open on a sudden, and the Glory of God will appear. A Glory surpassing the Sun in its greatest radiancy; which, tho' we cannot describe, we may suppose it will bear some resemblance or proportion with those representations that are made in Scripture, of *God upon his Throne.* This wonder in the Heavens, whatsoever its form may be, will presently attract the eyes of all the Christian World. Nothing can more affect them than an object so unusual and so illustrious; and that, (probably) brings along with it their last destiny, and will put a period to all humane affairs.

Some of the Ancients have thought that this coming of our Saviour would be in the dead of the night, and his first glorious appearance in the midst of darkness. God is often describ'd in Scripture as Light or Fire, with darkness round about him. *He bowed the Heavens and came down, and darkness was under his feet. He made darkness his secret place: His pavilion round about him were dark Waters and thick Clouds of the Skies. At the brightness that was before him, the thick Clouds passed.* And when God appear'd upon Mount *Sinai*, the *Mountain burnt with fire unto the midst of Heaven with darkness, clouds, and thick darkness*: Or, as the Apostle expresses it, with *blackness* and *darkness*, and *tempest.* Light is never more glorious than when surrounded with darkness; and it may be the Sun, at that time, will be so obscure, as to make little distinction of Day and Night. But

2 Pet. 3. 10.

Psal. 18. 9, 11, 12.
Psal. 97.

Deut. 4. 11.

Hebr. 12. 18.

however this Divine Light over-bears and distinguishes it self from common
Light, tho' it be at Mid-day. 'Twas about Noon that the Light shin'd from
Heaven and surrounded St. *Paul*. And 'twas on the Day-time that St. *Stephen*
saw the *Heavens opened; saw the glory of God, and Jesus standing at the right hand
of God*. This light, which flows from a more vital source, be it Day or Night,
will always be predominant.

Acts 22. 6.

Acts 7. 55, 56.

That appearance of God upon Mount *Sinai*, which we mention'd, if we reflect
upon it, will help us a little to form an Idea of this last appearance. When God
had declar'd, that he would come down in the sight of the People; The Text
says, *There were thunders and lightnings, and a thick Cloud upon the Mount, and
the voice of the Trumpet exceeding loud; so that all the people that was in the Camp
trembled. And Mount Sinai was altogether on a smoke, because the Lord descended
upon it in fire. And the smoke thereof ascended as the smoke of a furnace, and the
whole Mount quaked greatly.* If we look upon this Mount as an Epitome of the
Earth, this appearance gives us an imperfect resemblance of that which is to
come. Here are the several parts or main strokes of it; first, the Heavens and the
Earth in smoke and fire, then the appearance of a Divine Glory, and the sound
of a Trumpet in the presence of Angels. But as the second coming of our Saviour
is a Triumph over his Enemies, and an entrance into his Kingdom, and is acted
upon the Theater of the whole Earth; so we are to suppose, in proportion, all the
parts and circumstances of it, more great and magnificent.

When therefore this mighty God returns again to that Earth, where he had
once been ill treated, not Mount *Sinai* only, but all the Mountains of the Earth,
and all the Inhabitants of the World, will tremble at his presence. At the first
opening of the Heavens, the brightness of his Person will scatter the dark Clouds,
and shoot streams of light throughout all the Air. But that first appearance, being
far from the Earth, will seem to be onely a great mass of light, without any distinct
form; till, by nearer approaches, this bright Body shows it self to be an Army of
Angels, with this King of kings for their Leader. Then you may imagine how
guilty Mankind will tremble and be astonish'd; and while they are gazing at this
heavenly Host, the Voice of the *Archangel is heard*, the shrill sound of the Trumpet
reaches their ears. And this gives the general Alarum to all the World. *For he
cometh, for he cometh*, they cry, *to judge the Earth*. The crucified God is return'd
in Glory, to take Vengeance upon his Enemies: Not onely upon those that
pierc'd his Sacred Body, with Nails and with a Spear, at *Jerusalem*; but those also
that pierce him every day by their prophaneness and hard speeches, concerning his Person and his Religion. Now they see that God whom they have
mock'd, or blasphem'd, laugh't at his meanness, or at his vain threats; They see
Him, and are confounded with shame and fear; and in the bitterness of their
anguish and despair call for the Mountains to fall upon them. *Fly into the clefts
of the Rocks, and into the Caves of the Earth, for fear of the Lord, and the glory
of his Majesty, when he ariseth to shake terribly the Earth.*

Isa. 2. 19.
Rev. 6. 16, 17.

As it is not possible for us to express or conceive the dread and majesty of this
appearance; so neither can we, on the other hand, express the passions and
consternation of the People that behold it. These things exceed the measures of

humane affairs, and of humane thoughts; we have neither words, nor comparisons, to make them known by. The greatest pomp and magnificence of the Emperors of the East, in their Armies, in their triumphs, in their inaugurations, is but like the sport and entertainment of Children, if compar'd with this Solemnity. When God condescends to an external glory, with a visible Train and Equipage: When, from all the Provinces of his vast and boundless Empire, he summons his Nobles, as I may so say: The several orders of Angels and Arch-Angels, to attend his Person; tho' we cannot tell the form or manner of this Appearance, we know there is nothing in our experience, or in the whole history of this World, that can be a just representation of the least part of it. No Armies so numerous as the Host of Heaven: and in the midst of those bright Legions, in a flaming Chariot, will sit the Sun of Man, when he comes to be glorified in his Saints, and triumph over his Enemies. And instead of the wild noises of the rabble, which makes a great part of our worldly state: This blessed Company will breath their *Halleluiahs* into the open Air; and repeated acclamations of *Salvation to God, which sits upon the Throne, and to the Lamb. Now is come salvation and strength, and the kingdom of our God, and the power of his Christ.*

Apoc. 7. 10. & 12. 10.

But I leave the rest to our silent devotion and admiration. Onely give me leave, whilst this object is before our eyes, to make a short reflection upon the wonderful history of our Saviour; and the different states, which that Sacred Person, within the compass of our knowledge, hath undergone. We now see him coming in the Clouds in glory and triumph, surrounded with innumerable Angels. This is the same Person, who, so many hundred Years ago, enter'd *Jerusalem*, with another sort of Equipage: mounted upon an Asse's Colt, while the little people and the multitude cry'd, *Hosanna* to the *Son of David*. Nay, this is the same Person, that, at his first coming into this World, was laid in a Manger instead of a Cradle; A naked Babe dropt in a Crib at *Bethlehem*: His poor Mother not having wherewithall to get her a better Lodging, when she was to be deliver'd of this Sacred burthen. This helpless Infant, that often wanted a little Milk to refresh it, and support its weakness: That hath often cry'd for the Breast, with hunger and tears: now appears to be the Lord of Heaven and Earth. If this Divine Person had faln from the clouds in a mortal Body, cloath'd with Flesh and Bloud, and spent his life here amongst sinners; that alone had been an infinite condescension. But as if it had not been enough to take upon him humane Nature, he was content, for many months, to live the life of an Animal, or of a Plant, in the dark cell of a woman's Womb. *This is the Lord's doing, it is marvellous in our eyes.*

Luke 2. 12.

Neither is this all that is wonderful in the story of our Saviour. If the manner of his death be compar'd with his present glory, we shall think, either the one, or the other, incredible. Look up, first, into the Heavens: see how they bow under him, and receive a new light from the Glory of his Presence. Then look down upon the Earth, and see a naked Body hanging upon a cursed Tree in *Golgotha*: crucified betwixt two Thieves: wounded, spit upon, mock'd, abus'd. Is it possible to believe that one and the same person can act or suffer such different parts? That he, that is now Lord and Master of all Nature: not only of Death and Hell, and the powers of darkness: but of all Principalities in heavenly places: is the same Infant Jesus, the same crucified Jesus, of whose life and death the Christian records give us an account? The History of this person is the Wonder of this World; and not of this World only, but of the Angels above, that desire to look into it.

1 Pet. I. II, 12.

Let us now return to our subject. We left the Earth in a languishing condition, ready to be made a Burnt-offering, to appease the wrath of its offended Lord. When *Sodom* was to be destroy'd, *Abraham* interceded with God that he would spare it for the Righteous sake: And *David* interceded to save his guiltless People from God's Judgments and the Destroying Angel. But here is no Intercessor for mankind in this last extremity: None to interpose where the Mediator of our Peace is the party offended. Shall then *the righteous perish with the wicked? Shall not the Judge of all the Earth do right?* Or if the Righteous be translated and delivered from This Fire, what shall become of innocent children and Infants? Must these all be given up to the merciless flames, as a Sacrifice to *Moloch?* and their tender flesh, like burnt incense, send up fumes to feed the nostrils of evil Spirits? Can the God of *Israel* smell a sweet savour from such Sacrifices? The greater half of mankind is made up of Infants and Children: and if the wicked be destroyed, *yet these Lambs, what have they done?* are there no bowels of compassion for such an harmless multitude? But we leave them to their Guardian Angels, and to that Providence which watches over all things.

Gen. 18.
2 Sam. 24. 17.

Matt. 18. 10.

It only remains therefore, to let fall that Fire from Heaven, which is to consume this Holocaust. Imagine all Nature now standing in a silent expectation to receive its last doom: The Tutelary and Destroying Angels to have their instructions: Every thing to be ready for the fatal hour: And then, after a little silence, all the Host of Heaven to raise their voice and sing aloud, *LET GOD ARISE: Let his enemies be scattered. As smoak is driven away, so drive them away: As wax melteth before the fire, so LET the wicked perish at the presence of God.* And upon this, as upon a signal given, all the sublunary World breaks into Flames, and all the Treasuries of Fire are open'd, in Heaven and in Earth.

Thus the Conflagration begins. If one should now go about to represent *the World on Fire*, with all the confusions that necessarily must be, in Nature and in Mankind, upon that occasion, it would seem to most men a Romantick Scene. Yet we are sure there must be such a Scene. *The heavens will pass away with a noise, and the Elements will melt with fervent heat, and all the works of the Earth will be burnt up.* And these things cannot come to pass without the greatest disorders imaginable, both in the minds of Men and in external Nature: and the saddest spectacles that eye can behold. We think it a great matter to see a single person burnt alive: here are Millions, shrieking in the flames at once. 'Tis frightful to us to look upon a great City in flames, and to see the distractions and misery of the people: here is an Universal Fire through all the Cities of the Earth, and an Universal Massacre of their Inhabitants. Whatsoever the Prophets foretold of the desolations of *Judea, Jerusalem,* or *Babylon,* in the highest strains, is more than literally accomplish'd in this last and general Calamity: And those only that are Spectators of it, can make its History.

Isa. 24.
Jer. 51.
Lament.

The disorders in Nature and the inanimate World will be no less, nor less strange and unaccountable, than those in Mankind. Every Element, and every Region, so far as the bounds of this Fire extend, will be in a tumult and a fury, and the whole habitable World running into confusion. A World is sooner destroyed than made, and Nature relapses hastily into that Chaos-state, out of which she came by slow and leisurely motions. As an Army advances into the field by just and regular marches, but when it is broken and routed, it flies with precipitation, and one cannot describe its posture. Fire is a barbarous Enemy, it gives no mercy; there is nothing but fury, and rage, and ruine, and destruction, wheresoever it prevails. A storm or *Hurricano*, tho' it be but the force of Air, makes a strange havock where it comes; but devouring flames, or exhalations set on Fire, have still a far greater violence, and carry more terror along with them. Thunder and Earth-quakes are the Sons of Fire: and we know nothing in all Nature, more impetuous, or more irresistibly destructive than these two. And accordingly in this last war of the Elements, we may be sure, they will bear their parts, and do great execution in the several regions of the World. Earth-quakes and Subterraneous Eruptions will tear the body and bowels of the Earth; and Thunders and convulsive motions of the Air, rend the Skies. The waters of the Sea will boyl and struggle with streams of Sulphur that run into them; which will make them fume, and smoke, and roar, beyond all storms and tempests. And these noises of the Sea will be answered again from the Land by falling Rocks and Mountains. This is a small part of the disorders of that day.

But 'tis not possible, from any station, to have a full prospect of this last Scene of the Earth: for 'tis a mixture of fire and darkness. This new Temple is fill'd with smoak, while it is consecrating, and none can enter into it. But I am apt to think, if we could look down upon this burning World from above the Clouds, and have a full view of it, in all its parts, we should think it a lively representation of *Hell* it self. For, Fire and darkness are the two chief things by which that state, or that place, uses to be describ'd: and they are both here mingled together: with all other ingredients that make that Tophet that is prepar'd of old. Here *Isa.* 30. are Lakes of fire and brimstone: Rivers of melted glowing matter: Ten thousand Volcano's vomiting flames all at once. Thick darkness, and Pillars of smoke twisted about with wreaths of flame, like fiery Snakes. Mountains of Earth thrown up into the Air, and the Heavens dropping down in lumps of fire. These things will all be literally true, concerning that day, and that state of the Earth. And if we suppose *Beelzebub*, and his Apostate crew, in the midst of this fiery furnace: (and I know not where they can be else.) It will be hard to find any part of the Universe, or any state of things, that answers to so many of the properties and characters of *Hell*, as this which is now before us.

But if we suppose the storm over, and that the fire hath got an entire victory over all other bodies, and subdued every thing to it self, the Conflagration will end in a Deluge of fire: Or, in a Sea of fire, covering the whole Globe of the Earth. For, when the exterior region of the Earth is melted into a fluor, like molten glass, or running metal; it will, according to the nature of other Fluids, fill all vacuities and depressions, and fall into a regular surface, at an equal distance, every where, from its center. This Sea of fire, like the first Abyss, will cover the face of the whole Earth: make a kind of second Chaos: and leave a capacity for another World to rise from it. But that is not our present business. Let us onely, if you please, to take leave of this subject, reflect upon this occasion, on the Vanity and transient glory of all this habitable World. How, by the force of one Element, breaking loose upon the rest, all the Varieties of Nature, all the works of Art, all the labours of Men are reduc'd to nothing. All that we admir'd and ador'd before, as great and magnificent, is obliterated or vanish'd. And another form and face of things, plain, simple, and every where the same, overspreads the whole Earth. Where are now the great Empires of the World, and their great Imperial Cities? Their Pillars, Trophees, and Monuments of glory? Show me where they stood: read the Inscription, tell me the Victor's name. What remains, what impressions, what difference or distinction do you see in this mass of fire? *Rome* it self, *Eternal Rome*, the Great City, the Empress of the World, whose domination and superstition, *ancient and modern*, make a great part of the history of this Earth: What is become of her now? She laid her foundations deep, and her Palaces were strong and sumptuous: *She glorified her self, and liv'd deliciously: and said in her heart, I sit a Queen, and shall see no sorrow.* But her hour is come, she is wip'd away from the face of the Earth, and buried in everlasting oblivion. But 'tis not Cities onely, and works of men's hands, but the everlasting Hills, the Mountains and Rocks of the Earth, are melted as Wax before the Sun; and *their place is no where found.* Here stood the *Alpes*, a prodigious range of Stone, the Load of the Earth, that cover'd many Countries, and reach'd their armes from the Ocean to the *Black Sea*; This huge mass of Stone is soften'd and dissolv'd, as a tender Cloud into rain. Here stood the *African* Mountains, and *Atlas* with his top above the Clouds. There was frozen *Caucasus*, and *Taurus*, and *Imaus*, and the Mountains of *Asia*. And yonder towards the North stood the *Riphæan* Hills, cloath'd in Ice and Snow. All these are vanish'd, dropt away as the Snow upon their heads: and swallowed up in a

Revel. 15. 3.

red Sea of fire. *Great and marvellous are thy Works, Lord God Almighty: Just and true are thy ways, Thou King of Saints.* Hallelujah.

THE CONCLUSION

IF the Conflagration of the World be a reality, as, both by Scripture and Antiquity, we are assur'd it is: If we be fully perswaded and convinc'd of this: 'Tis a thing of that nature, that we cannot keep it long in our thoughts, without making some moral reflections upon it. 'Tis both great in it self, and of universal concern to all Mankind. Who can look upon such an Object, *A World in Flames*, without thinking with himself, Whether shall I be in the midst of these flames, or no? What is my security that I shall not fall under this fiery vengeance, which is the wrath of an angry God? St. *Peter*, when he had deliver'd

2 Epist. 3. 11.

the doctrine of the Conflagration, makes this pious reflection upon it: *Seeing then that all these things shall be dissolv'd, what manner of persons ought you to be, in holy conversation and godliness?* The strength of his argument depends chiefly upon what he had said before in the 7*th* Verse, where he told us, that the *present Heavens and Earth were reserv'd unto fire, against the Day of Judgment, and the perdition of irreligious men.* We must avoid the crime then, if we would escape the punishment. But this expression of *irreligious* or *ungodly men,* is still very general. St. *Paul,* when he speaks of this fiery indignation, and the Persons it is to fall upon, is more distinct in their characters. He seems to mark out for this destruction, three sorts of men chiefly, *The Atheists, Infidels, and the Tribe of Antichrist.* These are his words: *When the Lord Jesus shall be revealed from Heaven, with his mighty Angels, in flaming fire, taking vengeance on them that known not God: and that obey not the Gospel of our Lord Jesus Christ.* Then as for Antichrist and his adherents, he says, in the 2*d.* Chapt. and 8*th.* Verse, *The Lord shall consume that Wicked one with the Spirit of his mouth, and shall destroy him with the brightness of his coming,* or of his Presence. These, you see, all refer to the same time with St. *Peter:* namely, to the coming of our Saviour, at the Conflagration; and three sorts of Persons are characteriz'd as his Enemies, and set out for destruction at that time. First, those that know not God: that is, that acknowledge not God, that will not own the Deity. Secondly, those that hearken not to the Gospel; that is, that reject the Gospel and Christian Religion, when they are preach'd and made known to them. For you must not think that it is the poor barbarous and ignorant Heathens, that scarce ever heard of God, or the Gospel, that are threaten'd with this fiery vengeance. No, 'tis the Heathens that live amongst Christians; those that are Infidels, as to the existence of God, or the truth of Christian Religion, tho' they have had a full manifestation of both. These are properly the Adversaries of God and Christ. And such adversaries, St. *Paul* says in another place, *A fearful judgment, and fiery indignation shall devour:* which still refers to the same time, and the same Persons we are speaking of. Then as to the third sort of Men, Anti-christ and his Followers, besides this Text of St. *Paul* to the *Thessalonians,* 'tis plain to me in the Apocalypse, that *Mystical Babylon* is to be consum'd by fire: and the *Beast* and *False Prophet* to be thrown into the *Lake that burns with fire and brimstone*: Which Lake is no where to be found till the Conflagration.

You see then for whom *Tophet* is prepar'd of old. For Atheists, Infidels, and Anti-christian Persecutors. And they will have for their Companions, the Devil and his Angels, the heads of the Apostasie. These are all in open rebellion against God and Christ, and at defiance, as it were, with Heaven. Excepting Anti-christ, who is rather in a secret conspiracy, than an open rebellion. For, under a pretended Commission from Jesus Christ, He persecutes his Servants, dishonours his Person, corrupts his Laws and his Government, and makes War against his Saints. And this is a greater affront and provocation, if possible, than a barefac'd opposition would be.

There are other Men, besides these, that are unacceptable to God: All sorts of sinners and wicked persons: but they are not so properly the Enemies of God, as these we have mention'd. An intemperate Man is an Enemy to himself, and

2 Thess. I. 7, 8.

Heb. 10. 27.

an injust Man is an Enemy to his Neighbour: But those that deny God, or Christ, or persecute their Servants, are directly and immediately Enemies to God. And therefore when the Lord comes in flames of fire to triumph over his Enemies: To take vengeance upon all that are Rebels or Conspirators against him and his Christ; these Monsters of Men will be the first and most exemplary Objects of the divine wrath and indignation.

To undertake to speak to these three Orders of men, and convince them of their errour, and the danger of it, would be too much for the Conclusion of a short Treatise. And as for the third sort, the Subjects of Antichrist, none but the Learned amongst them are allow'd to be inquisitive, or to read such things as condemn their Church, or the Governors of it. Therefore I do not expect that this English Translation should fall into many of their hands. But those of them, that are pleas'd to look into the Latin, will find, in the Conclusion of it, a full and fair warning to come out of *Babylon*: which is there prov'd to be the Church of *Rome*. Then as to those that are Atheistically inclin'd, which I am willing to believe are not many, I desire them to consider, How mean a thing it is, to have hopes onely in this Life: and how uneasie a thing, to have nothing but fears as to the Future. Those, sure, must be little narrow Souls, that can make themselves a portion and a sufficiency out of what they enjoy here: That think of no more, that desire no more. For what is this life, but a circulation of little mean actions? We lie down and rise again: dress and undress: feed and wax hungry: work, or play, and are weary: and then we lie down again, and the circle returns. We spend the day in trifles, and when the Night comes, we throw our selves into the Bed of folly, amongst dreams and broken thoughts and wild imaginations. Our reason lies a-sleep by us; and we are, for the time, as arrant Brutes, as those that sleep in the Stalls, or in the Field. Are not the Capacities of Man higher than these? and ought not his ambition and expectations to be greater? Let us be Adventurers for another World: 'Tis, at least, a fair and noble Chance: and there is nothing in this, worth our thoughts or our passions. If we should be disappointed, we are still no worse than the rest of our fellow-mortals: and if we succeed in our expectations, we are eternally happy.

For my part, I cannot be perswaded, that any man of Atheistical inclinations can have a great and generous Soul. For there is nothing great in the World, if you take God out of it. Therefore such a person can have no great thought, can have no great aims, or expectations, or designs: for all must lie within the compass of this Life, and of this dull Body. Neither can he have any great instincts or noble passions: For if he had, they would naturally excite in him greater Ideas, inspire him with higher notions, and open the Scenes of the Intellectual World. Lastly, He cannot have any great sence of Order, Wisdom, Goodness, Providence, or any of the Divine Perfections. And these are the greatest things that can enter into the thoughts of man, and that do most enlarge and ennoble his mind. And therefore I say again, That, He that is naturally inclined to Atheism, being also naturally destitute of all these, must have a little and narrow soul.

But you'l say, it may be, This is to expostulate rather than to prove: or to upbraid us with our make and temper, rather than to convince us of an error in speculation. 'Tis an error it may be in practice, or in point of prudence; but we seek Truth, whether it make for us or against us: convince us therefore by just reasoning and direct arguments, that there is a God, and then wee'l endeavour to correct these defects in our natural complexion. You say well; and therefore I have endeavour'd to do this before, in another part of this Theory, in the *Second Book, ch.* 11. Concerning the *Author of Nature:* where you may see, that the Powers of Nature, or of the Material World, cannot answer all the Phænomena of the Universe, which are there represented. This you may consult at leisure. But, in the mean time, 'tis a good perswasive why we should not easily give our selves up to such inclinations or opinions, as have neither generosity, nor prudence on their side. And it cannot be amiss, that these persons should often take into their thoughts, this last scene of things, The *Conflagration* of the World. Seeing if there be a God, they will certainly be found in the number of his Enemies, and of those that will have their portion in the Lake that burns with Fire and Brimstone.

The Third sort of persons that we are to speak to, are the Incredulous, or such as do not believe the truth of *Christian Religion,* tho' they believe there is a God. These are commonly men of Wit and Pleasure, that have not patience enough to consider, coolely and in due order, the grounds upon which it appears, that Christian Religion is from Heaven, and of Divine Authority. They ought, in the first place, to examine *matter of Fact,* and the History of our Saviour: That there was such a Person, in the Reigns of *Augustus* and *Tiberius,* that wrought such and such Miracles in *Judæa;* taught such a Doctrine: was Crucified at *Jerusalem:* rise from the dead the Third Day, and visibly ascended into Heaven. If these matters of Fact be denied, then the controversie turns only to an Historical question, *Whether* the Evangelical History be a fabulous, or true History: which it would not be proper to examine in this place. But if matter of Fact recorded there, and in the Acts of the Apostles, and the first Ages of Christianity, be acknowledged, as I suppose it is, then the Question that remains is this, *Whether* such matter of Fact does not sufficiently prove the divine authority of Jesus Christ and of his Doctrine. We suppose it possible, for a person to have such Testimonials of divine authority, as may be sufficient to convince Mankind, or the more reasonable part of Mankind; And if that be possible, what, pray, is a-wanting in the Testimonies of Jesus Christ? The Prophecies of the Old Testament bear witness to him: His Birth was a miracle, and his Life a train of Miracles: not wrought out of levity and vain ostentation, but for useful and charitable purposes. His Doctrine and Morality not only blameless, but Noble: designed to remove out of the World the imperfect Religion of the *Jews,* and the false Religion of the *Gentiles*: All Idolatry and Superstition: and thereby to improve Mankind, under a better and more perfect dispensation. He gave an example of a spotless innocency in all his Conversation, free from Vice or any evil; and liv'd in a neglect of all the Pomp or Pleasures of this Life, referring his happiness wholly to another World. He Prophesied concerning his own Death, and his Resurrection: and concerning the destruction of *Jerusalem*: which all came to pass in a signal manner. He also

Prophesied of the Success of his Gospel: which, after his Death, immediately took root, and spread it self every way throughout the World: maugre all opposition or persecution, from *Jews* or *Heathens*. It was not supported by any temporal power for above three hundred Years: nor were any arts us'd, or measures taken, according to humane prudence, for the conservation of it. But, to omit other things, That grand article of his Rising from the Dead, Ascending visibly into Heaven, and pouring down the miraculous Gifts of the Holy Ghost, (according as he had promis'd) upon his Apostles and their followers: This alone is to me a Demonstration of his Divine Authority. To conquer Death: To mount, like an Eagle, into the Skies: and to inspire his followers with inimitable gifts and faculties, are things, without controversie, beyond all humane power: and may and ought be esteemed sure Credentials of a person sent from Heaven.

From these matters of Fact we have all possible assurance, that Jesus Christ was no Impostor or deluded person: (one of which two Characters all unbelievers must fix upon him) but Commission'd by Heaven to introduce a New Religion: to reform the World: to remove Judaism and Idolatry; The Beloved Son of God, the great Prophet of the latter Ages, the True Messiah that was to come.

It may be you will confess, that these are great arguments that the Author of our Religion was a Divine Person, and had supernatural powers: but withal, that there are so many difficulties in Christian Religion, and so many things unintelligible, that a rational man knows not how to believe it, tho' he be inclin'd to admire the person of Jesus Christ. I answer, If they be such difficulties as are made only by the Schools and disputacious Doctors, you are not to trouble your self about them, for they are of no Authority. But if they be in the very words of Scripture, then 'tis either in things practical, or in things meerly speculative. As to the Rules of Practice in Christian Religion, I do not know any thing in Scripture, obscure or unintelligible. And as to Speculations, great discretion and moderation is to be us'd in the conduct of them. If these matters of Fact, which we have alledg'd, prove the Divinity of the Revelation, keep close to the Words of that Revelation, asserting no more than it asserts, and you cannot err. But if you will expatiate, and determine modes, and forms, and consequences; you may easily be puzled by your own forwardness. For besides some things that are, in their own nature, Infinite and Incomprehensible, there are many other things in Christian Religion that are incompleatly reveal'd; the full knowledge whereof, it has pleased God to reserve to another life, and to give us only a summary account of them at present. We have so much deference for any Government, as not to expect that all their Councels and secrets should be made known to us, nor to censure every action whose reasons we do not fully comprehend; much more in the Providential administration of a World, we must be content to know so much of the Councels of Heaven and of supernatural Truths, as God has thought fit to reveal to us. And if these Truths be no otherwise than in a general manner, summarily and incompleatly revealed in this life, as commonly they are, we must not therefore throw off the Government, or reject the whole Dispensation: of whose Divine Authority we have otherways full proof and satisfactory evidence. For this would be, To lose the Substance in catching at a Shadow.

But men that live continually in the noise of the World, amidst business and pleasures, their time is commonly shar'd betwixt those two. So that little or nothing is left for Meditation; at least, not enough for such Meditations as require length, justness, and order. They should retire from the crowd for one Month or two, to study the truth of Christian Religion, if they have any doubt of it. They retire sometimes to cure a Gout, or other Diseases, and diet themselves according to rule: but they will not be at that pains, to cure a disease of the mind, which is of far greater and more fatal consequence. If they perish by their own negligence or obstinacy, the Physician is not to blame. Burning is the last remedy in some distempers: and they would do well to remember, that the World will flame about their heads one of these days: and whether they be amongst the Living, or amongst the Dead, at that time, the Apostle makes them a part of the Fewel, which that fiery vengeance will prey upon. Our Saviour hath been true to his word hitherto: whether in his promises, or in his threatnings; He promis'd the Apostles to send down the Holy Ghost upon them after his Ascension, and that was fully accomplish'd. He foretold and threaten'd the destruction of *Jerusalem*: and that came to pass accordingly, soon after he had left the World. And he hath told us also, that he will come again in *the Clouds of Heaven, with power and great glory*; and that will be to judge the World. *When the Son of Man shall come in his glory, and all the holy Angels with him, then shall he sit upon the Throne of his glory. And before him shall be gather'd all Nations,* and he will separate the good from the bad; and to the wicked and unbelievers he will say, *Depart from me ye cursed, into everlasting fire, prepared for the Devil and his Angels.* This is the same Coming, and the same Fire, with that which we mention'd before out of St. *Paul.* As you will plainly see, if you compare St. *Matthew*'s words with St. *Paul*'s, which are these, *When the Lord Jesus shall be revealed from heaven, with his mighty Angels: In flaming fire, taking vengeance on them that know not God, and that hearken not to the Gospel of our Lord Jesus Christ. Who shall be punished with everlasting destruction, from, or by the presence of the Lord, and the glory of his power.* This, me-thinks, should be an awakening thought, that there is such a threatening upon record, (by one who never yet fail'd in his word) against those that do not believe his Testimony. Those that reject him now as a Dupe, or an Impostor, run a hazard of seeing him hereafter coming in the Clouds to be their Judge. And it will be too late then to correct their errour, when the bright Armies of Angels fill the Air, and the Earth begins to melt at the Presence of the Lord.

Thus much concerning those three ranks of Men, whom the Apostle St. *Paul* seems to point at principally, and condemn to the flames. But, as I said before, the rest of sinners and vitious Persons amongst the Professors of Christianity, tho' they are not so directly the Enemies of God, as these are; yet being transgressors of his Law, they must expect to be brought to Justice. In every well-govern'd State, not onely Traitors and Rebels, that offend more immediately against the Person of the Prince, but all others, that notoriously violate the Laws, are brought to condign punishment, according to the nature and degree of their crime. So in this case, *The fire shall try every man's work, of what sort it is.* 'Tis

Matt. 24. 30. & 25. 31, &c.

Ver. 41.

2 *Thess.* 1. 7, 8, 9.

therefore the concern of every man to reflect often upon that Day, and to consider what his fate and sentence is likely to be, at that last Trial. The *Jews* have a Tradition that *Elias* sits in Heaven, and keeps a Register of all Men's actions, good or bad. He hath his Under-Secretaries for the several Nations of the World, that take minutes of all that passes: and so hath the history of every man's life before him, ready to be produc'd at the Day of Judgment. I will not vouch for the literal truth of this, but it is true in effect. Every man's fate shall be determin'd that Day, according to the history of his life: according to the works done in the flesh, whether good or bad. And therefore it ought to have as much influence upon us, as if every single action was formally register'd in Heaven.

If Men would learn to contemn this World, it would cure a great many Vices at once. And, me-thinks, St. *Peter*'s argument, from the approaching dissolution of all things, should put us out of conceit with such perishing vanities. Lust and Ambition are the two reigning Vices of great Men: and those little fires might be soon extinguish'd, if they would frequently and seriously meditate on this last and universal Fire; which will put an end to all passions and all contentions. As to Ambition, the Heathens themselves made use of this argument, to abate and repress the vain affectation of glory and greatness in this World. I told you before

P. 15.

the lesson that was given to *Scipio Africanus*, by his Uncle's Ghost, upon this Subject. And upon a like occasion and consideration, *Cæsar* hath a lesson given him by *Lucan*, after the Battle of *Pharsalia*; where *Pompey* lost the day, and *Rome* its liberty. The Poet says, *Cæsar* took pleasure in looking upon the dead Bodies, and would not suffer them to be buried, or, which was their manner of burying, to be burnt. Whereupon he speaks to Him in these words:

> *Hos*, Cæsar, *populos si nunc non usserit Ignis,*
> *Uret cum Terris, uret cum gurgite Ponti.*
> *Communis mundo superest Rogus, Ossibus astra*
> *Misturus. Quocunque Tuam Fortuna vocabit,*
> *Hæ quoque eunt Animæ; non altiùs ibis in auras,*
> *Non meliore loco Stygiâ sub nocte jacebis.*
> *Libera fortuna Mors est: Capit omnia Tellus*
> *Quæ genuit: Cælo tegitur Qui non habet urnam.*

Cæsar,

> *If now these Bodies want their fire and urn,*
> *At last, with the whole Globe, they'l surely burn.*
> *The World expects one general Fire: and Thou*
> *Must go where these poor Souls are wand'ring now.*
> *Thou'l reach no higher, in th' Ethereal plain,*
> *Nor 'mongst the shades a better place obtain.*
> *Death equals all: And He that has not room*
> *To make a Grave, Heav'ns Vault shall be his Tomb.*

These are mortifying thoughts to ambitious Spirits. And surely our own Mortality, and the Mortality of the World it self, may be enough to convince all considering Men, That, *Vanity of Vanities, all is Vanity under the Sun*: any otherwise than as they relate to a better Life.

312

THE
THEORY
OF THE
EARTH:

Containing an Account

OF THE

Original of the Earth,

AND OF ALL THE

GENERAL CHANGES

Which it hath already undergone,

OR

IS TO UNDERGO,

Till the CONSUMMATION of all Things.

THE FOURTH BOOK,

Concerning the NEW HEAVENS *and* NEW EARTH,

AND

Concerning the CONSUMMATION *of all* Things.

LONDON,

Printed by *R. Norton*, for *Walter Kettilby*, at the Bishop's-
Head in St. *Paul's* Church-Yard. 1690.

PREFACE
TO THE
READER

YOU see it is still my lot, to travel into New Worlds: having never found any great satisfaction in this. As an active people leaves their habitations in a barren soil, to try if they can make their fortune better elsewhere. I first lookt backwards, and waded through the Deluge, into the Primæval World: to see how they liv'd there, and how Nature stood in that original constitution. Now I am going forwards, to view the New Heavens and New Earth, that will be after the Conflagration. But, Gentle Reader, let me not take you any further, if you be weary. I do not love a querulous Companion. Unless your Genius therefore press you forwards, chuse rather to rest here, and be content with that part of the Theory which you have seen already. Is it not fair, to have followed Nature so far as to have seen her twice in her ruines? Why should we still pursue her, even after death and dissolution, into dark and remote Futurities? To whom therefore such disquisitions seem needless, or over-curious, let them rest here; and leave the remainder of this Work, which is a PROPHECY concerning the STATE of things after the Conflagration, to those that are of a disposition suited to such studies and enquiries.

Not that any part of this Theory requires much Learning, Art. or Science, to be Master of it; But a love and thirst after Truth, freedom of Judgment, and a resignation of our Understandings to clear Evidence, let it carry us which way it will. An honest English Reader that looks only at the Sence as it lies before him, and neither considers not cares whether it be New or Old, so it be true, may be a more competent Judge than a great Scholar full of his own Notions, and puff'd up with the opinion of his mighty knowledge. For such men think they cannot in honour own any thing to be true, which they did not know before. To be taught any new knowledge, is to confess their former ignorance; and that lessens them in their own opinion, and, as they think, in the opinion of the World; which are both uneasie reflections to them. Neither must we depend upon age only for soundness of Judgment: We seldom change our Opinions after threescore: especially if they be leading Opinions. It is then too late, we think, to begin the World again; and as we grow old, the Heart contracts, and cannot open wide enough to take in a great thought.

The Spheres of mens Understandings are as different, as Prospects upon the Earth. Some stand upon a Rock or a Mountain, and see far round about; Others are in an hollow, or in a Cave, and have no prospect at all. Some men consider nothing but what is present to their Senses: Others extend their thoughts both to what is past and what is future. And yet the fairest prospect in this Life is not to be compar'd to the least we shall have in another. Our clearest day here, is misty and hazy: We see not far, and what we do see is in a bad light. But when we have got better Bodies *in the first Resurrection, whereof we are going to Treat; better Senses and a better Understanding, a clearer light and an higher station, our Horizon will be enlarg'd every way, both as to the Natural World and as to the Intellectual.*

Two of the greatest Speculations that we are capable of in this Life, are, in my Opinion, The REVOLUTION OF WORLDS, and the REVOLUTION OF SOULS; one for the Material World, and the other for the Intellectual. Towards the former of these Our Theory is an Essay: and in this our Planet, (which I hope to conduct into a Fix'd Star, before I have done with it) we give an instance of what may be in other Planets. 'Tis true, we look to our rise no higher than the Chaos: because that was a known principle, and we were not willing to amuse the Reader with too many strange Stories: as that, I am sure, would have been thought one, TO HAVE brought this Earth from a Fix'd Star, and then carried it up again into the same Sphere. Which yet I believe, is the true circle of Natural Providence.

As to the Revolution of Souls, the footsteps of that Speculation are more obscure than of the former. For tho' we are assur'd by Scripture, that all good Souls will at length have Celestial Bodies; yet, that this is a returning to a Primitive State, or to what they had at their first Creation, that, Scripture has not acquainted us with. It tells us indeed that Angels fell from their Primitive Celestial Glory; and consequently we might be capable of a lapse as well as they, if we had been in that high condition with them. But that we ever were there, is not declared to us by any revelation. Reason and Morality would indeed suggest to us, that an innocent Soul, fresh and pure from the hands of its Maker, could not be immediately cast into Prison, before it had, by any act of its own Will, or any use of its own Understanding, committed either error or sin. I call this Body a Prison, both because it is a confinement and restraint upon our best Faculties and Capacities, and is also the seat of diseases and loathsomness; and, as prisons use to do, commonly tends more to debauch mens Natures, than to improve them.

But tho' we cannot certainly tell under what circumstances humane Souls were plac'd at first, yet all Antiquity agrees, Oriental and Occidental, concerning their pre-existence in general, in respect of these mortal Bodies. And our Saviour never reproaches or corrects the Jews, when they speak upon that supposition, Luk. 9. 18, Joh. 3. 13. & 6. *19. Joh. 9. 2. Besides, it seems to me beyond all controversie, that the Soul of the* 38. & 62. & 17. *Messiah did exist before the Incarnation, and voluntarily descended from Heaven to* 5. *take upon it a Mortal Body. And tho' it does not appear that all humane Souls were at first plac'd in Glory, yet, from the example of our Saviour, we see something greater in them: Namely, a capacity to be united to the Godhead. And what is possible to one, is possible to more. But these thoughts are too high for us: while we find our selves united to nothing, but diseased bodies and houses of clay.*

The greatest fault we can commit in such Speculations, is to be over-positive and Dogmatical. To be inquisitive into the ways of Providence and the works of God, is so far from being a fault, that it is our greatest perfection; We cultivate the highest principles and best inclinations of our Nature, while we are thus employ'd: and 'tis littleness or secularity of Spirit, that is the greatest Enemy to Contemplation. Those that would have a true contempt of this World, must suffer the Soul to be sometimes upon the Wing, and to raise her self above the sight of this little dark Point, which we now inhabit. Give her a large and free prospect of the immensity of God's works, and of his inexhausted wisdom and goodness, if you would make her Great and Good As the Poet said in his Rapture,

Give me a Soul so great, so high,
Let her dimensions stretch the Skie.
That comprehends within a thought,
The whole extent 'twixt God and Nought.
And from the World's first birth and date,
Its Life and Death can calculate:
With all th' adventures that shall pass,
To ev'ry Atome of the Mass.

But let Her be as GOOD as GREAT,
Her highest Throne a Mercy-Seat.
Soft and dissolving like a Cloud,
Losing her self in doing good.
A Cloud that leaves its place above,
Rather than dry, and useless move:
Falls in a showre upon the Earth,
And gives ten thousand Seeds a birth.
Hangs on the Flow'rs, and infant Plants,
Sucks not their Sweets, but feeds their Wants.
So let this mighty Mind diffuse
All that's her own to others use;
And free from private ends, retain
Nothing of SELF, but a bare Name.

THE
THEORY
OF THE
EARTH

BOOK IV
Concerning the new Heavens and new Earth,
AND
Concerning the Consummation of all things.

CHAPTER I

THE INTRODUCTION

*That the World will not be annihilated in the last Fire. That we are to expect,
according to Scripture and the Christian doctrine, New Heavens and a new
Earth, when these are dissolv'd or burnt up.*

WE are now so far advanc'd in the Theory of the Earth, as to have seen the
End of two Worlds: One destroy'd by Water, and another by Fire. It
remains onely to consider, whether we be yet come to the final period of Nature:
The last Scene of all things, and consequently the utmost bound of our enquiries.
Or, whether Providence, which is inexhausted in wisdom and goodness, will raise
up, from this dead Mass, New Heavens and a new Earth. Another habitable
World, better and more perfect than that which was destroyed. That, as the
first World began with a Paradise, and a state of Innocency, so the last may be
a kind of Renovation of that happy state; whose Inhabitants shall not die, but be
translated to a blessed Immortality.

I know 'tis the opinion of some, that this World will be annihilated, or reduc'd
to nothing, at the Conflagration: and that would put an end to all further enquiries. But whence do they learn this? from Scripture, or Reason, or their
own imagination? What instance or example can they give us, of this they call
Annihilation? Or what place of Scripture can they produce, that says the World,
in the last Fire, shall be reduc'd to nothing? If they have neither instance, nor
proof of what they affirm, 'tis an empty Imagination of their own: neither agreeable to Philosophy, nor Divinity. Fire does not consume any substance: It
changes the form and qualities of it, but the matter remains. And if the design
had been *Annihilation*, the employing of fire would have been of no use or effect.
For smoak and ashes are at as great a distance from *Nothing*, as the bodies themselves out of which they are made. But these Authors seem to have but a small
tincture of Philosophy, and therefore it will be more proper to confute their
opinion from the words of Scripture; which hath left us sufficient evidence, that
another World will succeed after the Conflagration of that we now inhabit.

The Prophets, both of the Old and New Testament, have left us their predictions concerning *New Heavens and a New Earth*. So says the Prophet *Isaiah*, ch. 65. 17. *Behold I create New Heavens and a New Earth, and the former shall not be remembred, or come into mind*. As not worthy our thoughts, in comparison of those that will arise when these pass away. So the Prophet St. *John*, in his *Apocalypse*, when he was come to the end of this World, says, *And I saw a new heaven and a new earth. For the first heaven and the first earth were passed away, and there was no more Sea*. Where he does not only give us an account of a New Heaven and a New Earth, in general: but also gives a distinctive character of the *New Earth*: that it shall have *no Sea*. And in the 5th ver. He that sat upon the Throne, says, *Behold I make all things New*; which, consider'd with the antecedents and consequents, cannot be otherwise understood than of a New World.

Apoc. 21. 1.

But some men make evasions here as to the words of the Prophets, and say they are to be understood in a figurate and allegorical sence: and to be applyed to the times of the Gospel, either at first or towards the latter end of the World. So as this *New Heaven and New Earth* signifie only a great change in the moral World. But how can that be, seeing St. *John* places them after the end of the World: and the Prophet *Isaiah* connects such things with his New Heavens and New Earth, as are not competible to the present state of Nature? However to avoid all shuffling and tergiversation in this point, let us appeal to St. *Peter*, who uses a plain literal style, and discourses down-right concerning the Natural World. In his 2d *Epist.* and 3d *chap.* when he had foretold and explained the Future Conflagration, he adds, But we expect *New Heavens and a New Earth according to his promises*. These Promises were made by the Prophets: and this gives us full authority to interpret their *New Heavens and New Earth* to be after the *Conflagration*. St. *Peter*, when he had describ'd the Dissolution of the World in the last Fire, in full and emphatical terms, as *the passing away of the Heavens with a noise: the melting of the Elements, and burning up all the works of the Earth:* he subjoyns, *Nevertheless*, notwithstanding this total dissolution of the present World, *We, according to his promises, look for new heavens and a new earth: wherein dwelleth Righteousness*. As if the Apostle should have said, Notwithstanding this strange and violent dissolution of the present Heavens and Earth, which I have described to you, we do not at all distrust God's Promises concerning New Heavens and a New Earth, that are to succeed these, and to be the seat of the Righteous.

ch. 65.

Here's no room for Allegories or allegorical expositions: unless you will make the Conflagration of the World an Allegory. For, as Heavens and Earth were destroy'd, so Heavens and Earth are restored: and if in the first place you understand the natural material World, you must also understand it in the second place: They are both Allegories, or neither. But to make the Conflagration an Allegory, is not only to contradict St. *Peter*, but all Antiquity, Sacred or Prophane. And I desire no more assurance that we shall have New Heavens and a New Earth, in a literal Sence, than we have that the present Heavens and Earth shall be destroyed in a literal Sence, and by material Fire. Let it therefore rest upon that issue, as to this first evidence and argument from Scripture.

Some will fancy, it may be, that we shall have New Heavens and Earth; and yet that these shall be annihilated; They would have These first reduc'd to nothing, and then others created, spick and span New, out of nothing. But why so, pray, what's the humour of that? lest Omnipotency should want employment, you would have it do, and undo, and do again. As if new-made Matter, like new Clothes, or new Furniture, had a better Gloss, and was more creditable. Matter never wears: as fine Gold, melt it down never so often, it loses nothing of its quantity. The substance of the World is the same, burnt or unburnt: and is of the same Value and Virtue, New or Old: and we must not multiply the actions of Omnipotency without necessity. God does not make, or unmake things, to try experiments: He knows before hand the utmost capacities of every thing, and does no vain or superfluous work. Such imaginations as these proceed only from want of true Philosophy, or the true knowledge of the Nature of God and of his Works; which should always be carefully attended to, in such Speculations as concern the Natural World. But to proceed in our Subject.

If they suppose part of the World to be annihilated, and to continue so, they Philosophize still worse and worse. How high shall this Annihilation reach? Shall the Sun, Moon, and Stars be reduc'd to nothing? but what have They done, that they should undergo so hard a fate? must they be turn'd out of Being for our faults? The whole material Universe will not be Annihilated at this bout, for we are to have Bodies after the Resurrection, and to live in Heaven. How much of the Universe then will you leave standing: or how shall it subsist with this great *Vacuum* in the heart of it? This shell of a World is but the fiction of an empty Brain: For God and Nature in their works never admit of such gaping vacuities and emptinesses.

If we consult Scripture again, we shall find that that makes mention of a *Restitution* and *Reviviscency* of all things: at the end of the World, or at the Coming of our Saviour. St. *Peter*, whose doctrine we have hitherto followed, in his Sermon to the *Jews* after our Saviour's Ascension, tells them that He will come again, and that there will be then a *Restitution of all things:* such as was promised by the Prophets. *The Heavens*, says he, *must receive him until the time of Restitution of all things: which God hath spoken by the mouth of his holy Prophets, since the world began.* If we compare this passage of St. *Peter*'s, with that which we alledged before out of his second Epistle, it can scarce be doubted but that he refers to the same Promises in both places: and what he there calls a *New Heaven* and a *New Earth*, he calls here a *Restitution of all things.* For the Heavens and the Earth comprehend all, and both these are but different phrases for the Renovation of the World. This gives us also light how to understand what our Saviour calls the *Regeneration* or *Reviviscency*, when he shall sit upon his Throne of Glory, and will reward his followers an hundred fold, for all their losses in this World: besides Everlasting Life as the Crown of all. I know, in our English Translation, we separate *the Regeneration* from *sitting upon his Throne:* but without any warrant from the Original. And seeing our Saviour speaks here of Bodily goods, and seems to distinguish them from *everlasting life*, which is to be the final reward of his Followers, This *Regeneration* seems to belong to his Second

Act. 3.

ver. 21.

Matt. 19. 28, 29.

coming, when the World shall be renew'd or regenerated: and the Righteous shall possess the Earth.

Other places of Scripture that foretel the fate of this material World, represent it always as a *Change*, not as an *Annihilation*. St. *Paul* says, *The Figure of this World passes away*: 1 Cor. 7. 31. The form, fashion, and disposition of its parts: but the substance still remains. As a Body that is melted down and dissolv'd, the Form perishes, but the Matter is not destroy'd. And the Psalmist says, The Heavens and the Earth shall be *chang'd*: which answers to this Transformation we speak of. The same Apostle, in the Eight Chapter to the *Romans*, shows also that this *change* shall be, and shall be for the better: and calls it a *Deliverance of the Creation from vanity and corruption:* and a participation of the *glorious liberty of the Children of God*. Being a sort of *Redemption*, as they have a *Redemption of their Bodies*.

Psal. 102. 26.

Ver. 21, 22, 23, 24.

But, seeing the *Renovation* of the World is a Doctrine generally receiv'd, both by ancient and modern Authors, as we shall have occasion to show hereafter: We need add no more, in this place, for confirmation of it. Some Men are willing to throw all things into a state of *Nothing* at the Conflagration, and bury them there, that they may not be oblig'd to give an account of that state of things, that is to succeed it. Those who think themselves bound in honour, to know every thing in Theology that is knowable: and find it uneasie to answer such questions and speculations, as would arise upon their admitting a new World, think it more adviseable to stifle it in the birth, and so to bound all knowledge at the Conflagration. But surely, so far as Reason or Scripture lead us, we may and ought to follow: otherwise we should be ungrateful to Providence, that sent us those Guides. Provided, we be always duly sensible of our own weakness: and, according to the difficulty of the subject, and the measure of light that falls upon it, proceed with that modesty and ingenuity, that becomes such fallible enquirers after Truth, as we are. And this rule I desire to prescribe to my self, as in all others Writings, so especially in this: where, tho' I look upon the principal Conclusions as fully prov'd, there are several particulars, that are rather propos'd to examination, than positively asserted.

CHAPTER II

The Birth of the new Heavens and the new Earth, from the second Chaos, or the remains of the old World. The form, order, and qualities of the new Earth, according to Reason and Scripture.

HAVING prov'd from Scripture, that we are to expect *New Heavens*, and a *New Earth*, after the Conflagration; it would be some pleasure and satisfaction to see how this new Frame will arise: and what foundation there is in Nature for the accomplishment of these promises. For, tho' the Divine Power be not bound to all the Laws of Nature, but may dispence with them when there is a necessity; yet it is an ease to us in our belief, when we see them both conspire in the same effect. And in order to this, we must consider in what posture we left the demolish'd World: what hopes there is of a Restauration. And we are not to be discourag'd, because we see things at present wrapt up in a confus'd Mass: for, according to the methods of Nature and Providence, in that dark Womb usually are the seeds and rudiments of an Embryo-World.

Neither is there, possibly, so great a confusion in this Mass, as we imagine. The Heart and interiour Body of the Earth is still entire: and that part of it that is consum'd by the fire, will be divided, of its own accord, into two Regions.

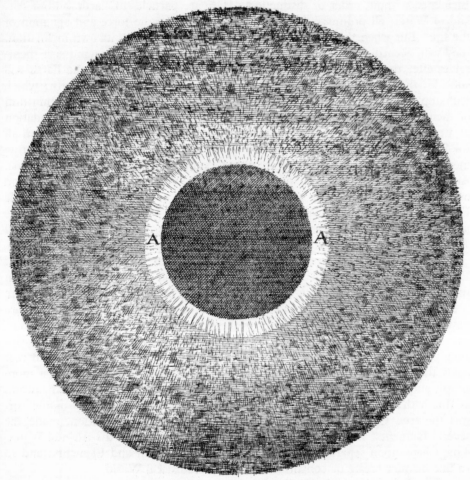

Fig. 1

What is dissolv'd and melted, being the heaviest, will descend as low as it can: and cover and enclose the kernel of the Earth round about, as a molten Sea or Abyss: according as is explain'd and set down in the precedent Book. But what is more light and volatile, will float in the Air: as fumes, smoak, exhalations, vapours of Water, and whatsoever terrestrial parts can be elevated and supported by the strength of fire. These all mingled together, of different sizes, figures, and motions, will constitute an opake Cloud, or thick region of darkness round the Earth: So as the Globe of the Earth, with its Atmosphere, after the Conflagration is finish'd, will stand in the form represented in this Scheme.

Now as to the lower of these two regions, the region of melted matter, A. A. we shall have little occasion to take notice of it: seeing it will contribute nothing to the formation of the new World. But the upper region, or all above that Orb of fire, is the true draught of a Chaos: or a mixture and confusion of all the Elements, without order or distinction. Here are particles of Earth, and of Air, and of Water, all promiscuously jumbled together, by the force and agitation of the fire. But when that force ceases, and every one is left to its own inclination, they will, according to their different degrees of gravity, separate and sort themselves after this manner. First, the heaviest and grossest parts of the Earth will subside; then the watery parts will follow; then a lighter sort of Earth; which will stop and rest upon the Surface of the Water, and compose there a thin film or membrane; this membrane or tender Orb is the first rudiment or foundation of a new habitable Earth. For according as terrestrial parts fall upon it, from all the regions and heighths of the Atmosphere, or of the Chaos, this Orb will grow more firm, strong, and immoveable: able to support it self and Inhabitants too. And having in it all the Principles of a fruitful Soil, whether for the production of Plants or of Animals, it will want no property or character of an habitable Earth. And particularly, will become such an Earth, and of such a form, as the first Paradisiacal Earth was. Which hath been fully describ'd in the first and second Books of this Theory.

There is no occasion of examining more accurately the formation of this Second Earth, seeing it is so much the same with that of the First; which is set down fully and distinctly in the *5th* Chapter of the first Book of this Theory. Nature here repeats the same work, and in the same method; onely the materials are now a little more refin'd and purg'd by the fire. They both rise out of a Chaos, and That, in effect, the same in both cases; For though in forming the first Earth, I suppos'd the Chaos or confus'd Mass to reach down to the Center, I did that onely for the ease of our imagination; that so the whole Mass might appear more simple and uniform. But in reality, that Chaos had a solid kernel of Earth within, as this hath; and that matter which fluctuated above in the regions of the Air, was the true Chaos, whose parts, when they came to a separation, made the several Elements, and the form of an habitable Earth betwixt the Air and Water. This Chaos upon separation, will fall into the same form and Elements: and so in like manner create or constitute a second Paradisiacal World.

I say a *Paradisiacal* World: For it appears plainly, that this new-form'd Earth must agree with that Primigenial Earth, in the two principal and fundamental properties. First, It is of an even, entire, uniform and regular Surface, without Mountains or Sea. Secondly, That it hath a straight and regular situation to the Sun, and the *Axis* of the *Ecliptick*. From the manner of its formation, it appears manifestly, that it must be of an even and regular Surface. For the Orb of liquid fire, upon which the first descent was made, being smooth and uniform every where, the matter that fell upon it would take the same form and mould. And so the second or third Region, that were superinduc'd, would still imitate the fashion of the first: there being no cause or occasion of any inequality. Then as to the situation of its *Axis*, this uniformity of figure would determine the center of its gravity to be exactly in the middle, and consequently there would be no inclination of one Pole more than another to the general center of its motion; But, upon a free libration in the liquid Air, its *Axis* would lie parallel with the *Axis* of the Ecliptick where it moves. But these things having been deduc'd more fully in the second Book about *Paradise* and *the Primigenial Earth*, they need no further explication in this place.

If Scripture had left us several distinct Characters of the *New Heavens*, and the *New Earth*, we might, by compare with those, have made a full proof of our Hypothesis. One indeed St. *John* hath left us in very express terms, *There was no Sea there*, He says. His words are these: *And I saw a New Heaven, and a New Earth: for the first Heaven and the first Earth were passed away; AND THERE WAS NO MORE SEA.* This character is very particular, and you see it exactly answers to our Hypothesis: for in the new-form'd Earth, the Sea is cover'd and inconspicuous: being an Abyss, not a Sea, and wholly lodg'd in the Womb of the Earth. And this one Character, being inexplicable upon any other supposition, and very different from the present Earth, makes it a strong presumption that we have hit upon the true model of the New Heavens and New Earth which St. *John* saw.

To this sight of the New Heavens and New Earth, St. *John* immediately subjoyns the sight of the *New Jerusalem*, ver. 2. as being contemporary, and in some respects the same thing. 'Tis true, the Characters of the New *Jerusalem* in these two last Chapters of the *Apocalypse*, are very hard to be understood: some of them being incompetible to a *Terrestrial* state, and some of them to a *Celestial*; so as it seems to me very reasonable to suppose, that the New *Jerusalem* spoken of by St. *John*, is twofold: That which he saw himself, ver. 2. and that which the Angel shewed him afterwards, ver. 9. For I do not see what need there was of an *Angel*, and of *taking him up into a great and high mountain*, only to shew him that which he had seen before, at the foot of the Mountain. However we are to consider in this place the Terrestrial New *Jerusalem* only, or that which is in the New Heavens and New Earth. And as St. *John* hath joyned these two together, so the Prophet *Isaiah* had done the same thing before; when he had promised *new Heavens and a new Earth*, he calls them, under another name, *Jerusalem*: and they both use the same character in effect, in the description of their *Jerusalem*. *Isaiah* says, *And I will rejoyce in Jerusalem, and joy in my people: and the voice of weeping shall be no more heard in her, nor the voice of crying.* St. *John* says also in his Jerusalem, *God shall dwell with them, and they shall be his people: And he shall wipe away all tears from their eyes: and there shall be no more death, neither sorrow, nor crying, neither shall there be any more pain.* Now in both these Prophets, when they treat upon this subject, we find they make frequent allusions to Paradise and a Paradisiacal state; so as that may be justly taken as a Scripture-Character of the *New Heavens and the New Earth*. The Prophet *Isaiah* seems

ch. 65. 17, 18.

ver. 19.
Apoc. 21. 3, 4.

325

plainly to point at a Paradisiacal state, throughout that Chapter, by an universal innocency, and harmlessness of animals; and peace, plenty, health, longævity or immortality of the inhabitants. St. *John* also hath several allusions to Paradise, in those two Chapters where he describes the New Jerusalem. And in his discourse to the seven Churches, in one place (ch. 2. 7.) *To him that overcometh* is promised *to eat of the tree of life, which is in the midst of the Paradise of God.* And in another place (ch. 3. 12.) *to him that overcometh* is promised, *to have the name of the New Jerusalem writ upon him.* These I take to be the same thing, and the same reward of Christian Victors, The *New Jerusalem* or the New Heavens and New Earth, and the *Paradise of God.* Now this being the general Character of the New Earth, That it is *Paradisiacal*: and the particular Character, That it *hath no Sea*: and both these agreeing with our Hypothesis, as apparently deducible from those principles and that manner of its formation which we have set down: We cannot but allow, that the Holy Scriptures and the Natural Theory agree in their Testimony, as to the conditions and properties of the *New Heavens and New Earth.*

From what hath been said in this and the precedent Chapter, it will not be hard to interpret what St. *Paul* meant by his *Habitable Earth to come:* which is to be subjected to our Saviour and not to the Angels. In the second chapter to the *Hebrews*, ver. 5. he says, *For unto the Angels hath he not put in subjection the WORLD TO COME:* So we read it, but, according to the strictest and plainest Translation, it should be *The habitable Earth to come.* Now what Earth is this, where our Saviour is absolute Soveraign: and where the Government is neither Humane, nor Angelical, but peculiarly Theocratical? In the first place, this cannot be the present World or the present Earth, because the Apostle calls it *Future*, or the *Earth to come.* Nor can it be understood of the days of the Gospel: seeing the Apostle acknowledges, *ver.* 8. that this subjection, whereof he speaks, is not yet made. And seeing Antichrist will not finally be destroy'd till the appearance of our Saviour, (2 *Thess.* 2. 8.) nor Satan bound, while Antichrist is in power: during the reign of these two, (who are the Rulers of the darkness of the World) our Saviour cannot properly be said to begin his reign here. 'Tis true, He exercises his Providence over his Church, and secures it from being destroy'd: He can, by a power paramount, stop the rage either of Satan or Antichrist; *Hitherto shall you go and no further.* As sometimes when he was upon Earth, he exerted a Divine Power, which yet did not destroy his state of Humiliation; so he interposes now when he thinks fit, but he does not finally take the power out of the hands of his Enemies, nor out of the hands of the Kings of the Earth. The *Kingdom is not deliver'd up to him,* and all *dominion, and power*; that all *Tongues and Nations should serve him.* For St. *Paul* can mean no less in this place than that Kingdom in *Daniel*: Seeing he calls it *putting all things in subjection under his feet,* and says that it is not yet done. Upon this account also, as well as others, our Saviour might truly say to *Pilate* (*Joh.* 18. 36.) *my kingdom is not of this World.* And to his Disciples, *The Son of man came not to be ministred unto, but to minister, Matt.* 20. 28. When he comes to receive his Kingdom, he comes in the clouds of Heaven (*Dan.* 7. 13, 14.) not in the womb of a Virgin. He comes

ch. 21. & *ch.* 22.

Τὴν οἰκουμένην
ᾗ μέλλουσαν.
πατὴρ τοῦ
μέλλονος αἰῶνος
Isa. 9. 6.

Ephes. 6. 12.

ch. 7. 13, 25, 26.
Hebr. 2. 8.

with the equipage of a King and Conqueror; with thousands and ten thousands of Angels: not in the form of a Servant, or of a weak Infant; as he did at his first coming.

Neither can this *World to come,* or this *Earth to come,* be understood of the Kingdom of Heaven. For the Greek word will not bear that sence, nor is it ever us'd in Scripture for *Heaven,* Besides, the Kingdom of Heaven, when spoken of as *future,* is not properly till the last resurrection and final judgment. Whereas *This World to come,* which our Saviour is to govern, must be before that time, and will then expire. For all his Government, as to this World, expires at the day of Judgment, and *he will then deliver up the kingdom into the hands of his father: that he may be all in all.* Having reigned first himself, and *put down all rule and all authority and power.* So that St. *Paul,* in these two places of his Epistles, refers plainly to the same time and the same reign of Christ: which must be in a *future World,* and before the *day of Judgment*: and therefore according to our deductions, in the New Heavens and the New Earth.

1 *Cor.* 15. 24, *&c.*

CHAPTER III

Concerning the Inhabitants of the New Earth. That Natural Reason cannot determine this point. That according to Scripture; The Sons of the first Resurrection, or the Heirs of the Millennium, *are to be the Inhabitants of the New Earth. The Testimony of the Philosophers, and of the Christian Fathers, for the Renovation of the World. The first Proposition laid down.*

THUS we have setled the true notion, according to Reason and Scripture, of the *New Heavens* and *New Earth.* But where are the Inhabitants, you'l say? You have taken the pains to make us a New World, and now that it is made, it must stand empty. When the first World was destroyed, there were eight persons preserv'd, with a Set of living Creatures of every kind, as a Seminary or foundation of another World: But the Fire, it seems, is more merciless than the Water; for in this destruction of the World, it does not appear that there is one living Soul left, of any sort, upon the face of the Earth. No hopes of posterity, nor of any continuation of Mankind, in the usual way of propagation. And Fire is a barren Element, that breeds no living Creatures in it, nor hath any nourishment proper for their food or sustenance.

We are perfectly at a loss, therefore, so far as I see, for a new race of Mankind, or how to people this new-form'd World. The Inhabitants, if ever there be any, must either come from Heaven, or spring from the Earth: There are but these two ways. But *Natural Reason* can determine neither of these: sees no tract to follow in these unbeaten paths, nor can advance one step further. Farewel then, dear Friend, I must take another Guide: and leave you here, as *Moses* upon Mount *Pisgah,* only to look into that Land, which you cannot enter. I acknowledge the good service you have done, and what a faithful Companion you have been, in a long journey; from the beginning of the World to this hour, in a tract of time of six thousand years. We have travel'd together through the dark regions of a First and Second *Chaos*: seen the World twice shipwrackt. Neither Water, nor Fire, could separate us. But now you must give place to other Guides.

Welcome, *Holy Scriptures*, The Oracles of God, a Light shining in darkness, a Treasury of hidden knowledge, and, where *humane faculties* cannot reach, a seasonable help and supply to their defects. We are now come to the utmost bounds of their dominion: They have made us a New World, but, how it shall be inhabited, they cannot tell: know nothing of the History or affairs of it. This we must learn from other Masters, inspir'd with the knowledge of things to come. And such Masters we know none, but the holy Prophets and Apostles. We must therefore now put our selves wholly under their conduct and instruction, and from them only receive our information concerning the moral state of the future habitable Earth.

Isa. 45. 18.

In the first place therefore, The Prophet *Isaiah* tells us, as a preparation to our further enquiries, *The Lord God created the Heavens, God himself that formed the Earth, He created it not in vain, he formed it to be inhabited*. This is true, both of the present Earth and the *Future*, and of every habitable World whatsoever. For to what purpose is it made habitable, if not to be inhabited? That would be, as if a man should manure, and plough, and every way prepare his ground for seed, but never sow it. We do not build houses that they should stand empty, but look out for Tenants as fast as we can; as soon as they are made ready, and become Tenantable. But if man could do things in vain and without use or design, yet God and Nature never do any thing *in vain*; much less so great a work as the making of a World. Which if it were in vain, would comprehend ten thousand vanities or useless preparations in it. *We* may therefore in the first place, safely conclude, *That the New Earth will be inhabited*.

But *by whom will it be inhabited?* This makes the second enquiry. St. *Peter* answers this question for us, and with a particular application to this very subject of the New Heavens and New Earth. They shall be inhabited, he says, by the *Just* or the *Righteous*. His words, which we cited before, are these. When he had describ'd the Conflagration of the World, he adds, But we *expect new Heavens and a new Earth, WHEREIN DWELLETH RIGHTEOUSNESS*. By *righteousness* here, it is generally agreed must be understood Righteous Persons. For Righteousness cannot be without righteous Persons: It cannot hang upon Trees, or grow out of the ground; 'Tis the endowment of reasonable Creatures. And these righteous Persons are eminently such, and therefore call'd Righteousness in the abstract, or purely righteous without mixture of Vice.

Apoc. 21. 27.

So we have found Inhabitants for the New Earth: Persons of an high and noble Character. Like those describ'd by St. *Peter*, (1 Epist. 2. 9.) *A chosen generation, a royal Priesthood, an holy Nation, a peculiar People*. As if into that World, as into St. *John*'s *New Jerusalem*, nothing impure or unrighteous was to be admitted. These being then the happy and holy Inhabitants: The next enquiry is, *Whence do they come?* From what off-spring, or from what Original? We noted before, that there was no remnant of Mankind left at the Conflagration, as there was at the Deluge: nor any hopes of a Restauration that way. Shall we then imagine that these new Inhabitants are a Colony wafted over from some

328

neighbouring World: as from the Moon, or Mercury, or some of the higher Planets. You may imagine what you please, but that seems to me not imaginary onely but impracticable; And that the Inhabitants of those Planets are Persons of so great accomplishments, is more than I know: but I am sure they are not the Persons here understood. For these must be such as inhabited this Earth before. WE look for new Heavens and new Earth, says the Apostle: Surely to have some share and interest in them; otherwise there would be no comfort in that expectation. And the Prophet *Isaiah* said before, I create new Heavens and a new Earth, and the former shall come no more into remembrance: But be *YOU glad and rejoyce for ever in that which I create*. The truth is, none can have so good pretensions to this spot of ground we call the Earth, as the Sons of Men, seeing they once possest it. And if it be restor'd again, 'tis their propriety and inheritance. But 'tis not Mankind in general that must possess this new World, but the *Israel of God*, according to the Prophet *Isaiah*; or the *Just*, according to St. *Peter*. And especially those that have suffer'd for the sake of their Religion. For this is that *Palingenesia*, as we noted before, that *Renovation*, or *Regeneration* of all things, where our Saviour says, Those, that suffer loss for his sake, shall be recompenced: *Matt.* 19. 28. 29.

But they must then be raised from the Dead. For all Mankind was destroy'd at the Conflagration: and there is no resource for them any other way, than by a Resurrection. 'Tis true: and St. *John* gives us a fair occasion to make this supposition, *That* there will be some raised from the Dead, before the General Day of Judgment. For he plainly distinguisheth of a *First* and *Second* Resurrection, and makes the first to be a thousand Years before the second, and before the general Day of Judgment. Now, if there be truly and really a two-fold Resurrection, as St. *John* tells us; and at a thousand Years distance from one another: It may be very rationally presum'd, that Those that are raised in the first Resurrection, are those *Just* that will inhabit the *new Heavens and new Earth*. Or whom our Saviour promis'd to reward in the Renovation of the World.

Apoc. 20.

For otherwise, who are those *Just* that shall inhabit the *new Earth*, and whence do they come? Or when is that Restauration which our Saviour speaks of, wherein those that suffer'd for the sake of the Gospel shall be rewarded? St. *John* says, the *Martyrs*, at this first Resurrection, shall live again and reign with Christ. Which seems to be the reward promis'd by our Saviour, to those that suffer'd for his sake: and the same Persons in both places. *And I saw the Souls of them* says St. *John, that were beheaded for the witness of Jesus, and for the Word of God: and which had not worshipped the Beast,* &c. *and They lived and reigned with Christ a thousand years.* These, I say, seem to be the same Persons to whom Christ had before promis'd and appropriated a particular reward. And this reward of theirs, or this Reign of theirs, is upon *Earth*: upon some Earth, new or old: not in Heaven. For, besides that we read nothing of their Ascension into Heaven after their Resurrection: There are several marks that shew it must necessarily be understood of a state upon Earth. For *Gog* and *Magog* came from the *four quarters of the Earth*, and besieged the *Camp of the Saints, and the beloved City*. That Camp and that City therefore were upon the Earth. And *fire*

Apoc. 20. 4.

Ver. 9.

came down from Heaven and devoured them. If it came down from Heaven, it came upon the Earth. Furthermore, those Persons that are rais'd from the Dead, Ver. 6. are said to be *Priests of God and of Christ, and to reign with him a thousand years.* Now these must be the same Persons with the *Priests* and *Kings,* mention'd in Ver. 10. the Fifth Chapter: which are there said expresly *to reign upon Earth,* or that they *should reign upon Earth.* It remains therefore onely to determine, *What Earth* this is, where the *Sons of the first Resurrection* will live and reign. It cannot be the present Earth, in the same state, and under the same circumstances it is now. For what happiness or priviledge would that be, to be call'd back into a mortal life, under the necessities and inconveniences of sickly Bodies, and an incommodious World? such as the present state of mortality is, and must continue to be, till some change be made in Nature. We may be sure therefore, that a change will be made in Nature before that time, and that the state they are rais'd into, and the Earth they are to inhabit, will be, at least, *Paradisiacal:* And consequently can be no other than the *new Heavens* and *new Earth,* which we are to expect after the Conflagration.

From these Considerations, there is a great fairness to conclude, both as to the Characters of the Persons, and of the place or state, that *the Sons of the first Resurrection,* will be Inhabitants of the *New Earth,* and reign there with Christ a thousand years. But seeing this is one of the principal and peculiar Conclusions of this Discourse, and bears a great part in this last Book of the Theory of the Earth, it will deserve a more full explication, and a more ample proof, to make it out. We must therefore take a greater compass in our discourse, and give a full account of that State which is usually call'd the *Millennium*: The Reign of the Saints a thousand years, or the Kingdom of Christ upon Earth. But before we enter upon this new Subject, give me leave to close our present Argument, about the *Renovation of the World,* with some Testimonies of the Ancient Philosophers, to that purpose. 'Tis plain to me, that there were amongst the Ancients several Traditions, or traditionary conclusions, which they did not raise themselves, by reason and observation, but receiv'd them from an unknown Antiquity. An instance of this is the *Conflagration of the World.* A Doctrine, as ancient, for any thing I know, as the World it self. At least as ancient as we have any Records. And yet none of those Ancients that tell us of it, give any argument to prove it. Neither is it any wonder, for they did not invent it themselves, but receiv'd it from others without proof, by the sole authority of Tradition. In like manner the *Renovation of the World,* which we are now speaking of, is an ancient Doctrine: both amongst the *Greeks* and *Eastern* Philosophers: but they shew us no method *how* the World may be *renew'd,* nor make any proof of its future Renovation; For it was not a discovery which they first made, but receiv'd it, with an implicite faith, from their Masters and Ancestors. And these Traditionary Doctrines were all fore-runners of that Light that was to shine more clearly at the opening of the Christian dispensation; to give a more full account of the fate and revolutions of the Natural World, as well as of the Moral.

The *Jews,* 'tis well known, held the *Renovation* of the World, and a *Sabbath* after six thousand years: according to the Prophecy that was currant amongst them, whereof we have given a larger account in the precedent Book, ch. 5. And

that future state they call'd *Olam Hava,* or the *World to come,* which is the very
same with St. *Paul's Habitable Earth to come, Heb.* 2. 6.   Neither can I easily
believe, that those constitutions of *Moses* that proceed so much upon a *Septenary,*
or the number Seven, and have no ground or reason, in the nature of the thing,
for that particular number: I cannot easily believe, I say, that they are either
accidental or humoursome: without design or signification.   But that they are
typical, or representative of some *Septenary* state, that does eminently deserve
and bear that Character.   *Moses,* in the History of the Creation, makes six days
work, and then a Sabbath.   Then, after six years, he makes a *Sabbath-year*: and
after a Sabbath of years a year of Jubilee, *Levit.* 25.   All these lesser revolutions
seem to me to point at the grand Revolution, the great *Sabbath* or *Jubilee,* after
six Millenaries, which as it answers the type in point of time, so likewise in the
nature and contents of it: Being a state of Rest from all labour and trouble and
servitude: a state of joy and triumph: and a state of *Renovation,* when things are
to return to their first condition and pristine order.   So much for the *Jews.*

    The Heathen Philosophers, both *Greeks* and *Barbarians,* had the same doctrine
of the *Renovation* of the *World,* currant amongst them.   And that under several
names and phrases; as of the *Great Year,* the *Restauration,* the *Mundane periods,*
and such like.   They suppos'd stated and fix'd periods of time, upon expiration
whereof there would always follow some great revolution of the World, and the
face of Nature would be renew'd.   Particularly after the Conflagration, the *Stoicks*
always suppos'd a new World to succeed, or another frame of Nature to be erected
in the room of that which was destroy'd.   And they use the same words and
phrases upon this occasion that Scripture useth; *Chrysippus* calls it *Apocatastasis,*
as St. *Peter* does, *Act.* 3. 21.   *Marcus Antoninus* in his *Meditations* several times
calls it *Palingenesia,* as our Saviour does, *Matt.* 19. 28.   And *Numenius* hath two
Scripture-words, *Resurrection* and *Restitution,* to express this renovation of the
World.   Then as to the *Platonicks,* that Revolution of all things hath commonly
been call'd the *Platonick* year, as if *Plato* had been the first author of that opinion;
But that's a great mistake; he receiv'd it from the *Barbarick* Philosophers, and
particularly from the *Ægyptian* Priests, amongst whom he liv'd several years, to
be instructed in their learning.   But I do not take *Plato* neither to be the first that
brought this doctrine into *Greece:* for, besides that the Sibylls, whose antiquity
we do not well know, sung this Song of old, as we see it copyed from them by
Vigil in his fourth Eclogue: *Pythagoras* taught it before *Plato:* and *Orpheus*
before them both.   And that's as high as the Greek Philosophy reaches.

    The Barbarick Philosophers were more ancient: namely the *Ægyptians, Persians,*
Chaldeans, Indian Brackmans, and other Eastern Nations.   Their Monuments
indeed are in a great measure lost, yet from the remains of them which the *Greeks*
have transcrib'd, and so preserv'd, in their writings, we see plainly they all had
this doctrine of the *Future Renovation.*   And to this day the posterity of the *Brack-*
mans in the East Indies, retain the same notion, *That* the World will be renewed
after the last Fire.   You may see the citations, if you please, for all these Nations,
in the *Latin* Treatise, ch. 5.   Which I thought would be too dry and tedious to
be render'd into English.

הבא עולם
ἡ οἰκουμένη
ἡ μέλλουσα.

Lact. l. 7. *c.* 23.
Euseb. præp. Ev.
l. 7. *c.* 23.

To these Testimonies of the Philosophers of all Ages, for the Future Renovation of the World, we might add the Testimonies of the Christian Fathers: Greek and Latin, ancient and modern. I will only give you a bare List of them, and refer you to the Latin Treatise for the words or the places. Amongst the Greek Fathers, *Justin Martyr, Irenæus, Origen,* The Fathers of the *Council of Nice, Eusebius, Basil*; The two *Cyrills,* of *Jerusalem* and *Alexandria*; The two *Gregorys, Nazianzen* and *Nyssen*; St. *Chrysostom, Zacharias Mitylenensis*; and of later date, *Damascen, Oecumenius, Futhymius,* and others. These have all set their hands and Seals to this doctrine. Of the Latin Fathers, *Tertullian, Lactantius,* St. *Hilary,* St. *Ambrose,* St. *Austin,* St. *Jerome*; and many later Ecclesiastical Authors. These, with the Philosophers before mentioned, I count good authority, Sacred and prophane: which I place here as an out-guard upon Scripture, where our principal force lies. And these three united and acting in conjunction, will be sufficient to secure this first post, and to prove our first Proposition, which is

this: *That after the Conflagration of this World, there will be New Heavens and a New Earth: and that Earth will be inhabited.*

CHAPTER IV

The proof of a Millennium, *or of a blessed Age to come, from Scripture. A view of the Apocalypse, and of the Prophecies of* Daniel, *in reference to this Kingdom of Christ and of his Saints.*

WE have given fair presumptions, if not proofs, in the precedent Chapter, That the Sons of the first Resurrection will be the persons that shall inhabit the *New Earth,* or the World to come. But to make that proof compleat and unexceptionable, I told you it would be necessary to make a larger compass in our discourse, and to examine what is meant by *That Reign with Christ a thousand years,* which is promis'd to the Sons of the *first Resurrection*; by St. *John* in the Apocalypse; and in other places of Scripture is usually call'd the *Kingdom of Christ,* and the reign of the Saints. And by Ecclesiastical Authors, in imitation of St. *John,* it is commonly styled the *Millennium.* We shall indifferently use any of these words or phrases; and examine, First, the truth of the Notion and Opinion; whether in Scripture there be such an happy state promised to the Saints, under the conduct of Christ. And then we will proceed to examine the nature, characters, place and time of it. And I am in hopes when these things are duly discuss'd and stated, you will be satisfied that we have found out the true Inhabitants of the New Heavens and New Earth: and the true mystery of that state which is call'd the *Millennium,* or the Reign of Christ and of his Saints.

We begin with St. *John*; whose words, in the twentieth chapter of the *Apocalypse,* are express, both as to the first Resurrection, and as to the reign of those Saints, that rise, with Christ, for a thousand years. Satan in the mean time being bound, or disabled from doing mischief and seducing mankind, The words of the Prophet

are these: *And I saw an Angel come down from heaven, having the key of the bottomless pit, and a great chain in his hand. And he laid hold on the Dragon, that old*

Serpent, which is the Devil and Satan; and bound him a thousand years. And I saw Thrones, and they sat upon them, and judgment was given unto them: and I saw the Souls of them that were beheaded for the witness of Jesus, and for the word of God, and which had not worshipped the beast, neither his image, neither had received his mark upon their fore-heads, or in their hands; and they lived and reigned with Christ a thousand years. But the rest of the dead lived not again until the thousand years were finished. This is the first Resurrection. Blessed and holy is he that hath part in the first Resurrection: on such the second death hath no power, but they shall be priests of God, and of Christ, and shall reign with him a thousand years. These words do fully express a Resurrection, and a reign with Christ a thousand years. As for that particular space of time, of a *thousand years*, it is not much material to our present purpose: but the Resurrection here spoken of, and the reign with Christ, make the substance of the controversie, and in effect prove all that we enquire after at present. This Resurrection, you see, is call'd the *First Resurrection*, by way of distinction from the second and general Resurrection; which is also taken notice of, and plac'd a thousand years after the first. And both this first Resurrection and the reign of Christ, seem to be appropriated to the Martyrs in this place. For the Prophet says, *The Souls of those that were beheaded for the witness of Jesus,* &c. *They lived and reigned with Christ a thousand years.* From which words, if you please, we will raise this Doctrine: That, *Those that have suffered for the sake of Christ and a good Conscience, shall be raised from the dead a thousand years before the general Resurrection, and reign with Christ, in an happy state.* This Proposition seems to be plainly included in the words of St. *John*, and to be the intended sence of this Vision; but you must have patience a little as to your enquiry into particulars, till, in the progress of our discourse, we have brought all the parts of this conclusion into a fuller light.

In the mean time, there is but one way, that I know of, to evade the force of these words, and of the conclusion drawn from them; and that is, by supposing that the *First Resurrection* here mentioned, is not to be understood in a literal sense, but is Allegorical and mystical; signifying only a Resurrection from sin to a Spiritual Life. As we are said to be *dead in sin*, and to be *risen with Christ*, by Faith and Regeneration. This is a manner of Speech which St. *Paul* does sometimes use: as *Ephes.* 2. 6. and 5. 14. and *Col.* 3. 1. But how can this be applyed to the present case? Were the Martyrs dead in sin? 'Tis they that are here rais'd from the dead. Or, after they were beheaded for the witness of Jesus, naturally dead and laid in their graves, were they then regenerate by Faith? There is no congruity in allegories so applyed. Besides, why should they be said to be regenerate a thousand years before the day of Judgment: Or, to reign with Christ, after this Spiritual Resurrection, such a limited time, a thousand years? why not to Eternity? For in this allegorical sence of *rising* and *reigning*, they will reign with him for everlasting. Then, after a thousand years must all the wicked be regenerate, and rise into a Spiritual Life? 'Tis said here, *The rest of the Dead* *ver. 5.* *lived not again, until the thousand years were finished.* That implyes, that at the end of these thousand years, the rest of the dead did live again; which, according to the Allegory must be, that, after a thousand years, all the wicked will be regenerate, and rais'd into a Spiritual Life. These absurdities arise upon an allegorical exposition of this Resurrection, if apply'd to single Persons.

But Dr. *Hammond*, a Learned and worthy Divine, (but one that loves to contract and cramp the sence of Prophecies) making this first Resurrection allegorical, applies it not to single Persons, but to the state of the Church in general; The Christian Church, he says, shall have a Resurrection for a thousand years: that is, shall rise out of Persecution, be in a prosperous condition, and an undisturb'd profession of the true Religion, for so long a time. But this agrees with the Prophecy as little as the former; If it be a state of the Church in general, and of the Church then in being, why is this Resurrection apply'd to the Martyrs? why are they said to rise? seeing the state they liv'd in, was a troublesome state of the Church, and it would be no happiness to have that reviv'd again. Then as to the Time of this Resurrection of the Church, where will you fix it? The Prophet *Daniel* places this Reign of Christ, at, or after the dissolution of the fourth Monarchy: and St. *John* places it a thousand years before the last Day of Judgment: How will you adjust the Allegorical Resurrection of the Church to these limits? Or if, in point of time, you was free, as to Prophecy; yet how would you adjust it to History? Where will you take these thousand years of happiness and prosperity to the Church? These Authors suppose them past, and therefore must begin them either from the first times of the Gospel, or from the time of *Constantine*. Under the first Ages of the Gospel, were, you know, the great Persecutions by the *Heathen* Emperours: Could those be call'd the Reign of Christ and of his Saints? Was Sathan then bound? or was this Epocha but a thousand years before the Day of Judgment? And if you begin this Resurrection of the Church from the days of *Constantine*, when the Empire became Christian, how will you reckon a thousand years from that time, for the continuance of the Church in *peace* and *purity*? for the reign of Christ and of his Saints must necessarily imply both those Characters. Besides, who are the *rest of the Dead*, that liv'd after the expiration of those thousand years, if they begun at *Constantine*? And why is not the second Resurrection and the Day of Judgment yet come? Lastly, you ought to be tender of interpreting the first Resurrection in an Allegorical sence, lest you expose the second Resurrection to be made an Allegory also.

Ver. 5.

To conclude, the words of the Text are plain and express for a literal Resurrection, as to the first, as well as the second; and there is no Allegorical interpretation that I know of, that will hold through all the particulars of the Text, consistently with it self and with History. And when we shall have prov'd this future Kingdom of Christ from other places of the Apocalypse, and of Holy Writ, you will the more easily admit the literal sence of this place: Which, you know, according to the receiv'd rule of Interpreters, is never to be quitted or forsaken, without necessity. But when I speak of confirming this Doctrine from other passages of Scripture, I do not mean as to that definite time of a *thousand years*, for that is no where else mention'd in the Apocalypse or in Scripture, that I know of; and seems to be mention'd here, in this close of all things, to mind us of that type that was propos'd in the beginning of all things, *Of Six days and a Sabbath*. Whereof each Day comprehends a thousand years, and the *Sabbath*,

which is the *Millennial state*, hath its thousand. According to the known Pro-
phecy of *Elias*, which, as I told you before, was not onely receiv'd amongst the   *Book* 3, *ch.* 5.
Jews, but also own'd by very many of the Christian Fathers.

To proceed therefore to other parts of St. *John*'s Prophecies, that set forth this
Kingdom of Christ. The Vision of the *Seven Trumpets* is one of the most remarkable in the Apocalypse; and the seventh Trumpet, which, plainly reaches to
the end of the World, and the Resurrection of the Dead, opens the Scene to the
Millennium. Hear the sound of it. *The seventh Angel sounded, and there were great*   *Chap.* 11. 15, 16,
voices in heaven, saying, The kingdoms of this world are become the kingdoms of our   17, 18.
Lord, and of his Christ, and he shall reign for ever and ever. And the four and
twenty Elders, which sat before God on their Seats, fell upon their faces, and wor-
shiped God: Saying, We give thee thanks, O Lord God Almighty, which art, and
wast, and art to come; because thou hast taken to thee thy great power and hast
reigned. And the Nations were angry, and thy wrath is come, and the time of the
Dead, that they should be judged, and that thou shouldest give reward unto thy
servants the Prophets, and to the Saints, and them that fear thy Name, small and
great, and shouldest destroy them that destroy the Earth, &c. This is manifestly
the kingdom of Christ: and with this is joyn'd the Resurrection of the Dead, and
the rewarding of the suffering Prophets and Saints; as in the *twentieth Chapter.*
This is that *mystery of God that was to be finish'd in the days of the voice of the*
seventh Angel: as is said in the 20*th.* Chap. ver. 7. *As he hath declared to his*
servants the Prophets. Namely, the mystery of this kingdom, which was foretold
by the Prophets of the Old Testament: and more especially by *Daniel*, as we shall
see hereafter.

The *new Jerusalem*, (as it is set down, *Apoc.* 21. 2, 3, 4, 5, 6, 7.) is another
instance or image of this kingdom of Christ. And the *Palm-bearing Company*,
Chap. 7. 9, &c. are some of the Martyrs that shall enjoy it. They are plainly
describ'd there as Christian Martyrs; (*ver.* 14.) And their reward, or the state
of happiness they are to enjoy, (*ver.* 15, 16, 17.) is the same with that of the Inhabitants of the *new Jerusalem:* Ch. 21. 2, 3, 4, &c. as, upon comparing those two
places, will easily appear. Furthermore, at the opening of the *Seals, Chap.* 5.
which is another principal Vision, and reaches to the end of the World, there is
a prospect given us of this kingdom of Christ, and of that reward of his Saints.
For when they sing the new Song to the Lamb, (*ver.* 9, 10.) they say, *Thou art*
worthy to take the Book, and to open the Seals thereof: For thou wast slain and
hast redeemed us to God, by thy bloud. And hast made us unto our God Kings and
Priests: and we shall reign on the Earth. This must be the same state, and the
same thousand-years-Reign mention'd in the 20*th* Chapter. Where 'tis said,
(*ver.* 6.) the partakers of it *shall be Priests of God and of Christ, and shall reign with*
him a thousand years.

Another completory Vision, that extends it self to the end of the World, is
that of the *seven Vials*, Ch. 15, & 16. And as at the opening of the Seals, so at
the pouring out of the Vials, a triumphal Song is sung, and 'tis call'd the *Song*
of Moses and of the Lamb. 'Tis plainly a Song of thanksgiving for a Deliverance: *ch.* 15. 3.
but I do not look upon this deliverance as already wrought, before the pouring

335

out of Vials, though it be plac'd before them: as often the grand design and issue of a Vision is plac'd at the beginning. It is wrought by the Vials themselves, and by their effusion, and therefore upon the pouring out of the last Vial, The voice came out of the Temple of Heaven, from the Throne, saying, *Consummatum est: It is done.* Now the Deliverance is wrought, now the work is at an end: or, *The mystery of God is finish'd*, as the phrase was before, concerning the 7*th* Trumpet: *Ch.* 10. 7. You see therefore this terminates upon the same time, and consequently upon the same state, of the *Millennium.* And that they are the same Persons that triumph here, and reign there, *Ch.* 20. You may see by the same Characters given to both of them. Here, those that triumph, are said *to have gotten the victory* over the Beast, and over his Image, *and over his mark, and over the number of his name.* And there, Those that reign with Christ, are said to be those *that had not worshipped the Beast, neither his Image, neither had received his mark upon their foreheads, or in their hands.* These are the same Persons therefore, triumphing over the same Enemies, and enjoying the same reward.

And you shall seldom find any *Doxology* or *Hallelujah* in the Apocalypse, but 'tis in prospect of the kingdom of Christ, and the *Millennial* state. That is still the burthen of the Sacred Song: The complement of every grand Vision, and the life and strength of the whole Systeme of Prophecies in that Book. Even those *Halleluja's* that are sung at the destruction of *Babylon*, in the 19*th*. Chapter, are rais'd upon the view of the succeeding state, *the Reign of Christ.* For the Text says, *And I heard as it were a voice of a great multitude, and as the voice of many waters, and as the voice of mighty thunders, saying, Hallelujah. FOR THE LORD GOD OMNIPOTENT REIGNETH. Let us be glad and rejoyce and give honour to him: FOR THE MARRIAGE OF THE LAMB IS COME, AND HIS WIFE HATH MADE HER SELF READY.* This appears plainly to be the *New Jerusalem*, if you consult the 21. ch. ver. 2. *And I John saw the Holy City, New Jerusalem, coming down from God out of Heaven, PREPARED AS A BRIDE ADORNED FOR HER HUSBAND.* 'Tis, no doubt, the same Bride and Bridegroom, in both places; the same marriage or preparations for marriage; which are compleated in the Millennial bliss, in the kingdom of Christ and of his Saints.

I must still beg your patience a little longer, in pursuing this argument throughout the Apocalypse. As towards the latter end of St. *John*'s Revelation this Kingdom of Christ shines out in a more full glory, so there are the dawnings of it in the very beginning and entrance into his Prophecies. As at the beginning of a Poem, we have commonly in a few words the design of the Work, in like manner St. *John* makes this Preface to his Prophecies, *From Jesus Christ, who is the faithful witness, the first begotten of the dead, and the Prince of the Kings of the Earth: unto him that loved us, and washed us from our sins in his own bloud: And hath made us Kings and Priests unto God and his Father; to him be glory and dominion for ever and ever, Amen. Behold, he cometh in the clouds,* &c. In this Prologue the grand argument is pointed at, and that happy Catastrophe and last Scene which is to crown the Work: The Reign of Christ and of his Saints at his second coming. He hath *made us Kings and Priests unto God*: This is always the

ch. 16. 17.

ch. 15. 2.

ch. 20. 4.

ch. 19. 6, 7.

ch. 1. 5, 6.

336

Characteristick of those that are to enjoy the Millennial happiness; as you may see at the opening of the Seals, *chap.* 5. 10. and in the Sons of the *First Resurrection, ch.* 20. 6. And this being joyned to the coming of our Saviour, puts it still more out of doubt. That expression also, of being *washt from our sins in his bloud,* is repeated again both at the opening of the Seals, *ch.* 5. 9. and in the *Palm-bearing* Company, *ch.* 7. 14. both which places we have cited before as referring to the Millennial State.

Give me leave to add further, that as in this general Preface, so also in the Introductory visions of the *Seven Churches,* there are, covertly or expresly, in the conclusion of each, glances upon the *Millennium.* As in the first to *Ephesus,* the *ch.* 2. 7. Prophet concludes, *He that hath an ear, let him hear, what the Spirit says to the Churches: TO HIM THAT OVERCOMETH WILL I GIVE TO EAT OF THE TREE OF LIFE, WHICH IS IN THE MIDST OF THE PARADISE OF GOD.* This is the Millennial happiness which is promised to the Conquerour; as we noted before concerning that phrase. In like manner in the second to *Smyrna,* He concludes: *He that overcometh, shall not be hurt of the second death.* *ch.* 2. 11. This implyes, he shall be partaker of the *first Resurrection,* for that's the thing understood; as you may see plainly by their being joyn'd in the 20*th ch. ver.* 6. *Blessed and holy is he that hath part in the first Resurrection: on such the second death hath no power: but they shall be Priests of God and of Christ, and shall reign with him a thousand years.* In the 3*d* to *Pergamus,* the promise is, *to eat of the* *ch.* 2. 17. *hidden Manna, to have a white stone, and a new name written in it.* But seeing the Prophet adds, *which no man knoweth saving he that receiveth it,* we will not presume to interpret that new state, whatsoever it is. In *Thyatira,* the reward is, *ch.* 2. 26, 27. *To have power over the nations,* and to have the *Morning Star.* Which is to reign with Christ, who is the morning Star, in his Millennial Empire: both these phrases being us'd in that sence in the close of this Book. In *Sardis* the promise *ch.* 3. 5. is, *To be clothed in white raiment, and not to be blotted out of the Book of Life.* And you see afterwards the *Palm-bearing* Company are clothed in *white robes*; and *ch.* 7. 9, 14. those that are admitted into the *New Jerusalem,* are such as are *written in the Lamb's book of life, ch.* 21. 27. Then as to *Philadelphia,* the reward promised *ch.* 3. 12. there does openly mark the Millennial state, by the *City of God, New Jerusalem which cometh down out of heaven from God:* compar'd with *chap.* 21. 2. Lastly, to the Church of *Laodicea* is said, *To him that overcometh will I grant to sit with* *ch.* 3. 21. *me in my Throne.* And that is the usual phrase to express the dignity of those that reign with Christ, in his Millennial kingdom: as you may see, *Apoc.* 20. 4. *Matt.* 19. 28. *Dan.* 7. 9, 13, 14. So all these promises to the Churches aim at one and the same thing, and terminate upon the same point; 'Tis the same reward express'd in different ways; and seeing 'tis still fixt upon a victory, and appropriated to those that overcome, it does the more easily carry our thoughts to the *Millennium,* which is the proper reward of Victors, that is, of Martyrs and Confessors.

Thus you see how this notion and mystery of the Millennial kingdom of Christ, does both begin and end the *Apocalypse,* and run thorough all its parts: As the Soul of that Body of Prophecies: A Spirit or ferment that actuates the whole

Y   337 mass. And if we could thoroughly understand that illustrious Scene at the opening of this Apocalyptical Theatre in the 4*th* and 5*th chap.* I do not doubt but we should find it a Representation of the Majesty of our Saviour in the Glory of his future Kingdom. But I dare not venture upon the explication of it, there are so many things of difficult and dubious interpretation, couch'd under those Schemes. Wherefore having made these observations upon the Prophecies of St. *John,* we will now add to them some reflections upon the Prophecies of *Daniel.* That by the agreement and concurrence of these two great Witnesses, the Conclusion we pretend to prove, may be fully established.

In the Prophecies of *Daniel* there are two grand Visions, that of the *Statue* or Image, *chap.* 2. and that of the four Beasts, *chap.* 7. And both these Visions terminate upon the *Millennium,* or the Kingdom of Christ. In the Vision of the Statue, representing to us the four great Monarchies of the World successively, (whereof, by the general consent of Interpreters, The *Roman* is the fourth and last) after the dissolution of the last of them, a fifth Monarchy, the Kingdom of

ch. 2. v. 44. Christ, is openly introduc'd, in these words: *And in the days of these kingdoms, shall the God of heaven set up a kingdom, which shall never be destroy'd, and the kingdom shall not be left to other people, but it shall break in pieces, and consume all those kingdoms, and it shall stand for ever.* This may be verified, in some measure, by the first coming of our Saviour in the days of the 4*th* kingdom; when his Religion from small beginnings, in a short time overspread the greatest part

ver. 34, 35. of the known World. As the *stone cut out without hands,* became a great *mountain and filled the whole Earth.* But the full and final accomplishment of this Prophecy cannot be till the second coming of our Saviour. For not till then, will he *break*

ver. 35. *in pieces and consume all those kingdoms; and that in such a manner, that they shall become like the chaff of the Summer threshing-floor, carried away by the wind: so as no place shall be found for them.* This, I say, will not be done, nor an everlasting Kingdom erected in their place, over all the Nations of the Earth, till his Second Coming, and his Millennial Reign.

But this Reign is declared more expresly, in the Vision of the four Beasts,

ch. 7. 13. *chap.* 7. For after the destruction of the fourth Beast, the Prophet says, *I saw in the night, Visions, and behold one like the Son of man, came with the clouds of heaven, and came to the Ancient of days, and they brought him near before him: And there was given him dominion, and glory, and a kingdom, that all people, nations, and languages should serve him: His dominion is an everlasting dominion, which shall not pass away: and his kingdom that which shall not be destroy'd.* Accordingly he says, ver. 21, 22. *The last Beast and the little Horn made war against the Saints, until the Ancient of days came, and judgment was given to the Saints of the most High; and the time came that the Saints possessed the kingdom.* And lastly, in pursuit still of the same argument, he concludes to the same effect in fuller words, ver. 26, 27. *But the Judgment shall sit, and they shall take away his dominion, to consume and to destroy it unto the end. And the kingdom and dominion, and the greatness of the kingdom under the whole heaven, shall be given to the people of the Saints of the most High: whose kingdom is an everlasting kingdom, and all dominions shall serve and obey him.*

Here is the end of the matter: says the Prophet. Here is the upshot and result　ch. 7. 28.
of all. Here terminate both the Prophecies of *Daniel* and St. *John:* and all the　ch. 12. 13.
affairs of the Terrestrial World. *Daniel* brings in, this kingdom of Christ, in the
conclusion of two or three Visions; but St. *John* hath interwoven it every where
with his Prophecies, from first to last. And you may as well open a Lock without
a Key, as interpret the Apocalypse without the *Millennium.* But after these two
great Witnesses, the one for the old Testament, the other for the new, we must
look into the rest of the Sacred Writers; for tho' every single Author there, is an
Oracle, yet the concurrence of Oracles is still a further demonstration, and takes
away all remains of doubt or incredulity.

CHAPTER V

*A view of other places of Scripture concerning the Millennium or future kingdom of
Christ. In what sence all the Prophets have born Testimony concerning it.*

THE Wife of *Zebedee* came to our Saviour, and begg'd of him, like a fond　Matt. 20. 21.
Mother, that her two Sons might sit, one at his right hand, th'other at his
left, when he came into his kingdom. Our Saviour does not deny the supposition,
or general ground of her request, that *he was to have a kingdom*; but tells her,
The honours of that kingdom were not then in his disposal. He had not drunk
his Cup, nor been baptiz'd with his last baptism: which were conditions, both
to him and others, of entring into that kingdom. Yet, in another place, our　Matt. 19. 28.
Saviour is so well assur'd of his interest and authority there, by the good will of
his Father, that he promises to his Disciples and followers, that for the losses
they should sustain here, upon his account, and for the sake of his Gospel, they
should receive there an hundred fold; and sit upon Thrones with him, judging
the Tribes of *Israel.* The words are these: *And Jesus said unto them, verily I say
unto you, that ye which have followed me,* in the Regeneration or Renovation,
*when the Son of man shall sit in the Throne of his glory, ye also shall sit upon twelve
thrones, judging the twelve tribes of Israel.* These Thrones, in all reason, must be
understood to be the same with those which we mention'd in the foregoing
Chapter, out of *Daniel* and the *Apocalypse:* and therefore mark the same time　Dan. 7. 9.
and the same state. And seeing, in those places, they plainly signified the *Millen-*　Apoc. 20. 4.
nial state, or the kingdom of Christ and of his Saints, they must here signifie
the same, in this promise of our Saviour to his suffering Followers. And as to
the word *Palingenesia,* which is here translated *Regeneration,* 'tis very well known,
that, both the *Greek* Philosophers, and *Greek* Fathers, use that very word for the
Renovation of the World. Which is to be, as we shall hereafter make appear, at
or before the *Millennial* state.

Our Saviour also, in his Divine Sermon upon the Mount, makes this one of
his *Beatitudes, Blessed are the Meek, for they shall inherit the Earth.* But *how,* I
pray, or *where,* or *when,* do the Meek inherit the Earth? neither at present, I am
sure, nor in any past Ages. 'Tis the Great Ones of the World, ambitious Princes
and Tyrants, that slice the Earth amongst them: and those that can flatter them

best, or serve them in their interests or pleasures, have the next best shares. But a meek, modest, and humble Spirit, is the most unqualified Person that can be for a Court, or a Camp: to scramble for Preferment, or Plunder. Both He, and his self-denying notions, are ridicul'd, as things of no use, and proceeding from meanness and poorness of Spirit. *David*, who was a Person of an admirable devotion, but of an unequal Spirit; subject to great dejections, as well as elevations of mind; was so much affected with the prosperity of the wicked in this World, that he could scarce forbear charging Providence with injustice. You may see several touches of a repining Spirit in his Psalms: and in the Seventy-third *Psalm*, compos'd upon that Subject, you have both the wound and the cure. Now this Beatitude pronounc'd here by our Saviour, was spoken before by *David*, *Psal.* 37. 11. The same *David* that was always so sensible of the hard usage of the Just in this life. Our Saviour also, and his Apostles, preach the Doctrine of the Cross every where, and foretell the sufferings that shall attend the Righteous, in this World. Therefore neither *David*, nor our Saviour, could understand this *inheritance of the Earth*, otherwise than of some future state, or of a state yet to come. But as it must be a future state, so it must be a Terrestrial state; for it could not be call'd the *inheritance of the Earth*, if it was not so. And 'tis to be a state of *peace*, as well as *plenty*, according to the words of the *Psalmist*, *But the meek shall inherit the Earth, and shall delight themselves in the abundance of peace.* It follows therefore from these premises, that, both our Saviour, and *David*, must understand some future state of the Earth, wherein the *Meek* will enjoy both peace and plenty. And this will appear to be the future kingdom of Christ, when, upon a fuller description, we shall have given you the marks and characters of it.

In the mean time, why should we not suppose, this Earth, which the Meek are to inherit, to be that *habitable Earth to come*, which St. *Paul* mentions (*Hebr.* 2. 6.) and represents as subject to our Saviour in a peculiar manner: at his disposal and under his government, as his kingdom; Why should not that Earth be the subject of this Beatitude: The promis'd Land, the Lot of the Righteous? This I am sure of, that both this Text and the former deserve our serious thoughts; and tho' they do not expresly, and in terms, prove the future kingdom of our Saviour, yet upon the fairest interpretations they imply such a state. And it will be very uneasie to give a satisfactory account, either of the *Regeneration* or *Renovation*, when our Saviour and his Disciples shall sit upon Thrones: Or of that *Earth* which the *Meek shall inherit:* Or lastly, of that *Habitable World*, which is peculiarly subject to the dominion of Jesus Christ, without supposing, on this side Heaven, some other reign of Christ and his Saints, than what we see, or what they enjoy, at present.

But to proceed in this argument. It will be necessary, as I told you, to set down some notes and characters of this Reign of Christ and of his Saints, whereby it may be distinguish'd from the present state, and present kingdoms of the World. And these characters are chiefly three, *Justice*, *Peace*, and *Divine Presence* or conduct, which uses to be called *Theocrasie*. By these characters it is sufficiently distinguish'd from the kingdoms of this World; which are generally unjust in

their titles or exercise: stain'd with bloud: and so far from being under a parti-́
cular divine conduct, that humane passions and humane vices, are the Springs
that commonly give motion to their greatest designs. But more particularly and
restrainedly, the Government of Christ, is opposed to the kingdom and government of Antichrist, whose characters are diametrically opposite to these, being
injustice, cruelty, and *humane or diabolical artifices.*

Upon this short view of the kingdom of Christ, let us make enquiry after it
amongst the Prophets of the Old Testament. And we shall find, upon examination, that there is scarce any of them, greater or lesser, but take notice of this
mystical kingdom; either expresly, or under the types of *Israel, Sion, Jerusalem,*
and such like. And therefore I am apt to think, that, when St. *Peter* in his Sermon
to the *Jews, Act.* 3. says, All the holy Prophets spoke of *The Restitution of all
things,* he does not mean the Renovation of the World separately from the kingdom of Christ, but complexly, as it may imply both. For there are not many of
the old Prophets that have spoken of the Renovation of the *Natural* World; but
a great many have spoken of the Renovation of the *Moral,* in the kingdom of
Christ. These are St. *Peter's* words: *Act.* 3. 19, 20, 21. *Repent ye therefore and
be converted, that your sins may be blotted out, when the times of refreshing shall
come from the presence of the Lord. And he shall send Jesus Christ which before was
preached unto you: whom the heavens must receive until the times of RESTITUTION
OF ALL THINGS.* The Apostle here mentions three things, The *Times of
refreshing,* The *Second Coming* of our Saviour, And the *Times* of *Restitution of
all things.* And to the last of these he immediately subjoins, *which God hath
spoken by the mouth of all his holy Prophets, since the world began.* This *Restitution
of all things,* I say, must not be understood abstractly from the reign of Christ,
but as in conjunction with it; and in that sence, and no other, it is the general
subject of the Prophets.

To enter therefore into the Schools of the Prophets, and enquire their sence
concerning this mystery, let us first address our selves to the Prophet *Isaiah,* and
the Royal Prophet *David;* who seem to have had many noble thoughts, or inspirations, upon this subject. *Isaiah* in the 65*th chap.* from the 17*th ver.* to the
end, treats upon this argument: and joyns together the Renovation of the Natural
and Moral World; as St. *Peter,* in the place forementioned, seems to do. And
accordingly the Prophet, having set down several natural characters of that State,
as indolency and joy, longevity, ease, and plenty, from *ver.* 18. to the 24*th.* He
there begins the moral characters, of divine favour, and such a particular protection, that they are heard and answer'd before they pray. And lastly, He represents it as a state of universal peace and innocency, *ver.* 23. *The Wolf and the
Lamb shall feed together,* &c.

This last character, which comprehends *Peace, Justice,* and *Innocency,* is more
fully display'd by the same Prophet, in the 11*th chap.* where he treats also of the
Kingdom of Christ. Give me leave to set down his words, *ver.* 4, 5, 6, 7, 8, 9.
*But with righteousness shall he judge the poor, and reprove with equity for the meek
of the Earth: and he shall smite the Earth with the rod of his mouth, and with the
breath of his lips shall he slay the wicked. And righteousness shall be the girdle of*

his loins, and faithfulness the girdle of his reins. The Wolf also shall dwell with the Lamb, and the Leopard shall lye down with the kid: and the Calf and the young Lyon, and the fatling together, and a little child shall lead them. And the Cow and the Bear shall feed, their young ones shall lie down together: and the Lyon shall eat straw like the Ox. And the suckling child shall play on the hole of the Asp, and the weaned child shall put his hand on the Cockatrice-den. They shall not hurt, nor destroy in all my holy mountain: for the Earth shall be full of the knowledge of the Lord, as the waters cover the Sea. Thus far the Prophet: Now if we joyn this to what we noted before, from his 65*th* chap. concerning the same state, 'twill be impossible to understand it of any order of things, that is now, or hath been hitherto in the World. And consequently it must be the Idea of some state to come, and particularly of that which we call the Future Kingdom of Christ.

The same pacifick temper, Innocency and Justice, are celebrated by this Prophet when the *Mountain of the Lord shall be established in the top of the mountains,* chap. 2. 2, 4. *And he shall judge amongst the nations, and shall rebuke many people; and they shall beat their swords into plow-shares, and their spears into pruning-hooks. Nation shall not lift up sword against nation, neither shall they learn war any more.* And as to righteousness, he says in the 23. chap. *Behold a king shall reign in righteousness, and Princes shall rule in judgment,* &c. These places, I know, usually are applyed to the first coming of our Saviour; the peaceableness of his doctrine, and the propagation of it through all the World. I willingly allow this to be a true sence, so far as it will go. But 'tis one thing to be a true sence, to such a degree; and another thing to be the final sence and accomplishment of a Prophecy. The affairs of the first and second coming of our Saviour are often mingled together in the Prophecies of the Old Testament; but in that mixture there are some characters whereby you may distinguish what belongs to his first, and what to his second coming: what to the time when he came to suffer, and what to the time when he shall come to reign. For instance, In these Prophecies recited, though there are many things very applicable to his first coming, yet that *Regality* which is often spoken of, and that universal Peace and Innocency that will accompany it, cannot be verified of his coming in the flesh. Seeing it is plain, that in his state of humiliation he did not come as a King, to rule over the nations of the Earth. And he says himself expresly, *That his Kingdom is not of this World. Joh.* 18. 36. And the Prayer of *Salome,* and of the good Thief upon the Cross, suppose it not then present, but to come. Then as to the establishment of *Peace* in his kingdom, it does not at all appear to me that there is more peace in the World now than there was before our Saviour came into it; or that the Christian parts of the World are more peaceable than the unchristian. Therefore these great promises of a *Pacifick kingdom,* which are exprest in terms as high and emphatical as can be imagin'd, must belong to some other days, and some other ages, than what we have seen hitherto.

You'l say, it may be, 'tis not the fault of the Gospel that the World is not peaceable, but of those that profess it, and do not practise it. This is true, but it does not answer the Prophecy; for that makes no such exception. And by such a reserve as this, you may elude any Prophecy. So the *Jews* say, Their *Messiah*

Matt. 20. 21.
Luke 23. 42.

342

defers his coming beyond the time appointed by Prophecy, because of their sins: but we do not allow this for a good reason. The *Israelites* had their promised *Canaan*, tho' they had render'd themselves unworthy of it; and by this method of interpreting Prophecies, all the happiness and glory promised in the Millennial kingdom of Christ may come to nothing, upon a pretended forfeiture. Threatnings indeed may have a tacit condition; God may be better than his word, and, upon repentance, divert his judgments; but he cannot be worse than his word, or fail of performance, when, without any condition exprest, he promises or prophesies good things to come. This would destroy all assurance of hope or faith. Lastly, This Prophecy concerning Pacifick times or a *Pacifick kingdom*, is in the 65*th* chap. subjoyn'd to the *Renovation of the Heavesn and the Earth*, and several marks of a change in the Natural World; which things we know did not come to pass at the first coming of our Saviour: there was no change of Nature then, nor has been ever since. And therefore this happy change, both in the Natural and Moral World, is yet to come. *Isa.* 65.

But, as we said before, we do not speak this exclusively of the first coming of our Saviour, as to other parts of these Prophecies; for no doubt that was one great design of them. And in the Prophecies of the old Testament, there are often three gradations, or gradual accomplishments; The first, in some King of *Israel*, or some Person or affair relating to *Israel*, as National onely. The second, in the Messiah at his first coming. And the last, in the Messiah, and his Kingdom at his second coming. And that which we affirm and contend for, is, that the Prophecies foremention'd have not a final and total accomplishment, either in the Nation of the *Jews*, or at the first coming of our Saviour. And this we 'bide by.

The next Prophet that we mention'd, as a witness of the future kingdom of Christ, is *David*. Who, in his Psalms, seems to be pleas'd with this subject above all others; And when he is most exalted in his thoughts and Prophetical raptures, the Spirit carries him into the kingdom of the Messiah, to contemplate its glory, to sing praises to its King, and triumph over his Enemies: *Psal. 68. Let God arise, let his enemies be scattered: Let them also that hate him flie before him. As smoke is driven away, so drive them away: as wax melteth before the fire, so let the wicked perish at the presence of God. But let the Righteous be glad, &c.* The plain ground he goes upon in this Psalm, is the Deliverance out of *Ægypt*, and bringing the *Israelites* into the Land of *Canaan*; But when he is once upon the wing, he soars to an higher pitch: from the type to the Antitype: To the days of the Messiah, the Ascension of our Saviour; and, at length, to his kingdom and dominion over all the Earth. The 45*th*. Psalm is an *Epithalamium* to Christ and the Church, or to the *Lamb* and his *Spouse*. And when that will be, and in what state, we may learn from St. *John*, *Apoc.* 19. 7, 8. and *ch.* 21. 2, 9. Namely, after the destruction of *Babylon*, in the *new Jerusalem* glory. The words and matter of the two Prophets answer to one another; Here, in this Psalm, there is a fight and victory celebrated, as well as a marriage: and so there is in that 19*th*. Chapter of St. *John*. Here, the Prophet says, *Gird thy Sword upon thy thigh, O most Mighty, with thy glory and thy majesty. And in thy Majesty ride prosperously, because of truth and meekness and righteousness: and thy right hand shall teach thee terrible things. Thy* *Ver.* 18. *Ver.* 32, *&c.*

Ps. 45. 3, 4, 6.

Throne, O God, is for ever and ever; The Scepter of thy kingdom is a right Scepter,
&c. There St. *John* says, having describ'd a Conquerour on a white Horse, *Out of his mouth goeth a sharp Sword, that with it he should smite the Nations: and he shall rule them with a rod of Iron: and he treadeth the Wine-press of the fierceness and wrath of Almighty God. And he hath on his Vesture and on his thigh a Name written, KING of KINGS, and LORD of LORDS.* This is the same glorious Conquerour and Bridegroom in both places: And this Victory is not gain'd, nor these Nuptials compleated till the second coming of our Saviour.

In many other Psalms, there are reflections upon this happy kingdom, and the triumph of Christ over his Enemies: as *Psal.* 2. *Psal.* 9. *Psal.* 21. and 24. and 47. and 85. and 110. and others. In these, and such like Psalms, there are lineaments and colours of a fairer state, than any we have yet seen upon Earth. Not but that in their first instances and grounds they may sometimes respect the state of *Israel*, or the Evangelical state: but the eye of the Prophet goes further, this does not terminate his sight: His Divine enthusiasme reaches into another World: A world of *Peace* and *Justice*, and *Holiness:* of Joy, and Victory, and Triumph over all the wicked: and consequently such a World, as neither we, nor our Fathers, have yet seen.

This is an account of two Prophets, *David* and *Isaiah:* and of what they have more openly declar'd concerning the future kingdom of Christ. But to verifie St. *Peter*'s words, in that foremention'd place, *Act.* 3. 21. *viz.* that all the *Holy Prophets since the World began*, have spoken of the Restauration of all things at the second coming of Christ. I say, to verifie this assertion of St. *Peter*'s, we must suppose, that, where the Prophets speak of the Restauration and future glory of *Judah* and *Jerusalem*, they do, under those Types, represent to us the glory and happiness of the Church in the future kingdom of Christ. And most of the Prophets, in this sence, and under these forms, have spoken of this kingdom: In foretelling the Restauration of *Jerusalem* and *Sion*; and happy days, peace, plenty, and prosperity to the People of *Israel*.

Most of the Prophets, I say, from *Moses* to *Malachy*, have spoken of this *Restauration. Moses* in the 30*th.* of *Deut. ver.* 4, 5, 9. *David*, in many of those Psalms we have cited. *Isaiah*, besides the places foremention'd, treats amply of this subject, *Chap.* 51. and in several other places.* So likewise the Prophet *Ezekiel, Daniel, Hosea, Joel, Amos, Obadiah, Micah, Zephany, Haggai, Zachary, Malachy.* All these have, either expresly, or under the types of *Jerusalem* and *Sion*, foretold happy days, and a glorious triumph to the Church of God. And seeing in the new Testament, and in the Prophecies of St. *John*, the Christian Church is still represented, as under persecution and distress, till the fall of Anti-christ, and the Millennial Kingdom; 'Tis then, and not till then, that we must expect the full accomplishment of these Prophecies; The *Restauration* that St. *Peter* says was spoken of, by *all the Prophets:* and the *mystery*, which St. *John* says, (*Apoc.* 10. 7.) was *declared by his Servants the Prophets*, and would be finish'd under the 7*th. Trumpet*, which ushers in the Kingdom of Christ.

---

* *Isaiah ch.* 11, *ch.* 43. *ch.* 49. 13, *&c. ch.* 66. *Ezekiel, ch.* 28. *ch.* 37. *Hos. ch.* 3, *& ch.* 14. *Joel* 3. 18. *Amos, ch.* 9. *Obad. ver.* 17, &c. *Mich. ch.* 4. *ch.* 5. *Zeph.* 3. 14, *&c. Haggai, ch.* 2. *Zac.* 2. 10, *&c. & ch.* 9. 9, *&c. & ch.* 14. *Mala. ch.* 3. *ch.* 4.

It would be too long to examine all these places in the Prophets, which you may consult at leisure. However it cannot seem strange that *Jerusalem* should be us'd in a typical or allegorical sence, seeing we often find such applications of it in the new Testament: as *Gal.* 4. 26. *Hebr.* 12. 22. *Apoc.* 3. 12. And 'tis very natural that *Jerusalem restor'd*, should signifie the same thing as *New Jerusalem*; and therefore that St. *John*, by his *New Jerusalem*, intended the same thing, or the same state, that the ancient Prophets did by their Restauration of *Jerusalem*. And if neither can be understood in a literal sence, which, I believe, you will not contend for: they must both be interpreted of the future happiness and glory of the Church in the Kingdom of Christ.

But to conclude this point wholly as to Scripture; If we make reflection upon all the passages alledg'd in this and the foregoing Chapter, whether out of the Old or New Testament, we must at least acknowledge thus much; That there are happy days, at one time or other: Days of Peace and Righteousness: of Joy and Triumph: of external Prosperity and internal Sanctity: when Vertue and Innocency shall be in the Throne, and Vice and vitious Men out of power or credit. That there are such happy days prophesied of in Scripture, and promised to the Church of God. Whether you call this the *Reign of Christ* and of his Saints, or by any other name, it is not material at present to determine; let the title be what you will, as to the substance it cannot be denied to be a general doctrine of Prophetical Scripture. And we must not imagine, that the Prophets writ like the Poets: feigned an Idea of a Romantick state, that never was, nor ever will be; only to please their own fancies, or the credulous people. Neither is it the state of Heaven and eternal life that is here meant or intended: For, besides that they had little or no light concerning those Notions, in the Old Testament: The Prophets generally in their description of this happiness, either express the Earth, or at least give plain marks of a Terrestrial state. Wherefore the only question that remains, is this, *Whether* these happy Days are past already, or to come: Whether this blessed state of the Church is behind us, or before us: whether our predecessors have enjoy'd it, or our posterity is to expect it? For we are very sure that it is not present; The World is full of Wars, and rumours of wars: of vice and knavery, of oppression and persecution: and these are things directly contrary to the genius and characters of the state which we look after.

And if we look for it in times past, we can go no further back than the beginning of Christianity. For St. *John*, the last of the Apostles, prophesied of these times, as to come: and plac'd them at the end of his systeme of Prophecies; whereby one might conclude that they are not only within the compass of the Christian ages, but far advanc'd into them. But however, not to insist upon that at present, where will you find a thousand years, from the birth of Christianity to this present age, that deserves the name, or answers to the characters of this *Pure* and *Pacifick* state of the Church. The first ages of Christianity, as they were the most pure, so likewise were they the least peaceable. Continually, more or less, under the Persecution of the Heathen Emperours; and so far from being the reign and Empire of Christ and his Saints over the Nations, that Christians were then, every where, in subjection or slavery; A poor, feeble, helpless people, thrust into Prisons, or thrown to the Lyons, at the pleasure of their Princes or Rulers. 'Tis true, when the Empire became Christian under *Constantine*, in the fourth Century, there was, for a time, peace and prosperity in the Church, and a good degree of Purity and Piety. But that peace was soon disturb'd, and that piety soon corrupted. The growing pride and ambition of the Ecclesiasticks, and their easiness to admit or introduce Superstitious Practices, destroy'd the purity of the Church. And as to the peace of it, Their contests about opinions and doctrines, tore the Christians themselves into pieces; and, soon after, an inundation of Barbarous People fell into Christendom, and put it all into flames and confusion. After this Eruption of the Northern Nations, *Mahometanism* rose in the East; and swarms of *Saracens*, like armies of Locusts, invaded, conquer'd, and planted their religion in several parts of the *Roman* Empire and of the Christianiz'd World. And can we call such times the Reign of Christ, or the imprisonment of Satan? In the following ages, the *Turks* over-run the Eastern Empire and the *Greek* Church, and still hold that miserable people in slavery. Providence seems to have so order'd affairs, that the Christian World should never be without a WOE upon it, lest it should fansie it self already in those happy days of Peace and Prosperity, which are reserv'd for future times. Lastly, whosoever is sensible of the corruptions and persecutions of the Church of *Rome*, since she came to her greatness; whosoever allows her to be *mystical Babylon*, which must fall before the kingdom of Christ comes on; will think that kingdom duly plac'd by St. *John* at the end of his Prophecies, concerning the Christian Church: and that there still *remains, according* to the words of St. *Paul*, (Hebr. 4. 9.) *a Sabbatism to the people of God*.

CHAPTER VI

The sence and testimony of the Primitive Church concerning the Millennium, *or future kingdom of Christ: from the times of the Apostles to the* Nicene *Council. The second Proposition laid down. When, by what means, and for what reasons, that doctrine was afterwards neglected or discountenanc'd.*

YOU have heard the voice of the *Prophets* and *Apostles*, declaring the future kingdom of Christ. Next to these, the *Primitive Fathers* are accounted of good authority; Let us therefore now enquire into their Sence concerning this Doctrine, that we may give satisfaction to all parties; And both those that are guided by Scripture alone, and those that have a Veneration for Antiquity, may find proofs suitable to their inclinations and judgment.

And to make few words of it, we will lay down this Conclusion, *That the Millennial kingdom of Christ was the general doctrine of the Primitive Church, from the times of the Apostles to the* Nicene *Council*; inclusively. St. *John* out-liv'd all the rest of the Apostles, and towards the latter end of his life, being banish'd into the Isle of *Pathmos*, he writ his *Apocalypse*; wherein he hath given us a more full and distinct account of the Millennial kingdom of Christ, than any of the Prophets or Apostles before him. *Papias*, Bishop of *Hierapolis*, and Martyr; one of

Iren.

lib. 5, *c.* 33.

St. *John's* Auditors, as *Irenæus* testifies; taught the same doctrine after St. *John.* He was the familiar friend of *Polycarp*, another of St. *John's* Disciples; and either from him, or immediately from St. *John's* mouth, he might receive this doctrine. That he taught it in the Church, is agreed on by all hands; both by those that are his followers, as *Irenæus*; and those that are not well-wishers to this doctrine, as *Eusebius* and *Jerome.*

There is also another chanel wherein this doctrine is traditionally deriv'd from St. *John,* namely by the Clergy of *Asia*; as *Irenæus* tells us in the same Chapter. For, arguing the point, he shows that the Blessing promis'd to *Jacob* from his Father *Isaac,* was not made good to him in this life, and therefore he says, *without doubt those words had a further aim and prospect upon the times of the kingdom*: (so they us'd to call the Millennial state) *when the Just rising from the dead, shall reign: and when Nature renew'd and set at liberty, shall yield plenty and abundance of all things; being blest with the dew of Heaven, and a great fertility of the Earth. According as has been related by those Ecclesiasticks or Clergy, who see St.* John, *the Disciple of Christ: and heard of him WHAT OUR LORD HAD TAUGHT CONCERNING THOSE TIMES.* This, you see, goes to the Fountain-head. The Christian Clergy receive it from St. *John,* and St. *John* relates it from the mouth of our Saviour.

So much for the Original authority of this doctrine, as a Tradition: that it was from St. *John,* and by him from Christ. And as to the propagation and prevailing of it in the primitive Church, we can bring a witness beyond all exception, *Justin Martyr,* contemporary with *Irenæus,* and his Senior. He says, *that himself, and all the Orthodox Christians of his time, did acknowledge the Resurrection of the flesh* (suppose the first resurrection) *and a thousand years reign in Jerusalem restor'd,* or in the new Jerusalem. *According as the Prophets, Ezekiel, and Isaiah, and Others, attest with common consent.* As St. *Peter* had said before, *Act.* 3. 21. *That all the Prophets had spoken of it.* Then he quotes the 65*th.* Chapter of *Isaiah,* which is a bulwork for this doctrine, that never can be broken. And to shew the *Jew,* with whom he had this discourse, that it was the sence of our Prophets, as well as of theirs, He tells him, that *a certain Man amongst us Christians, by name John, one of the Apostles of Christ, in a Revelation made to him did prophesie, that the faithful believers in Christ should live a thousand years in the new Jerusalem; and after that should be the general Resurrection and day of Judgment.* Thus you have the thoughts and sentiment of *Justin Martyr,* as to himself: as to all the reputed Orthodox of his time; As to the sence of the Prophets in the old Testament, and as to the sence of St. *John* in the *Apocalypse.* All conspiring in confirmation of the Millenary doctrine.

Dial. with Tryphon *the Jew.*

To these three witnesses, *Papias, Irenæus,* and *Justin Martyr,* we may add two more within the second age of the Church: *Melito,* Bishop of *Sardis,* and St. *Barnabas,* or whosoever was the Author of the Epistle under his name. This *Melito,* by some is thought to be the Angel of the Church of *Sardis,* to whom St. *John* directs the Epistle to that Church: *Apoc.* 3. 1. But I do not take him to be so ancient; However he was Bishop of that place, at least in the second Century, and a Person of great Sanctity and Learning. He writ many Books, as you may *de Script. Eccles.*

Dogm. Eccl. c. 55.

see in St. *Jerome*: and, as He notes out of *Tertullian, was by most Christians reputed a Prophet.* He was also a declar'd *Millenary,* and is recorded as such, both by *Jerome* and *Gennadius.* As to the Epistle of *Barnabas,* which we mention'd, it must be very ancient, whosoever is the Author of it, and before the third Century; seeing it is often cited by *Clemens Alexandrinus,* who was himself within the second Century. The genius of it is very much Millenarian, in the interpretation of the *Sabbath,* the *promis'd Land,* a *Day* for a *thousand years,* and concerning the *Renovation of the World.* In all which, He follows the foot-steps of the Orthodox of those times: that is, of the *Millenarians.*

So much for the first and second Centuries of the Church. By which short account it appears, that the Millenary doctrine was *Orthodox* and *Catholick* in those early days. For these Authors do not set it down as a private opinion of their own, but as a *Christian doctrine,* or an *Apostolical Tradition.* 'Tis remarkable what *Papias* says of himself, and his way of learning, In his Book call'd, *The* *De Scrip. Eccles.* *Explanation of the Words of the Lord,* as St. *Jerome* gives us an account of it: He says in his Preface, *He did not follow various opinions, but had the Apostles for his Authors.* And that he consider'd what Andrew, *what* Peter *said; what* Philip, *what* Thomas, *and other Disciples of the Lord.* As also what Aristion, *and* John *the Senior, Disciples of the Lord, what they spoke.* And that he did not profit so much by reading Books, *as by the living voice of these persons which resounded from them to that day.* This hath very much the air of truth and sincerity, and of a Man that, in good earnest, sought after the Christian doctrine, from those that were the most authentick Teachers of it. I know *Eusebius* in his *Ecclesiastical* *Vide Hieron. Epist. 28. ad Lucinium.* *History,* gives a double Character of this *Papias;* In one place, he calls him, *A very eloquent Man in all things, and skilful in Scripture;* and in another, he makes him a man of a *small understanding.* But what reason there is to suspect *Eusebius* of partiality in this point of the *Millennium;* we shall make appear hereafter. However, we do not depend upon the learning of *Papias,* or the depth of his understanding: allow him but to be an honest man, and a fair witness, and 'tis all we desire. And we have little reason to question his testimony in this point, seeing it is backt by others of good credit; and also because there is no counter-evidence, nor any witness that appears against him. For there is not extant, either the Writing, Name, or Memory, of any Person, that contested this doctrine in the first or second Century. I say, that call'd in question this Millenary doctrine, propos'd after a Christian manner; unless such Hereticks as deny'd the Resurrection wholly: or such Christians as deny'd the divine authority of the Apocalypse.

We proceed now to the third Century. Where you find *Tertullian, Origen, Victorinus,* Bishop and Martyr: *Nepos, Ægyptius, Cyprian,* and, at the end of it, *Lactantius:* All openly professing, or implicitly favouring the Millenary doctrine. We do not mention *Clemens Alexandrinus,* contemporary with *Tertullian,* because he hath not any thing, that I know of, expresly either for, or against the *Millennium.* But he takes notice that the *Seventh Day* hath been accounted *Sacred,* both by the Hebrews and Greeks, because of the *Revolution* of the *World,* and the *Renovation of all things.* And giving this as a reason why they kept that day

Holy, seeing there is not a Revolution of the World every seven days, it can be in no other sence than as the *Seventh Day* represents the *seventh Millenary*, in which the Renovation of the World and the kingdom of Christ, is to be. As to *Tertullian*, St. *Jerome* reckons him, in the first place, amongst the Latin *Millenaries*. And tho' his Book, about the *Hope* of the *Faithful*, as also that about *Paradise*, which should have given us the greatest light in this affair, be both lost or suppress'd; yet there are sufficient indications of his Millenary opinion in his Tracts against *Marcion*, and against *Hermogenes*. St. *Cyprian* was *Tertullian*'s admirer, and inclines to the same opinion, so far as one can judge, in this particular; for his period of *Six thousand years*, and making the *Seventh Millenary* the Consummation of all, is wholly according to the Analogy of the Millenary doctrine. As to the two Bishops, *Victorinus* and *Nepos*, St. *Jerome* vouches for them. The writings of the one are lost, and of the other so chang'd, that the sence of the Author does not appear there now. But *Lactantius*, whom we nam'd in the last place, does openly and profusely teach this doctrine, in his *Divine Institutions:* and with the same assurance that he does other parts of the Christian Doctrine. For he concludes thus, speaking of the *Millennium, This is the Doctrine of the Holy Prophets, which we Christians follow. This is our wisdom,* &c. Yet he acknowledges there that it was kept as a mystery or secret amongst the Christians, lest the Heathens should make any perverse or odious interpretation of it. And for the same or like reason, I believe, The Book of the *Apocalypse* was kept out of the hands of the Vulgar for some time, and not read publickly, lest it should be found to have spoken too openly of the fate of the *Roman* Empire, or of this Millennial State.

Book 7.

So much for the first, second, and third Century of the Church. But, by our conclusion, we engag'd to make out this proof as far as the *Nicene Council*, Inclusively. The *Nicene Council* was about the year of Christ 325. and we may reasonably suppose *Lactantius* was then living; at least he came within the time of *Constantine*'s Empire. But however the Fathers of that Council are themselves our witnesses in this point. For, in their *Ecclesiastical Forms* or *Constitutions*, in the *chapter about the Providence of God*, and *about the World*, they speak thus; *The World was made meaner or less perfect, providentially; for God foresee that man would sin. Wherefore we expect New Heavens and a New Earth, according to the holy Scriptures: at the appearance and kingdom of the great God, and our Saviour Jesus Christ.* And then, as *Daniel* says (ch. 7. 18.) *The Saints of the most High shall take the kingdom. And the Earth shall be pure, holy, the land of the living, not of the dead. Which* David *foreseeing by the eye of Faith*, cryes out (Ps. 27. 13.) *I believe to see the good things of the Lord, in the land of the living.* Our Saviour says, *Happy are the meek, for they shall inherit the Earth*, Matt. 5. 5. *and the* Prophet Isaiah *says, (chap.* 26. 6.) *the feet of the meek and lowly shall tread upon it.* So you see, according to the judgment of these Fathers, there will be a kingdom of Christ upon Earth; and moreover, that it will be in the *New Heavens* and the *New Earth*. And, in both these points, they cite the Prophets and our Saviour in confirmation of them.

Thus we have discharg'd our promise and given you an account of the doctrine of the *Millennium*, or future kingdom of Christ, throughout the three first Ages of the Church: before any considerable corruptions were crept into the Christian Religion. And those Authorities of single and successive Fathers, we have seal'd up all together, with the declaration of the *Nicene* Fathers, in a Body. Those that think Tradition a rule of Faith, or a considerable motive to it, will find it hard to turn off the force of these Testimonies. And those that do not go so far, but yet have a reverence for Antiquity and the Primitive Church, will not easily produce better authorities, more early, more numerous, or more uncontradicted, for any article that is not fundamental. Yet these are but Seconds to the Prophets and Apostles, who are truly the Principals in this cause. I will leave them altogether, to be examin'd and weigh'd by the impartial Reader. And because they seem to me to make a full and undeniable proof, I will now at the foot of the account set

Propos. 2.

down our second Proposition, which is this, *That there is a Millennial State, or a Future Kingdom of Christ and his Saints, Prophesied of and Promised, in the Old and New Testament; and receiv'd by the Primitive Church as a Christian and Catholick Doctrine.*

HAVING dispatch'd this main point, To conclude the Chapter and this head of our discourse, It will be some satisfaction possibly to see, *How* a Doctrine so generally receiv'd and approv'd, came to decay and almost wear out of the Church, in following Ages. The Christian Millenary doctrine was not call'd into question, so far as appears from History, before the middle of the third Century; when *Dionysius Alexandrinus* writ against *Nepos*, an *Ægyptian* Bishop, who had declar'd himself upon that subject. But we do not find that this Book had any great effect; for the declaration or constitution of the *Nicene Fathers* was after: and in St. *Jerome's* time, who writ towards the end of the fourth Century, this doctrine had so much Credit, that, He, who was its greatest adversary, yet durst not condemn it, as he says himself. *Quæ licet non sequamur, tamen damnare non possumus; quià multi Ecclesiasticorum virorum & Martyres ista dixerunt. Which things, or doctrines,* speaking of the Millennium, *tho' we do not follow, yet we cannot condemn. Because many of our Church-men, and Martyrs, have affirmed these things.* And when *Apollinarius* replyed to that Book of *Dionysius,* St. *Jerome* says, that, *not only those of his own Sect, but a great multitude of other Christians did agree with* Apollinarius *in that particular. Ut præsagâ mente jam cernam, quantorum in me rabies concitanda sit. That I now foresee, how many will be enrag'd against me, for what I have spoken against the Millenary doctrine.*

We may therefore conclude that in St. *Jerome's* time the Millenaries made the greater party in the Church; for a little matter would not have frighted him from censuring their opinion. St. *Jerome* was a rough and rugged Saint, and an unfair adversary, that usually run down, with heat and violence, what stood in his way. As to his unfairness, he shews it sufficiently in this very cause, for he generally represents the Millenary doctrine after a Judaical rather than a *Christian* manner.

And in reckoning up the chief Patrons of it, he always skips *Justin Martyr*. Who was not a man so obscure as to be overlook'd: and he was a man that had declar'd himself sufficiently upon this point, for he says, *both himself and all the Orthodox of his time, were of that judgment*, and applyes both the *Apocalypse* of St. *John*, and the 65*th chap.* of *Isaiah*, for the proof of it. As we noted before.

As St. *Jerome* was an open enemy to this doctrine, so *Eusebius* was a back friend to it; and represented every thing to its disadvantage, so far as was tolerably consistent with the fairness of an Historian. He gives a slight character of *Papias*, without any authority for it; and brings in one *Gaius* that makes *Cerinthus* to be the author of the *Apocalypse* and of the *Millennium*: and calls the Visions there *monstrous stories*. He himself is willing to shuffle off that Book from *John* the *Evangelist* to another *John* a *Presbyter*: and to shew his skill in the interpretation of it, he makes the *New Jerusalem* in the 21*st chap.* to be *Constantine*'s *Jerusalem*, when he turn'd the Heathen Temples there into Christian. A wonderful invention. As St. *Jerome* by his flouts, so *Eusebius* by sinister insinuations, endeavour'd to lessen the reputation of this doctrine; and the art they both us'd, was, to misrepresent it as *Judaical*. But we must not cast off every doctrine which the Jews believ'd, only for that reason; for we have the same Oracles which they had, and the same Prophets: and they have collected from them the same general doctrine that we have, namely, that *there will be an happy and pacifick state of the Church, in future times*. But as to the circumstances of this state we differ very much; They suppose the Mosaical Law will be restor'd, with all its pomp, rites, and ceremonies; whereas we suppose the Christian Worship, or something more perfect, will then take place. Yet St. *Jerome* has the confidence, even there where he speaks of the many Christian Clergy and Martyrs that held this doctrine: has the confidence, I say, to represent it, as if they held that *Circumcision, Sacrifices,* and all the Judaical rites, should then be restor'd. Which seems to me to be a great slander, and a great instance how far mens passions will carry them, in misrepresenting an opinion which they have a mind to disgrace.

But as we have reason to blame the partiality of those that opposed this doctrine, so, on the other hand, we cannot excuse the Patrons of it from all indiscretions. I believe they might partly themselves make it obnoxious; by mixing some things with it, from pretended traditions, or the Books of the Sibylls, or other private authorities, that had so sufficient warrant from Scripture; and things, sometimes, that Nature would not easily bear. Besides, in later ages, they seem to have dropt one half of the doctrine, namely, the *Renovation of Nature*, which *Irenæus, Justin Martyr*, and the Ancients, joyn inseparably with the Millennium. And by this omission, the doctrine hath been made less intelligible, and one part of it inconsistent with another. And when their pretensions were to reign upon this present Earth, and in this present state of Nature, it gave a jealousie to Temporal Princes, and gave occasion likewise to many of fanatical Spirits, under the notion of Saints, to aspire to dominion, after a violent and tumultuary manner. This I reckon as one great cause that brought the doctrine into discredit. But I hope by reducing of it to the true state, we shall cure this and other abuses, for the future.

Eccles. Hist. 3. 22.
τερατολογίας.

l. 3. 32. *de vit. Constan.*

Lastly, It never pleas'd the Church of *Rome;* and so far as the influence and authority of that would go, you may be sure it would be deprest and discountenanc'd. I never yet met with a Popish Doctor that held the *Millennium*; and *Baronius* would have it pass for an Heresie, and *Papias* for the Inventor of it; whereas, if *Irenæus* may be credited, it was receiv'd from St. *John*, and by him from the mouth of our Saviour. And neither St. *Jerome*, nor his friend Pope *Damasus*, durst ever condemn it for an *heresie*. It was always indeed uneasie, and gave offence, to the Church of *Rome*, because it does not suite to that Scheme of Christianity, which they have drawn. They suppose Christ reigns already, by his Vicar, the Pope: and treads upon the Necks of Emperours and Kings. And if they could but suppress the *Northern Heresie*, as they call it, they do not know what a Millennium would signifie, or how the Church could be in an happier condition than she is. The *Apocalypse* of St. *John* does suppose the true Church under hardship and persecution, more or less, for the greatest part of the Christian Ages: namely for 1260 years, while the witnesses are in Sack-cloth. But the Church of *Rome* hath been in prosperity and greatness, and the commanding Church in Christendom, for so long or longer, and hath rul'd the Nations with a Rod of Iron; so as that mark of the true Church, does not favour her at all. And the *Millennium* being properly a reward and triumph for those that come out of Persecution, such as have liv'd always in pomp and prosperity can pretend to no share in it, or benefit by it. This has made the Church of *Rome* have always an ill eye upon this doctrine, because it seem'd to have an ill eye upon her. And as she grew in splendor and greatness, she eclips'd and obscur'd it more and more: so that it would have been lost out of the World as an obsolete errour, if it had not been reviv'd by some of the Reformation.

CHAPTER VII

The true state of the Millennium, according to Characters taken from Scripture; some mistakes concerning it, examin'd.

WE have made sufficient proof of a Millennial state, from Scripture and Antiquity; and upon that firm Basis have setled our second Proposition. We should now determine the *Time* and *Place* of this future kingdom of Christ: Not whether it is to be in Heaven, or upon Earth: for that we suppose determin'd already; but whether it is to be in the present Earth, and under the present constitution of Nature, or in the *New Heavens* and *New Earth*, which are promis'd after the *Conflagration*. This is to make our *Third Proposition:* and I should have proceeded immediately to the examination of it, but that I imagine it will give us some light in this affair, if we enquire further into the true state of the *Millennium*, before we determine its Time and Place.

We have already noted some *moral* Characters of the *Millennial* state; And the great *Natural* Character of it, is this in general, That it will be *Paradisiacal*. Free from all inconveniences, either of external Nature, or of our own Bodies. For my part, I do not understand how there can be any considerable degree of happiness without *Indolency*: nor how there can be Indolency, while we have such Bodies as we have now, and such an external constitution of Nature. And as there must be *Indolency*, where there is happiness; so there must not be *Indigency*, or want of any due comforts of life. For where there is *Indigency*, there is solicitude, and distraction, and uneasiness, and fear: Passions, that do as naturally disquiet the Soul, as pain does the Body. Therefore Indolency and Plenty seem to be two essential Ingredients of every happy state; and these two in conjunction make that state we call *Paradisiacal*.

Now the Scripture seems plainly to exempt the Sons of the *New Jerusalem*, or of the *Millennium*, from all *pain* or *want*, in those words, Apoc. 21. 4. *And God shall wipe away all tears from their eyes. And there shall be no more death, neither sorrow, nor crying: neither shall there be any more pain: for the former things are passed away.* And the Lord of that kingdom, *He that sate upon the Throne*, said, *Behold I make all things new*, ver. 5. This Renovation is a restauration to some former state: and I hope not to that state of Indigency, and misery, and diseasedness, which we languish under at present. But to that pristine Paradisiacal state, which was the blessing of the first Heavens and the first Earth.

As Health and Plenty are the Blessings of Nature, so, in civil affairs, *Peace* is the greatest blessing. And this is inseparably annext to the *Millennium:* an indelible character of the kingdom of Christ. And by *Peace* we understand, not onely freedom from Persecution upon religious accounts, but that *Nation shall not rise up against Nation*, upon any account whatsoever. That bloody Monster, *War*, that hath devour'd so many Millions of the Sons of *Adam*, is now at length to be chain'd up: and the Furies, that run throughout the Earth, with their Snakes and Torches, shall be thrown into the Abyss, to sting and prey upon one another. All evil and mischievous passions shall be extinguish'd: and that not in men onely, but even in Brute creatures, according to the Prophets. *The Lamb and the Lyon shall lie down together, and the sucking Child shall play with the Basilisk.* Happy days, when not onely the Temple of *Janus* shall be shut up for a thousand years, and the *Nations shall beat their Swords into plowshares*: but all enmities and antipathies shall cease, all acts of hostility, throughout all nature. And this Universal Peace is a demonstration also of the former character, *Universal Plenty*: for where there is want and necessitousness, there will be quarrelling.

Fourthly, 'Tis a kingdom of Righteousness, as well as of Peace. These also must go together; for unrighteous Persons will not live long in peace, no more than indigent Persons. The *Psalmist* therefore joyns them together: and *Plenty* also, as their necessary preservative: in his description of the kingdom of Christ: Psal. 85. 10, 11, 12. *Mercy and truth are met together: Righteousness and peace have kissed each other. Truth shall spring out of the Earth, and righteousness shall look down from Heaven. Yea the Lord shall give good, and our Land shall yield her increase.* This will not be a medley-state, as the present World is, good and bad mingled together; but a *chosen generation, a royal Priesthood, an holy Nation, a peculiar people.* Those that have a part in the first Resurrection, the Scripture pronounceth them *Holy and Blessed*: and says, *the second death shall have no power over them.* Satan also is bound and shut up in the bottomless Pit, and has

Z

no liberty of tempting or seducing this people, for a thousand years: but at the
end of that time, he will meet with a degenerate crew, separate and aliens to the

Apoc. 5. 9.

Holy City, that will make war against it, and perish in the attempt. In a word,
those that are to enjoy this state, are always distinguish'd from the multitude, as

ch. 7. 14.
ch. 14. 3, 4.
ch. 21. 27.

People redeem'd from the Earth; That have wash'd their Robes, and made them
white in the blood of the Lamb; and are represented as Victors over the World;
with such other Characters as are incompetible to any but the righteous.

Fifthly, This will be a state under a peculiar divine presence and conduct. It
is not easie indeed to determine the manner of this presence, but the Scripture
plainly implies some extraordinary divine presence to enlighten and enliven that

Apoc. 21. 3.

state. When the *New Jerusalem* was come down, St. *John* says, *And I heard a
great voice out of Heaven, saying, Behold the Tabernacle of God is with men: and
he will dwell with them, and they shall be his people: and God himself shall be with
them and be their God.* And the like is promis'd to the Palm-bearing Company,
Chap. 7. 15. where they are admitted to the priviledges of the *New Jerusalem*.
When our Saviour was incarnate, and vouchsafed to dwell amongst the Children
of Men, the same phrase is us'd by this same Author, Joh. 1. 14. *The Word was*

ἐσκήγωση

made flesh, and Tabernacled amongst us: and we beheld his glory, &c. We read it,
He dwelt amongst us, but render'd more closely, it is, *He* set his *Tabernacle amongst*

שכינה
*Maimon. Mor.
Nev. par.* 1. *c.* 25

us. And that which the *Hebrews* call the *Shekinah,* or *divine presence,* comes from
this very word. Therefore there will be a *Shekinah* in that kingdom of Christ;
but as to the mode of it, I am very willing to confess my ignorance.

The last Character that belongs to this state, or rather to those that enjoy it, is,
that they are *Kings and Priests unto God.* This is a character often repeated in
Scripture, and therefore the more to be regarded. It occurs thrice in the Apocalypse in formal terms, *Ch.* 1. 6. *Ch.* 5. 10. *Ch.* 20. 6. And as to the Regal dignity
apart, that is further exprest, either by the *donation of a kingdom,* as in *Daniel*'s
phrase, *Chap.* 7. 18, 22, 27. Or by *placing upon Thrones,* with a judicial power;
which is the New Testament style, *Matt.* 19. 28. *Luk.* 22. 29, 30. *Revel.* 20. 4.
These two Titles, no doubt, are intended to comprehend the highest honours
that we are capable of: these being the highest dignities in every kingdom; and
such as were by the Ancients, both in the East and in the West, commonly united
in one and the same Person: Their Kings being Priests, like *Melchisedeck:* or as
the *Roman* Emperour was *Pontifex Maximus.* But as to the Sacerdotal character,
that seems chiefly to respect the temper of the mind; to signifie a People dedicated
to God and his Service: Separate from the World, and from secular affairs:
Spending their time in devotion and contemplation, which will be the great
employments of that happy state. For where there is ease, peace, and plenty of
all things: refin'd Bodies, and purified Minds, there will be more inclination to
intellectual exercises and entertainments: which they may attend upon, without
any distraction, having neither want, pain, nor worldly business.

The Title of *King* implies a confluence of all things that constitute temporal
happiness. 'Tis the highest thing we can wish any in this World, to be a King.
So as the *Regal* dignity seems to comprehend all the Goods of Fortune, or external felicity: And the *Sacerdotal,* the Goods of the Mind, or internal: Both

which concur in the constitution of true happiness. There is also a further force and emphasis in this notion, *of the Saints being made Kings*, if we consider it *comparatively*, with respect to what they were before in this World; where they were not only mean and despicable, in subjection and servility, but often under persecution, abus'd and trampled upon, by the secular and Ecclesiastical powers. But now the Scene is chang'd, and you see the reverse of Providence, according as *Abraham* said to the Rich *man, Son, remember that thou in thy life time receivedst the good things, and likewise Lazarus evil things. But now he is comforted, and thou art tormented.* Now they are set upon Thrones and Tribunals, who were before arraigned as Criminals, and brought before tyrannical Judicatures. They are now Laws and Law-givers to themselves: in a true state of Royal Liberty, neither under the domination of evil men, nor of their own evil passions.

Some possibly may think, that this high character of *being made Priests* and *Kings to God*, is not general to all that enjoy the *Millennium*, but a prerogative belonging to the Apostles and some of the chief Martyrs, who are eminently rewarded for their eminent services. But Scripture, as far as I perceive, applyes it to all that inherit that kingdom. *The redeemed out of every kindred, and tongue, and people, and nation,* are made *kings and priests to God, and shall reign on the earth, Apoc. 5. 9, 10.* And in the 20*th chap. ver.* 6. all the sons of the first Resurrection are made *Priests of God and shall reign with him a thousand years.* Here is no distinction or discrimination thus far. Not that we suppose an universal equality of conditions in the Millennial state, but as to all these characters which we have given of it, I do not perceive that they are restrain'd or confin'd by Scripture to single persons, but make the general happiness of that state, and are the portion of every one that is admitted into the New Jerusalem.

Others possibly may think that this priviledge of the *first Resurrection* is not common to all that enjoy the Millennial state. For tho' St. *John*, who is the only person that hath made express mention of the *first Resurrection*, and of the *thousand years reign* of Christ, does joyn these two as the same thing, and common to the same persons; yet I know there are some that would distinguish them as things of a different extent, and also of a different nature. They suppose the Martyrs only will rise from the dead; and will be immediately translated into Heaven, and there pass their *Millennium* in celestial glory. While the Church is still here below, in her *Millennium*, such as it is; a state indeed better than ordinary, and free from persecution: but obnoxious to all the inconveniences of our present mortal life, and a medly of good and bad people, without separation. This is such an Idea of the *Millennium*, as, to my eye, hath neither beauty in it, nor foundation in Scripture. That the Citizens of the *New Jerusalem* are not a miscellaneous company, but a Community of righteous persons, we have noted before: and that the state of nature will be better than it is at present. But, besides this, what warrant have they for this Ascension of the Martyrs into Heaven at that time? where do we read of that in Scripture? And in those things that are not matters of Natural Order, but of Divine Oeconomy, we ought to be very careful how we add to Scripture.

The Scripture speaks only of the Resurrection of the Martyrs, *Apoc.* 20. 45. but not a word concerning their ascension into heaven. Will that be visible ? We read of our Saviour's Resurrection and Ascension, and therefore we have reason to affirm them both. We read also of the Resurrection and Ascension of the *Witnesses,* (*Apoc.* 11.) in a figurate sence, and in that sence we may assert them upon good grounds. But as to the Martyrs, we read of their Resurrection only, without any thing exprest or imply'd about their Ascension. By what authority then shall we add this new notion to the history or scheme of the Millennium ? The Scripture on the contrary, makes mention of the descent of the *New Jerusalem, Apoc.* 21. 2. making the Earth the Theatre of all that affair. And the Camp of the Saints is upon the Earth, *ver.* 9. and these Saints are the same persons, so far as can be collected from the text, that rise *from the dead, and reign'd with Christ,* and were *Priests to God. ver.* 4, 5, 6. Neither is there any distinction made, that I find, by St. *John,* of two sorts of Saints in the *Millennium,* the one in Heaven, and the other upon Earth. Lastly, The four and twenty Elders, *ch.* 5. 10. tho' they were *Kings* and *Priests unto God,* were content to reign upon Earth. Now who can you suppose of a superiour order to these four and twenty Elders : Whether they represent the twelve Patriarchs and twelve Apostles, or whomsoever they represent, they are *chap.* 11. 16. plac'd next to him that sit upon the Throne, and they have Crowns of Gold upon their heads, *ch.* 4. 4. there can be no marks of honour and dignity greater than these are; and therefore seeing these highest Dignitaries in the Millennium or future kingdom of Christ, are to reign upon Earth, there is no ground to suppose the assumption of any other into Heaven upon that account, or upon that occasion.

This is a short and general draught of the Millennial state, or future Reign of the Saints, according to Scripture. Wherein I have endeavour'd to rectifie some mistakes or misconceptions about it: That viewing it in its true nature, we may be the better able to judge when and where it will obtain. Which is the next thing to be consider'd.

CHAPTER VIII

The Third Proposition laid down, concerning the time and place of the Millennium. *Several Arguments us'd to prove that it cannot be till after the Conflagration: and that the New Heavens and the New Earth are the true Seat of the blessed* Millennium.

WE come now to the Third and last head of our Discourse: To determine the *Time* and *Place* of the *Millennium.* And seeing it is indifferent whether the proofs lead or follow the Conclusion, we will lay down the Conclusion in the first place, that our business may be more in view; and back it with proofs in the *Propos.* 3. following part of the Chapter. Our Third and last Proposition therefore is this, *That the Blessed Millennium,* (properly so called) *according as it is describ'd in Scripture, cannot obtain in the present Earth, nor under the present constitution of Nature and Providence; but is to be celebrated in the New Heavens and New Earth,*

356

after the Conflagration. This Proposition, it may be, will seem a Paradox or singularity to many, even of those that believe a *Millennium*; We will therefore make it the business of this Chapter, to state it, and prove it; by such Arguments as are manifestly founded in Scripture and in Reason.

And to prevent mistakes, we must premise this in the first place; That, tho' the Blessed *Millennium* will not be in this Earth, yet we allow that the state of the Church here, will grow much better than it is at present. There will be a full *Resurrection of the Witnesses,* and an *Ascension* into power, and the tenth part of the City will fall; which things imply ease from Persecution, The Conversion of some part of the Christian World to the reformed Faith, and a considerable diminution of the power of Antichrist. But this still comes far short of the happiness and glory wherein the future Kingdom of Christ is represented. Which cannot come to pass till the *Man of Sin* be destroy'd, with a total destruction. After the Resurrection of the Witnesses, there is a Third *WOE yet* to come: and how long that will last, does not appear. If it bear proportion with the preceding *WOES*, it may last some hundreds of years. And we cannot imagine the *Millennium* to begin till that *WOE* be finish'd. As neither till the *Vials* be poured out, in the 15*th chap.* which cannot be all pour'd out till after the Resurrection of the Witnesses; those *Vials* being the last plagues that compleat the destruction of Antichrist. Wherefore allowing that the Church, upon the Resurrection and Ascension of the Witnesses, will be advanc'd into a better condition, yet that condition cannot be the Millennial state; where the Beast is utterly destroy'd, and Satan bound, and cast into the bottomless pit.

This being premis'd, let us now examine what grounds there are for the Translation of that blessed state into the New Heavens and New Earth: seeing that thought, it may be, to many persons, will appear new and extraordinary. In the first place, We suppose it out of dispute, that there will be New Heavens and a New Earth after the Conflagration. This was our first Proposition, and we depend upon it, as sufficiently prov'd both from Scripture and Antiquity. This being admitted, How will you stock this New Earth? What use will you put it to? 'Twill be a much nobler Earth, and better built than the present: and 'tis pity it should only float about, empty and useless, in the wild Air. If you will not make it the seat and habitation of the Just in the blessed *Millennium*, what will you make it? How will it turn to account? what hath Providence design'd it for? We must not suppose New Worlds made without counsel or design. And as, on the one hand, you cannot tell what to do with this New Creation, if it be not thus employ'd: so, on the other hand, it is every way fitted and suited to be an happy and Paradisiacal habitation, and answers all the natural Characters of the Millennial state; which is a great presumption that it is design'd for it.

But to argue this more closely upon Scripture-grounds. St. *Peter* says, the Righteous shall inhabit the new Heavens and the new Earth: 2 *Pet.* 3. 13. *Nevertheless, according to his promise, we look for new Heavens and new Earth, WHEREIN DWELLETH RIGHTEOUSNESS:* that is, a Righteous people, as we have shewn before. But who are these righteous People? that's the great question. If you compare St. *Peter*'s new Heavens and new Earth with St. *John*'s, *Apoc.* 21.

1, 2. it will go far towards the resolution of this question: For St. *John* seems plainly to make the Inhabitants of the *New Jerusalem* to be in this *New Earth*. *I saw*, says he, *new Heavens and a new Earth:* and the *New Jerusalem descending from God out of Heaven*; therefore descending into this *new Earth*, which he had mention'd immediately before. And there *the Tabernacle of God was with men*, *ver.* 3. and there He that sate upon the Throne, said, *Behold I make all things new*. Referring still to this new Heavens and new Earth, as the Theater where all these things are acted, or all these Scenes exhibited: from the first Verse to the eighth. Now the New Jerusalem state being the same with the Millennial, if the one be in the new Heavens and new Earth, the other is there also. And this interpretation of St. *John*'s words is confirm'd and fully assur'd to us by the Prophet *Isaiah*; who also placeth the joy and rejoycing of the *new Jerusalem* in the new Heavens and new Earth: Chap. 65. 17, 18. *For behold I create new Heavens and a new Earth: and the former shall not be remembred: but be you glad and rejoyce for ever in that which I create: for behold I create Jerusalem a rejoycing and her people a joy.* Namely in that new Heavens and new Earth. Which answers to St. *John*'s Vision of the new *Jerusalem* being let down upon the new Earth.

To these reasons, and deductions from Scripture, we might add the testimony of several of the Fathers; I mean of those that were Millenaries. For we are speaking now to such as believe the *Millennium*, but place it in the present Earth before the Renovation whereas the ancient Millenaries suppos'd the regeneration and renovation of the World before the kingdom of Christ came. As you may see in **Irenæus*, a *Justin Martyr*, b *Tertullian*, c *Lactantius*, and d the Author *ad Orthodoxos*. And the neglect of this, I look upon as one reason, as we noted before, that brought that doctrine into discredit and decay. For when they plac'd the kingdom of the Saints upon this Earth, it became more capable of being abus'd, by fanatical spirits, to the disturbance of the World, and the invasion of the rights of the Magistrates, Civil or Ecclesiastical, under that notion of Saints. And made them also dream of sensual pleasures, such as they see in this life: Or at least gave an occasion and opportunity to those, that had a mind to make the doctrine odious, of charging it with these consequences. All these abuses are cut off, and these scandals prevented, by placing the Millennium aright. Namely, not in this present life, or on this present Earth, but in the new Creation, where peace and righteousness will dwell. And this is our first argument why we place the Millennium in the new Heavens and new Earth: And 'tis taken partly, you see, from the reason of the thing it self, the difficulty of assigning any other use of the New Earth, and its fitness for this; and partly from Scripture-evidence, and partly from Antiquity.

The second argument for our opinion, is this; The present constitution of Nature will not bear that happiness, that is promis'd in the Millennium, or is not consistent with it. The diseases of our Bodies, the disorders of our passions, the incommodiousness of external Nature; Indigency, servility, and the unpeaceableness of the World; These are things inconsistent with the happiness that is promis'd in the kingdom of Christ. But these are constant attendants upon this life,

* *li.* 5, *ch.* 32, &c. a *Dial. cum* Tryph. b *Contra Marc.* c *Li.* 7. d *Quæst. & respon.* 93.

and inseparable from the present state of Nature. Suppose the Millennium was to begin Nine or Ten Years hence, as some pretend it will. How shall this World, all on a sudden, be metamorphos'd into that happy state? No more *sorrow, nor crying, nor pain, nor death*, says St. *John*: *All former things are past away*. But how past away? Shall we not have the same Bodies: and the same external Nature: and the same corruptions of the Air: and the same excesses and intemperature of Seasons? Will there not be the same barrenness of the ground: the same number of People to be fed: and must they not get their living by the sweat of their brows, with servile labour and drudgery? How then are all former evils past away? And as to publick affairs, while there are the same necessities of humane life, and a distinction of Nations, those Nations sometimes will have contrary interests, will clash and interfere one with another: whence differences, and contests, and Wars will arise, and the *Thousand Years Truce*, I am afraid, will be often broken. We might add also, that if our Bodies be not chang'd, we shall be subject to the same appetites, and the same passions: and upon those, vices will grow: as bad fruit upon a bad Tree. To conclude, so long as our Bodies are the same: external Nature the same: The necessities of humane life the same: which things are the roots of evil; you may call it a *Millennium*, or what you please, but there will be still diseases, vices, Wars, tears and cries, pain and sorrow in this *Millennium*; And if so, 'tis a *Millennium* of your own making; for that which the Prophets describe is quite another thing.

Furthermore, if you suppose the Millennium will be upon this Earth, and begin, it may be, ten or twenty years hence, How will it be introduc'd: how shall we know when we are in it, or when we enter upon it? If we continue the same, and all Nature continue the same, we shall not discern when we slip into the Millennium. And as to the Moral state of it, shall we all, on a sudden, *become Kings and Priests to God?* wherein will that change consist, and how will it be wrought? St. *John* makes the *First Resurrection* introduce the Millennium; and that's a conspicuous mark and boundary. But as to the modern or vulgar Millennium, I know not how 'tis usher'd in. Whether they suppose a visible resurrection of the Martyrs, and a visible Ascension: and that to be a Signal to all the World that the Jubilee is beginning: or whether 'tis gradual and creeps upon us insensibly: or the fall of the Beast marks it. These things need both explication and proof; for to me they seem either arbitrary, or unintelligible.

But to return more closely to our Subject. That which gives me the greatest scandal in this doctrine of the vulgar Millennium, is, their joyning things together that are really inconsistent; a natural World of one colour, and a moral World of another. They will make us happy in spight of Nature: as the Stoicks would make a man happy in *Phalaris his Bull*; so must the Saints be in full bliss in the Millennium, tho' they be under a fit of the Gout or of the Stone. For my part, I could never reconcile pain to happiness: It seems to me to destroy and drown all pleasure, as a loud noise does a still voice. It affects the Nerves with violence, and over-bears all other motions. But if, according to this modern supposition, they have the same Bodies, and breath the same air, in the Millennium, as we do now, there will be both private and Epidemical distempers, in the same

Apoc. 21. 4.

359

manner as now; Suppose then a Plague comes and sweeps away half an hundred thousand Saints in the Millennium, is this no prejudice or dishonour to the State? Or a War makes a Nation desolate: or, in single Persons, a lingring disease makes life a burthen: or a burning Fever, or a violent Colick tortures them to death. Where such evils as these reign, christen the thing what you will, it can be no better than a Mock-Millennium. Nor shall I ever be perswaded that such a state as our present life, where an akeing Tooth, or an akeing Head, does so discompose the Soul, as to make her unfit for business, study, devotion, or any useful employment: And that all the powers of the mind, all its vertue, and all its wisdom, are not able to stop these little motions, or to support them with tranquility: I can never perswade my self, I say, that such a state was designed by God or Nature, for a state of happiness.

Our third argument is this; The future kingdom of Christ will not take place, till the kingdom of Antichrist be wholly destroy'd. But that will not be wholly destroy'd till the end of the World, and the appearing of our Saviour. Therefore the Millennium will not be till then. Christ and Antichrist cannot reign upon Earth together: their kingdoms are opposite, as Light to darkness. Besides, the kingdom of Christ is universal, extends to all the Nations, and leaves no room for other kingdoms at that time. Thus it is describ'd in *Daniel*, in the place mention'd before, *Chap.* 7. 13, 14. *I saw in the Night visions, and behold, one like the Son of man, came with the Clouds of Heaven, and came to the Ancient of days; And there was given him dominion and glory, and a kingdom; that all People, Nations, and Languages, should serve him.* And again, ver. 27. *And the kingdom and dominion and the greatness of the kingdom under the whole heaven, shall be given to the people of the Saints of the most High; whose kingdom is an everlasting kingdom, and all dominions shall serve and obey him.* The same character of universality is given to the kingdom of Christ by *David, Isaiah,* and other Prophets. But the most direct proof of this, is from the *Apocalypse*: where the *Beast* and *false Prophet* are thrown into the Lake of Fire and Brimstone, (*Chap.* 19. 20) before the Millennium comes on: *ch.* 20. This, *being cast into a Lake of fire burning with brimstone,* must needs signifie utter destruction. Not a diminution of power onely, but a total perdition and consumption. And that this was before the Millennium, both the order of the narration shows, and its place in the Prophecy; And also because notice is taken, at the end of the Millennium, of the Beast and false Prophet's being in the Lake of fire, as of a thing past, and formerly transacted. For when Satan, at length, is thrown into the same Lake, 'tis said, He is thrown into the Lake of fire and brimstone, *where the Beast and false Prophet are: Apoc.* 20. 10. They were there before, it seems; namely, at the beginning of the Millennium; and now at the conclusion of it, the Devil is thrown in to them. Besides, the Ligation of Satan proves this point effectually. For so long as Antichrist reigns, Satan cannot be said to be bound; but he is bound at the beginning of the Millennium, therefore Antichrist's reign was then totally expir'd. Lastly, the destruction of *Babylon*, and the destruction of Antichrist go together: but you see *Babylon* utterly and finally destroy'd, (*Apoc.* 18. and 19.) before the Millennium comes on. I say *utterly and finally destroy'd.* For she is

Psal. 2. &
Psal. 72.
Isa. 2. 2.

not onely said to be made an utter desolation, but to be consum'd by fire: and absorpt as a Milstone thrown into the Sea: and that she shall be found no more at all, *Chap.* 18. 21. Nothing can express a total and universal destruction more effectually, or more emphatically. And this is before the Millennium begins; as you may see both by the order of the Prophecies, and particularly, in that upon this destruction, the Hallelujah's are sung, *Chap.* 19. and concluded thus, (*ver.* 6, 7.) *Hallelujah, for the God omnipotent reigneth. Let us be glad and rejoyce and give honour to him; for the marriage of the Lamb is come, and his wife hath made her self ready.* This, I suppose, every one allows to be the Millennial state, which now approaches, and is making ready, upon the destruction of *Babylon*.

Thus much for the first part of our argument, that the kingdom of Christ will not take place, till the kingdom of Antichrist be wholly destroyed. We are now to prove the second part: That the kingdom of Antichrist will not be wholly destroy'd till the end of the World, and the coming of our Saviour. This, one would think, is sufficiently prov'd from St. *Paul*'s words alone, 2 *Thess.* 2. 8. *The Lord shall consume the man of sin,* who is suppos'd the same with Antichrist, *with the Spirit of his mouth, and shall destroy him with the brightness of his coming.* He will not then be destroy'd before the coming of our Saviour: and that will not be till the end of the World. For St. *Peter* says, *Act.* 3. 21. *The Heaven must receive him,* speaking of Christ, *until the times of restitution of all things:* that is, the renovation of the World. And if we consider that our Saviour's coming will be in *flames of fire,* as the same Apostle St. *Paul* tells us, 2 *Thess.* 1. 7, 8. 'tis plain that his coming will not be till the Conflagration: in which last flames Antichrist, will be universally destroy'd. This manner of destruction agrees also with the *Apocalypse,* and with *Daniel,* and the Prophets of the old Testament. As to the Apocalypse, *Babylon,* the seat of Antichrist, is represented there as destroy'd by Fire, *chap.* 18. 8, 18. *ch.* 14. 11. *ch.* 19. 3, 20. And in *Daniel,* when the Beast is destroy'd, *ch.* 7. 11. *His body was given to the burning flame.* Then as to the other Prophets, they do not, you know, speak of Antichrist or the Beast in terms: but under the Types of *Babylon, Tyre,* and such like; and these places or Princes are represented by them as to be destroy'd by fire, *Isa.* 13. 19. *Jer.* 51. 25. *Ezek.* 28. 18.

So much for this third Argument. The fourth Argument is this: The Future Kingdom of Christ will not be till the day of Judgment and the Resurrection. But that will not be till the end of the World. Therefore neither the kingdom of Christ. By the day of Judgment here I do not mean the final and universal Judgment: Nor by the Resurrection, the final and universal Resurrection: for these will not be till after the Millennium. But we understand here the first day of Judgment and the first Resurrection, which will be at the end of this present World; according as St. *John* does distinguish them, in the 20*th chap.* of the *Apocalypse.* Now that the Millennium will not be till the day of Judgment in this sence, we have both the testimonies of *Daniel* and of St. *John. Daniel* in the 7*th chap.* supposes the Beast to rule *till judgment shall sit,* and then *they shall take away his dominion,* and it shall be given to the people of the Saints of the most High. St. *John* makes an explicit declaration of both these, in this 20*th chap.*

ver. 9, &c.
ver. 26, &c.

of the *Apocalypse*, which is the great Directory in this point of the Millennium; He says there were Thrones set, as for a judicature. Then there was a Resurrection from the Dead: and those that rise, reigned with Christ a Thousand years. Here's a Judicial Session, a Resurrection, and the reign of Christ joyned together. There is also another passage in St. *John*, that joyns the judgment of the Dead with the Kingdom of Christ. 'Tis in the 11*th chap.* under the seventh Trumpet. The words are these, *ver.* 15. *And the seventh Angel sounded, and there were great voices in heaven, saying, the kingdoms of this world are become the kingdoms of our Lord and of his Christ: and he shall reign for ever and ever. And the four and twenty Elders,* &c. *And the nations were angry, and thy wrath is come, and the time of the Dead, that they should be judged, and that thou shouldst give reward unto thy servants the Prophets, and to the Saints, and them that fear thy name.* Here are two things plainly express'd and link'd together, *The judging of the Dead*, and the *Kingdom of Christ*; wherein the Prophets and Saints are rewarded. Now as the *judging of the Dead* is not in this life, so neither is the reward of the Prophets and Saints in this life: as we are taught sufficiently in the Gospel and by the Apostles, (*Matt.* 19. 28. 1 *Thess.* 1. 7. 2 *Tim.* 4. 8. 1 *Pet.* 1. 7. *and ch.* 5. 4.) Therefore the Reign and Kingdom of Christ which is joyned with these two, cannot be in this life, or before the end of the world. And as a further testimony and confirmation of this, we may observe that St. *Paul* to *Timothy*, hath joyn'd together these three things; The *appearance of Christ, the Reign of Christ*, and the *judging of the Dead. I charge thee therefore before God, and the Lord Jesus Christ, who shall judge the quick and the dead, at his appearing, and his kingdom,* 2 *Tim.* 4. 1.

This might also be prov'd from the order, extent, and progress, of the Prophecies of the *Apocalypse*; whereof some are such as reach to the end of the World, and yet must be accomplish'd before the Millennium begin: as the Vials. Others are so far already advanc'd towards the end of the World, as to leave no room for a thousand years reign; as the Trumpets. But because every one hath his own interpretation of these Prophecies, and it would be tedious here to prove any single Hypothesis in contradistinction to all the rest, we will therefore leave this remark, to have more or less effect, according to the minds it falls upon. And proceed to our fifth Argument.

Fifthly, The *New Jerusalem*-state is the same with the Millennial state: But the *New Jerusalem*-state will not be till the end of the World, or till after the Conflagration: Therefore neither the Millennium. That the *New Jerusalem*-state is the same with the Millennium, is agreed upon, I think, by all Millenaries, Ancient and Modern. *Justin Martyr, Irenæus*, and *Tertullian*, speak of it in that sence; and so do the later Authors, so far as I have observ'd. And St. *John* seems to give them good authority for it. In the 20*th chap.* of the *Apocalypse*, he says, the *Camp of the Saints* and *the Beloved City* were besieg'd by Satan and his Gigantick crew at the end of the Millennium. That *Beloved City* is the *New Jerusalem*, and you see it is the same with the Camp of the Saints, or, at least, contemporary with it. Besides, the marriage of the Lamb was in the New Jerusalem, for that was the *Spouse of the Lamb, Apoc.* 21. 2. Now this Spouse was ready, and this marriage was said to be come, at the destruction of *Babylon*:

which was the beginning of the Millennium, *ch.* 18. 7. Therefore the New Jerusalem run all along with the Millennium, and was indeed the same thing under another name. Lastly, What is this New Jerusalem if it be not the same with the Millennial state? It is promis'd as a reward to the sufferers for Christ, *Apoc.* 3. 12. and you see its wonderful priviledges, *ch.* 21. 3, 4. and yet it is not heaven and eternal Life; for it is said to come down from God out of Heaven, *ch.* 21. 2. *and ch.* 3. 12. It can therefore be nothing but the glorious kingdom of Christ upon Earth, where the Saints shall reign with him a Thousand Years.

Now as to the second part of our Argument, that the New Jerusalem will not come down from Heaven till the end of the World: of this St. *John* seems to give us a plain proof or demonstration; for he places the New Jerusalem in the New Heavens and New Earth, which cannot be till after the Conflagration. Let us hear his words, *Apoc.* 21. 1, 2. *And I saw a New Heaven and a New Earth, for the first heaven and the first earth were passed away, and there was no more sea. And I John saw the Holy City, New Jerusalem, coming down from God out of heaven: prepared as a Bride adorned for her husband.* When the New Earth was made, he sees the New Jerusalem coming down upon it; and this renovation of the Earth not being till the Conflagration. The New Jerusalem could not be till then, neither. The Prophet *Isaiah* had long before said the same thing, though not in terms so express; He first says, *Behold I create new heavens and a new earth, wherein you shall rejoyce.* Then subjoyns immediately, *Behold, I create Jerusalem a rejoycing.* This rejoycing is still in the same place; in the New Heavens and New Earth, or in the New Jerusalem. And St. *John* in a like method first, sets down the New Earth, then the New Jerusalem; and expresses the mind of the Prophet *Isaiah* more distinctly. *Isa.* 65. 17, 18.

This leads me to a Sixth Argument to confirm our Conclusion. The time of the *Restitution* or *Restauration of all things*, spoken of by St. *Peter* and the Prophets, is the same with the Millennium: But that Restauration will not be till the coming of Christ, and the end of the World: Therefore neither the Millennium. That this Restitution of all things will not be till the coming of our Saviour, St. *Peter* declares in his Sermon, *Act.* 3. 21. and that the coming of our Saviour will not be till the end of the World, or till the Conflagration, both St. *Paul* and St. *Peter* signifie to us, 1 *Thess.* 1. 7, 8. 2 *Pet.* 3. 10. Therefore it remains only to prove, that this Restitution of all things spoken of here by the Apostle, is the same with the Millennium. I know that which it does directly and immediately signifie, is the Renovation of the World: but it must include the Moral World as well as the Natural: otherwise it cannot be truly said, as St. *Peter* does there, that all the Prophets have spoken of it. And what is the Renovation of the Natural and Moral World, but the New Jerusalem or the Millennium.

These Arguments, taken together, have, to me, an irresistible evidence for the proof of our Conclusion: That the Blessed Millennium cannot obtain in the present Earth, or before the Conflagration; But when Nature is renew'd, and the Saints and Martyrs rais'd from the Dead, then they shall reign together with Christ, in the New Heavens and New Earth, or in the New Jerusalem; Satan being bound for a thousand years.

CHAPTER IX

The chief employment of the Millennium, DEVOTION and CONTEMPLATION.

WE have now done with the substance of our Discourse: which is comprehended in these Three Propositions:

I.   *After the Conflagration of this World, there will be New Heavens and a
     New Earth: And that Earth will be inhabited.*

II. *That there is an happy Millennial state; Or a future kingdom of Christ and
     his Saints, prophesied of and promis'd in the Old and New Testament: and
     receiv'd by the Primitive Church, as a Christian and Catholick doctrine.*

III. *That this blessed Millennial state, according as it is describ'd in Scripture,
     cannot take place in the present Earth, nor under the present constitution of
     Nature and Providence: But is to be celebrated in the New Heavens and New
     Earth, after the Conflagration.*

These three Propositions support this Work; and if any of them be broken, I
confess my design is broken, and this Treatise is of no effect. But what remains
to be spoken to in these last Chapters, is more circumstantial or modal; and an
error or mistake in such things, does not wound any vital part of the argument.
You must now therefore lay aside your severity, and rigorous censures; we are
very happy, if, in this life, we can attain to the substance of truth: and make
rational conjectures concerning modes and circumstances; where every one hath
a right to offer his sence, with modesty and submission. Revelations made to us
from Heaven in this present state, are often incompleat, and do not tell us all: as
if it was on purpose to set our thoughts a work to supply the rest; which we may
lawfully do, provided it be according to the analogy of Scripture and Reason.

To proceed therefore; We suppose, as you see, the *new Heavens* and the *new
Earth* to be the seat of the *Millennium:* and that new Creation to be *Paradisiacal.*
Its Inhabitants also to be righteous Persons, the Saints of the most High. And
seeing the ordinary employments of our present life, will then be needless and
superseded, as Military affairs, Sea-affairs, most Trades and Manufactures, Law,
Physick, and the laborious part of Agriculture: it may be wonder'd, how this
happy People, will bestow their time: what entertainment they will find in a
state of so much ease, and so little action. To this one might answer in short, by
another question, *How* would they have entertain'd themselves in Paradise, if
man had continued in Innocency? This is a revolution of the same state, and
therefore they may pass their time as well now, as they could have done then.
But to answer more particularly, besides all innocent diversions, ingenuous con-
versations, and entertainments of friendship, the greatest part of their time will
be spent in *Devotion* and *Contemplation.* O happy employment, and next to that
of Heaven it self. What do the Saints above, but sing praises unto God, and
contemplate his Perfections. And how mean and despicable, for the most part,
are the employments of this present life, if compar'd with those intellectual
actions. If Mankind was divided into ten parts, nine of those ten employ their
time to get bread to their belly, and cloaths to their back; And what impertinences

are these to a reasonable Soul, if she was free from the clog of a mortal Body; or if that could be provided for, without trouble or loss of time? Corporeal labour is from need and necessity, but intellectual exercises are matter of choice, that please and perfect at the same time.

Devotion warms and opens the Soul, and disposes it to receive divine influences. It sometimes raises the mind into an heavenly ecstasie, and fills it with a joy that is not to be exprest. When it is pure, it leaves a strong impression upon the heart, of Love to God; and inspires us with a contempt of this World, having tasted the pleasures of the World to come. In the state which we speak of, seeing the *Tabernacle of God will be with men,* we may reasonably suppose that there will be greater effusions and irradiations of the Holy Spirit, than we have or can expect in this region of darkness: and consequently, all the strength and comfort that can arise from private devotion. *Apoc.* 21. 3.

And as to their publick Devotions, all beauties of holiness, all perfection of divine worship, will shine in their Assemblies. Whatsoever *David* says of *Sion* and *Jerusalem* are but shadows of this new *Jerusalem,* and of the glory that will be in those Solemnities. Imagine what a Congregation will be there of Patriarchs, Prophets, Apostles, Christian Martyrs, and Saints of the first rank, throughout all Ages. And these all known to one another by their Names and History. This very meeting together of such Persons, must needs create a joy unspeakable: But when they unite in their praises to God and to the Lamb, with pure hearts full of divine Love: when they sing their Halleluiah's to him that sits upon the Throne, that hath wash'd them in his blood, and redeem'd them out of every Kingdom, and Tongue, and People, and Nation. When, with their Psalms in their hands, they triumph over Sin, and Death, and Hell, and all the Powers of Darkness: can there be any thing, on this side Heaven, and a Quire of Angels, more glorious or more joyful? *Psal.* 84.
Psal. 87.

But why did I except Angels? Why may not they be thought to be present at these Assemblies? In a Society of Saints and purified Spirits, Why should we think their converse impossible? In the Golden Age, the gods were always represented, as having freer intercourse with Men; and before the Flood, we may reasonably believe it so. I cannot think, *Enoch* was translated into Heaven without any converse with its Inhabitants before he went thither. And seeing the Angels vouchsaf'd often, in former Ages, to visit the Patriarchs upon Earth, we may with reason judge, that they will much more converse with the same Patriarchs and holy Prophets, now they are risen from the Dead, and cleans'd from their sins, and seated in the new *Jerusalem.* I cannot but call to mind upon this occasion, that representation which St. *Paul* makes to us, of a glorious state and a glorious Assembly, too high for this present Earth: 'Tis *Hebr.* 12. 22, *&c.* in these words. *But you are come unto Mount Sion, and unto the City of the living God, the heavenly Jerusalem, and to an innumerable company of Angels; To the general Assembly and Church of the First-born, which are written in Heaven; and to God the Judge of all, and to the Spirits of just men made perfect.* This, I know, several apply to the Times and state of the Gospel, in opposition to that of the Law; and it is introduc'd in that manner; But here are several expressions too

high for any present state of things; They must respect a future state, either of
Heaven, or of the Millennial kingdom of Christ. And to the later of these the
expressions agree, and have a peculiar fitness and applicability to it. And what
follows in the context, *ver.* 26, 27, 28. *about shaking the Heavens and the Earth
once more:* Removing the former Scenes, and bringing on a new Kingdom that
cannot be shaken: All this, I say, answers to the kingdom of Christ, which is to
be establish'd in the new Heavens and new Earth.

But to proceed in their publick Devotions; Suppose this August Assembly,
inflam'd with all divine passions, met together to celebrate the name of God;
with Angels intermixt, to bear a part in this holy exercise. And let this concourse
be, not in any Temple made with hands, but under the great roof of Heaven,
(the true Temple of the most High,) so as all the Air may be fill'd with the chearful
harmony of their Hymns and Halleluiahs. Then, in the heighth of their devotion,
as they sing praises to the Lamb, and to him that sits upon the Throne, suppose
Apoc. 5. 11. the Heavens to open, and the Son of God to appear in his glory, with Thousands
and Ten Thousands of Angels round about him; That their eyes may see him,
who, for their sakes, was crucified upon Earth, now encircled with Light and
Majesty. This will raise them into as great transports as humane nature can
bear: They will wish to be dissolv'd, they will strive to fly up to him in the clouds,
ch. 5. 13. or to breath out their Souls in repeated doxologies of *Blessing, and honour, and
glory, and power, to him that sits upon the Throne, and to the Lamb, for ever and ever.*

But we cannot live always in the flames of Devotion. The weakness of our
nature will not suffer us to continue long under such strong Passions, and such
intenseness of Mind. The question is therefore, What will be the ordinary employment of that life? How will they entertain their thoughts, or spend their
time? For we suppose they will not have that multiplicity of frivolous business
that we have now: About our Bodies, about our Children: in Trades and Mechanicks: in Traffick and Navigation: or Wars by Sea or Land. These things being
swept away, wholly or in a great measure, what will come in their place? how
will they find work or entertainment for a long life? If, we consider, who they
are that will have a part in this first Resurrection, and be Inhabitants of that
World that is to come, we may easily believe that the most constant employment
of their life will be CONTEMPLATION. Not that I exclude any innocent
diversions, as I said before: The entertainments of friendship, or ingenuous
conversation, but the great business and design of that life is Contemplation: as
l. 5. *c.* 32. preparatory to heaven and eternal Glory. *Ut paulatim assuescant capere Deum,* as
Irenæus says: That they may, by degrees, enlarge their capacities, fit and *accustom
themselves to receive God.* Or, as he says in another place, *That they may become
capable of the glory of the Father,* that is, capable of bearing the glory and presence
of God: capable of the highest enjoyment of him, which is usually call'd the
Beatifical Vision; and is the condition of the blessed in Heaven.

It cannot be deny'd, that in such a Millennial state, where we shall be freed
from all the incumbrances of this life, and provided of better Bodies and greater
light of Mind: It cannot be doubted, I say, but that we shall then be in a disposition
to make great proficiency in the knowledge of all things, Divine and Intellectual:

and consequently of making happy preparations for entring upon a further state of glory. For there is nothing certainly does more prepare the mind of man for the highest perfections, than Contemplation: with that Devotion which naturally flows from it, as heat follows light. And this Contemplation hath always a greater or less effect upon the mind according to the perfection of its object. So as the Contemplation of the Divine Nature, is, of all others, the most perfective in it self, and to us, according to our capacities and degree of abstraction. An *Immense Being* does strangely fill the Soul: and Omnipotency, Omnisciency, and Infinite Goodness, do enlarge and dilate the Spirit, while it fixtly looks upon them. They raise strong passions of Love and Admiration, which melt our Nature, and transform it into the mould and image of that which we contemplate. What the Scripture says of our *Transformation* into the Divine likeness: what St. *John* and the *Platonists* say of our *Union* with God. And whatever is not Cant in the *Mystical Theology*, when they tell us of being Deified: all this must spring from these sources of Devotion and Contemplation. They will change and raise us from perfection to perfection, as from glory to glory: into a greater similitude and nearer station to the Divine Nature.

The Contemplation of God and his Works, comprehends all things. For, the one makes the uncreated World, and the other the Created. And as the divine Essence and Attributes are the greatest object that the mind of man can set before it self; so next to that are the effects and emanations of the Divinity, or the Works of the Divine Goodness, Wisdom, and Power, in the Created World. This hath a vast extent and variety, and would be sufficient to entertain their time, in that happy state, much longer than a thousand years. As you will easily grant, if you allow me but to point at the several heads of those Speculations.

The Contemplation of the *Created World* divides it self into three parts, that of the *Intellectual* World: that of the *Corporeal*: And the Government and Administration of both, which is usually call'd *Providence*. These three, drawn into one thought, with the reasons and proportions that result from them, compose that *GRAND IDEA*, which is the treasury and comprehension of all Knowledge. Whereof we have spoken more largely in the last Chapter of the Second Book of this Theory, under the name of the *Mundane Idea*. But at present we shall only mention such particulars, as may be thought proper subjects for the meditations and enquiries of those who shall enjoy that happy state which we now treat of.

As to the Intellectual World, excepting our own Souls, we know little, in this region of darkness where we are at present, more than bare names. We hear of Angels and Archangels, of Cherubins and Seraphins, of Principalities and Powers and Thrones and Dominions. We hear the sound of these words with admiration, but we know little of their natures; wherein their general notion, and wherein their distinction, consists: what peculiar excellencies they have, what offices and employments: of all this we are ignorant. Only in general, we cannot but suppose that there are more orders and degrees of Intellectual Beings, betwixt us and the Almighty, than there are kinds or species of living Creatures upon the face of the Earth: betwixt Man, their Lord and Master, and the least Worm that creeps upon the ground. Nay, than there are Stars in Heaven, or Sands upon the Sea shore. For there is an infinite distance and interval betwixt us and God Almighty: and all that, is fill'd with created Beings of different degrees of perfection, still approaching nearer and nearer to their Maker. And when this invisible World shall be open'd to us: when the Curtain is drawn, and the Celestial Hierarchy set in order before our eyes, we shall despise our selves, and all the petty glories of a mortal life, as the dirt under our feet.

As to the Corporeal Universe, we have some share already in the Contemplation and knowledge of that: tho' little in comparison of what will be then discover'd. The doctrine of the Heavens, fix'd Stars, Planets and Comets, both as to their matter, motion and form, will be then clearly demonstrated: and what are mysteries to us now, will become matter of ordinary conversation. We shall be better acquainted with our neighbouring Worlds, and make new discoveries as to the state of their affairs. The Sun especially, the Great Monarch of the Planetary Worlds: whose dominion reaches from Pole to Pole, and the greatness of his kingdom is under the whole heaven. Who sends his bright messengers every day through all the regions of his vast Empire: throwing his beams of light round about him, swifter and further than a thought can follow. This noble Creature, I say, will make a good part of their study in the succeeding World. *Eudoxus* the Philosopher, wish'd he might die like *Phaeton*, in approaching too near to the Sun; provided he could fly so near it, and endure it so long, till he had discover'd its beauty and perfection. Who can blame his curiosity: who would not venture far to see the Court of so great a Prince: who hath more Worlds under his command than the Emperors of the Earth have Provinces or Principalities. Neither does he make his Subjects slaves to his pleasure, or tributaries to serve and supply his wants; on the contrary, They live upon him, he nourishes and preserves them: gives them fruits every year, corn, and wine, and all the comforts of life. This glorious Body, which now we can only gaze upon and admire, will be then better understood. A mass of Light and Flame, and Ethereal matter, ten thousand times bigger than this Earth: Enlightning and enlivening an Orb that exceeds the bulk of our Globe, as much as that does the least sand upon the Sea shore, may reasonably be presum'd to have some great Being at the Centre of it. But what that is, we must leave to the enquiries of another life.

The *Theory of the Earth* will be a common lesson there: carried through all its vicissitudes and periods from first to last, till its entire revolution be accomplish'd. I told you in the Preface, The *Revolution of Worlds* was one of the greatest Speculations that we are capable of in this life: and this little World where we are, will be the first and easiest instance of it; seeing we have Records, Historical or Prophetical, that reach from the Chaos to the end of the new Heavens and new Earth: which course of time makes up the greatest part of the Circle or Revolution. And as what was before the Chaos, was but the first remove from a Fixt Star, so what is after the thousand years Renovation, is but the last step to it again.

The *Theory of humane Nature* is also an useful and necessary speculation, and will be carried on to perfection in that state. Having fixt the true distinction betwixt Matter and Spirit, betwixt the Soul and the Body, and the true nature and laws of their union: The original contract, and the terms ratified by Providence at their first conjunction: It will not be hard to discover the springs of action and passion: how the thoughts of our mind, and the motions of our body act in dependance one upon another. What are the primary differences of Genius's and complexions, and how our Intellectuals or Morals depend upon them. What is the Root of Fatality, and how far it extends. By these lights, they will see into their own and every Man's breast, and trace the foot-steps of the divine wisdom in that strange composition of Soul and Body.

This indeed is a mixt speculation, as most others are: and takes in something of both Worlds, Intellectual and Corporeal: and may also belong in part to the Third Head we mention'd, *Providence.* But there is no need of distinguishing these Heads so nicely, provided we take in, under some or other of them, what may be thought best to deserve our knowledge, now, or in another World. As to *Providence*, what we intend chiefly by it here, is the general œconomy of our Religion, and what is reveal'd to us in Scripture, concerning God, Angels, and Mankind. These Revelations, as most in Sacred Writ, are short and incompleat: as being design'd for practice more than for speculation, or to awaken and excite our thoughts, rather than to satisfie them. Accordingly we read in Scripture of a Triune Deity: of God made flesh, in the Womb of a Virgin: Barbarously crucified by the *Jews:* Descending into Hell: rising again from the Dead: visibly ascending into Heaven: And sitting at the right hand of God the Father, above Angels and Arch-Angels. These great things are imperfectly reveal'd to us in this life; which we are to believe so far as they are reveal'd: In hopes these mysteries will be made more intelligible, in that happy state to come, where Prophets, Apostles, and Angels, will meet in conversation together.

In like manner, how little is it we understand concerning the *Holy Ghost.* That he descended like a *Dove* upon our Saviour: Like cloven Tongues of fire upon the Apostles; The Place being fill'd with a rushing mighty Wind: That he over-shadowed the Blessed Virgin, and begot the Holy Infant. That He made the Apostles speak all sort of Tongues and Languages *ex tempore*, and pour'd out strange Vertues and miraculous Gifts upon the Primitive Christians. These things we know as bare matter of fact, but the method of these operations we do not at all understand. Who can tell us now, what that is which we call *INSPIRATION?* What change is wrought in the Brain, and what in the Soul: and how the effect follows? Who will give us the just definition of a *Miracle?* What the proximate Agent is above Man, and whether they are all from the same power? How the manner and process of those miraculous changes in matter, may be conceiv'd? These things we see darkly, and hope they will be set in a clearer light, and the Doctrines of our Religion more fully expounded to us, in that Future World. For as several things obscurely exprest in the Old Testament, are more clearly reveal'd in the New; So the same mysteries, in a succeeding state, may still receive a further explication.

The History of the Angels, Good or bad, makes another part of this Providential Systeme. Christian Religion gives us some notices, of both kinds, but very imperfect; What interest the Good Angels have in the government of the

Mat. 3. 16.
Act. 1.
Matt. 1. 18.
Luke 1. 35.

World, and in ordering the affairs of this Earth and Mankind: What subjection they have to our Saviour, and what part in his Ministery: Whether they are Guardians to particular Persons, to Kingdoms, to Empires: All that we know at present, concerning these things, is but conjectural. And as to the bad Angels, who will give us an account of their fall, and of their former condition? I had rather know the history of *Lucifer*, than of all the *Babylonian* and *Persian* Kings; Nay, than of all the Kings of the Earth. What the Birthright was of that mighty Prince: what his Dominions: where his Imperial Court and Residence? How he was depos'd: for what Crime, and by what Power? How he still wages War against Heaven, in his exile: What Confederates he hath: What is his Power over Mankind, and how limited? What change or damage he suffer'd by the coming of Christ, and how it alter'd the posture of his affairs. Where he will be imprison'd in the *Millennium:* and what will be his last fate and final doom: whether he may ever hope for a Revolution or Restauration? These things lie hid in the secret Records of Providence, which then, I hope, will be open'd to us.

With the Revolution of *Worlds*, we mention'd before the Revolution of *Souls*; which is another great Circle of Providence, to be studied hereafter. We know little here, either of the pre-existence or post-existence of our Souls. We know not what they will be, till the loud Trump awakes us, and calls us again into the Corporeal World. Who knows how many turns he shall take upon this stage of the Earth, and how many trials he shall have, before his doom will be finally concluded. Who knows where, or what, is the state of Hell: where the Souls of the wicked are said to be to Eternity. What is the true state of Heaven: what our Celestial Bodies: and what that sovereign happiness that is call'd the *Beatifical Vision?* Our knowledge and conceptions of these things, are, at present, very general and superficial; But in the future kingdom of Christ, which is introductory to Heaven it self, these imperfections, in a great measure, will be done away; and such preparations wrought, both in the will and understanding, as may fit us for the life of Angels, and the enjoyment of God in Eternal Glory.

Thus you see in general, what will be the employment of the Saints in the blessed *Millennium*. And tho' they have few of the trifling businesses of this life, they will not want the best and noblest of diversions. 'Tis an happy thing when a Man's pleasure is also his perfection: for most Men's pleasures are such as debase their nature. We commonly gratifie our lower faculties, our passions, and our appetites: and these do not improve, but depress the mind. And besides, they are so gross, that the finest tempers are surfeited in a little time. There is no lasting pleasure, but *Contemplation*. All others grow flat and insipid upon frequent use; And when a Man hath run thorough a Sett of Vanities, in the declension of his Age, he knows not what to do with himself, if he cannot Think. He saunters about, from one dull business to another, to wear out time: And hath no reason to value life, but because he's afraid of death. But Contemplation is a continual spring of fresh pleasures. Truth is inexhausted, and when you are once in the right way, the further you go, the greater discoveries you make, and with the greater joy. We are sometimes highly pleas'd, and even transported, with little inventions in Mathematicks, or Mechanicks, or natural Philosophy;

All these things will make part of their diversion and entertainment in that state; All the doctrine of sounds and harmony: Of light, colours, and perspective, will be known in perfection. But these I call Diversions, in comparison of their higher and more serious speculations, which will be the business and happiness of that life.

Do but imagine, that they will have the Scheme of all humane affairs lying before them: from the Chaos to the last period. The universal history and order of times. The whole œconomy of the Christian Religion, and of all Religions in the World. The Plan of the undertaking of the Messiah: with all other parts and ingredients of the Providence of this Earth. Do but imagine this, I say, and you will easily allow, that when they contemplate the beauty, wisdom, and goodness, of the whole design, it must needs raise great and noble passions, and a far richer joy than either the pleasures or speculations of this life can excite in us. And this being the last Act and close of all humane affairs, it ought to be the more exquisite and elaborate: that it may crown the work, satisfie the Spectators, and end in a general applause. The whole Theater resounding with the praises of the great Dramatist, and the wonderful art and order of the composition.

CHAPTER X

Objections against the Millennium, answer'd. With some Conjectures concerning the state of things after the Millennium: and what will be the final Consummation of this World.

YOU see how Nature and Providence have conspir'd, to make the *Millennium* as happy a state, as any Terrestrial state can be. For, besides health and Plenty: Peace, Truth, and Righteousness will flourish there, and all the evils of this life stand excluded. There will be no ambitious Princes, studying mischief one against another; or contriving methods to bring their own Subjects into slavery. No mercenary Statesmen, to assist and intrigue with them. No oppression from the powerful, no snares or traps laid for the innocent. No treacherous friends, no malicious Enemies. No knaves, cheats, hypocrites; the Vermin of this Earth, that swarm every where. There will be nothing but truth, candor, sincerity, and ingenuity: as in a Society or Commonwealth of Saints and Philosophers. In a word, 'twill be *Paradise Restor'd*: both as to innocency of temper, and the beauties of Nature.

I believe you will be apt to say, If this be not true, 'tis pity but that it should be true. For 'tis a very desirable state, where all good People would find themselves mightily at ease. What is it that hinders it then? It must be some ill *Genius*. For Nature tends to such a Renovation, as we suppose: and Scripture speaks loudly of an happy state to be, some time or other, on this side Heaven. And what is there, pray, in this present World, natural or moral, if I may ask with reverence, that could make it worth the while for God to create it, if it never was better, nor ever will be better? Is there not more misery than happiness: Is there not more vice than virtue, in this World? as if it had been made by a

Manichean God. The Earth barren, the Heavens inconstant: Men wicked, and God offended. This is the posture of our affairs: such hath our World been hitherto with wars and bloudshed, sickness and diseases, poverty, servitude and perpetual drudgery for the necessaries of a mortal life. We may therefore reasonably hope, from a God infinitely good and powerful, for better times and a better state, before the last period and consummation of all things.

But it will be objected, it may be, that, according to Scripture, the vices and wickedness of men will continue to the end of the World; and so there will be *Luke* 18. 8. no room for such an happy state, as we hope for. Our Saviour says, *When the son of man cometh, shall he find faith upon the Earth?* They shall *eat and drink and play*, as before the destruction of the *old World*, or of *Sodom*, (*Luk.* 17. 26, &c.) and the wickedness of those men, you know, continued to the last. This objection may pinch those that suppose the Millennium to be in the present Earth, and a thousand years before the coming of our Saviour: for his words seem to imply that the World will be in a state of wickedness even till his coming. Accordingly Antichrist or the *Man of Sin*, is not said to be destroy'd till the coming of our Saviour. 2 *Thess.* 2. 8. and till he be destroy'd, we cannot hope for a Millennium. Lastly, the Coming of our Saviour is always represented in Scripture as sudden, surprising and unexpected. As *Lightning* breaking suddenly out of the clouds, (*Luk.* 17. 24. and *ch.* 21. 34, 35.) or as a *thief in the night*, 1 *Thess.* 5. 2, 3, 4. 2 *Pet.* 3. 10. *Apoc.* 16. 15. But if there be such a forerunner of it as the Millennial state, whose bounds we know, according as that expires and draws to an end, men will be certainly advertis'd of the approaching of our Saviour. But this objection, as I told you, does not affect our hypothesis, for we suppose the Millennium will not be till after the coming of our Saviour, and the Conflagration. And also that his coming will be sudden and surprising: and that Antichrist will continue in being, tho' not in the same degree of power, till that time. So that they that place the Millennium in the present Earth, are chiefly concern'd to answer this first objection.

But you will object, it may be, in the second place, That this Millennium, wheresoever it is, would degenerate, at length, into sensuality, and a Mahometan Paradise. For where there are early pleasures and earthly appetites, they will not be kept always in order, without any excess or luxuriancy: especially as to the senses of touch and taste. I am apt to think this is true, if the Soul have no more power over the body than she hath at present: and our senses, passions, and appetites be as strong as they are now. But according to our explication of the Millennium, we have great reason to hope, that the Soul will have a greater dominion over the Resurrection-body, than she hath over this. And you know we suppose that none will truly inherit the Millennium, but those that rise from the Dead. Nor do we admit any propagation there, nor the trouble or weakness of Infants. But that all rise in a perfect age, and never die: being translated, at the final judgment, to meet our Saviour in the clouds, and to be with him for ever. Thus we easily avoid the force of this objection. But those that place the Millennium in this life, and to be enjoy'd in these Bodies, must find out some new preservatives against vice: otherwise they will be continually subject to degeneracy.

Another objection may be taken from the personal Reign of Christ upon Earth: which is a thing incongruous, and yet asserted by many modern Millenaries. That Christ should leave that right hand of his Father, to come and pass a thousand years here below: living upon Earth in an heavenly Body: This, I confess, is a thing I never could digest, and therefore I am not concern'd in this objection; not thinking it necessary that Christ should be personally present and resident upon Earth in the Millennium. I am apt to believe that there will be then a celestial presence of Christ, if I may so call it; as the Sun is present to the Earth, yet never leaves its place in the Firmament; so Christ may be visibly conspicuous in his heavenly Throne, as he was to St. *Steven*: and yet never leave the right   *Act.* 7. 55, 56. hand of his Father. And this would be a more glorious and illustrious presence, than if he should descend, and converse amongst men in a personal shape. But these things not being distinctly reveal'd to us, we ought not to determine any thing concerning them, but with modesty and submission.

We have thus far pretty well escap'd, and kept ourselves out of the reach of the ordinary objections against the Millennium. But there remains one, concerning a *double Resurrection*, which must fall upon every Hypothesis: and 'tis this. The Scripture, they say, speaks but of one Resurrection: whereas the doctrine of the Millennium supposes two; one at the beginning of the Millennium, for the Martyrs, and those that enjoy that happy state, and the other at the end of it; which is universal and final, in the last day of judgment. 'Tis true, Scripture generally speaks of the Resurrection in gross: without distinguishing first and second; and so it speaks of the *Coming* of our Saviour, without distinction of first or second; yet it does not follow from that, that there is but one coming of our Saviour: so neither that there is but one Resurrection. And seeing there is one place of Scripture that speaks expresly and distinctly of two Resurrections, namely the 20*th chap.* of the *Apocalypse*: that is to us a sufficient warrant for asserting two. As there are some things in one Evangelist that are not in another, yet we think them authentick if they be but in one. There are also some things in *Daniel*, concerning the *Messiah*, and concerning the *Resurrection*, that are not in the rest of the Prophets: yet we look upon his single testimony, as good authority. St. *John* writ the last of all the Apostles: and as the whole series of his Prophecies is new, reaching through the later times to the Consummation of all things; so we cannot wonder if he had something more particular reveal'd to him concerning the Resurrection; that which was spoken of before in general, being distinguish'd now into *First* and *Second*, or particular and universal, in this last Prophet. Some think St. *Paul* means no less, when he makes an *order* in the   *See* Mr. Mede. Resurrection: some rising sooner, some later: 1 *Cor.* 15. 23, 24. 1 *Thess.* 4. 14, 15, &c. but whether that be so or no, St. *John* might have a more distinct revelation concerning it, than St. *Paul* had, or any one before him.

After these Objections, a great many Quæries and difficulties might be propos'd relating to the Millennium. But that's no more than what is found in all other matters, remote from our knowledge. Who can answer all the Quæries that may be made concerning *Heaven*, or *Hell*, or *Paradise*? When we know a thing as to the substance, we are not to let go our hold, tho' there remain some difficulties unresolv'd; otherwise we should be eternally Sceptical in most matters of knowledge. Therefore, tho' we cannot, for example, give a full account of the distinction of habitations and inhabitants in the *Future Earth*: or, of the order of the *first Resurrection*; whether it be performed by degrees and successively, or all the Inhabitants of the New Jerusalem rise at once, and continue throughout the whole Millennium. I say, tho' we cannot give a distinct account of these, or such like particulars, we ought not therefore to deny or doubt whether there will be a *New Earth*, or a *First Resurrection*. For the Revelation goes clearly so far: and the obscurity is only in the consequences and dependances of it. Which Providence thought fit, without further light, to leave to our search and disquisition.

Scripture mentions one thing, at the end of the Millennium, which is a common difficulty to all; and every one must contribute their best thoughts and con-

Apoc. 20. 8, 9.   jectures towards the solution of it. 'Tis the strange doctrine of *Gog* and *Magog*; which are to rise up in rebellion against the Saints, and besiege the holy City, and the holy Camp. And this is to be upon the expiration of the thousand years, when Satan is loosen'd. For no sooner will his Chains be knock'd off, but he will put himself in the head of this Army of Gyants, or Sons of the Earth, and attack Heaven, and the Saints of the most High. But with ill success, for there will come down fire and lightning from Heaven, and consume them. This, methinks, hath a great affinity with the history of the Gyants, rebelling and assaulting Heaven, and struck down by thunder-bolts. But that of setting mountains upon mountains, or tossing them into the Skie, that's the Poetical part, and we must not expect to find it in the Prophecy. The Poets told their fable, as of a thing past, and so it was a fable; But the Prophets speak of it, as of a thing to come, and so it will be a reality. But how and in what sence it is to be understood and explain'd, every one has the liberty to make the best judgment he can.

ch. 38, & 39.   *Ezekiel* mentions *Gog* and *Magog:* which I take to be onely types and shadows of these which we are now speaking of: and not yet exemplified, no more than his Temple. And seeing this People is to be at the end of the *Millennium*, and in the same Earth with it, We must, according to our Hypothesis, plant them in the Future Earth; and therefore all former conjectures about the *Turks*, or *Scythians*, or other *Barbarians*, are out of doors with us, seeing the Scene of this action does not lie in the present Earth. They are also represented by the Prophet, as a People distinct and separate from the Saints, not in their manners onely, but also

Apoc. 20. 8, 9.   in their seats and habitations; For they are said to come up from the four corners of the Earth, upon the breadth of the Earth: and there to besiege the *Camp of the Saints and the beloved City:* This makes it seem probable to me, that there will be a double race of Mankind in that *Future Earth:* very different one from another, both as to their temper and disposition, and as to their origine. The one born from Heaven, Sons of God, and of the Resurrection: who are the true Saints and heirs of the *Millennium*. The others born of the Earth, Sons of the Earth, generated from the slime of the ground, and the heat of the Sun, as brute Creatures were at first. This second Progeny or Generation of Men in the Future Earth, I understand to be signified by the Prophet under these borrowed or feigned names of *Gog* and *Magog*. And this Earth-born race, encreasing and multiplying after the manner of Men, by carnal propagation, after a thousand years, grew numerous, as the Sand by the Sea; and thereupon made an irruption or inundation upon the face of the Earth, and upon the habitations of the Saints; As the barbarous Nations did formerly upon Christendom: Or as the Gyants are said to have made War against the Gods. But they were soon confounded in their impious and sacrilegious design, being struck and consum'd by fire from Heaven.

Some will think, it may be, that there was such a double race of Mankind in the first World also. *The Sons of Adam, and the Sons of God:* because it is said, Gen. 6. *When men began to multiply upon the face of the Earth,* that *the SONS OF GOD SAW THE DAUGHTERS OF MEN, that they were fair, and they took them Wives of all that they lik'd.* And it is added presently, *ver. 4. There were Gyants in the Earth in those days; and also after that, when the Sons of God came in unto the daughters of men, and they bare children to them: the same became mighty men, which were of old men of renown.* Here seem to be two or three orders or races in this Ante-diluvian World. *The Sons of God: The Sons and Daughters of Adam*: and a third sort arising from the mixture and copulation of these, which are call'd *Mighty men of old*, or Hero's. Besides, here are Gyants mention'd, and to which they are to be reduc'd, it does not certainly appear.

This mixture of these two Races, whatsoever they were, gave, it seems, so great offence to God, that he destroy'd that World upon it, in a Deluge of Water. It hath been matter of great difficulty to determine, who these *Sons of God* were, that fell in love with and married the daughters of men. There are two conjectures that prevail most: One, that they were Angels: and another, that they were of the Posterity of *Seth*, and distinguish'd from the rest, by their Piety, and the worship of the true God: so that it was a great crime for them to mingle with the rest of mankind, who are suppos'd to have been Idolaters. Neither of these opinions is to me satisfactory. For as to Angels; Good Angels neither *marry, nor are given in marriage; Matt.* 22. 30. and bad Angels are not call'd the *Sons of God.* Besides, if Angels were capable of those mean pleasures, we ought in reason to suppose, that there are female Angels, as well as male; for surely those capacities are not in vain through a whole *Species* of Beings. And if there be female Angels, we cannot imagine, but that they must be of a far more charming beauty than the dowdy daughters of men. Then as to the line of *Seth*, It does not appear that there was any such distinction of Idolaters and true Worshippers before the Flood, or that there was any such thing, as Idolatry, at that time: nor for some Ages after. Besides, it is not said that the Sons of God fell in love with the Daughters of *Cain*, or of any degenerate race, but with the Daughters of *Adam*: which may be the Daughters of *Seth*, as well as of any other. These conjectures therefore seem to be shallow and ill grounded. But what the distinction was of those two orders, remains yet very uncertain.

St. *Paul* to the *Galatians, (chap.* 4. 21, 22, *&c.*) makes a distinction also of a double Progeny: that of *Sarah*, and that of *Hagar*. One was born according to the flesh, after a natural manner: and the other by the divine power, or in vertue of the divine promise. This distinction of a natural and supernatural origine, and of a double progeny: the one born to servitude, the other to liberty: represents

very well either the manner of our present birth, and of our future, at the Resurrection: Or that double progeny and double manner of birth, which we suppose
in the *Future Earth*. 'Tis true, St. *Paul* applies this to the Law and the Gospel;
but Typical things, you know, have different aspects and completions: which are
not exclusive of one another: and so it may be here. But however this double
race of Mankind in the Future Earth, to explain the doctrine of *Gog* and *Magog*,
is but a conjecture: and does not pretend to be otherwise consider'd.

The last thing that remains to be consider'd and accounted for, is the upshot
and conclusion of all: namely, what will become of the Earth after the thousand
years expir'd? Or after the Day of Judgment past, and the Saints translated into
Heaven, what will be the face of things here below? There being nothing expresly reveal'd concerning this, we must not expect a positive resolution of it.
And the difficulty is not peculiar to our hypothesis: for though the *Millennium*,
and the final Judgment were concluded in the present Earth, the Quære would
still remain, *What* would become of this Earth after the Last Day. So that all
parties are equally concern'd, and equally free, to give their opinion, *What* will
be the *last state and Consummation* of this Earth. Scripture, I told you, hath not
defin'd this point: and the Philosophers say very little concerning it. The Stoicks
indeed speak of the final resolution of all things into *Fire*, or into *Æther*: which
is the purest and subtlest sort of fire. So that the whole Globe or Mass of the
Earth, and all particular bodies, will, according to them, be at last dissolv'd into
a liquid flame. Neither was this doctrine first invented by the Stoicks: *Heraclitus*
taught it long before them: and I take it to be as ancient as *Orpheus* himself: who
was the first Philosopher amongst the *Greeks*. And he deriving his notions from
the *Barbarick* Philosophers, or the Sages of the East, that School of wisdom may
be look'd upon as the true seminary of this doctrine: as it was of most other
natural knowledge.

But this dissolution of the Earth into Fire, may be understood two ways;
either that it will be dissolv'd into a loose flame, and so dissipated and lost as
Lightning in the Air, and vanish into nothing; or that it will be dissolv'd into a
fixt flame, such as the Sun is, or a fixt Star. And I am of opinion, that the Earth
after the last Day of Judgment, will be chang'd into the nature of a Sun, or of a
fixt Star: and shine like them in the Firmament. Being all melted down into a
mass of Æthereal matter, and enlightning a Sphere or Orb round about it. I
have no direct and demonstrative proof of this, I confess; But if Planets were
once fixt Stars, as I believe they were; their revolution to the same state again,
in a great circle of Time, seems to be according to the methods of Providence;
which loves to recover what was lost or decay'd, after certain periods: and what
Rom. 8. 21.   was originally good and happy, to make it so again; All Nature, at last, being
transform'd into a like glory with the Sons of God.

I will not tell you what foundation there is in Nature, for this change or transformation; from the interiour constitution of the Earth, and the instances we
have seen of new Stars appearing in the Heavens. I should lead the English
Reader too far out of his way, to discourse of these things. But if there be any
passages or expressions in Scripture, that countenance such a state of things after

the day of judgment, it will not be improper to take notice of them. That radiant and illustrious *Jerusalem,* describ'd by St. *John Apoc.* 21. *ver.* 10, 11, 12, *&c.* compos'd all of Gemms and bright materials, clear and sparkling, as a Star in the Firmament: Who can give an account what that is? Its foundations, walls, gates, streets, all the Body of it, resplendent as light or fire. What is there in Nature, or in this Universe, that bears any resemblance with such a Phænomenon as this, unless it be a Sun or a fixt Star? Especially if we add and consider what follows, That *the City had no need of the Sun, nor of the Moon, to shine in it.* And *ver.* 23. that *there was no night there.* This can be no Terrestrial Body; it must be a sub- *ver.* 25. stance luminous in it self, and a fountain of light, as a fixt Star. And upon such a change of the Earth, or transformation, as this, would *be brought to pass the saying that is written, DEATH IS SWALLOWED UP IN VICTORY.* Which indeed St. *Paul* seems to apply to our Bodies in particular, 1 *Cor.* 15. 54. But in the Eighth Chap. to the *Romans* He extends it to all Nature. *The Creation it* *ver.* 21. *self also shall be deliver'd from the bondage of Corruption, into the glorious liberty of the Sons of God.* And accordingly St. *John* speaking of the same time with St. *Paul* in that place to the *Corinthians,* namely of the general Resurrection and day of Judgment, says, *Death* and *Hades,* which we render Hell, *were cast into the* *Apoc.* 20. 14. *lake of fire.* This is their being *swallowed up in victory,* which St. *Paul* speaks of; when Death and Hades, that is, all the Region of mortality: The Earth and all its dependances: are absorpt into a mass of Fire; and converted, by a glorious Victory over the power of darkness, into a Luminous Body and a region of Light.

This great Issue and Period of the Earth, and of all humane affairs, tho' it seem to be founded in nature, and supported by several expressions of Scripture; yet we cannot, for want of full instruction, propose it otherwise than as a fair Conjecture. The Heavens and the Earth shall flie away at the day of Judgment, says the Text: *Apoc.* 20. 11. *And their place shall not be found.* This must be understood of our Heavens and our Earth. And their *flying away* must be their removing to some other part of the Universe; so as their place or residence shall not be found any more here below. This is the easie and natural sence of the Words; and this translation of the Earth will not be without some change pre- ceding, that makes it leave its place, and, with a lofty flight, take its seat amongst the Stars. . . . . . There we leave it; Having conducted it for the space of Seven Thousand Years, through various changes from a *dark Chaos* to a *bright Star.*

A
REVIEW
OF THE
THEORY
OF THE
EARTH,
And of its
PROOFS:
ESPECIALLY
IN REFERENCE TO
SCRIPTURE.

LONDON,

Printed by R. *Norton*, for *Walter Kettilby*, at the Bishop's-Head in St. *Paul's* Church-Yard. 1690.

A
REVIEW
OF THE
THEORY
OF THE
EARTH

TO take a review of this Theory of the Earth, which we have now finish'd, We must consider, first, the extent of it: and then the principal parts whereof it consists. It reaches, as you see, from one end of the World to the other: From the first Chaos to the last day, and the Consummation of all things. This, probably, will run the length of Seven Thousand Years: which is a good competent space of time to exercise our thoughts upon, and to observe the several Scenes which Nature and Providence bring into View within the compass of so many Ages.

The matter and principal parts of this Theory, are such things as are recorded in Scripture. We do not feign a Subject, and then descant upon it, for diversion; but endeavour to give an intelligible and rational account of such matters of Fact, past or future, as are there specified and declar'd. What it hath seem'd good to the Holy Ghost to communicate to us, by History or Prophecy, concerning the several States and general Changes of this Earth, makes the Argument of our Discourse. Therefore the Things themselves must be taken for granted, in one sence or other: seeing, besides all other proofs, they have the authority of a Revelation; and our business is only to give such an explication of them, as shall approve it self to the faculties of man, and be conformable to Scripture.

We will therefore first set down the things themselves, that make the subject matter of this Theory: and remind you of our explication of them. Then recollect the general proofs of that explication, from reason and nature: but more fully and particularly shew how it is grounded upon Scripture. The primary *Phænomena* whereof we are to give an account, are these Five or Six.

I. *The original of the Earth from a Chaos.*
II. *The state of Paradise, and the Ante-diluvian World.*
III. *The Universal Deluge.*
IV. *The Universal Conflagration.*
V. *The Renovation of the World, or the New Heavens and New Earth.*
VI. *The Consummation of all things.*

These are unquestionably in Scripture: and these all relate, as you see, to the several forms, states, and revolutions of this Earth. We are therefore oblig'd to give a clear and coherent account of these Phænomena, in that order and consecution wherein they stand to one another.

There are also in Scripture some other things, relating to the same Subjects, that may be call'd the secondary ingredients of this Theory, and are to be referr'd to their respective primary heads. Such are, for instance,

I. *The Longevity of the Ante-diluvians.*
II. *The Rupture of the Great Abyss, at the Deluge.*
III. *The appearing of the Rainbow after the Deluge: as a sign that there never should be a second Flood.*

These things Scripture hath also left upon record: as directions and indications how to understand the Ante-diluvian state, and the Deluge it self. Whosoever therefore shall undertake to write the Theory of the Earth, must think himself bound to give us a just explication of these secondary Phænomena, as well as of the primary; and that in such a dependance and connexion, as to make them give and receive light from one another.

This part of the Task is concerning the World behind us, Times and Things pass'd, that are already come to light. The remainder is concerning the World before us, Times and Things to come: that lie yet in the bosome of Providence, and in the seeds of Nature. And these are chiefly the *Conflagration* of the World, and the *Renovation* of it. When these are over and expir'd, then *comes the end,* as St. *Paul* says. Then *the Heavens and the Earth fly away,* as St. *John* says. Then is the *Consummation* of all things, and the last period of this sublunary World, whatsoever it is. Thus far the Theorist must go, and pursue the motions of Nature, till all things are brought to rest and silence. And in this latter part of the Theory, there is also a collateral Phænomenon, the *Millennium,* or Thousand years Reign of Christ and his Saints, upon Earth, to be consider'd. For this, according as it is represented in Scripture, does imply a change in the Natural World, as well as in the Moral: and therefore must be accounted for, in the Theory of the Earth. At least it must be there determin'd, whether that state of the World, which is singular and extraordinary, will be before or after the Conflagration.

1 Cor. 15.
Apoc. 20.

These are the Principals and Incidents of this Theory of the Earth, as to the matter and subject of it: which, you see, is both important, and wholly taken out of Scripture. As to our explication of these points, that is sufficiently known, being set down at large in four Books of this Theory. Therefore it remains only, having seen the matter of the Theory, to examine the Form of it, and the proofs of it: for from these two things it must receive its censure. As to the form, the characters of a regular Theory seem to be these three; *Few and easie Postulatums: Union of Parts:* and *a Fitness to answer, fully and clearly, all the Phænomena to which it is to be apply'd.*

We think our Hypothesis does not want any of these Characters. As to the First, we take but one single *Postulatum* for the whole Theory: and that an easie one, warranted both by Scripture and Antiquity: Namely, *That this Earth rise, at first, from a Chaos.* As to the second, *Union of parts,* The whole Theory is but one Series of Causes and Effects from that first Chaos. Besides, you can scarce admit any one part of it, first, last, or intermediate, but you must, in consequence of that, admit all the rest. Grant me but that the Deluge is truly explain'd, and I'le desire no more for proof of all the Theory. Or, if you begin at the other end, and grant the *New Heavens and New Earth* after the Conflagration, you will be led back again to the first Heavens and first Earth that were before the Flood. For St. *John* says, that *New Earth* was without a *Sea: Apoc.* 21. 1. And it was a *Renovation,* or *Restitution* to some former state of things: there was therefore some former Earth without a Sea; which not being the present Earth, it must be the Ante-diluvian. Besides, both St. *John,* and the Prophet *Isaias,* have represented the New Heavens and New Earth, as *Paradisiacal;* According as is prov'd, *Book the 4th. ch. 2.* And having told us the form of the New-future-Earth, that it will have *no Sea,* it is a reasonable inference that there was no Sea in the *Paradisiacal Earth.* However from the form of this Future Earth, which St. *John* represents to us, we may at least conclude, That an *Earth without a Sea* is no Chimæra, or impossibility: but rather a fit seat and habitation for the Just and the Innocent.

Thus you see the parts of the Theory link and hold fast one another: according to the second character. And as to the third, of being *suited to the Phænomena,* we must refer that to the next head, of *Proofs.* It may be truly said, that bare coherence and union of parts is not a sufficient proof; The parts of a Fable or Romance may hang aptly together, and yet have no truth in them. This is enough indeed to give the title of a just Composition to any work, but not of a true one: till it appear that the conclusions and explications are grounded upon good natural evidence, or upon good Divine authority. We must therefore proceed now to the third thing to be consider'd in a Theory, *What* its Proofs are: or the grounds upon which it stands, whether Sacred or Natural.

According to Natural evidence, things are proved from their Causes or their Effects. And we think we have this double order of proofs for the truth of our Hypothesis. As to the method of Causes, we proceed from what is more simple, to what is more compound: and build all upon one foundation. Go but to the Head of the Theory, and you will see the Causes lying in a train before you, from first to last. And tho' you did not know the Natural history of the World, past or future, you might, by intuition, foretell it, as to the grand revolutions and successive faces of Nature, through a long series of Ages. If we have given a true account of the motions of the Chaos, we have also truly form'd the first habitable Earth. And if that be truly form'd, we have thereby given a true account of the state of Paradise, and of all that depends upon it. And not of that onely, but also of the universal Deluge. Both these we have shewn in their causes: The one from the Form of that Earth, and the other from the Fall of it into the Abyss. And tho' we had not been made acquainted with these things by Antiquity, we might, in contemplation of the Causes, have truly conceiv'd them, as properties or incidents to the First Earth. But as to the Deluge, I do not say, that we might have calculated the Time, manner, and other circumstances of it: These things were regulated by Providence, in subordination to the Moral World. But that there would be, at one time or other, a disruption of that Earth, or of the Great Abyss: and in consequence of it, an universal Deluge: So far, I think, the light of a Theory might carry us.

Theor. book 3.
ch. 7, & 8.

Furthermore, In consequence of this disruption of the Primeval Earth, at the Deluge, the present Earth was made hollow and cavernous: and by that means, (due preparations being used) capable of *Combustion*, or of perishing by an universal Fire: Yet, to speak ingenuously, This is as hard a step to be made, in vertue of Natural causes, as any in the whole Theory. But in recompence of that defect, the Conflagration is so plainly and literally taught us in Scripture, and avow'd by Antiquity, that it can fall under no dispute, as to the thing it self. And as to a capacity or disposition to it in the present Earth, that I think is sufficiently made out.

Then, the Conflagration admitted, in that way it is explain'd in the 3*d*. Book: The Earth, you see, is, by that fire, reduc'd to a second Chaos. A Chaos truly so call'd. And from that, as from the First, arises another Creation, or *New Heavens* and a *New Earth*; By the same causes, and in the same form, with the Paradisiacal. This is the *Renovation* of the World: The *Restitution* of all things: mentioned both by Scripture and Antiquity: and by the Prophet *Isaiah*, St. *Peter* and St. *John*, call'd the *New Heavens* and *New Earth*. With this, as the last period, and most glorious Scene of all humane affairs, our Theory concludes, as to this method of Causes, whereof we are now speaking.

I say, here it ends as to the *method of Causes*. For tho' we pursue the Earth still further, even to its last Dissolution: which is call'd the Consummation of all things: yet all, that we have superadded upon that occasion, is but Problematical: and may, without prejudice to the Theory, be argued and disputed on either hand. I do not know, but that our conjectures there may be well grounded: but however, not springing so directly from the same root, or, at least, not by ways, so clear and visible, I leave that part undecided. Especially seeing we pretend to write no more than the *Theory of the Earth*, and therefore as we begin no higher than the *Chaos*, so we are not obliged to go any further than to the last state of a Terrestrial consistency: which is that of the New Heavens and the New Earth.

This is the first natural proof, From the order of Causes. The second is from the consideration of Effects. Namely of such effects as are already in being. And therefore this proof can extend onely to that part of the Theory, that explains the present and past form and Phænomena of the Earth. What is Future, must be left to a further trial, when the things come to pass, and present themselves to be examin'd and compar'd with the Hypothesis. As to the present Form of the Earth, we call all Nature to witness for us: The Rocks and the Mountains, the Hills and the Valleys, the deep and wide Sea, and the Caverns of the Ground: Let these speak, and tell their origine: How the Body of the Earth came to be thus torn and mangled: If this strange and irregular structure was not the effect of a ruine: and of such a ruine as was universal over the face of the whole Globe. But we have given such a full explication of this, in the first part of the Theory, from *Chapt. the 9th.* to the end of that Treatise, that we dare stand to the judgment, of any that reads those four Chapters; to determine if the Hypothesis does not answer all those Phænomena, easily and adequately.

The next Phænomenon to be consider'd, is the *Deluge*, with its adjuncts. This also is fully explain'd by our Hypothesis, in the 2*d.* 3*d.* and 6*th.* Chapters of the first Book. Where it is shewn, that the *Mosaical Deluge*, that is, an universal Inundation of the whole Earth, above the tops of the highest Mountains, made by a breaking open of the Great Abyss, (for thus far *Moses* leads us) is fully explain'd by this Hypothesis, and cannot be conceiv'd in any other method. There are no sources or stores of Water sufficient for such an effect: that may be drawn upon the Earth, and drawn off again, but by supposing such an Abyss, and such a Disruption of it, as the Theory represents.

Lastly, As to the Phænomena of Paradise and the Ante-diluvian World, we have set them down in order in the 2*d.* Book: and apply'd to each of them its proper explication, from the same Hypothesis. We have also given an account of that Character which Antiquity always assign'd to the first age of the World, or the Golden Age, as they call'd it: namely, *Equality of Seasons* throughout the Year, or a perpetual Equinox. We have also taken in all the adjuncts or con-comitants of these States, as they are mention'd in Scripture. *The Longevity* of the Ante-diluvians, and the declension of their age by degrees, after the Flood. As also that wonderful Phænomenon, the *Rainbow*: which appear'd to *Noah* for a Sign, that the Earth should never undergo a second Deluge. And we have shewn, wherein the force and propriety of that Sign consisted, for confirming *Noah*'s faith in the promise and in the divine veracity.

Theor. Book 2. chap. 5.

Thus far we have explain'd the past Phænomena of the Natural World. The rest are Futurities, which still lie hid in their Causes; and we cannot properly prove a Theory from effects that are not yet in being. But so far as they are foretold in Scripture, both as to substance and circumstance, in prosecution of the same Principles we have ante-dated their birth, and shew'd how they will come to pass. We may therefore, I think, reasonably conclude, That this Theory has performed its task and answer'd its title: having given an account of all the general changes of the Natural World, as far as either Sacred History looks back-wards, or Sacred Prophecy looks forwards. So far as the one tells us what is past in Nature, and the other what is to come. And if all this be nothing but an appearance of truth, 'tis a kind of fatality upon us to be deceiv'd.

SO much for Natural Evidence, from the Causes or Effects. We now proceed to Scripture, which will make the greatest part of this Review. The Sacred Basis upon which the whole Theory stands, is the doctrine of St. *Peter*, deliver'd in his *Second Epistle* and *Third Chapter*, concerning the *Triple Order* and Suc-cession of the Heavens and the Earth. That comprehends the whole extent of our Theory: which indeed is but a large Commentary upon St. *Peter*'s Text. The Apostle sets out a threefold state of the Heavens and Earth: with some general properties of each: taken from their different Constitution and different Fate. The Theory takes the same threefold state of the Heavens and the Earth: and explains more particularly, wherein their different Constitution consists: and how, under the conduct of Providence, their different fate depends upon it. Let us set down the Apostle's words, with the occasion of them: and their plain sence, according to the most easie and natural explication.

2 *Pet.* 3.

Ver. 3. *Knowing this first, that there shall come in the last days scoffers, walking after their own lusts.*

4. *And saying, Where is the promise of his coming? for since the fathers fell asleep, all things continue as they were from the beginning of the creation.*

5. *For this they willingly are ignorant of, that by the word of God, the heavens were of old, and the earth consisting of water and by water.*

6. *Whereby the world that then was, being overflowed with water, perished.*

7. *But the heavens and the earth that are now, by the same word, are kept in store, reserved unto fire against the day of judgment, and perdition of ungodly men. . . . .*

10. *The day of the Lord will come as a thief in the night, in the which the heavens shall pass away with a great noise, and the elements shall melt with fervent heat; the earth also and the works that are therein shall be burnt up.*

13. *Nevertheless we, according to his promise, look for new heavens and a new earth, wherein dwelleth righteousness.*

This is the whole Discourse so far as relates to our Subject. St. *Peter*, you see, had met with some that scoff'd at the future destruction of the World, and the coming of our Saviour; and they were men, it seems, that pretended to Philosophy and Argument; and they use this argument for their opinion, *Seeing there hath been no change in Nature, or in the World, from the beginning to this time, why should we think there will be any change for the future?*

The Apostle answers to this, That they willingly forget or are ignorant that there were Heavens of old, and an Earth, so and so constituted; consisting of Water and by Water; by reason whereof that World, or those Heavens and that Earth, perish'd in a Deluge of Water. But, saith he, the Heavens and the Earth that are now, are of another constitution, fitted and reserved to another fate, namely to perish by Fire. And after these are perish'd, there will be New Heavens and a New Earth, according to God's promise.

This is an easie Paraphrase, and the plain and genuine sence of the Apostle's discourse; and no body, I think, would ever look after any other sence, if this did not draw them into paths they do not know, and to conclusions which they do not fancy. This sence, you see, hits the objection directly, or the Cavil which these scoffers made; and tells them, that they vainly pretend that there hath been no change in the World since the beginning, for there was one sort of Heavens and Earth before the Flood, and another sort now; the first having been destroyed at the Deluge. So that the Apostle's argument stands upon this Foundation, That there is a diversity betwixt the present Heavens and Earth, and the Ante-diluvian Heavens and Earth; take away that, and you take away all the force of his Answer.

Then as to his *New Heavens* and *New Earth* after the Conflagration, they must be material and natural, in the same sence and signification with the former Heavens and Earth; unless you will offer open violence to the Text. So that this Triplicity of the Heavens and the Earth, is the first, obvious, plain sence of the Apostle's discourse: which every one would readily accept, if it did not draw after it a long train of Consequences, and lead them into other Worlds than they ever thought of before, or are willing to enter upon now.

But we shall have occasion by and by, to examine this Text more fully in all its circumstances. Give me leave in the mean time to observe, that St. *Paul* also implyes that *triple Creation* which St. *Peter* expresses. St. *Paul*, I say, in the *8th chap.* to the *Rom. ver.* 20, 21. tells us of a *Creation* that will be *redeem'd from Vanity:* which are the new Heavens and new Earth to come. *A Creation in subjection to Vanity:* which is the present state of the World. And a *Creation* that was subjected to Vanity, in hopes of being restor'd: which was the first Paradisiacal Creation. And these are the three states of the Natural World, which make the subject of our Theory.

To these two places of St. *Peter* and St. *Paul*, I might add that third in St. *John*, concerning the new Heavens and new Earth; with that distinguishing Character, that the Earth was *without a Sea*. As this distinguisheth it from the present Earth, so, being a *Restitution* or *Restauration*, as we noted before, it must be the same with some former Earth: and consequently, it implies that there was another precedent state of the natural World, to which this is a Restitution. These three places I alledge, as comprehending and confirming the Theory in its full extent. But we do not suppose them all of the same force and clearness. St. *Peter* leads the way, and gives light and strength to the other two. When a Point is prov'd by one clear Text, we allow others, as auxiliaries, that are not of the same clearness; But being open'd, receive light from the primary Text, and reflect it upon the Argument.

So much for the Theory in general. We will now take one or two principal heads of it, which vertually contain all the rest, and examine them more strictly and particularly, in reference to their agreement with Scripture. The two Heads we pitch upon, shall be, our Explication of the Deluge, and our Explication of the new Heavens and new Earth. We told you before, these two were as the Hinges, upon which all the Theory moves, and which holds the parts of it in firm union one with another. As to the Deluge, if I have explain'd that aright, by the Disruption of the Great Abyss, and the Dissolution of the Earth that cover'd it, all the rest follows in such a chain of consequences, as cannot be broken. Wherefore in order to the proof of that explication, and of all that depends upon it, I will make bold to lay down this Proposition, *That our Hypothesis concerning the universal Deluge, is not onely more agreeable to Reason and Philosophy than any other yet propos'd to the World, but is also more agreeable to Scripture.* Namely, to such places of Scripture, as reflect upon the *Deluge*, the *Abyss*, and the form of the *first Earth*. And particularly, to the *History of Noah's Flood*, as *recorded by Moses*. If I can make this good, it will, doubtless, give satisfaction to all intelligent Persons. And I desire their patience, if I proceed slowly.

We will divide our task into parts, and examine them separately: First, by Scripture in general, and then by *Moses* his history and description of the Flood.

Our Hypothesis of the Deluge consists of three principal Heads, or differs remarkably in three things from the common explication. First, in that we suppose the Antediluvian Earth to have been of another Form and constitution from the present Earth: with the Abyss placed under it.

Secondly, in that we suppose the Deluge to have been made, not by any inundation of the Sea, or overflowing of Fountains and Rivers: nor (principally) by any excess of rains: but by a real dissolution of the exteriour Earth, and disruption of the Abyss which it cover'd. These are the two principal points, to which may be added, as a Corollary.

Thirdly, that the Deluge was not in the nature of a standing Pool: the Waters lying every where level, of an equal depth and with an uniform Surface: but was made by a fluctuation and commotion of the Abyss upon the disruption: which commotion being over, the Waters retired into their Chanels, and let the dry Land appear.

These are the most material and fundamental parts of our Hypothesis: and these being prov'd consonant to Scripture, there can be no doubt of the rest.

We begin with the first: That the Ante-diluvian Earth was of another form and constitution from the present Earth, with the Abyss placed under it. This is confirm'd in Scripture, both by such places as assert a diversity in general: and by other places that intimate to us, wherein that diversity consisted, and what was the form of the first Earth. That discourse of St. *Peter*'s, which we have set before you, concerning the past, present, and future, Heavens and Earth, is so full a proof of this diversity in general, that you must either allow it, or make the Apostle's argumentation of no effect. He speaks plainly of the natural World, *The Heavens and the Earth*: And he makes a plain distinction, or rather opposition, betwixt those before and after the Flood: so that the least we can conclude from his words, is a diversity betwixt them; In answer to that Identity or immutability of Nature, which the Scoffers pretended to have been ever since the beginning.

But tho' the Apostle, to me, speaks plainly of the *Natural World*, and distinguishes that which was before the Flood, from the present: Yet there are some that will allow neither of these to be contain'd in St. *Peter*'s words; and by that means would make this whole Discourse of little or no effect, as to our purpose. And seeing we, on the contrary, have made it the chief Scripture-basis of the whole Theory of the Earth, we are oblig'd to free it from those false glosses or misinterpretations, that lessen the force of its testimony, or make it wholly ineffectual.

These Interpreters say, that St. *Peter* meant no more than to mind these Scoffers, that the World was once destroy'd by a Deluge of Water: meaning the *Animate World*, Mankind and living Creatures. And that it shall be destroy'd again by another Element, namely by Fire. So as there is no opposition or diversity betwixt the two Natural Worlds, taught or intended by the Apostle; but onely in reference to their different fate or manner of perishing, and not of their different nature or constitution.

Here are two main points, you see, wherein our interpretations of this discourse of the Apostles, differ. First, in that they make the Apostle (in that *sixth verse*) to understand onely the World *Animate,* or men and brute Creatures. That these were indeed destroy'd, but not the Natural World, or the form and constitution of the then Earth and Heavens. Secondly, that there is no diversity or opposition made by St. *Peter* betwixt the ancient Heavens and Earth, and the present, as to their form and constitution. We pretend that these are mis-apprehensions, or mis-representations of the sence of the Apostle in both respects, and offer these reasons to prove them to be so.

For the first point; That the Apostle speaks here of the natural World, particularly in the 6*th.* Verse; and that it perish'd, as well as the animate, these Considerations seem to prove.

First, because the argument or ground these Scoffers went upon, was taken from the natural World, its constancy and permanency in the same state from the beginning; therefore if the Apostle answers *ad idem,* and takes away their argument, he must understand the same natural World, and show that it hath been chang'd, or hath perish'd.

You will say, it may be, the Apostle doth not deny, nor take away the ground they went upon, but denies the consequence they made from it; that *therefore there would be no change, because there had been none.* No, neither doth he do this, if by the *World* in the 6*th.* Verse, he understands Mankind onely; for their ground was this, *there hath been no change in the natural World*; Their consequence, this, *therefore there will be none,* nor any Conflagration. Now the Apostle's answer, according to you, is this, *you forget that Mankind hath been destroyed in a Deluge.* And what then? what's this to the natural World, whereof they were speaking? this takes away neither antecedent nor consequent, neither ground nor inference; nor any way toucheth their argument, which proceeded from the natural World to the natural World. Therefore you must either suppose that the Apostle takes away their ground, or he takes away nothing.

Secondly, what is it that the Apostle tells these Scoffers they were ignorant of? that there was a Deluge, that destroyed Mankind? They could not be ignorant of that, nor pretend to be so; It was therefore the constitution of those old Heavens and Earth, and the change or destruction of them at the Deluge, that they were ignorant of, or did not attend to; and of this the Apostle minds them. These Scoffers appear to have been *Jews* by the phrase they use, *since the Fathers fell asleep,* which in both parts of it is a Judaical expression; And does St. *Peter* tell the *Jews* that had *Moses* read to them every Sabbath, that *they were ignorant that Mankind was once destroyed with a Deluge in the Days of Noah*? or could they pretend to be ignorant of that without making themselves ridiculous both to *Jews* and Christians? Besides, these do not seem to have been of the vulgar amongst them, for they bring a Philosophical argument for their opinion; and also in their very argument they refer to the History of the Old Testament,*

---

* There was a Sect amongst the *Jews* that held this perpetuity and immutability of Nature; and *Maimonides* himself was of this principle, and gives the same reason for it with the Scoffers here in the Text, *Quod mundus retinet & sequitur consuetudinem suam.* And as to those of the *Jews* that were *Aristoteleans,* it was very suitable to their principles to hold the incorruptibility of the World, as their Master did. *Vid. Med. in loc.*

in saying, *Since the Fathers fell asleep*, amongst which Fathers, *Noah* was one of the most remarkable.

Thirdly, the design of the Apostle is to prove to them, or to dispose them to the belief of the Conflagration, or future destruction of the World; which I suppose you will not deny to be a destruction of the natural World; therefore to prove or perswade this, he must use an argument taken from a precedent destruction of the natural World; for to give an instance of the perishing of Mankind onely, would not reach home to his purpose. And you are to observe here that the Apostle does not proceed against them barely by authority; for what would that have booted? If these Scoffers would have submitted to authority, they had already the authority of the Prophets and Apostles in this point: but he deals with them at their own weapon, and opposes reasons to reasons; What hath been done may be done, and if the natural World hath been once destroyed, 'tis not hard, nor unreasonable, to suppose those Prophecies to be true, that say it shall be destroyed again.

Fourthly, unless we understand here the natural World, we make the Apostle both redundant in his discourse, and also very obscure in an easie argument. If his design was onely to tell them that Mankind was once destroy'd in a Deluge, what's that to the Heavens and the Earth? the *5th.* Verse would be superfluous; which yet he seems to make the foundation of his discourse.. He might have told them how Mankind had perish'd before with a Deluge, and aggravated that destruction as much as he pleas'd, without telling them how the Heavens and the Earth were constituted then; what was that to the purpose, if it had no dependance or connection with the other? In the precedent Chapter, Verse *5th.* when he speaks onely of the Floods destroying Mankind, he mentions nothing of the Heavens or the Earth: and if you make him to intend no more here, what he says more is superfluous.

I also add, that you make the Apostle very obscure and operose in a very easie argument. How easie had it been for him, without this *Apparatus*, to have told them, as he did before, that God brought a Flood upon the World of the ungodly; and not given us so much difficulty to understand his sence, or such a suspicion and appearance, that he intended something more; for that there is at least a great appearance and tendency to a further sence, I think none can deny; And St. *Austin, Didymus, Alex. Bede*, as we shall see hereafter, understood it plainly of the natural World: Also modern Expositors and Criticks; as *Cajetan, Estius, Drusius, Heinsius*, have extended it to the natural World, more or less; tho' they had no Theory to mislead them, nor so much as an hypothesis to support them; but attended onely to the tenor of the Apostle's discourse, which constrain'd them to that sence, in whole or in part.

Fifthly, the opposition carries it upon the natural World. The opposition lies betwixt the οἱ ἔκπαλαι οὐρανοὶ καὶ γῆ and ὁι νῦν οὐρανοὶ καὶ γῆ, the Heavens that were of old, and the Earth, and the present Heavens and Earth, or the two natural Worlds. And if they will not allow them to be oppos'd in their natures (which yet we shall prove by and by) at least they must be oppos'd in their fate; and as This is to perish by fire, so That perish'd by water; And if it perish'd by water, it perish'd; which is all we contend for at present.

Lastly, if we would be as easily govern'd in the exposition of this place, as we are of other places of Scripture, it would be enough to suggest, that in reason and fairness of interpretation, the same World is destroy'd in the *6th verse*, that was describ'd in the foregoing *verse*; but it is the Natural World that is describ'd there, the Heavens and the Earth, so and so constituted; and therefore in fairness of interpretation they ought to be understood here; that World being the subject that went immediately before, and there being nothing in the words that restrains them to the animate World or to Mankind. In the *2d ch. ver. 5.* the Apostle does restrain the word κόσμος by adding ἀσεβῶν, *the World of the ungodly*; but here 'tis not only illimited, but according to the context, both preceding and following, to be extended to the Natural World. I say by the following context too, for so it answers to the World that is to perish by Fire; which will reach the frame of Nature as well as Mankind.

For a conclusion of this first point, I will set down St. *Austin*'s judgment in this case; who in several parts of his works hath interpreted this place of St. *Peter, of the natural world*. As to the heavens, he hath these words in his Exposition upon *Genesis, Hosetiam aerios cœlos quondam periisse Diluvio, in quâdam earum quæ Canonica appellantur, Epistolâ legimus. We read in one of the Epistles called Canonical,* meaning this of St. *Peter's that the aerial heavens perish'd in the Deluge.* And he concerns himself there to let you know that it was not the starry heavens that were destroy'd; the waters could not reach so high; but the regions of our air. Then afterwards he hath these words *Faciliùs eos* (cœlos) *secundum illius Epistolæ authoritatem credimus periisse, & alios, sicut ibi scribitur, repositos. We do more easily believe, according to the authority of* that *Epistle, those heavens to have perish'd; and others, as it is there written, substituted in their place.* In like manner, and to the same sence, he hath these words upon *Psal.* 101. *Aerii utique cœli perierunt ut propinqui Terris, secundum quod dicuntur volucres cœli; sunt autem & cœli cœlorum, superiores in Firmamento, sed utrùm & ipsi perituri sint igni, an hi soli, qui etiam diluvio perierunt, disceptatio est aliquanto scrupulosior inter doctos.* And in his Book *de Civ. Dei,* he hath several passages to the same purpose, *Quemadmodum in Apostolicâ illâ Epistolâ â toto pars accipitur, quod diluvio periisse dictus est mundus, quamvis sola ejus cum suis cœlis pars ima perierit.* These being to the same effect with the first citation, I need not make them English; and this last place refers to the Earth as well as the Heavens, as several other places in St. *Austin* do, whereof we shall give you an account, when we come to shew his judgment concerning the second point, *the diversity of the ante-diluvian and post-diluvian World.* This being but a foretaste of his good will and inclinations towards this doctrine.

These considerations alledg'd, so far as I can judge, are full and unanswerable proofs, that this discourse of the Apostle's comprehends and refers to the Natural World; and consequently they warrant our interpretation in this particular, and destroy the contrary. We have but one step more to make good, *That there was a change made in this natural world at the Deluge,* according to the Apostle; and this is to confute the second part of their interpretation, which supposeth that St. *Peter* makes no distinction or opposition betwixt the antediluvian Heavens and Earth, and the present Heavens and Earth, in that respect.

This second difference betwixt us, methinks, is still harsher than the first; and contrary to the very form, as well as to the matter of the Apostle's discourse. For there is a plain antithesis, or opposition made betwixt the Heavens and the Earth of old (*ver. the 5th*) and the Heavens and the Earth that are now (*verse the 7th*) οἱ ἔκπαλαι οὐρανοὶ καὶ ἡ γῆ and οἱ νῦν οὐρανοὶ καὶ ἡ γῆ , and the adversative particle, *but*, you see marks the opposition; so that it is full and plain according to Grammar and Logick. And that the parts or members of this opposition differ in nature from one another, is certain from this, because otherwise the Apostle's argument or discourse is of no effect, concludes nothing to the purpose; he makes no answer to the objection, nor proves any thing against the Scoffers, unless you admit that diversity. For they said, *All things had been the same from the beginning in the Natural World*, and unless he say, as he manifestly does, that there hath been a change in Nature, and that the Heavens and Earth that are now, are different from the ancient Heavens and Earth, which perish'd at the Flood, he says nothing to destroy their argument, nor to confirm the Prophetical doctrine of the future destruction of the Natural World.

This, I think, would be enough to satisfie any clear and free mind concerning the meaning of the Apostle; but because I desire to give as full a light to this place as I can, and to put the sence of it out of controversie, if possible, for the future, I will make some further remarks to confirm this exposition.

And we may observe that several of those reasons which we have given to prove, That the *Natural World* is understood by St. *Peter*, are double reasons; and do also prove the other point in question, a *diversity betwixt the two Natural Worlds*, the Anti-diluvian and the present. As for instance, unless you admit this diversity betwixt the two natural Worlds, you make the *5th verse* in this *Chapter* superfluous and useless: and you must suppose the Apostle to make an inference here without premises. In the *6th verse* he makes an inference, * *Whereby* the World, that then was, perish'd in a Deluge; what does this *whereby* relate to? *by reason* of what? sure of the particular constitution of the Heavens and the Earth immediately before describ'd. Neither would it have signified any thing to the Scoffers, for the Apostle to have told them how the Ante-diluvian Heavens and Earth were constituted, if they were constituted just in the same manner as the present.

Besides, what is it, as I ask'd before, that the Apostle tells these Scoffers they were ignorant of? does he not say formally and expresly (*ver. 5.*) that they were ignorant that the Heavens and the Earth were constituted so and so, before the Flood? but if they were constituted as these present Heavens and Earth are, they were not ignorant of their constitution; nor did pretend to be ignorant, for their own (mistaken) argument supposeth it.

But before we proceed any further, give me leave to note the impropriety of our Translation, in the *5th*. Verse, or latter part of it; Ἐξ ὕδατος καὶ δι᾽ ὑδάτων (vel δι᾽ ὕδατος) συνεϛῶσα, This we translate *standing in the water, and out of*

δὲ

---

* δι᾽ ὧν, *per que*. Vulgat. *Quamobrem*, Beza. *Quâ de causâ*, Grot. *Nemo interpretum reddidit* δι᾽ ὧν *per quas*; *subintelligendo* aquas. *Hoc enim argumentationem Apostolicam tolleret, supponeretque illusores illos ignorâsse quod olim fuerit Diluvium; Quod supponi non posse suprà ostendimus.*

the water, which is done manifestly in compliance with the present form of the Earth, and the notions of the Translators: and not according to the natural force and sence of the *Greek* words. If one met with this sentence * in a *Greek* Author, who would ever render it *standing in the water and out of the water?* nor do I know any *Latin* Translator that hath ventur'd to render them in that sence; nor any *Latin* Father; St. *Austin* and St. *Jerome* I'me sure do not, but *Consistens ex aquâ*, or *de aquâ*, & *per aquam:* for that later phrase also συνεϑάναι δἰ ὕδατος does not with so good propriety signifie *to stand in the water*, as to consist or subsist by water, or by the help of water, *Tanquam per causam sustinentem*; as St. *Austin* and *Jerome* render it. Neither does that instance they give from 1 *Pet.* 3. 20. prove any thing to the contrary, for the Ark was sustain'd by the waters, and the *English* does render it accordingly.

The Translation being thus rectified, you see the ante-diluvian Heavens and Earth consisted of Water, and by water; which makes way for a second observation to prove our sence of the Text; for if you admit no diversity betwixt those Heavens and Earth, and the present, shew us 'pray how the present Heavens and Earth consist of water, and by water. What watery constitution have they? The Apostle implies rather, that *The now Heavens and Earth* have a fiery constitution. We have now Meteors of all sorts in the air, winds, hail, snow, lightning, thunder, and all things engender'd of fiery exhalations, as well as we have rain; but according to our Theory, the ante-diluvian Heavens, of all these Meteors had none but dews and rain, or watery Meteors onely; and therefore might very aptly be said by the Apostle to be *constituted of water*, or to have a watery σύϑασις. Then the Earth was said to *consist by water*, because it was built upon it, and at first was sustain'd by it. And when such a Key as this is put into our hands, that does so easily unlock this hard passage, and makes it intelligible, according to the just force of the words, why should we pertinaciously adhere to an interpretation, that neither agrees with the words,† nor makes any sence that is considerable?

Book 2. c. 5, p. 233.

Thirdly, If the Apostle had made the ante-diluvian Heavens and Earth the same with the present, his apodosis in the 7*th.* Verse, should not have been ὅι δε νῦν οὐρανοὶ, but καὶ οἱ αὐτοὶ οὐρανοὶ καὶ ἡ γῆ τεθησαυρισμένοι εἰσί, &c. I say, it should not have been by way of antithesis, but of identity or continuation; *And the same Heavens and Earth are kept in store reserv'd unto fire, &c.* Accordingly we see the Apostle speaks thus, as to the Logos, or the *Word of God*, Verse 7. τῷ αὐτῷ λόγῳ, *by the same Word of God;* where the thing is the same, he expresseth it as the same; And if it had been the same Heavens and Earth, as well as the same Word of God, Why should he use a mark of opposition for the one, and of identity for the other? to this I do not see what can be fairly answer'd.

* This phrase or manner of speech συνιζάναι ἐκ vel ὅξ is not unusual in *Greek* Authors, and upon a like subject; *Plato* saith, τόν δε κόσμον συνιςάναι ἐκ πυρὲς, ὕδατος, ἄερος, γῆς, but he that should translate *Plato, The world stands out of fire, water, &c.* would be thought neither *Græcian*, nor Philosopher. The same phrase is us'd in reciting *Heraclitus* his opinion, τὰ πάντα ἐκ πυρὸς συνεςάναι, καὶ οἷς τοῦτο ἀναλίεως. And also in *Thales* his, which is still nearer to the subject, ἐκ τοῦ ὕδατός, φηοι, συνιζάναι πάντα, which *Cicero* renders, *ex aquâ, dixit, constare omnia.* So that it is easie to know the true importance of this phrase, and how ill it is render'd in the English, *standing out of the water.*

† Whether you refer the words ὅξ ὕδατ. καί δι ὕδατ. separately, to the Heavens and the Earth, or both to the Earth, or both to both, it will make no great difference as to our interpretation.

Fourthly, the ante-diluvian Heavens and Earth were different from the present, because, as the Apostle intimates, they were such, and so constituted, as made them obnoxious to a Deluge; whereas ours are of such a form, as makes them incapable of a Deluge, and obnoxious to a Conflagration; the just contrary fate.

Theor I *Book,*
c. 2.

If you say there was nothing of natural tendency or disposition in either World to their respective fate, but the first might as well have perish'd by fire, as water, and this by water as by fire, you unhinge all Nature and natural providence in that method, and contradict one main scope of the Apostle in this discourse. His first scope is to assert, and mind them of that diversity there was betwixt the ancient Heavens and Earth, and the present; and from that, to prove against those Scoffers, that there had been a change and revolution in Nature; And his second scope seems to be this, to show that diversity to be such, as, under the Divine conduct, leads to a different fate, and expos'd that World to a Deluge; for when he had describ'd the constitution of the first Heavens and Earth, he subjoyns, δι᾽ ὧν ὁ τότε κόσμος ὕδατι κατακλυσθεὶς ἀπόλετο. *Quià talis erat,* saith *Grotius, qualem diximus, constitutio & Terræ & Cœli. WHEREBY the then World perish'd in a Flood of Water.* This *whereby* notes some kind of causal dependance, and must relate to some means or conditions precedent. It cannot relate to Logos, or *the Word of God,* Grammar will not permit that; therefore it must relate to the state of the ante-diluvian Heavens and Earth immediately premis'd. And to what purpose indeed should he premise the description of those Heavens and Earth, if it was not to lay a ground for this inference?

Having given these Reasons for the necessity of this Interpretation; in the last place, let's consider St. *Austin*'s judgment, and his sence upon this place, as to the point in question. As also the reflections that some other of the Ancients have made upon this doctrine of St. *Peter*'s. *Didymus Alexandrinus,* who was for some time St. *Jerome*'s Master, made such a severe reflection upon it, that he said this Epistle was corrupted, and should not be admitted into the Canon, because it taught the doctrine of a *Triple* or *Triform World* in this third Chapter. As you may see in his *Enarr. in Epist. Canonicas.* Now this threefold World is first that in the 6*th* Verse, *The World that then was.* In the 7*th.* Verse, *The Heavens and the Earth, that are now.* And in the 13*th.* Verse, *We expect new Heavens and a new Earth, according to his promise.* This seems to be a fair account that St. *Peter* taught the doctrine of a triple World; And I quote this testimony, to show what St. *Peter*'s words do naturally import, even in the judgment of one that was not of his mind. And a Man is not prone to make an exposition against his own Opinion, unless he think the words very pregnant and express.

But St. *Austin* owns the authority of this Epistle, and of this doctrine, as deriv'd from it, taking notice of this Text of St. *Peter*'s in several Parts of his Works. We have noted three or four places already to this purpose, and we may further take notice of several passages in his Treatise, *de Civ. Dei,* which confirm our exposition. In his 20*th.* Book, *ch.* 24. he disputes against *Porphyry,* who had the same Principles with these Æternalists in the Text; or, if I may so call them, Incorruptarians; and thought the World never had, nor ever would undergo any change, especially as to the Heavens. St. *Austin* could not urge *Porphyry* with the authority of St. *Peter*, for he had no veneration for the Christian Oracles; but it seems he had some for the *Jewish*, and arguing against him, upon that Text in the Psalms, *Cœli peribunt*, he shows upon occasion how he understands St. *Peter*'s destruction of the Old World. *Legitur Cœlum & Terra transibunt, Mundus transit, sed puto quod præterit, transit, transibunt aliquantò mitiùs dicta sunt quàm peribunt. In Epistolâ quoque Petri Apostoli, ubi aquâ inundatus, qui tum erat, periisse dictus est Mundus, satis clarum est quæ pars mundi à toto significata est, & quatenùs periisse dicta sit, & qui cœli repositi igni reservandi.* This he explains more fully afterwards by subjoyning a caution (which we cited before) that we must not understand this passage of St. *Peter*'s, concerning the destruction of the ante-diluvian World, to take in the whole Universe, and the highest Heavens, but onely the aerial Heavens, and the sublunary World. *In Apostolicâ illâ Epistolâ à toto pars accipitur, quod Diluvio periisse dictus est mundus, quamvis sola ejus, cum suis cœlis, pars ima perierit.* In that Apostolical Epistle, a part is signified by the whole, when the World is said to have perish'd in the Deluge, although the lower part of it onely, with the Heavens belonging to it, perished: that is, the Earth with the regions of the Air that belong to it. And consonant to this, in his exposition of that hundred and first Psalm, upon those words, *The Heavens are the work of thy hands, They shall perish, but thou shalt endure.* This perishing of the Heavens, he says, St. *Peter* tells us, hath been once done already, namely, at the Deluge; *Apertè dixit hoc Apostolus Petrus, Cœli erant olim & Terra, de aquâ & per aquam constituti, Dei verbo; per quod qui factus est mundus, aquâ inundatus deperiit; Terra autem & cœli qui nunc sunt, igni reservantur. Jam ergo dixit periisse cœlos per Diluvium.*

These places shew us that St. *Austin* understood St. *Peter*'s discourse to aim at the natural World, and his *periit* or *periisse* (*verse 6.*) to be of the same force as *peribunt* in the Psalms, when 'tis said the Heavens *shall perish*; and consequently that the Heavens and the Earth, in this Father's opinion, were as really chang'd and transform'd at the time of the Flood, as they will be at the Conflagration. But we must not expect from St. *Austin* or any of the Ancients a distinct account of this Apostolical doctrine, as if they knew and acknowledg'd the Theory of the first World; that does not at all appear; but what they said was either from broken Tradition, or extorted from them by the force of the Apostle's words and their own sincerity.

There are yet other places in St. *Austin* worthy our consideration upon this subject; especially his exposition of this 3*d. chap.* of St. *Peter*, as we find it in that same Treatise *de Civ. Dei*. There he compares again, the destruction of the World at the Deluge, with that which shall be at the Conflagration, and supposeth both the Heavens and Earth to have perish'd. *Apostolus commemorans factum ante Diluvium, videtur admonuisse quodammodò quatenùs in fine hujus seculi mundum istum periturum esse credamus. Nam & illo tempore periisse dixit, qui tunc erat, mundum; nec solum orbem terræ, verùm etiam cœlos,* Then giving his usual caution, That the Stars and starry heavens should not be comprehended in that mundane destruction, He goes on, *Atque hoc modo* (penè totus aer) *cum terra perierat; cujus Terræ utique prior facies* (nempe ante-diluviana) *fuerat deleta Diluvio. Qui*

cap. 18.

395

autem nunc sunt cœli & terra eodem verbo repositi sunt igni reservandi; Proinde qui cœli & quæ Terra, id est, qui mundus, pro eo mundo qui Diluvio periit, ex eâdem aquâ repositus est, ipse igni novissimo reservatur. Here you see St. *Austin*'s sence upon the whole matter; which is this, That the natural World, the Earth with the Heavens about it, was destroyed and changed at the Deluge into the present Heavens and Earth; which shall again in like manner be destroyed and chang'd cap. 16. by the last fire. Accordingly in another place, to add no more, he saith the figure of the (sublunary) world shall be chang'd at the Conflagration, as it was chang'd at the Deluge. *Tunc figura hujus mundi,* &c. *cap.* 16.

Thus you see, we have St. *Austin* on our side, in both parts of our interpretation; that St. *Peter*'s discourse is to be referr'd to the natural inanimate World, and that the present natural World is distinct and different from that which was before the Deluge. And St. *Austin* having applyed this expresly to St. *Peter*'s doctrine by way of Commentary, it will free us from any crime or affectation of singularity in the exposition we have given of that place.

Venerable *Bede* hath followed St. *Austin*'s footsteps in this doctrine; for, interpreting St. *Peter*'s *Original World* (Ἀρχαῖος Κόσμος) 2 *Pet.* 2. 5. he refers both that and this (*chap.* 3. 6.) to the natural inanimate World, which he supposeth to have undergone a change at the Deluge. His words are these, *idem ipse mundus est* (nempe quoad materiam) *in uqo nunc humanum genus habitat, quem inhabitaverunt hi qui ante diluvium fuerunt, sed tamen rectè Originalis Mundus, quasi alius, dicitur; quia sicut in consequentibus hujus Epistolæ scriptum continetur, Ille tunc mundus aquâ inundatus periit. Cœlis videlicet qui erant priùs, id est, cunctis aeris hujus turbulenti spaciis, aquarum accrescentium altitudine consumptis, ac Terrâ in alteram faciem, excedentibus aquis, immutatâ. Nam etsi montes aliqui atque convalles ab initio facti creduntur, non tamen tanti quanti nunc in orbe cernuntur universo.* 'Tis the same *World* (namely, as to the matter and substance of it) *which mankind lives in now, and did live in before the Flood, but yet that is truly call'd the ORIGINAL WORLD, being as it were another from the present. For 'tis said in the sequel of this Epistle that the World that was then, perish'd in the Deluge; namely, the regions of the air were consumed by the height and excess of the waters, and by the same waters the Earth was chang'd into another form or face. For although some Mountains and Valleys are thought to have been made from the beginning, yet not such great ones as now we see throughout the whole Earth.*

You see this Author does not only own a change made at the Deluge, but offers at a further explication wherein that change consisted, *viz.* that the Mountains and inequalities of the Earth were made greater than they were before the Flood; and so he makes the change or the difference betwixt the two Worlds gradual, rather than specifical, if I may so term it. But we cannot wonder at that, if he had no principles to carry it further, or to make any other sort of change De 6 dier. creat. intelligible to him. *Bede* also pursues the same sence and notion in his interpretation of that *fountain, Gen.* 2. 5. that watered the face of the Earth before the Flood. And many other transcribers of Antiquity have recorded this Tradition concerning a difference, gradual or specifical, both in the Ante-diluvian heavens (*Gloss. Ordin. Gen.* 9. *de Iride. Lyran. ibid. Hist. Scholast. c.* 35. *Rab. Maurus &*

Gloss. Inter. Gen. 2. 5, 6. *Alcuin. Quæst. in Gen. inter.* 135.) and in the Ante-diluvian Earth, as the same Authors witness in other places. As *Hist. Schol.* c. 34. *Gloss. Ord. in Gen.* 7. *Alcuin. Inter.* 118, *&c.* Not to instance in those that tell us the properties of the Ante-diluvian World under the name and notion of Paradise.

Thus much concerning this remarkable place in St. *Peter*, and the true exposition of it; which I have the more largely insisted upon, because I look upon this place as the chief repository of that great natural mystery, which in Scripture is communicated to us, concerning the Triple state or revolution of the World. And of those men that are so scrupulous to admit the Theory we have propos'd, I would willingly know whether they believe the Apostle in what he says concerning the *New Heavens* and the *New Earth to come*, *ver.* 13. and if they do, why they should not believe him as much concerning the *Old Heavens* and the *Old Earth*, past; *ver.* 5, *&* 6. which he mentions as formally, and describes more distinctly than the other. But if they believe neither past nor to come, in a natural sence, but an unchangeable state of Nature from the Creation to its annihilation, I leave them then to their Fellow Eternalists in the Text, and to the character or censure the Apostle gives them, Κατὰ τὰς ἰδίας αὐτῶν ἐπιθυμίας πορευόμγυοι, men that go by their own private humour and passions, and prefer that to all other evidence.

They deserve this censure, I am sure, if they do not only disbelieve, but also scoff, at this Prophetick and Apostolick doctrine concerning the Vicissitudes of Nature and a triple World; The Apostle in this discourse does formally distinguish three Worlds (for 'tis well known that the *Hebrews* have no word to signifie the natural World, but use that Periphrasis, *The Heavens* and *the Earth*) and upon each of them engraves a name and title, that bears a note of distinction in it; He calls them the *Old Heavens and Earth*, the *Present Heavens and Earth*, and the *New Heavens and Earth*. 'Tis true, these three are one, as to matter and substance; but they must differ as to form and properties; otherwise what is the ground of this distinction and of these three different appelations? Suppose the *Jews* had expected *Ezekiel's* Temple for the Third, and last, and most perfect; and that in the time of the second Temple they had spoke of them with this distinction, or under these different names, The *Old Temple*, the *Present Temple*, and the *New Temple* we expect: Would any have understood those three of one and the same Temple; never demolish'd, never chang'd, never rebuilt; always the same both as to materials and form? no, doubtless, but of three several Temples succeeding one another. And have we not the same reason to understand this Temple of the World, whereof St. *Peter* speaks, to be threefold in succession? seeing he does as plainly distinguish it into the *Old* heavens and earth, the *Present* heavens and earth, and the *New* heavens and earth. And I do the more willingly use this comparison of the Temple, because it hath been thought an Emblem of the outward World.

I know we are naturally averse to entertain any thing that is inconsistent with the general frame and texture of our own thoughts; That's to begin the World again; and we often reject such things without examination. Neither do I wonder that the generality of Interpreters beat down the Apostle's words and sence to their own notions; They had no other grounds to go upon, and Men are not willing, especially in natural and comprehensible things, to put such a meaning upon Scripture, as is unintelligible to themselves; They rather venture to offer a little violence to the words, that they may pitch the sence at such a convenient height, as their Principles will reach to. And therefore though some of our modern Interpreters, whom I mention'd before, have been sensible of the natural tendency of this discourse of St. *Peter*'s, and have much ado to bear off the force of the words, so as not to acknowledge that they import a real diversity betwixt the two worlds spoken of; yet having no Principles to guide or support them in following that Tract, they are forc'd to stop or divert another way. 'Tis like entering into the mouth of a Cave, we are not willing to venture further than the light goes. Nor are they much to blame for this; the fault is onely in those Persons that continue wilfully in their darkness, and when they cannot otherwise resist the light, shut their eyes against it, or turn their head another way..... but I am afraid I have staid too long upon this argument: not for my own sake, but to satisfie others.

You may please to remember that all that I have said hitherto, belongs onely to the first Head: To prove a *Diversity in general* betwixt the Ante-diluvian Heavens and Earth, and the present: not expressing what their particular form was. And this general diversity may be argued also by observations taken from *Moses* his history of the World, before and after the Flood. From the Longevity of the Ante-diluvians: The Rain-bow appearing after the Deluge: and the breaking open an Abyss capable to overflow the Earth. The Heavens that had no Rainbow, and under whose benign and steddy influence, Men liv'd seven, eight, nine hundred years and upwards, must have been of a different aspect and constitution from the present Heavens. And that Earth that had such an Abyss, that the disruption of it made an universal Deluge, must have been of another form than the present Earth. And those that will not admit a diversity in the two worlds, are bound to give us an intelligible account of these Phænomena: How they could possibly be in Heavens and Earth, like the present. Or if they were there once, why they do not continue so still, if Nature be the same.

See Theor. Book 2. ch. 5.

We need say no more, as to the Ante-diluvian Heavens: but as to the Earth, we must now, according to the second Part of the first Head; enquire, If that *Particular Form*, which we have assign'd it before the Flood, be agreeable to Scripture. You know how we have describ'd the Form and situation of that Earth: namely, that it was built over the Abyss, as a regular Orb, covering and incompassing the waters round about: and founded, as it were, upon them. There are many passages of Scripture that favour this description: Some more expresly, others upon a due explication. To this purpose there are two express Texts in the Psalms: as *Psal.* 24. 1, 2. *The Earth is the Lords, and the fulness thereof: The habitable World, and they that dwell therein. FOR he has founded it upon* * *the Seas, and establish'd it upon the Floods.* An Earth founded upon the

* I know some would make this place of no effect by rendering the *Hebrew* particle על *juxta, by* or *near* to; so they would read it thus, *He hath founded the Earth by the Sea-side,* and establish'd it by the Floods. What is there wonderful in this, that the shores should lie by the Sea-side; Where could they lie else? What reason or argument is this, why the Earth should be the Lord's?

Seas, and establish'd upon the Waters, is not this the Earth we have describ'd? the first Earth, as it came from the hands of its Maker. Where can we now find in Nature, such an Earth as has the Seas and the Water for its foundation? Neither is this Text without a second, as a fellow-witness to confirm the same truth: For in the 136. *Psalm, ver.* 4, 5, 6, we read to the same effect, in these words: *To him, who alone does great wonders: To him that by wisdom made the Heavens: To him that stretched out the Earth above the Waters.* We can hardly express that form of the Ante-diluvian Earth, in words more determinate than these are; Let us then in the same simplicity of heart, follow the words of Scripture; seeing this literal sence is not repugnant to Nature, but, on the contrary, agreeable to it upon the strictest examination. And we cannot, without some violence, turn the words to any other sence. What tolerable interpretation can these admit of, if we do not allow the Earth once to have encompass'd and over-spread the face of the Waters? To be *founded* upon the waters, to be *establish'd* upon the waters, to be *extended* upon the waters, what rational or satisfactory account can be given of these phrases and expressions from any thing we find in the present situation of the Earth: or how can they be verified concerning it? Consult Interpreters, ancient or modern, upon these two places: see if they answer your expectation, or answer the natural importance of the words, unless they acknowledge another form of the Earth, than the present. Because a Rock hangs its nose over the Sea, must the body of the Earth be said to be *stretched over the waters?* Or because there are waters in some subterraneous cavities, is the Earth therefore *founded upon the Seas?* Yet such lame explications as these you will meet with; and while we have no better light, we must content our selves with them; but when an explication is offer'd, that answers the propriety, force, and extent of the words, to reject it, onely because it is not fitted to our former opinions, or because we did not first think of it, is to take an ill method in expounding Scripture. This *Foundation* or *Establishment* of the Earth upon the Seas, this *Extension* of it above the waters, relates plainly to the body, or whole circuit of the Earth, not to parcels and particles of it; as appears from the occasion, and its being joyn'd with the Heavens, the other part of the World. Besides, *David* is speaking of the Origin of the World, and of the Divine power and wisdom in the construction and situation of our Earth, and these attributes do not appear from the holes of the Earth, and broken Rocks; which have rather the face of a ruine, than of wisdom; but in that wonderful libration and expansion of the first Earth over the face of the waters, sustained by its own proportions, and the hand of his Providence.

The Earth is the Lord's *for* he hath founded it *near* the Seas, Where is the consequence of this? But if he founded it upon the Seas, which could not be done by any other hand but his, it shows both the Workman and the Master. And accordingly in that other place, *Psal.* 136. 6, if you render it, he *stretched* out the Earth *near* the Waters, How is that one of God's great wonders? as it is there represented to be. Because in some few places this particle is render'd otherwise, where the sense will bear it, must we therefore render it so when we please, and where the sence will not bear it? This being the most usual signification of it, and there being no other word that signifies *above* more frequently or determinately than this does, Why must it signifie otherwise in this place? Men will wriggle any way to get from under the force of a Text, that does not suit to their own Notions.

These two places in the Psalms being duly consider'd, we shall more easily understand a third place, to the same effect, in the *Proverbs*; delivered by *WISDOM*, concerning the Origin of the World, and the form of the first Earth, in these words, *Chap. 8. 27. When he prepared the Heavens I was there, when HE SET an Orb or Sphere upon the face of the Abyss.* We render it, when we set a *Compass* upon the face of the Abyss; but if we have rightly interpreted the Prophet *David*, 'tis plain enough what compass is here to be understood; not an imaginary circle, (for why should that be thought one of the wonderful works of God) but that exterior Orb of the Earth that was set upon the waters. That was the Masterpiece of the Divine art in framing of the first Earth, and therefore very fit to be taken notice of by *Wisdom*. And upon this occasion, I desire you to reflect upon St. *Peter*'s expression, concerning the first Earth, and to compare it with *Solomon*'s to see if they do not answer one another. St. *Peter* calls it γῆ καθεσῶσα δι' ὑδάτων, *An Earth consisting, standing,* or *sustained by the waters.* And *Solomon* calls it חוּג עַל פְּנֵי תְהוֹם.. *An Orb drawn upon the face of the Abyss.* And St. *Peter* says, that was done τῷ λόγῳ τοῦ Θεοῦ· by the *wisdom of God:* which is the same Λόγος or *wisdom*, that here declares her self, to have been present at this work. Add now to these two places, the two foremention'd out of the Psalmist; *An Earth founded upon the Seas,* (*Psal.* 24. 2.) and an *Earth stretched out above the waters:* (*Psal.* 136. 6.) Can any body doubt or question, but all these four Texts refer to the same thing? And seeing St. *Peter*'s description refers certainly to the Ante-diluvian Earth, they must all refer to it; and do all as certainly and evidently agree with our Theory concerning the form and situation of it.

The pendulous form and posture of that first Earth being prov'd from these four places, 'tis more easie and emphatical to interpret in this sence that passage in *Job* ch. 26. 7. *He stretcheth out the North over the Tohu,* (for so it is in the original) *and hangeth the Earth upon nothing.* And this strange foundation or no foundation of the exteriour Earth seems to be the ground of those noble questions propos'd to *Job* by God Almighty, *ch.* 38. *Where wast thou when I laid the foundations of the Earth? Declare if thou hast understanding. Whereupon are the foundations thereof fastned, and who laid the corner stone?* There was neither foundation, nor corner stone, in that piece of Architecture; and that was it which made the art and wonder of it. But I have spoken more largely to these places *Book* I. *p.* 88. in the Theory it self. And if the four Texts before-mentioned be consider'd without prejudice, I think there are few matters of natural Speculation that can be so well prov'd out of Scripture, as the Form which we have given to the Antediluvian Earth.

But yet it may be thought a just, if not a necessary appendix to this discourse, concerning the form of the ante-diluvian Earth, to give an account also of the *ante-diluvian Abyss,* and the situation of it according to Scripture; for the relation which these two have to one another, will be a further means to discover if we have rightly determin'd the form of that Earth. The *Abyss* or *Tehom-Rabbah* is a Scripture notion, and the word is not us'd, that I know of, in that distinct and peculiar sence in Heathen Authors. 'Tis plain that in Scripture it is not always taken for the Sea (as *Gen.* 1. 2. & 7. 11. & 49. 25. *Deut.* 33. 13. *Job* 28. 14. & 38. 16. *Ps.* 33. 7. & 71. 20. & 78. 15. & 135. 6. *Apoc.* 20. 1. 3.) but for some other mass of waters, or subterraneous storehouse. And this being observ'd, we may easily discover the nature, and set down the history of the Scripture-Abyss.

The Mother-Abyss is no doubt that in the beginning of *Genesis, ver.* 2. which had nothing but darkness upon the face of it, or a thick caliginous air. The next news we hear of this Abyss is at the Deluge, (*Gen.* 7. 11.) where 'tis said to be broke open, and the waters of it to have drowned the World. It seems then this Abyss was clos'd up some time betwixt the Creation and the Deluge, and had got another cover than that of darkness. And if we will believe *Wisdom,* (*Prov.* 8. 27.) who was there present at the formation of the Earth, an *Orb was set upon the face of the Abyss* at the beginning of the World.

That these three places refer to the same Abyss, I think, cannot be questioned by any that will compare them and consider them. That of the Deluge, *Moses* calls there *Tehom-Rabbah,* the *Great Abyss*; and can there be any greater than the forementioned Mother-Abyss? And *WISDOME,* in that place in the *Proverbs,* useth the same phrase and words with *Moses, Gen.* 1. 2. עַל פְּנֵי תְהוֹם *upon the face of the Deep* or of the *Abyss*; changing *darkness* for that *Orb* of the exteriour Earth which was made afterwards to inclose it. And in this vault it lay, and under this cover, when the Psalmist speaks of it in these words (*Ps.* 33. 7.) *He gathereth the waters of the Sea, as in a * bag; he layeth up the Abyss in storehouses.* Lastly, we may observe that 'twas this Mother-Abyss whose womb was burst at the Deluge, when the Sea was born, and broke forth as if it had issued out of a womb; as God expresseth it to *Job, ch.* 38. 8. in which place the *Chaldee* Paraphrase reads it, when it broke forth, *coming out of the Abyss.* Which disruption at the Deluge seems also to be alluded to *Job* 12. 14, 15, and more plainly, *Prov.* 3. 20. *by his knowledge the Abysses are broken up.*

Thus you have already a threefold state of the Abyss, which makes a short History of it; first, *Open,* at the beginning; then *covered,* till the Deluge. Then *broke open* again, as it is at present. And we pursue the History of it no further; but we are told, *Apoc.* 20. 3. That it shall be shut up again, and the great Dragon in it, for a Thousand years. In the mean time we may observe from this form and posture of the Ante-diluvian Abyss, how suitable it is and coherent with that form of the Ante-diluvian Earth which St. *Peter* and the *Psalmist* had describ'd, *sustain'd by the waters; founded upon the waters; strecht above the waters*; for if it was the cover of this Abyss (and it had some cover that was broke at the Deluge) it was spread as a Crust or Ice upon the face of those waters, and so made an *orbis Terrarum,* an habitable sphere of Earth about the Abyss.

S O much for the form of the Ante-diluvian Earth and Abyss; which as they aptly correspond to one another, so you see, our Theory answers and is adjusted to both; and, I think, so fitly, that we have no reason hitherto to be

---

* *This reading or translating is generally followed,* (Theor. book 1, p. 86.) *though the English translation read* on a heap, *unsuitably to the matter and to the sence.*

displeas'd with the success we have had in the examination of it, according to Scripture. We have dispatch'd the two main points in question, first, to prove a diversity in general betwixt the two natural Worlds, or betwixt the Heavens and the Earth before and after the Flood. Secondly, to prove wherein this diversity consisted; or that the particular form of the Ante-diluvian Heavens and Earth was such according to Scripture, as we have describ'd it in the Theory. You'l say, then the work is done, what needs more, all the rest follows of course; for if the Ante-diluvian Earth had such a form as we have propos'd and prov'd it to have had, there could be no Deluge in it but by a dissolution of its parts and exteriour frame: And a Deluge so made, would not be in the nature of a standing Pool, but of a violent agitation and commotion of the waters. This is true; These parts of the Theory are so cemented, that you must grant all, if you grant any. However we will try if even these two particulars also may be prov'd out of Scripture; That is, if there be any marks or memorandums left there by the Spirit of God, of such a fraction or dissolution of the Earth at the Deluge. And also such characters of the Deluge it self, as show it to have been by a fluctuation and impetuous commotion of the waters.

To proceed then; That there was a Fraction or Dissolution of the Earth at the Deluge, the history of it by *Moses* gives us the first account, seeing he tells us, as the principal cause of the Flood, that the Fountains of the *Great Abyss* were *cloven* or *burst asunder*; and upon this disruption the waters gush'd out from the bowels of the Earth, as from the widen'd mouths of so many Fountains. I do not take *Fountains* there to signifie any more than Sources or Stores of Water; noting also this manner of their eruption from below, or out of the ground, as Fountains do. Accordingly in the *Proverbs*, (*chap.* 3. 20.) 'tis onely said, the *Abysses were broken open*. I do not doubt but this refers to the Deluge, as *Bede*, and others understand it; the very word being us'd here, both in the *Hebrew* and Septuagint, the express'd the disruption of the Abyss at the Deluge.

נבקעו
ἐῤῥάγησάν.
c. 38.

And this breaking up of the Earth at that time, is elegantly exprest in *Job*, by the bursting of the Womb of Nature, when the Sea was first brought to light; when after many pangs and throes and dilacerations of her body, Nature was deliver'd of a burthen which she had born in her Womb Sixteen Hundred Years.

These three places I take to be memorials and proofs of the disruption of the Earth, or of the Abyss, at the universal Deluge. And to these we may add more out of the Prophets, *Job*, and the *Psalms*, by way of allusion (commonly) to the state of Nature at that time. The Prophet *Isaiah* in describing the future destruction of the World, *chap.* 24. 18, 19. seems plainly to allude and have respect to the past destruction of it at the Deluge; as appears by that leading expression, *the windows from on high are open*, אֲרֻבּוֹת סְמָרוֹס נִפְתָּחוּ, θυρίδες ὀκ τοῦ οὐρανοῦ ἠνεῴχθησαν, taken manifestly from *Gen.* 7. 11. Then see how the description goes on, *the windows from on high are open, and the foundations of the Earth do shake. The Earth is utterly broken down, the Earth is quite dissolv'd, the Earth is exceedingly moved.* Here are Concussions, and Fractions, and Dissolutions, as there were in the Mundane Earth-quake and Deluge; which we had exprest before only by *breaking open the Abyss*. By the Foundations of the Earth here and elsewhere, I perceive many understand the Centre; so by *moving* or *shaking* the foundations, or putting them out of course, must be understood a displacing of the Centre; which was really done at the Deluge, as we have shewn in its proper place. If we therefore remember that there was both a dislocation, as I may so say; and a fraction in the body of the Earth, by that great fall; a dislocation as to the centre, and a fraction as to the surface and exterior region, it will truly answer to all those expressions in the Prophet, that seem so strange and extraordinary. 'Tis true, this place of the Prophet respects also and foretells the future destruction of the World; but that being by Fire, when the *Elements shall melt with fervent heat, and the Earth with the works therein shall be burnt up*, these expressions of *fractions and concussions*, seem to be taken originally from the manner of the World's first destruction, and to be transferr'd, by way of application, to represent and signifie the second destruction of it, though, it may be, not with the same exactness and propriety. *Theor. book* 2. *p.* 194, 195.

There are several other places that refer to the dissolution and subversion of the Earth at the Deluge: *Amos* 9. 5, 6. *The Lord of Hosts is he that toucheth the Earth, and it shall melt, or be dissolv'd. . . . . . and it shall rise up wholly like a Flood, and shall be drowned as by the Flood of Ægypt.* By *this* and by *the next Verse* the Prophet seems to allude to the Deluge, and to the dissolution of the Earth that was then. This in *Job* seems to be call'd *breaking down the Earth, and overturning the Earth*, Chap. 12. 14, 15. *Behold he breaketh down and it cannot be built again, He shutteth upon man, and there can be no opening. Behold, he withholdeth the waters, and they dry up; also he sendeth them out, and they overturn the Earth*: Which place you may see paraphras'd, *Theor. Book* 1. *pp.* 91, 92. We have already cited, and shall hereafter cite, other places out of *Job*; And as that Ancient Author (who is thought to have liv'd before the Judaical Oeconomy, and nearer to *Noah* than *Moses*) seems to have had the *Præcepta Noachidarum*, so also he seems to have had the *Dogmata Noachidarum*; which were deliver'd by *Noah* to his Children and Posterity, concerning the mysteries of natural Providence, the origine and fate of the World, the Deluge and Ante-diluvian state, *&c.* and accordingly we find many strictures of these doctrines in the Book of *Job*. Lastly, in the Psalms there are Texts that mention the *shaking of the Earth*, and the *foundations* of the World, in reference to the Flood, if we judge aright; whereof we will speak under the next Head, *concerning* the raging of the Waters in the Deluge.

These places of Scripture may be noted, as left us to be remembrancers of that general ruine and disruption of the Earth at the time of the Deluge. But I know it will be said of them, that they are not strict proofs, but allusions onely. Be it so; yet what is the ground of those allusions? something must be alluded to, and something that hath past in nature, and that is recorded in Sacred History; And what is that, unless it be the universal Deluge, and that change and disturbance that was then in all nature. If others say, that these and such like places are to be understood morally and allegorically, I do not envy them their interpretation; but when nature and reason will bear a literal sence, the rule is, that we should not recede from the letter. But I leave these things to every one's thoughts; which the more calm they are, and the more impartial, the more easily they will feel the impressions of truth. In the mean time, I proceed to the last particular mention'd, *The form of the Deluge it self.*

This we suppose to have been not in the way of a standing Pool, the Waters making an equal Surface, and an equal heighth every where; but that the extreme heighth of the Waters was made by the extreme agitation of them; caus'd by the weight and force of great Masses or Regions of Earth falling at once into the Abyss; by which means, as the waters in some places were prest out, and thrown at an excessive height into the air, so they would also in certain places gape, and lay bare even the bottom of the Abyss; which would look as an open Grave ready to swallow up the Earth, and all it bore. Whilst the Ark, in the mean time, falling and rising by these gulphs and precipices, sometimes above water, and sometimes under, was a true Type of the state of the Church in this World; And to this time and state *David* alludes in the name of the Church, *Psal.* 42. 7. *Abyss calls unto Abyss at the noise of thy Cataracts or Water-spouts; All thy waves and billows have gone over me.* And again, *Psal.* 46. 2, 3. in the name of the Church. *Therefore will not we fear, tho' the Earth be removed, and tho' the mountains be carried into the midst of the Seas. The waters thereof roar and are troubled, the mountains shake with the swelling thereof.*

But there is no description more remarkable or more eloquent, than of that Scene of things represented, *Psal.* 18. 7, 8, 9, &c. which still alludes, in my opinion, to the Deluge-scene, and in the name of the Church. We will set down the words at large.

Ver. 6. *In my distress I called upon the Lord, and cried unto my God; He heard my voice out of his Temple, and my cry came before him into his ears.*

7. *Then the Earth shook and trembled, the foundations also of the hills moved and were shaken, because he was wroth.*

8. *There went up a smoke from his nostrils, and fire out of his mouth devoured; Coals were kindled by it.*

9. *He bowed the Heavens also and came down, and darkness was under his feet.*

10. *And he rode upon a Cherub and did flie, he did flie upon the wings of the wind.*

11. *He made darkness his secret place; his pavilion round about him was dark waters and thick clouds of the skie.*

12. *At the brightness before him the thick clouds passed, hail and coals of fire.*

13. *The Lord also thunder'd in the Heavens, and the Highest gave his voice, hail and coals of fire.*

14. *Yea, he sent out his arrows, and scatter'd them: and he shot out lightnings and discomfited them.*

15. *Then the Chanels of waters were seen, and the foundations of the World were discovered; at thy rebuke, O Lord, at the blast of the breath of thy nostrils.*

מַיִם רַבִּים

He sent from above, he took me; he drew me out of great waters.

This I think is a rough * draught of the face of the Heavens and the Earth at the Deluge, as the last Verses do intimate; and 'tis apply'd to express the dangers and deliverances of the Church: The Expressions are far too high to be apply'd

---

* See *Philo Judæus* his description of the Deluge, both as to the commotions of the Heavens, and the fractions of the Earth. In his first Treatise de *Abrahamo,* mihi *pa.* 279.

to *David* in his Person, and to his deliverance from *Saul*; no such agonies or disorders of nature as are here instanc'd in, were made in *David*'s time, or upon his account; but 'tis a scheme of the Church, and of her fate, particularly, as represented by the Ark, in that dismal distress, when all nature was in confusion. And though there may be some things here intermixt to make up the Scene, that are not so close to the subject as the rest, or that may be referr'd to the future destruction of the world: yet that is not unusual, nor amiss, in such descriptions, if the great strokes be fit and rightly plac'd. That there was smoke, and fire, and water, and thunder, and darkness, and winds, and Earth-quakes at the Deluge, we cannot doubt, if we consider the circumstances of it; Waters dash'd and broken make a smoke and darkness, and no Hurricano could be so violent as the motions of the Air at that time; Then the Earth was torn in pieces, and its Foundations shaken; And as to thunder and lightning, the encounters and collisions of the mighty Waves, and the cracks of a falling World, would make flashes and noises, far greater and more terrible, than any that can come from vapors and clouds. There was an universal Tempest, a conflict and clashing of all the Elements; and *David* seems to have represented it so; with God allmighty in the midst of it, ruling them all.

But I am apt to think some will say, all this is Poetical in the Prophet, and these are hyperbolical and figurate expressions, from which we cannot make any inference, as to the Deluge and the natural World. 'Tis true, those that have no Idea of the Deluge, that will answer to such a Scene of things, as is here represented, must give such a slight account of this Psalm. But on the other hand, if we have already an Idea of the Deluge that is rational, and also consonant to Scripture upon other proofs, and the description here made by the Prophet answer to that Idea, whether then is it not more reasonable to think that it stands upon that ground, than to think it a meer fancy and Poetical Scene of things: This is the true state of the case, and that which we must judge of. Methinks 'tis very harsh to suppose all this a bare fiction, grounded upon no matter of fact, upon no Sacred story, upon no appearance of God in nature. If you say it hath a moral signification, so let it have, we do not destroy that; it hath reference, no doubt, to the dangers and deliverances of the Church; but the question is, whether the words and natural sence be a fancy onely, a bundle of randome hyperboles: or whether they relate to the history of the Deluge, and the state of the Ark there representing the Church. This makes the sence doubly rich, historically and morally; and grounds it upon Scripture and reason, as well as upon fancy.

That violent eruption of the Sea out of the Womb of the Earth, which *Job* speaks of, is, in my judgment, another description of the Deluge; 'tis *Chap.* 38. 8, 9, 10, 11. *Who shut up the Sea with doors, when it broke forth, as if it had issued out of a Womb; When I made the cloud the garment thereof, and thick darkness a swadling band for it. And broke up for it my decreed place . . . . . hitherto shalt thou come, &c.* Here you see the birth and nativity of the Sea, or of *Oceanus*, describ'd;* how he broke out of the Womb, and what his first garment and

* *Utì comparatio præcedens || de ortu Telluris, sumitur ab ædificio, ita bæc altera de ortu maris, sumitur à partu; & exhibetur Oceanus, primùm, ut fœtus inclusus in utero, dein ut erumpens & prodeuns, denique ut fasciis & primis suis pannis involutus. Atque ex aperto Terræ utero prorupit aquarum moles, ut proluvies illa, quam simul cum fœtu profundere solet puerpera. || Ver. 4, 5, 6.*

swadling cloaths were; namely clouds and thick darkness. This cannot refer to any thing, that I know of, but to the face of Nature at the Deluge; when the Sea was born, and wrapt up in clouds and broken waves, and a dark impenetrable mist round the body of the Earth. And this seems to be the very same that *David* had exprest in his description of the Deluge, *Psal.* 18. 11. *He made darkness his secret place, his pavilion round about him were dark waters and thick clouds of the skies.* For this was truly the face of the World in the time of the Flood, tho' we little reflect upon it. And this dark confusion every where, above and below, arose from the violent and confus'd motion of the Abyss; which was dasht in pieces by the falling Earth, and flew into the air in misty drops, as dust flies up in a great ruine.

See Theor. Book I, *p.* 99.

But I am afraid, we have stayed too long upon this particular, *the form of the Deluge;* seeing 'tis but a Corollary from the precedent article about the dissolution of the Earth. However time is not ill spent about any thing that relates to natural Providence, whereof the two most signal instances in our Sacred Writings, are, the *Deluge* and the *Conflagration.* And seeing *Job* and *David* do often reflect upon the works of God in the external creation, and upon the administrations of Providence, it cannot be imagin'd that they should never reflect upon the Deluge; the most remarkable change of Nature that ever hath been, and the most remarkable judgment upon mankind. And if they have reflected upon it any where, 'tis, I think, in those places and those instances which I have noted; and if those places do relate to the Deluge, they are not capable, in my judgment, of any fairer or more natural interpretation than that which we have given them; which, you see, how much it favours and confirms our Theory.

I have now finisht the heads I undertook to prove, that I might shew our Theory to agree with Scripture in these three principal points; first, in that it supposeth a diversity and difference betwixt the Ante-diluvian Heavens and Earth, and the present Heavens and Earth. Secondly, in assigning the particular form of the Ante-diluvian Earth and Abyss. Thirdly, in explaining the Deluge by a dissolution of that Earth, and an eruption of the Abyss. How far I have succeeded in this attempt, as to others, I cannot tell; but I am sure I have convinc'd my self, and am satisfied that my thoughts, in that Theory, have run in the same tract with the holy writings: with the true intent and spirit of them. There are some persons that are wilfully ignorant in certain things, and others that are willing to be ignorant as the Apostle phraseth it; speaking of those Eternalists that denied the doctrine of the change and revolutions of the Natural World: And 'tis not to be expected but there are many still of the same humour; and therefore may be called *willingly ignorant,* that is, they will not use that pains and attention that is necessary for the examination of such a doctrine, nor impartiality in judging after examination; they greedily lay hold on all evidence on one side, and willingly forget, or slightly pass over, all evidence for the other; this I think is the character of those that are *willingly ignorant;* for I do not take it to be so deep as a down-right wilful ignorance, where they are plainly conscious to themselves of that wilfulness; but where an insensible mixture of humane passions inclines them one way, and makes them averse to the other; and in that method draws on all the consequences of a willing *ignorance.*

There remains still, as I remember, one Proposition that I am bound to make good; I said at first, that our Hypothesis concerning the Deluge was more agreeable not only to Scripture in general, but also to the particular History of the Flood left us by *Moses*; I say, more agreeable to it than any other Hypothesis that hath yet been propos'd. This may be made good in a few words. For in *Moses*'s history of the Deluge there are two principal points, The extent of the Deluge, and the Causes of it; and in both these we do fully agree with that sacred Author. *As to the extent of it,* He makes the Deluge universal; *All the high hills under the whole heaven were cover'd, fifteen cubits upwards*; We also make it universal, over the face of the whole Earth; and in such a manner as must needs raise the waters above the top of the highest hills every where. As *to the causes of it,* Moses makes them to be the disruption of the *Abyss*, and the *Rains*; and no more; and in this also we exactly agree with him; we know no other causes, nor pretend to any other but those two. Distinguishing therefore *Moses* his narration as to the substance and circumstances of it, it must be allowed that these two points make the substance of it, and that an Hypothesis that differs from it in either of these two, differs from it more than Ours; which, at the worst, can but differ in matter of circumstance. Now seeing the great difficulty about the Deluge is the quantity of Water required for it, there have been two explications proposed, besides ours, to remove or satisfie this difficulty; One whereof makes the Deluge not to have been universal, or to have reacht only *Judea* and some neighbouring Countreys; and therefore less water would suffice; The other owning the Deluge to be universal, supplies it self with Water from the Divine Omnipotency, and says *new* Waters were created then for the nonce, and again annihilated when the Deluge was to cease. Both these explications you see, (and I know no more of note that are not obnoxious to the same exceptions) differ from *Moses* in the substance, or in one of the two substantial points, and consequently more than ours doth. The first changeth the Flood into a kind of national inundation, and the second assigns other causes of it than *Moses* had assigned. And as they both differ apparently from the Mosaical history, so you may see them refuted upon other grounds also, in the third Chapter of the First Book of the Theory.

This may be sufficient as to the History of the Flood by *Moses*. But possibly it may be said the principal objection will arise from *Moses* his Six-days Creation in the first Chapter of *Genesis*: where another sort of Earth, than what we have form'd from the Chaos, is represented to us; namely, a Terraqueous Globe, such as our Earth is at present. 'Tis indeed very apparent, that *Moses* hath accommodated his Six-days Creation to the present form of the Earth, or to that which was before the eyes of the people when he writ. But it is a great question whether that was ever intended for a true Physical account of the origine of the Earth: or whether *Moses* did either Philosophize or Astronomize in that description. The ancient Fathers, when they answer the Heathens, and the adversaries of Christianity, do generally deny it; as I am ready to make good upon another occasion. And the thing it self bears in it evident marks of an accommodation and condescention to the vulgar notions concerning the form of the World. Those that think otherwise, and would make it literally and physically true in all the parts of it, I desire them, without entring upon the strict merits of the cause, to determine these Preliminaries. First, whether the whole universe rise from a Terrestrial Chaos. Secondly, what Systeme of the World this Six-days Creation proceeds upon: whether it supposes the Earth, or the Sun, for the Center. Thirdly, Whether the Sun and Fixt Stars are of a later date, and a later birth, than this Globe of Earth. And lastly, Where is the Region of the Super-celestial Waters. When they have determin'd these Fundamentals, we will proceed to other observations upon the Six-days work, which will further assure us, that 'tis a narration suited to the capacity of the people, and not to the strict and physical nature of things. Besides, we are to remember, that *Moses* must be so interpreted in the first Chapter of *Genesis*, as not to interfere with himself in other parts of his History; nor to interfere with St. *Peter*, or the Prophet *David*, or any other Sacred Authors, when they treat of the same matter. Nor lastly, so, as to be repugnant to clear and uncontested Science. For, in things that concern the natural World, that must always be consulted.

With these precautions, let them try if they can reduce that narrative of the Origine of the World, to physical truth; so as to be consistent, both with Nature, and with Divine Revelation every where. It is easily reconcileable to both, if we suppose it writ in a Vulgar style, and to the conceptions of the People: And we cannot deny that a Vulgar style is often made use of in the holy Writings. How freely and unconcernedly does Scripture speak of God Allmighty, according to the opinions of the vulgar? of his *passions, local motions, parts and members of his body.* Which all are things that do not belong, or are not compatible with the Divine nature, according to truth and Science. And if this liberty be taken, as to God himself, much more may it be taken as to his works. And accordingly we see, what motion the Scripture gives to the Sun: what figure to the Earth: what figure to the Heavens: All according to the appearance of sence and popular credulity; without any remorse for having transgressed the rules of intellectual truth.

This vulgar style of Scripture in describing the natures of things, hath been often mistaken for the real sence, and so become a stumbling block in the way of truth. Thus the *Anthropomorphites* of old contended for the humane shape of God, from the Letter of Scripture; and brought many express Texts for their purpose: but sound reason, at length, got the upper hand of Literal authority. Then, several of the Christian Fathers contended, that there were no *Antipodes:* and made that doctrine irreconcileable to Scripture. But this also, after a while, went off, and yielded to reason and experience. Then, the Motion of the Earth must by no means be allow'd, as being contrary to Scripture: for so it is indeed, according to the Letter and Vulgar style. But all intelligent Persons see thorough this argument, and depend upon it no more in this case, than in the former. Lastly, The original of the Earth from a Chaos, drawn according to the rules of Physiology, will not be admitted: because it does not agree with the Scheme of the Six-days Creation. But why may not this be writ in a Vulgar style, as well as the rest? Certainly there can be nothing more like a Vulgar style, than to set God to *work by the day*, and in Six-days to finish his task: as he is there represented. We may therefore probably hope that all these disguises of truth will at length fall off, and that we shall see God and his Works in a pure and naked Light.

Thus I have finish'd what I had to say in confirmation of this Theory from Scripture. I mean of the former part of it, which depends chiefly upon the Deluge, and the Ante-diluvian Earth. When you have collated the places of Scripture, on either side, and laid them in the balance, to be weigh'd one against another; If you do but find them equal, or near to an equal poise, you know in whether Scale the Natural Reasons are to be laid: and of what weight they ought to be in an argument of this kind. There is a great difference betwixt Scripture with Philosophy on its side, and Scripture with Philosophy against it: when the question is concerning the Natural World. And this is our Case: which I leave now to the consideration of the unprejudic'd Reader: and proceed to the Proof of the Second Part of the Theory.

THE later Part consists of the *Conflagration of the World*, and the *New Heavens* and *New Earth*. And seeing there is no dispute concerning the former of these two, our task will now lie in a little compass. Being onely this, To prove that there will be New Heavens, and a New Earth, after the Conflagration. This, to my mind, is sufficiently done already, in the first, second and third Chapters of the 4*th*. Book, both from Scripture and Antiquity, whether Sacred or prophane: and therefore, at present, we will onely make a short and easie review of Scripture-Testimonies, with design chiefly to obviate and disappoint the evasions of such, as would beat down solid Texts into thin Metaphors and Allegories.

The Testimonies of Scripture concerning the *Renovation of the World*, are either express, or implicit. Those I call express, that mention the New Heavens and New Earth: And those implicit, that signifie the same thing, but not in express terms. So when our Saviour speaks of a *Palingenesia*, or Regeneration, (*Matt.* 19. 28, 29.) Or St. *Peter* of an *Apocatastasis* or Restitution, (*Act.* 3. 21.) These being words us'd by all Authors, prophane or Ecclesiastical, for the *Renovation* of the World, ought, in reason, to be interpreted in the same sence in the holy Writings. And in like manner, when St. *Paul* speaks of his *Future Earth*, or an *habitable World to come*, Hebr. 2. 5. or of a *Redemption* or melioration of the present state of nature, *Rom.* 8. 21, 22. These lead us again, in other terms, to the same *Renovation* of the World. But there are also some places of Scripture, that set the *New Heavens* and *New Earth* in such a full and open view, that we must shut our eyes not to see them. St. *John* says, he saw them, and observ'd the form of the New Earth, *Apoc.* 21. 1. The Seer *Isaiah* spoke of them in express words, many hundred years before. And St. *Peter* marks the time when they are to be introduc'd, namely after the Conflagration, or after the Dissolution of the present Heavens and Earth: 2 *Pet.* 3. 12, 13.

ἡ εἰκουμίνη
ἡ μέλλουτα.

Isa. 65. 17.

These later Texts of Scripture, being so express, there is but one way left to elude the force of them; and that is, by turning the *Renovation of the World* into an Allegory: and making the New Heavens and New Earth to be Allegorical Heavens and Earth, not real and material, as ours are. This is a bold attempt of some modern Authors, who chuse rather to strain the Word of God, than their own notions. There are Allegories, no doubt, in Scripture, but we are not to allegorize Scripture without some warrant: either from an Apostolical interpretation, or from the necessity of the matter: and I do not know how they can pretend to either of these, in this case. However, that they may have all fair play, we will lay aside, at present, all the other Texts of Scripture, and confine our selves wholly to St. *Peter's* words: to see and examine whether they are, or can be turn'd into an Allegory, according to the best rules of interpretation.

2 *Pet.* 3. 11, 12, 13. St. *Peter's* words are these: *Seeing then all these things shall be dissolv'd, what manner of persons ought ye to be, in holy conversation and godliness? Looking for, and hasting the coming of the Day of God: wherein the Heavens being on fire shall be dissolv'd, and the Elements shall melt with fervent heat. NEVERTHELESS, we, according to his promise, look for New Heavens and a New Earth, wherein Righteousness shall dwell.* The Question is concerning this last Verse, *Whether the New Heavens and Earth* here promis'd, are to be real and material Heavens and Earth, or onely figurative and allegorical. The words, you see, are clear: And the general rule of interpretation is this, *That* we are not to recede from the letter, or the literal sence, unless there be a necessity from the subject matter; such a necessity, as makes a literal interpretation absurd. But where is that necessity in this Case? Cannot God make new Heavens and a new Earth, as easily as he made the Old ones? Is his strength decay'd since that time, or is Matter grown more disobedient? Nay, does not Nature offer her self voluntarily to raise a new World from the second Chaos, as well as from the first: and, under the conduct of Providence, to make it as convenient an habitation as the Primæval Earth? Therefore no necessity can be pretended of leaving the literal sence, upon an incapacity of the subject matter.

The second rule to determine an Interpretation to be Literal or Allegorical, is, the use of the same words or phrase in the Context, and the signification of them there. Let's then examine our case according to this rule. St. *Peter* had us'd the same phrase of *Heavens and Earth* twice before in the same Chapter. The *old Heavens and Earth*, *ver.* 5. The *present Heavens and Earth*, *ver.* 7. and now he uses it again, *ver.* 13. The *new Heavens and Earth.* Have we not then reason to suppose, that he takes it here in the same sence, that he had done twice before, for real and material Heavens and Earth? There is no mark set of a new signification, nor why we should alter the sence of the words. That he us'd them always before for the material Heavens and Earth, I think none will question: and therefore, unless they can give us a sufficient reason, why we should change the signification of the words, we are bound, by this second rule also, to understand them in a literal sence.

Lastly, The very form of the words, and the manner of their dependance upon the Context, leads us to a literal sence, and to material Heavens and Earth. *NEVERTHELESS*, says the Apostle, *we expect new Heavens*, &c. Why *Nevertheless!* that is, notwithstanding the dissolution of the present Heavens and Earth. The Apostle foresaw, what he had said, might raise a doubt in their minds, whether all things would not be at an end: Nothing more of Heavens and Earth, or of any habitable World, after the Conflagration; and to obviate this, he tells them, *Notwithstanding* that wonderful desolation that I have describ'd, we do, according to God's promises, expect new Heavens and a new Earth, to be an Habitation for the Righteous.

You see then the New Heavens and New Earth, which the Apostle speaks of, are substituted in the place of those that were destroy'd at the Conflagration; and would you substitute Allegorical Heavens and Earth in the place of Material? A shadow for a substance? What an Equivocation would it be in the Apostle, when the doubt was about the material Heavens and Earth, to make an answer about Allegorical. Lastly, the timeing of the thing determines the sence. When shall this new World appear? after the Conflagration, the Apostle says: Therefore it cannot be understood of any moral renovation, to be made at, or in the times of the Gospel, as these Allegorists pretend. We must therefore, upon all accounts, conclude, that the Apostle intended a literal sence: real and material Heavens, to succeed these after the Conflagration: which was the thing to be prov'd. And I know not what Bars the Spirit of God can set, to keep us within the Compass of a Literal sence, if these be not sufficient.

Thus much for the Explication of St. *Peter*'s Doctrine, concerning the new Heavens and new Earth: which secures the second Part of our Theory. For the Theory stands upon two Pillars, or two pedestals, The Ante-diluvian Earth and the Future Earth: or, in St. *Peter*'s phrase, The Old Heavens and Earth, and the New Heavens and Earth: And it cannot be shaken, so long as these two continue firm and immoveable. We might now put an end to this Review, but it may be expected possibly that we should say something concerning the *Millennium:* which we have, contrary to the general Sentiment of the modern *Millenaries*, plac'd in the *Future* Earth. Our opinion hath this advantage above others, that, all fanatical pretensions to power and empire in this World, are, by these means, blown away, as chaff before the wind. Princes need not fear to be dethron'd, to make way to the Saints: nor Governments unhing'd, that They may rule the World with a rod of Iron. These are the effects of a wild Enthusiasm; seeing the very state which they aim at, is not to be upon this Earth.

But that our sence may not be mistaken or misapprehended in this particular, as if we thought the Christian Church would never, upon this Earth, be in a better and happier posture than it is in at present: We must distinguish betwixt a *melioration* of the World, if you will allow that word: and a *millennium*. We do not deny a reformation and improvement of the Church, both as to Peace, Purity, and Piety. That knowledge may increase, mens minds be enlarg'd, and Christian Religion better understood: That the power of Antichrist shall be diminish'd, persecution cease, and a greater union and harmony establish'd amongst the Reformed. All this may be, and I hope will be, ere long. But the *Apocalyptical Millennium*, or the *New Jerusalem*, is still another matter. It differs not in degree only from the present state, but is a new order of things: both in the Moral World and in the Natural; and that cannot be till we come into the *New Heavens* and *New Earth*. Suppose what Reformation you can in this World, there will still remain many things inconsistent with the true Millennial state. Antichrist, tho' weakned, will not be finally destroy'd till the coming of our

Saviour, nor Satan bound. And there will be always poverty, wars, diseases, knaves and hypocrites, in this World: which are not consistent with the *New Jerusalem*, as St. *John* describes it. *Apoc.* 21. 2, 3, 4, &c.

You see now what our notion is of the Millennium, as we deny this Earth to be the Seat of it. 'Tis the state that succeeds the first Resurrection, when Satan is lockt up in the bottomless pit. The state when the Martyrs are to return into Life, and wherein they are to have the first lot and chief share. A state which is to last a thousand years. *And Blessed and Holy is he, that hath a part in it: on such the second death hath no power, but they shall be Priests of God and Christ, and shall reign with him a thousand years.* If you would see more particular reasons of our judgment in this case, why such a Millennium is not to be expected in this World: they are set down in the *8th* Chap. of the *4th* Book, and we do not think it necessary that they should be here repeated.

As to that dissertation that follows the Millennium, and reaches to the Consummation of all things, seeing it is but problematical, we leave it to stand or fall by the evidence already given. And should be very glad to see the conjectures of others, more learned, in Speculations so abstruse and remote from common knowledge. They cannot surely be thought unworthy or unfit for our Meditations, seeing they are suggested to us by Scripture it self. And to what end were they propos'd to us there, if it was not intended that they should be understood, sooner or later?

I have done with this Review: and shall only add one or two reflections upon the whole discourse, and so conclude. You have seen the state of the Theory of the Earth, as to the *Matter*, *Form*, and *Proofs* of it: both Natural and Sacred. If any one will substitute a better in its place, I shall think my self more obliged to him, than if he had shew'd me the Quadrature of the Circle. But it is not enough to pick quarrels here and there: that may be done by any writing, especially when it is of so great extent and comprehension. They must build up, as well as pull down; and give us another Theory instead of this, fitted to the same natural History of the Earth, according as it is set down in Scripture: and then let the World take their choice. He that cuts down a Tree, is bound in reason to plant two, because there is an hazard in their growth and thriving.

Then as to those that are such rigorous Scripturists, as to require plainly demonstrative and irresistible Texts for every thing they entertain or believe; They would do well to reflect and consider, whether, for every article in the three Creeds (which have no support from natural reason) they can bring such Texts of Scripture, as they require of others: or a fairer and juster evidence, all things consider'd, than we have done for the substance of this Theory. We have not indeed said all that might be said, as to Antiquity: that making no part in this Review, and being capable still of great additions. But as to Scripture and Reason I have no more to add. Those that are not satisfied with the proofs already produc'd upon these two heads, are under a fate, good or bad, which is not in my power to overcome.

BOOKS Printed for *Walter Kettilby.*

*H*Enrici Mori Cantabrigiensis Opera omnia, tum quæ Latinè, tum quæ Anglicè scripta sunt; nunc verò Latinitate donata Instigatu & Impensis Generosissimi Juvenis Johannis Cockshuti Nobilis Angli, 3. Vol. Fol.

. . . . .'s Exposition upon *Daniel.* quart.

. . . . .'s Exposition upon the *Revelations.* quart.

. . . . .'s Answer to several Remarks upon his Expositions upon *Daniel,* and the *Revelations.* quart.

. . . . .'s Notes upon *Daniel* and the *Revelations.* quart.

. . . . .'s *Paralipomena Prophetica,* containing several Supplements and Defences of his Expositions. quart.

. . . . .'s Confutation of Judiciary Astrology against *Butler.* quart.

. . . . .'s Brief Discourse of the Real Presence of the Body and Blood of Christ, in the Celebration of the Holy Eucharist. 40. stitch.

. . . . .'s Reply to the Answer to his Antidote against Idolatry. *oct.*

. . . . .'s Remarks upon Judge *Hales* of Fluid Bodies. *oct.*

The Theory of the Earth, &c. the two first Books, concerning the *Deluge,* and concerning *Paradise.* Fol.

Telluris Theoria Sacra, &c. *Libri duo Priores de Diluvio & Paradiso.* quarto.

Libri duo Posteriores de Conflagratione Mundi, & de futuro Rerum Statu. quart.

Dr. *Goodal's* Royal Colledge of Physicians. *quart.*

Sydenham Opera Universa Medica. oct.

Ent. de Circuitione Sanguinis. oct.

Charleton de Causis Catameniorum & uteri Rheumatismo. oct.

Mr. *L'Emery's* Course of Chymistry. *oct.*

An Answer to *Harvey's* Conclave of Physicians.

Dr. *Scott's Christian Life,* in 3. Vol.

Dr. *Falkner's Libertas Ecclesiastica.* oct.

. . . . .'s Vindication of Liturgies. *oct.*

. . . . .'s *Christian Loyalty.* oct.

Dr. *Fowler's Libertas Evangelica.* oct.

Dr. *Kidder's* Christian Sufferer. *oct.*

Mr. *W. Allen's* Twelve several Tracts, in 4. Vol. *oct.*

Lately Printed.

Mr. *W. Allen's* Nature, Series, and Order of Occurrences, as they are prophetically represented in the 11*th* Chapter of the *Revelations.* oct.

Mr. *Raymond's* Pattern of Pure and undefiled Religion. *oct.*

Dr. *Worthington's* Great duty of Self-resignation. *oct.* reprinted.

A Relation of the Proceedings at *Charter-House,* upon occasion of K. *James's* presenting a *Papist* to be admitted into that Hospital, by vertue of his Letters Dispensatory. *Fol.* stitch.

Mr. *Mariott's* Sermon, on *Easter*-day, before the Lord Mayor.

. . . . .'s Sermon at the Election of the Lord Mayor.

Dr. *Pellings* Sermon before the *K.* and *Q.* at *White-hall.* Dec. 8. 1689.